SQL

A Beginner's Guide

Fourth Edition

About the Author

Andrew (Andy) J. Oppel is a proud graduate of The Boys' Latin School of Maryland and of Transylvania University (Lexington, KY) where he earned a BA in computer science in 1974. Since then he has been continuously employed in a wide variety of information technology positions, including programmer, programmer/analyst, systems architect, project manager, senior database administrator, database group manager, consultant, database designer, data modeler, technical trainer, and data architect. In addition, he has been a part-time instructor with the University of California (Berkeley) Extension for more than 30 years and received the Honored Instructor Award for the year 2000. His teaching work included developing three courses for UC Extension, "Concepts of Database Management Systems," "Introduction to Relational Database Management Systems," and "Data Modeling and Database Design." He also earned his Oracle 9*i* Database Associate certification in 2003. He is currently employed as a technical program manager for GoodData Corporation. Aside from computer systems, Andy enjoys music (guitar and vocals) and amateur radio.

Andy has designed and implemented hundreds of databases for a wide range of applications, including medical research, banking, insurance, apparel manufacturing, telecommunications, wireless communications, human resources, and business intelligence. He is the author of *Databases Demystified* (McGraw-Hill Professional, 2010), *SQL Demystified* (McGraw-Hill Professional, 2005), and *Data Modeling: A Beginner's Guide* (McGraw-Hill Professional, 2010), and coauthor of *SQL: The Complete Reference, Third Edition* (McGraw-Hill Professional, 2009). His database product experience includes IMS, DB2, Sybase, Microsoft SQL Server, Microsoft Access, MySQL, HP Vertica, and Oracle.

About the Technical Editor

James Seymour is a graduate of the University of North Carolina at Chapel Hill with a BA in history and political science and the University of Kentucky with an MA in history. He first became involved with computer technology in 1965 with the mainframe environment at North Carolina. While in the United States Army during the Vietnam War, he was on the small team that worked with the mainframe setup at the Pentagon for various military strategic scenarios. Since 1972, he has been involved in many varied computer environments, including the second point-of-sale and inventory control project in the retail industry, analytical programs and database initiatives in the insurance and benefits industries, risk analysis and loss control start-ups, and many other application projects throughout many different industries.

From 1987 through 1995, Mr. Seymour was an instructor of database management in the community college system of the state of Kentucky. In this capacity, he created the first database management and C programming courses in the state of Kentucky and helped both public and private entities with urgent training needs, including the programming of guidance systems on cruise missiles for Desert Storm.

Before 1985 and through 1995, he was a system administrator, network administrator, programmer, and database administrator. Since 1985, Mr. Seymour has been a senior database administrator working primarily with DB2 and Oracle DBMSs on multiple platforms plus SQL Server beginning with version 7.0. In 2002, he became a senior data/database architect and one of the senior database administrators for a Fortune 100 company overseeing major projects in the United States, Canada, and the United Kingdom. While with this firm, he joined the author of this book, Andy Oppel, in writing many best practices and standards documents.

In 2010, Mr. Seymour began writing books on various topics in information technology and business. Currently, he has 26 small books on different topics for businesses, a large 460-page book on the enterprise in business and information technology, and a 280-page book on data archival and its importance. Additionally, Mr. Seymour has developed a ministry online to work with ministries around the world in various capacities; as of 2015, he works with nearly 3,800 ministries.

SQL
A Beginner's Guide
Fourth Edition

Andrew J. Oppel

New York Chicago San Francisco
Athens London Madrid Mexico City
Milan New Delhi Singapore Sydney Toronto

Library of Congress Cataloging-in-Publication Data

Oppel, Andrew J., author.
SQL : a beginner's guide / Andrew J. Oppel.—Fourth edition.
pages cm
Earlier edition by Andy Oppel, Robert Sheldon.
Includes index.
ISBN 978-0-07-184259-4—ISBN 0-07-184259-4 1. SQL (Computer program language) 2. Relational databases. I. Title.
QA76.73.S67S54 2016
005.75'65—dc23
2015034055

McGraw-Hill Education books are available at special quantity discounts to use as premiums and sales promotions, or for use in corporate training programs. To contact a representative, please visit the Contact Us pages at www.mhprofessional.com.

SQL: A Beginner's Guide, Fourth Edition

1 2 3 4 5 6 7 8 9 0 DOC/DOC 1 0 9 8 7 6 5

ISBN 978-0-07-184259-4
MHID 0-07-184259-4

Sponsoring Editor Brandi Shailer
Editorial Supervisor Jody McKenzie
Project Manager Raghavi Khullar, Cenveo® Publisher Services
Acquisitions Coordinator Amanda Russell
Technical Editor James Seymour
Copy Editor Surendra N. Shivam
Proofreader Lisa McCoy
Indexer James Minkin
Production Supervisor Pamela Pelton
Composition Cenveo Publisher Services
Illustration Cenveo Publisher Services
Art Director, Cover Jeff Weeks

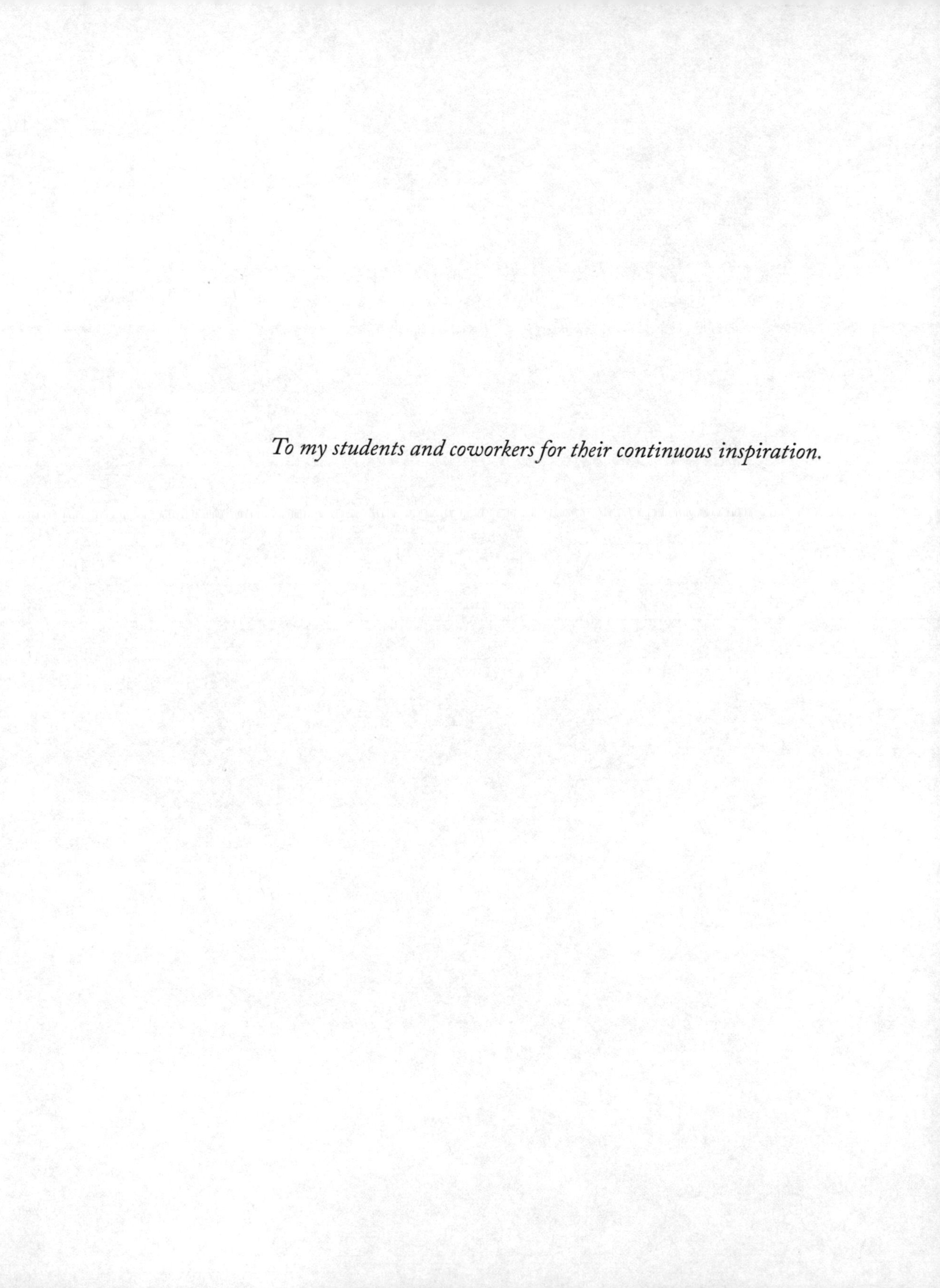

To my students and coworkers for their continuous inspiration.

Contents at a Glance

Contents

Acknowledgments

There were many people involved in the development of *SQL: A Beginner's Guide, Fourth Edition*, many of whom I do not know by name. First, the editors and staff at McGraw-Hill Education provided countless hours of support for this project. I wish to especially thank Editorial Coordinator Amanda Russell and Senior Acquisitions Editor Brandi Shailer as the individuals with whom I had direct contact throughout the writing and editing process. Your comments and suggestions, as well as quick and accurate answers to my many questions, made the writing tasks flow without a hitch; and your work behind the scenes kept the entire project moving smoothly. I also wish to thank the copy editor and all the other editors, proofreaders, indexers, designers, illustrators, and other participants whose names I do not know. My special thanks go to my friend and former colleague, Jim Seymour, the technical editor, for his attention to detail and his helpful input throughout the editing process. And I wish to acknowledge the work of Robert Sheldon, author of the first two editions, whose excellent writing made the revisions required for this edition so much easier to accomplish. Finally, my thanks to my family for their support and understanding as I fit the writing schedule into an already overly busy life.

Acknowledgments

[illegible]

Introduction

Relational databases have become the most common data storage mechanism for modern computer applications. Programming languages such as Java, C, and COBOL, and scripting languages such as Perl, VBScript, and JavaScript must often access a data source in order to retrieve or modify data. Many of these data sources are managed by a relational database management system (RDBMS), such as Oracle, Microsoft SQL Server, MySQL, and DB2, that relies on the Structured Query Language (SQL) to create and alter database objects, add data to and delete data from the database, modify data that has been added to that database, and, of course, retrieve data stored in the database for display and processing.

SQL is the most widely implemented language for relational databases. Much as mathematics is the language of science, SQL is the language of relational databases. SQL not only allows you to manage the data within the database, but also manage the database itself. By using SQL statements, you can access an SQL database directly by using an interactive client application or through an application programming language or scripting language. Regardless of which method you use to access a data source, a foundation in how to write SQL statements is required in order to access relational data. *SQL: A Beginner's Guide, Fourth Edition* provides you with such a foundation. It describes the types of statements that SQL supports and explains how they're used to manage databases and their data. By working through this book, you'll build a strong foundation in basic SQL and gain a comprehensive understanding of how to use SQL to access data in your relational database.

This fourth edition has been updated to include the provisions of the ISO SQL:2011 standard, along with technical corrigenda published in 2013. Chapter 13 has been added to cover the long-awaited temporal data features, which were added to the SQL standard in 2011. Other features added to the SQL standard in 2008 and 2011, including the TRUNCATE and MERGE statements, instead of triggers, and partitioned joins, have been added in the appropriate chapters. In addition, educators can contact their McGraw-Hill Education sales representative for access to an Instructor's Manual, written to aid in teaching a course with this book.

Who Should Read This Book

SQL: A Beginner's Guide is recommended for anyone trying to build a foundation in SQL programming based on the ISO SQL:2011 standard. The book is designed specifically for those who are new or relatively new to SQL; however, those of you who need a refresher in SQL will also find this book beneficial. Whether you're an experienced programmer, have had some web development experience, are a database administrator, or are new to programming and databases, *SQL: A Beginner's Guide* provides a strong foundation that will be useful to any of you wishing to learn more about SQL. In fact, any of the following individuals will find this book helpful when trying to understand and use SQL:

- The novice new to database design and SQL programming
- The analyst or manager who wants to better understand how to implement and access SQL databases
- The database administrator who wants to learn more about programming
- The technical support professional or testing/QA engineer who must perform ad hoc queries against an SQL data source
- The web developer writing applications that must access SQL databases
- The third-generation language (3GL) programmer embedding SQL within an application's source code
- Any other individual who wants to learn how to write SQL code that can be used to create and access databases within an RDBMS

Whichever category you might fit into, an important point to remember is that the book is geared toward anyone wanting to learn standard SQL, not a product-specific version of the language. The advantage of this is that you can take the skills learned in this book and apply them to real-world situations, without being limited to product standards. You will, of course, still need to be aware of how the product you work in implements SQL, but with the foundation provided by the book, you'll be able to move from one RDBMS to the next and still have a basic understanding of how SQL is used. As a result, this book is a useful tool to anyone new to SQL-based databases, regardless of the product used. SQL programmers need only adapt their knowledge to the specific RDBMS.

What Content the Book Covers

SQL: A Beginner's Guide is divided into three parts. Part I introduces you to the basic concepts of SQL and explains how to create objects within your database. Part II provides you with a foundation in how to retrieve data from a database and modify (add, change, and delete) the data that's stored in the database. Part III provides you with information about advanced data access techniques that allow you to expand on what you learned in Part I and Part II. In addition to the three parts, *SQL: A Beginner's Guide* contains appendixes that include reference material for the information presented in the three parts.

Description of the Book's Content

The following outline describes the contents of the book and shows how the book is broken down into task-focused chapters.

Part I: Relational Databases and SQL

Chapter 1: Introduction to Relational Databases and SQL This chapter introduces you to relational databases and the relational model, which forms the basis for SQL. You'll also be provided with a general overview of SQL and how it relates to RDBMSs.

Chapter 2: Working with the SQL Environment This chapter describes the components that make up the SQL environment. You'll also be introduced to the objects that make up a schema, and you'll learn how to create a schema within your SQL environment. You'll also be introduced to the concept of creating a database object in an SQL implementation that supports the creation of database objects.

Chapter 3: Creating and Altering Tables In this chapter, you'll learn how to create SQL tables, specify column data types, create user-defined types, and specify column default values. You'll also learn how to alter a table definition, delete a table definition from your database, and truncate a table.

Chapter 4: Enforcing Data Integrity This chapter explains how integrity constraints are used to enforce data integrity in your SQL tables. The chapter includes information on table-related constraints, assertions, and domain constraints. You will learn how to create NOT NULL, UNIQUE, PRIMARY KEY, FOREIGN KEY, and CHECK constraints.

Chapter 5: Creating SQL Views In this chapter, you'll learn how to add views to your SQL database. You'll also learn how to create updateable views and how to drop views from the database.

Chapter 6: Managing Database Security In this chapter, you'll be introduced to the SQL security model and learn how authorization identifiers are defined within the context of a session. You'll then learn how to create and delete roles, grant and revoke privileges, and grant and revoke roles.

Part II: Data Access and Modification

Part II explains how to access and modify data in an SQL database. You'll also learn how to use predicates, functions, and value expressions to manage that data. In addition, Part II describes how to join tables and use subqueries to access data in multiple tables.

Chapter 7: Querying SQL Data This chapter describes the basic components of the SELECT statement and how the statement is used to retrieve data from an SQL database. You'll learn how to define each clause that can be included in the SELECT statement and how those clauses are processed when querying a database.

Chapter 8: Modifying SQL Data In this chapter, you'll learn how to modify data in an SQL database. Specifically, you'll learn how to insert data, update data, delete data, and merge data. The chapter reviews each component of the SQL statements that allow you to perform these data modifications.

Chapter 9: Using Predicates In this chapter, you'll learn how to use predicates to compare SQL data, return null values, return similar values, reference additional sources of data, and quantify comparison predicates. The chapter describes the various types of predicates and shows you how they're used to retrieve specific data from an SQL database.

Chapter 10: Working with Functions and Value Expressions This chapter explains how to use various types of functions and value expressions in your SQL statements. You'll learn how to use set functions, value functions, value expressions, and special values in various clauses within an SQL statement.

Chapter 11: Accessing Multiple Tables This chapter describes how to join tables in order to retrieve data from those tables. You will learn how to perform basic join operations, join tables with shared column names, use the condition join, specify partitioned joins, and perform union operations.

Chapter 12: Using Subqueries to Access and Modify Data In this chapter, you'll learn how to create subqueries that return multiple rows and others that return only one value. You'll also learn how to use correlated subqueries and nested subqueries. In addition, you'll learn how to use subqueries to modify data.

Chapter 13: Working with Temporal Data This chapter introduces the temporal features that were added to the SQL:2011 standard. *Temporal data* is data that changes over time. You'll learn how to specify and use system-versioned tables, application-time period tables, and system-versioned application-time period tables, and to write queries containing new options that exploit the powerful capabilities of temporal tables.

Part III: Advanced Data Access

Part III introduces you to advanced data-access techniques such as SQL-invoked routines, triggers, and cursors. You'll also learn how to manage transactions, how to access SQL data from your host program, and how to incorporate XML data into your database.

Chapter 14: Creating SQL-Invoked Routines This chapter describes SQL-invoked procedures and functions and how you can create them in your SQL database. You'll learn how to define input parameters, add local variables to your routine, work with control statements, and use output parameters.

Chapter 15: Creating SQL Triggers This chapter introduces you to SQL triggers and explains how to create insert, update, and delete triggers in your SQL database, including the newly added instead of trigger feature. You'll learn how triggers are automatically invoked and what types of actions they can take.

Chapter 16: Using SQL Cursors In this chapter, you'll learn how SQL cursors are used to retrieve one row of data at a time from a result set. The chapter explains how to declare a cursor, open and close a cursor, and retrieve data from a cursor. You'll also learn how to use positioned UPDATE and DELETE statements after you fetch a row through a cursor.

Chapter 17: Managing SQL Transactions In this chapter, you'll learn how transactions are used to ensure the integrity of your SQL data. The chapter describes how to set transaction properties, start a transaction, set constraint deferrability, create savepoints in a transaction, and terminate a transaction.

Chapter 18: Accessing SQL Data from Your Host Program This chapter describes the four methods supported by the SQL standard for accessing an SQL database. You'll learn how to invoke SQL directly from a client application, embed SQL statements in a program, create SQL client modules, and use an SQL call-level interface to access data.

Chapter 19: Working with XML Data This chapter describes how XML data can be incorporated into an SQL database. You'll learn the basics of XML, how to use the XML data type to store XML in table column values, how to write SQL/XML functions that can be used to return data from the database formatted as XML, and the SQL/XML mapping rules that describe how SQL values are translated to XML values and vice versa.

Part IV: Appendices

The appendices include reference material for the information presented in the first three parts.

Appendix A: SQL:2011 Keywords This appendix lists the reserved and nonreserved keywords as they are used in SQL statements as defined in the SQL:2011 standard.

Appendix B: Answers to Self Tests This appendix provides the answers to the Self-Test questions listed at the end of each chapter and may be downloaded from http://www.mhprofessional.com by searching for the book's ISBN, 9780071842594.

Appendix C: SQL Code Used in the Book's Try This Exercises This appendix lists all the SQL code used in the book's Try This exercises, consolidated into one place for easy reference. Appendix C may be downloaded from http://www.mhprofessional.com by searching for the book's ISBN, 9780071842594. The code may also be downloaded by going to the same location and then selecting Source Code.

Chapter Content

As you can see in the outline, *SQL: A Beginner's Guide* is organized into chapters. Each chapter focuses on a set of related tasks. The chapter contains the background information you need to understand the various concepts related to those tasks, explains how to create the necessary SQL statements to perform the tasks, and provides examples of how those statements are created. In addition, each chapter contains elements to help you better understand the information covered in that chapter:

- **Ask the Expert** Each chapter contains one or two Ask the Expert sections that provide information on questions that might arise regarding the information presented in the chapter.
- **Self Test** Each chapter ends with a Self Test, which is a set of questions that tests you on the information and skills you learned in that chapter. The answers to the Self Test are included in Appendix B, available for download.

SQL Syntax

The syntax of an SQL statement refers to the structure and rules used for that statement, as outlined in the SQL standard. Most chapters will include the syntax for one or more statements so that you have an understanding of the basic elements contained in them. For example, the following syntax represents the information you need when you define a CREATE TABLE statement:

```
<table definition> ::=
CREATE [ { GLOBAL | LOCAL } TEMPORARY ] TABLE <table name>
( <table element> [ { , <table element> } . . . ] )
[ ON COMMIT { PRESERVE | DELETE } ROWS ]
```

Do not be concerned about the meaning of the SQL code at this time. This example is meant only to show you how SQL statements are represented in this book.

As you can see, a statement's syntax can contain many elements. Notice that most of the words used within the statement are shown in uppercase. The uppercase words are SQL keywords that are used to formulate the SQL statement. (For a complete list of SQL:2011 keywords, see Appendix A.) Although SQL does not require that keywords be written in uppercase, I use that convention in this book so that you can easily identify the keywords within a statement. In addition to the keywords, the syntax for an SQL statement includes a number of other elements that help define how a particular statement should be created:

- **Square brackets** The square brackets indicate that the syntax enclosed in those brackets is optional. For example, the ON COMMIT clause in the CREATE TABLE statement is optional.
- **Angle brackets** The angle brackets enclose information that represents a placeholder. When a statement is actually created, the placeholder is replaced by the appropriate SQL elements or identifiers. For example, you should replace the <table name> placeholder with a name for the table when you define a CREATE TABLE statement.

- **Curly brackets** The curly brackets are used to group elements together. The brackets tell you that you should first decide how to handle the contents within the brackets and then determine how they fit into the statement. For example, the PRESERVE | DELETE set of keywords is enclosed by curly brackets. You must first choose PRESERVE or DELETE and then deal with the entire line of code. As a result, your clause can read ON COMMIT PRESERVE ROWS, or it can read ON COMMIT DELETE ROWS.
- **Vertical bars** The vertical bar can be read as "or," which means that you should use either the PRESERVE option or the DELETE option.
- **Three periods** The three periods indicate that you can repeat the clause as often as necessary. For example, you can include as many table elements (represented by <table element>) as necessary.
- **Colons/equal sign** The ::= symbol (two consecutive colons plus an equal sign) indicates that the placeholder to the left of the symbol is defined by the syntax following the symbol. In the syntax example, the <table definition> placeholder equals the syntax that makes up a CREATE TABLE statement.

By referring to the syntax, you should be able to construct an SQL statement that creates database objects or modifies SQL data as necessary. However, in order to better demonstrate how the syntax is applied, each chapter also contains examples of actual SQL statements.

Examples of SQL Statements

Each chapter provides examples of how SQL statements are implemented when accessing an SQL database. For example, you might see an SQL statement similar to the following:

```
CREATE TABLE ARTISTS
( ARTIST_ID         INT,
  ARTIST_NAME       VARCHAR(60),
  ARTIST_DOB        DATE,
  POSTER_IN_STOCK   BOOLEAN );
```

Notice that the statement is written in special type to show that it is SQL code. Also notice that keywords and object names are all uppercase. (You don't need to be concerned about any other details at this point.)

The examples used in the book are pure SQL, meaning they're based on the SQL standard. You'll find, however, that in some cases your SQL implementation does not support an SQL statement in exactly the same way as it is defined in the standard. For this reason, you might also need to refer to the documentation for a particular product to be sure that your SQL statement conforms to that product's implementation of SQL. Sometimes it might be only a slight variation, but there might be times when the product statement is substantially different from the standard SQL statement.

The examples in each chapter are based on a database related to an inventory of compact discs. However, the examples are not necessarily consistent in terms of the names used for database objects and how those objects are defined. For example, two different chapters might contain examples that reference a table named CD_INVENTORY. However, you cannot assume that the tables used in the different examples are made up of the same columns or contain the same content. Because each example focuses on a unique aspect of SQL, the tables used in examples are defined in a way specific to the needs of that example, as you'll see as you get into the chapters. However, this is not the case for Try This exercises, which use a consistent database structure throughout the book.

Try This Exercises

Each chapter (except Chapter 2) contains one or two Try This exercises that allow you to apply the information that you learned in the chapter. Each exercise is broken down into steps that walk you through the process of completing a particular task. Many of the projects include related files that you can download from our web site at http://www.mhprofessional.com. The files usually include the SQL statements used within the Try This exercise. In addition, a consolidation of the SQL statements is included in Appendix C.

The Try This exercises are based on the INVENTORY database. You'll create the database, create the tables and other objects in the database, add data to those tables, and then manipulate that data. Because the projects build on one another, it is best that you complete them in the order that they're presented in the book. This is especially true for the chapters in Part I, in which you create the database objects, and Chapter 7, in which you insert data into the tables. However, if you do plan to skip around, you can refer to Appendix C, which provides all the code necessary to create the database objects and populate the tables with data.

To complete most of the Try This exercises in this book, you'll need to have access to an RDBMS that allows you to enter and execute SQL statements interactively. If you're accessing an RDBMS over a network, check with the database administrator to make sure that you're logging in with the credentials necessary to create a database and schema. You might need special permissions to create these objects. Also verify whether there are any parameters you should include when creating the database (for example, log file size), restrictions on the names you can use, or restrictions of any other kind. Be sure to check the product's documentation before working with any database product.

Part I

Relational Databases and SQL

Chapter 1

Introduction to Relational Databases and SQL

Key Skills & Concepts

- Understand Relational Databases
- Learn About SQL
- Use a Relational Database Management System

In 2011, the International Organization for Standardization (ISO) and the American National Standards Institute (ANSI) published revisions to their SQL standard, which I will call SQL:2011. As you will see later, the standard is divided in parts, and each part is approved and published on its own timeline, so different parts have different publication years; it is common to use the latest year as the collective name for the set of all parts published up through that year. The SQL:2011 standard, like its predecessors SQL:2008, SQL:2006, SQL:2003, SQL:1999 (also known as SQL3), and SQL-92, is based on the relational data model, which defines how data can be stored and manipulated within a relational database. Relational database management systems (RDBMSs) such as Oracle, Sybase, DB2, MySQL, and Microsoft SQL Server (or just SQL Server) use the SQL standard as a foundation for their technology, providing database environments that support both SQL and the relational data model. There is more information on the SQL standard later in this chapter.

Understand Relational Databases

Structured Query Language (SQL) supports the creation and maintenance of the relational database and the management of data within that database. However, before I go into a discussion about relational databases, I want to explain what I mean by the term *database.* The term itself has been used to refer to anything from a collection of names and addresses to a complex system of data retrieval and storage that relies on user interfaces and a network of client computers and servers. There are as many definitions for the word *database* as there are books about them. Moreover, different DBMS vendors have developed different architectures, so not all databases are designed in the same way. Despite the lack of an absolute definition, most sources agree that a database, at the very least, is a collection of data organized in a structured format that is defined by *metadata* that describes that structure. You can think of metadata as data about the data being stored; it defines how the data is stored within the database.

Over the years, a number of database models have been implemented to store and manage data. Several of the more common models include the following:

- **Hierarchical** This model has a parent–child structure that is similar to an inverted tree, which is what forms the hierarchy. Data is organized in *nodes*, the logical equivalent of tables in a relational database. A parent node can have many child nodes, but a child node can have only one parent node. Although the model has been highly implemented, it is often considered unsuitable for many applications because of its inflexible structure and lack of support for complex relationships. Still, some implementations such as IMS from IBM have introduced features that work around these limitations.

- **Network** This model addresses some of the limitations of the hierarchical model. Data is organized in *record types*, the logical equivalent of tables in a relational database. Like the hierarchical model, the network model uses an inverted tree structure, but record types are organized into a set structure that relates pairs of record types into owners and members. Any one record type can participate in any set with other record types in the database, which supports more complex queries and relationships than are possible in the hierarchical model. Still, the network model has its limitations, the most serious of which is complexity. In accessing the database, users must be very familiar with the structure and keep careful track of where they are and how they got there. It's also difficult to change the structure without affecting applications that interact with the database.
- **Relational** This model addresses many of the limitations of both the hierarchical and network models. In a hierarchical or network database, the application relies on a defined implementation of that database, which is then hard-coded into the application. If you add a new attribute (data item) to the database, you must modify the application, even if it doesn't use the attribute. However, a relational database is independent of the application; you can make nondestructive modifications to the structure without impacting the application. In addition, the structure of the relational database is based on the relation, or table, along with the ability to define complex relationships between these relations. Each relation can be accessed directly, without the cumbersome limitations of a hierarchical or owner/member model that requires navigation of a complex data structure. In the following section, "The Relational Model," I'll discuss the model in more detail.

Although still used in many organizations, hierarchical and network databases are now considered legacy solutions. The relational model is the most extensively implemented model in modern business systems, and it is the relational model that provides the foundation for SQL.

The Relational Model

If you've ever had the opportunity to look at a book about relational databases, you have quite possibly seen the name of E. F. (Ted) Codd referred to in the context of the relational model. In 1970, Codd published his seminal paper, "A Relational Model of Data for Large Shared Data Banks," in the journal *Communications of the ACM*, Volume 13, Number 6 (June 1970). Codd defines a relational data structure that protects data and allows that data to be manipulated in a way that is predictable and resistant to error. The relational model, which is rooted primarily in the mathematical principles of set theory and predicate logic, supports easy data retrieval, enforces *data integrity* (data accuracy and consistency), and provides a database structure independent of the applications accessing the stored data.

At the core of the relational model is the relation. A *relation* is a set of columns and rows collected in a table-like structure that represents a single entity made up of related data. An *entity* is a person, place, thing, event, or concept about which data is collected, such as a recording artist, a book, or a sales transaction. Each relation comprises one or more attributes (columns). An *attribute* is a unit fact that describes or characterizes an entity in some way. For example, in Figure 1-1, the entity is a compact disc (CD) with attributes of ARTIST_NAME (the name of the recording artist), CD_TITLE (the title of the CD), and COPYRIGHT_YEAR (the year the recording was copyrighted).

As you can see in Figure 1-1, each attribute has an associated domain. A *domain* defines the type of data that can be stored in a particular attribute; however, a domain is not the same thing as a data type. A *data type,* which is discussed in more detail in Chapter 3, is a specific kind of *constraint* (a control used to enforce data integrity) associated with a column, whereas a domain as it is used in the relational model has a much broader meaning and describes exactly what data can be included in an attribute associated with that domain. For example, the COPYRIGHT_YEAR attribute is associated with the Year domain. As you see in this example, it is common practice to include a class word that describes the domain in attribute names, but this is not at all mandatory. The domain can be defined so that the attribute includes only data whose values and format are limited to years, as opposed to days or months. The domain might also limit the data to a specific range of years. A data type, on the other hand, restricts the format of the data, such as allowing only numeric digits, but not the values, unless those values somehow violate the format.

Data is stored in a relation in tuples (rows). A *tuple* is a set of data whose values make up an instance of each attribute defined for that relation. Each tuple represents a record of related data. (In fact, the set of data is sometimes referred to as a *record.*) For example, in Figure 1-1, the second tuple from the top contains the value "Joe Bonamassa" for the ARTIST_NAME

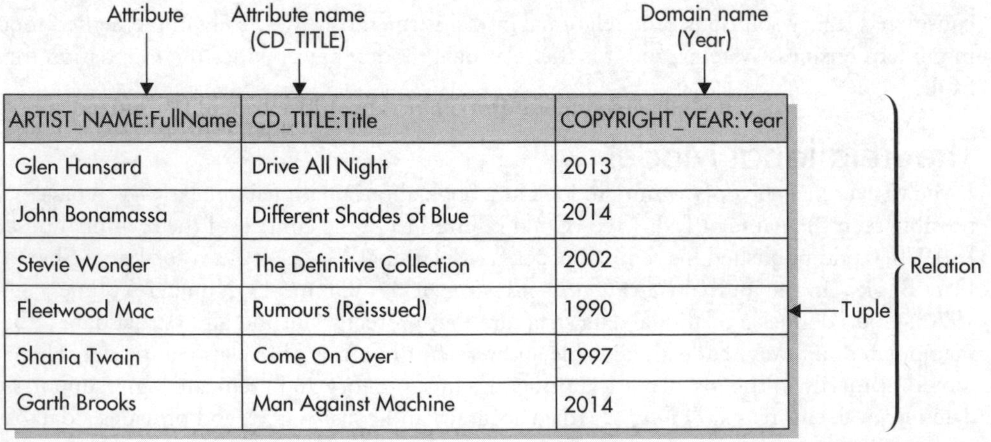

ARTIST_NAME:FullName	CD_TITLE:Title	COPYRIGHT_YEAR:Year
Glen Hansard	Drive All Night	2013
John Bonamassa	Different Shades of Blue	2014
Stevie Wonder	The Definitive Collection	2002
Fleetwood Mac	Rumours (Reissued)	1990
Shania Twain	Come On Over	1997
Garth Brooks	Man Against Machine	2014

Figure 1-1 Relation containing ARTIST_NAME, CD_TITLE, and COPYRIGHT_YEAR attributes

attribute, the value "Different Shades of Blue" for the CD_TITLE attribute, and the value "2014" for the COPYRIGHT_YEAR attribute. Together these three values form a tuple.

NOTE

The logical terms relation, attribute, and tuple are used primarily when referring to the relational model. SQL uses the physical terms table, column, and row to describe these items. Because the relational model is based on mathematical principles (a logical model) and SQL is concerned more with the physical implementation of the model, the meanings for the model's terms and the SQL language's terms are slightly different, but the underlying principles are the same. The SQL terms are discussed in more detail in Chapter 2.

The relational model is, of course, more complex than merely the attributes and tuples that make up a relation. Two very important considerations in the design and implementation of any relational database are the normalization of data and the associations of relations among the various types of data.

Normalizing Data

Central to the principles of the relational model is the concept of *normalization*, a technique for producing a set of relations that possesses a certain set of properties that minimizes redundant data and preserves the integrity of the stored data as data is maintained (added, updated, and deleted). The process was developed by E. F. Codd in 1972, and the name is a bit of a political gag because President Nixon was "normalizing" relations with China at that time. Codd figured if relations between countries could be normalized, then surely he could normalize database relations. Normalization defines sets of rules, referred to as *normal forms*, which provide specific guidelines on how data should be organized in order to avoid anomalies that lead to inconsistencies in and loss of data as the data stored in the database is maintained.

When Codd first presented normalization, it included three normal forms. Although additional normal forms have been added since then, the first three still cover most situations you will find in both personal and business databases, and since my primary intent here is to introduce you to the process of normalization, I'll discuss only those three forms.

Choosing a Unique Identifier A unique identifier is an attribute or set of attributes that uniquely identifies each row of data in a relation. The unique identifier will eventually become the primary key of the table created in the physical database from the normalized relation, but many use the terms *unique identifier* and *primary key* interchangeably. Each potential unique identifier is called a *candidate key*, and when there are multiple candidates, the designer will choose the best one, which is the one least likely to change values or the one that is the simplest and/or shortest. In many cases, a single attribute can be found that uniquely identifies the data in each tuple of the relation. However, when no single attribute can be found that is unique, the designer looks for several attributes that can be concatenated (put together) in order to form the unique identifier. In the few cases where no reasonable candidate keys can be found, the designer must invent a unique identifier called a *surrogate key*, often with values assigned sequentially or randomly as tuples are added to the relation.

While not absolutely required until second normal form, it is customary to select a unique identifier as the first step in normalization. It's just easier that way.

First Normal Form First normal form, which provides the foundation for second and third normal forms, includes the following guidelines:

- Each attribute of a tuple must contain only one value.
- Each tuple in a relation must contain the same number of attributes.
- Each tuple must be different, meaning that the combination of all attribute values for a given tuple cannot be the same as any other tuple in the same relation.

As you can see in Figure 1-2, the third tuple and the last tuple violate first normal form. In the third tuple, the CD_TITLE attribute and the COPYRIGHT_YEAR attribute each contain two values. In the last tuple, the ARTIST_NAME attribute contains two values. Also be on the lookout for repeating values in the form of repeating columns. For example, splitting the ARTIST_NAME attribute into three attributes called ARTIST_NAME_1 and ARTIST_NAME_2 is not an adequate solution because you will eventually find a need for a third name, then a fourth name, and so on. Moreover, repeating columns make queries more difficult because you must remember to search all the columns when looking for a specific value.

To normalize the relation shown in Figure 1-2, you would create additional relations that separate the data so that each attribute contains only one value, each tuple contains the same number of attributes, and each tuple is different, as shown in Figure 1-3. The data now conforms to first normal form.

Notice that there are duplicate values in the second relation; the ARTIST_ID value of 3003 is repeated and the CD_ID value of 108 is also repeated. However, when the

ARTIST_NAME	CD_TITLE	COPYRIGHT_YEAR
Glen Hansard	Drive All Night	2013
John Bonamassa	Different Shades of Blue	2014
Stevie Wonder	Innervisions; The Definitive Collection	2000; 2002
Fleetwood Mac	Rumours (Reissued)	1990
Shania Twain	Come On Over	1997
Garth Brooks	Man Against Machine	2014
Joshua Bell; Johannes Sebastian Bach	Bach	2014

Figure 1-2 Relation that violates first normal form

ARTIST_ID	ARTIST_NAME
3001	Glen Hansard
3002	John Bonamassa
3003	Stevie Wonder
3004	Fleetwood Mac
3005	Shania Twain
3006	Garth Brooks
3007	J. S. Bach
3008	Joshua Bell

ARTIST_ID	CD_ID
3001	101
3002	102
3003	103
3003	104
3004	105
3005	106
3006	107
3007	108
3008	108

CD_ID	CD_TITLE	COPYRIGHT_YEAR
101	Drive All Night	2013
102	Different Shades of Blue	2014
103	Innervisions (Remastered)	2000
104	The Definitive Collection	2002
105	Rumours (Reissued)	1990
106	Come On Over	1997
107	Man Against Machine	2014
108	Bach	2014

Figure 1-3 Relations that conform to first normal form

two attribute values in each tuple are taken together, the tuple as a whole forms a unique combination, which means that, despite the apparent duplications, each tuple in the relation is different.

Did you notice that the ARTIST_ID and CD_ID attributes were added? This was done because there were no other key candidates. ARTIST_NAME is not unique (two people with the same name could both be recording artists), and neither is CD_TITLE (two CDs could end up with the same name, although they would likely be from different record labels). ARTIST_ID is the primary key of the first relation, and CD_ID is the primary key of the third. The primary key of the second relation is the combination of ARTIST_ID and CD_ID.

Second Normal Form To understand second normal form, you must first understand the concept of *functional dependence*. For this definition, we'll use two arbitrary attributes, cleverly named A and B. Attribute B is *functionally dependent* (*dependent* for short) on attribute A if at any moment in time there is no more than one value of attribute B associated with a given value of attribute A. Lest you wonder what planet I lived on before this one, let's try to make the definition more understandable. If we say that attribute B is functionally dependent on attribute A, we are also saying that attribute A *determines* attribute B, or that A is a *determinant* (unique identifier) of attribute B. In Figure 1-4, COPYRIGHT_YEAR is dependent on CD_ID since there can be only one value of COPYRIGHT_YEAR for any given CD. Said the other way, CD_ID is a determinant of COPYRIGHT_YEAR.

Second normal form states that a relation must be in first normal form and that all attributes in the relation are dependent on the *entire* unique identifier. In Figure 1-4, if the combination of ARTIST_ID and CD_ID is selected as the unique identifier, then COPYRIGHT_YEAR violates second normal form because it is dependent only on CD_ID rather than the combination of CD_ID and ARTIST_ID. Even though the relation conforms to first normal form, it violates second normal form. Again, the solution is to separate the data into different relations, as you saw in Figure 1-3 where COPYRIGHT_YEAR is in a relation that has CD_ID as its primary key.

ARTIST_ID	CD_ID	COPYRIGHT_YEAR
3001	101	2013
3002	102	2014
3003	103	2000
3003	104	2002
3004	105	1990
3005	106	2014
3006	107	2014

(Unique Identifier: ARTIST_ID, CD_ID)

Figure 1-4 Relation that violates second normal form

Third Normal Form Third normal form, like second normal form, is dependent on the relation's unique identifier. To adhere to the guidelines of third normal form, a relation must be in second normal form and nonkey attributes (attributes that are not part of any candidate key) must be independent of each other and dependent on the unique identifier. For example, the unique identifier in the relation shown in Figure 1-5 is the ARTIST_ID attribute. The ARTIST_NAME and AGENCY_ID attributes are both dependent on the unique identifier and are independent of each other. However, the AGENCY_STATE attribute is dependent on the AGENCY_ID attribute, and therefore it violates the conditions of third normal form. This attribute would be better suited in a relation that includes data about agencies, most likely with AGENCY_ID as its primary key.

NOTE

In the theoretical world of relational design, the goal is to store data according to the rules of normalization. However, in the real world of database implementation, we must occasionally denormalize data, which means to deliberately violate the rules of normalization, particularly the second and third normal forms. Denormalization is used primarily to improve performance or reduce complexity in cases where an overnormalized structure complicates implementation. Still, the goal of normalization is to ensure data integrity, so denormalization should be performed with great care and as a last resort in databases that are updated by business transactions. On the other hand, databases that are not actively updated by business transactions, such as databases used by business intelligence applications, can be denormalized with less significant consequences.

Unique Identifier

ARTIST_ID	ARTIST_NAME	AGENCY_ID	AGENCY_STATE
3001	Glen Hansard	2305	NY
3002	John Bonamassa	2306	NY
3003	Stevie Wonder	2327	MI
3004	Fleetwood Mac	2345	CA
3005	Shania Twain	2367	TN
3006	Garth Brooks	2367	TN
3007	J. S. Bach		
3008	Joshua Bell	2305	NY

Figure 1-5 Relation with an attribute that violates third normal form

Relationships

So far, the focus in this chapter has been on the relation and how to normalize data. However, an important component of any relational database is how those relations are associated with each other. These associations, or *relationships*, link relations together in meaningful ways, which helps to ensure the integrity of the data so that an action taken in one relation does not negatively impact data in another relation.

There are three primary types of relationships:

- **One-to-one** A relationship between two relations in which a tuple in the first relation is related to, at most, one tuple in the second relation, and a tuple in the second relation is related to, at most, one tuple in the first relation.
- **One-to-many** A relationship between two relations in which a tuple in the first relation is related to zero, one, or more tuples in the second relation, but a tuple in the second relation is related to, at most, one tuple in the first relation.
- **Many-to-many** A relationship between two relations in which a tuple in the first relation is related to zero, one, or more tuples in the second relation, and a tuple in the second relation is related to zero, one, or more tuples in the first relation.

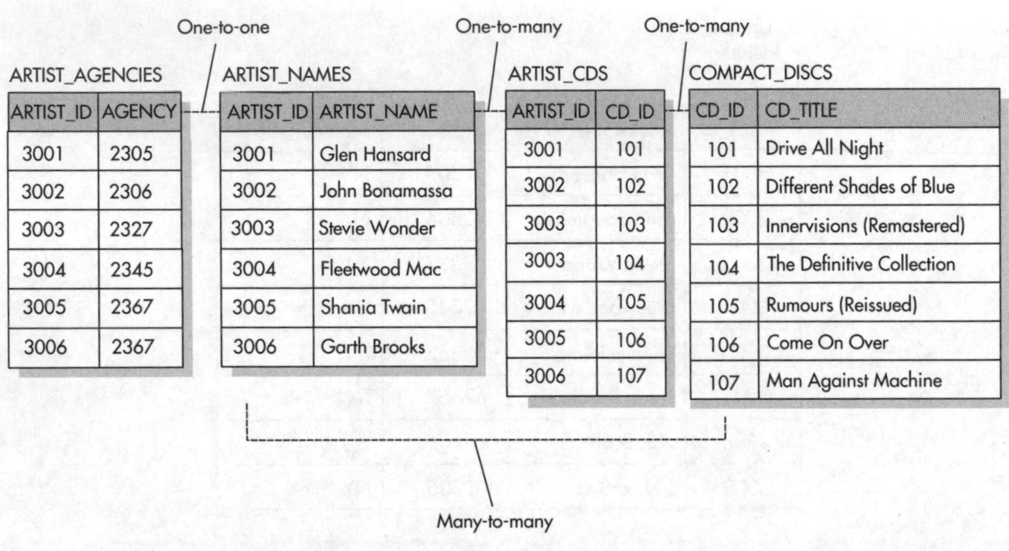

Figure 1-6 Types of relationships between relations

The best way to illustrate these relationships is to look at a data model of several relations (shown in Figure 1-6). The relations are named to make referencing them easier. As you can see, all three types of relationships are represented:

- A one-to-one relationship exists between the ARTIST_AGENCIES relation and the ARTIST_NAMES relation. For each artist listed in the ARTIST_AGENCIES relation, there can be only one matching tuple in the ARTIST_NAMES relation, and vice versa. This implies a business rule that an artist may work with only one agency at a time.
- A one-to-many relationship exists between the ARTIST_NAMES relation and the ARTIST_CDS relation. For each artist in the ARTIST_NAMES relation, zero, one, or more tuples for that artist can be listed in the ARTIST_CDS relation. In other words, each artist could have made zero, one, or more CDs. However, for each artist listed in the ARTIST_CDS relation, there can be only one related tuple for that artist in the ARTIST_NAMES relation because each artist can have only one tuple in the ARTIST_NAMES relation.
- A one-to-many relationship exists between the ARTIST_CDS relation and the COMPACT_DISCS relation. For each CD, there can be one or more artists; however, each tuple in ARTIST_CDS can match only one tuple in COMPACT_DISCS because each CD can appear only once in the COMPACT_DISCS relation.
- A many-to-many relationship exists between the ARTIST_NAMES relation and the COMPACT_DISCS relation. For every artist, there can be zero, one, or more CDs, and for every CD, there can be one or more artists.

NOTE

Relational databases only support one-to-many relationships directly. A many-to-many relationship is physically implemented by adding a third relation between the first and second relations to create two one-to-many relationships. In Figure 1-6, the ARTIST_CDS relation was added between the ARTIST_NAMES relation and the COMPACT_DISCS relation. A one-to-one relationship is physically implemented just like a one-to-many relationship, except that a constraint is added to prevent duplicate matching rows on the "many" side of the relationship. In Figure 1-6, a unique constraint would be added on the ARTIST_ID attribute to prevent an artist from appearing with more than one agency. (Constraints are rules that are formally defined in the database to preserve data integrity. I cover constraints in Chapter 4.)

Relationships are also classified by *minimum cardinality* (the minimum number of tuples that must participate in the relationship). If each tuple in one relation *must* have a matching tuple in the other, the relationship is said to be *mandatory* in that direction. Similarly, if each tuple in one relation does not require a matching tuple in the other, the relationship is said

Ask the Expert

Q: You mention that relationships between relations help to ensure data integrity. How do relationships make that possible?

A: Suppose your data model includes a relation (named ARTIST_NAMES) that lists all the artists who have recorded CDs in your inventory. Your model also includes a relation (named ARTIST_CDS) that matches artist IDs with compact disc IDs. If a relationship exists between the two relations, tuples in one relation will always correspond to tuples in the other relation. As a result, you could prevent certain actions that could compromise data. For example, you would not be able to add an artist ID to the ARTIST_CDS relation if that ID wasn't listed in the ARTIST_NAMES relation. Nor would you be able to delete an artist from the ARTIST_NAMES relation if the artist ID was referenced in the ARTIST_CDS relation.

Q: What do you mean by the term *data model*?

A: By data model, I'm referring to a design, often presented using diagrams, that represents the structure of a database. The model identifies the relations, attributes, keys, domains, and relationships within that database. Some database designers will create a logical model and a physical model. The logical model is based more on relational theory and applies the appropriate principles of normalization to the data. The physical model, on the other hand, is concerned with the actual implementation, as the data will be stored in an RDBMS. Based on the logical design, the physical design brings the data structure down to the real world of implementation.

to be *optional* in that direction. For example, the relationship between ARTIST_NAMES and ARTIST_AGENCIES is mandatory-mandatory because each artist must have one agency and each ARTIST_AGENCIES tuple must refer to one and only one artist. Business rules must be understood before minimum cardinality can be determined with certainty. For instance, can we have an artist in the database who at some point in time has no CDs in the database (that is, no matching tuples in ARTIST_CDS)? If so, then the relationship between ARTIST_NAMES and ARTIST_CDS is mandatory-optional; otherwise, it is mandatory-mandatory.

Try This 1-1 Normalizing Data and Identifying Relationships

As a beginning SQL programmer, it's unlikely that you'll be responsible for normalization of the database. Still, it's important that you understand these concepts, just as it's important that you understand the sorts of relationships that can exist between relations. Normalization and relationships, like the relations themselves, help to provide the foundation on which SQL is built. As a result, this Try This exercise focuses on the process of normalizing data and identifying the relationships between relations. To complete the exercise, you need only a paper and pencil on which to sketch the data model.

Step by Step

1. Review the relation in the following table:

CD_ID	CD_TITLE	CATEGORY
101	Drive All Night	Alternative Rock, Rock
102	Different Shades of Blue	Blues, Pop
103	Innervisions (Remastered)	R&B
104	The Definitive Collection	R&B, Rock
105	Rumours (Reissued)	Classic Rock, Pop
106	Come On Over	Country, Pop, Rock
107	Man Against Machine	Country

2. Identify any elements that do not conform to the three normal forms. You will find that the CATEGORY attribute contains more than one value for each tuple, which violates the first normal form.
3. Normalize the data according to the normal forms. Sketch out a data model that includes the appropriate relations, attributes, and tuples. Your model will include three tables: one for the list of CDs, one for the list of music categories (for example, Pop), and one that associates the CDs with the appropriate categories of music. View the Try_This_01-1a.jpg file online for an example of how your data model might look.
4. On the illustration you drew, identify the relationships between the relations. Remember that each CD can be associated with one or more categories, and each category can be associated with zero, one, or more CDs. View the Try_This_01-1b.jpg file online to view the relationships between relations.

Try This Summary

Data models are usually more specific than the illustrations shown in this Try This exercise. Relationships and keys are clearly marked with symbols that conform to a particular type of data modeling system, and relationships show only the attributes, but not the tuples. However, for the purposes of this chapter, it is enough that you have a basic understanding of normalization and the relationships between relations. The exercise is meant only as a way for you to better understand these concepts and how they apply to the relational model.

Learn About SQL

Now that you have a fundamental understanding of the relational model, it's time to introduce you to SQL and its basic characteristics. As you might recall from the "Understand Relational Databases" section earlier in this chapter, SQL is based on the relational model, although it is not an exact implementation. While the relational model provides the theoretical underpinnings of the relational database, it is the SQL language that supports the physical implementation of that database.

SQL, a nearly universally implemented relational language, is different from other computer languages such as C, COBOL, and Java, which are procedural. A procedural language defines *how* an application's operations should be performed and the order in which they are performed. A nonprocedural language, on the other hand, is concerned more with the results of an operation; the underlying software environment determines how the operations will be processed. This is not to say that SQL supports no procedural functionality. For example, stored procedures, added to many RDBMS products a number of years ago, are part of the SQL standard and provide procedural-like capabilities. (Stored procedures are discussed in Chapter 14.) Many of the RDBMS vendors added extensions to SQL to provide these procedural-like capabilities, such as Transact-SQL found in Sybase and Microsoft SQL Server and PL/SQL found in Oracle.

SQL still lacks many of the basic programming capabilities of most other computer languages. For this reason, SQL is often referred to as a data *sublanguage* because it is most often used in association with application programming languages such as C and Java, languages that are not designed for manipulating data stored in a database. As a result, SQL is used in conjunction with the application language to provide an efficient means of accessing that data, which is why SQL is considered a sublanguage.

The SQL Evolution

In the early 1970s, after E. F. Codd's groundbreaking paper had been published, IBM began to develop a language and a database system that could be used to implement that model. When it was first defined, the language was referred to as Structured English Query Language (SEQUEL). When it was discovered that SEQUEL was a trademark owned by Hawker-Siddeley Aircraft Company of the UK, the name was changed to SQL. As word got out that IBM was developing a relational database system based on SQL, other companies began to develop their own SQL-based products. In fact, Relational Software, Inc., now Oracle Corporation, released their database system before IBM got its product to market. As more vendors released their products, SQL began to emerge as the standard relational database language.

In 1986, the American National Standards Institute (ANSI) released the first published standard for the language (SQL-86), which was adopted by the International Organization for Standardization (ISO) in 1987. The standard was updated in 1989, 1992, 1999, 2003, 2006, 2008, and 2011 and work continues. It has grown over time—the original standard was well under 1000 pages, while the SQL:2011 version weighs in at more than 4050 pages. The standard was written in parts to permit more timely publication of revisions and to facilitate parallel work by different committees. Table 1-1 provides an overview of the parts and the current status of each.

RDBMS vendors had products on the market before there was a standard, and some of the features in those products were implemented differently enough that the standard could not accommodate them all when it was developed. We often call these *vendor extensions*. This may explain why there is no standard for a database. And as each release of the SQL standard comes out, RDBMS vendors have to work to incorporate the new standard into their products. For example, stored procedures and triggers were new in the SQL:1999 standard, but had been implemented in RDBMSs for many years. SQL:1999 merely standardized the language used to implement functions that already existed.

Part	Topic	Status
1	SQL/Framework	Completed in 1999, revised in 2003, corrections published in 2007, revised in 2008 and 2011, corrections published in 2013
2	SQL/Foundation	Completed in 1986, revised in 1999 and 2003, corrections published in 2007, revised in 2008 and 2011, corrections published in 2013
3	SQL/CLI	Completed in 1995, revised in 1999 and 2003, corrections published in 2005, revised in 2008
4	SQL/PSM	Completed in 1996, revised in 1999 and 2003, corrections published in 2007, revised in 2011, corrections published in 2013
5	SQL/Bindings	Established as a separate part in 1999, but merged back into Part 2 in 2003; there is currently no Part 5
6	SQL/Transaction	Project canceled; there is currently no Part 6
7	SQL/Temporal	Withdrawn; there is no Part 7. In SQL:2011, temporal features are included in Part 2.
8	SQL/Objects and Extended Objects	Merged into Part 2; there is no Part 8
9	SQL/MED	Started after 1999, completed in 2003, corrections published in 2005, revised in 2008, corrections published in 2010
10	SQL/OLB	Completed as ANSI standard in 1998, ISO version completed in 1999, revised in 2003, corrections published in 2007, revised in 2008, corrections published in 2010
11	SQL/Schemata	Extracted to a separate part in 2003, corrections published in 2007, revised in 2011
12	SQL/Replication	Project started in 2000, but subsequently dropped; there currently is no Part 12
13	SQL/JRT	Completed as ANSI standard in 1999, revision completed in 2003, corrections published in 2005, revised in 2008, corrections published in 2010
14	SQL/XML	Completed in 2003, expanded in 2006, corrections published in 2007, revised in 2011, corrections published in 2013

Table 1-1 Parts of the SQL Standard

NOTE

Although I discuss stored procedures in Chapter 14 and triggers in Chapter 15, I thought I'd give you a quick definition of each. A stored procedure is a set of SQL statements that are stored as an object in the database server but can be invoked by a client simply by calling the procedure. A trigger is similar to a stored procedure in that it is a set of SQL statements stored as an object in the database on the server. However, rather than being invoked from a client, a trigger is invoked automatically when some predefined event occurs, such as inserting or updating data.

Object Relational Model

The SQL language is based on the relational model, and up through SQL-92, so was the SQL standard. However, beginning with SQL:1999, the SQL standard extended beyond the pure relational model to include object-oriented constructs into the language. These constructs are based on the concepts inherent in *object-oriented programming*, a programming methodology that defines self-contained collections of data structures and routines (called *objects*). In object-oriented languages such as Java and C++, the objects interact with one another in ways that allow the language to address complex problems that were not easily resolved in traditional languages.

With the advent of object-oriented programming—along with advances in hardware and software technologies and the growing complexities of applications—it became increasingly apparent that a purely relational language was inadequate to meet the demands of the real world. Of specific concern was the fact that SQL could not support complex and user-defined data types or the extensibility required for more complicated applications.

Fueled by the competitive nature of the industry, RDBMS vendors took it upon themselves to augment their products and incorporate object-oriented functionality into their systems. The SQL standard follows suit and extends the relational model with object-oriented capabilities, such as methods, encapsulation, and complex user-defined data types, making SQL an *object-relational* database language. As shown in Table 1-1, Part 14 (SQL/XML) was created as part of SQL:2003, significantly expanded and republished with SQL:2006, and revised again with SQL:2011.

Conformance with the SQL Standard

Once SQL was standardized, it followed that the standard would also define what it took for an implementation of SQL (an RDBMS product) to be considered in conformance to that standard. For example, the SQL-92 standard provided three levels of conformance: entry, intermediate, and full. Most popular RDBMSs reached only entry-level conformance. Because of this, SQL takes a different approach to setting conformance standards. For a product to be in conformance with the SQL standard, it must support the Core SQL level of conformance. Core SQL in the SQL standard is defined as conformance to Part 2 (SQL/Foundation) and Part 11 (SQL/Schemata) of the standard.

In addition to the Core SQL level of conformance, vendors can claim conformance to any other part by meeting the minimum conformance requirements for that part.

NOTE

You can view information about the SQL standard by purchasing a copy of the appropriate standard document(s) published by ANSI and ISO. The standard is divided into nine documents (one part per document). The first document (ANSI/ISO/IEC 9075-1:2011) includes an overview of all nine parts. The suffix of each document name contains the year of publication, and different parts have different publication years because parts are updated and published independently by different committees. As you can see in Table 1-1, Parts 1, 2, 4, 11, and 14 were last published in 2011, while Parts 3, 9, 10, and 13 carry a 2008 publication date. You can purchase these documents online at the ANSI Electronic Standards Store (http://webstore.ansi.org/), the NCITS Standards Store (http://www.techstreet.com/ncitsgate.html), or the ISO Store (http://www.iso.org/iso/store.htm). On the ANSI site, note that there are two variants of each document with essentially identical content, named INCITS/ISO/IEC 9075 and ISO/IEC 9075. The ISO/IEC variants cost between $192 and $265 per document, while the INCITS/ISO/IEC variants cost only $60 per document. The ISO Store has the entire set of documents available on a convenient CD for 352 Swiss francs (about $377). Obviously, prices are subject to change at any time. Also available at no charge are corrections, called "Technical Corrigenda." As shown in Table 1-1, three parts had corrections published in 2005, six parts had corrections published in 2007, three parts had corrections in 2010, and four parts had corrections in 2013.

Types of SQL Statements

Although SQL is considered a sublanguage because of its nonprocedural nature, it is nonetheless a complete language in that it allows you to create and maintain database objects, secure those objects, and manipulate the data within the objects. One common method used to categorize SQL statements is to divide them according to the functions they perform. Based on this method, SQL can be separated into three types of statements:

- **Data Definition Language (DDL)** DDL statements are used to create, modify, or delete database objects such as tables, views, schemas, domains, triggers, and stored procedures. The SQL keywords most often associated with DDL statements are CREATE, ALTER, and DROP. Most SQL implementations also consider the TRUNCATE statement (added with SQL:2008) to be DDL. For example, you would use the CREATE TABLE statement to create a table, the ALTER TABLE statement to modify the table's properties, the TRUNCATE TABLE to empty all table contents, and the DROP TABLE statement to delete the table definition from the database.
- **Data Control Language (DCL)** DCL statements allow you to control who or what (a database user can be a person or an application program) has access to specific objects in your database. With DCL, you can grant or restrict access by using the GRANT or REVOKE statements, the two primary DCL commands. The DCL statements also allow you to control the type of access each user has to database objects. For example, you can determine which users can view a specific set of data and which users can manipulate that data.

- **Data Manipulation Language (DML)** DML statements are used to retrieve, add, modify, or delete data stored in your database objects. The primary keywords associated with DML statements are SELECT, INSERT, UPDATE, and DELETE, all of which represent the types of statements you'll probably be using the most. For example, you can use a SELECT statement to retrieve data from a table and an INSERT statement to add data to a table.

Most SQL statements that you'll be using fall neatly into one of these categories, and I'll be discussing a number of these statements throughout the remainder of the book.

NOTE

There are a number of ways you can classify statements in addition to how they're classified in the preceding list. For example, you can classify them according to how they're executed or whether or not they can be embedded in a standard programming language. The SQL standard provides 10 broad categories based on function. However, I use the preceding method because it is commonly used in SQL-related documentation and because it is a simple way to provide a good overview of the functionality inherent in SQL.

Types of Execution

In addition to defining how the language can be used, the SQL standard provides details on how SQL statements can be executed. These methods of execution, known as *binding styles,* not only affect the nature of the execution, but also determine which statements, at a minimum, must be supported by a particular binding style. The standard defines four methods of execution:

- **Direct invocation** By using this method, you can communicate directly from a front-end application, such as SQL Developer in Oracle or Management Studio in Microsoft SQL Server, to the database. (The front-end application and the database can be on the same computer, but often are not.) You simply enter your query into the application window and execute your SQL statement. The results of your query are returned to you as immediately as processor power and database constraints permit. This is a quick way to check data, verify connections, and view database objects. However, the SQL standard's guidelines about direct invocation are fairly minimal, so the methods used and SQL statements supported can vary widely from product to product.

- **Embedded SQL** In this method, SQL statements are encoded (embedded) directly in the host programming language. For example, you can embed SQL statements within C application code. Before the code is compiled, a preprocessor analyzes the SQL statements and splits them out from the C code. The SQL code is converted to a form the RDBMS can understand, and the remaining C code is compiled as it would be normally.

- **Module binding** This method allows you to create blocks of SQL statements (modules) that are separate from the host programming language. Once the module is created, it is combined into an application with a linker. A module contains, among other things, procedures, and it is the procedures that contain the actual SQL statements.
- **Call-level interface (CLI)** A CLI allows you to invoke SQL statements through an interface by passing SQL statements as argument values to subroutines. The statements are not precompiled as they are in embedded SQL and module binding. Instead, they are executed directly by the RDBMS.

Direct invocation, although not the most common method used, is the one I'll be using primarily for the examples and exercises in this book because it supports the submission of ad hoc queries to the database and generates immediate results. However, embedded SQL is currently the method most commonly used in business applications. I discuss this method, as well as module binding and CLI, in greater detail in Chapter 18.

SQL Standard versus Product Implementations

At the core of any SQL-based RDBMS is, of course, SQL itself. However, the language used is not pure SQL. Each product extends the language in order to implement vendor-defined features and enhanced SQL-based functionality. Moreover, a number of RDBMS products made it to market before there was a standard. Consequently, every vendor supports a slightly different variation of SQL, meaning that the language used in each product is implementation specific.

Ask the Expert

Q: You state that for an RDBMS to be in conformance with the SQL standard, it must comply with Core SQL. Are there any additional requirements to which a product must adhere?

A: Yes. In addition to Core SQL, an RDBMS must support either embedded SQL or module binding. Most products support only embedded SQL, with some supporting both. The SQL standard does not require RDBMS products to support direct invocation or CLI, although most do.

Q: What are the 10 categories used by the SQL standard to classify SQL statements?

A: The SQL standard classifies statements into the following categories: schema, data, data change, transaction, connection, control, session, diagnostics, dynamic, and embedded exception declaration. Keep in mind that these classifications are merely a tool that you can use to better understand the scope of the language and its underlying concepts. Ultimately, it is the SQL statements themselves—and what they can do—that is important.

Use a Relational Database Management System

Throughout this chapter, when discussing the relational model and SQL, I've often mentioned RDBMSs and how they use the SQL standard as the foundation for their products. A *relational database management system* is a program or set of programs that store, manage, retrieve, modify, and manipulate data in one or more relational databases. Oracle, Microsoft SQL Server, IBM's DB2, and the shareware product MySQL are all examples of RDBMSs. These products, like other RDBMSs, allow you to interact with the data stored in their systems. Although an RDBMS is not required to be based on SQL, most products on the market are SQL based and strive to conform to the SQL standard. At a minimum, these products claim entry-level conformance with the SQL-92 standard and are now working toward Core SQL conformance with the SQL standard.

In addition to complying with the SQL standard, most RDBMSs support other features, such as additional SQL statements, product-based administrative tools, and graphical user interface (GUI) applications that allow you to query and manipulate data, manage database objects, and administer the system and its structure. The types of functionality implemented and the methods used to deliver that functionality can vary widely from product to product. As databases grow larger, become more complicated, and are distributed over greater areas, the RDBMS products used to manage those databases become more complex and robust, meeting the demands of the market, as well as implementing new, more sophisticated technologies.

For example, SQL Server uses Transact-SQL, which encompasses both SQL and vendor extensions to provide the procedural statements necessary for triggers and stored procedures. On the other hand, Oracle provides procedural statements in a separate product component called PL/SQL. As a result, the SQL statements that I provide in the book might be slightly different in the product implementation that you're using.

Throughout the book, I will be using pure SQL in most of the examples and exercises. However, I realize that as a beginning SQL programmer, your primary interest is in implementing SQL in the real world. For that reason, I will at times use SQL Server (with Transact-SQL), Oracle (with PL/SQL), DB2 UDB, or MySQL to demonstrate or clarify a particular concept that can't be fully explained by pure SQL alone.

One of the advantages to using a product like Oracle or SQL Server is that they both support direct invocation through a front-end GUI application. SQL Server uses the Management Studio interface, shown in Figure 1-7. The GUI interface makes it possible for you to create ad hoc SQL queries, submit them to the DBMS for processing, and view the results, allowing you to apply what you're learning in the book to an actual SQL environment. Oracle has several solutions for a front-end GUI, including SQL Developer, shown in Figure 1-8.

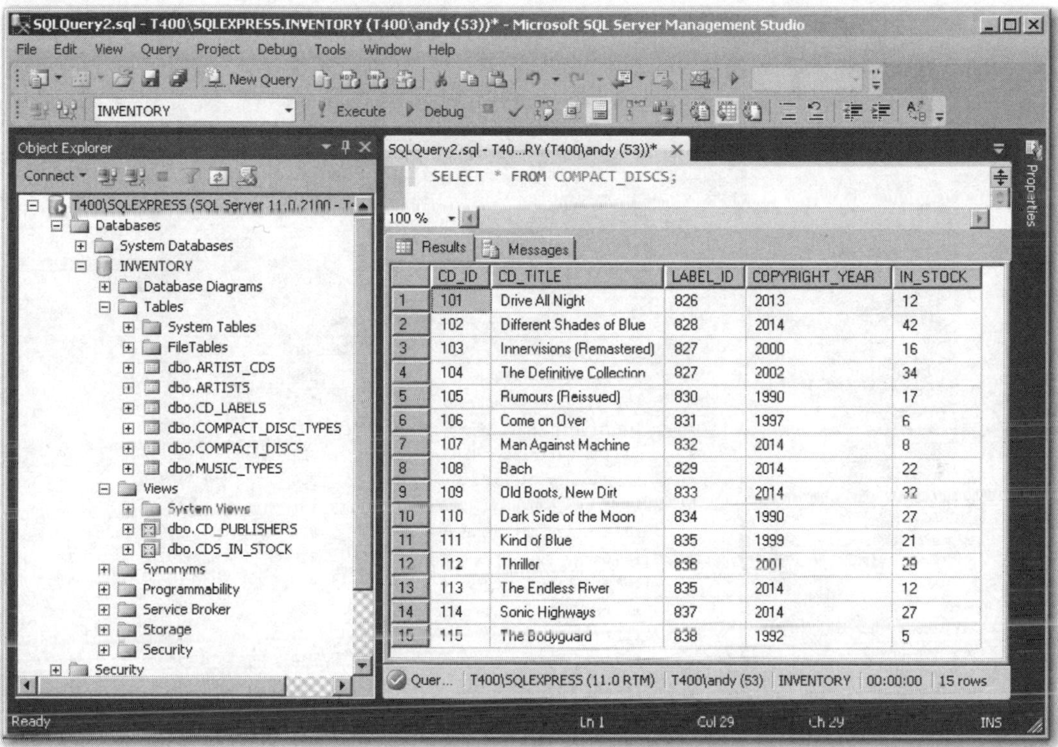

Figure 1-7 Using SQL Server Management Studio

In addition to GUI interfaces, most products include a command-line interface that can be used on older terminals that have no graphic capability. These interfaces are also useful for executing scripts containing SQL statements and for dial-up connections where graphical interfaces are too slow. Figure 1-9 shows the command-line interface for MySQL running on Microsoft Windows. MySQL also has a GUI interface called MySQL Workbench.

My use of these products by no means implies that I'm endorsing any of them over any other commercial products (such as Sybase or Informix) or shareware products (such as PostgreSQL), and indeed you're encouraged to use whatever RDBMS you have available, assuming it supports most of the functionality I'll be discussing in this book. However, I'm choosing MySQL, SQL Server, Oracle, and DB2 UDB for the majority of the examples in this book because I want to demonstrate how SQL is implemented in the real world and how SQL might differ from an implementation-specific version of the language, and these products supply me with the vehicles to do so. Keep in mind that in order for you to gain a full understanding of SQL and use it in various RDBMS products, you will need to understand both standard SQL and the language as it is implemented in the products you'll be using.

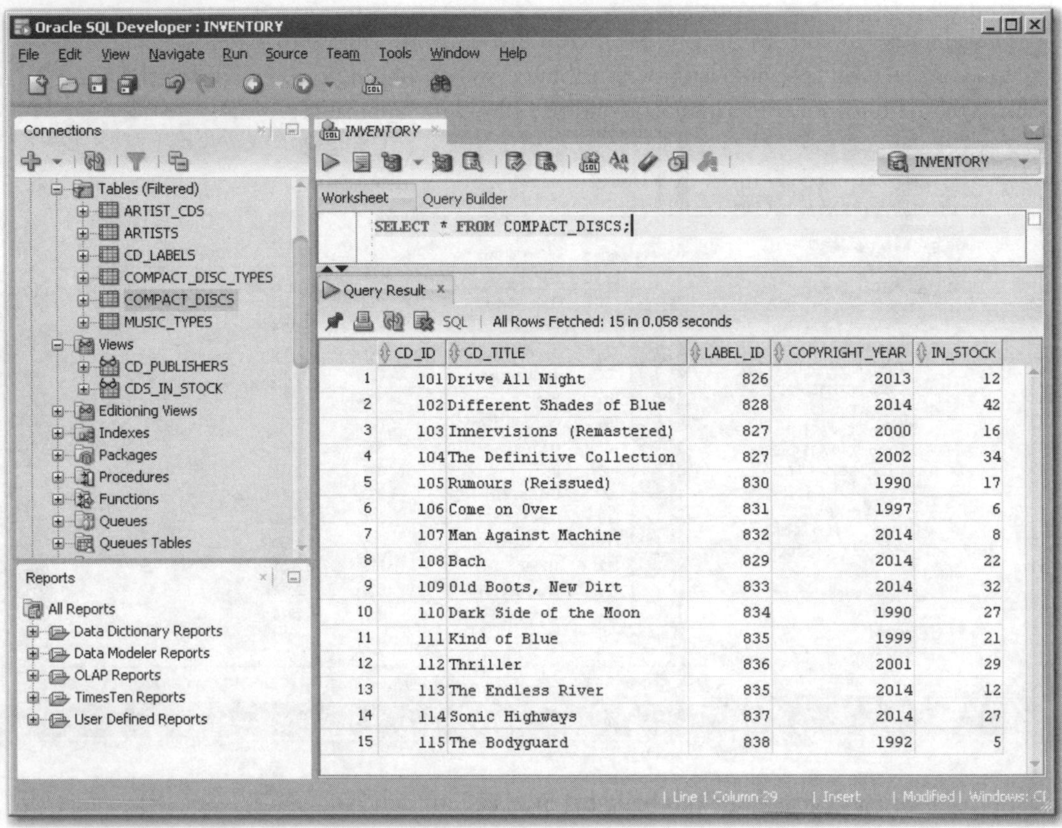

Figure 1-8 Using Oracle's SQL Developer

Try This 1-2 Connecting to a Database

Although this book focuses primarily on pure SQL, to try out the examples and do most of the exercises, you'll need access to an RDBMS in order to execute SQL statements. As a result, one of the first things you should do is make sure you're able to access an SQL environment. This exercise will help you do that; however, unlike most other exercises in the book, this one will require more effort on your part to go to resources outside the book to set yourself up with an RDBMS that allows you to invoke SQL statements directly. To that end, this exercise tries to get you started, but you must use your own initiative to ensure that you have an environment in which you're comfortable working.

```
C:\Program Files\MySQL\MySQL Server 5.1\bin\mysql.exe
mysql> use inventory
Database changed
mysql> SELECT * FROM COMPACT_DISCS;
+-------+---------------------------+----------+----------------+----------+
| CD_ID | CD_TITLE                  | LABEL_ID | COPYRIGHT_YEAR | IN_STOCK |
+-------+---------------------------+----------+----------------+----------+
|   101 | Drive All Night           |      826 |           2013 |       12 |
|   102 | Different Shades of Blue  |      828 |           2014 |       42 |
|   103 | Innervisions (Remastered) |      827 |           2000 |       16 |
|   104 | The Definitive Collection |      827 |           2002 |       34 |
|   105 | Rumours (Reissued)        |      830 |           1990 |       17 |
|   106 | Come on Over              |      831 |           1997 |        6 |
|   107 | Man Against Machine       |      832 |           2014 |        8 |
|   108 | Bach                      |      829 |           2014 |       22 |
|   109 | Old Boots, New Dirt       |      833 |           2014 |       32 |
|   110 | Dark Side of the Moon     |      834 |           1990 |       27 |
|   111 | Kind of Blue              |      835 |           1999 |       21 |
|   112 | Thriller                  |      836 |           2001 |       29 |
|   113 | The Endless River         |      835 |           2014 |       12 |
|   114 | Sonic Highways            |      837 |           2014 |       27 |
|   115 | The Bodyguard             |      838 |           1992 |        5 |
+-------+---------------------------+----------+----------------+----------+
15 rows in set (0.10 sec)

mysql>
```

Figure 1-9 Using the MySQL command-line interface

Step by Step

1. Identify the RDBMS you plan to use for the exercises in this book. Perhaps there is a system you're already familiar with or one that's available to you in your work environment. If you don't have anything available at work and you're not ready to purchase a product, check online to see what might be available. Most RDBMS vendors offer a free of charge, basic, restricted-use version of their product, often called the "Express Edition"; others offer a trial version that may be used free of charge for a limited time period. For example, you can download Oracle Express Edition for Linux or Windows at http://www.oracle.com/technetwork/database/database-technologies/express-edition/downloads/index.html, or you can download SQL Server Express (for Windows) at http://www.microsoft.com/en-us/server-cloud/products/sql-server-editions/sql-server-express.aspx. (You will need a high-speed Internet connection to download large files.)

   If you prefer a freeware product, MySQL Community Server Edition is a popular choice, particularly because it has versions for Mac OS X, Windows, and various versions of Linux and Unix. In fact, Yahoo! and Google both use MySQL extensively in a configuration known as LAMP (Linux, Apache, MySQL, and PHP). You can download the MySQL Community Server at no charge from http:// http://dev.mysql.com/downloads/mysql/. MySQL Enterprise Server, on the other hand, is a fee-based edition supported by the vendor. (MySQL is currently owned by Oracle Corporation.)

(continued)

Before you decide on a particular product, do the necessary research to make sure it supports direct invocation, preferably though a GUI application, and can run in your computer environment. Also check to see how much of the SQL standard it supports, and review any licensing agreements to make sure you're in compliance. If a system is available through your work, be sure to talk to database and network administrators to determine which server you should use, whether and how you should download a copy, and how to make your connection to the SQL server. You'll often need an account to connect to the RDBMS, so if this is the case, find out what username and password you should use.

2. Once you've established which RDBMS you'll be using, install it on your computer. If you'll be connecting to a system over the network, you'll need to install only the client tools on your local computer.

3. Open the client GUI that allows you to directly invoke SQL statements. When you open the GUI, you might be prompted for a username and password. When and if you're prompted varies depending on the product you're using, whether you're connecting over the network, whether the RDBMS is set up as a stand-alone system, and other variables specific to the product. In addition, a product such as SQL Server offers security integrated with the operating system, so you may be prompted for a server name only.

4. Execute a SELECT statement in the application input window. I realize that we haven't covered SELECT statements yet, but the basic syntax is relatively easy:

```
SELECT * FROM <table>
```

The <table> placeholder should be replaced with the name of a table in an existing database.

The purpose of this exercise is simply to verify that you have connectivity with the data stored in your RDBMS. Most products include sample data, and that is the data you're trying to connect to. Check product documentation or check with the database administrator to verify whether a database exists that you can access. If not, you can download the SQL for the INVENTORY database from the download site http://www.mhprofessional.com/getpage.php?c=computing_downloads.php&cat=112, and use it to create your database objects.

If you're working in Oracle and the sample schemas were installed, you can execute the following statement:

```
SELECT * FROM HR.EMPLOYEE;
```

Start SQL Developer, select SQL Worksheet from the Tools menu, and connect as the system user. To execute the SELECT statement, type it in the input window in SQL Developer and then click the execute icon (the green triangle).

If you're working in SQL Server with sample data installed, you can execute the following statements:

```
USE pubs
SELECT * FROM employee;
```

To execute the statements, type them in the SQL Query window of SQL Server Management Studio and then click Execute.

If you're working in a command-line interface, simply type the SQL statements and press ENTER.

Once you execute each statement, the results of your query appear in the output window. At this point, don't concern yourself with the meaning of each word in the SQL statement or with the query results. Your only concern is to make sure everything is working. If you can't execute the statement, check with your database administrator or the product documentation.

5. Close the GUI application without saving your query.

Try This Summary

As I said at the beginning of the exercise, it is different from most of the other ones in the book because you are basically on your own to establish connectivity with your RDBMS. Again, this is because SQL is a language standard, independent of RDBMS implementations, and vendor-specific issues are, for the most part, beyond the scope of this book. In addition, the methods used to connect to a database, the tools available to make those connections, and the way in which an RDBMS is set up vary from product to product, environment to environment, and even operating system to operating system. However, the time you take now to research which product you'll use and to make sure you can connect to data in an existing database will prove invaluable as you apply the information discussed in the rest of the book.

Chapter 1 Self Test

1. What is a database?

2. Which of the following objects make up a relation?

   A Data types

   B Tuples

   C Attributes

   D Forms

3. A(n) _______________ is a set of data whose values make up an instance of each attribute defined for that relation.

4. What are the differences between the first normal form and the second normal form?

5. A relation is in third normal form if it is in second normal form and if it complies with the other guidelines of that form. What are those guidelines?
6. What are the three primary types of relationships supported by a relational database?
7. In your data model, you have two relations associated with each other by a many-to-many relationship. How will this relationship be physically implemented in a relational database?
8. How does SQL differ from programming languages such as C, COBOL, and Java?
9. What factors have contributed to the SQL standard incorporating object-oriented capabilities?
10. Which level of conformance must an RDBMS support in order to comply with the SQL standard?

    A Entry

    B Core

    C Full

    D Intermediate
11. What are the differences between a DDL statement and a DML statement?
12. What method of executing SQL statements would you use if you want to communicate directly with an SQL database from a front-end application?
13. What four methods does the SQL standard support for the execution of SQL statements?
14. What is a relational database management system?
15. What is an example of an RDBMS?

Chapter 2

Working with the SQL Environment

Key Skills & Concepts

- Understand the SQL Environment
- Understand SQL Catalogs
- Name Objects in an SQL Environment
- Create a Schema
- Create a Database

In Chapter 1, I discuss relational theory, SQL, and relational database management systems (RDBMSs). In this chapter, I want to take this discussion one step further and introduce you to the SQL environment as it is defined in the SQL standard. The SQL environment provides the structure in which SQL is implemented. Within this structure, you can use SQL statements to define database objects and store data in those objects. However, before you start writing SQL statements, you should have a basic understanding of the foundations on which the SQL environment is built so you can apply this information throughout the rest of the book. In fact, you might find it helpful to refer back to this chapter often to help gain a conceptual understanding of the SQL environment and how it relates to the SQL elements you'll learn about in subsequent chapters.

Understand the SQL Environment

The *SQL environment* is, quite simply, the sum of all the parts that make up that environment. Each distinct part, or component, works in conjunction with other components to support SQL operations such as creating and modifying objects, storing and querying data, or modifying and deleting that data. Taken together, these components form a model on which an RDBMS can be based. This does not imply, however, that RDBMS vendors adhere strictly to this model; which components they implement and how they implement them are left, for the most part, to the discretion of those vendors. Even so, I want to provide you with an overview of the way in which the SQL environment is defined in terms of its distinct components as they are described in the SQL standard.

The SQL environment is made up of six types of components, as shown in Figure 2-1. The SQL client and SQL servers are part of the SQL implementation and are therefore subtypes of that component.

Notice that there is only one SQL agent and one SQL implementation, but there are multiple components for other types, such as catalogs and sites. According to SQL, there must be exactly one SQL agent and SQL implementation and zero or more SQL client modules, authorization identifiers, and catalogs. The standard does not specify how many sites are supported, but implies multiple sites.

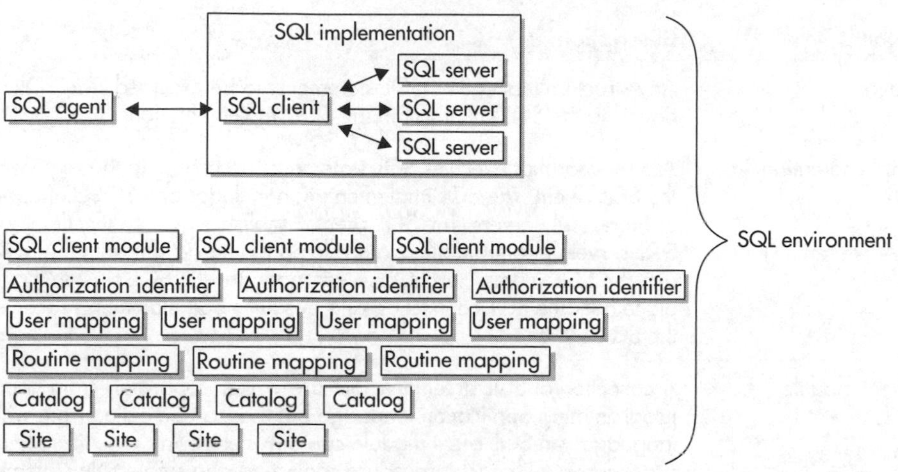

Figure 2-1 The components of the SQL environment

Each type of component performs a specific function within the SQL environment. Table 2-1 describes the eight types.

For the most part, you need to have only a basic understanding of the components that make up an SQL environment (in terms of beginning SQL programming). However, one of these components—the catalog—plays a more critical role than the others with regard to what you'll be learning in this book. Therefore, I will cover this topic in more detail and explain how it relates to the management of data and the objects that hold that data.

Understand SQL Catalogs

In the previous section, "Understand the SQL Environment," I state that an SQL environment is the sum of all parts that make up that environment. You can use the same logic to describe a *catalog*, in that a catalog is a collection of schemas and these schemas, taken together, define a namespace within the SQL environment.

NOTE

A namespace is a naming structure that identifies related components in a specified environment. A namespace is often depicted as an inverted tree configuration to represent the hierarchical relationship of objects. For example, suppose your namespace includes two objects: OBJECT_1 and OBJECT_2. If the namespace is called NAME_1, the full object names will be NAME_1.OBJECT_1 and NAME_1.OBJECT_2 (or some such naming configuration), thus indicating that they share the same namespace.

Component Type	Description
SQL agent	Any structure that causes SQL statements to be executed. The SQL agent is bound to the SQL client within the SQL implementation.
SQL implementation	A processor that executes SQL statements according to the requirements of the SQL agent. The SQL implementation includes one SQL client and one or more SQL servers. The SQL client establishes SQL connections with the SQL servers and maintains data related to interactions with the SQL agent and the SQL servers. An SQL server manages the SQL session that takes place over the SQL connection and executes SQL statements received from the SQL client.
SQL client module	A collection of SQL statements that are written separately from your programming application language but that can be called from within that language. An SQL client module contains zero or more externally invoked procedures, with each procedure consisting of a single SQL statement. SQL client modules reside within the SQL environment and are processed by the SQL implementation, unlike embedded SQL, which is written within the application programming language and precompiled before the programming language is compiled. SQL client modules are discussed in more detail in Chapter 18.
Authorization identifier	An identifier that represents a user or role that is granted specific access privileges to objects and data within the SQL environment. A user is an individual security account that can represent an individual, an application, or a system service. A *role* is a set of predefined privileges that can be assigned to a user or to another role. I discuss authorization identifiers, users, and roles in Chapter 6.
User mapping	A user mapping pairs an authorization identifier with a foreign server descriptor.
Routine mapping	A routine mapping pairs an SQL-invoked routine with a foreign server descriptor.
Catalog	A group of schemas collected together in a defined namespace. Each catalog contains the information schema, which includes descriptors of a number of schema objects. The catalog itself provides a hierarchical structure for organizing data within the schemas. (A *schema* is basically a container for objects such as tables, views, and domains, all of which I'll be discussing in greater detail in the next section, "Understand SQL Catalogs.")
Site	A group of base tables that contain SQL data, as described by the contents of the schemas. This data may be thought of as "the database," but keep in mind that the SQL standard does not include a definition of the term "database" because it has so many different meanings.

Table 2-1 The Component Types Supported in an SQL Environment

Another way to look at a catalog is as a hierarchical structure with the catalog as the parent object and the schemas as the child objects, as shown in Figure 2-2. At the top of the hierarchy is the SQL environment, which can contain zero or more catalogs (although an environment with zero catalogs wouldn't do you much good because the catalog is where you'll find the data definitions and SQL data). The schemas are located at the third tier, beneath the catalog, and the schema objects are at the fourth tier.

You can compare the relationships between the objects in a catalog to the relationships between files and directories in your computer's operating system. The catalog is represented by a directory off the root; the schemas, by subdirectories; and the schema objects, by files within the subdirectories.

Like the hierarchical structure of a file system, the structure of a catalog is *logical* in nature; that is, a file system is presented in a hierarchical form (like that of Windows Explorer), but that doesn't mean that the files are actually stored hierarchically on your hard disk. In the same

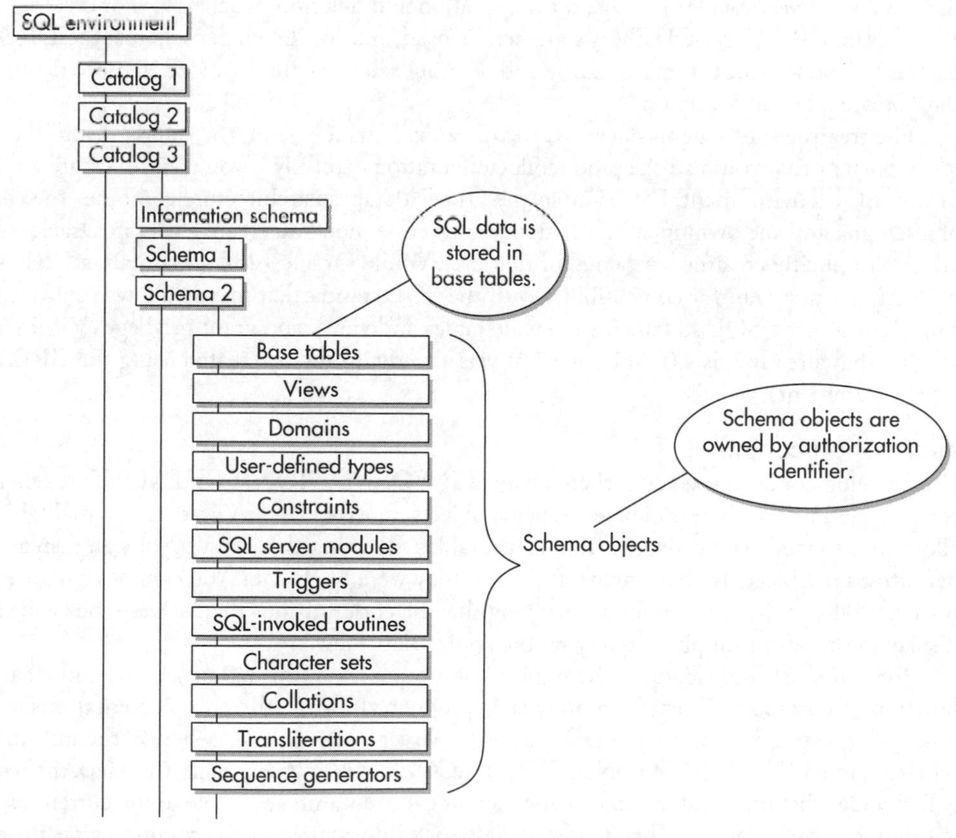

Figure 2-2 The components of a catalog

sense, the catalog hierarchy is merely a representation of the relationships between objects in your SQL environment. It doesn't imply any physical containment or organization. How these objects are actually implemented with regard to the catalog structure and which ones are implemented are left to the discretion of the RDBMS vendor. In fact, the SQL standard doesn't define language for the creation or deletion of catalogs; this, too, is left up to the vendors, and few systems even support catalogs.

Schemas

Each catalog contains one or more schemas. A *schema* is a set of related objects that are collected under a common namespace. The schema acts as a container for those objects, which in turn store the SQL data or perform other data-related functions. Each schema, the objects contained in the schema, and the SQL data within those objects are owned by the authorization identifier associated with that schema.

Unlike catalogs, schemas are widely implemented in RDBMS products. However, as with catalogs, SQL leaves most of the implementation details up to the vendor, although the standard does provide language for the creation and deletion of schemas. For creating a schema, the CREATE SCHEMA statement is used, and for deleting a schema, the DROP SCHEMA statement is used. Creating and deleting schemas are discussed in more detail in the "Create a Schema" section.

The treatment of schemas in an RDBMS can vary widely from the standard, and therefore, it's important that you read the product documentation carefully if you want to create a schema in your SQL environment. For example, the Oracle database architecture combines the concept of a schema and the owning authorization identifier—when you create a user in Oracle, you are also implicitly creating a schema for that user. While Oracle 12*c* does contain a CREATE SCHEMA statement for compatibility with the SQL standard, it merely allows you to execute a batch of specific SQL statements to create tables and views and grant privileges within a schema that already exists (that is, one that was already implicitly created using the CREATE USER statement).

Information Schema

Each catalog contains a special schema named INFORMATION_SCHEMA. This schema contains definitions for a number of schema objects, mostly views. A *view* is a virtual table that allows you to view data collected from actual tables. By using these views, you can display the definitions of objects in that catalog as though they were SQL data. You cannot change any of the data—if you did, you would be changing the object definitions themselves—but you can display information simply by querying the appropriate view.

As with most SQL features, the implementation of the information schema and what functions are supported vary from product to product, although these implementations are usually fairly straightforward. For example, SQL Server 2012 includes a view in the information schema named INFORMATION_SCHEMA.COLUMNS. If you query this view, the results will include a list that contains information about every column accessible to the current user within the current database. The results include such information as the column name, the data type assigned to that column, and the owner (authorization identifier) who owns that column.

Schema Objects

At the bottom tier of the catalog hierarchy sit the schema objects. The *schema objects* are a set of related components that are contained within a schema. This is the level where the SQL data is stored and, consequently, the level that concerns SQL programmers the most. By using SQL, you'll be able to define SQL objects, modify those definitions, and store and manipulate SQL data within the objects. In fact, most of what you'll be doing in this book from here on in has a direct impact on or is directly connected with the schema objects.

The SQL standard defines 12 types of schema objects. These objects, described in Table 2-2, provide the foundation for the SQL environment and the structure for the way in which data is stored within that environment. I'll be discussing most of these objects in greater detail later in the book; as a result, I've included references, where appropriate, to the applicable chapters.

Schema Object	Description
Base table	The basic unit of data management in the SQL environment. A table is made up of columns and rows and is analogous to a relation (with its attributes and tuples) in relational theory. Each column is associated with a data type and holds values that are somehow related to each other. For example, a table about customers would contain columns that contain data about those customers, such as their names and addresses. (See Chapter 3.)
View	A virtual table that is created when the view is invoked (by calling its name). The table doesn't actually exist—only the SQL statement that defines the table is stored in the database. When that statement is invoked, the view pulls data from base tables and displays the results as if you're viewing the results of a base table query. (See Chapter 5.)
Domain	A user-defined object that can be specified in place of a data type when defining a column (a process part of creating or altering a table definition). A domain is based on an SQL data type but can include a default value and a constraint, which further limits the values that can be stored in a particular column. (See Chapter 4.)
User-defined type (UDT)	A user-defined object that can be specified in place of a data type when defining a column. SQL supports two types of UDTs: distinct and structured. *Distinct* types are based on SQL data types and their defined values. *Structured* types are made up of attribute values, each of which is based on an SQL data type. (See Chapter 3.)
Constraint	A restriction defined on a table, column, or domain that limits the type of data that can be inserted into the applicable object. For example, you can create a constraint on a column (known as an *assertion* or *check constraint*) that restricts the values that can be inserted into that column to a specific range or list of numbers. (See Chapter 4.)

Table 2-2 The Types of Objects That Can Be Defined in Each Schema *(continued)*

Schema Object	Description
SQL Server module	A module that contains SQL-invoked routines. A *module* is an object that contains SQL statements, routines, or procedures. An SQL-invoked routine is a function or procedure that can be invoked from SQL. Both functions and procedures are types of SQL statements that can handle parameters (values passed to a statement when you invoke that statement). A *function* can receive input parameters and return a value based on the expression included in the function statement. A *procedure* can receive input and return output parameters. (See Chapter 14.)
Trigger	An object associated with a base table that defines an action to be taken when an event occurs related to that table. The action that caused the trigger to fire (execute) can be an insert into, delete from, or update of a base table. For example, a row deleted from one table might cause a trigger to fire that then deletes data from another table. (See Chapter 15.)
SQL-invoked routine	A function or procedure that can be invoked from SQL. An SQL-invoked routine can be a schema object or be embedded in a module, which is also a schema object. (See Chapter 14.)
Character set	A collection of character attributes that defines how characters are represented. A character set has three attributes: the repertoire, form-of-use, and default collation. The *repertoire* determines which characters can be expressed (for example, A, B, C, and so on). The *form-of-use* determines how the characters are represented as strings to hardware and software (for example, one byte per character, two bytes per character). The *default collation* determines how those strings compare with one another.
Collation	A set of rules that controls how character strings compare with one another within a particular repertoire. This information can then be used to order the characters (for example, A comes before B, B comes before C). A default collation is defined for each character set.
Transliteration	An operation that maps characters from one character set to characters in another set. Transliterations can include such operations as translating characters from uppercase to lowercase or from one alphabet into another.
Sequence generator	A mechanism for generating successive numeric data values (integers), one at a time. Sequence generators retain a *current base value,* which is used as the basis for generating the next sequential value.

Table 2-2 The Types of Objects That Can Be Defined in Each Schema

As I said, I'll be discussing most of the items in the table in greater detail later in the book. However, the last three items, which are all related to character sets, are covered only briefly. The character sets, collations, and translations supported by RDBMSs can vary from product to product, and so can the implementation of these features. Throughout this book, the examples and projects I'll be giving you all rely on whatever the default character set is for the

Ask the Expert

Q: You describe a domain as a user-defined object that is based on a data type but can include a default value and a constraint. How does this type of domain differ from a domain as you describe it in the relational model?

A: In many ways the two are the same, and for all practical purposes, you can think of an SQL domain as a counterpart to a domain in the relational model. There is one subtle difference, however—a domain in the relational model is merely a description of the data that can be included in an attribute (column) associated with that particular domain. An SQL domain, on the other hand, restricts the data that can be inserted into the column. An SQL domain does this through the use of constraints, which are validation rules that are part of the system of data integrity. The main idea to keep in mind is that a domain in the relational model is a logical concept, whereas an SQL domain is a physical one.

Q: When you talk about schema objects, you mention base tables. Does SQL support any other types of tables?

A: The SQL standard supports three types of tables: base tables, transient tables, and derived tables. The base table is a type of table whose data is actually stored somewhere. In other words, SQL data is stored in a base table. A transient table is a named table that is implicitly created during the evaluation of a query expression or the execution of a trigger. A derived table is the returned table that contains the result of a query (the set of data specific to the query).

product that you're using. If you want to change that character set, either at the default level or at the database or table level, you should first carefully review the product documentation to find out what is supported and how those features are implemented.

Then What Is a Database?

As you might have noticed, nowhere in the structure of the SQL environment or a catalog is there mention of a database. The reason for this is that nowhere in the SQL standard is the term "database" defined. In fact, the only mention of a database in terms of how it might fit into the structure of the SQL environment is that you can consider the sites to be the database, although this is offered more as a suggestion than an absolute definition. Although the standard uses the word to refer to SQL as a database language, it never actually defines the term.

This approach might be fine for the standard, but in the real world, it can be difficult for an RDBMS to create an SQL environment without creating some sort of component that users can point to and say, "Yes, there is the database." And indeed, most products allow you to create, alter, and delete objects that are called databases. In SQL Server, for example, an instance of the DBMS software can manage any number of databases, with each database being a logical collection of database objects that the designer chooses to manage together. Sybase, MySQL, and IBM's DB2 have similar architecture. SQL Server provides a management console called Microsoft SQL Server Management Studio to view and manipulate database objects. The Object Explorer panel along the left margin provides a hierarchical, directory-like structure that includes a Database node, with each database shown under it, and objects such as tables shown under each database. Figure 2-3 shows SQL Server Management Studio with the INVENTORY database expanded down to the columns of the ARTIST_CDS table.

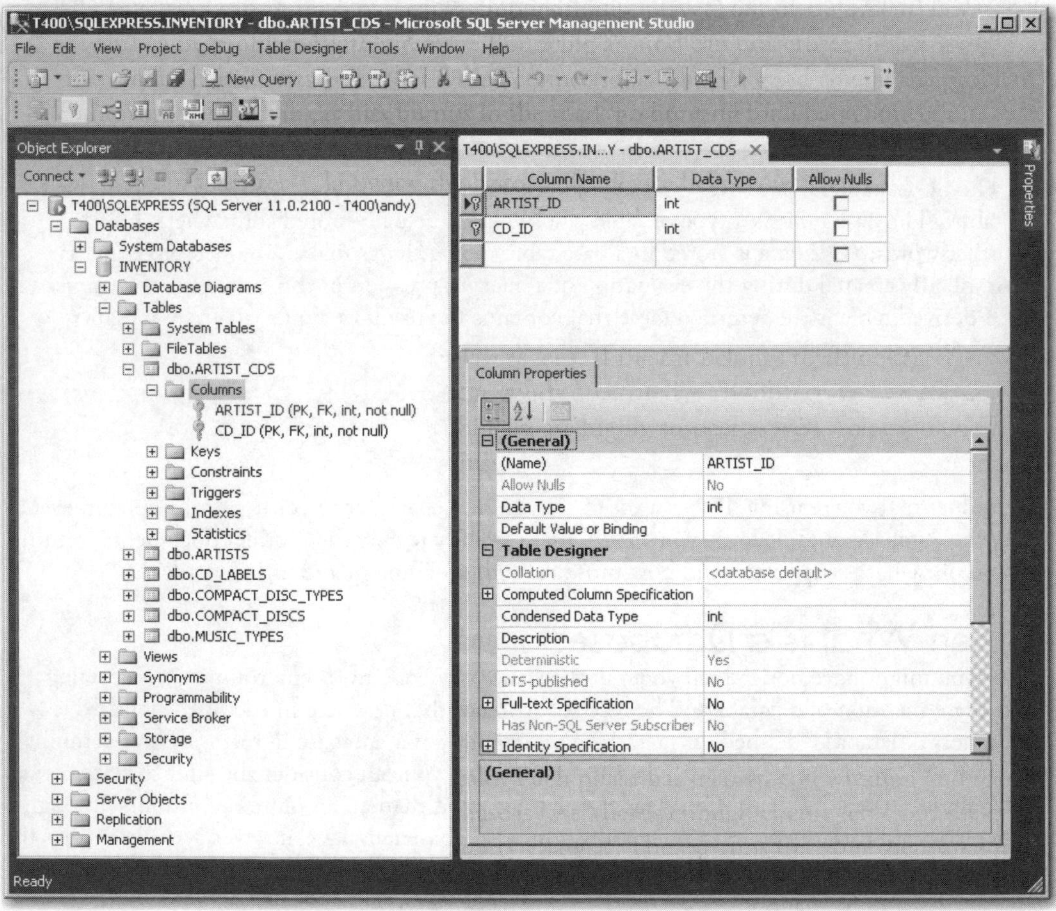

Figure 2-3 Microsoft SQL Server Management Studio with INVENTORY database expanded

The Oracle DBMS has a different architecture. Each instance of the DBMS software manages only one database. However, each database user gets a distinct schema for storage of database objects owned by that user. So, in Oracle a schema is much like what SQL Server calls a database. Oracle has a tool called SQL Developer that is functionally similar to the SQL Server Management Studio. Figure 2-4 shows SQL Developer with the INVENTORY schema expanded down to the columns in the ARTIST_CDS table. Oracle was the first commercially available RDBMS, and since it was created long before there was an SQL standard, it should be no surprise that it is architecturally different.

In Chapter 1, I stated that a database is a collection of data organized in a structured format that is defined by the metadata that describes that structure. In both SQL Server and Oracle you can see how this definition applies. Both systems (and any true RDBMS you're working with) collect the data in a structured format and define that data by the use of schemas, which contain the metadata. This definition can also be applied to the SQL standard and its construction of the SQL environment and catalogs. SQL data is stored in an organized format within base tables. These base tables are contained within a schema, which defines those tables, thereby defining the data. So even though the SQL standard doesn't actually define the term "database," it nonetheless supports the concept of a database, as do the RDBMS products that implement SQL.

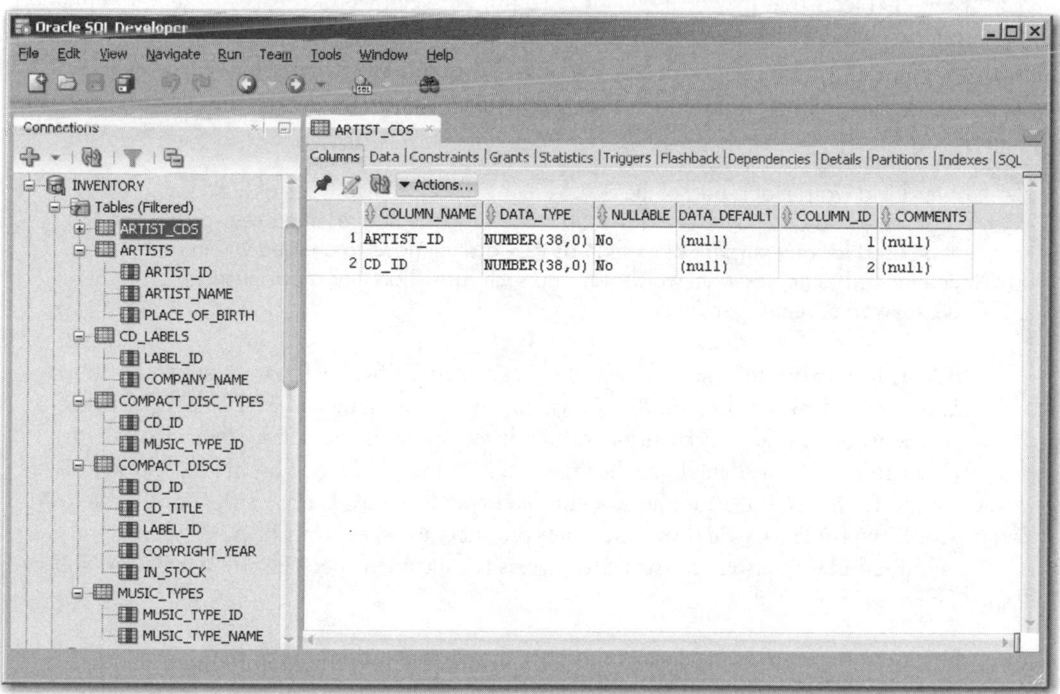

Figure 2-4 Oracle SQL Developer with INVENTORY schema expanded

Name Objects in an SQL Environment

Up to this point in the book, I have provided you with a lot of conceptual and background information. The reason for this is that I want you to have a basic foundation in SQL before you actually start writing SQL statements. I believe that with this information, you will be better able to grasp the logic behind the SQL code that you create and the reason for creating it, and I have no doubt that you're more than ready to start writing those statements.

However, before I actually start getting into the meat of SQL, there's one more topic that I need to cover briefly—object identifiers. An *identifier* is a name given to an SQL object. The name must contain fewer than 128 characters and must follow defined conventions. An identifier can be assigned to any object that you can create with SQL statements, such as domains, tables, columns, views, or schemas. The SQL standard defines two types of identifiers: regular identifiers and delimited identifiers.

Regular identifiers are fairly restrictive and must follow specific conventions:

- The names are not case sensitive. For example, Artist_Name is the same as ARTIST_NAME and artist_name.
- Only letters, digits, and underscores are allowed. For example, you can create identifiers such as First_Name, 1stName, or FIRST_NAME. Notice that the underscore is the only valid character that may be used as a separator between words. Spaces are not acceptable, nor are dashes (dashes are interpreted as subtraction operators).
- No SQL reserved keywords can be used.

NOTE

A keyword is a word that is part of the SQL lexicon. There are two types of SQL keywords: reserved and nonreserved. As the name suggests, the reserved keywords cannot be used for any purpose other than as they are intended to be used within an SQL statement. The nonreserved words have no such restriction. For a complete list of the SQL keywords, see Appendix A.

SQL is insensitive to case with regard to regular identifiers. All names are changed to uppercase by SQL when they are stored, which is why 1stName and 1STNAME are read as identical values. As already mentioned, case insensitivity is the default behavior in most RDBMSs and while the default can be changed in some products, I highly recommend that you don't change it because it's not consistent with the SQL standard, and it leads to compatibility problems should you use other products to access your data.

Delimited identifiers are not as restrictive as regular identifiers, but they still must follow specific conventions:

- The identifier must be enclosed in a set of double quotation marks, such as the "ArtistName" identifier.
- The quotation marks are not stored in the database, but all other characters are stored as they appear in the SQL statement.

- The names are case sensitive. For example, "Artist_Name" *is not* the same as "artist_name" or ARTIST_NAME, but "ARTIST_NAME" *is* the same as ARTIST_NAME and Artist_Name (because regular identifiers are converted to uppercase).
- Most characters are allowed, including spaces.
- SQL reserved keywords can be used.

When you're deciding how to name your SQL objects, there are a number of systems that you can follow. The first choice you'll have to make is whether you want to use regular or delimited identifiers. You'll also want to decide on other issues, such as case and the use of underscores, and whether your identifiers will be singular or plural. For example, you could name a table CompactDiscTypes, compact_disc_types, COMPACT_DISC_TYPES, "Compact Disc Types," or some other form of that name. The important part to remember is that you should choose a naming convention and stick with it throughout the coding for a particular database. You'll also want to take the RDBMS you are using into account. Earlier versions of the SQL standard allowed only uppercase letters in object names (a consequence of mainframe systems that used a character set called EBCDIC that in the early days contained only capital letters). As a result, many of the older RDBMS products, including Oracle and DB2, automatically fold lowercase names into uppercase. So, you may create a table named CompactDiscTypes, but it will appear as COMPACTDISCTYPES in the catalog, which is obviously not a very user-friendly name. By the way, MySQL follows the case sensitivity of the operating system, so on Windows it is case insensitive, but on Linux and Unix, it is case sensitive. And finally, take note of the maximum identifier length in the RDBMS product you are using. While SQL Server allows 128-character names (one character longer than the standard allows), Oracle allows up to 30 characters (8 for database names), and many others have maximum lengths that are shorter than 128.

NOTE

For the examples and projects in this book, I use regular identifiers with uppercase letters and underscores used to separate words (for example, COMPACT_DISC_TYPES). I do this because such identifiers are compatible with (and form user-friendly object names in) all RDBMS products. However, I acknowledge that SQL Server users in particular like to use mixed-case identifiers.

Qualified Names

All schema object identifiers are qualified by the logical way in which they fit into the hierarchical structure of the SQL environment. A fully qualified name includes the name of the catalog, the name of the schema, and the name of the schema object, each separated by a period. For example, suppose you have a table named ARTIST_CDS. The table is in the INVENTORY schema, which is in the MUSIC catalog. The fully qualified name for that table would be MUSIC.INVENTORY.ARTIST_CDS.

The way in which these naming conventions play out in various RDBMS products depends on how that product has implemented the structure of the SQL environment. For example, a fully qualified name in SQL Server is based on the server name, database name, owner name, and object name. In this case, a table named ARTISTS might have a fully qualified name of SERVER01.INVENTORY.DBO.ARTISTS, where SERVER01 is the name of the server, INVENTORY is the name of the database, and DBO (which refers to database owner) is the name of the object owner. To determine how fully qualified names are handled for a particular RDBMS, check the product documentation.

Create a Schema

Now that you have a fundamental understanding of how to use identifiers to name SQL objects, you're ready to start writing SQL statements. I'll begin with the CREATE SCHEMA statement because schemas are at the top of the SQL hierarchy in terms of which objects the SQL standard allows you to create. (Remember, the SQL standard doesn't provide any sort of CREATE CATALOG or CREATE DATABASE statement. It's left up to the RDBMS vendors to determine how and whether to implement these objects.) And as already mentioned, Oracle automatically creates a schema for each user, so while it has a CREATE SCHEMA statement, it is only there for compatibility with the SQL standard. In the next section, "Create a Database," I will slip out of SQL mode and discuss database creation because most RDBMS products support the creation of database objects, and you'll probably find that you'll want to create a database in order to try out the examples and projects in this book.

The place to start with any type of SQL statement is the syntax that defines the statements. The following syntax shows the basic components of the CREATE SCHEMA statement:

```
CREATE SCHEMA <schema name clause>
[ <schema character set or path> ]
[ <schema elements> ]
```

NOTE

The angle brackets contain information that serves as a placeholder for a value or clause related to that information. For example, <schema name clause> is a placeholder for keywords and values related to naming the schema. The square brackets, on the other hand, mean that the clause is optional. You do not have to specify a character set, path, or schema element.

Let's look at the syntax for the CREATE SCHEMA statement piece by piece. The SQL keywords CREATE SCHEMA alert the SQL implementation to the type of statement being executed. This is followed by the <schema name clause> placeholder, which can include a name for the schema, an authorization identifier (preceded by the AUTHORIZATION keyword), or both. As a result, the schema name clause can take any one of the following forms:

- <schema name>
- AUTHORIZATION <authorization identifier>
- <schema name> AUTHORIZATION <authorization identifier>

The <authorization identifier> value specifies who owns the schema and its objects. If none is specified, the value defaults to the current user. If no <schema name> value is specified, a name is created that's based on the authorization identifier.

The next clause, <schema character set or path>, allows you to set a default character set, a default path, or both. The name of the character set is preceded by the DEFAULT CHARACTER SET keywords and specifies a default character set for the new schema. The path specifies an order for searching for SQL-invoked routines (procedures and functions) that are created as part of the CREATE SCHEMA statement. (SQL-invoked routines are discussed in Chapter 14.)

The <schema elements> clause is made up of various types of other SQL statements that you can include in the CREATE SCHEMA statement. For the most part, this clause allows you to create schema objects such as tables, views, domains, and triggers. The advantage of this is that objects are added right to the schema when you create it, all in one step.

Now that you've seen the syntax for a CREATE SCHEMA statement, let's look at an example. The following code creates a schema named INVENTORY. The statement also specifies an authorization identifier name MNGR and a character set named Latin1.

```
CREATE SCHEMA INVENTORY AUTHORIZATION MNGR
DEFAULT CHARACTER SET Latin1
CREATE TABLE ARTISTS
( ARTIST_ID        INTEGER,
  ARTIST_NAME      VARCHAR(60),
  PLACE_OF_BIRTH   VARCHAR(60) ) ;
```

Notice that the code sample includes a CREATE TABLE statement. This is one of the elements that can be specified as part of the <schema elements> clause. You can include as many statements as you want. This particular statement creates a table named ARTISTS that contains the ARTIST_ID column, the ARTIST_NAME column, and the PLACE_OF_BIRTH column. (I discuss the CREATE TABLE statement in great detail in Chapter 3.)

In addition to defining a CREATE SCHEMA statement, SQL defines a DROP SCHEMA statement, as shown in the following syntax:

```
DROP SCHEMA <schema name>
CASCADE | RESTRICT
```

The first line is fairly straightforward: the named schema will be removed from the system. The second line has two options: CASCADE and RESTRICT.

NOTE

The vertical bar (|) symbol can be read as "or," which means that you should use either the CASCADE option or the RESTRICT option, but not both.

If the CASCADE option is specified, all schema objects and SQL data within those objects are deleted from the system. If the RESTRICT option is used, the schema is deleted only if no schema objects exist. This method is used as a safeguard against deleting any objects that you do not want deleted. It's meant as a way to make you verify that the objects you're deleting are what you want to delete before you actually delete the schema.

Now let's look at an example of the DROP SCHEMA statement. The following code removes the INVENTORY schema:

```
DROP SCHEMA INVENTORY CASCADE;
```

Notice that the CASCADE option is used, which means that all schema objects and SQL data will be removed.

Create a Database

Despite the fact that the SQL standard does not define what a database is, let alone provide a statement to create any sort of database object, there is a good possibility that you'll be working with an RDBMS that not only supports the creation of a database object, but also uses that object as the foundation for its hierarchical structure in the management of data objects. Consequently, you might find that, in order to work through the examples and projects in this book, you will want to create a test database so you have an environment in which you can create, alter, or delete data objects or data as necessary, without risking the loss of data definitions or data from an actual database. (Ideally, you'll be working with an RDBMS that is a clean installation, without any existing databases except preinstalled system and sample databases.)

If you've already worked with an RDBMS, you might be familiar with how database objects are organized within that system. For example, if you take a look again at Figure 2-3, you can see that SQL Server organizes the server's databases into a logical structure beneath the Databases node. Each database node (for example, INVENTORY) contains child nodes that represent the different types of objects associated with that particular database. As you can see, the INVENTORY database currently lists eight categories of objects: Database Diagrams, Tables, Views, Synonyms, Programmability, Service Broker, Storage, and Security. And under the ARTIST_CDS table, the categories are Columns, Keys, Constraints, Triggers, Indexes, and Statistics. For a definition of how SQL Server defines each of these types of objects, you should view the product documentation, which you should do for any RDBMS. Compare and contrast that with Oracle's categories of objects as shown in Figure 2-4.

Most products that support database objects also support language to create those objects. For example, Oracle, MySQL, and SQL Server all include the CREATE DATABASE statement in their SQL-based languages. In the case of MySQL 5.7, the CREATE DATABASE statement is considered a synonym for the CREATE SCHEMA statement, meaning the two statements have the same syntax and do exactly the same thing. There is considerable variance from product to product regarding which parameters can be defined when building the CREATE DATABASE statement, what permissions you need in order to execute the statement, and how a system implements the database object. Fortunately, most products use the same basic syntax to create a database object:

```
CREATE DATABASE <database name>
<additional parameters>
```

Before creating a database in any system, make sure to first read the product documentation and, if appropriate, consult with a database administrator to be sure that it is safe for you to add a database object to the SQL environment. Once you create the database, you can create schemas, tables, views, and other objects within that database and, from there, populate the tables with the necessary data.

Try This 2-1 Creating a Database and a Schema

In "Try This 1-2: Connecting to a Database," you established access to an RDBMS. In that project, you used a front-end application that allowed you to directly invoke SQL statements. You will be using that application for this project (and the rest of the projects in the book) to create a database and a schema, or whichever of these functions your system supports. Once you create the database, you should work within the context of that database for future examples and projects. If your system supports schema creation but not database creation, you should work within the context of that schema for the other projects.

Step by Step

1. Open the client application that allows you to directly invoke SQL statements. If applicable, check with the database administrator to make sure that you're logging in with the credentials necessary to create a database and schema. You might need special permissions to create these objects. Also verify whether there are any parameters you should include when creating the database (for example, log file size), restrictions on the name you can use, or restrictions of any other kind. Be sure to check the product documentation before going any further.

2. Create a database named INVENTORY (if your RDBMS supports this functionality—in Oracle, you'll want to create a user named INVENTORY, which will implicitly create a schema with the same name). Depending on the product you're using, you'll be executing a statement that's similar to the following:

   ```
   CREATE DATABASE INVENTORY;
   ```

   If you're required to include any additional parameters in the statement, they would most likely be included in the lines following the CREATE DATABASE clause. Once you execute the statement, you should receive some sort of message telling you that the statement has been executed successfully.

3. Connect to the new database. The method for doing that will vary from product to product. In Oracle, you can connect to a database by entering the appropriate logon information in any of several tools, such as SQL*Plus, *i*SQL*Plus, and SQL Developer. In SQL Server, it's simply a matter of selecting the appropriate database from the Connect drop-down list of

(continued)

databases in the SQL Server Management Studio toolbar, or you can execute the following statement (MySQL uses this same syntax):

```
USE Inventory
```

4. Create a schema named INVENTORY (if your RDBMS supports this functionality). Note that if you already created a database named INVENTORY, you may have to use a different name for the schema, such as INVTRY. (In MySQL, you should run either the CREATE DATABASE statement or the CREATE SCHEMA statement, but not both because the two statements produce the same result.) Create the schema under your current authorization identifier. Do not include any schema elements at this time. In most cases, you will be executing a statement that looks similar to the following:

```
CREATE SCHEMA INVENTORY;
```

Try This Summary

Step-by-step exercises of this sort can be complicated because they're so dependent on how RDBMS products have implemented various features. As a result, you must rely heavily on product documentation (which you should be using anyway) and, if applicable, database administrators. However, now that you've gotten through this exercise and have created the necessary database and/or schema environment, you should be ready to move on to the examples and projects in the rest of the book. Because you've laid the necessary foundation, you're now ready to create, alter, and drop data objects, and insert, modify, and delete the data stored in those objects.

Chapter 2 Self Test

1. What are the differences between an SQL agent and an SQL implementation?
2. Which component of an SQL environment represents a user or role that is granted specific access privileges to objects and data?

   A Catalog

   B Authorization identifier

   C SQL client module

   D SQL agent
3. A(n) _______________ is a collection of schemas that form a namespace within the SQL environment.
4. What is a schema?

5. Which statement do you use to add a schema to an SQL environment?

   A ADD SCHEMA

   B INSERT SCHEMA

   C CREATE SCHEMA

6. What is the name of the schema that contains definitions for schema objects in a catalog?

7. What are the 11 types of schema objects that can be contained in a schema?

8. What is a view?

9. Which schema objects provide the basic unit of data management in the SQL environment?

   A Views

   B Domains

   C Base tables

   D Character sets

10. How does the SQL standard define a database?

11. A(n) _______________ is a name given to an SQL object.

12. How is a regular identifier distinguished from a delimited identifier in an SQL statement?

13. Which type of identifier permits spaces to be used as part of the name of an object?

14. Your SQL environment includes a catalog named RETAIL. In that catalog is a schema named INVENTORY, and in that schema is a table named ARTISTS. What is the qualified name of that table?

15. What three forms can the <name clause> component of a CREATE SCHEMA statement take?

16. What are the differences between the CASCADE option and the RESTRICT option in a DROP SCHEMA statement?

17. Within the hierarchy of the SQL environment, how is a domain related to a catalog?

18. Which type of identifier allows you to use a reserved keyword?

Chapter 3

Creating and Altering Tables

Key Skills & Concepts

- Create SQL Tables
- Specify Column Data Types
- Create User-Defined Types
- Specify Column Default Values
- Specify Identity Column and Generation Options
- Alter SQL Tables
- Drop SQL Tables
- Truncate SQL Tables

In an SQL environment, tables are the basic unit of data management. Most SQL programming you do is related either directly or indirectly to those tables. As a result, before you can insert data into your database or modify that data, the appropriate tables must have been created or you must create them. The SQL standard provides four statements that allow you to define, change, and delete table definitions in an SQL environment. You can use the CREATE TABLE statement to add a table, the ALTER TABLE statement to modify that definition, the DROP TABLE statement to delete the table and its data from your database, and the TRUNCATE TABLE statement to delete the data in the table while leaving the table definition intact. Of these four statements, the CREATE TABLE statement has the most complex syntax. Not only is this because of the various types of tables supported by SQL, but also because a table definition can include many elements. However, despite these complexities, table creation is a fairly straightforward process once you understand the basic syntax.

Create SQL Tables

As you might recall from Chapter 2, SQL supports three types of tables: base tables, derived tables, and transient tables. Most base tables are schema objects that hold SQL data. Derived tables are the results you see when you request (query) data from the database. Transient tables are named tables that are implicitly created during the evaluation of a query expression or the execution of a trigger.

In this chapter, you'll be working with base tables. In fact, most of what you'll be directly working with throughout this book (as well as throughout your programming career) are base tables; however, not all base tables are the same. Some are persistent (permanent) and some are temporary. Some are schema objects and some are contained in modules. All module base tables are also temporary tables. SQL supports five types of base tables:

- **Regular persistent base tables** A named schema object defined by a table definition in a CREATE TABLE statement that specifies neither the WITH SYSTEM VERSIONING nor TEMPORARY options. Regular persistent base tables hold the SQL data that is stored in your database. This is the most common type of base table and is often what is being referred to when people mention base tables or tables. A regular persistent base table always exists as long as the table definition exists, and can be called from within any SQL session.
- **System-versioned tables** A named schema object defined by a table definition that specifies the WITH SYSTEM VERSIONING option. System-versioned tables, which are part of the temporal features added to the SQL:2011 version of the SQL standard, contain both current and historical versions of table rows. I describe the temporal features of the SQL standard in Chapter 13.
- **Global temporary tables** A named schema object defined by a table definition in a CREATE GLOBAL TEMPORARY TABLE statement. Although the table definition is a part of the schema, the actual table exists only when referenced within the context of the SQL session in which it was created. When the session ends, the table no longer exists. A global temporary table created in one session cannot be accessed from another SQL session. The contents are distinct within each SQL session.
- **Created local temporary tables** A named schema object defined by a table definition in a CREATE LOCAL TEMPORARY TABLE statement. Like a global temporary table, the created local temporary table can be referenced only within the context of the SQL session in which it was created and cannot be accessed from another SQL session. However, a global temporary table can be accessed from anywhere within the associated SQL session, whereas a created local temporary table can be accessed only within the associated module. The contents are distinct within that module.
- **Declared local temporary tables** A table declared as part of a procedure in a module. The table definition is not contained in the schema and does not exist until that procedure is executed. Like other temporary tables, the declared local temporary table can be referenced only within the context of the SQL session in which it was created.

NOTE

An SQL session refers to the connection between a user and an SQL agent. During this connection, a sequence of consecutive SQL statements is invoked by this user and then executed. A module is an object that contains SQL statements, routines, or procedures. Modules are discussed in Chapters 14 and 18.

As you can see, you can use a form of the CREATE TABLE statement to create all base table types except declared local temporary tables. Throughout the rest of the chapter, I will primarily be discussing persistent base tables, although I'll be touching on the subject of temporary tables in subsequent chapters. In the meantime, let's take a look at the syntax in a CREATE TABLE statement:

```
CREATE [ { GLOBAL | LOCAL } TEMPORARY ] TABLE <table name>
( <table element> [ { , <table element> } . . . ] )
[ WITH SYSTEM VERSIONING]
[ ON COMMIT { PRESERVE | DELETE } ROWS ]
```

NOTE

The curly brackets are used to group elements together. For example, in the first line of syntax, the GLOBAL | LOCAL keywords are grouped together. The brackets tell you that you should first decide how to handle the contents within the brackets and then determine how they fit into the clause. In the first line, you should use either GLOBAL or LOCAL along with TEMPORARY. However, the entire clause is optional. The three periods (in the second line) tell you that you can repeat the clause as often as necessary. In this case, you could add as many <table element> clauses as your definition requires.

The syntax I've shown here provides only the basics of the CREATE TABLE statement, which is actually far more complex. (The syntax and its explanations take up over 30 pages of the SQL standard.) Even so, the syntax provided here is enough of a foundation for you to create the majority of tables that you're likely to be using.

In the first line of the syntax, you designate whether the table is temporary and you provide a name for the table, so you have three options:

- CREATE TABLE <table name>
- CREATE GLOBAL TEMPORARY TABLE <table name>
- CREATE LOCAL TEMPORARY TABLE <table name>

Depending on the RDBMS in which you're working, you might have to qualify the table name by including a schema name, authorization identifier, or database name (for example, INVENTORY.ARTISTS).

NOTE

There are a number of implementation-specific variations regarding temporary tables that are worth mentioning here. Oracle (through 12*c*) has no LOCAL option for creating a temporary table; data in a temporary table is private to the expressed session. IBM DB2 UDB through 10.1 uses the command CREATE GLOBAL TEMPORARY TABLE to create a global temporary table that can be shared by multiple SQL sessions, as well as the command DECLARE GLOBAL TEMPORARY TABLE to create a global temporary table that is only visible to a single session (the equivalent of what the SQL standard refers to as a local temporary table). In SQL Server (through 2014), temporary tables are created with the typical CREATE TABLE command, but local temporary table names are prefixed with a single number sign (#table_name), and global temporary table names are prefixed with a double number sign (##table_name).

The second line of the syntax allows you to specify the parts that make up the table, such as columns. (I'll return to that in a moment.) The third line of the syntax applies only if you're creating a temporary table. The clause allows you to specify whether or not the table should be emptied when a COMMIT statement is executed. A COMMIT statement is used in a transaction to commit changes to the database. I discuss transactions in Chapter 17.

You can think of the <table element> clauses as the meat of a CREATE TABLE statement. It is here that you define columns, constraints, and other elements specific to the table you're creating. You can define one or more <table element> clauses. If you define more than one, you must separate them with commas. Of the elements that you can create, we'll be focusing primarily on columns (in this chapter) and constraints (in Chapter 4). Let's take a closer look at the syntax that is used to define a column:

```
<column name> { <data type> | <domain> }
[ <default clause> |
  <identity column specification> |
  <generation clause> |
  <system time period start column specification> |
  <system time period end column specification> ]
[ <column constraint> ] [ COLLATE <collation name> ]
```

In the first line of the syntax, you must provide a column name and declare a data type or user-defined domain. I discuss data types in the "Specify Column Data Types" section later in this chapter, and I discuss domains in Chapter 4.

In the second line of the syntax, you have the option to provide a default value (see the "Specify Column Default Values" section).

In the third and fourth lines of the syntax, you have the option of specifying automatic generation of unique values for each new row added to the table. I discuss these options in the "Specify Identity Column and Generation Options" section later in this chapter.

In the fifth and sixth lines of the syntax, you have the option of specifying begin and end columns for time periods in which row history will be tracked. These are part of the temporal data features added to the SQL:2011 version of the standard and which I discuss in Chapter 13.

In the last line of the syntax, you have the option of specifying column constraints (see Chapter 4), and/or a collation (see Chapter 2).

At its most basic, a CREATE TABLE statement might look something like the following:

```
CREATE TABLE ARTISTS
( ARTIST_ID     INTEGER,
  ARTIST_NAME   CHARACTER(60) );
```

In this statement, I'm creating a table named ARTISTS, a column named ARTIST_ID, and a column named ARTIST_NAME. The ARTIST_ID column is associated with the INTEGER data type, and the ARTIST_NAME column is associated with the CHARACTER data type. Notice that the two column definitions are separated by a comma.

ARTIST_ID: INTEGER	ARTIST_NAME: CHARACTER(60)
3001	Glen Hansard
3002	Joe Bonamassa
3003	Stevie Wonder
3004	Fleetwood Mac
3005	Shania Twain
3006	Garth Brooks

Figure 3-1 The ARTIST_ID and ARTIST_NAME columns of the ARTISTS table

Also notice that I have placed the two column definitions on separate lines and aligned the data types by adding extra spaces—all of this is to improve readability, but is otherwise unnecessary (when SQL statements are processed, extra spaces and new lines are simply ignored). If you execute the CREATE TABLE statement, your table will look similar to the table shown in Figure 3-1.

Ask the Expert

Q: When you discussed the various types of tables that SQL supports, you talked briefly about temporary tables. What is the purpose of temporary tables?

A: Temporary tables provide you with a way to store temporary results within the context of your session. You might find that you need a place to store data in order to take a certain course of action. You can explicitly create a persistent base table, store data in it, and then drop the table when you're finished, but the temporary table allows you to do the same without having to explicitly destroy the table each time you use it. In other words, the temporary table is a useful tool when you need to store data for only a specific period of time. For example, suppose you have an application that allows you to generate a quarterly report based on your inventory at the end of the reporting period. The application might need to gather the data into a meaningful collection to generate the report; however, once the report is generated, the application no longer needs to store that data, so the table can be deleted. One of the advantages of using a temporary table is that because it is unique to a session, the table cannot interact with other users or sessions. As a result, the RDBMS doesn't have to take special steps to lock the data to prevent other users from applying conflicting updates to the temporary tables, and bypassing locking can result in better performance.

NOTE

The rows of data shown would not be in a table until you have actually added that data. The rows are shown here merely to give you an idea of the type of table that this statement would create.

Before we go any further with the discussion of creating a table, let's take a closer look at data types, which play an integral role in any column definition.

Specify Column Data Types

Whenever you define a column in a CREATE TABLE statement, you must, at the very least, provide a name for the column and an associated data type or domain. The data type or domain (discussed in Chapter 4) restricts the values that can be entered into that column. For example, some data types limit a column's values to numbers, while other data types allow any character to be entered. SQL supports three types of data types:

- **Predefined** Predefined data types, sometimes called "built-in" data types, are the most common. Each predefined data type is a named element (using an SQL keyword) that limits values to the restrictions defined by that database. SQL includes five types of predefined data types: string, numeric, datetime, interval, and Boolean.
- **Constructed** Constructed data types are also a named element but tend to be more complex than predefined data types because they can hold multiple values. Constructed types allow you to *construct* more complicated structures than more traditional data types. A thorough discussion of these types is beyond the scope of this book, but I wanted to mention them so you know that they exist.
- **User-defined** User-defined data types are based on predefined types or attribute definitions and are added as schema objects to the SQL environment. SQL supports two types of user-defined data types: distinct and structured. The distinct type is based on a predefined data type, and the structured type is based on attribute definitions. I discuss user-defined types in the "Create User-Defined Types" section later in this chapter.

Although all implementations of SQL support data types, which data types are supported varies from product to product. However, as a beginning SQL programmer, you'll find that most implementations support the basic (more traditional) data types, which are the ones I will be using in the examples and exercises throughout the book. These more traditional data types, sometimes known as primitive types, are all part of the SQL predefined data types, which I describe in the following sections. Don't try to memorize each of these types, but start becoming familiar with the differences between them. You'll find that as you start using specific data types, you'll become more comfortable with them. In the meantime, refer back to the following sections as often as necessary whenever you're working with table definitions or SQL data.

String Data Types

The string data types are made up of types that permit values based on character sets or on data bits. The values permitted by string types can be fixed in length or varying, depending on the specific type. SQL defines four types of string data types:

- **Character strings** Permitted values must be drawn from a specific character set, either the default set or a set defined at the time the column is being defined. Character string data types include CHARACTER, CHARACTER VARYING, CHARACTER LARGE OBJECT, and XML.
- **National character strings** Permitted values are similar to character strings except that the character set associated with these data types is defined by the implementation. As a result, when a national character string data type is specified, the values associated with that data type must be based on the character set specified by the relational database management system (RDBMS) for national character strings. These are useful for storing character strings in various human languages in the same database. The national character string data types include NATIONAL CHARACTER, NATIONAL CHARACTER VARYING, and NATIONAL CHARACTER LARGE OBJECT.
- **Binary strings** Permitted values are based on strings of data bits (binary digits), rather than character sets or collations, which means these data types allow only values of 0 or 1. As a result, no character sets or collations are associated with them. The data bits are organized into bytes, where each byte contains 8 bits, which is why the SQL standard uses the term octet. The binary string data types include BINARY, BINARY VARYING, and BINARY LARGE OBJECT. These types are useful for storing pure binary data such as sound clips or images in the database.

Now that you have an overview of the types of string data types, let's take a closer look at each one. Table 3-1 describes each of these data types and provides an example of a column definition that uses the specific type.

Numeric Data Types

As you probably guessed by the name, the values specified by the numeric data types are numbers. All numeric data types have a precision and some have a scale. The *precision* refers to the number of digits (within a specific numeric value) that can be stored. The *scale* refers to the number of digits in the fractional part of that value (the digits to the right of the decimal point). For example, the number 435.27 has a precision of 5 and a scale of 2. The decimal point is implied (not stored as part of the number) and thus is not counted when determining the precision of the number; however, some of the early RDBMS products did count the decimal point as part of the precision. A scale cannot be a negative number or be larger than

Data Type	Description/Example
CHARACTER	Specifies the exact number of characters (which must be from a character set) that will be stored for each value. For example, if you define the number of characters as 10, but the value contains only six characters, the remaining four characters will be spaces. The data type can be abbreviated as CHAR. Example: `ARTIST_NAME  CHAR(60)`
CHARACTER VARYING	Specifies the greatest number of characters (which must be from a character set) that can be included in a value. The number of characters stored is exactly the same number as the value entered, so no spaces are added to the value. The data type can be abbreviated as CHAR VARYING or VARCHAR. Example: `ARTIST_NAME  VARCHAR(60)`
CHARACTER LARGE OBJECT	Stores large groups of characters, up to the specified amount. The number of characters stored is exactly the same number as the value entered, so no spaces are added to the value. The data type can be abbreviated as CLOB. Example: `ARTIST_BIO  CLOB(200K)`
XML	The Extensible Markup Language (XML) is a general-purpose markup language used to describe documents in a format that is convenient for display on web pages and for exchanging data between different parties. The specifications for storing XML data in SQL databases were added to the SQL standard in version SQL:2003 and are covered in Chapter 19. Example: `ARTIST_BIO  XML(DOCUMENT(UNTYPED))`
NATIONAL CHARACTER	Operates just like the CHARACTER data type, except that it's based on an implementation-defined character set. The data type can be abbreviated as NATIONAL CHAR and NCHAR. Example: `ARTIST_NAME  NCHAR(60)`
NATIONAL CHARACTER VARYING	Operates just like the CHARACTER VARYING data type, except that it's based on an implementation-defined character set. The data type can be abbreviated as NATIONAL CHAR VARYING or NCHAR VARYING. Example: `ARTIST_NAME  NCHAR VARYING (60)`
NATIONAL CHARACTER LARGE OBJECT	Operates just like the CHARACTER LARGE OBJECT data type, except that it's based on an implementation-defined character set. The data type can be abbreviated as NCHAR LARGE OBJECT or NCLOB. Example: `ARTIST_BIO  NCLOB(200K)`
BINARY	Specifies the exact number of bytes of binary data that will be stored for each value. Example: `ARTIST_SIGNATURE_IMAGE  BINARY(32)`

Table 3-1 String Data Types with Example Column Definitions *(continued)*

Data Type	Description/Example
BINARY VARYING	Specifies the greatest number of binary bytes that can be included in a value. The number of bytes stored is exactly the same number as the value entered, so no spaces are added to the value. Example: `ARTIST_SIGNATURE_IMAGE  BINARY VARYING(32)`
BINARY LARGE OBJECT	Stores large groups of bytes, up to the specified amount. The number of bytes stored is exactly the same number as the value entered, so no spaces are added to the value. The data type can also be referred to as BLOB. Example: `ARTIST_PIC  BLOB(1M)`

Table 3-1 String Data Types with Example Column Definitions

the precision. A scale of 0 indicates that the number is an integer and contains no fractional component. SQL defines two types of numeric data types:

- **Exact numerics** Permitted values have a precision and scale, which for some numeric data types, are defined by the implementation. Exact numeric data types include NUMERIC, DECIMAL, INTEGER, BIGINT, and SMALLINT.
- **Approximate numerics** Permitted values have a precision but no scale. As a result the decimal point can float. A *floating-point* number is one that contains a decimal point, but the decimal point can be located at any place within that number, which is why an approximate numeric is said to have no scale. Approximate numeric data types include REAL, DOUBLE PRECISION, and FLOAT.

Table 3-2 describes each of the numeric data types and provides an example of a column definition that uses the specific type.

Datetime Data Types

As the name implies, datetime data types are concerned with tracking dates and times. SQL defines three datetime types—DATE, TIME, and TIMESTAMP—and variations on these types. These variations are related to Coordinated Universal Time (UTC), which used to be called Greenwich Mean Time (GMT), and the various time zones. Table 3-3 describes each of the SQL standard datetime data types and provides an example of a column definition that uses the specific type.

You will find considerable implementation variations for datetime data types because early relational databases didn't have them at all. That seems odd until you realize that they were built by computer scientists who didn't know how much business applications rely on dates and times. As business users demanded date and time capabilities, commercial RDBMS vendors of the day (long before there was an SQL standard) rushed to deliver the new

Data Type	Description/Example
NUMERIC	Specifies the precision and the scale of a numeric value. You can specify only the precision and use the implementation-defined (default) scale, or you can specify the precision and scale. If you specify neither the precision nor the scale, the implementation will provide defaults for both values. Example: `ARTIST_RATE NUMERIC(5,2)`
DECIMAL	Specifies values similar to those of the NUMERIC data type. However, if the implementation-defined precision is higher than the specified precision, values with the higher precision will be accepted, but the scale will always be what you specify. Example: `ARTIST_ROYALTY DECIMAL(5,2)`
INTEGER	Specifies a value with an implementation-defined precision and a 0 scale, meaning that only integers are accepted and you do not specify any parameters with this data type. The data type can also be abbreviated as INT. Example: `ARTIST_ID INT`
SMALLINT	Specifies a value similar to an INTEGER data type. However, the precision defined by the implementation must be smaller than the INTEGER precision. Example: `ARTIST_ID SMALLINT`
BIGINT	Specifies a value similar to an INTEGER data type. However, the precision defined by the implementation must be larger than the INTEGER precision. Example: `ARTIST_ID BIGINT`
FLOAT	Specifies the precision of a numeric value, but not the scale. Example: `ARTIST_ROYALTY FLOAT(6)`
REAL	Specifies a value with an implementation-defined precision, but without a scale. The precision must be smaller than the precision defined for a DOUBLE PRECISION data type. Example: `ARTIST_ROYALTY REAL`
DOUBLE PRECISION	Specifies a value with an implementation-defined precision, but without a scale. The precision must be greater than the precision defined for the REAL data type. The implication is that the value of the precision should be double that of the REAL data type, but each implementation defines *double* differently. Example: `ARTIST_ROYALTY DOUBLE PRECISION`

Table 3-2 Numeric Data Types with Example Column Definitions

features, and thus implemented them in very different ways. For example, Oracle's DATE data type always includes a time component (hour, minutes, and seconds), and SQL Server uses the TIMESTAMP data type for a completely different purpose, with a data type called DATETIME operating like the SQL TIMESTAMP data type. So, as always, consult your vendor documentation.

Data Type	Description/Example
DATE	Specifies the year, month, and day value of a date. The year is four digits and supports the values 0001 through 9999; the month is two digits and supports the values 01 through 12; and the day is two digits and supports the values 01 through 31. Example: `DATE_HIRED  DATE`
TIME	Specifies the hour, minute, and second values of a time. The hour is two digits and supports the values 00 through 23; the minute is two digits and supports the values 00 through 59; and the second is at least two digits and supports values 00 through 61.999 (to accommodate leap seconds). The data type includes no fractional digits unless you specify them. For example, TIME(3) would give you three fractional digits. The data type can also be referred to as TIME WITHOUT TIME ZONE. Example: `EVENT_TIME  TIME(2)`
TIME WITH TIME ZONE	Specifies the same information as the TIME data type except that the value also includes information specific to UTC and time zones. The values added to the data type range from –11:59 to +12:00. Example: `EVENT_TIME  TIME WITH TIME ZONE (2)`
TIMESTAMP	Combines the values of TIME and DATE. The only difference is that with the TIME data type, the default number of fractional digits is 0, but with the TIMESTAMP data type, the default number is 6. You can specify a different number of fractional digits by including a parameter, such as TIMESTAMP(4). The data type can also be referred to as TIMESTAMP WITHOUT TIME ZONE. Example: `PURCHASE_DATE  TIMESTAMP(3)`
TIMESTAMP WITH TIME ZONE	Specifies the same information as the TIMESTAMP data type except that the value also includes information specific to UTC and time zones. The values added to the data type range from –11:59 to +12:00. Example: `PURCHASE_DATE  TIMESTAMP WITH TIME ZONE (2)`

Table 3-3 Datetime Data Types with Example Column Definitions

Interval Data Type

The interval data type is closely related to the datetime data types. The value of an interval data type represents the difference between two datetime values. SQL supports two types of intervals:

- **Year-month intervals** The interval data type specifies intervals between years, months, or both. You can use only the YEAR and MONTH fields in a year-month interval.
- **Day-time intervals** The interval data type specifies intervals between any of the following values: days, hours, minutes, or seconds. You can use only the DAY, HOUR, MINUTE, and SECOND fields in a day-time interval.

You cannot mix one type of interval with the other. For example, you cannot define an interval data type that uses the YEAR field and the HOUR field.

The interval data type uses the keyword INTERVAL followed by an <interval qualifier> clause. The clause is a complex series of rules that describe how the INTERVAL data type can be defined to express intervals involving years, months, days, hours, minutes, or seconds. In addition, the leading field (the first word) in the clause can be defined with a precision (*p*). The precision is the number of digits that will be used in the leading field. If a precision isn't specified, the default is 2. For year-month intervals, you can specify one of the following interval data types:

- INTERVAL YEAR
- INTERVAL YEAR(*p*)
- INTERVAL MONTH
- INTERVAL MONTH(*p*)
- INTERVAL YEAR TO MONTH
- INTERVAL YEAR(*p*) TO MONTH

There are many more options for day-time intervals because there are more fields from which to choose. For example, you can specify any of the following interval types using the DAY field as a leading field or stand-alone field:

- INTERVAL DAY
- INTERVAL DAY(*p*)
- INTERVAL DAY TO HOUR
- INTERVAL DAY(*p*) TO HOUR
- INTERVAL DAY TO MINUTE
- INTERVAL DAY(*p*) TO MINUTE
- INTERVAL DAY TO SECOND
- INTERVAL DAY(*p*) TO SECOND
- INTERVAL DAY TO SECOND(*x*)
- INTERVAL DAY(*p*) TO SECOND(*x*)

When the trailing field (the last word) is SECOND, you can specify an additional precision (*x*), which defines the number of digits after the decimal point. As you can see from these examples, there are many more day-time interval data types that can be defined. Keep in mind, however, that the leading field must always be a greater time unit than the trailing field. For example, the YEAR field is greater than MONTH, and HOUR is greater than MINUTE.

If you were going to use an interval data type in a column definition, it might look something like the following:

```
DATE_RANGE INTERVAL YEAR(4) TO MONTH
```

In this example, a value in this column will include four digits for the year, a hyphen, and then two digits for the month, such as 2014-08. If a precision were not specified for the year, the year range could include only two digits (00 through 99).

Boolean Data Type

The Boolean data type (unlike the interval data types) is very straightforward and easy to apply. The data type supports a true/false construct that permits only three values: true, false, or unknown. A null value evaluates to unknown. (In SQL, a *null* value is used to signify that a value is undefined or not known. I discuss null values in Chapter 4.)

The values in the Boolean data type can be used in SQL queries and expressions for comparison purposes. (I discuss comparisons in Chapter 9.) Boolean comparisons follow specific logic:

- True is greater than false.
- A comparison involving an unknown (null) value will return an unknown result.
- A value of unknown can be assigned to a column only if it supports null values.

To use the Boolean data type, you must use the BOOLEAN keyword with no parameters, as shown in the following example:

```
ARTIST_HAS_AGENT BOOLEAN
```

The ARTIST_HAS_AGENT column will accept only the values of true, false, and unknown.

NOTE

The Boolean data type is based on a specific type of computer logic known as Boolean (named for 19th-century mathematician George Boole), which evaluates conditions of true or false in a given operation or expression. Many programming languages support Boolean logic through the use of logical operators such as AND, OR, and NOT, for example, "ITEM_A IS NOT FALSE" or "ITEM_A AND ITEM_B OR ITEM_C IS TRUE." In SQL, Boolean logic is implemented through the use of comparison operators to compare values within various data types. I discuss these operators in Chapter 9.

Using SQL Data Types

Now that you've taken a look at the various predefined data types, let's look at a CREATE TABLE statement that defines a table with columns that use different data types. In the

Ask the Expert

Q: How do the predefined data types in SQL compare to the data types you find in other programming languages?

A: For the most part, it is unlikely that data types from two different languages will be the same. A set of data types in one language can vary in structure and semantics from a set of data types in another language. These differences, sometimes called impedance mismatch, can lead to the loss of information when an application draws data from an SQL database. In fact, it's often a good idea to know which language will be used for applications as the database is being designed. In some cases, the database design can affect which application language you can most easily use to manipulate data in an SQL database. However, SQL includes a data conversion expression named CAST. The CAST expression allows you to convert data from one data type to another data type, allowing the host language to access values that it wouldn't have been able to handle in its original form. The CAST expression is discussed in more detail in Chapter 10.

Q: Can SQL data types be assigned to objects other than columns?

A: Every SQL data value, or literal, belongs to a data type. For example, data types can be assigned to the parameters of externally invoked procedures. ***Externally invoked procedures*** are procedures that are contained within an SQL client module. A procedure is an SQL statement (or series of statements) that can be called from another element in the code, which in the case of externally invoked procedures is external code. A parameter, which is the literal that belongs to a data type, is a value that is passed to the procedure and used as the procedure is processed. The parameter acts as a placeholder for that value. SQL client modules are discussed in Chapter 18.

following example, the statement is creating a table named ARTISTS that includes four columns:

```
CREATE TABLE ARTISTS
( ARTIST_ID          INT,
  ARTIST_NAME        VARCHAR(60),
  ARTIST_DOB         DATE,
  POSTER_IN_STOCK    BOOLEAN );
```

As you can see, the ARTIST_ID column is a numeric data type, the ARTIST_NAME column is a string data type, the ARTIST_DOB column is a datetime data type, and the POSTER_IN_STOCK column is a Boolean data type. Figure 3-2 illustrates how this table might look. You may notice that one of the ARTIST_DOB column values is null (displayed as <null> in Figure 3-2), along with one of the POSTER_IN_STOCK column values. As you will learn in Chapter 4, null values can apply to columns of any data type.

ARTIST_ID: INT	ARTIST_NAME: VARCHAR(60)	ARTIST_DOB: DATE	POSTER_IN_STOCK: BOOLEAN
3001	Glen Hansard	1970-04-21	True
3002	Joe Bonamassa	1977-05-08	False
3003	Stevie Wonder	1950-05-13	True
3004	Fleetwood Mac	<null>	True
3005	Shania Twain	1965-08-28	False
3006	Garth Brooks	1962-02-07	<null>

Figure 3-2 The ARTISTS table defined with different data types

Create User-Defined Types

In Chapter 1, I mentioned that the SQL standard has incorporated some of the principles of object-oriented programming (OOP) into its language. One example of this is the user-defined type, sometimes referred to as the user-defined data type. The *user-defined type* is a type of data type (stored as a schema object) that is in part defined by the programmer and in part based on one or more data types. SQL supports two types of user-defined types:

- **Structured types** These types are made up of one or more attributes that are each based on another data type, including predefined types, constructed types, and other structured types. In addition to being associated with a data type, each attribute can include a default clause and can specify a collation. A structured type can include methods in its definition. A *method* is a type of function that's associated with a user-defined type. A *function* is a named operation that performs predefined tasks that you can't normally perform by using SQL statements alone. It is a type of routine that takes input parameters (which are sometimes optional) and returns a single value based on those parameters.
- **Distinct types** These types are simply based on predefined data types and whatever parameters are defined for that data type, if parameters are required or desired.

SQL provides a CREATE TYPE statement for defining user-defined types. However, the language used for creating a user-defined type can vary from product to product. The features that are supported in a user-defined type also vary widely. For example, SQL Server 2000 and earlier versions do not support a CREATE TYPE statement, but SQL Server 2005 and later versions do.

Despite the differences with and limitations of product implementations, I want to at least provide an example of how the CREATE TYPE statement is used to create a distinct type.

In the following statement, I create a user-defined type that is based on the NUMERIC data type:

```
CREATE TYPE SALARY AS NUMERIC(8,2)
FINAL;
```

This simple example is straightforward enough, creating a type named SALARY with a data type of NUMERIC(8,2). However, the keyword FINAL is probably new to you. When FINAL is specified, it tells SQL that no subtypes will be defined for this type. The alternative is to specify NOT FINAL, which means that subtypes may be defined for the type. Once you've created the type, you can use it in a column definition as you would a predefined data type:

```
CREATE TABLE EMPLOYEES
( EMPLOYEE_ID        INTEGER,
  EMPLOYEE_SALARY    SALARY );
```

Any values you add to the EMPLOYEE_SALARY column would have to conform to the specifications of the NUMERIC data type with a precision of 8 and a scale of 2. As a result, a value could be anything from –999999.99 to 999999.99. The nice part is that you can then use the SALARY user-defined type in any other tables that require similar values.

NOTE

As you see, numeric types allow negative numbers as well as zero and positive numbers. If negative numbers are not desired (which would obviously be the case for someone's salary), the data type alone won't do the job, but you can use a CHECK constraint for this purpose. I discuss CHECK constraints in Chapter 4.

Specify Column Default Values

Another valuable feature that SQL supports is the ability to specify a default value for a column when you're using the CREATE TABLE statement to create a table. The syntax for a simple column definition with a default value looks like this:

```
<column name> <data type> DEFAULT <default value>
```

The <column name> and <data type> placeholders, which should now be familiar, are followed by the DEFAULT keyword. After the DEFAULT keyword, you must specify a value for the <default value> placeholder. This value can be a literal, which is an SQL data value (such as the string "To be determined" or the number 0); a datetime value function, which is a function that allows you to perform operations related to dates and times (discussed in Chapter 10); or a session-related user function, which is a function that returns user-related information (discussed in Chapter 10).

Whichever type of value you use for the <default value> placeholder, it must conform to the data requirements of the data type specified in the column definition. For example, if you

ARTIST_ID: INT	ARTIST_NAME: VARCHAR(60)	PLACE_OF_BIRTH: VARCHAR(60)
3001	Glen Hansard	Ballymun, Dublin, Ireland
3002	Joe Bonamassa	Unknown
3003	Stevie Wonder	Saginaw, Michigan, USA
3004	Fleetwood Mac	Unknown
3005	Shania Twain	Windsor, Ontario, Canada
3006	Garth Brooks	Tulsa, Oklahoma, USA

Figure 3-3 A default value of "Unknown" for the PLACE_OF_BIRTH column

define a column with an INT data type or a CHAR(4) data type, you cannot specify a default value of "Unknown." In the first case, INT requires a numeric value, and in the second case, CHAR(4) requires that the value contain no more than four characters.

In the following example, I use the CREATE TABLE statement to define a table named ARTISTS, which contains three columns:

```
CREATE TABLE ARTISTS
( ARTIST_ID         INT,
  ARTIST_NAME       VARCHAR(60),
  PLACE_OF_BIRTH    VARCHAR(60)    DEFAULT 'Unknown' );
```

Notice that the PLACE_OF_BIRTH column includes the default value "Unknown." The value is acceptable because it conforms to the data requirements of the VARCHAR(60) data type. Also notice that the default value is enclosed in single quotes. You must use single quotes for character string values. Figure 3-3 illustrates what this table might look like if it were populated with rows of data.

If you were to insert any new rows into this table and you didn't know the artist's place of birth, the system would automatically insert a value of "Unknown."

Specify Identity Column and Generation Options

In some situations, you may find it useful to have unique values generated sequentially using what is known as a *sequencer* and assigned to column values automatically as you insert new rows into tables. The <identity column specifications> or <generation clause> clause in the <table element> clause (described in the "Create SQL Tables" section) can be used for this purpose. The two clauses are mutually exclusive, meaning you can only use one of them for any given column. Also, you can define no more than one column per table using the <identity column specifications> or <generation clause>.

Here is the syntax of the <identity column specifications> clause.

```
GENERATED { ALWAYS | BY DEFAULT } AS IDENTITY
    [ <common sequence generator options ] |
```

In the first line of the syntax, you must choose between ALWAYS and BY DEFAULT. If you choose the ALWAYS option, you will not be able to specify a value for the identity column in any SQL statement—the value will always be generated by the RDBMS. If instead you choose the BY DEFAULT option, the RDBMS only generates a value for the identity column when the SQL statement does not provide one. The <common sequence generator options> allow you to specify values for the following in a comma-separated list that is enclosed in parentheses:

- **Increment by** The value to be added to each new value generated by the sequencer, with a default value of 1.
- **Maxvalue option** The maximum value to be generated by the sequencer, which has no limit by default.
- **Minvalue option** The minimum value to be generated by the sequencer, with a default value of 1.
- **Cycle option** The keyword CYCLE instructs the sequencer to start over when the maximum value is reached. If NO CYCLE is specified, the sequencer raises an error when attempts are made to assign values beyond the maximum value.

Here is the syntax of the <generation clause>:

```
GENERATED ALWAYS AS <generation expression>
```

The <generation expression> clause is similar to the <common sequence generation options> clause. The most notable difference is that the <generation expression> clause also permits specification of a starting value, allowing the sequence to be started anywhere between the minimum and maximum values, inclusive.

In the following example, I use the CREATE TABLE statement to define a table named ARTISTS, which contains three columns, with identity generation options specified for the ARTIST_ID column:

```
CREATE TABLE ARTISTS
( ARTIST_ID        INT     GENERATED ALWAYS AS IDENTITY
                           (INCREMENT BY 1,
                            MAXVALUE 999999999,
                            MINVALUE 1,
                            CYCLE),
  ARTIST_NAME      VARCHAR(60),
  PLACE_OF_BIRTH   VARCHAR(60)    DEFAULT 'Unknown' );
```

NOTE

Support for identity column and generation options varies widely across SQL implementations. For example, Oracle provides sequence generation using completely different syntax, while DB2 adheres closely to the syntax of the standard. Always check your vendor documentation for details.

Maintaining Independent Sequence Generators

The SQL standard provides syntax for creating, altering, and dropping sequence generators (commonly known as *sequences*) as database objects that are independent of the tables that can use them. The main advantage of independent sequences is the same sequence can be used with multiple tables. You simply refer to the sequence when you use the INSERT statement to add new rows into a table. I discuss the SQL INSERT statement in Chapter 8.

Here is the syntax for creating a sequence:

```
CREATE SEQUENCE <sequence generator name>
   [ AS <data type> ]
   [ START WITH <start value> ]
   [ <common sequence generator options ]
```

In the first line of the syntax, you must give the sequence a name that is unique within the schema or database. The second line of the syntax allows for optional specification of a data type to be used when the sequence generates numeric values. The data type must be an exact numeric type with a scale of 0 (usually INTEGER, SMALLINT, or BIGINT). If other exact numeric types are permitted by the SQL implementation, such as DECIMAL or NUMBER, the scale must be 0 because sequences must generate whole numbers. The third line of the syntax allows you to specify the starting value for the sequence. If you do not specify a starting value, the default is 1. The fourth line of the syntax allows for optional common sequence generator options, which are the same options discussed in the preceding "Specify Identity Column and Generation Options" section, except that the list of options is not separated by commas.

In the following example, I create a sequence named ARTIST_ID_SEQ with a data type of INTEGER and include some optional sequence generator options.

```
CREATE SEQUENCE ARTIST_ID_SEQ
    AS INTEGER
    INCREMENT BY 1
    MAXVALUE 999999999
    MINVALUE 1
    CYCLE);
```

Once sequences are created, the ALTER SEQUENCE statement can be used to restart the sequence at a specific value, or specify new values for any of the sequence generator options. In the following example, I restart the ARTIST_ID_SEQ sequence at the value of 100 and change the sequence to NO CYCLE.

```
ALTER SEQUENCE ARTIST_ID_SEQ
    RESTART WITH 100
    NO CYCLE;
```

When you no longer need a sequence, you can delete it with the DROP SEQUENCE statement. In the following example, I drop the ARTIST_ID_SEQ sequence.

```
DROP SEQUENCE ARTIST_ID_SEQ;
```

Support for sequences varies across SQL implementations. Oracle and DB2 support the CREATE SEQUENCE, ALTER SEQUENCE, and DROP SEQUENCE statements, but MySQL and SQL Server do not. As always, check your product documentation for syntax variations.

Try This 3-1 Creating SQL Tables

You've probably noticed that I've been using CD-related data for the examples I've shown you so far. We will be carrying this theme throughout the book as we begin to build a database that tracks the CD inventory of a small business. In this exercise, you will create three tables that are related to the INVENTORY database, which you created in Chapter 2, Try This 2-1. Before you begin, take a look at a simple data model (Figure 3-4) that shows the three tables you'll be creating. Each table is represented by a rectangle, with the name of the table above the rectangle and the name of the columns, along with their data types, listed within the rectangle.

We will be using the data model throughout the book—as it evolves into a more complex structure—to define the objects in our database. You can also download the Try_This_03.txt file, which contains the SQL statements used in this Try This exercise.

Step by Step

1. Open the client application for your RDBMS and connect to the INVENTORY database. You will be creating all objects within that database. (If your RDBMS doesn't support the creation of a database and instead you created the CD_INVENTORY schema, you should create all your objects within that schema.)
2. The first table that you will create is the COMPACT_DISCS table. Notice that it includes three columns, two of which have an INT data type and one that has a VARCHAR(60) data type. This table will hold data about the compact discs in your inventory. The COMPACT_DISC_ID column will contain numbers that uniquely identify each CD.

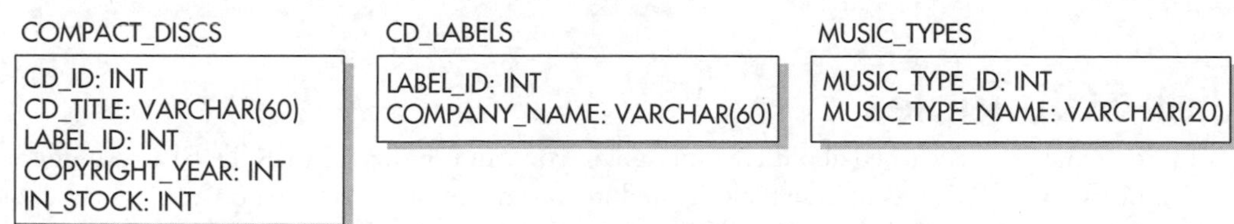

Figure 3-4 Simple data model of the INVENTORY database

(continued)

The CD_TITLE column will contain the actual names of the CDs. The LABEL_ID column will contain numbers that identify the companies that published the CDs. Enter the following SQL statement into your client application's input window:

```
CREATE TABLE COMPACT_DISCS
( CD_ID             INT,
  CD_TITLE             VARCHAR(60),
  LABEL_ID             INT );
```

3. Verify that you have entered the correct information and execute the statement. You should receive a message confirming that the statement has been successfully executed.

4. The next table that you will create is the CD_LABELS table. The table includes the LABEL_ID column, which uniquely identifies each company that publishes the CDs, and the COMPANY_NAME column, which lists the actual names of the companies. Enter and execute the following code:

```
CREATE TABLE CD_LABELS
( LABEL_ID       INT,
  COMPANY_NAME   VARCHAR(60) );
```

5. The final table that you will create is the MUSIC_TYPES table. The table includes the TYPE_ID column, which uniquely identifies each category of music, and the TYPE_NAME column, which lists the actual names of the categories of music (for example, Blues or Jazz). Enter and execute the following code:

```
CREATE TABLE MUSIC_TYPES
( MUSIC_TYPE_ID     INT,
  MUSIC_TYPE_NAME   VARCHAR(20) );
```

6. Close the client application.

Try This Summary

Your database should now contain three new tables. These tables will serve as a foundation for other Try This exercises in the book. As you progress through these exercises, you will modify these tables, create additional tables, insert data into the tables, and then query and manipulate that data. By the time you've completed all the exercises, you'll have created and populated a small database that stores data about an inventory of compact discs.

Alter SQL Tables

Taking what you've learned about creating tables, you can use the ALTER TABLE statement to modify the definitions of base tables stored in your database (as schema objects). At its most basic, the syntax for the ALTER TABLE statement looks like this:

```
ALTER TABLE <table name>
   ADD [COLUMN] <column definition>
|  ALTER [COLUMN] <column name>
```

```
    { SET DEFAULT <default value> | DROP DEFAULT }
|  DROP [COLUMN] <column name> { CASCADE | RESTRICT }
```

The statement allows you to take three different actions: adding columns, altering columns, or dropping columns.

NOTE

The ALTER TABLE statement also allows you to add or drop table constraints. A table constraint is a rule that restricts what data can be entered into the table. The table constraint is part of the table definition, but is not part of any specific column definitions. Constraints are discussed in detail in Chapter 4.

The <column definition> placeholder in the ADD [COLUMN] clause is similar to the column definition section of the CREATE TABLE statement. You provide a column name and a data type or domain. You also have the option of adding a default clause, a column constraint, or a collation. For example, you can use the following statement to alter the ARTISTS table so that it includes an ARTIST_DOB column:

```
ALTER TABLE ARTISTS
  ADD COLUMN ARTIST_DOB DATE;
```

Unlike the ADD [COLUMN] clause, the ALTER [COLUMN] clause is limited to two actions: setting a default or deleting the default (although there are product implementations that permit changes to other properties such as data type or precision and scale). For example, suppose your ARTISTS table includes a PLACE_OF_BIRTH column, but no default has been defined for that column. You can add a default by using the following statement:

```
ALTER TABLE ARTISTS
   ALTER COLUMN PLACE_OF_BIRTH SET DEFAULT 'Unknown';
```

You can also drop the default by using the following statement:

```
ALTER TABLE ARTISTS
   ALTER COLUMN PLACE_OF_BIRTH DROP DEFAULT;
```

The final clause in the syntax—DROP [COLUMN]—provides two options for deleting a column and its data from a table: the CASCADE keyword and the RESTRICT keyword. You might remember these keywords from the discussion about the DROP SCHEMA statement in Chapter 2. If the CASCADE option is specified, the column and the data within the column are deleted regardless of whether other objects reference the column. Any views, constraints, routines, or triggers that reference the column are also dropped. If the RESTRICT option is used, the column is deleted only if no views, constraints, routines, or triggers reference the column. For example, the following statement deletes the PLACE_OF_BIRTH column and the data stored in the column, regardless of dependencies:

```
ALTER TABLE ARTISTS
 DROP COLUMN PLACE_OF_BIRTH CASCADE;
```

In general, the ALTER TABLE statement is a handy one to know because invariably, table definitions are going to change, and so, too, are the types of data stored in those tables. However, this statement, like most SQL statements, can vary widely from implementation to implementation in terms of how the specifics of the statement are applied. For example, SQL Server does not support the CASCADE and RESTRICT keywords. In Oracle, CASCADE must be written as CASCADE CONSTRAINTS, and RESTRICT (which is the default behavior) is not explicitly supported. As always, be sure to check your product documentation.

Drop SQL Tables

As you might imagine, the process of dropping (destroying) a table and its stored data is very straightforward. The following syntax shows you how easy this process is:

```
DROP TABLE <table name> { CASCADE | RESTRICT }
```

The only real decision you need to make when deleting the table is whether to choose the CASCADE option or the RESTRICT option. As in previous syntax examples, the two options determine whether you should delete the table and its data if the table is being referenced by other objects. If CASCADE is used, the table and its data are deleted, along with any views, constraints, routines, or triggers that reference the table. If RESTRICT is used, the table is deleted only if no such dependencies exist. (As with the DROP COLUMN clause, SQL Server does not support CASCADE or RESTRICT, and Oracle permits only CASCADE CONTRAINTS.) For example, the following statement deletes the ARTISTS table and the data stored in the column, regardless of dependencies:

```
DROP TABLE ARTISTS CASCADE;
```

Truncate SQL Tables

The TRUNCATE TABLE statement allows you to quickly and efficiently remove all the data from an SQL table while leaving the table definition intact. Although the statement has been in use in various SQL implementations for many years, it was added to the SQL standard as of version SQL:2008. The syntax of the TRUNCATE TABLE statement is as follows:

```
TRUNCATE TABLE <table name>
  [ CONTINUE IDENTITY | RESTART IDENTITY ];
```

As you can see, the syntax is very simple. The only options to choose apply only to tables that have an identity column. (See the "Specify Identity Column and Generation Options" section.) As the keywords suggest, CONTINUE IDENTITY causes the sequencer to continue with the next sequential value as new rows are inserted after the table data has been truncated, while RESTART IDENTITY causes the sequencer to start the sequence over from the minimum value (or starting value if one was specified) when a row is inserted after the table data has been truncated.

Ask the Expert

Q: What if you want to delete only some of the data in a table?

A: The SQL DELETE statement, which I discuss in more detail in Chapter 8, can be used to selectively delete rows from a table. Although the DELETE statement can be used to delete all the rows in the table, the TRUNCATE statement is a far more efficient way of doing so.

Q: You state that when a default value is defined for a column, the value is automatically inserted into the column when you add a row to the table but don't specify a value for that particular column. What happens if your column definition doesn't include a default and you try to insert that row?

A: The action taken depends on whether null values are permitted within the column. A null value means that the value is not known. This is not the same as a zero, blank, or default. If a null value is present, then the data is not available. By default, all columns permit null values, although you can override the default (discussed in Chapter 4). If you try to insert a row without specifying a value, a null value will be inserted into that column if the column permits null values. If the column does not permit null values, you will not be able to insert a row without defining a specific value for that column.

Q: I've often heard the term "indexes" discussed in relation to creating SQL tables. How do you create indexes?

A: Oddly enough, the SQL standard does not support the creation and maintenance of indexes, nor does it provide a definition or mention them in any other way. For those of you not familiar with them, an index is a set of search values and pointers (in a subsidiary table) that correspond to rows in a table. Indexes speed up queries and improve performance, making data access much more efficient, much like using the index of a book helps you find things more quickly than sequentially searching the pages. As a result, nearly every RDBMS supports some form of indexing, and indeed they are an important part of that product. However, the method used to implement indexing varies greatly, so each product provides its own system to set up and maintain their indexes. For example, the CREATE INDEX statement is available in most products; however, the syntax for the statement can vary considerably. As always, be sure to review the product documentation.

Try This 3-2 Altering and Deleting SQL Tables

Throughout the life cycle of nearly any database, the likelihood that business requirements will change and the database will have to be altered is almost a foregone conclusion. As a result, you will no doubt run into situations in which table definitions have to be modified or dropped. In this Try This exercise, you will create a table, drop it, re-create it, and then change it by deleting a column. By the time you are finished, you will have added one more table to the INVENTORY database and will be making use of that table in later exercises. You can download the Try_This_03.txt file, which contains the SQL statements used in this exercise.

Step by Step

1. Open the client application for your RDBMS and connect to the INVENTORY database (or CD_INVENTORY schema).
2. You will create a table named COMPACT_DISC_TYPES. The table will include the COMPACT_DISC_ID column and the MUSIC_TYPE_ID column. Both columns will be assigned an INT data type. Enter and execute the following code:

```
CREATE TABLE COMPACT_DISC_TYPES
( COMPACT_DISC_ID  INT,
  MUSIC_TYPE_ID    INT );
```

3. You will now delete the table from the database. Enter and execute the following code:

```
DROP TABLE COMPACT_DISC_TYPES CASCADE;
```

4. You will now re-create the table you created in step 2, only this time you'll include a third column named CD_TITLE with a data type of VARCHAR(60). Enter and execute the following code:

```
CREATE TABLE COMPACT_DISC_TYPES
( COMPACT_DISC_ID  INT,
  CD_TITLE         VARCHAR(60),
  MUSIC_TYPE_ID    INT );
```

5. Your next step will be to delete the CD_TITLE column. Enter and execute the following code:

```
ALTER TABLE COMPACT_DISC_TYPES
 DROP COLUMN CD_TITLE CASCADE ;
```

6. The COMPACT_DISC_TYPES table should now contain only the COMPACT_DISC_ID column and the MUSIC_TYPE_ID column. Close the client application.

Try This Summary

The INVENTORY database should now contain four tables: COMPACT_DISCS, CD_LABELS, MUSIC_TYPES, and COMPACT_DISC_TYPES. The COMPACT_DISC_TYPES table, which you just created, contains two columns, COMPACT_DISC_ID and TYPE_ID, both of which are defined with the INT data type. In subsequent Try This exercises, you will continue to build on this database by adding new tables and modifying existing ones.

Chapter 3 Self Test

1. Which kinds of base tables can you create by using a CREATE TABLE statement?

   A Persistent base tables

   B Global temporary base tables

   C Created local temporary tables

   D Declared local temporary tables

2. What is the primary difference between a global temporary table and a created local temporary table?

3. You're creating a table named AGENTS. The table includes the AGENT_ID column, which has an INT data type, and the AGENT_NAME column, which has a CHAR(60) data type. What SQL statement should you use?

4. What are the three data types that SQL supports?

5. What are the three string data types?

6. A(n) ________________ data type permits values that are based on data bits rather than character sets or collations. This type of data type allows only values of 0 and 1.

7. What are the precision and the scale of the number 5293.472?

8. What are the differences between exact numeric data types and approximate numeric data types?

9. Which data types are exact numeric data types?

   A DOUBLE PRECISION

   B DECIMAL

   C REAL

   D SMALLINT

10. A(n) ______________ data type specifies the year, month, and day values of a date.
11. What are the two types of interval data types that SQL supports?
12. Which data type should you use to support a true/false construct that can be used for comparing values?
13. You are creating a distinct user-defined type named CITY. The user type is based on the CHAR(40) data type. Which SQL statement should you use?
14. You're creating a table named CUSTOMERS. The table includes the CUSTOMER_NAME column and the CUSTOMER_CITY column. Both columns have a VARCHAR(60) data type. The CUSTOMER_CITY column also has a default value of *Seattle*. Which SQL statement should you use?
15. Which SQL statement should you use to delete a column from an existing table?
16. Which SQL statement should you use to delete a table definition and all its SQL data from a database?
17. Your database includes a table named OPERA_SINGERS. You want to add a column named NATIONALITY to the table. The column should have a VARCHAR(40) data type. What SQL statement should you use?
18. You want to delete the table definition for the OPERA_SINGERS table from your database. You also want to delete all the data and any dependencies on the table. What SQL statement should you use?
19. Which statement should you use to quickly and efficiently remove all rows from the OPERA_SINGERS table?
20. You want to create a table named EMPLOYEES with columns EMPLOYEE_ID and EMPLOYEE_NAME. The EMPLOYEE_ID column should have the INT data type, and you want the column data values to be automatically assigned by the RDBMS whenever you don't provide a value for the column when inserting new rows. The EMPLOYEE_NAME column should have the VARCHAR(60) data type. What SQL statement should you use?

Chapter 4

Enforcing Data Integrity

Key Skills & Concepts

- Understand Integrity Constraints
- Use NOT NULL Constraints
- Add UNIQUE Constraints
- Add PRIMARY KEY Constraints
- Add FOREIGN KEY Constraints
- Define CHECK Constraints

An SQL database must do more than just store data. It must ensure that the data it stores is correct. If the integrity of the data is compromised, the data might be inaccurate or inconsistent, bringing into question the reliability of the database itself. In order to ensure the integrity of the data, SQL provides a number of *integrity constraints,* rules that are applied to base tables to constrain the values that can be placed into those tables. You can apply constraints to individual columns, to individual tables, or to multiple tables. In this chapter, I discuss each type of constraint and explain how you can apply them to your SQL database.

Understand Integrity Constraints

SQL integrity constraints, which are usually referred to simply as constraints, can be divided into three categories:

- **Table-related constraints** A type of constraint that is defined within a table definition. The constraint can be defined as part of the column definition or as an element in the table definition. Constraints defined at the table level can apply to one or more columns.
- **Assertions** A type of constraint that is defined within an assertion definition (separate from the table definition). An assertion can be related to one or more tables.
- **Domain constraints** A type of constraint that is defined within a domain definition (separate from the table definition). A domain constraint is associated with any column that is defined within the specific domain.

Of these three categories of constraints, table-related constraints are the most common and include the greatest number of constraint options. Table-related constraints can be divided into two subcategories: table constraints and column constraints. The constraints in both these subcategories are defined in the table definition. A column constraint is included with the column definition, and a table constraint is included as a table element, similar to the way columns are defined as table elements. (Chapter 3 discusses table elements and column definitions.) Both column constraints and table constraints support a number of different types of constraints. This is not the case for assertions and domain constraints, which are limited to only one type of constraint. Figure 4-1 provides an overview of the types of constraints that can be created.

At the top of the illustration, you can see the three categories of constraints. Beneath the Table-Related Constraints category are the Column Constraints subcategory and the Table Constraints subcategory, each of which contains specific types of constraints. For example, table constraints can include unique (UNIQUE constraints and PRIMARY KEY constraints), referential (FOREIGN KEY constraints), and CHECK constraints, while column constraints can include the NOT NULL constraint as well as unique, referential, and CHECK constraints. However, domains and assertions support only CHECK constraints.

NOTE

In some places, the SQL standard uses the term "table constraint" to refer to both types of table-related constraints. I use the term "table-related" to avoid confusion.

As Figure 4-1 shows, there are five different types of constraints: NOT NULL, UNIQUE, PRIMARY KEY, FOREIGN KEY, and CHECK. In SQL, UNIQUE constraints and

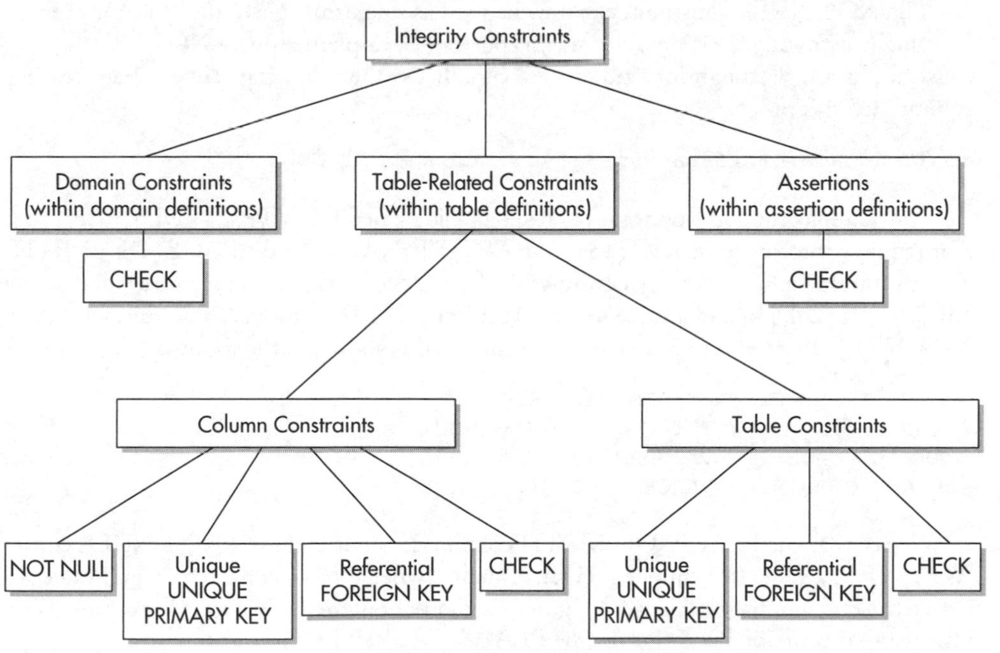

Figure 4-1 Types of SQL integrity constraints

PRIMARY KEY constraints are both considered unique constraints, and FOREIGN KEY constraints are considered referential constraints. The rest of the chapter is devoted to explaining what each of these constraints means and how to apply them.

Use NOT NULL Constraints

In Chapter 3, I told you that *null* signifies that a value is undefined or not known. This is not the same as a zero, a blank, an empty string, or a default value. Instead, it indicates that a data value is absent. You can think of a null value as being a flag. (A *flag* is a character, number, or bit that indicates a certain fact about a column. The flag serves as a marker that designates a particular condition or existence of something.) In the case of null, if no value is provided for a column, the flag is set, indicating that the value is unknown, or null. Every column has a *nullability* characteristic that indicates whether the column will accept null values. By default, all columns accept null values. However, you can override the default nullability characteristic by using a NOT NULL constraint, which indicates that the column will *not* accept null values.

NOTE

Some RDBMSs allow you to change the default nullability of any new column you create. In addition, most systems support a NULL constraint, which you can use to designate that a column will accept null values.

The NOT NULL constraint can only be used as a column constraint. It is not supported for table constraints, assertions, or domain constraints. Implementing a NOT NULL constraint is a very straightforward process. Simply use the following syntax when creating a column definition:

```
<column name> { <data type> | <domain> } NOT NULL
```

For example, suppose you want to create a table named COMPACT_DISC_ARTISTS that requires three columns: ARTIST_ID, ARTIST_NAME, and PLACE_OF_BIRTH. You want to make sure that any new rows that are added to the table include a value for the ARTIST_ID column and a value for the ARTIST_NAME column. To do this, you add a NOT NULL constraint to both column definitions, as shown in the following SQL statement:

```
CREATE TABLE COMPACT_DISC_ARTISTS
( ARTIST_ID        INT          NOT NULL,
  ARTIST_NAME      VARCHAR(60)  NOT NULL,
  PLACE_OF_BIRTH   VARCHAR(60) );
```

Notice that the PLACE_OF_BIRTH column does not include a NOT NULL constraint. As a result, if a value isn't supplied for this column (when a row is inserted), a null value will be inserted. (The null flag will be set.) Figure 4-2 shows how the table might look if rows were inserted that contained no value for the PLACE_OF_BIRTH column.

ARTIST_ID: INT	ARTIST_NAME: VARCHAR(60)	PLACE_OF_BIRTH: VARCHAR(60)
3001	Glen Hansard	Ballymun, Dublin, Ireland
3002	Joe Bonamassa	<null>
3003	Stevie Wonder	Saginaw, Michigan, USA
3004	Fleetwood Mac	<null>
3005	Shania Twain	Windsor, Ontario, Canada
3006	Garth Brooks	Tulsa, Oklahoma, USA

Figure 4-2 Null values appearing in the PLACE_OF_BIRTH column in the COMPACT_DISC_ARTISTS table

NOTE

SQL clients display null values in different ways, with many of them showing nothing, which makes it visually impossible to distinguish between columns containing blanks and those set to null values. To avoid such confusion, I show null values as "<null>" in all the figures in this book. Just keep in mind that nothing other than the null flag is actually stored in the database for a column containing a null value.

As you can see, the ARTIST_ID and ARTIST_NAME columns do not—and cannot—contain null values. The PLACE_OF_BIRTH column, on the other hand, contains two null values.

Add UNIQUE Constraints

If you refer back to Figure 4-1, you'll see that both column constraints and table constraints support unique constraints. You'll also see that there are two types of unique constraints: UNIQUE and PRIMARY KEY. In this section, I focus on the UNIQUE constraint. The PRIMARY KEY constraint is discussed in the "Add PRIMARY KEY Constraints" section later in this chapter.

The UNIQUE constraint allows you to require that a column or set of columns contains unique values, meaning values that are different from all other rows in the same table. For example, take a look at Figure 4-3, which shows the CD_INVENTORY table. The table contains three columns: ARTIST_NAME, CD_TITLE, and COPYRIGHT_YEAR.

You might decide that you want the values in the CD_TITLE column to be unique so that no two CD titles can be alike. If you applied a UNIQUE constraint to the column, you would not be able to insert a row that contained a CD_TITLE value that already existed in the table. Now suppose that you realize that making the CD_TITLE values unique is not a good idea because it is possible for more than one CD to share the same title. You decide

ARTIST_NAME: VARCHAR(40)	CD_TITLE: VARCHAR(60)	COPYRIGHT_YEAR: INT
Glen Hansard	Drive All Night	2013
Joe Bonamassa	Different Shades of Blue	2014
Stevie Wonder	Innervisions (Remastered)	2000
Stevie Wonder	The Definitive Collection	2002
Fleetwood Mac	Rumours (Remastered)	1990
Shania Twain	Come On Over	1997

Figure 4-3 The CD_INVENTORY table with the ARTIST_NAME, CD_TITLE, and COPYRIGHT_YEAR columns

to take another approach and use a UNIQUE constraint on the ARTIST_NAME and CD_TITLE columns. That way, no ARTIST_NAME/CD_TITLE pair can be repeated. You can repeat an ARTIST_NAME value or a CD_TITLE value, but you cannot repeat the exact same combination of the two. For example, the table already contains a row with an ARTIST_NAME value of Joe Bonamassa and a CD_TITLE value of Different Shades of Blue. If a UNIQUE constraint had been applied to these two columns, you could not add another row that contained *both* of these values.

NOTE

I should point out that the tables used for illustration of concepts in this chapter are not necessarily good designs. For example, names of people and things are seldom good choices to uniquely identify rows of data because they are rather long (compared to numbers), tend to change, and are prone to problems with duplicate values. However, these tables were chosen because they illustrate the concepts well.

Now that you have a basic understanding of how UNIQUE constraints are applied, let's take a look at the syntax that you use to create them. Remember, I said that you can create a UNIQUE constraint that is either a column constraint or a table constraint. To create a column constraint, add it as part of the column definition, as shown in the following syntax:

```
<column name> { <data type> | <domain> } UNIQUE
```

If you want to add a unique constraint as a table constraint, you must add it as a table element in the table definition, as shown in the following syntax:

```
[ CONSTRAINT <constraint name> ]
UNIQUE ( <column name> [ {, <column name> } . . . ] )
```

As you can see, applying a UNIQUE constraint as a column constraint is a little simpler than applying it as a table constraint. However, if you apply the constraint at the column level, you can apply it to only one column. Regardless of whether you use column constraints or table constraints, you can define as many UNIQUE constraints as necessary in a single table definition.

Now let's return to the table in Figure 4-3 and use it to create code examples for applying UNIQUE constraints. In the first example, I apply a UNIQUE constraint to the CD_TITLE column:

```
CREATE TABLE CD_INVENTORY
( ARTIST_NAME       VARCHAR(40),
  CD_TITLE          VARCHAR(60) UNIQUE,
  COPYRIGHT_YEAR    INT );
```

I can also apply UNIQUE constraints to other columns, but that would not have the same effect as combining two columns into one table constraint, as shown in the following example:

```
CREATE TABLE CD_INVENTORY
( ARTIST_NAME        VARCHAR(40),
  CD_TITLE           VARCHAR(60),
  COPYRIGHT_YEAR     INT,
  CONSTRAINT UN_ARTIST_CD UNIQUE ( ARTIST_NAME, CD_TITLE ) );
```

The ARTIST_NAME column and CD_TITLE column must now contain unique combinations of values in order for a row to be added to the CD_INVENTORY table.

Until now, I have told you that a UNIQUE constraint prevents duplicate values from being entered into a column or columns defined with that constraint. However, there is one exception to this—the null value. A UNIQUE constraint permits multiple null values in a column. As with other columns, null values are permitted by default. You can always override the default by using the NOT NULL constraint in conjunction with the UNIQUE constraint. For example, you can add NOT NULL to the CD_TITLE column definition:

```
CREATE TABLE CD_INVENTORY
( ARTIST_NAME       VARCHAR(40),
  CD_TITLE          VARCHAR(60)  NOT NULL  UNIQUE,
  COPYRIGHT_YEAR    INT );
```

You can also add NOT NULL to a column definition that's referenced by a table constraint:

```
CREATE TABLE CD_INVENTORY
( ARTIST_NAME       VARCHAR(40),
  CD_TITLE          VARCHAR(60)  NOT NULL,
  COPYRIGHT_YEAR    INT,
  CONSTRAINT UN_ARTIST_CD UNIQUE (CD_TITLE) );
```

In each case, both the NOT NULL constraint and the UNIQUE constraint are applied to the CD_TITLE column, which means the CD_TITLE values must be unique and without null values.

As always, check the documentation of the SQL implementation you are using. There are a few SQL implementations, such as DB2, that do not permit null values in columns that are included in UNIQUE constraints.

Add PRIMARY KEY Constraints

As I mentioned in the "Add UNIQUE Constraints" section, a PRIMARY KEY constraint, like the UNIQUE constraint, is a type of SQL unique constraint. Both types of constraints permit only unique values in the specified columns, both types can be applied to one or more columns, and both types can be defined as either column constraints or table constraints. However, PRIMARY KEY constraints have two restrictions that apply only to them:

- A column that is defined with a PRIMARY KEY constraint cannot contain null values. It doesn't matter whether or not the column definition specifies NOT NULL—the column cannot contain null values because of the PRIMARY KEY constraint.
- Only one PRIMARY KEY constraint can be defined for each table.

The reason for these restrictions is the role that a primary key (unique identifier) plays in a table. As you might recall from Chapter 1, each row in a table must be unique. This is important because SQL cannot differentiate between two rows that are completely identical, so you cannot update or delete one duplicate row without doing the same to the other. The primary key for a table is chosen by the database designer from available candidate keys. A *candidate key* is a set of one or more columns that uniquely identify each row. For example, in Figure 4-4, the only reasonable candidate key in the CD_ARTISTS table is the ARTIST_ID column. Each value in the column will be unique. That way, even if the ARTIST_NAME values and AGENCY values are duplicated, the row is still unique because the ARTIST_ID value is always unique.

The uniqueness of a candidate key can be enforced with either a UNIQUE constraint or a PRIMARY KEY constraint. However, each table should include a primary key even if no UNIQUE constraints are defined. This is considered an industry best practice because a primary key cannot accept null values, which makes it the definitive measure by which a row's uniqueness can be ensured. Primary keys are also useful when one table references another through the use of foreign keys. (See the "Add FOREIGN KEY Constraints" section later in this chapter.) Furthermore, some RDBMSs require the definition of primary keys under certain circumstances, such as when a table column is included in a full text index.

To define the primary key, you must use the PRIMARY KEY constraint to specify which column or columns will serve as the table's primary key. The process of defining a PRIMARY KEY constraint is very similar to that of defining a UNIQUE constraint. If you want to add a PRIMARY KEY constraint to a column definition, use the following syntax:

```
<column name> { <data type> | <domain> } PRIMARY KEY
```

Candidate Key

ARTIST_ID INT	ARTIST_NAME VARCHAR(60)	AGENCY_ID INT
3001	Glen Hansard	2305
3002	John Bonamassa	2306
3003	Stevie Wonder	2327
3004	Fleetwood Mac	2345
3005	Shania Twain	2367
3006	Garth Brooks	2367
3007	J. S. Bach	<null>
3008	Joshua Bell	2305

Figure 4-4 The candidate key in the CD_ARTISTS table

If you want to add a PRIMARY KEY constraint as a table constraint, you must add it as a table element in the table definition, as shown in the following syntax:

```
[ CONSTRAINT <constraint name> ]
PRIMARY KEY ( <column name> [ {, <column name> } . . . ] )
```

As with the UNIQUE constraint, you can use a column constraint to define a primary key if you're including only one column in the definition. For example, if you were to define a PRIMARY KEY constraint for the table shown in Figure 4-4, you would use the following SQL statement:

```
CREATE TABLE CD_ARTISTS
( ARTIST_ID     INT           PRIMARY KEY,
  ARTIST_NAME   VARCHAR(60),
  AGENCY_ID     INT );
```

If you want to apply the constraint to multiple columns—or you simply want to keep it as a separate definition—then you must use a table constraint:

```
CREATE TABLE CD_ARTISTS
( ARTIST_ID     INT,
  ARTIST_NAME   VARCHAR(60),
  AGENCY_ID     INT,
  CONSTRAINT PK_ARTIST_ID PRIMARY KEY ( ARTIST_ID, ARTIST_NAME ) );
```

This method creates a primary key on the ARTIST_ID and ARTIST_NAME columns, so that the combined values of both columns must be unique, although duplicates can exist within the individual column. An experienced database designer will quickly point out to you that this is a *superkey*, which means that it has more columns in it than the minimum needed to form a primary key. And that is true—ARTIST_ID by itself is unique, and we really don't need to add ARTIST_NAME to it in order to form a primary key, and we want to be sure that duplicate values of ARTIST_ID are not entered into the table, which means we should have a primary key with only ARTIST_ID in it. It was only done here to illustrate that a primary key can contain multiple columns and to define one that way, a table constraint must be used.

You might find that you want to define both PRIMARY KEY and UNIQUE constraints in a table. To do so, you simply define the constraints as you normally would. For example, the following SQL statement defines a PRIMARY KEY constraint on the ARTIST_ID column and a UNIQUE constraint on the ARTIST_NAME column:

```
CREATE TABLE CD_ARTISTS
( ARTIST_ID     INT             PRIMARY KEY,
  ARTIST_NAME   VARCHAR(60),
  AGENCY_ID     INT,
  CONSTRAINT UN_ARTIST_NAME UNIQUE (ARTIST_NAME) );
```

You would achieve the same results with the following code:

```
CREATE TABLE CD_ARTISTS
( ARTIST_ID     INT,
  ARTIST_NAME   VARCHAR(60)   UNIQUE,
  AGENCY_ID     INT,
  CONSTRAINT PK_ARTIST_ID PRIMARY KEY (ARTIST_ID) );
```

NOTE

I used a UNIQUE constraint in these SQL statements only as a way to demonstrate how the constraint can be used in a table with a primary key. Most likely, you would not want to use a UNIQUE constraint for the ARTIST_NAME column because it is possible for two artists to share the same name. (For example, two different blues artists, both of whom lived in the earlier part of the last century, went by the name of Sonny Boy Williamson.)

Add FOREIGN KEY Constraints

Up to this point, the types of constraints that I've discussed have had to do primarily with ensuring the integrity of data within a table. The NOT NULL constraint prevents the use of null values within a column, and the UNIQUE and PRIMARY KEY constraints ensure the uniqueness of values within a column or set of columns. However, the FOREIGN KEY constraint is different in that it is concerned with how data in one table relates to data in another table, which is why it is known as a *referential constraint*—it references another table.

Ask the Expert

Q: Can the columns in a table belong to both a UNIQUE constraint and a PRIMARY KEY constraint?

A: Yes, as long as the constraints are not on the exact same columns. For example, suppose you have a table that includes three columns: ARTIST_ID, ARTIST_NAME, and PLACE_OF_BIRTH. You can define a PRIMARY KEY constraint that includes the ARTIST_ID and ARTIST_NAME columns, which would ensure unique value pairs in those two columns, but values within the individual columns could still be duplicated. However, you can then define a UNIQUE constraint that includes only the ARTIST_NAME column to ensure that those values are unique as well. (This certainly isn't the best design, but it illustrates my point.) You can also create a UNIQUE constraint that includes the ARTIST_NAME and PLACE_OF_BIRTH columns to ensure unique value pairs in those two columns. The only thing you can't do is create a UNIQUE constraint that includes the exact same columns as an existing PRIMARY KEY constraint and vice versa.

Q: You state that a column that is included in a PRIMARY KEY constraint will not accept null values. What happens if that column is configured with a NOT NULL constraint as well?

A: Nothing different happens. The table is still created in the same way. A column definition that includes PRIMARY KEY is saying the same thing as a column definition that includes NOT NULL PRIMARY KEY. In fact, prior to SQL-92, the NOT NULL keywords were required on all columns included in a PRIMARY KEY constraint. The same was true for UNIQUE constraints. It wasn't until SQL-92 that null values were permitted in columns included in a UNIQUE constraint, which clearly set them apart from PRIMARY KEY constraints. Also, be wary of variations across vendor implementations. For example, Oracle will automatically add NOT NULL constraints to columns included in a PRIMARY KEY constraint, while SQL Server (or at least some versions of it) will display an error if you attempt to create a PRIMARY KEY constraint using columns that have not been specified with a NOT NULL constraint.

(Actually, there is an exception called a *recursive relationship* where the foreign key refers to another row in the same table, but I'm going to ignore this special case for now in order to focus on the basics.)

You might recall from Chapter 1 that tables in a relational database are linked together in a meaningful way in order to ensure the integrity of the data. This association between tables forms a relationship that provides *referential integrity* between tables. Referential integrity prevents the manipulation of data in one table from adversely affecting data in another table. Let's take a look at an example that illustrates this point. Figure 4-5 shows two tables

COMPACT_DISCS

CD_ID: INT	CD_TITLE: VARCHAR(60)	LABEL_ID: INT
101	Drive All Night	826
102	Different Shades of Blue	828
103	Innervisions (Remastered)	827
104	The Definitive Collection	827
105	Rumours (Remastered)	830
106	Come On Over	831

CD_LABELS

LABEL_ID: INT	COMPANY_NAME: VARCHAR(60)
826	ANTI Records
827	Motown / Universal
828	J&R Adventures
830	Warner Bros.
831	Mercury

Figure 4-5 The relationship between the COMPACT_DISCS and CD_LABELS tables

(COMPACT_DISCS and CD_LABELS) that are each defined with a primary key. The CD_ID column in the COMPACT_DISCS table is configured with a PRIMARY KEY constraint, as is the LABEL_ID column in the CD_LABELS table. Both these columns are shaded in the illustration.

Notice that the COMPACT_DISCS table contains a column named LABEL_ID. This column includes values from the LABEL_ID column of the CD_LABELS table. In fact, the LABEL_ID values in the COMPACT_DISCS table should include only values that come from the LABEL_ID column in the CD_LABELS table. You should not be able to insert a row into COMPACT_DISCS if the LABEL_ID value is not listed in the CD_LABELS table. At the same time, if you alter or delete a LABEL_ID value in the CD_LABELS table, you should be able to predict the outcome of your action if those same values exist in the COMPACT_DISCS table. Under no circumstances would you want to delete a label and leave LABEL_ID values in the COMPACT_DISCS table that reference a label that no longer exists. These results can be achieved by using a FOREIGN KEY constraint. A FOREIGN KEY constraint enforces referential integrity between two tables by ensuring that no action is taken on either table that adversely affects the data protected by the constraint.

In the tables shown in Figure 4-5, the FOREIGN KEY constraint must be configured on the LABEL_ID column of the COMPACT_DISCS table. The FOREIGN KEY constraint restricts the values in that column to the values of a candidate key (usually the primary key) in the related table. Only valid data values are permitted in the FOREIGN KEY column or columns.

NOTE

The table that contains the foreign key is the referencing table (sometimes called the *child* table). The table that is being referenced by the foreign key is the referenced table (sometimes called the *parent* table). Likewise, the column or columns that make up the foreign key in the referencing table are referred to as the referencing columns. The columns being referenced by the foreign key are the referenced columns.

When creating a FOREIGN KEY constraint, you must follow several guidelines:

- The referenced columns must be defined with either a UNIQUE or PRIMARY KEY constraint on them. As you might guess, the primary key is most commonly used for the referenced columns.
- A FOREIGN KEY constraint can be created as a table constraint or column constraint. If you create the foreign key as a column constraint, you can include only one column. If you create the foreign key as a table constraint, you can include one or more columns.
- The foreign key in the referencing table must include the same number of columns that are being referenced, and the referencing columns must each be configured with the same data types as their referenced counterparts. However, the referencing columns do not have to have the same names as the referenced columns.
- If you don't specify the referenced columns when you define a FOREIGN KEY constraint, then the columns defined in the primary key of the referenced table are used as the referenced columns.

These guidelines will become clearer as I explain how to implement a foreign key. First, let's take a look at the basic syntax used to create that constraint. If you want to add a FOREIGN KEY constraint as a column constraint, you must add the constraint to a column definition, as shown in the following syntax:

```
<column name> { <data type> | <domain> } [ NOT NULL ]
REFERENCES <referenced table> [ ( <referenced columns> ) ]
[ MATCH { FULL | PARTIAL | SIMPLE } ]
[ <referential triggered action> ]
```

If you want to add a FOREIGN KEY constraint as a table constraint, you must add it as a table element in the table definition, as shown in the following syntax:

```
[ CONSTRAINT <constraint name> ]
FOREIGN KEY ( <referencing column > [ {, <referencing column> } . . . ] )
REFERENCES <referenced table> [ ( <referenced columns> ) ]
[ MATCH { FULL | PARTIAL | SIMPLE } ]
[ <referential triggered action> ]
```

As you can see, a FOREIGN KEY constraint is a bit more complicated than the constraint syntax you've looked at so far. However, creating a basic FOREIGN KEY constraint is a relatively straightforward process. Let's take a look at one first, and then we'll go on to the more complex language elements.

In the following example, I use a CREATE TABLE statement to create the COMPACT_DISCS table (shown in Figure 4-5) and define a column constraint:

```
CREATE TABLE COMPACT_DISCS
( CD_ID        INT,
```

```
  CD_TITLE      VARCHAR(60),
  LABEL_ID INT REFERENCES CD_LABELS );
```

This statement defines a FOREIGN KEY constraint on the LABEL_ID column. Notice that in order to add a column constraint, all you have to do is add the REFERENCES keyword and the name of the referenced table. Also notice that the foreign key contains the same number of columns as the primary key in the referenced table, and the referenced and referencing columns are the same data type. Remember, if you're not referencing the primary key in the referenced table, you must also include the name of the column or columns—for example, REFERENCES CD_LABELS (LABEL_ID).

NOTE

Before you can create a foreign key on a table, the referenced table must already exist and a UNIQUE or PRIMARY KEY constraint must be defined for that table.

In the next example, I create a foreign key that is a table constraint. Unlike the previous example, I include the name of the referenced column in this constraint definition, even though it isn't necessary:

```
CREATE TABLE COMPACT_DISCS
( CD_ID          INT,
  CD_TITLE       VARCHAR(60),
  LABEL_ID       INT,
  CONSTRAINT FK_LABEL_ID FOREIGN KEY (LABEL_ID)
    REFERENCES CD_LABELS (LABEL_ID) );
```

The last two lines of code are the constraint definition. The name of the constraint, FK_LABEL_ID, follows the CONSTRAINT keyword. Constraint names aren't necessary because the DBMS will assign a system-generated name if one is not supplied. However, it's a good practice to supply your own because constraint names often appear in error messages when SQL statements attempt to violate constraints, and names you supply will be easier to recognize than ones the DBMS supplied for you. Following the constraint name, the FOREIGN KEY keywords indicate the type of constraint, which is followed by the referencing column name, LABEL_ID. This is the name of the column on which the constraint is being placed. If there were multiple column names, they would be separated by commas. The name of the referencing column is then followed by the REFERENCES keyword, which is followed by the name of the referenced table, CD_LABELS. The name of the referenced column follows the name of the referenced table.

That's all there is to it. Once the constraint is defined, you would not be able to place values in the LABEL_ID column of the COMPACT_DISCS table unless those values already existed in the primary key of the CD_LABELS table. You should note, however, that the values in the foreign key do not have to be unique, as they must be in the CD_LABELS primary key. Values in the foreign key can be repeated any number of times, unless the column is limited by a unique constraint.

Before I move on to discussing the other elements of the FOREIGN KEY syntax, let's take a quick look at a foreign key that includes multiple columns. In Figure 4-6, there are two tables: PERFORMING_ARTISTS and ARTISTS_MUSIC_TYPES.

The primary key on the PERFORMING_ARTISTS table is defined on the ARTIST_NAME and ARTIST_DOB columns. The following SQL statement creates the ARTISTS_MUSIC_TYPES table, which includes a foreign key made up of the ARTIST_NAME and DOB columns:

```
CREATE TABLE ARTISTS_MUSIC_TYPES
( ARTIST_NAME   VARCHAR(60),
  DOB           DATE,
  TYPE_ID       INT,
  CONSTRAINT FK_CD_ARTISTS FOREIGN KEY ( ARTIST_NAME, DOB )
     REFERENCES PERFORMING_ARTISTS (ARTIST_NAME, ARTIST_DOB) );
```

In this statement, there are two referencing columns (ARTIST_NAME and DOB) and two referenced columns (ARTIST_NAME, ARTIST_DOB). The ARTIST_NAME columns in the two tables have the same data type, and the DOB column has the same data type as the ARTIST_DOB column. As you can see, one of the referencing columns (DOB) has a different name than its referenced counterpart (ARTIST_DOB).

PERFORMING_ARTISTS

ARTIST_NAME: VARCHAR(60)	ARTIST_DOB: DATE	PLACE_OF_BIRTH: VARCHAR(60)	POSTER_IN_STOCK: BOOLEAN
Glen Hansard	1970-04-21	Ballymun, Dublin, Ireland	True
Joe Bonamassa	1977-05-08	Unknown	False
Stevie Wonder	1950-05-13	Saginaw, Michigan, USA	True
Fleetwood Mac	<null>	Unknown	True
Shania Twain	1965-08-28	Windsor, Ontario, Canada	False
Garth Brooks	1962-02-07	Tulsa, Oklahoma, USA	<null>

ARTISTS_MUSIC_TYPES

ARTIST_NAME: VARCHAR(60)	DOB: DATE	TYPE_ID: INT
Glen Hansard	1970-04-21	11
Glen Hansard	1970-04-21	20
Joe Bonamassa	1977-05-08	12
Joe Bonamassa	1977-05-08	17
Stevie Wonder	1950-05-13	19
Stevie Wonder	1950-05-13	20
Fleetwood Mac	<null>	14
Shania Twain	1965-08-28	15
Shania Twain	1965-08-28	17
Shania Twain	1965-08-28	20
Garth Brooks	1962-02-07	15

Figure 4-6 A foreign key made up of multiple columns

Ask the Expert

Q: In Figure 4-6 and in the preceding examples, you created a FOREIGN KEY constraint on the ARTIST_NAME and DOB columns in the ARTISTS_MUSIC_TYPES table. What would the primary key be for this table?

A: Remember that a primary key must uniquely identify each row in a table. However, because pairs of values in the ARTIST_NAME and DOB columns can be repeated (which means that they can be repeated in the individual columns as well), those two columns cannot be used by themselves as a primary key for this table. On the other hand, the TYPE_ID column can have repeating values as well, so that column cannot be used by itself. In addition, you probably wouldn't want to combine the TYPE_ID column with one of the other two columns because it is conceivable that you would have repeating rows (for example, two artists with the same name performing the same types of music, such as the two blues musicians named Sonny Boy Williamson, or two artists with the same date of birth performing the same type of music). As a result, your best solution (aside from adding another column to the table) is to roll all three columns into the primary key. Together, the three columns would uniquely identify each row because it is highly unlikely that anyone would share the same name, date of birth, and type of music (although anything is possible, which is why, ultimately, adding another column that is guaranteed to be unique is the very best way to go).

The MATCH Clause

Now that you have an understanding of how to define a basic FOREIGN KEY constraint, let's look at another line of the FOREIGN KEY syntax:

```
[ MATCH { FULL | PARTIAL | SIMPLE } ]
```

You can tell from the brackets that this is an optional clause. And in fact, very few vendor products currently support this clause (it's not supported by SQL Server 2014, Oracle 12*c*, or MySQL prior to version 5.0, for example), so you won't see it used much at all. Starting with MySQL version 5.0, the MATCH clause can be specified, but it currently has no effect. (MATCH SIMPLE is always in force, even if you specify otherwise.) However, the clause is described in the SQL standard, which means we can expect more vendor product support in the future. Its purpose is to allow you to decide how to treat null values in the foreign key columns with regard to permitting values to be inserted into the referencing columns. If the columns do not permit null values, then the MATCH clause does not apply. You have three options that you can use in the MATCH clause:

1. If MATCH FULL is specified, all referencing columns must have a null value or none of these columns can have a null value.

2. If MATCH PARTIAL is specified, one or more referencing columns can have null values as long as the remaining referencing columns have values that equal their corresponding referenced columns.
3. If MATCH SIMPLE is specified and one or more referencing columns have null values, then the remaining referencing columns can have values that are not contained in the corresponding referenced columns. The SIMPLE option is implied if the MATCH clause is not included in the FOREIGN KEY constraint definition.

The best way to illustrate each of these MATCH options is through examples of valid and invalid data that can be inserted in the referencing columns. Going back to our example shown in Figure 4-6, you can see that the foreign key in the ARTISTS_MUSIC_TYPES table is made up of two referencing columns: ARTIST_NAME and DOB. Table 4-1 provides examples for data that can and cannot be inserted into the foreign key columns. The examples are based on data in the primary key columns of the PERFORMING_ARTISTS table.

NOTE

You probably wouldn't want to permit null values in your referencing columns in the ARTISTS_MUSIC_TYPES table, particularly for the ARTIST_NAME column. And if either of these columns were used in the primary key, you would not be able to permit null values. However, in order to demonstrate how the MATCH options work, let's assume that null values are permitted.

MATCH Option	Valid Data Examples	Invalid Data Examples
FULL	Glen Hansard, 1970-04-21 NULL, NULL	NULL, 1970-04-21 Glen Hansard, NULL Glen Hansard, 1802-08-03
PARTIAL	Joe Bonamassa, 1977-05-08 NULL, 1977-05-08 Joe Bonamassa, NULL NULL, NULL	NULL, 1802-08-03 Henryk Górecki, NULL Joe Bonamassa, 1965-02-07
SIMPLE	Stevie Wonder, 1950-05-13 NULL, 1950-05-13 Stevie Wonder, NULL NULL, 1802-08-03 Henryk Górecki, NULL NULL, NULL	Stevie Wonder, 1802-08-03 Stevie Wonder, 1965-02-07 Henryk Górecki, 1965-02-07

Table 4-1 Valid and Invalid Examples of the MATCH Clause Options

If you decide to use the MATCH clause, you simply add it to the end of your FOREIGN KEY constraint definition, as shown in the following SQL statement (assuming your implementation of SQL supports it):

```
CREATE TABLE ARTISTS_MUSIC_TYPES
( ARTIST_NAME  VARCHAR(60),
  DOB          DATE,
  TYPE_ID      INT,
  CONSTRAINT FK_CD_ARTISTS FOREIGN KEY ( ARTIST_NAME, DOB )
     REFERENCES PERFORMING_ARTISTS (ARTIST_NAME, ARTIST_DOB)
     MATCH FULL );
```

To insert data into the referencing columns (ARTIST_NAME and DOB), both values have to be null or they must be valid data values from the referenced columns in the PERFORMING_ARTISTS table.

The <referential triggered action> Clause

The final clause in the FOREIGN KEY constraint syntax is the optional <referential triggered action> clause. The clause allows you to define what types of actions should be taken when attempting to update or delete data from the referenced columns—if that attempt would cause a violation of the data in the referencing columns. For example, suppose you try to delete data from a table that has a primary key. If that primary key is referenced by a foreign key and if the data to be deleted is stored in the foreign key, then deleting the data from the primary key would cause a violation of the FOREIGN KEY constraint. Data in referencing columns must always be included in the referenced columns.

The point to remember about the <referential triggered action> clause is that you are including in the definition of the referencing table (through the foreign key) an action that should be taken as a result of something being done to the referenced table. This can be clarified by taking a look at the syntax for the <referential triggered action> clause:

```
ON UPDATE <referential action> [ ON DELETE <referential action> ]
| ON DELETE <referential action> [ ON UPDATE <referential action> ]
<referential action> ::=
CASCADE | SET NULL | SET DEFAULT | RESTRICT | NO ACTION
```

NOTE

The ::= symbol (two consecutive colons plus an equals sign) is used in the SQL standard to separate a placeholder in the angle brackets from its definition. In the preceding syntax, the <referential action> placeholder is defined. The placeholder is used in the code preceding the definition. You would then take the definition (the five keywords) and use them in place of the <referential action> placeholder as it is used in the ON UPDATE and ON DELETE clauses.

As you can see from the syntax, you can define an ON UPDATE clause, an ON DELETE clause, or both, and you can define them in any order. For each of these clauses, you can choose one of five referential actions:

1. If CASCADE is used and data is updated or deleted in the referenced columns, the data in the referencing columns is updated or deleted.
2. If SET NULL is used and data is updated or deleted in the referenced columns, the values in the corresponding referencing columns are set to null. Null values have to be supported in the referencing columns for this option to work.
3. If SET DEFAULT is used and data is updated or deleted in the referenced columns, the values in the corresponding referencing columns are set to their default values. Default values must be assigned to the referencing columns for this option to work.
4. If RESTRICT is used and you try to update or delete data in your referenced columns that would cause a foreign key violation, you are prevented from performing that action. Data in the referencing columns can never violate the FOREIGN KEY constraint, not even temporarily.
5. If NO ACTION is used and you try to update or delete data in your referenced columns that would cause a foreign key violation, you are prevented from performing that action. However, data violations can occur temporarily under certain conditions during the execution of an SQL statement, but the data in the foreign key is never violated in its final state (at the end of that execution). The NO ACTION option is the default used for both updates and deletes if no referential triggered action is specified.

If you decide to use the <referential triggered action> clause, you simply add it to the end of your FOREIGN KEY constraint definition, as shown in the following SQL statement:

```
CREATE TABLE ARTISTS_MUSIC_TYPES
( ARTIST_NAME  VARCHAR(60),
  DOB          DATE,
  TYPE_ID      INT,
  CONSTRAINT FK_CD_ARTISTS FOREIGN KEY ( ARTIST_NAME, DOB )
     REFERENCES PERFORMING_ARTISTS ON UPDATE CASCADE ON DELETE CASCADE
);
```

If you update data in or delete data from the referenced columns in PERFORMING_ARTISTS, those changes will be made to the referencing columns in the ARTISTS_MUSIC_TYPES table.

Try This 4-1 Adding NOT NULL, Unique, and Referential Constraints

In Chapter 3, Try This 3-1 and Try This 3-2, you created several tables that you added to the INVENTORY database (or the CD_INVENTORY schema). In this Try This exercise, you will add a number of constraints to the tables and create new tables that are also defined with constraints. However, rather than use the ALTER TABLE statement to modify the tables that you already created, you will be re-creating those tables. The advantage to this is that you'll be able to see the complete table definition as it relates to the updated data model, shown in Figure 4-7.

The data model incorporates a few more elements than you have seen before. It identifies tables, columns within those tables, data types for those columns, constraints, and relationships between tables. You should already be familiar with how tables, columns, and data types are represented, so let's take a look at constraints and relationships:

- The columns included in the primary key are in the top section of the table, and the other columns lie in the bottom section. For example, in the COMPACT_DISCS table, the CD_ID column is the primary key. In some cases, as in the COMPACT_DISC_TYPES table, all columns are included in the primary key.
- Each foreign key is represented by an [FK].

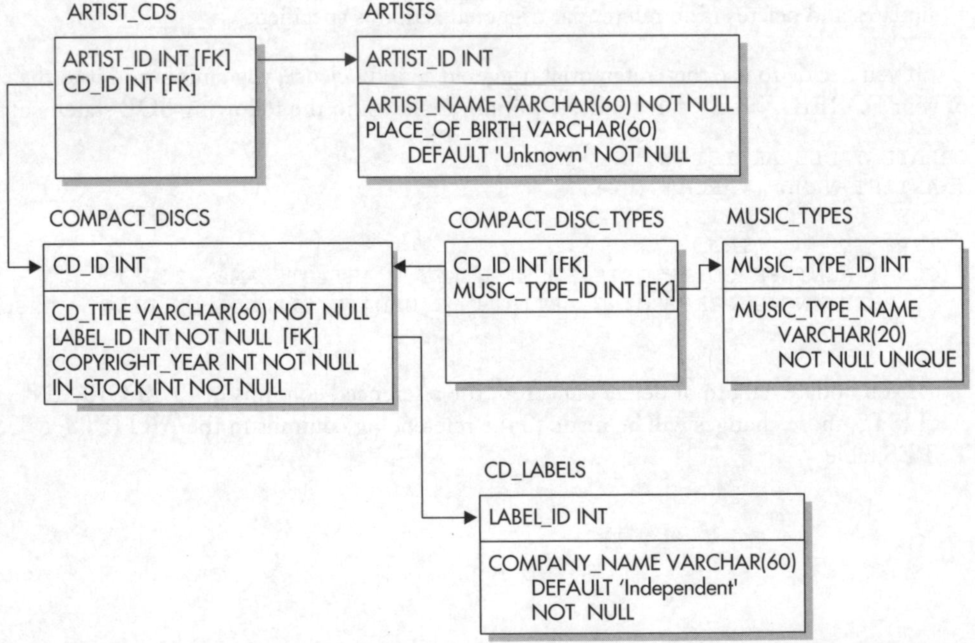

Figure 4-7 Data model for the INVENTORY database

- Defaults, UNIQUE constraints, and NOT NULL constraints are identified with each applicable column.
- Relationships, as defined by foreign keys, are represented by lines that connect the foreign key in one table to the candidate key (usually the primary key) in another table.

You'll find this data model useful not only for this exercise, but for other Try This exercises in the book, all of which will continue to build upon or use the INVENTORY database. You can also download the Try_This_04.txt file, which contains the SQL statements used in this exercise.

NOTE

Data models come in many varieties. The model I use here is specific to the needs of the book. You'll find in the real world that the models will differ from what you see here. For example, relationships between tables might be represented differently, and column definition information might not be quite as extensive.

Step by Step

1. Open the client application for your RDBMS and connect to the INVENTORY database.
2. You first need to drop the four tables (COMPACT_DISC_TYPES, COMPACT_DISCS, MUSIC_TYPES, and CD_LABELS) that you already created. Enter and execute the following SQL statements:

```
DROP TABLE COMPACT_DISC_TYPES CASCADE;
DROP TABLE COMPACT_DISCS      CASCADE;
DROP TABLE MUSIC_TYPES        CASCADE;
DROP TABLE CD_LABELS          CASCADE;
```

NOTE

If you created either the ARTISTS table or the ARTIST_CDS table when trying out examples or experimenting with CREATE TABLE statements, be sure to drop those as well.

NOTE

The CASCADE option is not supported by SQL Server, and in Oracle must be written as CASCADE CONSTRAINTS.

Now you can begin to re-create these tables and create new ones. You should create the tables in the order outlined in this exercise because the tables referenced in foreign keys will have to exist—with primary keys created—before you can create the foreign keys. Be sure to refer to the data model in Figure 4-7 for details about each table that you create.

(continued)

3. The first table that you're going to create is the MUSIC_TYPES table. It contains two columns: TYPE_ID and TYPE_NAME. You'll configure the TYPE_ID column as the primary key, and you'll configure a UNIQUE constraint and NOT NULL constraint on the TYPE_NAME column. Enter and execute the following SQL statement:

```
CREATE TABLE MUSIC_TYPES
( MUSIC_TYPE_ID     INT,
  MUSIC_TYPE_NAME   VARCHAR(20)  NOT NULL,
  CONSTRAINT UN_TYPE_NAME UNIQUE (MUSIC_TYPE_NAME),
  CONSTRAINT PK_MUSIC_TYPES PRIMARY KEY (MUSIC_TYPE_ID) );
```

4. The next table that you'll create is the CD_LABELS table. The table includes the LABEL_ID column, which will be defined as the primary key, and the COMPANY_NAME column, which will be defined with a default and the NOT NULL constraint. Enter and execute the following SQL statement:

```
CREATE TABLE CD_LABELS
( LABEL_ID       INT,
  COMPANY_NAME   VARCHAR(60)  DEFAULT 'Independent'  NOT NULL,
  CONSTRAINT PK_CD_LABELS PRIMARY KEY (LABEL_ID) );
```

5. Now that you've created the CD_LABELS table, you can create the COMPACT_DISCS table. The COMPACT_DISCS table contains a foreign key that references the CD_LABELS table. This is why you created CD_LABELS first. Enter and execute the following SQL statement:

```
CREATE TABLE COMPACT_DISCS
( CD_ID              INT,
  CD_TITLE           VARCHAR(60)  NOT NULL,
  LABEL_ID           INT          NOT NULL,
  COPYRIGHT_YEAR     INT          NOT NULL,
  CONSTRAINT PK_COMPACT_DISCS PRIMARY KEY (CD_ID),
  CONSTRAINT FK_LABEL_ID FOREIGN KEY (LABEL_ID)
     REFERENCES CD_LABELS (CD_ID) );
```

6. The next table, COMPACT_DISC_TYPES, includes two foreign keys, along with its primary key. The foreign keys reference the COMPACT_DISCS table and the MUSIC_TYPES table, both of which you've already created. Enter and execute the following SQL statement:

```
CREATE TABLE COMPACT_DISC_TYPES
( CD_ID            INT,
  MUSIC_TYPE_ID    INT,
  CONSTRAINT PK_COMPACT_DISC_TYPES
     PRIMARY KEY (CD_ID, MUSIC_TYPE_ID),
  CONSTRAINT FK_CD_ID_01 FOREIGN KEY (CD_ID)
     REFERENCES COMPACT_DISCS (CD_ID),
  CONSTRAINT FK_MUSIC_TYPE_ID FOREIGN KEY (MUSIC_TYPE_ID)
     REFERENCES MUSIC_TYPES (MUSIC_TYPE_ID) );
```

7. Now you can create the ARTISTS table. Enter and execute the following SQL statement:

```
CREATE TABLE ARTISTS
( ARTIST_ID INT,
  ARTIST_NAME      VARCHAR(60)                          NOT NULL,
  PLACE_OF_BIRTH   VARCHAR(60)   DEFAULT 'Unknown'      NOT NULL,
  CONSTRAINT PK_ARTISTS PRIMARY KEY (ARTIST_ID) ) ;
```

8. The last table you'll create (at least for now) is the ARTIST_CDS table. Enter and execute the following SQL statement:

```
CREATE TABLE ARTIST_CDS
( ARTIST_ID          INT,
  CD_ID  INT,
  CONSTRAINT PK_ARTIST_CDS PRIMARY KEY ( ARTIST_ID, CD_ID ),
  CONSTRAINT FK_ARTIST_ID FOREIGN KEY (ARTIST_ID)
     REFERENCES ARTISTS (ARTIST_ID),
  CONSTRAINT FK_CD_ID_02 FOREIGN KEY (CD_ID)
   REFERENCES COMPACT_DISCS (CD_ID) ) ;
```

9. Close the client application.

Try This Summary

Your database now has six tables, each one configured with the necessary defaults and constraints. In this Try This exercise, we followed a specific order for creating the tables in order to more easily implement the foreign keys. However, you could have created the tables in any order, without their foreign keys—unless the referenced table was already created—and then added in the foreign keys later, but this would have added extra steps. In fact, had you wanted to, you could have altered the tables that had existed prior to this exercise (rather than dropping them and then re-creating them), as long as you created primary keys (or UNIQUE constraints) on the referenced tables before creating foreign keys on the referencing tables. Regardless of the approach you take, the end result should be that your database now has the necessary tables to begin moving on to other components of SQL.

Define CHECK Constraints

Earlier in the chapter, in the "Understand Integrity Constraints" section, I discussed the various constraint categories and the types of constraints they support. (Refer back to Figure 4-1 for an overview of these categories.) One type of constraint—the CHECK constraint—can be defined as table constraints, column constraints, domain constraints, or within assertions. A CHECK constraint allows you to specify what values can be included in a column. You can define a range of values (for example, between 10 and 100), a list of values (for example, blues, jazz, pop, country), or a number of other conditions that restrict exactly what values are permitted in a column.

CHECK constraints are the most flexible of all the constraints and are often the most complicated. Despite this, the basic syntax used for a CHECK constraint is relatively simple. To create a column CHECK constraint, use the following syntax in a column definition:

```
<column name> { <data type> | <domain> } CHECK ( <search condition> )
```

To create a table CHECK constraint, use the following syntax in a table definition:

```
[ CONSTRAINT <constraint name> ] CHECK ( <search condition> )
```

I'll be discussing domain constraints and assertions later in this section.

As you can see by the syntax, a CHECK constraint is relatively straightforward. However, the values used for the <search condition> clause can be very extensive and, consequently, quite complex. The main concept is that the <search condition> is tested (one could say "checked") for any SQL statement that attempts to modify the data in a column covered by the CHECK constraint, and if it evaluates to TRUE, the SQL statement is allowed to complete; if it evaluates to FALSE, the SQL statement fails and an error message is displayed. The best way for you to learn about the clause is by looking at examples. However, most <search condition> components are based on the use of predicates in order to create the search condition. A *predicate* is an expression that operates on values. For example, a predicate can be used to compare values (for instance, COLUMN_1 > 10). The greater-than symbol (>) is a comparison predicate, sometimes referred to as a *comparison operator*. In this case, the predicate verifies that any value inserted into COLUMN_1 is greater than 10.

Many <search condition> components also rely on the use of subqueries. A *subquery* is an expression that is used as a component within another expression. Subqueries are used when an expression must access or calculate multiple layers of data, such as having to search a second table to provide data for the first table.

Both predicates and subqueries are complicated enough subjects to be beyond the scope of a discussion about CHECK constraints, and indeed each subject is treated separately in its own chapter. (See Chapter 9 for information about predicates and Chapter 12 for information about subqueries.) Despite the fact that both topics are discussed later in the book, I want to provide you with at least a few examples of CHECK constraints to give you a feel for how they're implemented in an SQL environment.

The first example we'll look at is a CHECK constraint that defines the minimum and maximum values that can be inserted into a column. The following table definition in this example creates three columns and one CHECK constraint (as a table constraint) that restricts the values of one of the columns to a range of numbers between 0 and 30:

```
CREATE TABLE COMPACT_DISCS
( CD__ID          INT,
  CD_TITLE        VARCHAR(60)  NOT NULL,
  IN_STOCK        INT          NOT NULL,
  CONSTRAINT CK_IN_STOCK CHECK ( IN_STOCK > 0 AND IN_STOCK < 30 ) );
```

If you were to try to enter a value into the IN_STOCK column other than 1 through 29, you would receive an error. You can achieve the same results by defining a column constraint:

```
CREATE TABLE COMPACT_DISCS
( CD_ID              INT,
  CD_TITLE           VARCHAR(60)  NOT NULL,
  IN_STOCK           INT          NOT NULL
     CHECK ( IN_STOCK > 0 AND IN_STOCK < 30 ) ),
```

Let's take a closer look at the <search condition> clause in these statements, which in this case is (IN_STOCK > 0 AND IN_STOCK < 30). The clause first tells us that any value entered into the IN_STOCK column must be greater than 0 (IN_STOCK > 0). The AND keyword tells us that the conditions defined on either side of AND must be applied. Finally, the clause tells us that the value must be less than 30 (IN_STOCK < 30). Because the AND keyword is used, the value must be greater than 0 *and* less than 30.

Another way that a CHECK constraint can be used is to explicitly list the values that can be entered into the column. This is a handy option if you have a limited number of values and they're not likely to change (or will change infrequently). The following SQL statement creates a table that includes a CHECK constraint that defines in which decade the music belongs:

```
CREATE TABLE COMPACT_DISCS
( CD_ID              INT,
  CD_TITLE           VARCHAR(60)  NOT NULL,
  ERA                CHAR(5),
  CONSTRAINT CK_ERA CHECK ( ERA IN ( '1950s', '1960s',
     '1970s', '1980s', '1990s', '2000s', '2010s' ) ) );
```

The value entered into the ERA column must be one of the seven decades represented by the search condition. If you tried to enter a value other than a null value or one of these seven, you would receive an error. Notice that the IN operator is used to designate that the ERA column values must be one of the set of values enclosed by parentheses following the keyword IN.

If the number of parentheses starts to confuse you, you can separate your code into lines that follow the embedding of those parentheses. For example, the preceding statement can be written as follows:

```
CREATE TABLE COMPACT_DISCS
(
   CD_ID              INT,
   CD_TITLE           VARCHAR(60)  NOT NULL,
   ERA                CHAR(5),
   CONSTRAINT CK_ERA CHECK
```

```
    (
      ERA IN
      (
          '1950s', '1960s', '1970s', '1980s', '1990s', '2000s', '2010s'
      )
    )
);
```

Each set of parentheses and its content is indented to a level that corresponds to the level of embedding for that particular clause, just like an outline. Using this method tells you exactly which clauses are enclosed in which set of parentheses, and the statement is executed just the same as if you hadn't separated out the lines. The downside is that it takes up a lot of room (which is why I don't use this method in this book), although it might be a helpful tool for you for those statements that are a little more complicated.

Now let's look at one other example of a CHECK constraint. This example is similar to the first one we looked at, only this one is concerned with values between certain numbers:

```
CREATE TABLE COMPACT_DISCS
( CD_ID             INT,
  CD_TITLE          VARCHAR(60)  NOT NULL,
  IN_STOCK          INT          NOT NULL,
  CONSTRAINT CK_IN_STOCK CHECK
   ( ( IN_STOCK BETWEEN 0 AND 30 ) OR
     ( IN_STOCK BETWEEN 49 AND 60 ) ) ) ;
```

In this statement, you use the BETWEEN operator to specify a range which *includes* the endpoints. Because you are creating two different ranges, you enclose each range specification in parentheses: (IN_STOCK BETWEEN 0 AND 30) and (IN_STOCK BETWEEN 49 AND 60). These two range specifications are then connected by an OR keyword, which indicates that either one *or* the other condition must be met. As a result, any value entered into the IN_STOCK column must be from 0 through 30 or from 49 through 60.

As I said earlier, you will learn more about search conditions in Chapter 9. At that time, you'll see just how flexible the CHECK constraint is. And when used with subqueries (see Chapter 12), they provide a powerful tool for explicitly defining what values are permitted in a particular column.

Defining Assertions

An assertion is merely a type of CHECK constraint that can be applied to multiple tables. For this reason, an assertion must be created separately from a table definition. Unfortunately, most vendor products, including Oracle 12*c*, SQL Server 2014, and MySQL 5.7, don't yet support assertions. To create an assertion, use the following syntax:

```
CREATE ASSERTION <constraint name> CHECK <search conditions>
```

Creating an assertion is very similar to creating a table CHECK constraint. After the CHECK keyword, you must provide the necessary search condition(s). Now let's take a look at an example. Suppose the COMPACT_DISCS table includes a column for the number of compact discs in stock. You want the total for that table to always be less than the maximum inventory you want to carry. In the following example, I create an assertion that totals the values in the IN_STOCK column and verifies that the total is less than 5000:

```
CREATE ASSERTION LIMIT_IN_STOCK CHECK
   ( ( SELECT SUM (IN_STOCK) FROM COMPACT_DISCS ) < 5000 );
```

In this statement, I am using a subquery, (SELECT SUM (IN_STOCK) FROM COMPACT_DISCS), and comparing it to 5000. The subquery begins with the SELECT keyword, which is used to query data from a table. The SUM function adds the values in the IN_STOCK column, and the FROM keyword specifies which table the column is in. The results of this subquery are then compared (using the less-than comparison operator) to 5000. If you try to add a value to the IN_STOCK column that would cause the total to exceed 5000, you will receive an error.

Creating Domains and Domain Constraints

The last type of CHECK constraint is the kind that you insert into a domain definition. For the most part, the constraint definition is similar to what you've seen before, except that you do not tie the constraint to a specific column or table. In fact, domain constraints use the VALUE keyword when referring to the value within a column defined with that particular domain. Let's look at the syntax for creating a domain:

```
CREATE DOMAIN <domain name> [ AS ] <data type>
[ DEFAULT <default value> ]
[ CONSTRAINT <constraint name> ] CHECK ( <search condition> )
```

You should already be familiar with most of the elements in this syntax. I discuss data types and default clauses in Chapter 3, and the constraint definition is similar to what you've seen so far in this chapter.

In the following example, I create a domain that's based on the INT data type and that requires all values to be between 0 and 30:

```
CREATE DOMAIN STOCK_AMOUNT AS INT
  CONSTRAINT CK_STOCK_AMOUNT CHECK (VALUE BETWEEN 0 AND 30 );
```

The only really new item here (other than the CREATE DOMAIN clause) is the keyword VALUE, which, as I said, refers to the value of the column defined with the STOCK_AMOUNT domain. As a result, if you try to insert a value into one of those columns that is not between 0 and 30, you will receive an error.

Try This 4-2 Adding a CHECK Constraint

In this Try This exercise, which is relatively short, you will be using the ALTER TABLE statement to modify the COMPACT_DISCS table. You will be adding a column to the table and then defining a CHECK constraint that restricts the values that can be entered into the column. The additional column and constraint will have no impact on other tables in the INVENTORY database or on the relationship between tables. You can download the Try_This_04.txt file, which contains the SQL statements used in this exercise.

Step by Step

1. Open the client application for your RDBMS and connect to the INVENTORY database.
2. You're going to modify the COMPACT_DISCS table by adding the IN_STOCK column. Enter and execute the following SQL statement:

```
ALTER TABLE COMPACT_DISCS
  ADD COLUMN IN_STOCK  INT  NOT NULL;
```

NOTE

For Oracle and SQL Server, omit the keyword COLUMN.

3. Now that the column exists, you can add a CHECK constraint to the table definition. You could have entered the constraint as a column constraint, but adding it separately as a table constraint allows you to do each step separately so you can see the results of your actions. The CHECK constraint limits the values that can be entered into the IN_STOCK column. Each value must be greater than 0, but less than 50. Enter and execute the following SQL statement:

```
ALTER TABLE COMPACT_DISCS
  ADD CONSTRAINT CK_IN_STOCK CHECK ( IN_STOCK > 0 AND IN_STOCK < 50
);
```

4. Close the client application.

Try This Summary

The new column, IN_STOCK, tracks the number of each compact disc listed in the COMPACT_DISCS table. The CK_IN_STOCK constraint restricts the number per row to an amount between 0 and 50. Now that the table has been updated, you cannot add any values that would violate the constraint.

Chapter 4 Self Test

1. What are the three categories of integrity constraints?
2. What are the differences between a column constraint and a table constraint?
3. What types of constraints can you include in a column definition?
4. What is the difference between a table constraint and an assertion?
5. What does a null value signify?
6. Which of the following types of constraints support NOT NULL constraints?
   - **A** Table constraints
   - **B** Column constraints
   - **C** Domain constraints
   - **D** Assertions
7. You are creating a table that includes a column that allows null values but whose non-null values should be unique. Which type of constraint should you use?
8. You're creating a table that includes the TYPE_NAME column. The column is defined with the CHAR(10) data type and requires a UNIQUE constraint, which you'll define as a column constraint. What SQL code should you use for the column definition?
9. What two restrictions apply to PRIMARY KEY constraints but not to UNIQUE constraints?
10. You're creating a PRIMARY KEY constraint named PK_ARTIST_MUSIC_TYPES on the ARTIST_MUSIC_TYPES table. The primary key includes the ARTIST_NAME and ARTIST_DOB columns. What SQL code should you use for a table constraint?
11. How does a referential constraint differ from a unique constraint?
12. A(n) _______________ constraint enforces referential integrity between two tables by ensuring that no action is taken to either table that affects the data protected by the constraint.
13. You're creating a table that includes a column named BUSINESS_TYPE_ID, with a data type of INT. The column will be defined with a FOREIGN KEY constraint that references the primary key in a table named BUSINESS_TYPES. The foreign key will be added as a column constraint. What SQL code should you use for the column definition?
14. What three options can you use in the MATCH clause of a FOREIGN KEY constraint?

15. What are the two types of referential triggered actions that can be defined in a FOREIGN KEY constraint?

16. You're creating a FOREIGN KEY constraint and want the values in the referencing column to be updated if values in the referenced column are updated. Which <referential triggered action> clause should you use?

    A ON UPDATE RESTRICT

    B ON UPDATE NO ACTION

    C ON UPDATE CASCADE

    D ON UPDATE SET DEFAULT

17. What syntax should you use for a CHECK constraint that you're defining as a table constraint?

18. What types of constraints can you define within an assertion?

19. You're creating a CHECK constraint on the NUMBER_IN_STOCK column. You want to limit the values that can be entered into the column to the range of 11 through 29. What should you use for the <search condition> clause of the constraint?

Chapter 5

Creating SQL Views

Key Skills & Concepts

- Add Views to the Database
- Create Updateable Views
- Drop Views from the Database

As you learned in Chapter 3, persistent base tables store the SQL data in your database. However, these tables are not always in a useful form if you only want to look at specific data from one table or data from multiple tables. For this reason, the SQL standard supports the use of viewed tables, or views. A *view* is a virtual table whose definition exists as a schema object. Unlike persistent base tables, there is no data stored in the view. In fact, the viewed table does not actually exist—only the definition that defines it exists. It is this definition that allows you to select specific information from one or more tables, based on the query statements in that definition. Once you create a view, you simply invoke it by calling its name in a query as you would a base table. The data is then presented as though you were looking at a base table.

Add Views to the Database

Before I go too deeply into the specifics of views, I want to quickly review some of what I discussed in Chapters 2 and 3. SQL supports three types of tables: base tables, derived tables, and transient tables. Of these three types, it is the base tables that hold the actual SQL data. Most base tables are schema objects and come in five types: persistent base tables, system-versioned tables, global temporary tables, created local temporary tables, and declared local temporary tables. Derived tables, on the other hand, are merely the results you see when you query data from the database. For example, if you request data from the COMPACT_DISCS table, the results of your request are displayed in a table-like format, which is known as the derived table. A viewed table is a named derived table defined by a *view definition*.

In some ways, a view is like a cross between a persistent base table and a derived table. It is like a persistent base table in that the view definition is stored as a schema object using a unique name (within the schema) that can be accessed as you would a base table. However, a view is more like a derived table in that no data is stored in association with the view, and is therefore classified as a derived table. Derived tables, including views, can be thought of as *virtual* tables. The data is selected from one or more base tables when you invoke the view. The data results that you see when you access a view are not stored anywhere but are derived from existing base tables. This is what makes a view a named derived table, with the view definition stored in the schema.

Views can be useful tools when accessing different types of data. One of the main advantages of using views is that you can define complex queries and store them within the view definition. Instead of re-creating those queries every time you need them, you can simply invoke the view. Moreover, views can be a handy way to present information to users without providing them with more information than they need or information they should not see. For example, you might want users in your organization to have access to certain employee records, but you might not want information such as Social Security numbers or pay rates available to those users, so you can create a view that provides only the information that they should see. Views can also be used to synthesize complex structures and present information in a way that is easier for some users to understand, which in effect hides the underlying structure and complexity of the database from the users.

Now that you have an overview of what views are, let's take a look at a few examples that illustrate how data is extracted from base tables into the type of derived table that is presented by a view definition. The first example we'll look at, shown in Figure 5-1, is based on the COMPACT_DISC_INVENTORY table, which includes six columns. Suppose you want to view only the CD_TITLE, COPYRIGHT, and IN_STOCK columns. You can create a view that extracts these three columns from the table and organizes them as if the data existed in its own table, as shown in Figure 5-1. The COMPACT_DISCS_IN_STOCK view contains a query that defines exactly what data should be returned by the view.

You might have noticed that one of the column names in the view (COMPACT_DISC) is different from the corresponding column name of the COMPACT_DISC_INVENTORY table (CD_TITLE), even though the data within the columns is the same. This is because you can assign names to view columns that are different from the originating table if you wish. If you don't assign any names, the view columns inherit the names from the originating table. The view columns inherit their data types from their respective table columns. For example, the COMPACT_DISC column in the COMPACT_DISCS_IN_STOCK view inherits the VARCHAR(60) data type from the CD_TITLE column of the COMPACT_DISC_INVENTORY table. You don't specify the VARCHAR(60) data type anywhere within the view definition.

As you can see, a view allows you to define which columns are returned when you invoke the view. The definition for the COMPACT_DISCS_IN_STOCK view specifies three columns; however, it could have specified any of the columns from the COMPACT_DISC_INVENTORY table. In addition to columns, a view definition can specify which rows are returned. For example, Figure 5-2 shows the CDS_IN_STOCK_2010S view. Notice that it contains the same columns as the COMPACT_DISCS_IN_STOCK view (shown in Figure 5-1), but there are fewer rows. In this case, the view definition not only specifies the same three columns from the COMPACT_DISC_INVENTORY table, but also specifies that only rows with values between 2010 and 2019 (inclusive) in the COPYRIGHT column are to be returned. This illustrates one of the beauties of views—as new rows are added to the base table (COMPACT_DISC_INVENTORY) with years greater than 2009 and less than 2020, they will *automatically* appear in the CDS_IN_STOCK_2010S view the next time it is accessed, without the need for special commands to update or refresh the view. And, of course, the view behaves this way because it does not actually store any rows of data, but rather relies on the base table to supply the rows of data.

COMPACT_DISC_INVENTORY

CD_ID: INT	CD_TITLE: VARCHAR(60)	COPYRIGHT_YEAR: INT	LABEL_ID: INT	DISC_ID: INT	IN_STOCK: INT
101	Drive All Night	2013	826	1299	12
102	Different Shades of Blue	2014	828	1232	42
103	Innervisions (Remastered)	2000	827	1287	16
104	The Definitive Collection	2002	827	1292	34
105	Rumours (Reissued)	1990	830	1255	17
106	Come On Over	1997	831	1216	6
107	Man Against Machine	2014	832	1210	8
108	Bach	2014	829	1276	22
109	Old Boots, New Dirt	2014	833	1266	32

COMPACT_DISCS_IN_STOCK

COMPACT_DISC	COPYRIGHT_YEAR	IN_STOCK
Drive All Night	2013	12
Different Shades of Blue	2014	42
Innervisions (Remastered)	2000	16
The Definitive Collection	2002	34
Rumours (Reissued)	1990	17
Come On Over	1997	6
Man Against Machine	2014	8
Bach	2014	22
Old Boots, New Dirt	2014	32

Figure 5-1 The COMPACT_DISCS_IN_STOCK view, based on the COMPACT_DISC_INVENTORY table

CDS_IN_STOCK_2010S

COMPACT_DISC	COPYRIGHT_YEAR	IN_STOCK
Drive All Night	2013	12
Different Shades of Blue	2014	42
Man Against Machine	2014	8
Bach	2014	22
Old Boots, New Dirt	2014	32

Figure 5-2 The CDS_IN_STOCK_2010S view, based on the COMPACT_DISC_INVENTORY table

In the previous two examples, we looked at views that derive data from only one table; however, you can create views based on multiple tables. This is particularly useful if you want to display related information that spans more than one table. Let's take a look at Figure 5-3, which includes the CD_INVENTORY table and the LABELS table. The CD_INVENTORY table contains a list of CDs in your inventory, and the LABELS table contains a list of companies that publish CDs. I am briefly introducing multiple table access here because it is a great way to demonstrate how well views can hide query complexity. The topic is covered in detail in Chapter 11.

Suppose you have users who want to be able to see the names of the CD and the publisher, but who are not interested in the CD_ID or LABEL_ID values. And they certainly aren't interested in having to look in two different locations to compare LABEL_ID values in order to match up CDs with company names. One solution is to create a view that matches up this information for them, while at the same time displaying only the information that is useful to them. In the case of the CD_INVENTORY and LABELS tables, you can create a view (named CD_PUBLISHERS in Figure 5-3) that bridges (*joins*) this data for the users, while hiding the underlying structure and extraneous data.

A view of this sort is possible by taking advantage of the relationships between tables. In the case of the CD_INVENTORY and LABELS tables, a foreign key has been defined on the LABEL_ID column of the CD_INVENTORY table that references the LABEL_ID column of the LABELS table. The query contained in the CD_PUBLISHERS view definition matches the values in the LABEL_ID column of the CD_INVENTORY table to the values in the LABEL_ID column of the LABELS table. For every match that is found, a row is returned. For example, the Drive All Night row includes a LABEL_ID value of 826. In the LABELS table, you can see that this value matches the ANTI Records row. As a result, the view contains a row with the Drive All Night value and the ANTI Records value.

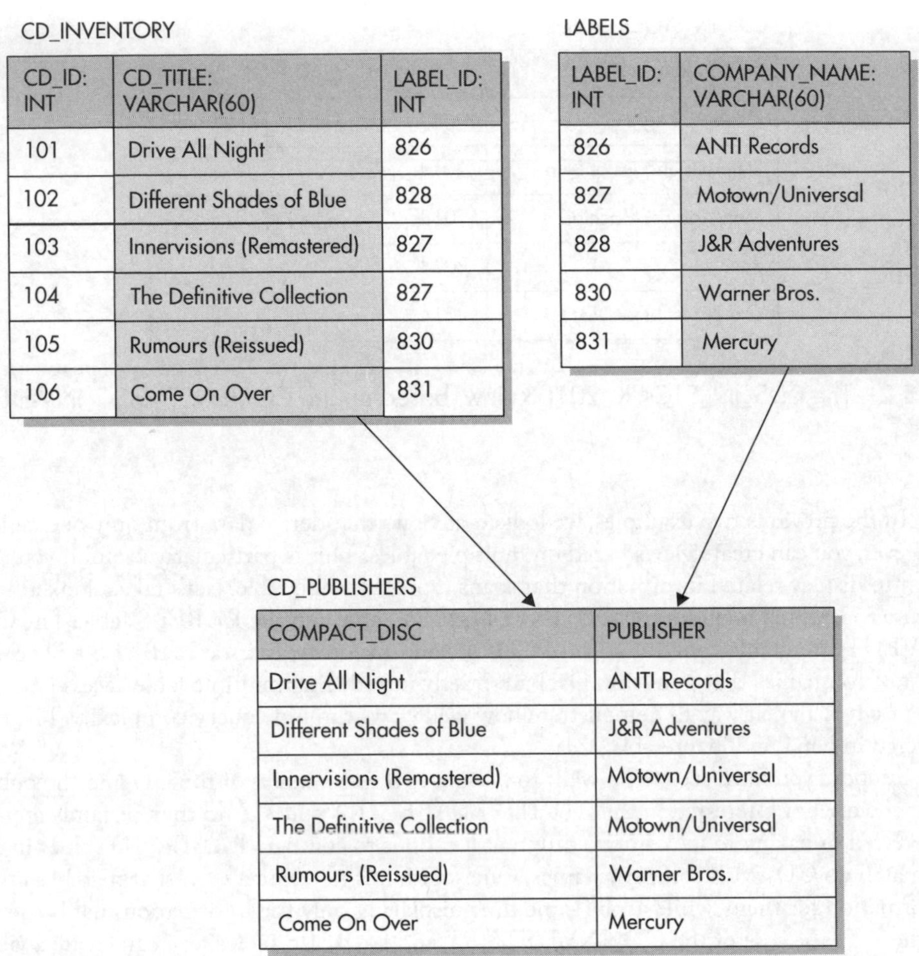

CD_INVENTORY

CD_ID: INT	CD_TITLE: VARCHAR(60)	LABEL_ID: INT
101	Drive All Night	826
102	Different Shades of Blue	828
103	Innervisions (Remastered)	827
104	The Definitive Collection	827
105	Rumours (Reissued)	830
106	Come On Over	831

LABELS

LABEL_ID: INT	COMPANY_NAME: VARCHAR(60)
826	ANTI Records
827	Motown/Universal
828	J&R Adventures
830	Warner Bros.
831	Mercury

CD_PUBLISHERS

COMPACT_DISC	PUBLISHER
Drive All Night	ANTI Records
Different Shades of Blue	J&R Adventures
Innervisions (Remastered)	Motown/Universal
The Definitive Collection	Motown/Universal
Rumours (Reissued)	Warner Bros.
Come On Over	Mercury

Figure 5-3 The COMPACT_DISC_PUBLISHERS view, based on the LABELS and CD_INVENTORY tables

NOTE

You don't necessarily have to use a foreign key relationship to join tables. Any two columns from different tables that store the same information can be used. This might mean using all the columns in a foreign key (if the foreign key includes multiple columns), using only one of the columns, or not using a foreign key at all. I discuss joining multiple tables in Chapter 11.

In addition to joining information from different tables, you can use views to modify the data that is pulled from a table column and presented in the view column. This allows you to take such actions as performing calculations, finding averages, determining minimum and maximum values, and completing countless other operations. You can then take the results of these operations and include them in a column within the view. In Figure 5-4, for example, the CD_DISCOUNTS view deducts a 10 percent discount from the retail price and presents the result in the DISCOUNT_PRICE column.

The CD_DISCOUNTS view includes three columns. The COMPACT_DISC column pulls data directly from the CD_TITLE column. The RETAIL_PRICE and DISCOUNT PRICE columns in the view both pull their data from the RETAIL_PRICE column in the INVENTORY table. The RETAIL_PRICE column in the view copies the values just as they

INVENTORY

CD_ID: INT	CD_TITLE: VARCHAR(60)	COPYRIGHT_YEAR: INT	RETAIL_PRICE: NUMERIC(5,2)	IN_STOCK: INT
101	Drive All Night	2013	5.99	12
102	Different Shades of Blue	2014	11.99	42
103	Innervisions (Remastered)	2000	10.00	16
104	The Definitive Collection	2003	8.39	34
105	Rumours (Reissued)	1990	7.99	17
106	Come On Over	1997	5.99	6
107	Man Against Machine	2014	9.99	8

CD_DISCOUNTS

COMPACT_DISC	RETAIL_PRICE	DISCOUNT_PRICE
Drive All Night	5.99	5.39
Different Shades of Blue	11.99	10.79
Innervisions (Remastered)	10.00	9.00
The Definitive Collection	8.39	7.55
Rumours (Reissued)	7.99	7.19
Come On Over	5.99	5.39
Man Against Machine	9.99	8.99

Figure 5-4 The CD_DISCOUNTS view, based on the INVENTORY table

are. However, for the DISCOUNT_PRICE column, the values pulled from the RETAIL_PRICE column in the INVENTORY table are multiplied by 0.9.

As you can see, you can specify many types of operations in a view and then simply invoke the view when you need the information. Most of what can be included in a regular query can be included in a view. In fact, it is the query, or query expression, that forms the nucleus of the view. However, before we look at query expressions, I want to first discuss the syntax used for creating views.

Defining SQL Views

The simplest type of view to create is one that references only one table and retrieves data from columns within the table without modifying that data. The more complicated the view, the more complicated the query expression underlying the view. At its most basic, the syntax for a view is as follows:

```
CREATE VIEW <view name> [ ( <view column names> ) ]
AS <query expression>
[ WITH CHECK OPTION ]
```

For now, we'll focus only on the first two lines of the syntax and leave the WITH CHECK OPTION for later, in the "Create Updateable Views" section. As shown in the first line of the syntax, you must provide a name for the view. In addition, you must provide names for the columns in the following circumstances:

- If any column values are based on some sort of operation that calculates the value to be inserted in the column, rather than the value being copied directly from the table. (See Figure 5-4.)
- If table column names are duplicated, which can happen when joining tables together.

Even if you aren't required to provide column names, you still can if you wish. For example, you might find that you want to rename them so the names are more logical for your particular users. If, however, you do provide column names using the <view column names> syntax, you must provide names for all columns.

NOTE

There is also a way to provide alternative column names using the AS keyword within the query expression itself, which I discuss in Chapter 7. Also, many RDBMS products will automatically assign names to view columns derived using some sort of calculation, but it is always a best practice to provide your own names in these cases so the names are as meaningful as possible.

The second line of the syntax includes the AS keyword, which is required, and the <query expression> placeholder. The <query expression> placeholder, although it appears straightforward, can involve a complex structure of query statements that can perform a number of operations, including retrieving data from multiple tables, calculating data, limiting the type of data returned, and performing virtually any other type of operation supported by a query expression. Because of the complexity of query expressions, I spend the majority of Part II of this book discussing various ways to query data. What this implies, then, is that it would be very difficult to condense a thorough discussion of query expressions into the topic of views. Still, I want to provide you with a number of examples that illustrate how you can create views that perform various functions. With each example, I'll include a cursory explanation of the query expression used in the view definition. Know, however, that I will be going into the details of query expressions in greater depth later in the book, beginning with Chapter 7. Also note that the base tables used in these examples have not been created in previous Try This exercises, so if you want to try the examples, you will have to create the base tables first. The figures show the information you need to do that.

The first example we'll look at is based on the view shown in Figure 5-1. The COMPACT_DISCS_IN_STOCK view derives data from the COMPACT_DISC_INVENTORY table and includes three columns from that table. To create the view, use the following CREATE VIEW statement:

```
CREATE VIEW COMPACT_DISCS_IN_STOCK
  ( COMPACT_DISC, COPYRIGHT_YEAR, IN_STOCK ) AS
   SELECT CD_TITLE, COPYRIGHT_YEAR, IN_STOCK
     FROM COMPACT_DISC_INVENTORY;
```

This view is the simplest of all types of views to create. It is based on one table and pulls three of the six columns from that table. Keep in mind that while SQL usually requires clauses to be in a particular order, there are no restrictions as to spaces and line breaks. For example, when creating views, I prefer to put the column name list (when present) on a new line and to place the AS keyword at the end of the line that precedes the query expression. Others prefer the AS keyword on a line by itself, and still others prefer to place it at the beginning of the first line of the query expression. Your RDBMS is not going to care which way you do it, but adopting a style and sticking to it will make your SQL easier to read, understand, and maintain.

Dissecting the statement a bit, the first line provides a name for the view, COMPACT_DISCS_IN_STOCK. The second line provides a name for each of the three columns: COMPACT_DISC, COPYRIGHT_YEAR, and IN_STOCK, and ends with the AS keyword. If the column names were omitted, the view columns would inherit their names from the table columns. The third and fourth lines of the CREATE VIEW statement contain the query expression, which in this case is the following SELECT statement:

```
SELECT CD_TITLE, COPYRIGHT_YEAR, IN_STOCK
  FROM COMPACT_DISC_INVENTORY
```

The SELECT statement is one of the most common statements (if not *the* most common statement) you'll be using as an SQL programmer. It is also one of the most extensive and flexible statements you'll be using, allowing you to form intricate queries that can return exactly the type of data you want to retrieve from your database.

The SELECT statement used in the COMPACT_DISCS_IN_STOCK view definition is a SELECT statement at its most basic. The statement is divided into two clauses: the SELECT clause and the FROM clause. The SELECT clause identifies which columns to return (CD_TITLE, COPYRIGHT_YEAR, and IN_STOCK), and the FROM clause identifies the table from which to pull the data (COMPACT_DISC_INVENTORY). When you invoke the COMPACT_DISCS_IN_STOCK view, you are essentially invoking the SELECT statement that is embedded in the view definition, which in turn pulls data from the applicable base table(s).

In the next example, which is based on the view in Figure 5-2, the CREATE VIEW statement is nearly the same as the previous example, except that an additional clause has been added to the statement:

```
CREATE VIEW CDS_IN_STOCK_2010S
  ( COMPACT_DISC, COPYRIGHT_YEAR, IN_STOCK ) AS
    SELECT CD_TITLE, COPYRIGHT_YEAR, IN_STOCK
      FROM COMPACT_DISC_INVENTORY
     WHERE COPYRIGHT_YEAR > 2009 AND COPYRIGHT_YEAR < 2020;
```

The WHERE clause defines a condition that must be met in order for data to be returned. As in the previous example, you're still pulling data from the CD_TITLE, COPYRIGHT_YEAR, and IN_STOCK columns of the COMPACT_DISC_INVENTORY table, only this time you're limiting the data to those rows whose COPYRIGHT_YEAR values are greater than 2009 but less than 2020 (COPYRIGHT_YEAR > 2009 AND COPYRIGHT_YEAR < 2020). You might recognize the comparison operators greater than (>) and less than (<) from Chapter 4 in the discussion about CHECK constraints. They're used to limit which values will be included in the view.

NOTE

The operators used in the WHERE clause (or any condition defined in the clause) have no effect on the data stored in the base tables. They affect only the data returned when the view is invoked. I discuss these types of operators in greater detail in Chapter 9.

You can use the WHERE clause in a SELECT statement to define a wide variety of conditions. For example, the WHERE clause can be used to help join tables together, as shown in the following CREATE VIEW statement:

```
CREATE VIEW COMPACT_DISC_PUBLISHERS
 ( COMPACT_DISC, PUBLISHER ) AS
  SELECT CD_INVENTORY.CD_TITLE, LABELS.COMPANY_NAME
    FROM CD_INVENTORY, LABELS
   WHERE CD_INVENTORY.LABEL_ID = LABELS.LABEL_ID;
```

This statement creates the view that you see in Figure 5-3. The name of the view is COMPACT_DISC_PUBLISHERS and it includes the COMPACT_DISC column and the

PUBLISHER column. The view pulls information from two sources: the CD_TITLE column in the CD_INVENTORY table and the COMPANY_NAME column in the LABELS table.

Let's first take a look at the SELECT clause. Notice that the name of each column is qualified by the name of its respective table (for example, CD_INVENTORY.CD_TITLE). When joining two or more tables, you must qualify the column names if there's any possibility that the column names could be confused, which would be the case if you included columns with the same name. If, however, there is no possibility the column names could be confused, then you can omit the table names. For example, the SELECT clause could read as follows:

```
SELECT CD_TITLE, COMPANY_NAME
```

Despite the fact that the qualified names are not always necessary, many programmers prefer to use them in all cases because it's easier to know what table is being referenced if you ever need to modify the database structure or the view definition at a later time.

The next clause in the SELECT statement is the FROM clause. When joining tables together, you must include the names of all the participating tables, separated by commas. Other than the issue of multiple names, the FROM clause is similar to what you've seen in other examples.

The WHERE clause, which is the final clause in the SELECT statement, is what matches rows together. The WHERE clause is necessary because, without it, there would be no way of knowing how to match up the values from the different tables. The WHERE clause specifies how this is to be done. In the COMPACT_DISC_PUBLISHERS view definition, the value in the LABEL_ID column of the CD_INVENTORY table must equal the value in the LABEL_ID column of the LABELS table for a row to be returned. For example, if you refer again to Figure 5-3, you can see that the Different Shades of Blue row in the CD_INVENTORY table has a value of 828 in the LABEL_ID column, which is matched up with the J&R Adventures row in the LABELS table. Notice that, once again, the column names are qualified by the table names, which is essential in this case because the columns share the same name. Without the table names, SQL would not know whether it was comparing values with itself or with the other table.

You can also expand the WHERE clause to further qualify your query. In the following example, the WHERE clause limits the rows returned to only those that contain a value of 827 in the LABEL_ID column of the CD_INVENTORY table:

```
CREATE VIEW COMPACT_DISC_PUBLISHERS
 ( COMPACT_DISC, PUBLISHER ) AS
   SELECT CD_INVENTORY.CD_TITLE, LABELS.COMPANY_NAME
     FROM CD_INVENTORY, LABELS
    WHERE CD_INVENTORY.LABEL_ID = LABELS.LABEL_ID
      AND CD_INVENTORY.LABEL_ID = 827;
```

If you were then to invoke the COMPACT_DISC_PUBLISHERS view, you would see only the CDs that are produced by Motown/Universal.

NOTE

Use of the WHERE clause is the original method of matching data values when joining tables in SQL. However, newer and more flexible syntax in the form of the JOIN clause was added to the SQL standard as of version SQL-92. I describe the JOIN clause in detail in Chapter 11.

Now let's look at another example, which is based on the view in Figure 5-4. Like the first two examples we looked at, this view derives data from only one table. However, this view actually performs calculations that return data that has been modified. The CREATE VIEW statement looks like this:

```
CREATE VIEW CD_DISCOUNTS
  ( COMPACT_DISC, RETAIL_PRICE, DISCOUNT_PRICE ) AS
    SELECT CD_TITLE, RETAIL_PRICE, RETAIL_PRICE * 0.9
      FROM INVENTORY;
```

The CD_DISCOUNTS view includes three columns: COMPACT_DISC, RETAIL_PRICE, and DISCOUNT_PRICE. The DISCOUNT_PRICE column contains the calculated values. The SELECT clause identifies the table columns that contain the source data. The first two columns are defined in the same manner as you've seen in previous examples. Data is copied from the CD_TITLE and RETAIL_PRICE columns in the INVENTORY table to the COMPACT_DISC and RETAIL_PRICE columns of the CD_DISCOUNTS view. However, the third column definition (RETAIL_PRICE * 0.9) is a little different. Values are again taken from the RETAIL_PRICE column, only this time the values are multiplied by 0.9 (90 percent) to arrive at the discounted prices that appear in the DISCOUNT_PRICE column of the view.

You can also add a WHERE clause to the SELECT statement used in the CD_DISCOUNTS view definition:

```
CREATE VIEW CD_DISCOUNTS
  ( COMPACT_DISC, RETAIL_PRICE, DISCOUNT_PRICE ) AS
    SELECT CD_TITLE, RETAIL_PRICE, RETAIL_PRICE * 0.9
      FROM INVENTORY
     WHERE IN_STOCK > 10;
```

The WHERE clause restricts the query to only those rows whose IN_STOCK value is greater than 10. Notice that you can use a comparison operator on a table column (IN_STOCK) whose values are not even returned by the view.

As you can see from all these examples of view definitions, there are a great many things that you can do with views as a result of the flexibility and extensibility of the SELECT statement. Later in the book, when you become more familiar with the various types of SELECT statements you can create and the operations you can perform, you will be able to create views that are far more complex than anything we've looked at so far.

Create Updateable Views

In SQL, some types of views are updateable. In other words, you can use the view to modify the data (change existing data and/or insert new rows) in the underlying table. Whether a view is updateable depends on the SELECT statement that is defined within the view definition. Typically, the more complex the statement, the less likely the view will be updateable. There is no syntax within the CREATE VIEW statement that explicitly designates a view as being updateable. Instead, it is determined strictly by the nature of the SELECT statement, which must adhere to specific requirements in order for the view to be updateable.

Up to this point in the chapter, I have implied that the <query expression> placeholder in the CREATE VIEW syntax is made up of a SELECT statement. To be more precise, a query expression can be one of several types of expressions. The most common of these, and the one you'll be concerned with in this book, is the query specification. A *query specification* is an SQL expression that begins with the SELECT keyword and includes a number of elements that form that expression, as you have seen in the view examples we've looked at. A query specification is updateable if it meets the numerous guidelines outlined in the SQL standard. For the sake of simplicity, I refer to the query specification as the SELECT statement, which is often how it's referred to in various types of SQL-related and product-related documentation.

The issue of query specifications and the complexity of the SQL standards aside, the point I'm trying to make is that the syntax rules that determine the updatability of a view are not simple, clear-cut guidelines, particularly in light of the fact that I have yet to cover the SELECT statement in depth (which I do beginning in Chapter 7). However, there are some logical underpinnings that can be gleaned from these guidelines:

- Data within the view cannot be summarized, grouped together, or automatically eliminated.
- At least one column in the source table must be updateable.
- Each column in the view must be traceable to exactly one source column in one table.
- Each row in the view must be traceable to exactly one source row in one table. However, note that many vendor products permit modifications (but not inserts) to views created from multiple tables, provided that the update only references columns that trace to a single base table.

In many cases, you'll be able to determine the updatability of a view simply by applying common sense. Let's take a look at an example. Suppose that you decide to add information about your employees to your database because you want to track CD sale commissions earned. You decide to create the EMPLOYEE_COMMISSIONS table, shown in Figure 5-5, which lists the total amount of commissions each employee earned during a 3-year period.

Now suppose you want to know the average commission for each year for all the employees. You can create a view that determines the average for each year and displays those

EMPLOYEE_COMMISSIONS

EMPLOYEE_ID: INT	YEAR_2012: NUMERIC(7,2)	YEAR_2013: NUMERIC(7,2)	YEAR_2014: NUMERIC(7,2)
99301	126.32	11.28	16.86
99302	16.27	90.20	198.14
99303	354.34	16.32	1237.56
99304	112.11	87.56	14.14

Figure 5-5 Annual commission earnings in the EMPLOYEE_COMMISSIONS table

averages in three separate columns. To do so, you would use the following CREATE VIEW statement:

```
CREATE VIEW EMP_COMM ( AVG_2012, AVG_2013, AVG_2014 ) AS
  SELECT AVG(YEAR_2012), AVG(YEAR_2013), AVG(YEAR_2014)
    FROM EMPLOYEE_COMMISSIONS;
```

As you can see from the statement, the EMP_COMM view contains three columns: AVG_2012, AVG_2013, and AVG_2014. The SELECT clause pulls information from three columns in the EMPLOYEE_COMMISSIONS table—YEAR_2012, YEAR_2013, and YEAR_2014—and uses the AVG function to find the average for all the values in each column, as shown in Figure 5-6. For example, the AVG function first averages the four values in the YEAR_2012 column and then enters that average in the AVG_2012 column of the EMP_COMM view.

Now suppose you want to update the commission amounts in the EMPLOYEE_COMMISSIONS table. You could not do so through the view because values in the view are based on calculations performed on values in the table. For example, if you tried to update the value in the AVG_2012 column, the RDBMS would not know how many rows were affected or how to distribute the values within those rows. In other words, the row in the view is not traceable back to exactly one source row.

EMP_COMM

AVG_2012	AVG_2013	AVG_2014
152.26	51.34	366.68

Figure 5-6 The EMP_COMM view, based on the average of annual commission earnings

EMP_COMM

EMPLOYEE_ID	YEAR_2012	YEAR_2013
99301	126.32	11.28
99302	16.27	90.20
99303	354.34	16.32
99304	112.11	87.56

Figure 5-7 The EMP_COMM view, based on annual commission earnings for 2012 and 2013

You could, however, create a view that simply extracts information from the EMPLOYEE_COMMISSIONS table:

```
CREATE VIEW EMP_COMM AS
  SELECT EMPLOYEE_ID, YEAR_2012, YEAR_2013
    FROM EMPLOYEE_COMMISSIONS;
```

In this statement, you are creating a view that displays only three of the four columns of the table. No calculations are performed, and only one table is used. Figure 5-7 shows how this view would look.

This view, unlike the last one, is updateable. You can modify and insert data because no data has been summarized or grouped together, each column is traceable to exactly one source column in one table, and each row is traceable to exactly one source row in one table. In addition, no data is summarized or grouped together. Of course, if you were to update or insert data through the view, it is the data in the underlying table that is actually modified. That means any data modifications must still adhere to the constraints placed on that table. For example, you could not insert a row through the EMP_COMM view if null values were not allowed in the YEAR_2014 column of the table. The view would not have the capacity to accept a value for that column, and the table would not allow you to insert a row without supplying that value.

You can often determine whether a table is updateable just by looking at the outcome of any modification attempts. If your goal is to create views that allow users to update data in the underlying tables, then you must consider the complexities of those views and the functions that they are to perform. Also keep in mind that the constraints placed on the underlying tables affect your ability to modify and insert data through a view.

Using the WITH CHECK OPTION Clause

Now let's return to the CREATE VIEW syntax that I introduced earlier in the section "Defining SQL Views." The last line of the syntax includes the following clause:

```
[ WITH CHECK OPTION ]
```

The WITH CHECK OPTION clause applies to updateable views that include a WHERE clause in the SELECT statement. The best way to illustrate how this works is through an example. Let's modify the last view definition we looked at:

```
CREATE VIEW EMP_COMM  AS
  SELECT EMPLOYEE_ID, YEAR_2012, YEAR_2013
    FROM EMPLOYEE_COMMISSIONS
   WHERE YEAR_2012 > 100;
```

The WHERE clause specifies that only rows with YEAR_2012 values greater than 100 should be returned. This in itself is straightforward enough. However, suppose you want to update this view by setting a YEAR_2012 value to be less than or equal to 100. Because the view is updateable, it will allow you to do so. However, if you were to then invoke the view, the row you updated would no longer be visible, nor could you update it further.

To work around this problem, you can add the WITH CHECK OPTION clause to your view definition, as in the following example:

```
CREATE VIEW EMP_COMM  AS
  SELECT EMPLOYEE_ID, YEAR_2012, YEAR_2013
    FROM EMPLOYEE_COMMISSIONS
   WHERE YEAR_2012 > 100
  WITH CHECK OPTION;
```

Now if you tried to update a YEAR_2012 value to an amount less than or equal to 100, you would receive an error message telling you that the change could not be made. As you can see, the WITH CHECK OPTION is a handy way to ensure that your users don't perform updates that will prevent them from effectively using the views that you create.

Drop Views from the Database

You will no doubt run into situations when you want to remove a view definition from your database. The syntax for doing this is quite simple:

```
DROP VIEW <view name>
```

When you execute the DROP VIEW statement, the view definition is removed; however, none of the underlying data (which is stored in the base tables) is affected. Once the view is dropped, you can re-create the view or create a different view with the same name. Now let's look at a quick example:

```
DROP VIEW EMP_COMM;
```

This statement removes the EMP_COMM view from your database but leaves the underlying data untouched.

Ask the Expert

Q: You discuss creating views and dropping views, but you do not mention altering views. Does SQL support any sort of ALTER VIEW statement?

A: No, the SQL standard does not support altering views. However, some RDBMSs support an ALTER VIEW statement. Be aware, though, that the functionality supported by these statements can vary from product to product. For example, SQL Server, MySQL, and DB2 have ALTER VIEW statements that are fairly robust and allow you to change many aspects of the view definition, including the SELECT statement. On the other hand, the ALTER VIEW statement in Oracle is used to manually recompile a view to avoid runtime overhead or to modify certain constraints that Oracle supports on views. To actually alter an Oracle view, you must first drop it and then re-create it, as is the case with the SQL standard. However, Oracle has a CREATE OR REPLACE VIEW statement that essentially allows you to drop and re-create a view in a single step. MySQL supports the CREATE OR REPLACE VIEW statement as well as the ALTER VIEW statement, and the two statements are functionally equivalent.

Q: In the examples that you use to show how views are created, you use one or two tables for your source data. Can views be based on more than two tables?

A: Yes, a view can be based on as many tables as can be logically queried in the SELECT statement. For example, suppose you want to create a view in the INVENTORY database. (The INVENTORY database is the one you've been working with for the Try This exercises in this book.) The view might display artists' names alongside CD titles. To do that, however, your SELECT statement would have to join together three tables. You would have to match the ARTIST_ID values in the ARTISTS table and the ARTIST_CDS table, and you would have to match the CD_ID values in the COMPACT_DISCS table and the ARTIST_CDS table. The result would be a view that displays a list of artists and their CDs. (In Chapter 11, I will discuss how you can join these tables together in your SELECT statement.)

Q: In the examples that you use to show how views are created, all the views reference base tables. Are all views created only on base tables?

A: No, views can be created using query expressions that pull data from other views. Also, it is possible to create a view that contains only calculated data and thus has no data that maps back to a base table.

Try This 5-1 Adding Views to Your Database

In this Try This exercise, you will create two views in the INVENTORY database. The views will be based on tables you created in previous Try This exercises. The first view will be based on a single table, and the second view will be based on two tables. You'll create the second view two different times. You'll create it once, then drop the view definition from the database, and then re-create a modified version of the view. You can download the Try_This_05.txt file, which contains the SQL statements used in this exercise.

Step by Step

1. Open the client application for your RDBMS and connect to the INVENTORY database.
2. The first view that you'll create is named CDS_IN_STOCK. The view is based on the CD_TITLE and IN_STOCK columns in the COMPACT_DISCS table. You want the view to include only those rows whose values in the IN_STOCK column are greater than 10. The view will use the same column names as the table and will include the WITH CHECK OPTION to prevent values less than or equal to 10 from being added to the IN_STOCK column. Enter and execute the following SQL statement:

```
CREATE VIEW CDS_IN_STOCK AS
 SELECT CD_TITLE, IN_STOCK
   FROM COMPACT_DISCS
  WHERE IN_STOCK > 10 WITH CHECK OPTION;
```

3. Next, you will create a view named CD_PUBLISHERS that will contain the CD_TITLE column and the PUBLISHER column. The view will be based on the CD_TITLE column in the COMPACT_DISCS table and the COMPANY_NAME column of the CD_LABELS table. You will need to use a WHERE clause to match rows in the two tables. The WHERE clause will also limit the rows included in the view to those whose LABEL_ID value in the CD_LABELS table is either 826 or 827. Enter and execute the following SQL statement:

```
CREATE VIEW CD_PUBLISHERS
 ( CD_TITLE, PUBLISHER ) AS
   SELECT COMPACT_DISCS.CD_TITLE, CD_LABELS.COMPANY_NAME
     FROM COMPACT_DISCS, CD_LABELS
    WHERE COMPACT_DISCS.LABEL_ID = CD_LABELS.LABEL_ID
      AND CD_LABELS.LABEL_ID = 826 OR CD_LABELS.LABEL_ID = 827;
```

4. You decide that you do not want to limit the rows to specific values in the LABEL_ID column, so you must drop the view definition from the database and re-create the view without the value restrictions. Enter and execute the following SQL statement:

```
DROP VIEW CD_PUBLISHERS;
```

5. Now you can re-create the CD_PUBLISHERS view. Enter and execute the following SQL statement:

```
CREATE VIEW CD_PUBLISHERS
  ( CD_TITLE, PUBLISHER ) AS
    SELECT COMPACT_DISCS.CD_TITLE, CD_LABELS.COMPANY_NAME
      FROM COMPACT_DISCS, CD_LABELS
     WHERE COMPACT_DISCS.LABEL_ID = CD_LABELS.LABEL_ID;
```

6. Close the client application.

Try This Summary

In addition to the six tables created in earlier Try This exercises, your database should now include the CDS_IN_STOCK view and the CD_PUBLISHERS view. Later in this book, you'll use those views to query data from the base tables and update that data. Once you have a better understanding of how to create SELECT statements, you'll be able to define views that are even more extensive and provide an even greater level of detail than the views you've created so far.

Chapter 5 Self Test

1. What are two advantages of using views?
2. A viewed table (view) is classified as which type of SQL table?
   - **A** Base table
   - **B** Transient table
   - **C** Derived table
   - **D** System-versioned table
3. What happens if you don't assign column names to a view?
4. How do you assign data types to view columns?
5. In what circumstances must you provide the view column names in a view definition?
6. You're creating a view named EMP_BIRTHDAYS. The view is based on the EMP_NAME column and the BIRTHDAY column of the EMPLOYEES table. The view column names will be the same as the table column names. What SQL code should you use to create the view?
7. You're creating a view based on the COMPACT_DISCS table in the INVENTORY database. You want the view to include only those rows whose value in the LABEL_ID column is 832. What clause—in addition to the SELECT clause and the FROM clause—should be included in the SELECT statement for the view?

8. You're creating a view that references the EMPLOYEE table and the JOB_TITLE table. The data in the two tables is matched together by the JOB_TITLE_ID column in each table. How should you write the WHERE clause in the view's SELECT statement?
9. You're creating a view that references the EMPLOYEE table and the JOB_TITLE table. The data in the two tables is matched together by the JOB_TITLE_ID column in each table. You want the view to display only those rows whose value in the JOB_TITLE_ID column of the JOB_TITLE table is 109. How should you write the WHERE clause in the view's SELECT statement?
10. What is a query specification?
11. Which guidelines should you follow if you want to create an updateable view?
    - **A** Data within the view cannot be summarized, grouped together, or automatically eliminated.
    - **B** At least one column in the source table must be updateable.
    - **C** Each column in the view must be traceable to exactly one source column in one table.
    - **D** Each row in the view must be traceable to exactly one source row in one table.
12. You create the following view based on the COMPACT_DISCS table in the INVENTORY database:

```
CREATE VIEW IN_STOCK_AVERAGE AS
  SELECT AVG(IN_STOCK)
    FROM COMPACT_DISCS;
```

    How do you insert data through this view?
13. What type of view does the WITH CHECK OPTION clause apply to?
14. You create the following view definition:

```
CREATE VIEW EMP_COMM AS
  SELECT EMPLOYEE_ID, YEAR_2012, YEAR_2013
    FROM EMPLOYEE_COMMISSIONS
   WHERE YEAR_2012 > 100;
```

    You want to use the view to update data. What happens if you change the YEAR_2012 value to an amount less than or equal to 100?
15. You want to alter the EMP_COMM view definition in your database. How do you alter that definition?
16. You want to drop the EMP_BIRTHDAYS view definition from your database. What SQL statement should you use?
17. What happens to the SQL data when you drop a view from the database?

Chapter 6

Managing Database Security

Key Skills & Concepts

- Understand the SQL Security Model
- Create and Delete Roles
- Grant and Revoke Privileges
- Grant and Revoke Roles

A critical component of any database is the ability to protect the data from unauthorized access and malicious attacks. A database must ensure that no unauthorized users can view or change data that they should not be viewing or changing. At the same time, authorized users should not be prevented from accessing any information that should be available to them. The ideal balance is to give every database user exactly the privileges they need to do their job, nothing more and nothing less. In order to support these capabilities, SQL defines a security model that allows you to determine which users can access specific data and what they can do with that data. At the core of this model is the authorization identifier. An *authorization identifier*, as you learned in Chapter 2, is an object in the SQL environment that represents a user or group of users that are granted specific access privileges to objects and data within the SQL environment. Privileges on schema objects are granted to authorization identifiers. The type of privilege granted determines the type of access. In this chapter, we will look at the SQL security model, how it uses authorization identifiers, and how to set up privileges on objects in your SQL database.

Understand the SQL Security Model

Authorization identifiers provide the foundation for your database's security. Access to all objects is permitted through these identifiers. If the authorization identifier doesn't have the appropriate privileges to access a specific object, such as a table, the data within that table is unavailable to that user. In addition, each authorization identifier can be configured with different types of privileges. For example, you can permit some authorization identifiers to view the data within a specific table, while permitting other authorization identifiers to both view and modify that data.

SQL supports two types of authorization identifiers: user identifiers (or users) and role names (or roles). A *user identifier* is an individual security account that can represent an individual, an application, or a system service (all of which are considered database users). The SQL standard does not specify how an SQL implementation should create a user identifier. The identifier might be tied to the operating system on which the relational database management system (RDBMS) is running, or it might be explicitly created within the RDBMS environment.

A *role name* is a defined set of privileges that can be assigned to a user or to another role. If a role name is granted access to a schema object, then all user identifiers and role names that have been assigned the specified role name are granted the same access to that object whenever the role name is the current authorization identifier. For example, in Figure 6-1 the MRKT_DEPT role name has been assigned to the ACCT_DEPT role name and to four user identifiers: Ethan, Max, Linda, and Emma. If the MRKT_DEPT role name is the current authorization identifier and it has been granted access to the CD_PUBLISHERS table, the ACCT_DEPT role name and all four user identifiers have access to the CD_PUBLISHERS table. Note that, unlike a user identifier, SQL *does* specify how to create a role name, which I discuss in the "Create and Delete Roles" section later in this chapter.

Role names are commonly used as a mechanism for granting a uniform set of privileges to authorization identifiers that should have the same privileges, such as people who work in the same department. They also have the distinct advantage of being existence independent of user identifiers, which means they can be created prior to the user identifiers, and they persist even after the user identifiers referencing them are deleted. This is very helpful when administering privileges for a fluid workforce.

In addition to user identifiers and role names, SQL supports a special built-in authorization identifier named PUBLIC, which includes everyone who uses the database. Just as with any other authorization identifier, you can grant access privileges to the PUBLIC account. For example, suppose you wanted all potential customers to be able to view your list of CDs. You could grant the necessary privileges to the PUBLIC account for the appropriate tables and columns. Obviously, PUBLIC should be used with great care because it can open the door for people with ill intentions. In fact, many organizations ban its use completely.

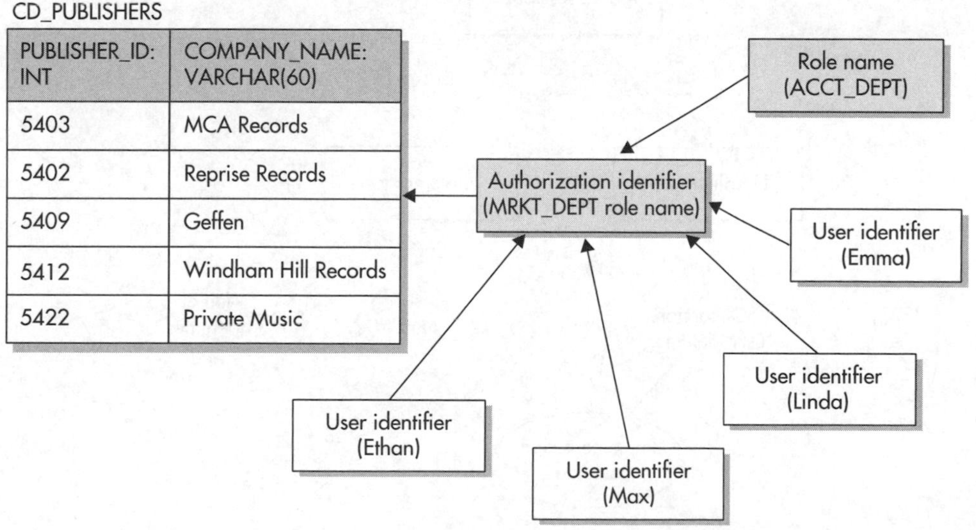

CD_PUBLISHERS

PUBLISHER_ID: INT	COMPANY_NAME: VARCHAR(60)
5403	MCA Records
5402	Reprise Records
5409	Geffen
5412	Windham Hill Records
5422	Private Music

Figure 6-1 The MRKT_DEPT role assigned to four user identifiers and one role

SQL Sessions

Each SQL session is associated with a user identifier and role name. An *SQL session* is the connection between some sort of client application and the database. The session provides the context in which the authorization identifier executes SQL statements during a single connection. Throughout this connection, the SQL session maintains its association with a user identifier/role name pair.

Let's take a look at Figure 6-2, which shows the user identifier/role name pair associated with a session. When a session is first established, the user identifier is always the *SQL session user identifier*, which is a special type of user identifier that remains associated with the session throughout the connection. It is up to the SQL implementation to determine how a specific account becomes the SQL session user identifier, although it can be an operating system user account or an account specific to the RDBMS. Whatever method is used to associate an account with the SQL session user identifier, it is this account that acts as the current user identifier.

As you can also see in Figure 6-2, the role name is a null value. The role name is always null when a session is first established. In other words, whenever you log onto an SQL database and establish a session, the initial user identifier will always be the SQL session user identifier and the role name will always be a null value.

At any instance during a connection, the session is associated with a user identifier/role name pair; however, it is not always the same pair throughout the length of the session. For example, embedded SQL statements, SQL client modules, and SQL-invoked routines can specify an authorization identifier. If a new identifier is specified, it becomes the current

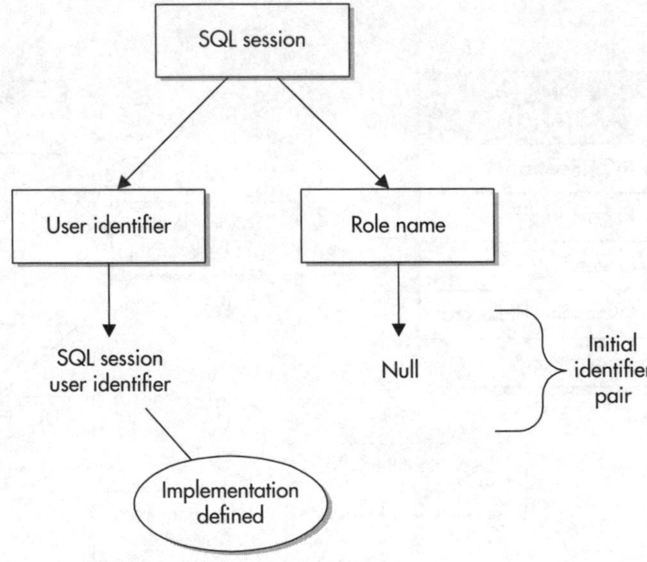

Figure 6-2 SQL session with user identifier and role name

authorization identifier until the transactions have completed, and access to objects is granted based on the current user identifier/role name pair.

For any user identifier/role name pair that is current, one of the two values is almost always null. In other words, if a user identifier is specified, then the role name must be null; if a role name is specified, then the user identifier must be null. Whichever value is not null is the authorization identifier.

When more than one user identifier/role name pair is used during a session, an authorization stack is created that reflects the current authorization identifier. The pair at the top of the stack is the current authorization identifier. Figure 6-3 shows an example of an authorization stack that can be created during a session.

In this example, the initial user identifier/role name pair is at the bottom of the stack. As you would expect, the user identifier is the SQL session user identifier and the role name is a null value. Access to database objects is based on the privileges granted to the SQL session user identifier when it is current.

During the session, an embedded SQL statement specifies an authorization identifier of App_User, which is a user identifier. When the embedded statement is executed, App_User becomes the current authorization identifier, and access privileges are based on that account.

Suppose one of the embedded SQL statements then calls an SQL-invoked routine that specifies an authorization of ROUTINE_ROLE, which is a role name. ROUTINE_ROLE then becomes the current authorization identifier and is at the top of the authorization stack. Once the routine runs, the current authorization identifier reverts to App_User until the embedded statements run, after which the authorization identifier reverts to the SQL session user identifier.

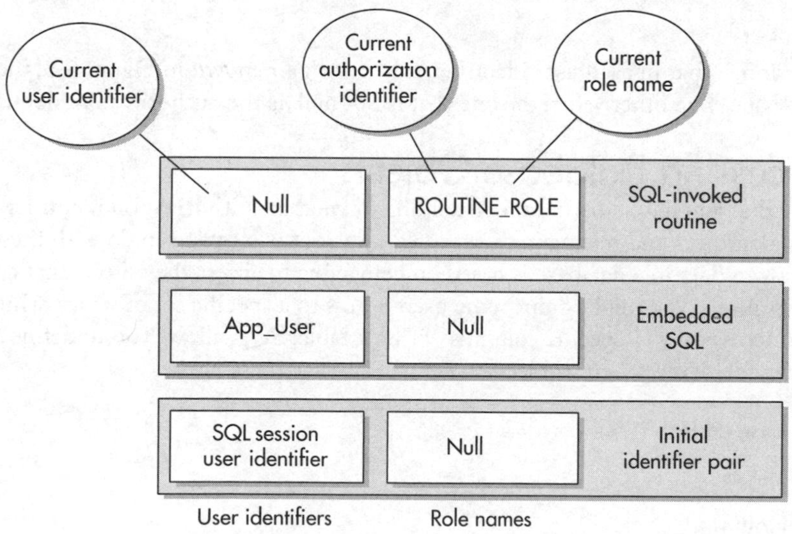

Figure 6-3 Authorization stack created during an SQL session

Ask the Expert

Q: You state that the current authorization identifier can change. How can you determine the current authorization user and role name at any time during a session?

A: SQL supports several special values that allow you to determine the current values of the various types of users. The special values act as placeholders for the actual user-related value. You can use these special values in expressions to return the value of the specific type of user. For example, you can use the CURRENT_USER special value to return the value of the current user identifier. SQL supports five of these special values: CURRENT_USER, USER, CURRENT_ROLE, SESSION_USER, and SYSTEM_USER. CURRENT_USER and USER mean the same thing and return a value equal to the current user identifier. CURRENT_ROLE returns the current role name, and SESSION_USER returns the SQL session user identifier. If the SQL session user identifier is the current user identifier, then CURRENT_USER, USER, and SESSION_USER all have the same value, which can occur if the initial identifier pair is the only active user identifier/role name pair (the pair at the top of the authorization stack). The last function, SYSTEM_USER, returns the operating system user who invoked an SQL module. As we get further into this chapter, you'll see how the CURRENT_USER and CURRENT_ROLE special values are used to identify the current authentication identifier when creating roles and granting privileges. (See the sections "Create and Delete Roles," "Grant and Revoke Privileges," and "Grant and Revoke Roles.") In addition, you'll find more information about special values in Chapter 10.

Notice that in each user identifier/role name pair shown in Figure 6-3, there is exactly one null value. The other value, the one that is not null, is the authorization identifier.

Accessing Database Objects

Now that you have a better understanding of what an authorization identifier is—along with user identifiers and role names—let's take a look at what you can do with these identifiers. Access to data in a database is based on being able to access the objects that contain the data. For example, you might grant some users access to a specific set of tables, while other users have access only to specific columns within a table. SQL allows you to define access privileges on the following schema objects:

- Base tables
- Views
- Columns
- Domains

- Character sets
- Collations
- Translations
- User-defined types
- Table/method pairs
- SQL-invoked routines
- Sequences

For each type of object, you can assign specific types of privileges that vary by object type. These assigned privileges are associated with specific authorization identifiers. In other words, you can assign one or more privileges for an object to one or more authorization identifiers. For example, you can assign the SELECT privilege for a table to the PUBLIC authorization identifier. This would allow all database users to view the contents of that table.

SQL defines nine types of privileges that you can assign to a schema object. Table 6-1 describes each of these privileges and lists the types of objects to which the privilege can be assigned.

Privilege	Description	Objects
SELECT	Allows specified authorization identifiers to query data in the object. For example, if UserA is granted the SELECT privilege on the CD_ARTISTS table, that user can view data in that table.	Tables Views Columns Methods (in structured types)
INSERT	Allows specified authorization identifiers to insert data into the object. For example, if UserA is granted the INSERT privilege on the CD_ARTISTS table, that user can add data to that table.	Tables Views Columns
UPDATE	Allows specified authorization identifiers to update data in the object. For example, if UserA is granted the UPDATE privilege on the CD_ARTISTS table, that user can modify data in that table. However, this privilege does not allow the user to change the table definition.	Tables Views Columns
DELETE	Allows specified authorization identifiers to delete data from the object. For example, if UserA is granted the DELETE privilege on the CD_ARTISTS table, that user can remove data from that table. However, this privilege does not allow the user to drop the table definition from the database.	Tables Views

Table 6-1 Security Privileges Assigned to Database Objects *(continued)*

Privilege	Description	Objects
REFERENCES	Allows specified authorization identifiers to define objects (such as referential constraints) that reference the table configured with the REFERENCES privilege. For example, if UserA is granted the REFERENCES privilege on the CD_ARTISTS table, that user can create other objects that reference the CD_ARTISTS table, as would be the case with foreign keys. (Note that UserA must also have the authorization to create the other object.)	Tables Views Columns
TRIGGER	Allows specified authorization identifiers to create triggers on the table. For example, if UserA is granted the TRIGGER privilege on the CD_ARTISTS table, that user can create triggers on that table.	Tables
USAGE	Allows specified authorization identifiers to use the object in a column definition. For example, if UserA is granted the USAGE privilege on the MONEY domain, that user can include the domain in a column definition when creating a table. (Note that UserA must also have the authorization to create a table.)	Domains Character sets Collations Translations User-defined types Sequences
EXECUTE	Allows specified authorization identifiers to invoke an SQL-invoked routine. For example, if UserA is granted the EXECUTE privilege on the UPDATE_CD_LISTING stored procedure, that user would be able to invoke that stored procedure.	SQL-invoked routines
UNDER	Allows specified authorization identifiers to define a direct subtype on a structured type. A *direct subtype* is a structured type that is associated with another structured type as a child object of that type. For example, if UserA is granted the UNDER privilege on the EMPLOYEE structured type, that user can define direct subtypes such as MANAGER or SUPERVISOR.	Structured types

Table 6-1 Security Privileges Assigned to Database Objects

Privileges are granted on database objects by using the GRANT statement to specify the objects as well as the authorization identifier that will acquire the privileges. You can also revoke privileges by using the REVOKE statement. I will be going into greater detail about both these statements as we move through the chapter. However, before I discuss how to grant or revoke privileges, I want to first discuss how to create a role name. (Remember, the SQL standard doesn't support the creation of a user identifier, only role names. The process for creating user identifiers is implementation specific.)

Create and Delete Roles

For the most part, creating a role is a very straightforward process. The statement includes only one mandatory clause and one optional clause, as shown in the following syntax:

```
CREATE ROLE <role name>
[ WITH ADMIN { CURRENT_USER | CURRENT_ROLE } ]
```

Notice that the only required part of the syntax is the CREATE ROLE clause, which means that all you really need to do is specify a name for your role. The WITH ADMIN clause is optional and you will rarely need to use this. It is necessary only if the current user identifier/role name pair contains no null values. The clause allows you to designate either the current user identifier (CURRENT_USER) or the current role name (CURRENT_ROLE) as the authentication identifier allowed to assign the role to user identifiers or role names. If the WITH ADMIN clause is not specified, the current authentication identifier, whether the current user identifier or the current role name, is allowed to assign the role.

NOTE

You'll probably find that you rarely need to use the WITH ADMIN clause of the CREATE ROLE statement, particularly as a beginning SQL programmer, and it isn't widely supported in RDBMS products. As a result, I keep my discussion of the clause brief.

Now let's look at creating a role. In the following example, I use the CREATE ROLE statement to create the CUSTOMERS role:

```
CREATE ROLE CUSTOMERS;
```

That's all there is to it. Once the role is created, you can grant the role to user identifiers or other role names. I discuss granting and revoking roles in the "Grant and Revoke Roles" section later in this chapter.

Dropping a role is just as easy as creating one. The syntax you use is as follows:

```
DROP ROLE <role name>
```

In this case, you merely need to identify the name of the role, as in the following example:

```
DROP ROLE CUSTOMERS;
```

The role is removed from the database. However, before removing a role, be sure that it is a role that you no longer need or that it is one you specifically want to delete (for security reasons).

As you can see, creating and dropping roles is a very simple process, and it can make managing your users a lot easier. Roles essentially allow you to group together those users who require the same privileges on the same objects. Now let's take a look at granting and revoking privileges to authentication identifiers, including both user identifiers and role names.

NOTE

Support for the CREATE ROLE and DROP ROLE statements varies from implementation to implementation. For example, Oracle and SQL Server (2005 and later) support both statements, but not the WITH ADMIN option. MySQL 5.7 does not appear to support the concept of roles.

Grant and Revoke Privileges

When you grant privileges on an object, you are associating one or more privileges with one or more authorization identifiers. This set of privileges and authorization identifiers is assigned to the object, which allows the authorization identifiers to have access to the object according to the type of privileges defined. To grant privileges, you must use the GRANT statement, as shown in the following syntax:

```
GRANT { ALL PRIVILEGES | <privilege list> }
ON <object type> <object name>
TO { PUBLIC | <authorization identifier list> }
[ WITH HIERARCHY OPTION ]
[ WITH GRANT OPTION ]
[ GRANTED BY { CURRENT_USER | CURRENT_ROLE } ]
```

The statement, as you can see, includes three required clauses—GRANT, ON, and TO—and three optional clauses—WITH HIERARCHY OPTION, WITH GRANT OPTION, and GRANTED BY. I will discuss each clause individually except for the WITH HIERARCHY and GRANTED BY clauses. The WITH HIERARCHY clause allows the granting of privileges to all the subobjects of the object(s) to which the privileges are granted. Object hierarchies is an advanced topic that you will not need to worry about until you master the basics of SQL.

The GRANTED BY clause is similar to the WITH ADMIN clause in the CREATE ROLE statement. Like the WITH ADMIN clause, the GRANTED BY clause applies only in those situations where the current user identifier/role name pair contains no null values, and it is not widely implemented in RDBMSs. As a beginner in SQL programming, you do not need to be concerned with the GRANTED BY clause.

NOTE

Many vendor implementations contain provisions for assigning system privileges such as starting and stopping the database to authorization identifiers using the GRANT statement. Since the syntax of these variants is entirely implementation specific, I do not cover them here.

You must have the necessary privileges on an object to grant privileges on that object. If you created the object, then you are the owner, which means that you have complete access to the object. (All privileges have been granted to you, including the ability to assign privileges to other authorization identifiers.)

Now let's take a look at the GRANT clause. The clause includes two options: ALL PRIVILEGES and the <privilege list> placeholder. If you use the ALL PRIVILEGES keywords, you are granting all available privileges to that object according to the privileges that you have been granted on the object. For example, assume for a moment that you created a table and are the owner. As a result, you are automatically granted the SELECT, INSERT, UPDATE, DELETE, TRIGGER, and REFERENCES privileges. (These are the only privileges that apply to a table. Refer back to Table 6-1 for a list of privileges and the objects to which they apply.) You are also automatically granted the ability to assign these privileges. In this situation, if you use the ALL PRIVILEGES keywords, you would be granting these six privileges to the authorization identifiers in the GRANT statement. It is always best to grant only the minimum privileges required, and therefore the use of ALL PRIVILEGES is usually not the best practice.

If you decide not to use the ALL PRIVILEGES option, you must then list each privilege that should be applied to the user identifiers. However, you can list only those privileges that can be applied to the specific object. For example, you cannot list the DELETE privilege if you are granting a privilege on a domain. Also note, if you list more than one privilege, you must separate the privilege names with commas.

The next clause we'll look at is the ON clause, which includes two placeholders: <object type> and <object name>. The <object type> placeholder simply refers to the type of object on which you're granting permissions. SQL supports the following values for the <object type> placeholder:

- TABLE (includes views)
- DOMAIN
- COLLATION
- CHARACTER SET
- TRANSLATION
- TYPE
- SEQUENCE
- Special designator for SQL-invoked routines

A value for the <object type> designator is required, unless the value is TABLE, in which case you can leave that off. If you provide the name of an object without specifying a type, SQL assumes that the <object type> value is TABLE. As noted in the list, the TABLE keyword also includes views. And, of course, not all implementations support all the object types included in the SQL standard, and some include types not covered by the standard—all of which leads to implementation-specific SQL variations.

NOTE

In Oracle, the TABLE keyword must be omitted. On the other hand, in DB2, it is optional, but highly recommended by the vendor. SQL Server does not support any of the <object type> keywords from the SQL standard in the GRANT statement, but instead permits a class keyword followed by a separator <::>, so instead of TABLE, you can write OBJECT:: (OBJECT being the keyword for database objects such as tables and views). The obvious lesson here is to always consult the documentation for your specific SQL implementation.

The <object name> placeholder in the ON clause refers to the name of the specific object. This value is always required.

The next clause is the TO clause. Like the GRANT clause, the TO clause has two options: PUBLIC and the <authorization identifier list> placeholder. If you use PUBLIC, all database users are granted access to the object. If you use the <authorization identifier list> option, then you must provide the name of one or more authorization identifiers. If you provide more than one, they must be separated by commas.

The last clause that I am going to discuss is the WITH GRANT OPTION clause. This clause grants the authorization identifiers permission to grant whatever privileges they're being granted in the GRANT statement. For example, suppose you're granting the EmmaW user identifier the SELECT privilege on one of your tables. If you use the WITH GRANT OPTION, EmmaW will be able to grant the SELECT privilege to another user. If you do not use the WITH GRANT OPTION, EmmaW will not be able to grant the privilege to another user. Incidentally, most security experts recommend that you never use this option because you quickly lose control over who has which privileges.

Now that we've taken a look at the syntax, let's look at a few examples. In the first example, we'll look at a GRANT statement that grants the SELECT privilege to the PUBLIC authorization identifier. The privilege is granted on a view named AVAILABLE_CDS, which lists the CDs that you currently have in stock. To grant the privilege, use the following statement:

```
GRANT SELECT ON TABLE AVAILABLE_CDS TO PUBLIC;
```

The SELECT privilege allows all database users (PUBLIC) to view data in the AVAILABLE_CDS view. However, because PUBLIC has not been granted any other privileges, users can view the data, but not take any action. In addition, because the WITH GRANT OPTION clause is not included in the statement, users cannot assign the SELECT privilege to any other users (which is a moot point in this case because everyone can already access the AVAILABLE_CDS view).

Now let's look at another example. This time, I'm granting the SELECT, UPDATE, and INSERT privileges to the SALES role and the ACCOUNTING role so that they have access to the CD_INVENTORY table:

```
GRANT SELECT, UPDATE, INSERT
   ON TABLE CD_INVENTORY
   TO SALES, ACCOUNTING WITH GRANT OPTION;
```

Notice that the privileges are separated by commas, as are the roles. As a result of this statement, the users associated with the SALES role and the ACCOUNTING role can view, update, and insert information into the CD_INVENTORY table. In addition, these users can assign the SELECT, UPDATE, and INSERT privileges to other users who need to access the CD_INVENTORY table.

The next example we will examine is a slight variation on this last one. Everything is the same, except that this time, I specify which column can be updated:

```
GRANT SELECT, UPDATE (CD_TITLE), INSERT
   ON TABLE CD_INVENTORY
   TO SALES, ACCOUNTING WITH GRANT OPTION;
```

Notice that you can add a column name after the specific privilege. You can add column names only to the SELECT, INSERT, UPDATE, and REFERENCES privileges. If you add more than one column name, you must separate them with commas.

The GRANT statement in this example still allows the Sales and Accounting users to view and insert information into the CD_INVENTORY table, but they can only update values in the CD_TITLE column. They cannot update any other column values in the table. In addition, although they can still assign privileges to other users, they can assign the UPDATE privilege only on the CD_TITLE column.

Let's take a look at one more example that grants SELECT privileges to the PUBLIC authorization identifier:

```
GRANT SELECT (CD_TITLE, IN_STOCK) ON CD_INVENTORY TO PUBLIC;
```

The PUBLIC authorization identifier allows all users to view data in the CD_TITLE and IN_STOCK columns of the CD_INVENTORY table, but they cannot view any other information in that table and they cannot modify the data in any way. Notice in this statement that the keyword TABLE isn't included. As I said earlier, TABLE is not required.

The GRANT statement, when used in conjunction with the available privileges and the authorization identifiers, provides a strong foundation for your database security. However, each SQL implementation is different with regard to how security is implemented and maintained. Therefore, when it comes to matters of security, it is important that you work closely with network and database administrators and carefully read the product documentation.

Revoking Privileges

Now that you know how to grant privileges to authorization identifiers, it's time to learn how to revoke those privileges. The statement that you use to revoke privileges is the REVOKE statement, as shown in the following syntax:

```
REVOKE [ GRANT OPTION FOR ] { ALL PRIVILEGES | <privilege list> }
ON <object type> <object name>
FROM { PUBLIC | <authorization identifier list>
[ GRANTED BY { CURRENT_USER | CURRENT_ROLE } ]
{ RESTRICT | CASCADE }
```

You probably recognize many of the syntax elements from the GRANT statement or from other statements. In fact, the only new component, other than the REVOKE keyword, is the GRANT OPTION FOR clause. Let's take a look at that one first, since it's at the beginning of the REVOKE statement. This clause applies only when the WITH GRANT OPTION clause was used in the GRANT statement. If a privilege was granted with this clause, you can use the GRANT OPTION FOR clause to remove that particular permission. If you do use it, the privileges are preserved, but the user can no longer grant those privileges to other users. However, very few RDBMS products support this clause.

Forgetting the GRANT OPTION FOR clause for a moment, let's look at the REVOKE clause itself, which is used to revoke either all privileges on an object (ALL PRIVILEGES) or only the defined privileges (<privilege list>). Both of these options have the same meaning they did in the GRANT statement; you can either use ALL PRIVILEGES or you can list each privilege separated by a comma.

The ON clause and GRANTED BY clause in the REVOKE statement are exactly the same as the ON clause and GRANTED BY clause in the GRANT statement. For the ON clause, you must specify values for the <object type> placeholder and the <object name> placeholder; however, if the <object type> value is TABLE, then you can leave that off (and, as before, you must omit it in Oracle and SQL Server). As for the GRANTED BY clause, assuming your RDBMS supports it (most do not), you can choose one of two options (CURRENT_USER or CURRENT_ROLE).

The FROM clause in the REVOKE statement can also be compared to the GRANT statement. The only difference is that in the GRANT statement, you use the TO keyword, but in the REVOKE statement you use the FROM keyword. In either case, you must either use PUBLIC as your authorization identifier, or you must list the specific user identifiers and role names.

The last elements of the statement to discuss are the RESTRICT keyword and the CASCADE keyword. You might recall these keywords from Chapters 2, 3, and 4. If you specify RESTRICT, the privilege will not be revoked if it had been passed on to other users—in other words, if there are any dependent privileges. (This would mean that the WITH GRANT OPTION had been used in the GRANT statement and that the authorization identifier that had been granted the privilege had then granted the privilege to someone else.) If you specify CASCADE, the privilege will be revoked, as will any privileges that were passed on to other users.

NOTE

Vendor implementations vary. In Oracle, CASCADE must be specified as CASCADE CONSTRAINTS. In both Oracle and SQL Server, RESTRICT cannot be specified, but rather is the default behavior when CASCADE is not specified. MySQL does not allow either to be specified.

Now let's take a look at some examples of revoking privileges. The following statement revokes a SELECT privilege that was granted to the PUBLIC authorization identifier on the AVAILABLE_CDS view:

```
REVOKE SELECT ON TABLE AVAILABLE_CDS FROM PUBLIC CASCADE;
```

As you can see, this statement is very similar to a GRANT statement. You must identify the privileges, the authorization identifiers, and the object. In addition, you may specify RESTRICT or CASCADE.

The next example is based on privileges that have been granted on a table named CD_INVENTORY. The SALES role and ACCOUNTING role have been granted the following privileges on this table: GRANT, SELECT, and INSERT. To revoke these privileges, use the following REVOKE statement:

```
REVOKE SELECT, UPDATE, INSERT ON TABLE CD_INVENTORY
  FROM SALES, ACCOUNTING CASCADE;
```

Notice that you simply specify the privileges you want to revoke, the name of the objects, and the name of the authorization identifiers. However, since you are revoking all the privileges that had been granted, you could have simplified the statement by using the ALL PRIVILEGES keywords, as shown in the following example:

```
REVOKE ALL PRIVILEGES ON TABLE CD_INVENTORY
  FROM SALES, ACCOUNTING CASCADE;
```

If you do not want to revoke all privileges, but instead want to revoke only the UPDATE and INSERT privileges, you can specify only those privileges, as shown in the following example:

```
REVOKE UPDATE, INSERT ON TABLE CD_INVENTORY
  FROM SALES, ACCOUNTING CASCADE;
```

You can also choose to revoke privileges for only one of the role names, rather than both. In addition, you can use the RESTRICT keyword rather than CASCADE.

Now suppose the same privileges had been granted as in the preceding example but in addition to those, the WITH GRANT OPTION had been specified when granting privileges. If you want to revoke only the ability of the Sales and Accounting roles to grant privileges to other users, you can use the following statement:

```
REVOKE GRANT OPTION FOR ALL PRIVILEGES ON CD_INVENTORY
  FROM SALES, ACCOUNTING CASCADE;
```

This statement revokes only the ability to grant privileges; the Sales and Accounting roles still have access to the CD_INVENTORY table. If you want to revoke all their privileges, you would have to execute this statement without the GRANT OPTION FOR clause. Notice in this statement that the TABLE keyword wasn't used before the name of the table. The REVOKE statement, like the GRANT statement, doesn't require the TABLE keyword when specifying a table or view.

NOTE

The vendor implementation variances noted with the use of the TABLE keyword in the GRANT statement (earlier in this chapter) apply in the same way to the REVOKE statement. In general, vendors support identical syntax between their GRANT and REVOKE statements except that TO in the GRANT statement becomes FROM in the REVOKE statement.

Grant and Revoke Roles

Now that you know how to create and delete roles and grant and revoke privileges, let's look at granting and revoking roles. We'll start with granting roles. To grant a role, you must use a GRANT statement to assign one or more role names to one or more authorization identifiers, as shown in the following syntax:

```
GRANT <role name list>
TO { PUBLIC | <authorization identifier list> } [ WITH ADMIN OPTION ]
[ GRANTED BY { CURRENT_USER | CURRENT_ROLE } ]
```

By now, most of this syntax should look quite familiar to you, except for a few variations. The GRANT clause allows you to specify a list of one or more role names. If you specify more than one name, you must separate them with commas. The TO clause allows you to specify one or more authorization identifiers. Again, if there are more than one, you must separate them with commas. You can also specify the PUBLIC authorization identifier to grant a role to all database users. The WITH ADMIN OPTION clause, which is optional, allows the authorization identifiers to grant the role to other users. And the GRANTED BY clause, which is also optional (and only supported in a few RDBMS products), is used in those rare instances when the user identifier/role name pair does not contain a null value.

Let's look at an example. Suppose you have created a role named MANAGERS and you want to assign that role to a user identifier named LindaN. You would use the following syntax:

```
GRANT MANAGERS TO LindaN;
```

Now suppose you want to give LindaN the ability to grant the MANAGERS role to other users. To do this, you simply add the WITH ADMIN OPTION clause, as in the following example:

```
GRANT MANAGERS TO LindaN WITH ADMIN OPTION;
```

You can also grant multiple roles to multiple user identifiers. The user identifiers can be user identifiers or other role names. In the following example, I grant the MANAGERS role and ACCOUNTING role to the LindaN user identifier and the MARKETING role name:

```
GRANT MANAGERS, ACCOUNTING TO LindaN, MARKETING WITH ADMIN OPTION;
```

Now that you know how to grant roles to authorization identifiers, it's time to learn how to revoke those roles.

Revoking Roles

Revoking roles is a lot like revoking privileges. The statement that you use to revoke privileges is the REVOKE statement, as shown in the following syntax:

```
REVOKE [ ADMIN OPTION FOR ] <role name list>
FROM { PUBLIC | <authorization identifier list> }
[ GRANTED BY { CURRENT_USER | CURRENT_ROLE } ]
{ RESTRICT | CASCADE }
```

As you can see, there is nothing new in the syntax except for the ADMIN OPTION FOR clause, which is similar to the GRANT OPTION FOR clause used when revoking privileges. It allows you to revoke the ability to assign roles to other users, without revoking the role itself.

NOTE

The same Oracle, SQL Server, and MySQL variances mentioned with revoking privileges apply to this use of the REVOKE statement.

Let's take a look at an example of revoking a role. Suppose you've granted the MANAGERS role to the LindaN user identifier. You can revoke that role by using the following REVOKE statement:

```
REVOKE MANAGERS FROM LindaN CASCADE;
```

If you had granted the MANAGERS role and the ACCOUNTING role to LindaN and the MARKETING role, your REVOKE statement would look like the following:

```
REVOKE MANAGERS, ACCOUNTING FROM LindaN, MARKETING CASCADE;
```

Now that we've looked at how to grant and revoke roles, you can see how similar this is to granting and revoking privileges. Again, I must stress that not all implementations are alike with regard to how they grant and revoke privileges and roles, so be sure to review your product documentation and work closely with the database administrator.

Try This 6-1 Managing Roles and Privileges

In this Try This exercise, you will create two roles in the INVENTORY database, grant privileges to the PUBLIC authorization identifier and to one of the roles you created, grant one of the roles to the other role, and then revoke all the privileges and roles. Finally, you will drop the two roles that you created. Your ability to follow all the steps in this exercise will depend on the type of security-related statements supported in the SQL implementation you're using. However, the exercise is designed so that any roles you create or privileges you assign are dropped by the end of the exercise. You will not be using these roles for any Try This

(continued)

exercises later in the book. If for any reason this exercise might affect the security of the system on which you're working, you should discuss this exercise with a database administrator or skip it altogether. You can download the Try_This_06.txt file, which contains the SQL statements used in this Try This exercise.

Step by Step

1. Open the client application for your RDBMS and connect to the INVENTORY database.
2. The first thing you'll do is create the MRKT role. Enter and execute the following SQL statement:

```
CREATE ROLE MRKT;
```

3. Next you'll create the SALES_STAFF role. Enter and execute the following SQL statement:

```
CREATE ROLE SALES_STAFF;
```

4. You'll now grant the SELECT privilege on the CDS_IN_STOCK view. The privilege will be assigned to the PUBLIC authorization identifier. Enter and execute the following SQL statement:

```
GRANT SELECT ON CDS_IN_STOCK TO PUBLIC;
```

5. The next privileges you grant will be to the SALES_STAFF role that you created in step 3. You'll be granting the SELECT, INSERT, and UPDATE privileges on the COMPACT_DISCS table. For the UPDATE privilege you will specify the CD_TITLE column. You will also allow the SALES_STAFF role to grant these privileges to other users. Enter and execute the following SQL statement:

```
GRANT SELECT, INSERT, UPDATE(CD_TITLE) ON COMPACT_DISCS
   TO SALES_STAFF WITH GRANT OPTION;
```

6. You'll now grant the SALES_STAFF role to the MRKT role. Enter and execute the following SQL statement:

```
GRANT SALES_STAFF TO MRKT;
```

7. Your next step is to revoke the SELECT privilege that you granted to the PUBLIC authorization identifier. Enter and execute the following SQL statement:

```
REVOKE SELECT ON CDS_IN_STOCK FROM PUBLIC CASCADE;
```

8. Now you'll revoke the privileges that you granted to the SALES_STAFF role. Because you're revoking all privileges, you can use the ALL PRIVILEGES keyword. You also want to ensure that any dependent privileges are revoked, so you'll use the CASCADE keyword. Enter and execute the following SQL statement:

```
REVOKE ALL PRIVILEGES ON COMPACT_DISCS FROM SALES_STAFF CASCADE;
```

9. You can now revoke the SALES_STAFF role from the MRKT role. Enter and execute the following SQL statement:

```
REVOKE SALES_STAFF FROM MRKT CASCADE;
```

10. Your next step is to drop the MRKT role. Enter and execute the following SQL statements:

```
DROP ROLE MRKT;
```

11. Finally, you need to drop the SALES_STAFF role. Enter and execute the following SQL statements:

```
DROP ROLE SALES_STAFF;
```

12. Close the client application.

Try This Summary

The INVENTORY database should now be set up the same way it was before you started this Try This exercise. The permissions and roles you granted should have been revoked, and the roles you created should have been dropped. This way, you will not have to worry about security considerations for other Try This exercises. For the remaining Try This exercises in the book, you should continue to work within the same security context in which you've been working for this exercise and for all Try This exercises preceding this one.

Chapter 6 Self Test

1. What is the difference between a user identifier and a role name?
2. What is the name of the special authorization identifier that grants access to all database users?
3. Each ________________ is associated with a user identifier and role name.
4. An SQL session is associated with which of the following?
   - **A** Privilege
   - **B** User identifier
   - **C** PUBLIC
   - **D** Role name
5. When an SQL session is first established, the user identifier is always the ______________.
6. What is the value of the current role name when an SQL session is first established?
7. What is an authorization identifier?
8. What two types of authorization identifiers does SQL support?

9. Which privilege should you grant on an object if you want to allow an authorization identifier to query data in that object?
10. You establish an SQL session with your database. The current user identifier is EthanW. The current role name is null. What is the current authorization identifier?
11. On which schema objects can you define access privileges?
12. On which types of database objects can you assign the DELETE privilege?
    - **A** Tables
    - **B** Views
    - **C** Columns
    - **D** Domains
13. On which types of database objects can you assign the TRIGGER privilege?
    - **A** Tables
    - **B** Views
    - **C** Columns
    - **D** Domains
14. You're creating a role named ACCOUNTING. Which SQL statement should you use?
15. You're granting all privileges on the CD_NAMES view to everyone who uses the database. Which SQL statement should you use?
16. You're granting the SELECT privilege to the SALES_CLERK role on a table in your database. You want the SALES_CLERK role to be able to assign the SELECT privilege to other users. What clause should you include in your GRANT statement?
17. You want to grant the ACCT role to the MaxN user authorization. You do not want the user to be able to grant the role to other users. What SQL statement should you use to grant the role?

Part II

Data Access and Modification

Chapter 7

Querying SQL Data

Key Skills & Concepts

- Use a SELECT Statement to Retrieve Data
- Use the WHERE Clause to Define Search Conditions
- Use the GROUP BY Clause to Group Query Results
- Use the HAVING Clause to Specify Group Search Conditions
- Use the ORDER BY Clause to Sort Query Results

Once the objects in a database have been created and the base tables populated with data, you can submit queries that allow you to retrieve specific information from the database. These queries, which usually take the form of SELECT statements, can range in complexity from a simple statement that returns all columns from a table to a statement that joins multiple tables, calculates values, and defines search conditions that restrict exactly which rows of data should be returned. The SELECT statement is made up of a flexible series of clauses that together determine which data will be retrieved. In this chapter, you will learn how to use each of these clauses to perform basic data retrieval, define search conditions, group query results, specify group search conditions, and order search results.

Use a SELECT Statement to Retrieve Data

In Chapter 5, when discussing views, I introduce you to the SELECT statement. As you might recall, the SELECT statement allows you to form intricate queries that can return exactly the type of data you want to retrieve. It is one of the most common statements you'll be using as an SQL programmer, and it is also one of the most flexible and extensive statements in the SQL standard.

The SELECT statement is a query expression that begins with the SELECT keyword and includes a number of elements that form the expression. The basic syntax for the SELECT statement can be split into several specific clauses that each help to refine the query so that only the required data is returned. The syntax for the SELECT statement can be shown as follows:

```
SELECT [ DISTINCT | ALL ] { * | <select list> }
FROM <table reference> [ { , <table reference> | <JOIN subclause> } . . . ]
[ WHERE <search condition> ]
[ GROUP BY <grouping specification> ]
[ HAVING <search condition> ]
[ ORDER BY <order condition> ]
```

As you can see, the only required clauses are the SELECT clause and the FROM clause. All other clauses are optional.

The FROM, WHERE, GROUP BY, and HAVING clauses are referred to as the table expression. This portion of the SELECT statement is always evaluated first when a SELECT statement is processed. Each clause within the table expression is evaluated in the order listed in the syntax. The result of that evaluation is a virtual table that is used in the subsequent evaluation. In other words, the results from the first clause evaluated are used in the next clause. The results from that clause are then used in the following clause, until each clause in the table expression is evaluated. For example, the first clause to be evaluated in a SELECT statement is the FROM clause. Because this clause is required, it is always the first clause evaluated. The results from the FROM clause are then used in the WHERE clause, if a WHERE clause is specified. If the clause is not specified, then the results of the FROM clause are used in the next specified clause, either the GROUP BY clause or the HAVING clause. Once the final clause in the table expression is evaluated, the results are then used in the SELECT clause. After the SELECT clause is evaluated, the ORDER BY clause is evaluated.

To sum all this up, the clauses of the SELECT statement are applied in the following order:

- FROM clause
- WHERE clause (optional)
- GROUP BY clause (optional)
- HAVING clause (optional)
- SELECT clause
- ORDER BY clause (optional)

Having a basic understanding of the order of evaluation is important as you create more complex SELECT statements, especially when working with joins and subqueries (discussed in Chapters 11 and 12, respectively). This understanding is also helpful when discussing each clause individually because it explains how one clause relates to other clauses. As a result, it is a good idea for you to keep this order of evaluation in mind throughout this chapter and in subsequent chapters that build upon various aspects of the SELECT statement.

The SELECT Clause and FROM Clause

Now that you have a basic overview of how the SELECT statement is executed, let's take a closer look at the SELECT clause and the FROM clause, the two required clauses in the statement. I'll discuss the other clauses in separate sections throughout the remainder of the chapter.

Let's begin with the SELECT clause. The SELECT clause includes the optional DISTINCT and ALL keywords. The DISTINCT keyword is used if you want to eliminate duplicate rows from the query results, and the ALL keyword is used if you want to return all rows in the query results. For example, suppose your database includes a table named

Ask the Expert

Q: You state that you can use an asterisk to include all columns in the query result. Does this ever present a problem if the number of columns changes?

A: Yes, this can present a problem. In fact, it is generally recommended that you use the asterisk only when you're accessing an SQL database through direct invocation. If you use the asterisk in embedded SQL and the number of columns changes, you might find that your application no longer responds correctly because the application program was coded to expect a specific response. If an asterisk is used and specific columns are expected to be returned, then you could run into a number of surprises if the database has been changed. For this reason, you should avoid the asterisk unless directly invoking a SELECT statement. However, in the case of direct invocation, the asterisk is a handy way to return all columns without having to specify the name of each one. In fact, many of the examples in the chapter use the asterisk to avoid having to repeat column names unnecessarily.

PERFORMER_CDS. The table includes the ARTIST_NAME column and the CD_NAME column. Because a CD can include more than one performer, the CD name can appear more than one time in the table. Now suppose that you want to query the table for the name of the CDs only, but you don't want the names repeated. You can use the DISTINCT keyword to ensure that your query returns the name of each CD only one time, or you can use the ALL keyword to specify that all rows be returned, even if there are duplicates. If you don't specify either of the keywords, the ALL keyword is assumed.

In addition to the DISTINCT and ALL keywords, the SELECT clause includes the asterisk (*) and the <select list> placeholder. You must specify one of these options in the clause. If you specify the asterisk, all applicable columns are included in the query result.

If you don't specify an asterisk in the SELECT clause, you must specify each column as it is derived from its source. The <select list> placeholder can be broken down into the following syntax:

```
<derived column> [ [ AS ] <column name> ]
[ { , <derived column> [ [ AS ] <column name> ] } . . . ]
```

Let's take a look at the first line of this syntax. (The second line is merely a repeat—as many times as necessary—of the first line.) The <derived column> placeholder in most cases refers to the name of the column in the source table. If more than one column is specified, then they must be separated with commas. However, the <derived column> placeholder might also refer to a column or set of columns that are in some way part of an expression. For instance, in Chapter 5, I discuss the AVG function, which averages the values in a specified column. The example I show in that chapter uses a SELECT statement to query data from the EMPLOYEE_COMMISSIONS table, which lists the total amount of commissions each employee made during a three-year period. The SELECT statement averages the values in three different columns, as shown in the following SELECT statement:

```
SELECT AVG(YEAR_1999), AVG(YEAR_2020), AVG(YEAR_2001)
  FROM EMPLOYEE_COMMISSIONS;
```

In this case, there are three expressions that are used for the <derived column> placeholder: AVG(YEAR_1999), AVG(YEAR_2020), and AVG(YEAR_2001). Notice that each derived column expression is separated by a comma, as would be the case if each value were simply a column name. The following example shows the same SELECT statement as in the preceding example, except that it uses only column names as the derived columns:

```
SELECT YEAR_1999, YEAR_2020, YEAR_2001
  FROM EMPLOYEE_COMMISSIONS;
```

If you were to execute this SELECT statement, your query would return all the values in the three columns, rather than averaging those values.

The SELECT clause also allows you to provide a column name for each derived column. To do this, add the AS keyword and the new column name after the derived column, as shown in the following example:

```
SELECT AVG(YEAR_1999) AS AVERAGE_1999
  FROM EMPLOYEE_COMMISSIONS;
```

In this SELECT statement, the value that is returned from the YEAR_1999 column is placed in a column named AVERAGE_1999. This is the name of the column that's returned as part of a virtual table in the query results. If you don't specify an AS subclause, the column name in the virtual table is the same as the column name in the source table. If a column name cannot be inherited naturally (for example, when adding two column values together), and you do not specify a name using the AS subclause, the column name is implementation specific (starting with SQL:2008), which means the SQL implementation will either assign a column name using an internal rule or terminate the query with an error condition.

Notice that in the previous examples the FROM clause is used to specify the table (EMPLOYEE_COMMISSIONS) that contains the columns referred to in the SELECT clause. The FROM clause includes the FROM keyword and one or more table references. If there are multiple table references, they must be separated using commas. In most cases, the table reference is either the name of a table or of joined tables, although it can also be a type of subquery. Alternatively, the JOIN subclause can be used to specify additional table references to be joined. I discuss joined tables in Chapter 11 and subqueries in Chapter 12. For this chapter, the FROM clause is used primarily to reference table names, as I have defined the clause in the two previous examples (where <table reference> equals EMPLOYEE_COMMISSIONS).

Together the SELECT clause and the FROM clause form the foundation for the SELECT statement, which can be as simple as querying every row and every column of a table, as shown in the following example:

```
SELECT * FROM ARTISTS;
```

In this statement, I specify that every column in the ARTISTS table should be returned. In addition, every row will be returned because no other clauses have been specified. Let's take a closer look at this. The ARTISTS table includes the ARTIST_ID, ARTIST_NAME, and PLACE_OF_BIRTH columns, as shown in Figure 7-1.

If you execute the SELECT statement shown in the previous example, your query results would look similar to the following:

```
ARTIST_ID  ARTIST_NAME              PLACE_OF_BIRTH
---------  -----------------------  --------------------------
3001       Glen Hansard             Ballymun, Dublin, Ireland
3002       Joe Bonamassa            New Hartford, New York, USA
3003       Stevie Wonder            Saginaw, Michigan, USA
3004       Fleetwood Mac            London, England
3005       Shania Twain             Windsor, Ontario, Canada
3006       Garth Brooks             Tulsa, Oklahoma, USA
3007       Johannes Sebastian Bach  Eisenarch, Saxe-Eisenarch
3008       Joshua Bell              Bloomington, Indiana, USA
3009       Jason Aldean             Macon, Georgia, USA
```

Notice that every row and every column is returned in the query results. If you use the asterisk in your SELECT clause, you do not have to specify the column names.

Now suppose you want to return only the ARTIST _NAME and PLACE_OF_BIRTH columns. You could modify your SELECT statement to look like the following:

```
SELECT ARTIST_NAME AS NAME, PLACE_OF_BIRTH
  FROM ARTISTS;
```

ARTIST_ID: INT	ARTIST_NAME: VARCHAR(60)	PLACE_OF_BIRTH: VARCHAR (60)
3001	Glen Hansard	Ballymun, Dublin, Ireland
3002	Joe Bonamassa	New Hartford, New York, USA
3003	Stevie Wonder	Saginaw, Michigan, USA
3004	Fleetwood Mac	London, England
3005	Shania Twain	Windsor, Ontario, Canada
3006	Garth Brooks	Tulsa, Oklahoma, USA
3007	Johannes Sebastian Bach	Eisenarch, Saxe-Eisenach
3008	Joshua Bell	Bloomington, Indiana, USA
3009	Jason Aldean	Macon, Georgia, USA

Figure 7-1 The ARTIST_ID, ARTIST_NAME, and PLACE_OF_BIRTH columns of the ARTISTS table

Your query results will now contain only two columns, as shown in the following:

```
NAME                        PLACE_OF_BIRTH
-----------------------     ----------------------------
Glen Hansard                Ballymun, Dublin, Ireland
Joe Bonamassa               New Hartford, New York, USA
Stevie Wonder               Saginaw, Michigan, USA
Fleetwood Mac               London, England
Shania Twain                Windsor, Ontario, Canada
Garth Brooks                Tulsa, Oklahoma, USA
Johannes Sebastian Bach     Eisenarch, Saxe-Eisenarch
Joshua Bell                 Bloomington, Indiana, USA
Jason Aldean                Macon, Georgia, USA
```

Notice that the name of the first column is NAME, rather than ARTIST_NAME. This is because the AS subclause (specifying NAME) is defined as part of the ARTIST_NAME derived column. If you were to specify the DISTINCT keyword in this particular situation, you would still receive the same number of rows, although they might not be returned in the same order as they were when you didn't use the keyword, depending on the SQL implementation. The reason that the DISTINCT keyword would make no difference in the query results is that there are no duplicate rows in the table. However, using the DISTINCT keyword can affect performance, particularly if your RDBMS has to sort through a large number of rows, so be sure to use the keyword only when necessary.

Now let's take a look at an example that uses the DISTINCT keyword. Suppose your database includes a table that matches artists to types of music, as shown in Figure 7-2.

ARTIST_NAME: VARCHAR(60)	ARTIST_TYPE: VARCHAR(20)
Glen Hansard	Alternative Rock
Joe Bonamassa	Blues
Joe Bonamassa	Pop
Stevie Wonder	R&B
Stevie Wonder	Rock
Stevie Wonder	Pop
Fleetwood Mac	Classic Rock
Fleetwood Mac	Pop

Figure 7-2 The ARTIST_NAME and ARTIST_TYPE columns of the ARTIST_TYPE table

If your SELECT statement includes both (all) columns in the SELECT clause, as shown in the following example, your query will return all rows:

```
SELECT * FROM ARTIST_TYPE;
```

It does not matter if you specify the DISTINCT keyword in this case because your query results include no duplicate rows. The results would be the same whether you include the ALL keyword, rather than DISTINCT, or whether you specify neither of the two qualifiers. In either case, the query results would include the same information that is shown in the table in Figure 7-2.

Now let's take a look at the same statement, only this time it specifies the DISTINCT keyword and only one of the two columns:

```
SELECT DISTINCT ARTIST_NAME
  FROM ARTIST_TYPE;
```

Notice that this statement includes only the ARTIST_NAME column, which includes duplicate values. By using the DISTINCT keyword, your query results will include only one instance of each value. If you execute the SELECT statement in the preceding example, your query results will look similar to the following:

```
ARTIST_NAME
-------------------------
Glen Hansard
Joe Bonamassa
Stevie Wonder
Fleetwood Mac
```

Although there are eight rows in the ARTIST_TYPE table, only four rows are returned because there are only four unique values in the ARTIST_NAME column and the other values are duplicates.

As you can see, the SELECT clause and the FROM clause are fairly straightforward, at least at this level of coding. Once we get into more complex structures, you'll find that both these clauses can at times become more complicated. However, the important thing to remember right now is that these clauses act as the foundation for the rest of the SELECT statement. In terms of execution, the SELECT statement, for all practical purposes, begins with the FROM clause and ends with the SELECT clause. (The ORDER BY clause is used primarily for display purposes and doesn't affect which information is actually returned. The ORDER BY clause is discussed in more detail in the "Use the ORDER BY Clause to Sort Query Results" section later in this chapter.)

Use the WHERE Clause to Define Search Conditions

The next clause in the SELECT statement is the WHERE clause. The WHERE clause takes the values returned by the FROM clause (in a virtual table) and applies the search condition that is defined within the WHERE clause. The WHERE clause acts as a filter on the results returned by the FROM clause. Each row is evaluated against the search condition. Those rows that evaluate to true are returned as part of the query result. Those that evaluate to unknown or false are not included in the results.

For a better understanding of how each row is evaluated, let's take a closer look at the <search condition> placeholder. The search condition is made up of one or more predicates that are used to test the contents returned by the FROM clause. A *predicate* is an SQL expression that defines a fact about any row returned by the SELECT statement. You have already seen examples of predicates in Chapters 4 and 5. For instance, one example of a view definition (in Chapter 5) includes the following SELECT statement:

```
SELECT CD_TITLE, COPYRIGHT_YEAR, IN_STOCK
  FROM COMPACT_DISC_INVENTORY
 WHERE COPYRIGHT_YEAR > 2009 AND COPYRIGHT_YEAR < 2020;
```

This statement is querying three columns in the COMPACT_DISC_INVENTORY table. The SELECT clause specifies the columns to be returned, and the FROM clause specifies the source table. The WHERE clause determines which rows (based on the FROM clause) are included in the results. In this case, the WHERE clause contains two predicates that are connected by the AND keyword. The first predicate (COPYRIGHT_YEAR > 2009) specifies that all rows included in the query results must contain a value greater than 2009 in the COPYRIGHT_YEAR column. The second predicate (COPYRIGHT_YEAR < 2020) specifies that all rows included in the query results must contain a value less than 2020 in the COPYRIGHT_YEAR column.

As rows are evaluated, each predicate is evaluated on an individual basis to determine whether the row meets the condition defined by that predicate. Returning to the last example, the first predicate sets the condition that values must be greater than 2009. If the COPYRIGHT_YEAR value for a particular row is more than 2009, the condition is met and the predicate evaluates to true. If the value is not greater than 2009, the predicate evaluates to false. If SQL cannot determine whether or not the value meets the condition (as would be the case if the value is null), the predicate evaluates to unknown.

Every predicate evaluates to true, false, or unknown. If more than one predicate is included in the WHERE clause, they are joined together by the OR keyword or the AND keyword. If OR is used, then at least one of the predicates on either side of OR must evaluate to true for the row to pass the filter, and therefore appear in the query results. If AND is used, then predicates on either side must evaluate to true for the row to pass the filter. For instance, the WHERE clause in the last example includes two predicates that are connected by the AND keyword. This means that the first predicate must evaluate to true *and* the second predicate must evaluate to true. If OR had been used instead of AND, then only one of the predicates must evaluate to true, which is a bit nonsensical in this case because all values except null are either above 2009 or below 2020.

Ultimately, the WHERE clause as a whole must evaluate to true in order for a row to be included in the query results. If the WHERE clause includes more than one predicate, SQL follows specific guidelines for how the statement as a whole is evaluated. Let's start by looking at the OR keyword. Table 7-1 lists the evaluation of a search condition if the OR keyword is

	True	False	Unknown
True	True	True	True
False	True	False	Unknown
Unknown	True	Unknown	Unknown

Table 7-1 Evaluating Predicates Connected by OR

used to separate two predicates. To use the table, match a condition in the left column to a condition in the top row. The result (where a row and column intersect to form a cell) shows how the search condition is evaluated based on how each predicate is evaluated.

As the table shows, if both predicates evaluate to true, then the search condition evaluates to true. If both are false, then the search condition evaluates to false. A condition is provided for each possible match. For example, suppose your SELECT statement includes the following WHERE clause:

```
WHERE ARTIST_TYPE = 'Blues' OR ARTIST_TYPE = 'Pop'
```

Now suppose that the first predicate in this example (ARTIST_TYPE = 'Blues') evaluates to true and the second predicate (ARTIST_TYPE = 'Pop') evaluates to false. This means that the row being evaluated contains the Blues value in the ARTIST_TYPE column, but does not contain the Pop value in that column. Now refer back to Table 7-1. If you select True from the first column, select False from the top row, and then match these two values together (by picking where they intersect), you can see that the search condition evaluates to true, so the row will be included in the query results.

You can do the same thing with the AND keyword as you did with the OR keyword. Table 7-2 matches the nine possible outcomes of two predicates.

Again, you simply match up how each predicate is evaluated to determine whether the search condition will be evaluated to true, false, or unknown. Remember, the search condition must evaluate to true for the row to be included in the query results. As you can see, the AND keyword is a lot less forgiving than the OR keyword. The only way for the search condition to evaluate to true is for both predicates to evaluate to true.

	True	False	Unknown
True	True	False	Unknown
False	False	False	False
Unknown	Unknown	False	Unknown

Table 7-2 Evaluating Predicates Connected by AND

NOTE

Comparison operators and predicates in general are discussed in greater detail in Chapter 9.

If a search condition includes more than two predicates, the predicates are evaluated in an order chosen by the RDBMS, unless parentheses are used to separate combinations of predicates. While the SQL standard does not specify the order in which multiple predicates are to be evaluated, most RDBMS products evaluate AND before OR. For example, you might have a SELECT statement that includes the following WHERE clause:

```
WHERE IN_STOCK = 42 OR IN_STOCK = 16 AND LABEL_ID = 828 OR LABEL_ID = 827
```

Notice that there are four predicates in this clause and no parentheses. Assuming that AND is evaluated before OR, the previous WHERE clause would be evaluated as if it was written this way:

```
WHERE IN_STOCK = 42 OR (IN_STOCK = 16 AND LABEL_ID = 828) OR LABEL_ID = 827
```

In order to evaluate to true, a row must contain one of the following values or set of values:

- IN_STOCK value of 42
- IN_STOCK value of 16 and LABEL_ID value of 828
- LABEL_ID value of 827

When you include both the AND and OR keywords in the same WHERE clause, it is *always* a good idea to include parentheses to make sure you are getting the filtering you intend, keeping in mind that predicates within parentheses are always evaluated first. If the RDBMS makes other assumptions, or if parentheses are used around other sets of predicates, the results will be different from what we've seen. For example, suppose you use parentheses as follows:

WHERE (IN_STOCK = 42 OR IN_STOCK = 16) AND (LABEL_ID = 828 OR LABEL_ID = 827)

The predicates are first evaluated within the context of the parentheses and then compared to other predicates accordingly. In this case, a row must contain one of the two IN_STOCK values *and* the row must contain one of the two LABEL_ID values. As a result, a row must contain one of the following sets of values to evaluate to true:

- IN_STOCK value of 42 and LABEL_ID value of 828
- IN_STOCK value of 42 and LABEL_ID value of 827
- IN_STOCK value of 16 and LABEL_ID value of 828
- IN_STOCK value of 16 and LABEL_ID value of 827

NOTE

SQL includes three operators that you can use if a search condition becomes too complicated. These operators are IS TRUE, IS FALSE, and IS UNKNOWN. For example, you can specify the following search condition: (ARTIST_NAME = 'Stevie Wonder' AND ARTIST_TYPE = 'R&B') IS TRUE. This means that the ARTIST_NAME value of a returned row must be Stevie Wonder and the ARTIST_TYPE value must be R&B. In other words, they must evaluate to true. If you specify IS FALSE in this situation, the predicate pair would have to evaluate to false, meaning that at least one of the two predicates had to be false (could not be Stevie Wonder or could not be R&B).

Another keyword that you might find useful is the NOT keyword, which can be used alone or along with the AND keyword and the OR keyword to specify the inverse of a predicate. For example, your SELECT statement might include the following WHERE clause:

```
WHERE ARTIST_NAME = 'Stevie Wonder'
   OR NOT ARTIST_NAME = 'Fleetwood Mac'
```

In this case, the ARTIST_NAME value can be Stevie Wonder or it can be any value other than Fleetwood Mac. Of course, Stevie Wonder is not equal to Fleetwood Mac, so that predicate is redundant and you get the same result if you remove the first predicate. Furthermore, you would get the same result if you used the not equal (<>) comparison operator, so the entire WHERE clause can be rewritten more simply as:

```
WHERE ARTIST_NAME <> 'Fleetwood Mac'
```

Defining the WHERE Clause

Now that you have an overview of how to define a WHERE clause, let's put it together with the SELECT clause and FROM clause and take a look at a few examples. The examples that we'll be looking at are based on the INVENTORY table, shown in Figure 7-3. The INVENTORY table contains five columns, some of which we'll be using to define our search conditions.

The first example that we'll be looking at includes a WHERE clause that defines which rows can be returned based on the IN_STOCK values:

```
SELECT * FROM INVENTORY
 WHERE IN_STOCK < 20;
```

If you execute this statement, your query results will be similar to the following:

```
CD_ID  CD_TITLE                  COPYRIGHT_YEAR  RETAIL_PRICE  IN_STOCK
-----  ------------------------  --------------  ------------  --------
101    Drive All Night           2013                5.99      12
103    Innervisions (Remastered) 2000               10.00      16
105    Rumours (Reissued)        1990                7.99      17
106    Come On Over              1997                5.99       6
107    Man Against Machine       2014                9.99       8
```

INVENTORY

CD_ID: INT	CD_TITLE: VARCHAR(60)	COPYRIGHT_YEAR: INT	RETAIL_PRICE: NUMERIC(5,2)	IN_STOCK: INT
101	Drive All Night	2013	5.99	12
102	Different Shades of Blue	2014	11.99	42
103	Innervisions (Remastered)	2000	10.00	16
104	The Definitive Collection	2003	8.39	34
105	Rumours (Reissued)	1990	7.99	17
106	Come On Over	1997	5.99	6
107	Man Against Machine	2014	9.99	8

Figure 7-3 The INVENTORY table containing CD-related data

As you can see, all but two rows are included in the query results. The rows not included contain IN_STOCK values greater than or equal to 20. In other words, these two rows evaluated to false.

Now let's take that same SELECT statement and refine the WHERE clause even further. In the new statement, the WHERE clause includes two predicates that are connected by the AND keyword, as shown in the following example:

```
SELECT * FROM INVENTORY
 WHERE IN_STOCK < 20 AND RETAIL_PRICE < 8.50;
```

When you execute this statement, you receive the following results:

```
CD_ID  CD_TITLE                    COPYRIGHT_YEAR  RETAIL_PRICE  IN_STOCK
-----  --------------------------  --------------  ------------  --------
101    Drive All Night             2013             5.99         12
105    Rumours (Reissued)          1990             7.99         17
106    Come On Over                1997             5.99          6
```

Notice that only three rows meet the search condition. In other words, only these three rows have an IN_STOCK value of less than 20 *and* a RETAIL_PRICE value of less than 8.50. Because the AND keyword is used, both predicates must evaluate to true, which they do for these three rows.

Now let's make one small modification to the SELECT statement. In the WHERE clause, I have changed the AND keyword to the AND NOT keywords, as shown in the following example:

```
SELECT * FROM INVENTORY
 WHERE IN_STOCK < 20 AND NOT RETAIL_PRICE < 8.50;
```

The NOT keyword changes the query results. As you can see, two rows are returned:

```
CD_ID  CD_TITLE                    COPYRIGHT_YEAR  RETAIL_PRICE  IN_STOCK
-----  --------------------------  --------------  ------------  --------
103    Innervisions (Remastered)   2000            10.00         16
107    Man Against Machine         2014             9.99          8
```

The returned rows each contain an IN_STOCK value of less than 20 *and* a RETAIL_PRICE value that is *not* less than 8.50, or 8.50 or greater.

Next we'll look at the same SELECT statement, only this time the two predicates are connected by the OR keyword, as shown in the following example:

```
SELECT * FROM INVENTORY
 WHERE IN_STOCK < 20 OR RETAIL_PRICE < 8.50;
```

The query results for this statement include many more rows than when the AND keyword was used. By its very nature, the OR keyword permits greater opportunities for a search clause to evaluate to true. As you can see, six rows have now been returned:

```
CD_ID  CD_TITLE                    COPYRIGHT_YEAR  RETAIL_PRICE  IN_STOCK
-----  --------------------------  --------------  ------------  --------
101    Drive All Night             2013             5.99         12
103    Innervisions (Remastered)   2000            10.00         16
104    The Definitive Collection   2003             8.39         34
105    Rumours (Reissued)          1990             7.99         17
106    Come On Over                1997             5.99          6
107    Man Against Machine         2014             9.99          8
```

Each row in the query results contains an IN_STOCK value of less than 20 *or* a RETAIL_PRICE value of less than 8.50. Because the OR keyword is being used, only one of the predicates needs to evaluate to true, although it's acceptable if both predicates evaluate to true.

In the next example, I add one more predicate that limits the rows returned to those with an IN_STOCK value greater than 10, along with parentheses to make my intentions clear:

```
SELECT * FROM INVENTORY
 WHERE (IN_STOCK < 20 AND IN_STOCK > 10) OR RETAIL_PRICE < 8.50;
```

For a row to be returned, the IN_STOCK value must fall between the range of 10 and 20 *or* the RETAIL_PRICE value must be less than 8.50. The query results from this SELECT statement would be as follows:

```
CD_ID  CD_TITLE                    COPYRIGHT_YEAR  RETAIL_PRICE  IN_STOCK
-----  --------------------------  --------------  ------------  --------
101    Drive All Night             2013             5.99         12
105    Rumours (Reissued)          1990             7.99         17
```

Now let's make one more change to the WHERE clause. Suppose you want the IN_STOCK value to be less than 20 and greater than 10 or the IN_STOCK value to be less than 20 and the RETAIL_PRICE value to be less than 8.50. One way to do this is to place parentheses around the last two predicates:

```
SELECT * FROM INVENTORY
 WHERE IN_STOCK < 20 AND (IN_STOCK > 10 OR RETAIL_PRICE < 8.50);
```

The results you receive this time are different because two other rows now evaluate to true:

```
CD_ID  CD_TITLE                    COPYRIGHT_YEAR  RETAIL_PRICE  IN_STOCK
-----  --------------------------  --------------  ------------  --------
101    Drive All Night             2013             5.99         12
103    Innervisions (Remastered)   2000            10.00         16
105    Rumours (Reissued)          1990             7.99         17
106    Come On Over                1997             5.99          6
```

By combining predicates together, you can create a variety of search conditions that allow you to return exactly the data you need. The key to writing effective search conditions is a thorough understanding of predicates and the operators used to form those predicates. Chapter 9 takes you through many of the operators you can use and the types of predicates you can create. With that information, you can create effective, concise search conditions.

Use the GROUP BY Clause to Group Query Results

The next clause in the SELECT statement is the GROUP BY clause. The GROUP BY clause has a function very different from the WHERE clause. As the name implies, the GROUP BY clause is used to group together types of information in order to summarize related data. The GROUP BY clause can be included in a SELECT statement whether or not the WHERE clause is used.

As you saw in the "Use a SELECT Statement to Retrieve Data" section, the syntax for the GROUP BY clause, as it appears in the SELECT statement syntax, looks like the following:

```
[ GROUP BY <grouping specification> ]
```

However, the <grouping specification> placeholder can be broken down into smaller elements:

```
<column name> [ { , <column name> } . . . ]
| { ROLLUP | CUBE } ( <column name> [ { , <column name> } . . . ] )
| GROUPING SETS ( <grouping set> [ { , <grouping set> } . . . ] )
```

In actuality, the <grouping specification> syntax, like some of the other syntax in this book, is even more complex than what I'm presenting here; however, for the purposes of this chapter, this syntax will provide you with all the details you need to use the GROUP BY clause effectively.

Now let's look at the syntax itself. The first line should be self-explanatory. You specify one or more column names that contain values that should be grouped together. This normally applies to columns that represent some sort of categories whose values are repeated within the table. For example, your database might include a table that lists the employees in your organization. Suppose that the table includes a job title for each employee. You might find that you want to group together information in the table by job title, with one row in the result set for each job title value, perhaps to determine such things as the average salary of each job or number of employees holding each job title. If you need to specify more than one column name, be sure to separate them with a comma following each name (except the last).

As you can see from the syntax, you can specify the second line rather than the first or the third line instead of either the first or second lines. Using the syntax on the second line, you can use either the ROLLUP or CUBE keyword, along with the list of column names, enclosed in parentheses. Again, be sure to separate column names with commas. Or following the syntax on the third line, you can use the GROUPING SETS keywords along with one or more grouping sets, each of which is a list of column names.

With regard to ROLLUP, CUBE, and GROUPING SETS, the best way to understand these operators is through the use of examples. In fact, the best way to understand the entire GROUP BY clause is through examples. However, before we get into those, let's take a look at the table on which the examples will be based. Figure 7-4 shows the COMPACT_DISC_COST

COMPACT_DISC: VARCHAR(60)	CATEGORY: VARCHAR(15)	COST: NUMERIC(5,2)	ON_HAND: INT
Drive All Night	Vocal	4.50	12
Different Shades of Blue	Vocal	5.50	42
Innervisions (Remastered)	Vocal	5.50	16
The Definitive Collection	Vocal	4.50	34
Rumours (Reissued)	Vocal	4.50	17
Come On Over	Vocal	4.50	6
Man Against Machine	Vocal	5.50	8
Bach	Instrumental	5.50	22
Old Boots, New Dirt	Vocal	5.50	32
Dark Side of the Moon	Vocal	7.75	27
Kind of Blue	Instrumental	4.50	21
Thriller	Vocal	4.50	29
The Endless River	Vocal	7.75	12
Sonic Highways	Vocal	5.50	27

Figure 7-4 CD information in the COMPACT_DISC_COST table

table, which contains a list of CDs, whether they're vocal or instrumental, the wholesale cost, and how many of each title are currently in stock.

Now we can get on with the examples. In the first one we'll look at, I use the GROUP BY clause to group rows based on the CATEGORY column of the COMPACT_DISC_COST table, as shown in the following SELECT statement:

```
SELECT CATEGORY, SUM(ON_HAND) AS TOTAL_ON_HAND
  FROM COMPACT_DISC_COST
 GROUP BY CATEGORY;
```

First, let's take a look at the GROUP BY clause, which specifies that the rows should be grouped together based on the CATEGORY column. If you look at Figure 7-4, you'll see that the column contains only two values: Vocal and Instrumental. As a result, the SELECT statement will return only two rows, one for Instrumental and one for Vocal:

```
CATEGORY      TOTAL_ON_HAND
------------  -------------
Instrumental  43
Vocal         262
```

Now let's look at the SELECT clause in the preceding SELECT statement example. Notice that the select list includes the SUM function, which adds data in the ON_HAND column. The resulting column is then named TOTAL_ON_HAND. The only other column included in the select list is the CATEGORY column. The select list can include only those columns that are specified in the GROUP BY clause or that can somehow be summarized.

What this statement does, then, is add together the total ON_HAND values for each value in the CATEGORY column. In this case, there are 43 total CDs in stock that are categorized as Instrumental, and 262 in stock that are categorized as Vocal. If there were another category, then a row would appear for that one as well.

If you only want the total number of CDs in stock without any grouping, you can write the query very simply as shown in the following SELECT statement:

```
SELECT SUM(ON_HAND) AS TOTAL_ON_HAND
  FROM COMPACT_DISC_COST;
```

Even though you did not use the GROUP BY clause, the DBMS still must group the rows in the table in order to produce the results. The only difference in this case is that there is one group consisting of all the rows in the table. The result is a single row like the following:

```
TOTAL_ON_HAND
-------------
 305
```

Ask the Expert

Q: Are there performance considerations regarding the use of GROUP BY?

A: Yes, the use of GROUP BY can cause performance issues because the RDBMS usually must perform a sort in order to properly group the rows, and sorts of large numbers of rows (tens of thousands or more) can consume considerable resources. But also be aware that the ORDER BY clause (presented later in this chapter) and the DISTINCT keyword also usually require sorts and thus have similar performance considerations. That doesn't mean you should be afraid to use them, but rather that you should strive to learn the performance impact of your SQL statements as you gain experience, and thus become more skilled at writing statements that perform best on your particular vendor implementation. For example, in Oracle, a GROUP BY that lists all columns in the SELECT clause is more efficient than using the DISTINCT keyword, and yet the query results of the two approaches are identical. Most SQL implementations have tuning guidelines for various SQL queries, so you should also consult the manuals for the particular DBMS and version you are using.

As I said earlier, you can still use the WHERE clause in a SELECT statement that includes a GROUP BY clause. For example, suppose you want to view totals only for CDs that cost less than $5.00. To do this, simply modify your SELECT statement as follows:

```
SELECT CATEGORY, SUM(ON_HAND) AS TOTAL_ON_HAND
  FROM COMPACT_DISC_COST
 WHERE COST < 5.00
 GROUP BY CATEGORY;
```

Your query results from this statement will be slightly different than if the WHERE clause had not been included:

```
CATEGORY      TOTAL_ON_HAND
------------  -------------
Instrumental  21
Vocal         98
```

Notice that with CDs that cost $5.00 or more excluded, your results now show only 21 instrumental CDs and 98 vocal CDs.

In the previous two examples, the GROUP BY clause specified only one column. However, you can specify additional columns as necessary. This allows you to create subgroups that group data within the scope of the main groups. For example, suppose you want to group data not only according to the values in the CATEGORY column, but also according to the values in the COST column. To do this, you should include the COST column in the select list as well as the GROUP BY clause, as shown in the following SELECT statement:

```
SELECT CATEGORY, COST, SUM(ON_HAND) AS TOTAL_ON_HAND
  FROM COMPACT_DISC_COST
 GROUP BY CATEGORY, COST;
```

Now your query results will include five rows, rather than two:

```
CATEGORY      COST   TOTAL_ON_HAND
------------  -----  -------------
Instrumental  4.50   21
Instrumental  5.50   22
Vocal         4.50   98
Vocal         5.50   125
Vocal         7.75   39
```

Notice that for each CATEGORY value, there is one for each of the COST values. For example, in the Instrumental group, there are 21 CDs at 4.50, and 22 CDs at 5.50. The number of rows depends on how many different values there are in the columns specified in the GROUP BY clause. In this example, there are two different values in the CATEGORY column and three different values in the COST column, which would lead you to believe that six (two times three) rows will be returned. However, there are no CDs in the Instrumental group with a cost of $7.75, so only five rows are actually returned.

NOTE

The order in which your query results are returned can vary from implementation to implementation. For example, some products might return all the Instrumental rows together, followed by all the Vocal rows. However, regardless of how the information appears in your user interface, the end results should be the same. Most implementations permit you to add an ORDER BY clause (discussed later in this chapter) to sort the summarized rows and thus control the order in which your query results are returned.

Now let's take a look at the ROLLUP and CUBE operators. Both operators are similar in function in that they return additional data in your query results when added to the GROUP BY clause. The main difference between the two is that the CUBE operator returns more information than the ROLLUP operator. Let's start with an example of the ROLLUP operator so I can demonstrate the difference.

In the following SELECT statement, the GROUP BY clause applies the ROLLUP operator to the CATEGORY and COST columns:

```
SELECT CATEGORY, COST, SUM(ON_HAND) AS TOTAL_ON_HAND
  FROM COMPACT_DISC_COST
 GROUP BY ROLLUP (CATEGORY, COST);
```

NOTE

Implementations can vary with regard to how they support the ROLLUP and CUBE operators. For example, in SQL Server implementations prior to 2008, you must add WITH ROLLUP or WITH CUBE to the end of the GROUP BY clause, rather than defining the clause in the way the SQL standard specifies. Therefore, in the previous example, you must write GROUP BY CATEGORY, COST WITH ROLLUP. MySQL (through version 5.7) also requires the WITH ROLLUP syntax, but there is no support for the CUBE operator in MySQL 5.7. Be sure to check your product documentation to determine how these operators are supported.

Now when you execute the SELECT statement, the query results include an additional row for each value in the CATEGORY column, plus a grand total row at the end:

```
CATEGORY      COST    TOTAL_ON_HAND
------------  ------  -------------
Instrumental  4.50    21
Instrumental  5.50    22
Instrumental  <NULL>  43
Vocal         4.50    98
Vocal         5.50    125
Vocal         7.75    39
Vocal         <NULL>  262
<NULL>        <NULL>  305
```

The two additional CATEGORY rows provide totals for each value in the CATEGORY column. In the preceding example, the Instrumental group includes a total of 43 CDs, and the Vocal group includes a total of 262 CDs. Notice that the COST column includes a null value for these particular rows. A value cannot be calculated for this column because all the subgroups (all possible values from the COST column) are represented here. The last row (the one with <NULL> for both the CATEGORY and COST columns) contains a grand total of all CDs counted by the query (all category groups and all cost subgroups).

The CUBE operator returns the same data as the ROLLUP operator, and then some. Notice that in the following SELECT statement, I've merely replaced the CUBE keyword for ROLLUP:

```
SELECT CATEGORY, COST, SUM(ON_HAND) AS TOTAL_ON_HAND
  FROM COMPACT_DISC_COST
 GROUP BY CUBE (CATEGORY, COST);
```

This statement returns the following query results:

```
CATEGORY      COST    TOTAL_ON_HAND
------------  ------  -------------
Instrumental  4.50    21
Instrumental  5.50    22
Instrumental  <NULL>  43
Vocal         4.50    98
```

```
Vocal          5.50     125
Vocal          7.75     39
Vocal          <NULL>   262
<NULL>         4.50     119
<NULL>         5.50     147
<NULL>         7.75     39
<NULL>         <NULL>   305
```

You can see that three additional rows have been added to the query results, one row for each different value in the COST column. Unlike the ROLLUP operator, the CUBE operator summarizes the values for each subgroup. Also notice that a null value is shown for the CATEGORY column for these rows. This is because both Vocal and Instrumental values are included in each subgroup summary.

Now let's look at the GROUPING SETS syntax introduced in SQL:2006. The GROUPING SET syntax is considerably more powerful than the GROUP BY options we have seen thus far because it allows you to precisely specify the aggregations you want in your query. Recall that the general syntax for grouping sets is as follows:

```
GROUPING SETS ( <grouping set> [ { , <grouping set> } . . . ] )
```

The syntax looks deceptively simple. The keywords GROUPING SETS are followed by a left parenthesis, a comma-separated list of grouping sets, and finally a right parenthesis. However, the syntax of each grouping set is as follows:

```
(<column name> [ { , <column name> } . . . ] ) | ()
```

Each grouping set must also be enclosed in parentheses and may contain any number of column names, separated by commas. Optionally, the grouping set may be empty, which is specified as a pair of parentheses that enclose nothing: `()`. The empty set specifies a group that contains all the rows selected from the table, resulting in the addition of a grand total row in the query results.

This somewhat complex syntax is worth knowing because it provides great flexibility. With grouping sets, you can simply list the groupings you want, with each set consisting of a single column name, a list of column names, or the empty set.

NOTE

As of version 5.7, MySQL does not yet support grouping sets.

ROLLUP and CUBE are actually shorthand notation for two commonly used forms of GROUPING SETS. For example, the following queries show the ROLLUP syntax we used earlier and the equivalent query written using the GROUPING SETS syntax:

```
SELECT CATEGORY, COST, SUM(ON_HAND) AS TOTAL_ON_HAND
  FROM COMPACT_DISC_COST
 GROUP BY ROLLUP (CATEGORY, COST);
```

```
SELECT CATEGORY, COST, SUM(ON_HAND) AS TOTAL_ON_HAND
  FROM COMPACT_DISC_COST
 GROUP BY GROUPING SETS ( (CATEGORY, COST), (CATEGORY), () );
```

The two queries in this example produce identical results (refer back to the previous example of the ROLLUP query for a listing of the query results). The GROUPING SETS clause in the later query contains a list of three grouping sets, each enclosed in a pair of parentheses. The first specifies the CATEGORY and COST columns, which specifies subtotals for each value of the CATEGORY column and each value of the COST column. This grouping set is the same as if you had written a simple GROUP BY and listed the two column names. The second grouping set specifies subtotals for each value of the CATEGORY column. The rows returned by this grouping set have null values in the COST column because the rows total the total on hand for the category across all possible COST column values. The third grouping set returns a single row containing the grand total row with null values in both the CATEGORY and COST columns.

The flexibility of grouping sets can best be demonstrated by another example. In the following example, I remove the second grouping set from the previous example, as shown in the following SELECT statement:

```
SELECT CATEGORY, COST, SUM(ON_HAND) AS TOTAL_ON_HAND
 FROM COMPACT_DISC_COST
GROUP BY GROUPING SETS ((CATEGORY, COST), ());
```

If you executed this query, the results would be similar to the following:

```
CATEGORY      COST    TOTAL_ON_HAND
------------  ------  -------------
Instrumental  4.50    21
Instrumental  5.50    22
Vocal         4.50    98
Vocal         5.50    125
Vocal         7.75    39
<NULL>        <NULL>  305
```

The results now contain the number of CDs on hand for each combination of category and cost and the grand total of all CDs on hand, but there are no subtotals by category. The flexibility of grouping sets should now be clear because you cannot obtain this exact result set using other forms of the GROUP BY clause, including the ROLLUP or CUBE syntax.

The GROUPING SETS syntax can also be used to accomplish the same results as the CUBE syntax. For example, the following queries show the CUBE syntax we used earlier and the equivalent query written using the GROUPING SETS syntax:

```
SELECT CATEGORY, COST, SUM(ON_HAND) AS TOTAL_ON_HAND
  FROM COMPACT_DISC_COST
 GROUP BY CUBE (CATEGORY, COST);
```

```
SELECT CATEGORY, COST, SUM(ON_HAND) AS TOTAL_ON_HAND
  FROM COMPACT_DISC_COST
GROUP BY GROUPING SETS ((CATEGORY, COST), (CATEGORY), (COST), ());
```

As you can see, the GROUP BY clause can be a valuable tool when trying to summarize data, particularly when you make use of the many functions available in SQL, such as SUM and AVG. In Chapter 10, I discuss these and many other functions that you can use to make your SELECT statement more robust and applicable to your needs.

Use the HAVING Clause to Specify Group Search Conditions

The HAVING clause is similar to the WHERE clause in that it defines a search condition. However, unlike the WHERE clause, the HAVING clause is concerned with groups, not individual rows:

- If a GROUP BY clause is specified, the HAVING clause is applied to the groups created by the GROUP BY clause.
- If a WHERE clause is specified and no GROUP BY clause is specified, the HAVING clause is applied to the output of the WHERE clause and that output is treated as one group.
- If no WHERE clause and no GROUP BY clause are specified, the HAVING clause is applied to the output of the FROM clause and that output is treated as one group.

The best way to understand the HAVING clause is to remember that the clauses in a SELECT statement are processed in a definite order. A WHERE clause can receive input only from a FROM clause, but a HAVING clause can receive input from a GROUP BY, WHERE, or FROM clause. This is a subtle, yet important, distinction, and the best way to illustrate it is to look at a couple of examples.

In the first example, which is based on the COMPACT_DISC_COST table in Figure 7-4, I use a WHERE clause to specify that the query results should include only rows whose ON_HAND value is less than 22, as shown in the following SELECT statement:

```
SELECT CATEGORY, AVG(COST) AS AVG_COST
  FROM COMPACT_DISC_COST
 WHERE ON_HAND < 22
 GROUP BY CATEGORY;
```

The statement returns two columns: CATEGORY and AVG_COST, which is the average of all prices for each category. The averages include only those rows where ON_HAND values are less than 22. If you executed this statement, the results would look similar to the following:

```
CATEGORY       AVG_COST
------------   ---------
```

```
Instrumental  4.5000000
Vocal         5.3750000
```

As you would expect, the query result returns two rows—one for the Instrumental group and one for the Vocal group.

If you were to use the HAVING clause rather than the WHERE clause to limit values to less than 22, you might use the following SELECT statement:

```
SELECT CATEGORY, AVG(COST) AS AVG_COST
  FROM COMPACT_DISC_COST
 GROUP BY CATEGORY
HAVING ON_HAND < 22;
```

However, if you were to try to execute this statement, you would receive an error because you cannot apply individual ON_HAND values to the groups. For a column to be included in the HAVING clause, it must be a grouped column or it must be summarized in some way.

Now let's take a look at another example that uses the HAVING clause. In this case, the clause includes a summarized column:

```
SELECT COST, CATEGORY, SUM(ON_HAND) AS TOTAL_ON_HAND
  FROM COMPACT_DISC_COST
 GROUP BY COST, CATEGORY
HAVING SUM(ON_HAND) < 100;
```

The HAVING clause in this statement will work because the ON_HAND values are being added together, which means they can work within the group structure. The query results would be as follows:

```
COST   CATEGORY      TOTAL_ON_HAND
-----  ------------  -------------
4.50   Instrumental  21
5.50   Instrumental  22
4.50   Vocal         98
7.75   Vocal         39
```

The HAVING clause is applied to the results after they have been grouped together (in the GROUP BY clause). For each group, the ON_HAND values are added together, but only groups with TOTAL_ON_HAND values less than 100 are included. If the HAVING clause were not included, the query results would include an additional row for the 5.50/Vocal group with a TOTAL_ON_HAND value of 125.

For the most part, you'll probably find that you'll be using the HAVING clause in conjunction with the GROUP BY clause. By using these two together, you can group together relevant data and then filter that data to refine your search even further. The HAVING clause also has the advantage of allowing you to use set functions such as AVG or SUM, which you cannot use in a WHERE clause unless you place them within a subquery. The important points to keep in mind with the HAVING clause are that it is the last clause in the table expression to be applied and that it is concerned with grouped data, rather than individual rows.

Use the ORDER BY Clause to Sort Query Results

The ORDER BY clause, when it is used in a SELECT statement, is the last clause to be processed. The ORDER BY clause takes the output from the SELECT clause and orders the query results according to the specifications within the ORDER BY clause. The clause does not group rows together, as they're grouped by the GROUP BY clause, nor does it filter out rows, as they're filtered by the WHERE clause or the HAVING clause. You can, however, specify whether the rows are organized in an ascending order (by using the ASC keyword) or in descending order (by using the DESC keyword).

To use the ORDER BY clause, simply specify one or more columns and the optional ASC or DESC keywords (one per column). If a keyword is not specified, ASC is assumed. The rows are organized according to the column you specify. If you define more than one column in the ORDER BY clause, the rows are organized in the order in which the columns are specified.

Let's take a look at a few examples to clarify how the ORDER BY clause works. (The examples are based on the COMPACT_DISC_COST table in Figure 7-4.) In the first example, I order the rows based on the COST column:

```
SELECT * FROM COMPACT_DISC_COST
 WHERE COST < 7.00
 ORDER BY COST;
```

Notice that the COST column is specified in the ORDER BY clause. Also notice that neither the ASC nor the DESC keyword has been specified, so the ASC keyword will be assumed. If you execute this query, you will receive results similar to the following:

```
COMPACT_DISC                  CATEGORY      COST  ON_HAND
---------------------------   ------------  ----- --------
The Definitive Collection     Vocal         4.50  34
Rumours (Reissued)            Vocal         4.50  17
Come On Over                  Vocal         4.50  6
Drive All Night               Vocal         4.50  12
Kind of Blue                  Instrumental  4.50  21
Thriller                      Vocal         4.50  29
Sonic Highways                Vocal         5.50  27
Different Shades of Blue      Vocal         5.50  42
Innervisions (Remastered)     Vocal         5.50  16
Man Against Machine           Vocal         5.50  8
Bach                          Instrumental  5.50  22
Old Boots, New Dirt           Vocal         5.50  32
```

The rows are listed according to the COST column. The values in the COST column appear in ascending order (lowest price to highest price). Because the WHERE clause was specified, no rows with prices above 6.99 are included in the query results. Also, since only the COST column was included in the ORDER BY clause, the order of rows that have the same price is unpredictable. For example, the six rows with a COST of 4.50 will all appear before those with a COST of 5.50, but those six rows might appear in any order.

Ask the Expert

Q: How does the ORDER BY clause affect query results in embedded SQL and SQL modules?

A: You can use the ORDER BY clause only in direct invocation and when defining cursors. (I discuss cursors in Chapter 16.) You cannot use an ORDER BY clause in other situations. This is because of limitations in application languages—they cannot handle an unknown number of rows in a query result. Application languages do not know what to do with this sort of uncertainty. And because the ORDER BY clause applies only to multirow query results, the clause is not applicable to environments that require rows to be returned one at a time. However, cursors offer a way for application languages to deal with that uncertainty, allowing the ORDER BY clause to be used in cursor definitions. Cursors are discussed in more detail in Chapter 16.

In the next example, the SELECT statement is nearly the same as the last statement, except that an additional column is specified in the ORDER BY clause:

```
SELECT * FROM COMPACT_DISC_COST
 WHERE COST < 7.00
 ORDER BY COST, ON_HAND DESC;
```

In this case, the ON_HAND column is followed by the DESC keyword, which means that the rows will be listed in descending order. However, because there are two columns, the rows are first ordered by the COST column and then by the ON_HAND column. If you execute this SELECT statement, you'll receive the following results:

```
COMPACT_DISC                  CATEGORY      COST   ON_HAND
----------------------------  ------------  -----  --------
The Definitive Collection     Vocal         4.50   34
Thriller                      Vocal         4.50   29
Kind of Blue                  Instrumental  4.50   21
Rumours (Reissued)            Vocal         4.50   17
Drive All Night               Vocal         4.50   12
Come On Over                  Vocal         4.50   6
Different Shades of Blue      Vocal         5.50   42
Old Boots, New Dirt           Vocal         5.50   32
Sonic Highways                Vocal         5.50   27
Bach                          Instrumental  5.50   22
Innervisions (Remastered)     Vocal         5.50   16
Man Against Machine           Vocal         5.50   8
```

As you can see, the rows are listed according to the order of the COST values, which are in ascending order. In addition, the ON_HAND values are listed in descending order for each price. So for the set of 4.50 COST values, the rows start with a value of 34 in the ON_HAND column and end with a value of 6. Then we jump to the next group of COST values: 5.50. Once again, the largest ON_HAND value for the 5.50 COST range is listed first and the last row contains the smallest ON_HAND value for the 5.50 COST range.

Whenever you're using the ORDER BY clause, you must be aware of the order in which you list column names within that clause. In the preceding example, the COST column is listed first, so the rows are ordered first by the COST column and then by the ON_HAND column. However, you can reverse the column names, as shown in the following SELECT statement:

```
SELECT * FROM COMPACT_DISC_COST
 WHERE COST < 7.00
 ORDER BY ON_HAND, COST DESC;
```

This time, the ON_HAND column is listed first and the COST column listed second, and the COST column is assigned the DESC keyword. As a result, the rows will be sorted by the ON_HAND column first, as shown in the following query results:

```
COMPACT_DISC                     CATEGORY      COST   ON_HAND
---------------------------      ------------  -----  --------
Come On Over                     Vocal         4.50   6
Man Against Machine              Vocal         5.50   8
Drive All Night                  Vocal         4.50   12
Innervisions (Remastered)        Vocal         5.50   16
Rumours (Reissued)               Vocal         4.50   17
Kind of Blue                     Instrumental  4.50   21
Bach                             Instrumental  5.50   22
Sonic Highways                   Vocal         5.50   27
Thriller                         Vocal         4.50   29
Old Boots, New Dirt              Vocal         5.50   32
The Definitive Collection        Vocal         4.50   34
Different Shades of Blue         Vocal         5.50   42
```

Notice that the ON_HAND values are in ascending order. The rows are then ordered according to the COST value. However, because there are no rows that share the same ON_HAND value, the second ORDER BY column (COST) does not affect the order of the query results.

The ORDER BY clause is a convenient tool for organizing your query results, but remember, it doesn't affect which data is displayed. Only the other clauses can actually name, filter, and group data. The ORDER BY clause is merely an organizer for what already exists. And in fact, while it is not a very sound practice, you can include columns in the ORDER BY clause that are not in the SELECT clause, thereby sorting on columns that are not visible in the query results.

Try This 7-1 Querying the Inventory Database

For the Try This exercises in previous chapters, you created a number of persistent base tables that are capable of storing data. In this chapter, you learned how to create SELECT statements that allow you to query data in base tables. As a result, this exercise focuses on creating SELECT statements that query data in the tables that you created. However, before you can actually query those tables, data must be stored within them. While I do not cover inserting data until Chapter 8, I do provide the statements you need to insert the data in the Try_This_07.txt file, which you can download from our web site. The file contains a series of INSERT statements that allow you to populate the tables, along with the SELECT statements used in this exercise. You can also view these statements in Appendix C.

If you look at the Try_This_07.txt file, you'll see a series of INSERT statements that are grouped together according to the tables that you created in the INVENTORY database. For example, the first set of INSERT statements are for the CD_LABELS table, as shown in the following statements:

```
--Insert data into the CD_LABELS table
INSERT INTO CD_LABELS VALUES ( 826, 'ANTI Records' );
INSERT INTO CD_LABELS VALUES ( 827, 'Motown / Universal' );
INSERT INTO CD_LABELS VALUES ( 828, 'J&R Adventures' );
INSERT INTO CD_LABELS VALUES ( 829, 'Sony Classical' );
INSERT INTO CD_LABELS VALUES ( 830, 'Warner Bros.' );
INSERT INTO CD_LABELS VALUES ( 831, 'Mercury' );
INSERT INTO CD_LABELS VALUES ( 832, 'Sony Music Nashville' );
INSERT INTO CD_LABELS VALUES ( 833, 'Broken Bow' );
INSERT INTO CD_LABELS VALUES ( 834, 'Capitol Records' );
INSERT INTO CD_LABELS VALUES ( 835, 'Columbia' );
INSERT INTO CD_LABELS VALUES ( 836, 'Epic' );
INSERT INTO CD_LABELS VALUES ( 837, 'RCA' );
INSERT INTO CD_LABELS VALUES ( 838, 'Arista' );
--End inserts for the CD_LABELS table
```

You will need to copy these statements into your client application and execute them. Each INSERT statement adds one row of data to the applicable table. For example, the first INSERT statement listed in the preceding code adds one row of data to the CD_LABELS table. The values that are added are 826 (for the LABEL_ID column) and ANTI Records (for the COMPANY_NAME column). Again, I present the INSERT statement in greater detail in Chapter 8. If you are uncomfortable inserting this data before reading about the INSERT statement, I suggest that you review the information in Chapter 8 before working on this Try This exercise and then return here to perform each step. However, if you decide to do this exercise now, then you simply need to execute each statement, as described in the following steps.

NOTE

As you probably noticed, each block of INSERT statements begins and ends with a line that starts off with double hyphens (--). Double hyphens indicate that the line of text that follows is a comment. Your SQL implementation will simply skip over these lines. The comments are there only to provide information to the SQL programmers so they can better understand the code.

Step by Step

1. Open the client application for your RDBMS and connect to the INVENTORY database.
2. Open the Try_This_07.txt file and copy the INSERT statements into your client application. Most applications will allow you to execute blocks of statements, rather than having to enter the data one row at a time. If your application supports executing multiple statements, execute the statements one table at a time by copying and pasting blocks of statements into your client application. You should enter data for each table in the order that the data appears in the Try_This_07.txt file. For example, you should insert values into the CD_LABELS table before the COMPACT_DISCS table.

   For each INSERT statement that you execute, you should receive a message acknowledging that the row has been inserted into the table. After you've populated each table with data, you're ready to move on to the next step.
3. You will now query all the data in the ARTISTS table. Enter and execute the following SQL statement:

   ```
   SELECT *
     FROM ARTISTS;
   ```

   Your query results should include the ARTIST_ID, ARTIST_NAME, and PLACE_OF_BIRTH columns. There should be 14 rows of data in all.
4. Now let's create a query that specifies which columns to include in the query results. For the next SELECT statement, you will query the COMPACT_DISC table, but return only the CD_TITLE and IN_STOCK columns. Enter and execute the following SQL statement:

   ```
   SELECT CD_TITLE, IN_STOCK
     FROM COMPACT_DISCS;
   ```

   Your query results should include only the two columns you specified in the SELECT statement. In addition, the query should return 15 rows of data.
5. In Chapter 5, Try This 5-1, you created the CD_IN_STOCK view. The view returns the same data as specified in the SELECT statement in step 4, except that it limits the results

(continued)

to rows with IN_STOCK values greater than 10. You will now query that view. Enter and execute the following SQL statement:

```
SELECT *
  FROM CDS_IN_STOCK;
```

Notice that your SELECT statement is the same as it would have been for a persistent base table. You can even specify the view column names if you want. (In fact, you should if you're querying the view in any way other than through direct invocation.) In the last SELECT statement, the query returned 15 rows, but this query returns only 12 rows because the IN_STOCK values must be over 10. The nice part about the view is that it is already set up to return exactly the information you want, without having to define the WHERE clause.

6. Now let's query the COMPACT_DISCS table but refine our SELECT statement by using a WHERE clause. Enter and execute the following SQL statement:

```
SELECT CD_TITLE, IN_STOCK
  FROM COMPACT_DISCS
 WHERE IN_STOCK > 10 AND IN_STOCK < 30;
```

Because the WHERE clause has been added, your query results should now include only 9 rows, and each row should contain an IN_STOCK value between 10 and 30.

7. The next SELECT statement that you create groups together information in the COMPACT_DISCS table. Enter and execute the following SQL statement:

```
SELECT LABEL_ID, SUM(IN_STOCK) AS TOTAL_IN_STOCK
  FROM COMPACT_DISCS
 GROUP BY LABEL_ID;
```

One row is returned for each different LABEL_ID value, and for each of those values, the total for the IN_STOCK values is returned. There are 13 rows in all. Notice that in your query results, the name of the column with the IN_STOCK totals is TOTAL_IN_STOCK. When you learn more about joining tables, you'll be able to group data based on more complex queries. Joining tables is discussed in Chapter 11.

8. Now you'll add a HAVING clause to the SELECT statement you just executed. Enter and execute the following SQL statement:

```
SELECT LABEL_ID, SUM(IN_STOCK) AS TOTAL_IN_STOCK
  FROM COMPACT_DISCS
 GROUP BY LABEL_ID
HAVING SUM(IN_STOCK) > 10;
```

The HAVING clause limits the rows that are returned to those whose TOTAL_IN_STOCK values are greater than 10. Now only 10 rows are returned.

9. You can also execute a SELECT statement that orders the data returned by your query. Enter and execute the following SQL statement:

```
SELECT *
  FROM COMPACT_DISCS
 WHERE IN_STOCK > 10
 ORDER BY CD_TITLE DESC;
```

Your query results should be organized according to the CD_TITLE column, with the columns listed in descending order. Because the WHERE clause is used, only 12 rows should have been returned.

10. Close the client application.

Try This Summary

In this Try This exercise, you inserted data into the tables of the INVENTORY database. You then created SELECT statements that allowed you to query data in those tables. You should feel free to experiment with SELECT statements and try different types of queries. As you become more comfortable with using the SELECT statement and learn more advanced techniques for querying data, you'll be able to write SELECT statements that access multiple tables, calculate data, and summarize information. However, even the more advanced techniques rely on the basic foundation that you have demonstrated in this exercise. Everything else builds on this.

Chapter 7 Self Test

1. Which clauses in a SELECT statement are part of the table expression?

   A SELECT

   B FROM

   C WHERE

   D ORDER BY

2. In what order are the clauses of a SELECT statement applied?

3. You are writing a SELECT statement that retrieves the CD_TITLE column and all rows from the INVENTORY table. Which SELECT statement should you use?

4. You are writing a SELECT statement that retrieves the CD_TITLE column and all rows from the INVENTORY table. You want the column in the query results to be named COMPACT_DISC. Which SELECT statement should you use?

5. Which clauses in a SELECT statement are required?

   A SELECT

   B FROM

   C WHERE

   D GROUP BY

6. Which keyword should you add to the SELECT clause to ensure that each row of the query result is unique?

   A ALL

   B ROLLUP

   C DISTINCT

   D CUBE

7. You're creating a SELECT statement for the INVENTORY table and you want to ensure that only rows with a RETAIL_PRICE value of less than $16.00 are included in the query results. What WHERE clause should you use?

8. You're creating a SELECT statement that includes a WHERE clause. The WHERE clause contains two predicates. You want the condition of either one of the predicates to be met, but it's not necessary for both conditions to be met. What keyword should you use to connect the two predicates?

9. Each predicate in a WHERE clause is evaluated to which of the following?

   A True

   B Not

   C False

   D Unknown

10. Which clause allows you to group together values in a specified column?

   A ROLLUP

   B HAVING

   C ORDER BY

   D GROUP BY

11. Which operators can you use in a GROUP BY clause to return additional summary data in a query result?

    A ROLLUP

    B HAVING

    C CUBE

    D GROUPING SETS

12. You're writing a SELECT statement that retrieves the CATEGORY and COST columns from the COMPACT_DISC_COST table. You want to group data together first by the CATEGORY column and then by the COST column. Which SELECT statement should you use?

13. You're writing a SELECT statement that retrieves the CATEGORY and COST columns from the COMPACT_DISC_COST table. You want to group together data first by the CATEGORY column and then by the COST column. You then want to filter out any groups that have a COST value over 4.99. Which SELECT statement should you use?

14. You're creating a SELECT statement that includes a SELECT clause, FROM clause, WHERE clause, GROUP BY clause, and HAVING clause. From which clause will the HAVING clause receive output?

    A SELECT

    B FROM

    C WHERE

    D GROUP BY

15. How does the HAVING clause differ from the WHERE clause?

16. From which clause does the ORDER BY clause receive output?

17. Which keyword should you add to an ORDER BY clause to sort data in descending order?

Chapter 8

Modifying SQL Data

Key Skills & Concepts

- Insert SQL Data
- Update SQL Data
- Delete SQL Data
- Merge SQL Data

One of the primary functions of any database is to be able to manipulate the data stored within its tables. Designated users must be able to insert, update, and delete data as necessary in order to keep the database current and ensure that only the appropriate data is being stored. SQL provides three statements for basic data manipulation: INSERT, UPDATE, and DELETE. Also, SQL provides the more powerful MERGE statement that can be used to apply inserts and updates (or deletes) to a table based on the contents of another table. In this chapter, I will examine each of these statements and demonstrate how they can be used in an SQL environment to modify data in the database.

Insert SQL Data

In Chapter 7, Try This 7-1, I introduce you briefly to the INSERT statement. As you can see from that exercise, the INSERT statement allows you to add data to the various tables in your database. I present the basic syntax in this section and an alternate syntax in the next section "Inserting Values from a SELECT Statement." The syntax for a basic INSERT statement is relatively straightforward:

```
INSERT INTO <table name>
[ ( <column name> [ { , <column name> } . . . ] ) ]
VALUES ( <value> [ { , <value> } . . . ] )
```

Only the first and last lines in the syntax are required. The second line is optional. Both the first and second lines are part of the INSERT INTO clause. In this clause, you must identify the name of the table (or view) into which you will be inserting data. The table name follows the INSERT INTO keywords. You then have the option of identifying the column names in the table that will be receiving the data. This is the purpose of the second line in the syntax. You can specify one or more columns, all of which must be enclosed in parentheses. If you specify more than one column, they must be separated using commas.

NOTE

Most SQL implementations support inserts into views. However, there are restrictions. For example, you cannot insert into a view if there are table columns that are not included in the view and those columns do not allow null values and do not have a default value defined. Furthermore, if the view has more than one base table, you may not be able to insert into it at all, but if you can, you will be required to name columns from only one of the base tables because an insert can affect only one base table. Always check your vendor documentation.

In the third line of syntax, which is the VALUES clause, you must specify one or more values that will be inserted into the table. The list of values must be enclosed in parentheses and, if more than one is specified, they must be separated using commas. In addition, the values must meet the following requirements:

- If the column names are not specified in the INSERT INTO clause, then there must be one value for each column in the table and the values must be in the same order as they are defined in the table.
- If the column names are specified in the INSERT INTO clause, then there must be exactly one value per specified column and those values must be in the same order in which they are defined in the INSERT INTO clause. However, the column names and values do not have to be in the same order as the columns in the table definition.
- You must provide a value for each column in the table *except* for columns that either allow null values or have a default value defined.
- Each value with a character string data type must be enclosed in single quotes.
- You may use the keyword NULL (or null) as the data value in the VALUES clause to assign a null value to any column that allows nulls.
- You may use the keyword DEFAULT (or default) as the data value in the VALUES clause to assign the default value to any column that has a default value defined.
- You may use the keywords NEXT VALUE FOR followed by a sequence generator name in the VALUES clause to assign the next value from an independent sequence generator to any column that is defined with a compatible numeric data type. I discuss sequence generators in the "Maintaining Independent Sequence Generators" section in Chapter 3.

NOTE

Many SQL programmers prefer to specify the column names in the INSERT INTO clause, whether or not it's necessary to do so, because it provides a method for documenting which columns are supposed to be receiving data. This practice also makes the INSERT statement less prone to errors and other problems should columns be added or the column order be changed at some future time. For these reasons, many organizations require the use of the column names in all INSERT statements.

Now let's take a look at some examples of the INSERT statement. For these examples, I will use the CD_INVENTORY table. The table is based on the following table definition:

```
CREATE TABLE CD_INVENTORY
  ( CD_NAME      VARCHAR(60)                          NOT NULL,
    MUSIC_TYPE   VARCHAR(30),
    PUBLISHER    VARCHAR(50)  DEFAULT 'Independent'   NOT NULL,
    IN_STOCK     INT                                  NOT NULL );
```

The first example I'll show you inserts values into every column in the CD_INVENTORY table:

```
INSERT INTO CD_INVENTORY
 VALUES ( 'Drive All Night', 'Alternative Rock', 'ANTI Records', 12 );
```

Notice that the INSERT INTO clause includes only the name of the CD_INVENTORY table, but does not specify any columns. In the VALUES clause, four values have been specified. The values are separated by commas, and the values with character string data types are enclosed in single quotes. If you refer back to the table definition, you'll see that the values specified in the VALUES clause are in the same order as the column definitions.

When you execute the INSERT statement shown in the example, the data is added to the CD_INVENTORY table, as shown in Figure 8-1.

If you had tried to execute an INSERT statement like the last example, but included only three values rather than four, you would have received an error. For example, you would not be able to execute the following statement:

```
INSERT INTO CD_INVENTORY
 VALUES ( 'Different Shades of Blue', 'J&R Adventures', 42 );
```

In this example, only three values have been specified. In this case, the missing value is for the MUSIC_TYPE column. Even though this column accepts null values, the SQL implementation has no way of knowing which value is being omitted, so an error is returned.

Instead of leaving the value out of the VALUES clause, you can specify a null value, as shown in the following example:

```
INSERT INTO CD_INVENTORY
 VALUES ('Different Shades of Blue ', null, 'J&R Adventures', 42 );
```

CD_NAME: VARCHAR(60)	MUSIC_TYPE: VARCHAR(30)	PUBLISHER: VARCHAR(50)	IN_STOCK: INT
Drive All Night	Alternative Rock	ANTI Records	12

Figure 8-1 The CD_INVENTORY table with the new row of data

CD_NAME: VARCHAR(60)	MUSIC_TYPE: VARCHAR(30)	PUBLISHER: VARCHAR(50)	IN_STOCK: INT
Drive All Night	Alternative Rock	ANTI Records	12
Different Shades of Blue	<null>	J&R Adventures	42

Figure 8-2 The CD_INVENTORY table with two rows of data

If you execute the INSERT statement, your table will now include an additional row. Figure 8-2 shows what the table would look like, assuming that the two INSERT statements have been executed.

The null value was inserted into the MUSIC_TYPE column, and the other values were inserted into the appropriate columns. If a null value were not permitted in the MUSIC_TYPE column, you would have had to specify a value.

NOTE

Figure 8-2 shows the new row being inserted after the existing row in the table. However, the row might be inserted at any place in a table, depending on how the SQL implementation inserts rows. The SQL standard does not specify where a row should be inserted in a table. In fact, you should never rely on the rows in a table being in any particular order—you should use the ORDER BY clause whenever the results of a SELECT need to be in a particular sequence.

Rather than having to provide a value for every column when you insert a row, you can specify which columns receive values. For example, you can specify values for the CD_NAME, PUBLISHER, and IN_STOCK columns of the CD_INVENTORY table, as shown in the following example:

```
INSERT INTO CD_INVENTORY ( CD_NAME, PUBLISHER, IN_STOCK )
 VALUES ( 'Innervisions (Remastered)', 'Motown / Universal', 16 );
```

In this case, one value has been specified for each of the columns identified in the INSERT INTO clause, and the values are specified in the same order as the columns in the INSERT INTO clause. Notice that the INSERT statement doesn't include the MUSIC_TYPE column in the INSERT INTO clause or in the VALUES clause. You can omit this column because null values are permitted in that column. If you were to execute this statement, your CD_INVENTORY table would now have a third row (shown in Figure 8-3).

Once again, the null value is automatically added to the MUSIC_TYPE column. If a default value had been defined for the column, that value would have been added. For example,

CD_NAME: VARCHAR(60)	MUSIC_TYPE: VARCHAR(30)	PUBLISHER: VARCHAR(50)	IN_STOCK: INT
Drive All Night	Alternative Rock	ANTI Records	12
Different Shades of Blue	<null>	J&R Adventures	42
Innervisions (Remastered)	<null>	Motown/Universal	16

Figure 8-3 The CD_INVENTORY table with three rows of data

the following INSERT statement omits the PUBLISHER column rather than the MUSIC_TYPE column:

```
INSERT INTO CD_INVENTORY ( CD_NAME, MUSIC_TYPE, IN_STOCK )
 VALUES ( 'The Definitive Collection', 'R&B', 34 );
```

When the row is added to the CD_INVENTORY table, the default value (Independent) is added to the PUBLISHER column, as shown in Figure 8-4.

If you try to execute an INSERT statement that omits a column that does not permit null values and is not defined with a default value, you will receive an error. When you insert a new row, the RDBMS must get a value for each column from somewhere, so if nulls are not permitted, then the value must come from either a default value (if defined) or the VALUES clause of the INSERT statement.

An alternative way to write the INSERT used in the previous example is to explicitly specify that the PUBLISHER column is to be assigned its default value using the DEFAULT keyword. The statement would look like this:

```
INSERT INTO CD_INVENTORY
 VALUES ( 'The Definitive Collection', 'R&B', DEFAULT, 34 );
```

CD_NAME: VARCHAR(60)	MUSIC_TYPE: VARCHAR(30)	PUBLISHER: VARCHAR(50)	IN_STOCK: INT
Drive All Night	Alternative Rock	ANTI Records	12
Different Shades of Blue	<null>	J&R Adventures	42
Innervisions (Remastered)	<null>	Motown/Universal	16
The Definitive Collection	R&B	Independent	34

Figure 8-4 The CD_INVENTORY table with four rows of data

NOTE

The values that you specify in the VALUES clause must conform to all restrictions placed on a table. This means that the values must conform to the data types or domains associated with a column. In addition, the values are limited by any constraints defined on the table. For example, a foreign key constraint would prevent you from adding any values that violate the constraint, or a check constraint may limit the range of values that can be inserted into the table. Be sure that you're familiar with the restrictions placed on a table before trying to insert data into that table. You can learn more about data types in Chapter 3. You can learn more about domains and constraints in Chapter 4.

You can, of course, specify all columns in the INSERT INTO clause. If you do this, you must be sure to specify the same number of values, in the same order in which the columns are specified. The following INSERT statement inserts values into all columns of the CD_INVENTORY table:

```
INSERT INTO CD_INVENTORY ( CD_NAME, MUSIC_TYPE, PUBLISHER, IN_STOCK )
 VALUES ( 'Rumours (Reissued)', 'Classic Rock', 'Warner Bros.', 17 );
```

When you execute this statement, a row is added to the CD_INVENTORY table, with a value for each column. Figure 8-5 shows the new row, along with the other four rows we have inserted. If you were to omit one of the values from the VALUES clause—even if null values were allowed for the related column—you would receive an error when you executed that statement.

Inserting Values from a SELECT Statement

Earlier in this chapter, at the beginning of the "Insert SQL Data" section, I say that the VALUES clause is mandatory and that you need to specify at least one value. There is, however, an alternative to the VALUES clause. You can use a SELECT statement to specify the values that you want to insert into a table. The key to using a SELECT statement, just as with using the VALUES clause, is to make sure that the number of values returned by the

CD_NAME: VARCHAR(60)	MUSIC_TYPE: VARCHAR(30)	PUBLISHER: VARCHAR(50)	IN_STOCK: INT
Drive All Night	Alternative Rock	ANTI Records	12
Different Shades of Blue	<null>	J&R Adventures	42
Innervisions (Remastered)	<null>	Motown/Universal	16
The Definitive Collection	R&B	Independent	34
Rumours (Reissued)	Classic Rock	Warner Bros.	17

Figure 8-5 The CD_INVENTORY table with five rows of data

SELECT statement matches the required number of values and that those values conform to any restriction on the target table. Let's look at an example.

Suppose that, in addition to the CD_INVENTORY table I've been using in previous examples, your database includes a second table named CD_INVENTORY_2, which includes two columns, as shown in the following table definition:

```
CREATE TABLE CD_INVENTORY_2
  ( CD_NAME_2    VARCHAR(60)   NOT NULL,
    IN_STOCK_2  INT            NOT NULL );
```

The CD_NAME_2 column in the CD_INVENTORY_2 table has the same data type as the CD_NAME column in the CD_INVENTORY table, and the IN_STOCK_2 column in the CD_INVENTORY_2 table has the same data type as the IN_STOCK column in the CD_INVENTORY table. As a result, values taken from the two columns in one table can be inserted into the two columns in the second table.

NOTE

A column in one table does not have to be the same data type as a column in another table for values to be copied from one to the other, as long as the values inserted into the target table conform to the data restrictions of that table.

By using an INSERT statement, you can copy values from the CD_INVENTORY table to the CD_INVENTORY_2 table. The following INSERT statement includes a SELECT statement that queries the CD_INVENTORY table:

```
INSERT INTO CD_INVENTORY_2
  SELECT CD_NAME, IN_STOCK
    FROM CD_INVENTORY;
```

As you can see, no columns are specified in the INSERT INTO clause; as a result, values will be inserted into both columns in the CD_INVENTORY_2 table. In the second line of the statement, a SELECT statement is used to pull values from the CD_NAME and IN_STOCK columns of the CD_INVENTORY table. The values will then be inserted into their respective columns in the CD_INVENTORY_2 table, as shown in Figure 8-6.

Notice that the CD_INVENTORY_2 table contains the same five rows of data that are shown in Figure 8-5, only the CD_INVENTORY_2 table contains only two columns: CD_NAME_2 and IN_STOCK_2.

Like any other SELECT statement, the SELECT statement that you use in an INSERT statement can contain a WHERE clause. In the following INSERT statement, the SELECT statement contains a WHERE clause that limits the IN_STOCK values to an amount greater than 15:

```
INSERT INTO CD_INVENTORY_2
  SELECT CD_NAME, IN_STOCK
    FROM CD_INVENTORY
   WHERE IN_STOCK > 15;
```

CD_NAME: VARCHAR(60)	IN_STOCK: INT
Drive All Night	12
Different Shades of Blue	42
Innervisions (Remastered)	16
The Definitive Collection	34
Rumours (Reissued)	17

Figure 8-6 The CD_INVENTORY_2 table with five rows of data

If you were to execute this statement, only four rows would be added to the CD_INVENTORY_2 table, rather than the five rows we saw in the previous example. The WHERE clause in this case works just like the WHERE clause in any SELECT statement. As a result, any row with an IN_STOCK value that is not greater than 15 is eliminated from the query results. Those new filtered results are then inserted into the CD_INVENTORY_2 table.

Update SQL Data

As its name implies, the UPDATE statement allows you to update data in your SQL database. With the UPDATE statement, you can modify data in one or more rows for one or more columns. The syntax for the UPDATE statement can be shown as follows:

```
UPDATE <table name>
SET <set clause expression> [ { , <set clause expression> } . . . ]
[ WHERE <search condition> ]
```

Ask the Expert

Q: If INSERT statements attempt to create duplicate rows, will executing the statements result in an error?

A: As I discuss in Chapter 4, if you define PRIMARY KEY or UNIQUE constraints on the table, the DBMS will reject any attempt to create duplicate values in the column or set of columns named in the constraints. However, the CD_INVENTORY and CD_INVENTORY_2 tables I have used in this chapter do not have such constraints defined, which means duplicate values would be allowed in all columns. Obviously, this would be confusing, which is why defining a primary key whenever possible is a best practice.

As you can see, the UPDATE clause and the SET clause are required and the WHERE clause is optional. In the UPDATE clause, you must specify the name of the table (or view) that you're updating. In the SET clause, you must specify one or more set clause expressions, which I discuss in more detail later in this chapter. In the WHERE clause, as with the WHERE clause in a SELECT statement (see Chapter 7), you must specify a search condition. The WHERE clause works here in much the same way as it does in the SELECT statement. You specify a condition or set of conditions that act as a filter for the rows that are updated. Only the rows that meet these conditions are updated. In other words, only rows that evaluate to true are updated.

NOTE

SQL supports using view names in UPDATE statements. However, if the view is based on multiple tables, all columns being updated must come from a single base table, and there may be other restrictions as described in your DBMS documentation.

Now let's return to the SET clause. As you can see, the clause includes the <set clause expression> placeholder. You must specify one or more set clause expressions. If you specify more than one, you must separate them with a comma. The syntax of the <set clause expression> placeholder can be broken down as follows:

```
<column name> = <value expression>
```

Basically, you must specify a column name (from the table that you're updating) and provide a value that the value in the column should equal. For example, suppose you want a value in the IN_STOCK column to be changed to 37. (It doesn't matter what the current value is.) The set clause expression would be as follows: IN_STOCK = 37. In this case, the value expression is 37; however, the value expression can be more complicated than that. For example, you can base the new value on an old value: IN_STOCK = (IN_STOCK + 1). In this case, the value expression is IN_STOCK + 1, which adds the current value in the IN_STOCK column to 1 to give you a new value. In this case, if the original value was 37, the new value will be 38.

Now that we've taken a look at the various parts of the UPDATE statement, let's put it all together using some examples. The examples we'll be looking at are based on the CD_INVENTORY table, which is shown in Figure 8-5.

In the first example, I use the UPDATE statement to change the values of the IN_STOCK column to 40, as shown in the following SQL statement:

```
UPDATE CD_INVENTORY
   SET IN_STOCK = 40;
```

This statement does exactly what you might expect: changes every row in the CD_INVENTORY table so that the IN_STOCK column for each row contains a value of 40. This is fine if that's what you want, but it is unlikely that you'll want to change every row in a table so that one of the column values is the same in every row. More likely than not, you'll want to qualify the update by using a WHERE clause.

In the next example, I modify the previous UPDATE statement to include a WHERE clause:

```
UPDATE CD_INVENTORY
   SET IN_STOCK = 40
 WHERE CD_NAME = 'Different Shades of Blue';
```

The UPDATE statement still changes the IN_STOCK column to a value of 40, but it does so only for the rows that meet the search condition in the WHERE clause. In this case, only one row meets that condition: Different Shades of Blue.

You might find that you want to change a value based on a value that already exists, such as the amount of inventory in stock. For example, you can add 2 to the value in the IN_STOCK column:

```
UPDATE CD_INVENTORY
   SET IN_STOCK = (IN_STOCK + 2)
 WHERE CD_NAME = 'Different Shades of Blue';
```

If the Different Shades of Blue row contains the value 40 in the IN_STOCK column and you execute this UPDATE statement, the new value will be 42. If you execute this statement without the WHERE clause, 2 will be added to the IN_STOCK value for every row in the table.

The WHERE clause also allows you to specify more than one predicate, as you can do with a WHERE clause in a SELECT statement. In the following example, I subtract 2 from the IN_STOCK value for any row that contains a MUSIC_TYPE value of R&B *and* an IN_STOCK value greater than 30:

```
UPDATE CD_INVENTORY
   SET IN_STOCK = (IN_STOCK - 2)
 WHERE MUSIC_TYPE = 'R&B' AND IN_STOCK > 30;
```

Only one row (The Definitive Collection) conforms to the search conditions specified in the WHERE clause. The IN_STOCK value for that row has been changed from 34 to 32.

You can also specify multiple expressions in the SET clause. In other words, you can change the values of more than one column at a time. For example, suppose you want to change the PUBLISHER value and IN_STOCK value for the The Definitive Collection row. Your UPDATE statement might look something like the following:

```
UPDATE CD_INVENTORY
   SET PUBLISHER = 'Motown / Universal',
       IN_STOCK  = (IN_STOCK * 2)
 WHERE CD_NAME = 'The Definitive Collection';
```

Notice that the two expressions in the SET clause are separated by a comma. When you execute this statement, the PUBLISHER value is changed from Independent to Motown / Universal, and the IN_STOCK value is changed from 32 to 64. (The 32 value is multiplied by 2.)

One thing you cannot do, however, is change the value for the same column for two different rows if you're trying to put different values in those rows. Let's look at an example to make this clearer. Suppose you want to update the MUSIC_TYPE value for the Different Shades of Blue row and the Innervisions (Remastered) row, but you want to update these rows with different values. Different Shades of Blue row should have a MUSIC_TYPE value of Blues, and the Innervisions (Remastered) row should have a MUSIC_TYPE value of R&B. As a result, you might try to execute a statement similar to the following:

```
UPDATE CD_INVENTORY
   SET MUSIC_TYPE = 'Blues',
       MUSIC_TYPE = 'R&B'
 WHERE CD_NAME = 'Different Shades of Blue'
    OR CD_NAME = 'Innervisions (Remastered)';
```

If you tried to execute this statement, the SQL implementation would not know which MUSIC_TYPE value to put into which row, and you would either receive an error or, worse yet, it would update both rows to a MUSIC_TYPE value of R&B (the last value mentioned in the SET clause). To handle a situation like this, you would need to create two separate UPDATE statements:

```
UPDATE CD_INVENTORY
   SET MUSIC_TYPE = 'Blues'
 WHERE CD_NAME = 'Different Shades of Blue';
UPDATE CD_INVENTORY
   SET MUSIC_TYPE = 'R&B'
 WHERE CD_NAME = 'Innervisions (Remastered)';
```

Updating Values from a SELECT Statement

In the "Inserting Values from a SELECT Statement" section earlier in this chapter, I told you that you can use a SELECT statement in place of the VALUES clause. You can also use a SELECT statement in the SET clause of the UPDATE statement. The SELECT statement returns the value that is defined in the <value expression> portion of the set clause expression. In other words, the SELECT statement is added to the right of the equal sign.

Let's take a look at a few examples to see how this works. The following examples are based on the original data in the CD_INVENTORY table (shown in Figure 8-5) and the CD_INVENTORY_2 table (shown in Figure 8-6). Suppose you want to update data in the CD_INVENTORY_2 table by using values from the CD_INVENTORY table. You might create an UPDATE statement that is similar to the following:

```
UPDATE CD_INVENTORY_2
   SET IN_STOCK_2 =
     ( SELECT AVG(IN_STOCK)
         FROM CD_INVENTORY );
```

The SELECT statement calculates the average of the IN_STOCK values in the CD_INVENTORY table, which is 24.2, but since the IN_STOCK column has an INT data type, the set clause expression is interpreted as follows: IN_STOCK_2 = 24. As a result, all IN_STOCK_2 values in the CD_INVENTORY_2 table are set to 24. Of course, you probably don't want all your IN_STOCK_2 values to be the same, so you can limit which rows are updated by adding a WHERE clause to the UPDATE statement:

```
UPDATE CD_INVENTORY_2
   SET IN_STOCK_2 =
       ( SELECT AVG(IN_STOCK)
           FROM CD_INVENTORY )
 WHERE CD_NAME_2 = 'Rumours (Reissued)';
```

Now only the Rumours (Reissued) row will be updated and the IN_STOCK_2 value will be changed to 24.

You can even add a WHERE clause to the SELECT statement, as shown in the following example:

```
UPDATE CD_INVENTORY_2
   SET IN_STOCK_2 =
       ( SELECT IN_STOCK
           FROM CD_INVENTORY
          WHERE CD_NAME = 'Rumours (Reissued)' )
 WHERE CD_NAME_2 = 'Rumours (Reissued)';
```

In this case, the IN_STOCK value of 17 is taken directly from the Rumours (Reissued) row of the CD_INVENTORY table and used as the <value expression> portion of the set clause expression. As a result, the set clause expression can be interpreted as the following: IN_STOCK_2 = 17. (Of course, the value in the CD_INVENTORY_2 table won't change if it is already 17, but if it were something other than 17, it would have been updated to 17.)

You can add one more layer of complexity to the UPDATE statement by modifying the SET clause even further. For example, suppose you want to increase the value by 2 before inserting it into the IN_STOCK_2 column. To do so, you can change the value expression to the following:

```
UPDATE CD_INVENTORY_2
   SET IN_STOCK_2 =
       ( SELECT IN_STOCK
           FROM CD_INVENTORY
          WHERE CD_NAME = 'Rumours (Reissued)' ) + 2
 WHERE CD_NAME_2 = 'Rumours (Reissued)';
```

Again, the SELECT clause pulls the value of 17 from the IN_STOCK column of the CD_INVENTORY table, but this time, 2 is added to the value returned by the SELECT statement, resulting in a total of 19. As a result, the new set clause expression can be represented as follows: IN_STOCK_2 = (17) + 2. If you execute this statement, the IN_STOCK_2 value will be changed to 19 in the Orlando row of the CD_INVENTORY_2 table.

By combining the SET clause with the WHERE clause, you can create UPDATE statements that can calculate very specific values that can be used to modify any number of rows and columns that you need to update. However, as with the INSERT statement, any values that you modify must conform to the restrictions of that table. In other words, the new values must abide by applicable data types, domains, and constraints.

Delete SQL Data

Of all the data modification statements supported by SQL, the DELETE statement is probably the simplest. It contains only two clauses, only one of which is mandatory. The following syntax shows you just how basic the DELETE statement is:

```
DELETE FROM <table name>
[ WHERE <search condition> ]
```

As you can see, the DELETE FROM clause requires that you specify the name of the table (or view) from which you are deleting rows. The WHERE clause, which is similar to the WHERE clause in a SELECT statement and an UPDATE statement, requires that you specify a search condition. If you don't include a WHERE clause in your DELETE statement, all rows are deleted from the specified table. Be sure you understand that the DELETE statement does not delete the table itself, only rows in the table—the DROP TABLE statement, as described in Chapter 3, is used to remove table definitions from the database.

NOTE

SQL supports referencing views in the DELETE statement, but the actual delete is done to rows in the base table. In nearly all implementations you cannot delete rows using views that reference more than one base table—see your vendor documentation for specifics.

Notice in the DELETE statement that no column names are specified. This is because you cannot delete individual column values from a table. You can delete only rows. If you need to remove a specific column value, you should use an UPDATE statement to set the value to null. But you can do this only if null values are supported for that column.

Now let's take a look at a couple of examples of the DELETE statement. The first example deletes all data (all rows) from the CD_INVENTORY table, shown in Figure 8-5:

```
DELETE FROM CD_INVENTORY;
```

That's all there is to it. Of course, you would use this statement only if you want to delete *all* data from the CD_INVENTORY. Although you might run into some occasions where it's necessary to delete every row from a table, it is more likely that you'll want to use the WHERE clause to specify which rows to delete. Let's modify the statement we just looked at to delete only rows where the MUSIC_TYPE value is Alternative Rock:

```
DELETE FROM CD_INVENTORY
 WHERE MUSIC_TYPE = 'Alternative Rock';
```

When you execute this statement, all rows whose MUSIC_TYPE value is Alternative Rock will be deleted from the CD_INVENTORY table, which in this case is the Drive All Night row.

Now let's modify this DELETE statement a little further by including two predicates in the WHERE clause:

```
DELETE FROM CD_INVENTORY
 WHERE MUSIC_TYPE = 'Classic Rock'
    OR PUBLISHER  = 'Independent';
```

This statement will delete any rows in the CD_INVENTORY table that include a MUSIC_TYPE value of Classic Rock *or* a PUBLISHER value of Independent, which means that the Rumours (Reissued) row and The Definitive Collection row will be deleted.

As you can see, the number of rows that are deleted from any table depends on the search conditions defined within the WHERE clause. When a WHERE clause is not specified, all rows evaluate to true and are deleted from the table. The WHERE clause allows you to specify exactly which rows should be deleted from the table.

Merge SQL Data

The MERGE statement is a powerful statement that combines the ability to insert new rows into a table and to update or delete existing rows. SQL programmers often use the term *upsert* (a blended word formed for the words update and insert) when referring to merge operations. The merge is accomplished by comparing the rows in a source table with the rows in the target table. When matches are found, the MERGE statement can specify which columns should be updated in the target table, or that the matching row in the target table should be deleted. When matches are not found, the MERGE statement can specify the insert of the new row in the target table. The best way to understand the MERGE statement is by looking at an example.

Figure 8-7 shows the MERGE_INVENTORY table along with the CD_INVENTORY table that was shown in Figure 8-5 and the way the CD_INVENTORY table will look once the merge operation is complete. We want to use the data in the MERGE_INVENTORY table to apply changes to the CD_INVENTORY table. The MERGE_INVENTORY table includes rows for three CDs that are already included in the CD_INVENTORY table: Different Shades of Blue, Innervisions (Remastered), and The Definitive Collection. Some of the data in these rows is different and we want to apply those differences to the CD_INVENTORY table. The MERGE_INVENTORY table also includes rows for two CDs that are not in the CD_INVENTORY table: Come On Over and Man Against Machine. We want the merge operation to insert both of these rows into CD_INVENTORY. Note that there are CDs in the CD_INVENTORY table that are not included in the MERGE_INVENTORY table. We want those rows to remain exactly the way they are, untouched by the merge operation. At the bottom of the figure, the CD_INVENTORY table is shown as it will be after the merge operation with any updated columns or inserted rows shaded gray.

MERGE_INVENTORY

MERGE_CD_NAME: VARCHAR(60)	MERGE_MUSIC_TYPE: VARCHAR(30)	MERGE_PUBLISHER: VARCHAR(50)	MERGE_IN_STOCK: INT
Different Shades of Blue	Blues	J&R Adventures	42
Come On Over	Country	Mercury	6
Innervisions (Remastered)	R&B	Motown/Universal	18
The Definitive Collection	R&B	Motown/Universal	34
Man Against Machine	<null>	Warner Bros.	8

CD_INVENTORY (Before Merge)

CD_NAME: VARCHAR(60)	MUSIC_TYPE: VARCHAR(30)	PUBLISHER: VARCHAR(50)	IN_STOCK: INT
Drive All Night	Alternative Rock	ANTI Records	12
Different Shades of Blue	<null>	J&R Adventures	42
Innervisions (Remastered)	<null>	Motown/Universal	16
The Definitive Collection	R&B	Independen	34
Rumours (Reissued)	Classic Rock	Warner Bros.	17

Merge

CD_INVENTORY (After Merge)

CD_NAME: VARCHAR(60)	MUSIC_TYPE: VARCHAR(30)	PUBLISHER: VARCHAR(50)	IN_STOCK: INT
Drive All Night	Alternative Rock	ANTI Records	12
Different Shades of Blue	Blues	J&R Adventures	42
Innervisions (Remastered)	R&B	Motown/Universal	18
The Definitive Collection	R&B	Motown/Universal	34
Rumours (Reissued)	Classic Rock	Warner Bros.	17
Come On Over	Country	Mercury	6
Man Against Machine	<null>	Warner Bros.	8

Figure 8-7 MERGE_INVENTORY and CD_INVENTORY merge operation

The syntax of the MERGE statement can be shown as follows:

```
MERGE INTO <target table name>
 USING <source table reference>
    ON <search condition>
 WHEN MATCHED [ AND <search condition> ]
    THEN { UPDATE SET <set clause list> } | DELETE
 WHEN NOT MATCHED [ AND <search condition> ]
    THEN INSERT
       [ ( <column name> [ { , <column name> } . . . ] ) ]
       VALUES ( <value> [ { , <value> } . . . ] )
```

As you can see in the first line of the syntax, the keywords MERGE INTO are required, followed by the name of the target table (the table to which changes will be applied). The second line shows the required USING keyword followed by a reference to the source table. The source table reference is usually a table name, but it can be a query. (Recall that all SQL queries produce results in the form of a table.) The source table does not have to be identical in structure with the target table, but in practice it is usually quite similar in design. The third line shows the mandatory keyword ON followed by the search condition that specifies how rows in the source table are to be matched with rows in the target table. This search condition follows the same syntax conventions as the search condition used in the WHERE clause I describe in Chapter 7. The matching of the rows between the two tables is essentially a join operation. (I describe table joins in Chapter 11.) In most cases, you will be matching the primary key column(s) in the target table with the same columns in the source table. However, you can theoretically match on any column(s) you wish, provided each row in the source table matches no more than one row in the target table.

The WHEN MATCHED clause specifies the action to be taken when a row in the source table has a matching row in the target table. In most situations, you will want to update the row in the target table using data from the source table, which is done with the THEN UPDATE SET syntax. The <set clause list> has syntax identical to the SET clause I describe with the UPDATE statement in the "Update SQL Data" section in this chapter. In rare situations, you may wish to delete the matching rows from the target table, which is specified using the THEN DELETE syntax.

The WHEN NOT MATCHED clause specifies the insert to be performed when rows in the source table are not found in the target table. The syntax should look familiar because the optional column name list and mandatory VALUES clause follow the syntax conventions used in the INSERT statement (see the "Insert SQL Data" section in this chapter).

You must include either the WHEN MATCHED clause or the WHEN NOT MATCHED clause in the MERGE statement, but in most cases, you will want to include both of them. If you omit the WHEN MATCHED clause, then no action is taken when matching rows are found in the source and target tables, and similarly, if you omit the WHEN NOT MATCHED clause, no action is taken when nonmatching rows are found in the source table.

NOTE

The MERGE statement was introduced in the SQL:2003 standard and expanded in the SQL:2008 standard. This means it has been around long enough that you can expect it to be supported by nearly all SQL implementations. However, MySQL 5.7 does not support the MERGE statement, but offers similar capability through optional ON DUPLICATE KEY UPDATE syntax within the INSERT statement. As always, check your vendor documentation.

Let's look at the actual SQL statements that accomplish the merge operation shown in Figure 8-7. Here is the SQL to create and load the MERGE_INVENTORY table:

```
CREATE TABLE MERGE_INVENTORY
  ( MERGE_CD_NAME      VARCHAR(60)       NOT NULL,
    MERGE_MUSIC_TYPE   VARCHAR(30),
    MERGE_PUBLISHER    VARCHAR(50)       NOT NULL,
    MERGE_IN_STOCK     INT               NOT NULL );

INSERT INTO MERGE_INVENTORY
 VALUES ('Different Shades of Blue', 'Blues', 'J&R Adventures', 42);

INSERT INTO MERGE_INVENTORY
 VALUES ('Come On Over', 'Country', 'Mercury', 6);

INSERT INTO MERGE_INVENTORY
 VALUES ('Innervisions (Remastered)', 'R&B', 'Motown/Universal', 18);

INSERT INTO MERGE_INVENTORY
 VALUES ('The Definitive Collection', 'R&B', 'Motown/Universal', 34);

INSERT INTO MERGE_INVENTORY
 VALUES ('Man Against Machine', null, 'Sony Music Nashville', 8);
```

Here is the syntax for the MERGE statement that applies the data in the MERGE_INVENTORY table to the CD_INVENTORY table:

```
MERGE INTO CD_INVENTORY
 USING MERGE_INVENTORY ON (CD_NAME = MERGE_CD_NAME)
 WHEN MATCHED THEN
    UPDATE SET MUSIC_TYPE = MERGE_MUSIC_TYPE,
               PUBLISHER  = MERGE_PUBLISHER,
               IN_STOCK   = MERGE_IN_STOCK
WHEN NOT MATCHED THEN
    INSERT  (CD_NAME, MUSIC_TYPE, PUBLISHER, IN_STOCK)
     VALUES (MERGE_CD_NAME, MERGE_MUSIC_TYPE,
             MERGE_PUBLISHER, MERGE_IN_STOCK);
```

MERGE statements are complex enough that it is worth reviewing the contents of this example. The MERGE statement specifies that we are merging into the CD_INVENTORY table. The USING statement indicates we are using the data contained in the MERGE_INVENTORY table to identify and apply any required changes, and the ON condition says we are matching the CD_NAME column (in the CD_INVENTORY table) and the MERGE_CD_NAME column (in the MERGE_INVENTORY table) in order to determine which rows in CD_INVENTORY need to be updated or inserted. The WHEN MATCHED THEN UPDATE clause specifies the updates to be performed for matched rows, and the SET clauses call for replacing the MUSIC_TYPE value with the MERGE_MUSIC_TYPE value, the PUBLISHER value with the MERGE_PUBLISHER value, and the IN_STOCK value with the MERGE_IN_STOCK value. The WHEN NOT MATCHED THEN INSERT clause specifies the inserts to be done (into CD_INVENTORY) for nonmatching rows, forming the values for CD_NAME, MUSIC_TYPE, PUBLISHER, and IN_STOCK from the values for MERGE_CD_NAME, MERGE_MUSIC_TYPE, MERGE_PUBLISHER, and MERGE_IN_STOCK, respectively.

As you can see, the MERGE statement is a powerful and flexible way to apply many changes to an SQL table using data contained in another SQL table.

Try This 8-1 Modifying SQL Data

In this Try This exercise, you will use the data modification statements discussed in this chapter to modify data in the INVENTORY database. You will use the INSERT statement to add data, the UPDATE statement to modify data, and the DELETE statement to remove the data from the database. Because you will be working only with data, you will not affect the underlying structure of the tables. You can download the Try_This_08.txt file, which contains the SQL statements used in this exercise.

Step by Step

1. Open the client application for your RDBMS and connect to the INVENTORY database.
2. First you will add a new company to the CD_LABELS table. The company is Atlantic and it will have a LABEL_ID value of 839. Enter and execute the following SQL statement:

```
INSERT INTO CD_LABELS
 VALUES ( 839, 'Atlantic' );
```

One row will be added to the CD_LABELS table.

(continued)

3. Now let's add a new CD to the COMPACT_DISCS table. The CD is named *X,* which has a COMPACT_DISC_ID value of 116. There are 14 of these CDs in stock, the Copyright Year is 2014, and the LABEL_ID value should be 838. (This is not the correct LABEL_ID value, but we will use it here for the purposes of this exercise.) Enter and execute the following SQL statement:

```
INSERT INTO COMPACT_DISCS
 VALUES ( 116, 'X', 838, 2014, 14 );
```

   One row will be added to the COMPACT_DISCS table. The LABEL_ID value of 838 represents Artista.

4. Now let's insert another row into the COMPACT_DISCS table; only this time, your INSERT statement will specify the column names of the target table. You will insert a CD named In The Lonely Hour. The new row will contain a CD_ID value of 117, a LABEL_ID value of 834 (Capital Records), a COPYRIGHT_YEAR of 2014, and an IN_STOCK value of 21. Enter and execute the following SQL statement:

```
INSERT INTO COMPACT_DISCS
        ( CD_ID, CD_TITLE, LABEL_ID, COPYRIGHT_YEAR, IN_STOCK)
 VALUES ( 117, 'In The Lonely Hour', 834, 2014, 21 );
```

   One row will be inserted into the COMPACT_DISCS table.

5. After you enter the In The Lonely Hour row, you realize that the IN_STOCK value is incorrect, and you want to update that value to 25. Enter and execute the following SQL statement:

```
UPDATE COMPACT_DISCS
   SET IN_STOCK = 25
 WHERE CD_ID = 117;
```

   The IN_STOCK value of the In The Lonely Hour row will be changed to 25.

6. You now realize that you entered the wrong LABEL_ID value for the X row. However, you want to be able to modify the existing value by specifying the company name rather than the LABEL_ID value. The company name is Atlantic, which you added to the CD_LABELS table in step 2. Enter and execute the following SQL statement:

```
UPDATE COMPACT_DISCS
   SET LABEL_ID =
       ( SELECT LABEL_ID
           FROM CD_LABELS
          WHERE COMPANY_NAME = 'Atlantic' )
WHERE CD_ID = 116;
```

   In this statement, you used a SELECT statement to pull the LABEL_ID value from the CD_LABELS table. The statement returned a value of 839. The value 839 was then used as the LABEL_ID value for the COMPACT_DISCS table. Note that you would not have been able to enter the value of 839 into the LABEL_ID column of the

COMPACT_DISCS table if it did not already exist in the CD_LABELS table. Not only is this because a SELECT statement was used to pull that value, but also because the LABEL_ID column in the COMPACT_DISCS table is a foreign key that references the CD_LABELS table. As a result, the value must exist in the referenced table before it can be added to the referencing table. See Chapter 4 for more information about foreign keys.

7. Now let's take a look at the data that you've entered and updated. Enter and execute the following SQL statement:

```
SELECT *
  FROM COMPACT_DISCS
 WHERE CD_ID = 116
    OR CD_ID = 117;
```

The SELECT statement requests data from all columns in the COMPACT_DISCS table, but only for those rows that have a COMPACT_DISC_ID value of 116 *or* 117. Your query results should include two rows. Verify that the information in those rows is correct. The X row should have a LABEL_ID value of 839, a COPYRIGHT_YEAR value of 2014, and an IN_STOCK value of 14, and the In The Lonely Hour row should have a LABEL_ID value of 834, a COPYRIGHT_YEAR value of 2014, and an IN_STOCK value of 25.

8. Now let's delete the two rows you added to the COMPACT_DISCS table. Enter and execute the following SQL statement:

```
DELETE FROM COMPACT_DISCS
 WHERE CD_ID = 116
    OR CD_ID = 117;
```

The X row and the In The Lonely Hour row should have been deleted from the COMPACT_DISCS table.

9. Next delete the row you added to the CD_LABELS table. Enter and execute the following SQL statement:

```
DELETE FROM CD_LABELS
 WHERE LABEL_ID = 839;
```

The Atlantic row should have been deleted from the CD_LABELS table.

NOTE

If you had tried to delete this row before deleting the X row in the COMPACT_DISCS table, you would have received an error because the LABEL_ID value in COMPACT_DISCS references the Atlantic row in CD_LABELS. The X row had to be deleted first, or the LABEL_ID value had to be changed to another value that conformed to the foreign key constraint.

10. Close the client application.

(continued)

Try This Summary

In this Try This exercise, you added one row to the LABEL_ID table and two rows to the COMPACT_DISCS table. You then updated the two rows in the COMPACT_DISCS table. After that, you deleted all the rows that you created. By the time you finished the exercise, the INVENTORY database should have been the same as when you began. As you can see, modifying data within tables is a very straightforward process; however, individual data modification statements can become far more complex. When you learn more advanced techniques for querying data, you'll be able to refine your statements to an even greater degree, providing you with more flexibility in inserting, updating, and deleting data.

Chapter 8 Self Test

1. Which SQL statement should you use to add data to a table?

   A SELECT

   B INSERT

   C UPDATE

   D DELETE

2. What two clauses are mandatory in an INSERT statement?

3. In which clause in the INSERT statement do you identify the table that will receive the new data?

4. You create the following INSERT statement to add data to the PERFORMING_ARTISTS table:

   ```
   INSERT INTO PERFORMING_ARTISTS VALUES ( 12, 'Frank Sinatra' );
   ```

   The PERFORMING_ARTISTS table includes three columns. What will happen when you try to execute this statement?

5. What information must you specify in the VALUES clause of an INSERT statement?

6. What requirements must be met by the values in a VALUES clause?

7. You're creating an INSERT statement to insert data into the ARTIST_TYPES table. The table includes only two columns: ART_ID and TYPE_NAME. You want to insert one row that includes the ART_ID value of 27 and the TYPE_NAME value of Gospel. Which SQL statement should you use?

8. You're creating an INSERT statement that inserts values taken from another table. Which type of statement or clause can you use in place of the VALUES clause to pull data from that other table?

   A UPDATE

   B SET

   C SELECT

   D WHERE

9. Which statement should you use to modify existing data in one or more rows in a table?

   A SELECT

   B INSERT

   C UPDATE

   D DELETE

10. Which clauses in an UPDATE statement are mandatory?

11. What is the purpose of the WHERE clause in an UPDATE statement?

12. You're creating an UPDATE statement to update data in the PERFORMING_ARTISTS table. You want to update the ART_ID value in the row that contains the PERF_ART_ID value of 139. The new ART_ID value is 27. Which SQL statement should you use?

13. You're creating an UPDATE statement to update data in the PERFORMING_ARTISTS table. You want to update the ART_ID value of every row to 27. Which SQL statement should you use?

14. You're updating two columns in the CD_INVENTORY table. You want to change the PUBLISHER value to MCA Records and you want to double the IN_STOCK value. Which SET clause should you use?

15. You're creating an UPDATE statement that includes a SET clause with one value expression. You want the value expression to pull a value from another table in the database. Which statement or clause can you use as a value expression to choose data from another table?

   A SELECT

   B WHERE

   C UPDATE

   D INSERT

16. Which clause in a DELETE statement is required?

17. Which statement or clause do you use in a DELETE statement to specify which rows are deleted from a table?

18. Which clauses are mandatory in the MERGE statement?

    A USING

    B ON

    C WHEN MATCHED

    D WHEN NOT MATCHED

    E Either WHEN MATCHED or WHEN NOT MATCHED

Chapter 9

Using Predicates

Key Skills & Concepts

- Compare SQL Data
- Return Null Values
- Return Similar Values
- Reference Additional Sources of Data
- Quantify Comparison Predicates

Up to this point in the book, I have presented a great deal of information about various aspects of database objects and the data they store. In relation to this, I discussed querying data (Chapter 7) and modifying data (Chapter 8). Now I want to take a step back and focus on one aspect of these discussions: the WHERE clause. The WHERE clause, as you might recall, allows you to specify a search condition that filters out those rows that you do not want returned by a SELECT statement or modified by an UPDATE or DELETE statement. The search condition includes one or more predicates that each state a fact about any row that is to be returned or modified. SQL supports a number of types of predicates, all of which allow you to test whether a condition is true, false, or unknown. In this chapter, I focus on those predicates that are most commonly used by SQL programmers, and I provide examples of how they're used to view and modify data in an SQL database.

Compare SQL Data

The first types of predicates that I plan to discuss are those that compare data. These predicates, like any predicate, are included in the WHERE clause. You can include a WHERE clause in a SELECT, UPDATE, or DELETE statement, and in each case, the clause can contain one or more comparison predicates.

Each predicate in the WHERE clause (whether a comparison predicate or another type) is evaluated on an individual basis to determine whether it meets the condition defined by that predicate. After the predicates are evaluated, the WHERE clause is evaluated as a whole. The clause must evaluate to true in order for a row to be included in a search result, be updated, or be deleted. If the clause evaluates to false or unknown, the row is not included or is not modified. For a complete discussion of how predicates and the WHERE clause are evaluated, see Chapter 7.

A comparison predicate is a type of predicate that compares the values in a specified column to a specified value. A comparison operator is used to compare those values. You have

Operator	Symbol	Example
Equal to	=	IN_STOCK = 47
Not equal to	<>	IN_STOCK <> 47
Less than	<	IN_STOCK < 47
Greater than	>	IN_STOCK > 47
Less than or equal to	<=	IN_STOCK <= 47
Greater than or equal to	>=	IN_STOCK >= 47

Table 9-1 SQL Comparison Operators

already seen a number of comparison operators (and, subsequently, comparison predicates) throughout the book. Table 9-1 lists the six comparison operators supported by SQL and provides an example of each one.

You no doubt recognize several of these operators, and even those you don't recognize should be fairly self-explanatory. But let's take a quick look at the examples in Table 9-1 to make sure you understand how a comparison predicate works. In the first row in the table (the Equal to row), the example predicate is IN_STOCK = 47. If this were to appear in a WHERE clause, it would look like the following:

```
WHERE IN_STOCK = 47
```

IN_STOCK is the name of the column in the table identified in the statement that contains the WHERE clause. The equals sign (=) is the comparison operator that is used to compare the values in the IN_STOCK column to the value to the right of the equals sign, which in this case is 47. Therefore, for a row to be evaluated to true, the IN_STOCK value for that row must be 47. All six comparison operators work in the same way. In each case, the WHERE clause must evaluate to true in order for the row to be returned in the query results or to be modified.

While it is traditional to place the column name to the left of the comparison operator and the constant value to the right, you can reverse them and form an equivalent statement, assuming you also adjust the comparison operator if needed. For example, the following two WHERE clauses are logically identical, each selecting rows with IN_STOCK values greater than 5:

```
WHERE IN_STOCK > 5
WHERE 5 < IN_STOCK
```

CD_TITLE: VARCHAR(60)	COPYRIGHT: INT	RETAIL_PRICE: NUMERIC(5,2)	INVENTORY: INT
Drive All Night	2013	5.99	12
Different Shades of Blue	2014	11.99	42
Innervisions (Remastered)	2000	10.00	16
The Definitive Collection	2002	8.39	34
Rumours (Reissued)	1990	7.99	17
Come On Over	1997	5.99	6
Man Against Machine	2014	9.99	8

Figure 9-1 Comparing data in the CDS_ON_HAND table

NOTE

As you learned in Chapter 7, you can combine predicates by using the AND keyword or the OR keyword to join together two or more predicates in a WHERE clause. You can also use the NOT keyword to create an inverse condition for a particular predicate. Remember, no matter how many predicates are included in the WHERE clause, the clause must still evaluate to true for a given row to be selected.

Now that you have an overview of the six types of comparison predicates, let's take a look at some examples. These examples are based on Figure 9-1, which shows the data stored in the CDS_ON_HAND table.

In the first example we'll look at, the WHERE clause uses an equal to operator to compare the values in the CD_TITLE column with one of the CD titles:

```
SELECT CD_TITLE, COPYRIGHT
  FROM CDS_ON_HAND
 WHERE CD_TITLE = 'Different Shades of Blue';
```

This statement will return one row with only two values (one for each column specified in the SELECT clause), as shown in the following query results:

```
CD_TITLE                    COPYRIGHT
------------------------    ---------
Different Shades of Blue    2014
```

Now let's change this SELECT statement a bit. Instead of using the equal to operator, I'll use the not equal to operator:

```
SELECT CD_TITLE, COPYRIGHT
  FROM CDS_ON_HAND
 WHERE CD_TITLE <> 'Different Shades of Blue';
```

When you execute this statement, six rows are returned:

```
CD_TITLE                          COPYRIGHT
-----------------------------     ---------
Drive All Night                   2013
Innervisions (Remastered)         2000
The Definitive Collection         2002
Rumours (Reissued)                1990
Come On Over                      1997
Man Against Machine               2014
```

Notice that all rows except the Different Shades of Blue row are included in the query results. In this case, the WHERE clause evaluates to true only when the CD_TITLE value does not equal Different Shades of Blue. Note, however, that if a row contained a null value for CD_TITLE, that row would not appear in either of the prior result sets. Keep in mind that a comparison with a null value will *always* evaluate to unknown (null)—the DBMS cannot tell what it is either equal to or not equal to because the value is unknown. As you will see later in the "Return Null Values" section, there are special operators used for dealing with null values.

Now let's take a look at the less than operator and the greater than operator. In the next example, I combine two comparison predicates together by using the AND keyword:

```
SELECT CD_TITLE, INVENTORY
  FROM CDS_ON_HAND
 WHERE INVENTORY > 6
   AND INVENTORY < 34;
```

As you can see, the rows returned by this SELECT statement must contain an INVENTORY value between 6 and 34, not including the end points. If you execute this statement, four rows are returned:

```
CD_TITLE                     INVENTORY
-------------------------    ---------
Drive All Night              12
Innervisions (Remastered)    16
Rumours (Reissued)           17
Man Against Machine          8
```

When defining the predicates in a WHERE clause, you're not limited to using only one column. For instance, if you want to select rows based on both the INVENTORY and RETAIL_PRICE column values, you can modify the last SELECT statement as shown in the following example:

```
SELECT CD_TITLE, INVENTORY
  FROM CDS_ON_HAND
 WHERE INVENTORY > 6
   AND INVENTORY < 34
   AND RETAIL_PRICE <> 7.99;
```

Because the conditions are connected using AND, any row returned in the query results must meet all three conditions defined in the WHERE clause. As a result, only three rows are returned when you execute this statement:

```
CD_TITLE                     INVENTORY
-------------------------    ---------
Drive All Night              12
Innervisions (Remastered)    16
Man Against Machine          8
```

Notice that the query results do not include the RETAIL_PRICE column. That is because this column is not specified in the SELECT clause. Even so, you can still use that column in a predicate in the WHERE clause to define a search condition.

Now let's take a look at the less than or equal to operator and the greater than or equal to operator. In the following example, both operators are used to limit the rows returned to those with a COPYRIGHT value that falls within the range of 1997 through 2013, inclusive.

```
SELECT CD_TITLE, COPYRIGHT
  FROM CDS_ON_HAND
 WHERE COPYRIGHT >= 1997
   AND COPYRIGHT <= 2013;
```

This statement will return slightly different results than what would be returned if you simply used the greater than and less than operators. By using the greater than or equal to operator and the less than or equal to operator, values that equal the specified value are also returned, as shown in the following query results:

```
CD_TITLE                          COPYRIGHT
------------------------------    ---------
Drive All Night                   2013
Innervisions (Remastered)         2000
The Definitive Collection         2002
Come On Over                      1997
```

Notice that the Come On Over row includes a COPYRIGHT value of 1997. This would not have been included if you had merely used the greater than operator.

Up to this point, the examples I've shown you have all been based on SELECT statements. However, you can add a WHERE clause to an UPDATE statement or a DELETE statement. Suppose you want to increase the INVENTORY value for the Man Against Machine row. You can use the following UPDATE statement:

```
UPDATE CDS_ON_HAND
   SET INVENTORY = 10
 WHERE CD_TITLE = 'Man Against Machine';
```

When you execute this statement, the INVENTORY value is increased to 10 for the Man Against Machine row but not for any other row because the WHERE clause evaluates to true only for that row. You could have just as easily added this WHERE clause to a DELETE statement, in which case the Man Against Machine row would have been deleted.

As with the WHERE clause in a SELECT statement, you can combine two or more predicates to form a search condition:

```
UPDATE CDS_ON_HAND
   SET INVENTORY = 8
 WHERE CD_TITLE = 'Man Against Machine'
   AND COPYRIGHT = 2014;
```

When you specify the AND keyword, both predicates must evaluate to true in order for the WHERE clause to evaluate to true. If you specify the OR keyword instead of AND, then only one of the predicates must evaluate to true for the row to be selected.

Using the BETWEEN Predicate

Strictly speaking, the BETWEEN predicate is not a comparison predicate, at least not as it is presented in the SQL standard. It is, however, so similar in function to a combination of the greater than or equal to operator and the less than or equal to operator that it's worth discussing here.

The BETWEEN predicate is used in conjunction with the AND keyword to identify a range of values that can be included as a search condition in the WHERE clause. Values in the identified column must fall within that range in order to evaluate to true. When you use the BETWEEN clause, you must specify the applicable column, the low end of the range, and the high end of the range. The following example (which is based on the CDS_ON_HAND table in Figure 9-1) specifies a range from 5.99 through 8.99:

```
SELECT CD_TITLE, RETAIL_PRICE
  FROM CDS_ON_HAND
 WHERE RETAIL_PRICE BETWEEN 5.99 AND 8.99;
```

The RETAIL_PRICE value for each selected row must fall within that range, including the end points. If you execute this statement, only four rows are included in the query results:

```
CD_TITLE                     RETAIL_PRICE
--------------------------   ------------
Drive All Night              5.99
The Definitive Collection    8.39
Rumours (Reissued)           7.99
Come On Over                 5.99
```

Now let's take a look at a query similar to the one in the last example, only this time using comparison predicates rather than the BETWEEN predicate:

```
SELECT CD_TITLE, RETAIL_PRICE
  FROM CDS_ON_HAND
 WHERE RETAIL_PRICE >= 5.99
   AND RETAIL_PRICE <= 8.99;
```

Notice that two predicates are used: one with the greater than or equal to operator and one with the less than or equal to operator. This SELECT statement will produce the same query results as the previous SELECT statement.

Now let's return to the BETWEEN predicate. As with any predicate, you can combine the BETWEEN predicate with other predicates. In the following statement, the WHERE clause includes a BETWEEN predicate and a comparison predicate:

```
SELECT CD_TITLE, RETAIL_PRICE
  FROM CDS_ON_HAND
 WHERE RETAIL_PRICE BETWEEN 5.99 AND 8.99
   AND INVENTORY > 12;
```

As a result of both predicates, the query results can include only those rows with a RETAIL_PRICE value that falls within the range of 5.99 through 8.99 *and* with an INVENTORY value greater than 12. When you execute this query, only two rows are returned:

```
CD_TITLE                     RETAIL_PRICE
-------------------------    ------------
The Definitive Collection    8.39
Rumours (Reissued)           7.99
```

Again, you will notice that the query results don't include the INVENTORY column even though that column is specified in a predicate in the WHERE clause. You'll also notice that more than one column is referenced in the WHERE clause.

In addition to what you've seen so far with the BETWEEN predicate, you can also use the clause to specify the inverse of a condition. This is done by using the NOT keyword within the predicate. For example, suppose you change the last example to the following:

```
SELECT CD_TITLE, RETAIL_PRICE
  FROM CDS_ON_HAND
 WHERE RETAIL_PRICE NOT BETWEEN 5.99 AND 8.99;
```

The rows returned in the query result will include all rows that do not have a RETAIL_PRICE value within the range of 5.99 through 8.99. When you execute the statement, three rows are returned:

```
CD_TITLE                        RETAIL_PRICE
-----------------------------   ------------
Different Shades of Blue        11.99
Innervisions (Remastered)       10.00
Man Against Machine             9.99
```

Notice that all values within the specified range have been excluded from the query results. If you find the NOT keyword confusing (as many people do), you can write an equivalent WHERE clause using the OR keyword and the greater than and less than operators as follows:

```
WHERE RETAIL_PRICE < 5.99
   OR RETAIL_PRICE > 8.99;
```

Return Null Values

As you might recall from Chapter 4, a null value is used in place of a value when that value is undefined or not known. A null indicates that the value is absent. This is not the same as a zero, a blank, or a default value. By default, SQL allows nulls to be used in place of regular values (although you can override the default by including a NOT NULL constraint in your column definition). In those cases where null values are permitted, you might find it necessary to specify that null values be returned when you query a table. For this reason, SQL provides the NULL predicate, which allows you to define search conditions that return null values.

The NULL predicate is very straightforward to implement. Used in conjunction with the IS keyword, the predicate is added to a WHERE clause in the same way any other predicate is added, and it applies only to null values that might exist in the column that you query. The best way to illustrate this is through the use of examples. In these examples, I use the ARTISTS_BIO table, shown in Figure 9-2.

The first example is a SELECT statement that returns rows with a PLACE_OF_BIRTH value of null:

```
SELECT *
  FROM ARTISTS_BIO
 WHERE PLACE_OF_BIRTH IS NULL;
```

PERFORMER_NAME: VARCHAR(60)	PLACE_OF_BIRTH: VARCHAR(60)	YEAR_BORN: INT
Glen Hansard	Ballymun, Dublin, Ireland	1970
Joe Bonamassa	New Hartford, New York, USA	1977
Stevie Wonder	Saginaw, Michigan, USA	1950
Fleetwood Mac	<null>	<null>
Shania Twain	Windsor, Ontario, Canada	1965
Garth Brooks	Tulsa, Oklahoma, USA	1962
Johannes Sebastian Bach	<null>	1685
Joshua Bell	Bloomington, Indiana, USA	1967
Jason Aldean	Macon, Georgia, USA	1977

Figure 9-2 Returning null values from the ARTISTS_BIO table

The statement returns all columns from the ARTISTS_BIO table; however, it returns only two rows, as you can see in the following query results (your results may look different depending on how your SQL client application displays null values):

```
PERFORMER_NAME             PLACE_OF_BIRTH   YEAR_BORN
-----------------------    --------------   ---------
Fleetwood Mac              <null>           <null>
Johannes Sebastian Bach    <null>           1685
```

The fact that the YEAR_BORN column contains a null value for the Fleetwood Mac row has no bearing on the fact that a NULL predicate is used. The NULL predicate in this case identifies the PLACE_OF_BIRTH column only, not the YEAR_BORN column. You can, however, replace the PLACE_OF_BIRTH column in the predicate with the YEAR_BORN column, in which case the rows returned will be those with a YEAR_BORN value of null. Notice, however, that only the Fleetwood Mac row has a null value in the YEAR_BORN column.

According to the SQL standard, you can also specify both columns in the NULL predicate, as shown in the following example:

```
SELECT *
  FROM ARTISTS_BIO
 WHERE (PLACE_OF_BIRTH, YEAR_BORN) IS NULL;
```

When you include both columns, the PLACE_OF_BIRTH column and YEAR_BORN column must both return null values in order for a row to be returned, which in the case of the ARTISTS_BIO table would only be one row.

NOTE

Although the SQL standard permits you to specify multiple columns in the NULL predicate, many implementations do not support this. Instead you must specify two NULL predicates connected with the AND keyword.

As an alternative to including both columns in one predicate, you can write your SELECT statement as follows:

```
SELECT *
  FROM ARTISTS_BIO
 WHERE PLACE_OF_BIRTH IS NULL
   AND YEAR_BORN IS NULL;
```

If you execute this statement, you'll receive the following query results:

```
PERFORMER_NAME             PLACE_OF_BIRTH   YEAR_BORN
-----------------------    --------------   ---------
Fleetwood Mac              <null>           <null>
```

SQL supports another feature in the NULL predicate. You can use the NOT keyword to find the inverse results of the predicate. For example, suppose you want to return all rows that include an actual value in the PLACE_OF_BIRTH column, rather than a null value. Your statement might look like the following:

```
SELECT *
  FROM ARTISTS_BIO
 WHERE PLACE_OF_BIRTH IS NOT NULL;
```

Your query results will now include eight rows, all of which contain values in the PLACE_OF_BIRTH column:

```
PERFORMER_NAME              PLACE_OF_BIRTH                 YEAR_BORN
--------------------------  -----------------------------  ---------
Glen Hansard                Ballymun, Dublin, Ireland      1970
Joe Bonamassa               New Hartford, New York, USA    1977
Stevie Wonder               Saginaw, Michigan, USA         1950
Shania Twain                Windsor, Ontario, Canada       1965
Garth Brooks                Tulsa, Oklahoma, USA           1962
Joshua Bell                 Bloomington, Indiana, USA      1967
Jason Aldean                Macon, Georgia, USA            1977
```

Notice that null values can still exist in other columns. Because only the PLACE_OF_BIRTH column is specified in the NULL predicate, only that column must contain a value (instead of being null) in order for a row to be returned.

As with the predicates we looked at earlier in the chapter, you can combine the NULL predicate with other types of predicates. For example, you can modify the last example to limit the YEAR_BORN values to certain years, as shown in the following example:

```
SELECT *
  FROM ARTISTS_BIO
 WHERE PLACE_OF_BIRTH IS NOT NULL
   AND YEAR_BORN > 1968;
```

Now any rows returned must include a value in the PLACE_OF_BIRTH column *and* the YEAR_BORN value must be greater than 1968. If you execute this query, you'll receive the following results:

```
PERFORMER_NAME   PLACE_OF_BIRTH                 YEAR_BORN
---------------  -----------------------------  ---------
Glen Hansard     Ballymun, Dublin, Ireland      1970
Joe Bonamassa    New Hartford, New York, USA    1977
Jason Aldean     Macon, Georgia, USA            1977
```

As you can see, only three rows are returned. No rows with a PLACE_OF_BIRTH value of null are returned because null evaluates to unknown, and only WHERE clauses that evaluate to true can be included in the query results.

Return Similar Values

If any predicate can be fun, it is the LIKE predicate. The LIKE predicate provides a flexible environment in which you can specify values that are only *similar* to the values stored in the database. This is particularly advantageous if you know only part of a value but still need to retrieve information based on that value. For example, suppose you don't know the entire title of a CD, but you do know part of that title. Or perhaps you know only part of a performer's name. By using the LIKE predicate, you can ask for values that are similar to what you do know and from those results determine if the information you need is there.

Before we take a look at the LIKE predicate itself, let's look at two symbols used within the predicate. The LIKE predicate uses two special characters, the percentage sign (%) and the underscore (_), to help define the search condition specified in the predicate. The percentage sign represents zero or more unknown characters, and the underscore represents exactly one unknown character. You can use these characters at the beginning of a value, in the middle, or at the end, and you can combine them with each other as necessary. The way in which you use these two characters determines the type of data that is retrieved from the database.

Table 9-2 provides a number of examples of how these special characters can be used in a LIKE predicate.

As you can see, the percentage sign and underscore special characters provide a great deal of flexibility and allow you to query a wide range of data.

Sample Value	Possible Query Results
'S%'	Stevie Wonder, Shania Twain
'%Blue'	Different Shades of Blue, Kind of Blue
'%Blue%'	Different Shades of Blue, Kind of Blue, Famous Blue Raincoat
'%Shades%Blue'	Different Shades of Blue
'201_'	2013, 2014
'20__'	2000, 2002, 2013, 2014
'Josh___Bell'	Joshua Bell
'9__01'	90201, 91401, 95501, 99301, 99901
'9_3%'	9032343, 903, 95312, 99306, 983393300333

Table 9-2 Using Special Characters in a LIKE Predicate

NOTE

Some vendor implementations can be configured to be case insensitive for data comparisons, meaning that lowercase letters and uppercase letters compare as the same. In fact, this is the default behavior for SQL Server and Sybase; however, Oracle is always case sensitive. MySQL varies by platform, but is generally case insensitive on Windows, but case sensitive on Unix, Linux, and Mac OS X. Looking at Table 9-2, uppercase letters in the Sample Value column can be changed to lowercase with the same results whenever the DBMS is configured as case insensitive. For example, a LIKE predicate value of %blue will still select the Different Shades of Blue and Kind of Blue rows in a case-insensitive implementation.

Now that you have an understanding of the special characters, let's take a look at the LIKE predicate as a whole. The LIKE predicate includes the column name, the LIKE keyword, and a value enclosed in a set of single quotation marks, which is then enclosed in a set of parentheses (the parentheses are optional in most vendor implementations). For example, the following WHERE clause includes one LIKE predicate:

```
WHERE CD_TITLE LIKE ('%Over')
```

The predicate includes the CD_TITLE column, the LIKE keyword, and a value of %Over. Only rows that contain the correct value in the CD_TITLE column are returned in the query results. The CD_TITLE column is part of the CDS table, which is shown in Figure 9-3. I will

CD_ID: INT	CD_TITLE: VARCHAR(60)
101	Drive All Night
102	Different Shades of Blue
103	Innervisions (Remastered)
104	The Definitive Collection
105	Rumours (Reissued)
106	Come On Over
107	Man Against Machine
108	Bach
109	Old Boots, New Dirt
110	Dark Side of the Moon
111	Kind of Blue

Figure 9-3 Returning similar values from the CDS table

Ask the Expert

Q: You've provided examples that use the LIKE predicate to search columns with character data types. Can I use the LIKE predicate to search columns with other data types, such as numeric and date columns?

A: As you noticed, the LIKE predicate uses a character string comparison technique, and therefore operates as if the table column being searched has a character data type. The SQL standard permits search predicates to be used on columns that have data types other than the one expected by the predicate, and the standard goes on to state that the column data should be implicitly converted to the appropriate data type by the SQL implementation. However, that does not mean it is a good practice, and in fact, it is *always* better to use matching data types, for two reasons: First, the SQL implementation may not support the implicit data type conversion required by the predicate, or even if it does, it may not carry out the conversion the same way you think it will. For example, some SQL implementations add one or more leading spaces when converting numeric column values to character strings. Second, in some SQL implementations, implicit data conversions are notorious for slow performance. For example, a query that runs well on MySQL may run significantly slower on Oracle due to implicit data type conversion. You can use conversion functions, such as CAST, to explicitly convert column data values into the required data type. I cover SQL functions, including CAST, in Chapter 10.

be using this table for the examples in this section. Notice that, based on the LIKE predicate defined in the preceding WHERE clause, only one row can be returned by this clause, the row with a CD_TITLE value of Come On Over.

Now let's take a look at a few examples of SELECT statements that include a LIKE predicate. Suppose you want to find any CDs that contain the word Against in the title. You can create the following SELECT statement to query the CDS table:

```
SELECT *
  FROM CDS
 WHERE CD_TITLE LIKE ('%Against%');
```

Your query results will include only one row:

```
CD_ID    CD_TITLE
------   -----------------------
107      Man Against Machine
```

If you had included only one percentage sign, no rows would have been returned. For example, if you had eliminated the first percentage sign, your SQL implementation would have interpreted this to mean that the value must begin with the word Against, which it does not. Similarly, if you had eliminated the second percentage sign, your implementation would have assumed that Against must be the last word in the character string. In addition, if no percentage signs were used, no rows would have been returned because no values would have matched Against exactly.

You can also add the NOT keyword to a LIKE predicate if you want all rows returned except those specified by the predicate. Take, for instance, the last example. If you add the NOT keyword, it will look like the following:

```
SELECT *
  FROM CDS
 WHERE CD_TITLE NOT LIKE ('%Against%');
```

This time, your query results include all rows that do not include the word Against:

```
CD_ID  CD_TITLE
-----  ------------------------------
101    Drive All Night
102    Different Shades of Blue
103    Innvervisions (Remastered)
104    The Definitive Collection
105    Rumours (Reissued)
106    Come On Over
108    Bach
109    Old Boots, New Dirt
110    Dark Side of the Moon
111    Kind of Blue
```

Notice that the Man Against Machine row is now among the missing.

You can also combine one LIKE predicate with another LIKE predicate. Suppose, for example, you still want to exclude the Against value, but you want to include the Blue value, as shown in the following example:

```
SELECT *
  FROM CDS
 WHERE CD_TITLE NOT LIKE ('%Against%')
   AND CD_TITLE LIKE ('%Blue%');
```

The WHERE clause in this SELECT statement eliminates any rows that have the word Against appearing anywhere in the CD_TITLE value. In addition, the CD_TITLE value must include the word Blue. As a result, only two rows are returned.

```
CD_ID  CD_TITLE
-----  ------------------------------
102    Different Shades of Blue
111    Kind of Blue
```

But what happens if the CD title includes both words? For example, Michael Martin Murphey's *Blue Sky-Night Thunder/Swans Against the Sun* is available on CD. The AND keyword used to connect the predicates means that *both* predicates must be true in order for a row to be returned. Even if a Blue Sky-Night Thunder/Swans Against the Sun row existed in the CDS table, it would not be included in the query results because the first predicate (the NOT LIKE one) would evaluate to false.

Try This 9-1 Using Predicates in SQL Statements

Before we move on to other predicates, I think it's a good idea to review those predicates that have already been discussed. These include the six types of comparison predicates, the BETWEEN predicate, the NULL predicate, and the LIKE predicate. In this Try This exercise, you will try a number of these predicates through the use of SELECT statements that will include the appropriate WHERE clauses. You will be querying tables that you created in the INVENTORY database. Because you will be using only SELECT statements, you won't be modifying the tables or the database structure in any way. You'll simply request data based on the predicates that you define. You can download the Try_This_09.txt file, which contains the SQL statements used in this exercise.

Step by Step

1. Open the client application for your RDBMS and connect to the INVENTORY database.
2. In the first statement you create, you'll query the MUSIC_TYPES table to return the names of those rows whose TYPE_ID value is equal to 11 or 12. Enter and execute the following SQL statement:

```
SELECT TYPE_ID, TYPE_NAME
  FROM MUSIC_TYPES
 WHERE TYPE_ID = 11
    OR TYPE_ID = 12;
```

   The statement should return two rows, one for Alternative Rock and one for Blues. Notice that the OR keyword is used to indicate that either value is acceptable.

3. Now you'll query the ARTISTS table and look for artists other than Shania Twain and Jason Aldean. Enter and execute the following SQL statement:

```
SELECT ARTIST_NAME, PLACE_OF_BIRTH
  FROM ARTISTS
 WHERE ARTIST_NAME <> 'Shania Twain'
   AND ARTIST_NAME <> 'Jason Aldean';
```

   Your query should return 12 rows and should not include the Shania Twain row or the Jason Aldean row.

4. Now let's combine a couple of comparison predicates to create a different sort of search condition. In this statement, you'll again query the ARTISTS table, but you'll request only those rows whose ARTIST_ID values lie between 3004 and 3014 (excluding the end points). Enter and execute the following SQL statement:

```
SELECT ARTIST_ID, ARTIST_NAME
  FROM ARTISTS
 WHERE ARTIST_ID > 3004
   AND ARTIST_ID < 3014;
```

Your query should return nine rows.

5. Now let's modify the SELECT statement that you just executed. You should use a BETWEEN predicate rather than the two comparison predicates. Enter and execute the following SQL statement:

```
SELECT ARTIST_ID, ARTIST_NAME
  FROM ARTISTS
 WHERE ARTIST_ID BETWEEN 3004 AND 3014;
```

You should now see 11 rows, rather than the 9 that were returned in the previous step because BETWEEN always includes the end points. Had you used the greater than or equal to operator and the less than or equal to operator in the last step, your query results would have been the same as in this step.

6. Now let's query the ARTISTS table once more, only this time we'll use the NULL predicate. Enter and execute the following SQL statement:

```
SELECT *
  FROM ARTISTS
 WHERE PLACE_OF_BIRTH IS NULL;
```

Your query will return no results because the PLACE_OF_BIRTH column contains no null values.

7. Let's try the same query as in the last step, only this time we'll add the NOT keyword to the NULL predicate. Enter and execute the following SQL statement:

```
SELECT *
  FROM ARTISTS
 WHERE PLACE_OF_BIRTH IS NOT NULL;
```

Your query should now return every row in the table (14 in all).

8. In the next statement, you will use the LIKE predicate to find CD titles that include the word Blue or the word Moon. Your predicate will reference the CD_TITLE column of the COMPACT_DISCS table. Enter and execute the following SQL statement:

```
SELECT CD_TITLE, IN_STOCK
  FROM COMPACT_DISCS
```

(continued)

```
WHERE CD_TITLE LIKE ('%Blue%')
   OR CD_TITLE LIKE ('%Moon%');
```

Your query should return three rows. In all those rows, the CD_TITLE value should contain the words Blue or Moon.

9. Next you'll modify the statement in the previous step to include the NOT keyword in both predicates. You should also change the OR keyword to AND. Enter and execute the following SQL statement:

```
SELECT CD_TITLE, IN_STOCK
  FROM COMPACT_DISCS
 WHERE CD_TITLE NOT LIKE ('%Blue%')
   AND CD_TITLE NOT LIKE ('%Moon%');
```

Your query results should now include 12 rows. If you had not changed the OR keyword to AND, your results would have included all 15 rows. This is because the statement would *always* evaluate to true—the first predicate would evaluate to true for a row containing Moon; the second predicate would evaluate to true for a row containing Blue; and both predicates would evaluate to true for any other row.

10. Close the client application.

Try This Summary

In this Try This exercise, you created a number of SELECT statements that included various predicates. The predicates were contained in WHERE clauses that were part of the SELECT statements; however, these clauses could also have been part of UPDATE and DELETE statements. As you move through the rest of this chapter, you will learn about other predicates and how they can be used in various types of statements. These predicates can be used in conjunction with the ones I've already discussed or used by themselves to create more complex search conditions and return more precise results.

Reference Additional Sources of Data

SQL supports several types of predicates that allow you to reference sources other than the main table that you're querying or modifying. As a result, you can create search conditions that compare data between tables in order to determine which rows should be included in your query results, which rows should be updated, or which ones deleted. In this section, I look at two important predicates that you can use to reference other tables: the IN predicate and the EXISTS predicate.

Both predicates can use subqueries to reference data in the table being queried or modified, or more commonly, in other tables. I first introduce the topic of subqueries in Chapter 4. As you might recall from that chapter, a subquery is an expression that is used as a component within another expression. In its most common usage, a subquery is simply a SELECT statement embedded within another statement. When used in a predicate, a subquery becomes part of that predicate and consequently is embedded in the WHERE clause of a SELECT, UPDATE, or DELETE statement. Although subqueries are discussed in detail in Chapter 12, I mention them here because they're an integral part of the predicates I'll be discussing in the remaining part of this chapter. In each of these predicates, subqueries are used to reference data in other tables. For the purposes of this chapter, I keep my examples of subqueries simple, but know that they can be far more elaborate than what you see here, and once you complete Chapter 12, you'll be able to apply that knowledge to the predicates you learn about in this chapter.

Using the IN Predicate

The IN predicate allows you to determine whether the values in the specified column of one table are contained in a defined list or contained within another table. In the first case, you specify the column name, the IN keyword, and a list of values that are compared to the values in the specified column. In the second case, you specify the column name, the IN keyword, and a subquery, which references the second table. In either case, if the column value matches one of the values in the list or in the subquery results, the predicate evaluates to true, and the row is returned in the query results.

The best way to illustrate both of these methods is through examples. However, before we look at those, refer to the tables shown in Figure 9-4. These are the tables I'll be using for the examples.

As I mentioned, the first method for using the IN predicate is to define a list. Your list should include all values that are to be compared to the values in the specified column. For example, suppose you want to limit your query results to rows in the COMPACT_DISC_INVENTORY table that have an IN_STOCK value of 12, 22, 32, or 42. You can create a SELECT statement that looks like the following:

```
SELECT CD_NAME, IN_STOCK FROM COMPACT_DISC_INVENTORY
WHERE IN_STOCK IN ( 12, 22, 32, 42 );
```

This statement returns only three rows because those are the only rows that have the correct IN_STOCK values:

```
CD_NAME                    IN_STOCK
------------------------   --------
Drive All Night             12
Different Shades of Blue    42
Endless River               12
```

As you can see, using the IN predicate to define a list is a fairly straightforward process and a useful one when you know exactly which values you want to compare your columns to.

COMPACT_DISC_INVENTORY

CD_NAME: VARCHAR (60)	IN_STOCK: INT
Drive All Night	12
Different Shades of Blue	42
Innervisions (Remastered)	16
The Definitive Collection	34
Rumours (Reissued)	17
Come On Over	6
Man Against Machine	8
Endless River	12
Sonic Highways	27

COMPACT_DISC_ARTISTS

TITLE: VARCHAR(60)	ARTIST: VARCHAR(60)
Drive All Night	Glen Hansard
Different Shades of Blue	Joe Bonamassa
Innervisions (Remastered)	Stevie Wonder
The Definitive Collection	Stevie Wonder
Rumours (Reissued)	Fleetwood Mac
Come On Over	Shania Twain
Bach	Joshua Bell
Old Boots, New Dirt	Jason Aldean
Man Against Machine	Garth Brooks
Dark Side of the Moon	Pink Floyd
Kind of Blue	Miles Davis
Endless River	Pink Floyd
Sonic Highways	Foo Fighters

Figure 9-4 Querying data from the COMPACT_DISC_INVENTORY table and the COMPACT_DISC_ARTISTS table

It also is a simpler method than defining separate predicates for each value, as in the following example:

```
SELECT CD_NAME, IN_STOCK
  FROM COMPACT_DISC_INVENTORY
 WHERE IN_STOCK = 12
    OR IN_STOCK = 22
    OR IN_STOCK = 32
    OR IN_STOCK = 42;
```

This statement will return the same results as the SELECT statement in the previous example; however, as you can see, it's much more cumbersome.

Now let's take a look at a SELECT statement that uses a subquery in the IN predicate. Suppose you want to create a query that returns CD names and their artists. You want your query results to include only those CDs that have more than 10 copies in stock. If you refer back to Figure 9-4, you'll see that the COMPACT_DISC_ARTISTS table includes the CD names and their artists. However, as you can also see, the IN_STOCK values are stored in the COMPACT_DISC_INVENTORY table, which means you'll need to reference that table in order to return the correct rows. To do so, you can create the following SELECT statement:

```
SELECT TITLE, ARTIST
  FROM COMPACT_DISC_ARTISTS
 WHERE TITLE IN
   ( SELECT CD_NAME
       FROM COMPACT_DISC_INVENTORY
      WHERE IN_STOCK > 10 );
```

If you execute this statement, you'll receive the following results:

```
TITLE                          ARTIST
-------------------------      ----------------
Drive All Night                Glen Hansard
Different Shades of Blue       Joe Bonamassa
Innervisions (Remastered)      Stevie Wonder
The Definitive Collection      Stevie Wonder
Rumours (Reissued)             Fleetwood Mac
Endless River                  Pink Floyd
Sonic Highways                 Foo Fighters
```

Notice that only seven rows have been returned. These are the seven CDs listed in the COMPACT_DISC_INVENTORY table that have an IN_STOCK value greater than 10.

Now let's take a closer look at the SELECT statement in order to give you a better understanding of how the IN predicate works. The WHERE clause contains only one predicate. It begins with the name of the column (TITLE) whose values you want to verify. The TITLE column is followed by the IN keyword. The keyword is then followed by a subquery, which is enclosed in parentheses. The subquery consists of the following SELECT statement:

```
SELECT CD_NAME
  FROM COMPACT_DISC_INVENTORY
 WHERE IN_STOCK > 10
```

If you were to execute this statement by itself, you would receive the following results:

```
CD_NAME
-------------------------
Drive All Night
Different Shades of Blue
Innervisions (Remastered)
The Definitive Collection
Rumours (Reissued)
Endless River
Sonic Highways
```

Each row in the query results, which are derived from the COMPACT_DISC_INVENTORY table, contains an IN_STOCK value greater than 10. The values in the TITLE column of the COMPACT_DISC_ARTISTS table are then compared against these results. Any row that contains a TITLE value that matches one of seven CD_NAME values (in the subquery results) is included in the query results of the main SELECT statement.

NOTE

When including a subquery in an IN predicate, the SELECT clause of the subquery must return only one column of data. If you specify more than one column in the result set or you specify an asterisk, you will receive an error.

Like many other predicates, the IN predicate allows you to specify the inverse of a condition by using the NOT keyword. Suppose you rewrite the SELECT statement in the last example to include the NOT keyword in the IN predicate:

```
SELECT TITLE, ARTIST
  FROM COMPACT_DISC_ARTISTS
 WHERE TITLE NOT IN
     ( SELECT CD_NAME
         FROM COMPACT_DISC_INVENTORY
        WHERE IN_STOCK > 10 );
```

Your query results will include all those rows that were not returned by the last SELECT statement and will exclude all those rows that were returned, as shown in the following results:

```
TITLE                      ARTIST
-------------------------  ----------------
Come On Over               Shania Twain
Bach                       Joshua Bell
Old Boots, New Dirt        Jason Aldean
Man Against Machine        Garth Brooks
Dark Side of the Moon      Pink Floyd
Kind of Blue               Miles Davis
```

As you can see, the IN predicate is a very flexible tool for comparing values in a specified column to data in other tables. You'll find this extremely useful as you learn more about subqueries and can create more complex predicates.

Using the EXISTS Predicate

Although similar to an IN predicate, the EXISTS predicate has a slightly different focus. It is concerned only with determining whether or not the subquery returns any rows. If it returns one or more rows, the predicate evaluates to true; otherwise, the predicate evaluates to false. The predicate is made up of the EXISTS keyword and a subquery. For the subquery to be of any real value (and subsequently the EXISTS predicate itself), it should include a predicate that matches two columns in different tables. For example, in Figure 9-4, the COMPACT_

DISC_INVENTORY table includes the CD_NAME column, and the COMPACT_DISC_ARTISTS table includes the TITLE column. The two columns can be matched together to ensure that only relevant rows are returned by the subquery. Let's take a look at an example to help clarify this issue.

Suppose you want to retrieve rows from the COMPACT_DISC_INVENTORY table so you can determine how many Stevie Wonder CDs you have in stock. You want to display only the CD names and the number of CDs in stock. You do not want to display the artist's name, and you do not want to display CDs by other artists. To accomplish this, you can use the following SELECT statement:

```
SELECT *
  FROM COMPACT_DISC_INVENTORY
 WHERE EXISTS
     ( SELECT TITLE
         FROM COMPACT_DISC_ARTISTS
        WHERE ARTIST = 'Stevie Wonder'
          AND COMPACT_DISC_INVENTORY.CD_NAME =
              COMPACT_DISC_ARTISTS.TITLE );
```

If you execute this statement, you'll receive the following query results:

```
CD_NAME                    IN_STOCK
-------------------------  --------
Innervisions (Remastered)  16
The Definitive Collection  34
```

The best way to understand how this statement works is to look at how individual rows are evaluated. As you will learn in Chapter 12, subqueries like this one are called *correlated subqueries* because the subquery is executed for each row returned in the main SELECT statement. Because the subquery WHERE clause matches the CD_NAME value to the TITLE value, the TITLE value in the row being evaluated (in the subquery) must match the CD_NAME value in order for that row to be returned. For example, the first row in the COMPACT_DISC_INVENTORY table contains a CD_NAME value of Drive All Night. When this row is tested against the EXISTS predicate, the Drive All Night value is matched with the Drive All Night value of the TITLE column in the COMPACT_DISC_ARTISTS table. In addition, the Stevie Wonder value is matched against the ARTIST value for the Drive All Night row. Because the ARTIST value is Glen Hansard and not Stevie Wonder, the search condition specified in the subquery WHERE clause evaluates to false, so no subquery row is returned for the Drive All Night row. As a result, the WHERE clause in the main SELECT statement evaluates to false for the Drive All Night row of the COMPACT_DISC_INVENTORY table, and the row is not included in the query results.

This process is repeated for each row in the COMPACT_DISC_INVENTORY table. If the WHERE clause in the subquery evaluates to true, then the EXISTS predicate evaluates to true, which means that the WHERE clause in the main SELECT statement evaluates to true. In the case of our last example SELECT statement, only two rows meet this criteria.

NOTE

It does not matter what columns or how many columns you specify in the SELECT clause of the subquery in an EXISTS predicate. This type of predicate is concerned only with whether rows are being returned, rather than the content of those rows. You can specify any column names or just an asterisk.

The EXISTS predicate, as you might expect, allows you to test the inverse of the predicate condition by using the NOT keyword:

```
SELECT *
  FROM COMPACT_DISC_INVENTORY
 WHERE NOT EXISTS
     ( SELECT TITLE
         FROM COMPACT_DISC_ARTISTS
        WHERE ARTIST = 'Stevie Wonder'
          AND COMPACT_DISC_INVENTORY.CD_NAME =
              COMPACT_DISC_ARTISTS.TITLE );
```

In this case, all CDs *except* the Stevie Wonder CDs are included in the query results. This means that if the WHERE clause of the subquery evaluates to true (which means that the subquery returns a row), the predicate itself evaluates to false and no row is returned. On the other hand, if the subquery does not return a row, the predicate evaluates to true and the row is returned in the query results of the main SELECT statement.

Ask the Expert

Q: You've provided examples that show there is often more than one way to achieve the same outcome. How do you know which option to select when you're writing an SQL statement?

A: You'll find that as you learn more about SQL programming and gain a better understanding of the nuances of each statement, there will often be more than one way to achieve the same results. In these cases, your choice of methods will often depend on which statement is the simplest to write or which one performs the best in a particular SQL implementation. As your understanding of SQL grows, so too will your ability to choose the method that's best for your situation. In many cases, the difference between one method and another will not be very great, and your choice might merely depend on your personal preference. However, you might also run into situations in which the SQL implementation in which you're working does not support all the methods provided in the SQL standard. Therefore, you must select the method that can be implemented in your particular environment. Whichever methods you might ultimately use in any given environment, it is best for now that you have as complete a foundation as possible in the basics of SQL. That way you'll be more prepared for various situations and be better equipped to move from implementation to implementation. In addition, you should learn about performance issues related to the implementation with which you're working. You should consider issues of performance when making a decision about which SQL statements to use.

Q: When you provided examples of the EXISTS predicate, your subqueries always matched columns within the subquery WHERE clause. Is this necessary?

A: You can, if you want, create an EXISTS predicate that does not match columns in the subquery, such as in the following statement:

```
SELECT TITLE, ARTIST
  FROM COMPACT_DISC_ARTISTS
 WHERE EXISTS
     ( SELECT CD_NAME
         FROM COMPACT_DISC_INVENTORY
        WHERE IN_STOCK > 10 );
```

In this case, your subquery merely checks to see whether any rows exist in the COMPACT_DISC_INVENTORY table with an IN_STOCK value greater than 10. If those rows exist, the predicate evaluates to true, which means the WHERE clause in the main SELECT statement evaluates to true. As a result, all rows in the COMPACT_DISC_ARTISTS table are returned. Using this sort of subquery is generally not very useful because it offers little advantage over a simple SELECT statement. When using EXISTS, matching columns from different tables within the subquery is essential to providing meaningful filtering for the main SELECT statement.

Quantify Comparison Predicates

SQL includes another type of predicate called a *quantified comparison predicate,* which is a type of predicate used in conjunction with a comparison operator to determine whether *any* or *all* returned values meet the search requirement. SQL supports three quantified comparison predicates: SOME, ANY, and ALL. The SOME and ANY predicates are referred to as *existential quantifiers* and are concerned with whether any returned values meet the search requirements. These two predicates are identical in meaning and can be used interchangeably. The ALL predicate is referred to as a *universal quantifier* and is concerned with whether *all* returned values meet the search requirements. Now let's take a closer look at each one.

Using the SOME and ANY Predicates

As I mentioned, the SOME and ANY predicates return identical results. For each row, the predicates compare the value in a specified column to the results of a subquery. If the comparison evaluates to true for *any* of the results, the condition has been satisfied and that row is returned. To create one of these predicates, you must specify the column name that contains the values you want to compare, the comparison operator (see the "Compare SQL Data" section), the SOME or ANY keyword, and the subquery. Although you can use either keyword, I prefer ANY because it seems more intuitive to me, but feel free to use either one.

Now let's take a look at an example to give you a better feel for how these predicates work. The example is based on the CD_RETAIL table and the CD_SALE table, which are shown in Figure 9-5.

Keep in mind that many of the tables I use to illustrate SQL concepts are not necessarily good table designs. In the case of Figure 9-5, an experienced database designer would point out that it would make more sense to combine the tables, which is true. However, these examples are designed to illustrate key SQL concepts and are not intended to illustrate good database design practices.

In this example, I want to query data from the CD_SALE table. I want to return only those rows that have a SALE value less than some of the RETAIL values in the CD_RETAIL table. The RETAIL values should be from rows that have an IN_STOCK value greater than 12. In other words, the query should return only those CDs whose sale price is less than *any* retail price of those CDs in which there are more than nine in stock. To accomplish this, I will use the following SELECT statement:

```
SELECT TITLE, SALE
  FROM CD_SALE
 WHERE SALE < ANY
     ( SELECT RETAIL
         FROM CD_RETAIL
        WHERE IN_STOCK > 12 );
```

CD_RETAIL

CD_NAME: VARCHAR(60)	RETAIL: NUMERIC(5,2)	IN_STOCK: INT
Drive All Night	5.99	12
Different Shades of Blue	11.99	42
Innervisions (Remastered)	10.00	16
The Definitive Collection	8.39	34
Rumours (Reissued)	7.99	17
Come On Over	5.99	6
Man Against Machine	9.99	8

CD_SALE

TITLE: VARCHAR(60)	SALE: NUMERIC(5,2)
Drive All Night	5.99
Different Shades of Blue	11.99
Innervisions (Remastered)	8.99
The Definitive Collection	7.99
Rumours (Reissued)	7.99
Come On Over	5.99
Man Against Machine	9.99

Figure 9-5 Using qualified comparison predicates on the CD_RETAIL and CD_SALE tables

If you want, you can use the SOME keyword rather than the ANY keyword. The query results would be the same, as shown in the following results:

```
TITLE                      SALE
-------------------------  -----
Drive All Night            5.99
Innervisions (Remastered)  8.99
The Definitive Collection  7.99
Rumours (Reissued)         7.99
Come On Over               5.99
Man Against Machine        9.99
```

Now let's look at the SELECT statement more closely. The ANY predicate contains the following subquery:

```
SELECT RETAIL
  FROM CD_RETAIL
 WHERE IN_STOCK > 12
```

If you were to execute this subquery on its own, you would receive the following results:

```
RETAIL
-------
11.99
10.00
8.39
7.99
```

The SALE value in each row in the CD_SALE table is then compared to the subquery results. For example, the The Definitive Collection row has a SALE value of 7.99. This value is compared to the subquery results to see whether 7.99 is less than *any* value. Because it is less than 11.99, 10.00, and 8.39, the predicate evaluates to true, and the row is returned. The only row that does not evaluate to true is the Different Shades of Blue row because the SALE value is 11.99, and this is not less than any of the values returned by the query results.

You can use any of the six comparison operators in an ANY or SOME predicate. If you use the greater than operator to find rows with a SALE value greater than any row in the subquery results, the results would look like this:

```
TITLE                      SALE
-------------------------  -----
Different Shades of Blue   5.99
Innervisions (Remastered)  8.99
Man Against Machine        9.99
```

NOTE

The quantified comparison predicates do not support an inverse condition like other predicates. In other words, you cannot add the NOT keyword before ANY or SOME. However, you can achieve the same results using the not equal to (<>) operator.

Using the ALL Predicate

The ALL predicate works much like the ANY and SOME predicates in that it compares column values to the subquery results. However, rather than the column values having to evaluate to true for *any* of the result values, the column values must evaluate to true for *all* the result values; otherwise, the row is not returned.

Let's return to the previous example we looked at, only this time substitute the keyword ALL for the keyword ANY. Your new SELECT statement will look like the following:

```
SELECT TITLE, SALE
  FROM CD_SALE
 WHERE SALE < ALL
     ( SELECT RETAIL
         FROM CD_RETAIL
        WHERE IN_STOCK > 12 );
```

Ask the Expert

Q: In your discussions about quantified comparison predicates, you included examples on how to use these predicates; however, the examples included only one predicate in the WHERE clause. Can you use multiple predicates when using a quantified comparison predicate?

A: Yes, you can use multiple predicates. As with any other sort of predicate, you simply connect the predicates using the AND keyword or the OR keyword. But you must make sure that the logic you're using not only makes sense in terms of the data being returned, but also in the sense of being able to understand the statement itself. As a result, the best way to treat these sorts of situations is to set off each predicate in parentheses and then connect the parenthetical expressions with AND or OR. For example, suppose you want to take the example in the section "Using the SOME and ANY Predicates" and add a LIKE predicate to it. (The example is based on Figure 9-5.) You can create a SELECT statement similar to the following:

```
SELECT TITLE, SALE
  FROM CD_SALE
 WHERE ( SALE < ANY ( SELECT RETAIL
                        FROM CD_RETAIL
                       WHERE IN_STOCK > 12 ) )
   AND ( TITLE LIKE ('%Reissued%') );
```

Notice that each predicate has been enclosed in a set of parentheses and that they are joined together by AND. If you execute this statement, your query results will meet the condition of the ANY predicate and the LIKE predicate, which specifies that the TITLE value include the word Reissued. If you wanted to, you could write these statements without enclosing the predicates in parentheses, but then the statements can start to get confusing and, in more complex structures, can start producing unexpected results.

If you execute this statement, you'll find that your query results are quite different from what they were in the previous example:

```
TITLE                      SALE
-----------------------    -----
Drive All Night            5.99
Come On Over               5.99
```

This time, only two rows are returned because they are the only ones that meet the condition of the WHERE predicate.

If you take a closer look at the statement, you'll find that the subquery returns the same values as it does in the previous examples. However, the SALE value for each row in the CD_SALE table must now be less than all the values in the subquery results. For example, the Drive All Night row contains a SALE value of 5.99. The subquery results include the values 11.99, 10.00, 8.39, and 7.99. The 5.99 value is less than all three of the subquery result values, which means that the predicate evaluates to true, so that row is included in the query results. On the other hand, the Innervisions (Remastered) row contains a SALE value of 8.99, which is not less than the 11.99 subquery value, so that row is not included in the query results.

As with the ANY and SOME predicates, you can use any of the six comparison operators in an ALL predicate. In addition, you can create any type of subquery, as long as it fits in logically with the main SELECT statement. The point to remember is that the column value must be true for all subquery results, not just some of them.

Try This 9-2 Using Subqueries in Predicates

This Try This exercise basically picks up where you left off in Try This 9-1. Once more, you'll be working with predicates, only this time it will be those that use subqueries. These are the predicates that were discussed since the last exercise. They include the IN, EXISTS, ANY, and ALL predicates. As with the previous Try This exercise, you'll apply these predicates to the tables you created in the INVENTORY database. You can download the Try_This_09.txt file, which contains the SQL statements used in this exercise.

Step by Step

1. Open the client application for your RDBMS and connect to the INVENTORY database.
2. In your first statement, you'll use an IN predicate to query data from the COMPACT_DISCS table. You want to view CD and inventory information for CDs published by Columbia. To find out which CDs these are, you must create a subquery that queries data from the CD_LABELS table. Enter and execute the following SQL statement:

```
SELECT CD_TITLE, IN_STOCK
  FROM COMPACT_DISCS
 WHERE LABEL_ID IN
```

(continued)

```
( SELECT LABEL_ID
    FROM CD_LABELS
   WHERE COMPANY_NAME = 'Columbia' );
```

Your query results should include only two rows. Both these rows have a LABEL_ID value of 835, which is the value returned by the subquery.

3. Now you will try a SELECT statement similar to the one in step 2, only this time you'll use an EXISTS predicate to return data. In addition, you will have to add a predicate to the subquery WHERE clause that matches the LABEL_ID value in the COMPACT_DISCS table to the LABEL_ID value in the CD_LABELS table. Enter and execute the following SQL statement:

```
SELECT CD_TITLE, IN_STOCK FROM COMPACT_DISCS
WHERE EXISTS
( SELECT LABEL_ID FROM CD_LABELS
  WHERE COMPACT_DISCS.LABEL_ID = CD_LABELS.LABEL_ID
    AND LABEL_ID > 832 );
```

Notice that one of the predicates in the subquery WHERE clause uses a comparison operator to look for LABEL_ID values greater than 832. If you were to look at the CD_LABELS table, you would see that six rows contain LABEL_ID values greater than 832. If you were then to match these six values to the LABEL_ID values in the COMPACT_DISCS table, you would find seven rows that would evaluate to true. These are the seven rows returned by your SELECT statement.

4. In this statement, you'll use an ANY predicate to compare LABEL_ID values in the CD_LABELS table to LABEL_ID values in the COMPACT_DISCS table that are included in rows with an IN_STOCK value greater than 25. The LABEL_ID values in the CD_LABELS table can match any values in the subquery results. Enter and execute the following SQL statement:

```
SELECT LABEL_ID, COMPANY_NAME
  FROM CD_LABELS
 WHERE LABEL_ID = ANY
     ( SELECT LABEL_ID
         FROM COMPACT_DISCS
        WHERE IN_STOCK > 25 );
```

Your query should return only six rows.

5. Now try creating the same SELECT statement in step 4, only use an ALL predicate rather than an ANY predicate. Enter and execute the following SQL statement:

```
SELECT LABEL_ID, COMPANY_NAME
  FROM CD_LABELS
 WHERE LABEL_ID = ALL
     ( SELECT LABEL_ID
         FROM COMPACT_DISCS
        WHERE IN_STOCK > 25 );
```

You'll find that no rows are returned by this query. This is because the subquery returns eight rows with five different values. The LABEL_ID value for each row in the CD_LABELS table cannot match all values, only one or some of them. The only way you would return any rows in this case would be if the subquery returned only one row or returned multiple rows all with the same value.

6. Now try modifying the SELECT statement by changing the comparison predicate in the subquery WHERE clause to greater than 40. Enter and execute the following SQL statement:

```
SELECT LABEL_ID, COMPANY_NAME
  FROM CD_LABELS
 WHERE LABEL_ID = ALL
     ( SELECT LABEL_ID
         FROM COMPACT_DISCS
        WHERE IN_STOCK > 40 );
```

   Your query results will now return one row. This is because the subquery returns only one row, which meets the condition of the ALL predicate.

7. Close the client application.

Try This Summary

In this Try This exercise, you used the IN, EXISTS, ANY, and ALL predicates to query data from the INVENTORY database. You could have also used the SOME predicate in place of the ANY predicate. Combined with the steps in Try This 9-1, your statements here should have allowed you to try a large variety of predicates. As you learn more about subqueries, you will be able to create even more elaborate predicates, ones that you can use not only in SELECT statements, but in UPDATE and DELETE statements as well. In the meantime, I suggest that you experiment with various types of SELECT statements and try different predicates within those statements to see exactly what types of query results you can receive.

Chapter 9 Self Test

1. In which SELECT statement clause do you include predicates?
2. Which comparison operator symbol should you use to express a not equal condition?

   A <=

   B >=

   C <>

   D =<

3. Which keywords can you use to combine predicates in a WHERE clause?

4. You want to query a table that includes the PRICE column. You want to ensure that all rows returned have a PRICE value of 13.99. What predicate should you use?

5. You create the following SQL statement:

```
SELECT CD_TITLE, RETAIL_PRICE
  FROM CDS_ON_HAND
 WHERE RETAIL_PRICE >= 14
   AND RETAIL_PRICE <= 16;
```

   What predicate can you use in place of the two predicates shown in this statement?

6. What keyword can you add to a BETWEEN predicate to find the inverse of the condition specified by the predicate?

7. When is a null value used in a column?

8. You want to query a table to determine which values are null. What type of predicate should you use?

9. You're creating a SELECT statement that queries the ARTISTS_BIO table. You want to return all columns in the table, but you want to return only those rows that do not contain null values in the PLACE_OF_BIRTH column. Which SELECT statement should you use?

10. You're querying the CD_INVENTORY table. You want to view all columns, but you want to view only rows that contain the word Blue in the name of the CD. The names are stored in the CD_TITLE column. Which SELECT statement should you use?

11. What is the difference between a percentage sign and an underscore when used in a LIKE predicate?

12. What two types of data sources can you use in an IN predicate?

13. Which type of predicate is concerned only with determining whether or not a subquery returns any rows?

14. What column names must be specified in an EXISTS predicate?

15. You're creating a SELECT statement that includes a predicate in the WHERE clause. You want to use a comparison operator to compare the values in one of the columns to the results of a subquery. You want the predicate to evaluate to true for any of the subquery results. Which type of predicate should you use?

    A EXISTS

    B ANY

    C ALL

    D IN

16. What is the difference between a SOME predicate and an ANY predicate?

17. How does the ALL predicate differ from the SOME predicate?

Chapter 10

Working with Functions and Value Expressions

Key Skills & Concepts

- Use Set Functions
- Use Value Functions
- Use Value Expressions
- Use Special Values

In earlier parts of the book, you have been briefly introduced to various value-related functions and expressions. These values and expressions are used in examples and Try This exercises in a number of chapters to demonstrate different components of SQL. In this chapter, I take a closer look at many of these values and expressions, focusing on those that you are most likely to use as a beginning SQL programmer. You should keep in mind, however, that this chapter covers only a portion of the many types of functions and expressions supported by SQL. In addition, SQL implementations can vary greatly with regard to which SQL functions and expressions they support, how those values and expressions are implemented, and what nonstandard functions and expressions they include in their products in addition to the standard ones. Be sure to check the product documentation to determine what functionality is supported. In general, I include in this chapter those functions and expressions most commonly supported by SQL implementations.

Use Set Functions

In Chapter 3, I introduce the concept of a function. As you might recall, a function is a named operation that performs predefined tasks that you can't normally perform by using SQL statements alone. It is a type of routine that takes input parameters, which are enclosed in parentheses, and returns values based on those parameters. An important property of functions is that each execution of a function returns exactly one data value, and this is why functions can be used in place of table column names in the SELECT list of a query—the function returns a single value for each row processed by the query. You have already seen examples of functions, such as SUM and AVG. Both of these functions are known as set functions. A *set function*, sometimes referred to as an *aggregate* function, processes or calculates data and returns the appropriate values. Set functions require that the data be grouped in some way, such as would be the case if the GROUP BY clause were used in a SELECT statement. If the rows are not explicitly grouped in some way, the entire table is treated as one group.

In this section, I discuss five set functions: COUNT, MAX, MIN, SUM, and AVG. These functions are all commonly supported in SQL implementations. For all the set functions, I provide examples of how you would use them in the SELECT clause of a SELECT statement. The examples are based on the table shown in Figure 10-1.

ARTIST_NAME: VARCHAR(60)	CD_NAME: VARCHAR(60)	NUMBER_SOLD: INT
Glen Hansard	Drive All Night	23
Joe Bonamassa	Different Shades of Blue	45
Stevie Wonder	Innervisions (Remastered)	34
Stevie Wonder	The Definitive Collection	23
Fleetwood Mac	Rumours (Reissued)	34
Shania Twain	Come On Over	54
Garth Brooks	Man Against Machine	12
Joshua Bell	Bach	20
Pink Floyd	Dark Side of the Moon	29
Miles Davis	Kind of Blue	18

Figure 10-1 The ARTIST_CD_SALES table

Using the COUNT Function

The first set function that we'll look at is the COUNT function. As the name implies, the COUNT function counts the number of rows in a table or the number of values in a column, as specified in a SELECT statement. When you use the COUNT function, you must specify a column name to count the number of non-null values in a column, or an asterisk to count all the rows in a table regardless of null values. For example, if you want to know the total number of rows in the ARTIST_CD_SALES table, you can use the following SELECT statement:

```
SELECT COUNT(*) AS TOTAL_ROWS
  FROM ARTIST_CD_SALES;
```

In this statement, the COUNT function is used with an asterisk—in parentheses—to count every row in the ARTIST_CD_SALES table and return the total count. The returned value is listed in the TOTAL_ROWS column, a name given to the column returned in the query results, as shown in the following results:

```
TOTAL_ROWS
----------
10
```

As you can see, the query results include only one value (one row with one column), as can be expected of a set function used without any row grouping. The value of 10 indicates that the ARTIST_CD_SALES table contains 10 rows.

As with any other sort of SELECT statement, you can qualify your query results by adding the necessary clauses to the statement. For example, suppose you want to find out how many rows include a NUMBER_SOLD value greater than 20. You can modify your SELECT statement to include a WHERE clause:

```
SELECT COUNT(*) AS TOTAL_ROWS
  FROM ARTIST_CD_SALES
 WHERE NUMBER_SOLD > 20;
```

The value returned will now be 7 rather than 10 because only seven rows meet the search condition specified in the WHERE clause.

You might find that instead of querying the number of rows in a table, you want to know the number of values in a given column (excluding null values). In this case, you would specify the column name rather than the asterisk. For example, suppose you modify the SELECT statement shown in the last example to count values in the ARTIST_NAME column:

```
SELECT COUNT(ARTIST_NAME) AS TOTAL_ARTISTS
  FROM ARTIST_CD_SALES
 WHERE NUMBER_SOLD > 20;
```

When you execute this query, the value returned is again 7. This means that seven ARTIST_NAME values have a NUMBER_SOLD value greater than 20. However, this statement doesn't account for ARTIST_NAME values that might be duplicated. If you want to arrive at a count that takes into consideration duplicate values, you can add the DISTINCT keyword to the COUNT function:

```
SELECT COUNT(DISTINCT ARTIST_NAME) AS TOTAL_ARTISTS
  FROM ARTIST_CD_SALES
 WHERE NUMBER_SOLD > 20;
```

This time, a value of 6 is returned rather than 7. This is because the ARTIST_NAME column includes two instances of the Stevie Wonder value. The column contains only six unique values that meet the condition set forth in the search criteria.

NOTE

Keep in mind that the SELECT statement is processed in a specific order: first the FROM clause, then the WHERE clause, and then the SELECT clause. As a result, the COUNT function applies only to the rows that meet the search condition defined in the WHERE clause. Rows that are not included in the results of the WHERE clause have no bearing on the COUNT function. For more information about the SELECT statement, see Chapter 7.

As already mentioned, if the column specified in the COUNT function contains null values, those values are not included in the count. For example, if we were to add a row to the ARTIST_CD_SALES table with an ARTIST_NAME value of null and a NUMBER_SOLD value greater than 20, the SELECT statement shown in the previous example would still return a value of 6 because the null value would not be counted. However, if you use an asterisk rather than a column name in the COUNT function, all rows are counted, even if some contain null values.

Using the MAX and MIN Functions

The MAX and MIN functions are so similar that it is worth discussing them together. The MAX function returns the highest value from the specified column, and the MIN function returns the lowest value. Both functions require that you specify a column name. For example, suppose you want to return the highest value from the NUMBER_SOLD column in the ARTIST_CD_SALES table. Your SELECT statement would look like the following:

```
SELECT MAX(NUMBER_SOLD) AS MAX_SOLD
  FROM ARTIST_CD_SALES;
```

When you execute this statement, your query results will include only one value (one row and one column), as shown in the following results:

```
MAX_SOLD
--------
54
```

This result, by itself, is not particularly helpful. It would be nice if your query results also included the name of the artist and the CD. However, SQL does not support a SELECT statement such as the following:

```
SELECT ARTIST_NAME, CD_NAME, MAX(NUMBER_SOLD)
  FROM ARTIST_CD_SALES;
```

Because set functions treat data as groups, you cannot specify the artist name and CD name without somehow grouping the data together. As it stands now, the MAX function treats the entire table as one group; however, neither the ARTIST_NAME values nor the CD_NAME values are grouped together in any way, so the SELECT clause becomes illogical.

NOTE

MySQL releases prior to 5.7.5 will actually process the statement shown in the previous example, but the values of ARTIST_NAME and CD_NAME will likely not be the correct values for the row in the ARTIST_CD_SALES table that contains the maximum value for NUMBER_SOLD. This nonstandard behavior could be disabled using a startup parameter. Fortunately, starting with release 5.7.5, MySQL follows the SQL standard and rejects SELECT statements that contain a mixture of set functions and ordinary column expressions when the GROUP BY clause fails to properly group the rows in the table. (I discuss the GROUP BY clause in more detail a little later in this section.)

Whenever you include a set function in an SQL statement, then every argument in the SELECT list must either be a set function or be included in a group (using the GROUP BY clause described a little later in this topic). One way around this is to use a subquery in the WHERE clause to return the maximum value and then return the necessary information based on that value, as shown in the following example:

```
SELECT ARTIST_NAME, CD_NAME, NUMBER_SOLD
  FROM ARTIST_CD_SALES
 WHERE NUMBER_SOLD = ( SELECT MAX(NUMBER_SOLD)
                          FROM ARTIST_CD_SALES );
```

The subquery finds the maximum value (54) and uses that value as a condition in the WHERE clause. The NUMBER_SOLD value must equal 54 as long as that is the highest NUMBER_SOLD value in the table. Once you define the necessary search condition in the WHERE clause, you can then use these results to return the information you need. If you execute this statement, one row is returned (assuming only one row contains the value 54 in the NUMBER_SOLD column):

```
ARTIST_NAME    CD_NAME                    NUMBER_SOLD
------------   -----------------------    -----------
Shania Twain   Come On Over               54
```

As you can see, you now have all the information you need to determine which artist and CD have sold the greatest number.

As I said earlier, the MAX and MIN functions are very similar. If you replace MIN for MAX in the previous example, your query results will look like the following:

```
ARTIST_NAME        CD_NAME                 NUMBER_SOLD
----------------   --------------------    -----------
Garth Brooks       Man Against Machine     12
```

The Man Against Machine row is returned because that is the row with the lowest NUMBER_SOLD value and there are no other rows with the same value.

The MAX and MIN functions are not limited to numeric data. You can also use them to compare character strings. For example, suppose you want to know which artist comes first alphabetically. The following statement will return Fleetwood Mac:

```
SELECT MIN(ARTIST_NAME) AS LOW_NAME
  FROM ARTIST_CD_SALES;
```

If you use the MAX function, the statement will return Stevie Wonder.

NOTE

It is more common for database designers to place first names and last names in separate columns because this is a more flexible design. I've included both names in one column to provide you with simple examples of how various statements work. If the names were separated into two columns, the MIN or MAX function would need to be used with the appropriate column.

Now let's back up a little and return to the idea of grouping data. As I mentioned, a set function treats a table as one group if no grouping has been implemented. However, you can easily use a GROUP BY clause to group data. Suppose you want to know the maximum amount sold by each artist. You can group data based on the ARTIST_NAME values:

```
SELECT ARTIST_NAME, MAX(NUMBER_SOLD) AS MAX_SOLD
  FROM ARTIST_CD_SALES
 WHERE NUMBER_SOLD > 20
 GROUP BY ARTIST_NAME;
```

The WHERE clause returns only those rows with a NUMBER_SOLD value greater than 20. These rows are then grouped together according to the ARTIST_NAME values. Once they're grouped together, the maximum amount is returned for each artist, as shown in the following query results:

```
ARTIST_NAME     MAX_SOLD
-------------   --------
Fleetwood Mac   34
Glen Hansard    23
Joe Bonamassa   45
Pink Floyd      29
Shania Twain    54
Stevie Wonder   34
```

The GROUP BY clause creates six groups, one for each artist that meets the search condition defined in the WHERE clause. Of these six groups, only one is made up of duplicate values: Stevie Wonder. Because there are two Stevie Wonder rows in the ARTIST_CD_SALES table, there are two NUMBER_SOLD values: 34 and 23. As you can see, the highest value is 34, which is the value that's included in the query results for the Stevie Wonder group. If the MIN function had been used in the SELECT statement, the 23 value would have been returned. As for the other five artist groups, because there is only one value for each of them, the same value is returned regardless of whether the MAX or the MIN function is used.

Using the SUM Function

Unlike the MIN and MAX functions, which select the lowest and highest values from a column, the SUM function adds column values together. This is particularly handy when you want to find the totals for grouped data (although the SUM function, like any other set function, treats the entire table as a single group if data hasn't been explicitly grouped together).

To better understand the SUM function, let's take the last example we looked at and modify it slightly:

```
SELECT ARTIST_NAME, SUM(NUMBER_SOLD) AS TOTAL_SOLD
  FROM ARTIST_CD_SALES
 WHERE NUMBER_SOLD > 20
 GROUP BY ARTIST_NAME;
```

As you saw before, the WHERE clause returns only those rows with a NUMBER_SOLD value greater than 20. These rows are then grouped together according to the ARTIST_NAME values. Once they're grouped together, the total amount for each artist group is returned in the query results:

```
ARTIST_NAME     TOTAL_SOLD
-------------   ----------
Fleetwood Mac   34
Glen Hansard    23
Joe Bonamassa   45
Pink Floyd      29
Shania Twain    54
Stevie Wonder   57
```

Notice that the query results include the same six groups that were returned in the previous example. The only difference is that the TOTAL_SOLD value in the Stevie Wonder row is 57, as opposed to 34 or 23. The SUM function adds these two values together and returns a value of 57. Because the other five groups are each made up of only one entry, their TOTAL_SOLD values are the same as their NUMBER_SOLD values in the ARTIST_CD_SALES table.

You do not have to use a GROUP BY clause in a SELECT statement that uses a SUM function. You can create a SELECT statement as simple as the following:

```
SELECT SUM(NUMBER_SOLD) AS TOTAL_SOLD
  FROM ARTIST_CD_SALES;
```

This statement merely adds together all the values in the NUMBER_SOLD column and returns a value of 292. By itself, this is not always the most helpful information, which is why using the function along with a GROUP BY clause is far more effective.

Using the AVG Function

As you probably realize, the AVG function merely averages the values in a specified column. Like the SUM function, it is most effective when used along with a GROUP BY clause, although it can be used without the clause, as shown in the following example:

```
SELECT AVG(NUMBER_SOLD) AS AVG_SOLD
  FROM ARTIST_CD_SALES;
```

This statement returns a value of 29, which is based on the NUMBER_SOLD values in the ARTIST_CD_SALES table. (A few implementations, such as MySQL, will display 29.2 instead of 29, while most implementations will truncate the value to an integer to match the data type of the NUMBER_SOLD column.) This means that for all the CDs listed in the table, an average of 29 for each one has been sold. Although you might find this information helpful, it might be more useful to you if you were to create a statement that groups data together:

```
SELECT ARTIST_NAME, AVG(NUMBER_SOLD) AS AVG_SOLD
  FROM ARTIST_CD_SALES
```

```
WHERE NUMBER_SOLD > 20
GROUP BY ARTIST_NAME;
```

If you execute this statement, you will receive the following query results:

```
ARTIST_NAME     AVG_SOLD
-------------   --------
Fleetwood Mac   34
Glen Hansard    23
Joe Bonamassa   45
Pink Floyd      29
Shania Twain    54
Stevie Wonder   28
```

As in the previous examples, six groups are created, and for each group, an average is calculated based on the values in the NUMBER_SOLD column. For the Stevie Wonder row, this average is based on the NUMBER_SOLD values of 34 and 23. For the other two rows, the average is the same as the NUMBER_SOLD value because there is only one row for each artist.

NOTE

The precision of the values returned by the AVG function depends on the column's data type, whether decimals are used, and how the SQL implementation averages numbers. For example, the exact average for the Stevie Wonder row is 28.5, but because the NUMBER_SOLD column is configured with an INT (integer) data type, most SQL implementations drop the .5 to show the result as a whole number, as shown in my latest sample query results. MySQL, on the other hand, displays the decimal value 28.5, and some other implementations may round 28.5 up to 29. Most SQL implementations include functions for rounding and truncating, which provide more control over the precision of the returned numeric values.

Use Value Functions

Value functions are a type of function that allow you to return a value that in some way calculates or derives information from the data stored within your tables or from the SQL implementation itself. Value functions are similar to set functions in the sense that they perform some sort of behind-the-scenes action to arrive at that value. However, value functions are different from set functions in that they do not require that data be grouped together.

SQL supports a number of value functions. Which functions are supported in which SQL implementations can vary widely. In addition, the meaning of a function name can sometimes vary from one implementation to the next. Still, there are some consistencies among the various implementations, and those are the value functions on which I focus.

The value functions that I discuss fall into two categories: string value functions and datetime value functions. In order to illustrate how these functions work, I use the SALES_DATES table, shown in Figure 10-2.

COMPACT_DISC: VARCHAR(60)	DATE_SOLD: TIMESTAMP
Drive All Night	2015-10-22 10:58:05.120
Different Shades of Blue	2015-01-22 12:02:05.033
Innervisions (Remastered)	2015-01-22 16:15:22.930
The Definitive Collection	2015-01-23 11:29:14.223
Rumours (Reissued)	2015-01-23 13:32:45.547
Come On Over	2015-01-23 15:51:15.730
Man Against Machine	2015-01-23 17:01:32.270
Bach	2015-01-24 10:46:35.123
Dark Side of the Moon	2015-01-24 12:19:13.843
Kind of Blue	2015-01-24 14:15:09.673

Figure 10-2 The SALES_DATES table

Working with String Value Functions

A string value function allows you to manipulate character string data to produce a precise value that is based on the original character string. When using a string value function, you must supply the character string as a parameter of the function. That parameter is then converted to a new value according to the purpose of that function and any other parameters that might be specified. In this section, I introduce you to three string value functions: SUBSTRING, UPPER, and LOWER.

Using the SUBSTRING String Value Function

The SUBSTRING string value function extracts a defined number of characters from an identified character string in order to create a new string. That original character string can be derived from a column or can be explicitly stated. In both cases, the character string is passed as a parameter of the SUBSTRING function, along with a start point and, optionally, a length specification. For example, suppose you want to return only the first 10 characters of the values in the COMPACT_DISC column in the SALES_DATES table. You can create a SELECT statement similar to the following:

```
SELECT SUBSTRING(COMPACT_DISC FROM 1 FOR 10) AS SHORT_NAME
  FROM SALES_DATES;
```

The SUBSTRING function includes three parameters. The first is the name of the column, COMPACT_DISC, which identifies the source used for the character string. The next parameter, FROM 1, indicates that the function will start counting at the first character. The third parameter, 10, follows the FOR keyword. The FOR 10 parameter, which is optional, indicates that up to 10 characters will be included in the new character string.

NOTE

Most implementations, including SQL Server and Oracle, do not use the keywords FROM and FOR—you simply separate the parameters using commas. Also, in Oracle, the function is named SUBSTR. Here is the same statement modified for Oracle:

```
SELECT SUBSTR(COMPACT_DISC, 1, 10) AS SHORT_NAME
  FROM SALES_DATES;
```

Here is the same statement modified for implementations (such as SQL Server) that do not accept the FROM and FOR keywords in the SUBSTRING function:

```
SELECT SUBSTRING(COMPACT_DISC, 1, 10) AS SHORT_NAME
  FROM SALES_DATES;
```

If you execute this SELECT statement, you'll receive the following query results:

```
SHORT_NAME
----------
Drive All
Different
Innervisio
The Defini
Rumours (R
Come On Ov
Man Agains
Bach
Dark Side
Kind of Bl
```

Notice that only the first 10 characters of each COMPACT_DISC value are included in the results. For those values less than 10 characters, the full name appears.

The FROM parameter can accept a negative number or a zero as a parameter, assuming your SQL implementation allows it. When using a negative number or a zero, keep in mind that 1 represents what you would think of as a normal starting position. The next character to the left of 1 is 0. The character to the left of 0 is –1, and so on. The FOR parameter counts characters starting at the starting point. If a zero or a negative number is used, the SUBSTRING function acts as though characters actually exist in those places. For example, suppose you modify the preceding SELECT statement as follows:

```
SELECT SUBSTRING(COMPACT_DISC FROM -2 FOR 10) AS SHORT_NAME
  FROM SALES_DATES;
```

If you execute this statement, only the first seven characters of each name would be returned. If you use a zero instead, only the first nine characters will be returned. It is only when you use a FROM parameter of 1 that you return exactly the number of characters (from the character string) that are specified by the FOR parameter.

NOTE

MySQL and Oracle handle FROM parameter values that are less than 1 differently. If you specify a FROM (starting position) value of 0, the result will begin with the last position of the string; a FROM value of –1 will start with the next to the last position in the string, and so forth. In other words, FROM values less than 1 wrap backward, starting with the end of the string. If the previous example is run in MySQL or Oracle, the FROM value of –2 and TO value of 10 will return rows containing only the last 3 positions of each COMPACT_DISC column value. (For Oracle, recall the function name must be SUBSTR instead of SUBSTRING, and the FROM and TO keywords have to be removed with the parameters separated by commas.)

The SUBSTRING function is not limited to the SELECT clause. In fact, using it in a WHERE clause can be quite useful when defining a search condition. For example, the following SELECT statement uses the SUBSTRING function to return rows that start with D:

```
SELECT COMPACT_DISC, DATE_SOLD
  FROM SALES_DATES
 WHERE SUBSTRING(COMPACT_DISC FROM 1 FOR 1) = 'D';
```

In this statement, the SUBSTRING function returns the first character of the COMPACT_DISC values and compares them to the D value. Only three rows are included in the query results:

```
COMPACT_DISC               DATE_SOLD
------------------------   -----------------------
Drive All Night            2015-01-22 10:58:05.120
Different Shades of Blue   2015-01-22 12:02:05.033
Dark Side of the Moon      2015-01-24 12:19:13.843
```

All three rows in the query results have a COMPACT_DISC value that starts with D. No other rows meet the search condition specified in the WHERE clause.

NOTE

The handling of datetime data varies considerably across SQL implementations, so the results from your DBMS may look quite different with respect to the DATE_SOLD column. For example, MySQL will truncate the fractional parts of a second (the last four positions of the DATE_SOLD column values).

Using the UPPER and LOWER String Value Functions

The UPPER and LOWER string value functions are quite similar in that they are both used to convert characters from one case to another. The UPPER function allows you to convert a character string to all uppercase. The LOWER function allows you to convert a string to all lowercase. For example, suppose you want to modify the SELECT statement shown in the last example to return all COMPACT_DISC values in uppercase. Your SELECT statement would now include an UPPER function:

```
SELECT UPPER(COMPACT_DISC) AS TITLE, DATE_SOLD
  FROM SALES_DATES
 WHERE SUBSTRING(COMPACT_DISC FROM 1 FOR 1) = 'D';
```

Your query results are the same as in the last example, only this time the CD titles are all in uppercase, as shown in the following results:

```
COMPACT_DISC                DATE_SOLD
-------------------------   -----------------------
DRIVE ALL NIGHT             2015-01-22 10:58:05.120
DIFFERENT SHADES OF BLUE    2015-01-22 12:02:05.033
DARK SIDE OF THE MOON       2015-01-24 12:19:13.843
```

If you had used the LOWER function instead of the UPPER, the CD titles would all be in lowercase, with no initial capitalization at the beginning of the words. These functions are also quite useful for comparing data in case-sensitive implementations when you don't know what case was used in storing the data, or when you want to be sure data appears in a particular case when you are inserting, updating, or converting data from one database to another.

Working with Datetime Value Functions

Datetime value functions provide information about the current date and time. Each function returns a value based on the time or date (or both) as they are configured in the operating system. SQL supports five datetime value functions, which are described in Table 10-1.

Value Function	Description
CURRENT_DATE	Returns a value that represents the current date.
CURRENT_TIME	Returns a value that represents the current time. The value includes information about the current time zone, relative to Coordinated Universal Time (UTC), which used to be called Greenwich Mean Time (GMT).
CURRENT_TIMESTAMP	Returns a value that represents the current date and time. The value includes information about the current time zone, relative to UTC.
LOCALTIME	Returns a value that represents the current time.
LOCALTIMESTAMP	Returns a value that represents the current date and time.

Table 10-1 Datetime Value Functions Supported by SQL

NOTE

SQL implementations vary widely with regard to how they implement datetime functionality; consequently, the implementation of datetime functions also varies. For example, SQL Server supports only the CURRENT_TIMESTAMP datetime value function. On the other hand, Oracle supports the CURRENT_DATE, CURRENT_TIMESTAMP, and LOCALTIMESTAMP datetime value functions, but not the CURRENT_TIME and LOCALTIME functions. Yet MySQL supports all five of them. In addition, the exact values generated by these functions can vary from implementation to implementation. For example, the query results will not always include information about the current time zone, and some might represent time using a 24-hour clock rather than A.M. and P.M.

Because the CURRENT_TIMESTAMP datetime value function is supported by SQL Server, MySQL and Oracle, let's take a closer look at implementing that one. However, keep in mind that implementing any of the SQL datetime functions is the same process, depending on which functions are supported by the specific SQL implementation in which you're working. By understanding how the CURRENT_TIMESTAMP function works, you'll gain a better understanding of how all functions work. However, be sure to check your implementation's documentation for more information on any of the functions that are supported by that product.

Depending on the SQL implementation, you can use the CURRENT_TIMESTAMP function in a SELECT statement to simply retrieve the current timestamp information. As you might expect with anything related to datetime functionality, the way in which you call a function can vary. However, in some cases you might be able to use a statement as basic as the following:

```
SELECT CURRENT_TIMESTAMP;
```

This statement will retrieve the current time and date in some implementations.

NOTE

Some implementations, including Oracle, require a FROM clause in all SELECT statements. Oracle provides a dummy table named DUAL to be used in situations where a query contains only a value function. Here is the previous SELECT statement modified to run on Oracle:

```
SELECT CURRENT_TIMESTAMP FROM DUAL;
```

Regardless of how you need to write your SELECT statement, in all likelihood using a CURRENT_TIMESTAMP function in this way is not very useful. You'll probably make better use of datetime functions by using them to compare data or to insert data automatically.

NOTE

Most SQL implementations have special functions for handling datetime data. For example, SQL Server provides the getdate function to return the current date, while Oracle provides the SYSDATE special value for the same purpose. The earliest SQL implementations did not include any support for datetime data types, but as soon as relational databases became popular in business applications, users demanded them. This left vendors scrambling to add the new features, and since there was no SQL standard to follow, wide variation across implementations was the result. Products such as MySQL that were developed after the standard have fewer such variations. As always, check your vendor documentation for details.

Suppose, for example, you wanted the SALES_DATES table (shown in Figure 10-2) to insert the current time and date automatically in your table each time you add a new row. Your table definition might look something like the following:

```
CREATE TABLE SALES_DATES
( COMPACT_DISC  VARCHAR(60),
  DATE_SOLD     TIMESTAMP     DEFAULT CURRENT_TIMESTAMP );
```

In this table definition, the DATE_SOLD column has been assigned a default value that is based on the CURRENT_TIMESTAMP function. Each time a row is added to the table, the datetime value is inserted into the DATE_SOLD column for that row. As a result, you can create INSERT statements that specify only the COMPACT_DISC value. The current date and time are then automatically added to the DATE_SOLD column at the time the row is added.

NOTE

SQL Server uses the TIMESTAMP data type for an entirely different purpose than what is described in the SQL Standard. Therefore, to create the SALES_DATES table in SQL Server, the DATE_SOLD column must have a data type of DATETIME instead of TIMESTAMP.

Use Value Expressions

A value expression is a type of expression that returns a data value. The expression can include column names, values, mathematical operators, keywords, or other elements that together create a sort of formula or expression that returns a single value. For example, you can combine the values in two columns to create one value, or you can perform operations on the value in one column to create a new value.

In this section, we will look at numeric value expressions as well as the CASE and CAST value expressions. To demonstrate how several of these expressions work, we will use the CD_TRACKING table, shown in Figure 10-3.

CD_NAME: VARCHAR(60)	CD_CATEGORY: CHAR(4)	IN_STOCK: INT	ON_ORDER: INT	SOLD: INT
Drive All Night	ALTR	19	16	23
Different Shades of Blue	BLUS	28	22	45
Innervisions (Remastered)	RNBL	12	11	34
The Definitive Collection	RNBL	6	17	23
Rumours (Reissued)	CROK	14	14	34
Come On Over	CTRY	15	18	54
Man Against Machine	CTRY	8	5	12
Bach	CLAS	6	8	20
Dark Side of the Moon	CROK	10	6	29
Kind of Blue	JAZZ	11	10	18

Figure 10-3 The CD_TRACKING table

Working with Numeric Value Expressions

Numeric value expressions are expressions that use mathematic operators to perform calculations on numeric data values stored in your tables. You can use these operators to add, subtract, multiply, and divide these values. Table 10-2 shows the four operators that you can use to create numeric value expressions.

You can build numeric value expressions in much the same way as you build mathematical formulas. The basic principles are the same. For example, multiplication and division take precedence over addition and subtraction, and elements that should be calculated first are

Expression	Operator	Example
Addition	+	IN_STOCK + ON_ORDER
Subtraction	–	SOLD – (IN_STOCK + ON_ORDER)
Multiplication	*	IN_STOCK * 2
Division	/	SOLD / 2

Table 10-2 Using Numeric Value Expressions to Calculate Data

enclosed in parentheses; otherwise, each operation is calculated according to precedence and the order in which it is written. For example, the formula 2 + 2 * 5 / 4 equals 4.5; however, the formula (2 + 2) * 5 / 4 equals 5. In the first formula, 2 is multiplied by 5, then divided by 4, and then added to 2. In the second formula, 2 is added to 2, then multiplied by 5, and then divided by 4.

Now let's take a look at an example of a numeric value expression. Suppose you want to add the IN_STOCK column to the ON_ORDER column in the CD_TRACKING table. You can create a SELECT statement similar to the following:

```
SELECT CD_NAME, IN_STOCK, ON_ORDER, (IN_STOCK + ON_ORDER) AS TOTAL
  FROM CD_TRACKING;
```

As you can see, the SELECT clause first specifies three column names: CD_NAME, IN_STOCK, and ON_ORDER. These are then followed by a numeric value expression: (IN_STOCK + ON_ORDER). Values from the IN_STOCK and ON_ORDER columns are added together and included in the query results under a column named TOTAL, as shown in the following results:

```
CD_NAME                         IN_STOCK  ON_ORDER  TOTAL
------------------------------  --------  --------  -----
Drive All Night                 19        16        35
Different Shades of Blue        28        22        50
Innervisions (Remastered)       12        11        23
The Definitive Collection       6         17        23
Rumours (Reissued)              14        14        28
Come On Over                    15        18        33
Man Against Machine             8         5         13
Bach                            6         8         14
Dark Side of the Moon           10        6         16
Kind of Blue                    11        10        21
```

For each row, a value has been added to the TOTAL column that adds together the values in the IN_STOCK column and the ON_ORDER column.

Numeric value expressions are not limited to the SELECT clause. For example, you can use one in a WHERE clause to specify a search condition. Suppose you want to return the same results as in the previous SELECT statement but only for those CDs with a TOTAL value greater than 25. It is tempting to try to use the column alias (TOTAL in this example) in the WHERE clause, but you cannot. Remember that the SELECT clause is processed *after* the FROM and WHERE clauses, which means that the column name TOTAL is not defined at the time the WHERE clause is processed. Instead you need to repeat the value expression in the WHERE clause. You can modify your statement as follows:

```
SELECT CD_NAME, IN_STOCK, ON_ORDER, (IN_STOCK + ON_ORDER) AS TOTAL
  FROM CD_TRACKING
 WHERE (IN_STOCK + ON_ORDER) > 25;
```

Now your search results include only four rows, as shown in the following:

```
CD_NAME                          IN_STOCK  ON_ORDER  TOTAL
-------------------------------  --------  --------  -----
Drive All Night                  19        16        35
Different Shades of Blue         28        22        50
Rumours (Reissued)               14        14        28
Come On Over                     15        18        33
```

Numeric value operators can also be combined with each other to create more complex expressions. In the next example, I include an additional expression that calculates three sets of values and combines them into one column in the query results:

```
SELECT CD_NAME, IN_STOCK, ON_ORDER, (IN_STOCK + ON_ORDER) AS TOTAL,
       SOLD, (SOLD - (IN_STOCK + ON_ORDER)) AS SHORTAGE
  FROM CD_TRACKING
 WHERE (IN_STOCK + ON_ORDER) > 25;
```

This statement allows you to calculate how many CDs you have available (IN_STOCK + ON_ORDER) as compared to how many you sold. The difference is then placed in the SHORTAGE column in the query results. If you have sold more CDs than are available, a positive number is placed in the SHORTAGE column. If, on the other hand, there are enough CDs available, a negative number is created. The following query results show the amounts calculated when you execute the SELECT statement:

```
CD_NAME                          IN_STOCK  ON_ORDER  TOTAL  SOLD  SHORTAGE
-------------------------------  --------  --------  -----  ----  --------
Drive All Night                  19        16        35     23    -12
Different Shades of Blue         28        22        50     45    -5
Rumours (Reissued)               14        14        28     34    6
Come On Over                     15        18        33     54    21
```

The query results now include two calculated columns: TOTAL and SHORTAGE. All other values (IN_STOCK, ON_ORDER, and SOLD) are taken directly from the table.

As you can see, numeric value expressions are quite flexible and can be used in many different ways. In addition to the methods we've looked at so far, you can combine column values with specified values. For example, suppose you want to see how many CDs you would have available if you doubled the amount you had on order for those CDs where there are fewer than 15 available:

```
SELECT CD_NAME, IN_STOCK, ON_ORDER, (IN_STOCK + ON_ORDER) AS TOTAL,
      (IN_STOCK + ON_ORDER * 2) AS DOUBLE_ORDER
  FROM CD_TRACKING
 WHERE (IN_STOCK + ON_ORDER) < 15;
```

The second numeric value expression in this statement multiplies the ON_ORDER value by 2, adds it to the IN_STOCK value, and inserts the total into the DOUBLE_ORDER column of the query results, as shown in the following results:

```
CD_NAME                    IN_STOCK  ON_ORDER  TOTAL  DOUBLE_ORDER
-------------------------  --------  --------  -----  ------------
Man Against Machine        8         5         13     18
Bach                       6         8         14     22
```

The query results include only two rows that meet the condition of the WHERE clause. For each of these rows, the IN_STOCK and ON_ORDER columns are calculated to provide you with data that can be useful to you, depending on your needs. The nice part is that these values do not have to be stored in the database. Instead, they're calculated when you execute the SELECT statement, rather than having to maintain tables with additional data.

Using the CASE Value Expression

A CASE value expression allows you to set up a series of conditions that modify specified values returned by your SQL statement. You can change the way a value is represented or calculate a new value. Each value is modified according to the condition specified within the CASE value expression. A CASE value expression includes the CASE keyword and a list of conditions. The last condition provides a default condition if none of the previous conditions have been met. The value expression is then closed by using the END keyword.

Let's take a look at an example to give you a better idea of how this works. Suppose you want to increase the number of CDs you have on order, but you want to increase the amount for only certain CDs. In addition, you want to base how many CDs you add to the order on the current amount. Before you actually update the table, you can look at what the new values would be by creating a SELECT statement that queries the CD_TRACKING table, as shown in the following example:

```
SELECT CD_NAME, ON_ORDER,
 CASE
  WHEN ON_ORDER < 6 THEN ON_ORDER + 4
  WHEN ON_ORDER BETWEEN 6 AND 8 THEN ON_ORDER + 2
  ELSE ON_ORDER
 END AS NEW_ORDERS
  FROM CD_TRACKING
 WHERE ON_ORDER < 11;
```

In this statement, three columns are specified: CD_NAME, ON_ORDER, and NEW_ORDERS. The NEW_ORDERS column is the column created for the query results. It will contain the values updated by the CASE value expression. The expression itself is made up of the CASE keyword, two WHEN/THEN clauses, one ELSE clause, and the END keyword. The expression is followed by the AS keyword and the column name NEW_ORDERS, which is the column name that appears in the query results. Each WHEN/THEN clause represents one of the conditions. For example, the first clause specifies that if the ON_ORDER value is less than 6, then 4 should be added to the value. The second WHEN/THEN clause specifies that if the ON_ORDER value falls within the range of 6 though 8, then 2 should be added to the value.

After the WHEN/THEN clauses, the ELSE clause specifies the final condition. If the value does not meet the conditions defined in the WHEN/THEN clauses, the ELSE clause specifies a default condition. In the case of the preceding SELECT statement, the ELSE clause merely refers to the ON_ORDER column, without specifying any modifications. (It would be the same as saying ON_ORDER + 0.) In other words, if none of the WHEN/THEN conditions are met, the ON_ORDER value stays the same. If you were to execute the SELECT statement, you would receive the following results:

```
CD_NAME                      ON_ORDER  NEW_ORDERS
---------------------------  --------  ----------
Man Against Machine          5         9
Bach                         8         10
Dark Side of the Moon        6         8
Kind of Blue                 10        10
```

As you can see, the Man Against Machine row is increased by 4, the Kind of Blue row is not increased at all, and the other two rows are increased by 2.

In addition to modifying values, you can use a CASE value expression to replace column values, sometimes known as *recoding* column values. This is particularly useful if your query results include values that are not easily recognizable. For example, suppose you want to create a query that returns data from the CD_CATEGORY column of the CD_TRACKING table. You can recode the values in the column so that the information returned is more understandable to users, as shown in the following SELECT statement:

```
SELECT CD_NAME,
  (CASE
    WHEN CD_CATEGORY = 'ALTR' THEN 'Alternative Rock'
    WHEN CD_CATEGORY = 'BLUS' THEN 'Blues'
    WHEN CD_CATEGORY = 'CLAS' THEN 'Classical'
    WHEN CD_CATEGORY = 'CROK' THEN 'Classic Rock'
    WHEN CD_CATEGORY = 'CTRY' THEN 'Country'
    WHEN CD_CATEGORY = 'JAZZ' THEN 'Jazz'
    WHEN CD_CATEGORY = 'RNBL' THEN 'Rhythm and Blues'
    ELSE NULL
  END) AS CD_CATEGORY
  FROM CD_TRACKING;
```

NOTE

You do not have to put the various components of the CASE value expression on separate lines, as I have done here. I do it this way to clearly show you each component. It also makes the code more readable to anyone reviewing it. In this example, I also enclosed the entire CASE expression in a pair of parentheses to improve readability.

In this SELECT statement, the different values in the CD_CATEGORY column are recoded to more useful category names. Notice that you do not need to repeat the column names to the right of the THEN keyword. The predicate construction is assumed by the context of the clause. When you execute this statement, you receive the following query results:

```
CD_NAME                          CD_CATEGORY
------------------------------   ---------------
Drive All Night                  Alternative Rock
Different Shades of Blue         Blues
Innervisions (Remastered)        Rhythm and Blues
The Definitive Collection        Rhythm and Blues
Rumours (Reissued)               Classic Rock
Come On Over                     Country
Man Against Machine              Country
Bach                             Classical
Dark Side of the Moon            Classic Rock
Kind of Blue                     Jazz
```

As you can see, only user-friendly values appear in the CD_CATEGORY column. If any of the original values had not met the condition defined in the WHEN/THEN clauses, a null value would be inserted in the query results.

Ask the Expert

Q: Can you use a CASE value expression anywhere other than a SELECT statement?

A: Another handy use for the CASE value expression is in the SET clause of an UPDATE statement. For example, suppose you want to update the values in the ON_ORDER column in the CD_TRACKING table (shown in Figure 10-3). You can update those values by specifying certain conditions in a CASE expression:

```
UPDATE CD_TRACKING
   SET ON_ORDER =
  CASE
   WHEN ON_ORDER < 6 THEN ON_ORDER + 4
   WHEN ON_ORDER BETWEEN 6 AND 8 THEN ON_ORDER + 2
   ELSE ON_ORDER
  END;
```

This statement will add 4 to the ON_ORDER values that are less than 6, and it will add 2 to the ON_ORDER values that fall within the range of 6 through 8. Otherwise, no additional rows will be changed.

(continued)

Q: Can you reference more than one column in a CASE value expression?

A: Yes, you can reference more than one column. Suppose you want to update ON_ORDER values but base those updates on CD_CATEGORY values. You can create a statement similar to the following:

```
UPDATE CD_TRACKING
   SET ON_ORDER =
  CASE
   WHEN CD_CATEGORY = 'CROK' THEN ON_ORDER * 3
   WHEN CD_CATEGORY = 'BLUS' THEN ON_ORDER * 2
   ELSE ON_ORDER
  END;
```

In this statement, ON_ORDER values are multiplied by 3 when CD_CATEGORY values equal CROK, and ON_ORDER values are multiplied by 2 when CD_CATEGORY values equal BLUS. Otherwise, no values are changed.

Q: Are there any performance implications when using a CASE value expression?

A: While there are no inherent performance issues regarding the use of CASE value expressions, it is possible to get carried away. In general, the more complex the statement, especially in terms of nesting and elaborate conditional logic, the more resources that will be required to parse and execute the statement.

Using the CAST Value Expression

The CAST value expression serves a much different purpose than the CASE expression. The CAST expression allows you to change a value's data type for a literal value or when retrieving that value from your database. However, it does not change the data type of the source column. This is particularly useful when working with programming languages in which data types do not match up and you need to use a common denominator to work with the value.

To use the CAST value expression, you must specify the CAST keyword and, in parentheses, provide the column name, the AS keyword, and the new data type, in that order. To illustrate this, let's return to the SALES_DATES table shown in Figure 10-2. The table includes the COMPACT_DISC column and the DATE_SOLD column. The DATE_SOLD column is defined with the TIMESTAMP data type. Suppose you want to change the datetime values to character strings. You can use the CAST expression in your SELECT clause, as shown in the following statement:

```
SELECT COMPACT_DISC, CAST(DATE_SOLD AS CHAR(30)) AS CHAR_DATE
  FROM SALES_DATES
 WHERE COMPACT_DISC LIKE ('%Blue%');
```

This statement converts the DATE_SOLD values from TIMESTAMP values to CHAR values. As you can see, all you need to do is specify the CAST keyword, followed by the parenthetical parameters that identify the source column and the new data type, along with the AS keyword. When you execute this statement, you receive query results similar to what you would see if you had not used CAST:

```
COMPACT_DISC                CHAR_DATE
------------------------    -------------------
Different Shades of Blue    2015-01-22 12:02:05
Kind of Blue                2015-01-24 14:15:09
```

Notice that you can assign a name to the column that contains the new datetime results. In this case, the new column name is CHAR_DATE.

NOTE

You might find that in your SQL implementation, when a datetime value is converted, the format changes slightly. For example, in SQL Server, a datetime value is expressed numerically and a time value is expressed in a 24-hour clock (military time), but when the value is converted to a CHAR data type, the date and time are expressed in alphanumeric characters with the time expressed in a 12-hour clock (A.M. and P.M.). Therefore, in the previous query, SQL Server would display the CHAR_DATE value for Different Shades of Blue as Jan 22 2015 12:02 P.M.

Use Special Values

In Chapter 6, I discuss special values that SQL supports that allow you to determine the current users. A special value exists for each type of user. These values act as placeholders for the actual user-related value. You can use them in expressions to return the value of the specific user. SQL supports five special values, which are described in Table 10-3. (See Chapter 6 for more information about the various types of SQL users.)

The special values can be used in different ways in an SQL database, such as for establishing connections or running a stored procedure. The special value, rather than the actual user name, is embedded in the code to allow the code to remain flexible from one situation to another. Another way in which a special value can be used is to store user data in a table. To illustrate this, let's take a look at the CD_ORDERS table in Figure 10-4.

Each time a row is added to the table, a value for CURRENT_USER is inserted into the ORDERED_BY column. This makes it handy to track which user has placed the order. If you were to look at the table definition, you would see that a default value has been defined for the ORDERED_BY column, as shown in the following CREATE TABLE statement:

```
CREATE TABLE CD_ORDERS
( CD_TITLE     VARCHAR(60),
  ORDERED      INT,
  ORDERED_BY   CHAR(30) DEFAULT USER);
```

Value	Description
CURRENT_USER	Identifies the current user identifier. If the SQL-session user identifier is the current user identifier, then CURRENT_USER, USER, and SESSION_USER all have the same value, which can occur if the initial identifier pair is the only active user identifier/role name pair (the pair at the top of the authentication stack).
USER	Identifies the current user identifier. USER means the same thing as CURRENT_USER.
SESSION_USER	Identifies the current SQL-session user identifier.
CURRENT_ROLE	Identifies the current role name.
SYSTEM_USER	Identifies the current operating system user who invoked an SQL module.

Table 10-3 Using SQL Special Values

NOTE

Oracle allows USER to be specified as a column default value, but it does not support CURRENT_USER as a default value. SQL Server supports either USER or CURRENT_USER as a default value. MySQL 5.7 does not support either USER or CURRENT_USER as a default value.

CD_TITLE: VARCHAR(60)	ORDERED: INT	ORDERED_BY: VARCHAR(30)
Drive All Night	16	Mngr
Different Shades of Blue	22	AsstMngr
Innervisions (Remastered)	11	Mngr
The Definitive Collection	17	AsstMngr
Rumours (Reissued)	14	Mngr
Come On Over	18	AsstMngr
Man Against Machine	5	AsstMngr
Bach	8	Mngr
Dark Side of the Moon	6	Mngr
Kind of Blue	10	Mngr

Figure 10-4 The CD_ORDERS table

If you were to insert data into this table, you would have to specify only a CD_TITLE value and an ORDERED value. The ORDERED_BY value would be inserted automatically, and that value would be the current user identifier. If you do not specify a default value for the ORDERED_BY column, you can use the special value to insert the user. For example, the following INSERT statement inserts a row into the CD_ORDERS table:

```
INSERT INTO CD_ORDERS
VALUES ( 'Rhythm Country and Blues', 14, CURRENT_USER );
```

When you execute the statement, a value representing the current user identifier (such as Mngr) is inserted into the ORDERED_BY column.

To determine the extent to which you can use the special values, you should review the product documentation for your SQL implementation. You'll find that the ways in which you can use these values will vary from one implementation to the next. For example, in the previous example, Oracle supports USER, but not CURRENT_USER. Once you're comfortable with using special values in your implementation, you'll find them a useful tool as you become more proficient with programming SQL.

Try This 10-1 Using Functions and Value Expressions

In this chapter, you learned about many of the functions and value expressions supported by SQL. Now you will try out these functions and expressions by querying data from the INVENTORY database. Specifically, you will create SELECT statements that contain the COUNT, MIN, SUM, SUBSTRING, and UPPER functions and ones that contain numerical, CASE, and CAST value expressions. You can download the Try_This_10.txt file, which contains the SQL statements used in this exercise.

Step by Step

1. Open the client application for your RDBMS and connect to the INVENTORY database.
2. In the first statement, you will determine the number of unique ARTIST_NAME values in the ARTISTS table. Enter and execute the following SQL statement:

   ```
   SELECT COUNT(DISTINCT ARTIST_NAME) AS ARTISTS
     FROM ARTISTS;
   ```

   Your query should return a count of 14.
3. In the next statement, you will determine the minimum number of CDs in stock, as listed in the COMPACT_DISCS table. You'll name the column in the query results MIN_STOCK. Enter and execute the following SQL statement:

   ```
   SELECT MIN(IN_STOCK) AS MIN_STOCK
     FROM COMPACT_DISCS;
   ```

(continued)

Your query results should include only one column and one row, and show a value of 5. That means that 5 is the least number of CDs you have in stock for any one CD.

4. Now you will determine the total number of CDs in stock. However, this time you will group these totals according to the LABEL_ID values. Enter and execute the following SQL statement:

```
SELECT LABEL_ID, SUM(IN_STOCK) AS TOTAL
  FROM COMPACT_DISCS
 GROUP BY LABEL_ID;
```

Your query should return 13 rows, one for each LABEL_ID value. The TOTAL value for each row represents the total number of CDs for that particular LABEL_ID group.

5. In the preceding steps, you used set functions when querying data from the INVENTORY database. You'll now try a couple of value functions. The first of these is SUBSTRING. In this SELECT statement, you'll extract data from the PLACE_OF_BIRTH column in the ARTISTS table. You want to extract eight characters, starting with the first character in the string. Enter and execute one of the following SQL statements:

For MySQL, use the following statement:

```
SELECT ARTIST_NAME,
       SUBSTRING(PLACE_OF_BIRTH FROM 1 FOR 8) AS BIRTH_PLACE
  FROM ARTISTS;
```

For SQL Server, use the following SQL statement:

```
SELECT ARTIST_NAME,
       SUBSTRING(PLACE_OF_BIRTH, 1, 8) AS BIRTH_PLACE
  FROM ARTISTS;
```

For Oracle, use the following SQL statement:

```
SELECT ARTIST_NAME,
       SUBSTR(PLACE_OF_BIRTH, 1, 8) AS BIRTH_PLACE
  FROM ARTISTS;
```

Your query results should return 14 rows and include two columns: ARTIST_NAME and BIRTH_PLACE. The BIRTH_PLACE column contains the extracted values, which are based on the table's PLACE_OF_BIRTH column.

6. The next value function you'll try is the UPPER function. In this SELECT statement, you'll convert the names of the CDs to all uppercase. Enter and execute the following SQL statement:

```
SELECT UPPER(CD_TITLE) AS CD_NAME
  FROM COMPACT_DISCS;
```

This statement should return 15 rows with only one column that lists the name of the CDs in the COMPACT_DISCS table. The CD titles should all be in uppercase.

7. Now you will move on to numeric value expressions. The next statement you try creates two columns in the query results that double and triple the values in the IN_STOCK column of the COMPACT_DISCS table. However, the statement returns values only for those rows with an IN_STOCK value less than 25. Enter and execute the following SQL statement:

```
SELECT CD_TITLE, IN_STOCK,
       (IN_STOCK * 2) AS DOUBLED, (IN_STOCK * 3) AS TRIPLED
  FROM COMPACT_DISCS
 WHERE IN_STOCK < 25;
```

   Your SELECT statement should return nine rows that each include IN_STOCK values that have been multiplied by 2 and by 3.

8. The next value expression you'll try is the CASE expression. The statement will provide updated IN_STOCK values in the TO_ORDER column of the query results. For IN_STOCK values less than 10, the values will be doubled. For IN_STOCK values that fall within the range of 10 through 15, 3 will be added to the values. All other IN_STOCK values will remain the same. The statement operates only on those rows whose original IN STOCK value is less than 20. Enter and execute the following SQL statement:

```
SELECT CD_TITLE, IN_STOCK,
  CASE
   WHEN IN_STOCK < 10 THEN IN_STOCK * 2
   WHEN IN_STOCK BETWEEN 10 AND 15 THEN IN_STOCK + 3
   ELSE IN_STOCK
  END AS TO_ORDER
  FROM COMPACT_DISCS
 WHERE IN_STOCK < 20;
```

   Your query results should include only seven rows, and the TO_ORDER column of the query results should contain the updated values.

9. Now you will try the CAST value expression. You will query the MUSIC_TYPES table but will convert the data type of the MUSIC_TYPE_ID column in your query results. Enter and execute the following SQL statement:

```
SELECT CAST(MUSIC_TYPE_ID AS CHAR(3)) AS ID,
       MUSIC_TYPE_NAME
  FROM MUSIC_TYPES;
```

   Your query should return 11 rows. The query results should include the ID column that contains the converted values.

10. Close the client application.

(continued)

Try This Summary

You should now be fairly comfortable with the various functions and value expressions that we reviewed in this chapter. Remember that each SQL implementation supports different functions and value expressions, usually many more than what you have seen here. In fact, in many cases, the functions and value expressions you saw in this chapter represent only the tip of the iceberg. Be sure to review your product documentation to find out what functions and value expressions are supported and how they're implemented. You'll find them useful tools in a variety of situations and well worth the effort you invest now.

Chapter 10 Self Test

1. What is a set function?
2. You're creating a SELECT statement that queries the ARTIST_CD_SALES table. The table includes the ARTIST_NAME and CD_NAME columns. You want your statement to return the total number of rows in the table. Which COUNT function should you include in your SELECT clause?

   A COUNT(*)

   B COUNT(ARTIST_NAME)

   C COUNT(CD_NAME)

   D COUNT(ARTIST_NAME, CD_NAME)
3. Which set function should you use to add together the values in a column?

   A MAX

   B COUNT

   C SUM

   D AVG
4. Set functions require that the data be ________________ in some way.
5. What are value functions?
6. You're using the SUBSTRING function to extract characters from the COMPACT_DISC column of the SALES_DATES table. You want to start with the third character and extract eight characters. What parameters should you use in the SUBSTRING function?
7. You're using the LOWER function on the Drive All Night value of the CD_NAME column. What value will be returned?

8. Which function returns a value that represents the current date and time as well as information related to UTC?

   A LOCALTIMESTAMP

   B CURRENT_DATE

   C LOCALTIME

   D CURRENT_TIMESTAMP

9. What are four types of operators that you use in a numeric value expression?

10. You are querying data from the CD_TRACKING table. You want to add values in the IN_STOCK column to values in the ON_ORDER column. You then want to double the column totals. How do you set up the numeric value expression?

11. Which value expression do you use to set up a series of conditions that modify values?

12. You're creating a SELECT statement that includes a CASE value expression. You want one of the conditions to specify that any ON_ORDER values greater than 10 should be increased by 5. How should you set up the WHEN/THEN clause?

13. What is the last word in a CASE value expression?

14. What is a CAST value expression?

15. You're querying the DATE_SOLD column in the SALES_DATES table. You want to convert the values to a CHAR (30) data type, and you want the data displayed in the CHAR_DATE column in the query results. How do you define the CAST value expression?

16. Which special value can you use to identify the current SQL session user identifier?

Chapter 11

Accessing Multiple Tables

Key Skills & Concepts

- Perform Basic Join Operations
- Join Tables with Shared Column Names
- Use the Condition Join
- Perform Union Operations

An important component of any relational database is the relationship that can exist between any two tables. This relationship allows you to tie data in one table to data in another table. These sorts of relationships are particularly useful when you want to query related data from more than one table and you want to retrieve that data in a meaningful way so that the relationships between the tables are, for all practical purposes, invisible. One method that SQL supports for querying data in this manner is to join the tables in one statement. A *join* is an operation that matches rows in one table with rows in another so that columns from both tables may be placed side by side in the query results as if they all came from a single table. SQL defines several types of join operations. The type you can use in any given situation depends on your SQL implementation (with regard to statements supported and how performance might be impacted), which data you want returned, and how the tables have been defined. In this chapter, I discuss a number of operations that combine data from multiple tables, including joins and unions, and provide details about how they're implemented and the results you can expect when you use them.

Perform Basic Join Operations

One of the simplest types of joins to implement is the comma-separated join. In this type of operation, you're required only to supply a list of tables (separated by commas) in the FROM clause of the SELECT statement. You can, of course, qualify the join in the WHERE clause—which you would want to do to obtain meaningful data from the tables—but you're not required to do so. However, before I discuss the WHERE clause, let's first take a look at the comma-separated join at its most basic.

Suppose you want to display data from the CD_INVENTORY table and the PERFORMERS table, shown in Figure 11-1. (The figure also includes the PERF_TYPE table, which we'll be using in the "Creating Joins with More than Two Tables" section.) You can view the data in the CD_INVENTORY and PERFORMERS tables by querying each table separately, or you can join the tables in one statement.

To join the two tables, you can create a SELECT statement as simple as the following one:

```
SELECT CD_NAME, IN_STOCK, PERF_NAME, TYPE_ID
  FROM CD_INVENTORY, PERFORMERS;
```

CD_INVENTORY

CD_NAME: VARCHAR(60)	PERF_ID: INT	IN_STOCK: INT
Drive All Night	3001	12
Different Shades of Blue	3002	42
Innervisions (Remastered)	3003	16
The Definitive Collection	3003	34
Rumours (Reissued)	3004	17
Come On Over	3005	6
Man Against Machine	3006	8
Bach	3008	22
Old Boots, New Dirt	3009	32
Dark Side of the Moon	3010	27
Kind of Blue	3011	21

PERFORMERS

PERF_ID: INT	PERF_NAME: VARCHAR(60)	TYPE_ID: INT
3001	Glen Hansard	10
3002	Joe Bonamassa	12
3003	Stevie Wonder	13
3004	Fleetwood Mac	11
3005	Shania Twain	16
3006	Garth Brooks	16
3008	Joshua Bell	14
3009	Jason Aldean	16
3010	Pink Floyd	11
3011	Miles Davis	15

PERF_TYPE

TYPE_ID: INT	TYPE_NAME: CHAR(20)
10	Alternative Rock
11	Classic Rock
12	Blues
13	R&B
14	Classical
15	Jazz
16	Country

Figure 11-1 Joining the CD_INVENTORY, PERFORMERS, and PERF_TYPE tables

The query produces what is known as a *Cartesian product table* (named after French mathematician and philosopher René Descartes), which is a list of each row in one table joined together with each row in the other table, as shown (in part) in the following query results:

```
CD_NAME                     PERF_ID  IN_STOCK  PERF_ID  PERF_NAME      TYPE_ID
--------------------------  -------  --------  -------  -------------  -------
Drive All Night             3001     12        3001     Glen Hansard   10
Drive All Night             3001     12        3002     Joe Bonamassa  12
Drive All Night             3001     12        3003     Stevie Wonder  13
Drive All Night             3001     12        3004     Fleetwood Mac  11
Drive All Night             3001     12        3005     Shania Twain   16
Drive All Night             3001     12        3006     Garth Brooks   16
Drive All Night             3001     12        3008     Joshua Bell    14
Drive All Night             3001     12        3009     Jason Aldean   16
Drive All Night             3001     12        3010     Pink Floyd     11
Drive All Night             3001     12        3011     Miles Davis    15
Different Shades of Blue    3002     42        3001     Glen Hansard   10
Different Shades of Blue    3002     42        3002     Joe Bonamassa  12
Different Shades of Blue    3002     42        3003     Stevie Wonder  13
Different Shades of Blue    3002     42        3004     Fleetwood Mac  16
Different Shades of Blue    3002     42        3005     Shania Twain   16
Different Shades of Blue    3002     42        3006     Garth Brooks   16
```

Actually, the preceding SELECT returns far more rows than are shown here. These results represent only a partial list. Because the CD_INVENTORY table contains 11 rows and the PERFORMERS table contains 10 rows, the entire query results would contain 110 rows. Let's take a closer look at this. The Drive All Night row in the CD_INVENTORY table has been joined with each row in the PERFORMERS table, which totals 10 rows. Each of the remaining 10 rows in the CD_INVENTORY table is matched to each row in the PERFORMERS table in the same way. As a result, there are 110 rows (11 × 10 = 110).

NOTE

Recall that when queries do not include the ORDER BY clause, the order of rows in the result set is not predictable. Therefore, if you try the queries in this chapter yourself, the order of the rows may not match the results shown in the chapter.

As you can see, these query results are not the most useful. However, you can generate more meaningful results if you use a WHERE clause to create an *equi-join* (also written as *equijoin*), which is a type of join that equates the values in one or more columns in the first table to the values in one or more corresponding columns in the second table. As you might guess from the name, the comparison operator in an equi-join is always an equal to (=) operator. For example, you can qualify the previous SELECT statement in the following way:

```
SELECT *
  FROM CD_INVENTORY, PERFORMERS
 WHERE CD_INVENTORY.PERF_ID = PERFORMERS.PERF_ID;
```

Now your query results will include only those rows in which the value in the PERF_ID column of the CD_INVENTORY table matches the value in the PERF_ID column of the PERFORMERS table. Notice that you have to qualify the column names by adding the table names. You must do this whenever columns from different tables have the same name. If you execute this statement, you'll receive the following query results:

```
CD_NAME                     PERF_ID  IN_STOCK  PERF_ID  PERF_NAME      TYPE_ID
--------------------------  -------  --------  -------  -------------  -------
Drive All Night             3001     12        3001     Glen Hansard   10
Different Shades of Blue    3002     42        3002     Joe Bonamassa  12
Innervisions (Remastered)   3003     16        3003     Stevie Wonder  13
The Definitive Collection   3003     34        3003     Stevie Wonder  13
Rumours (Reissued)          3004     17        3004     Fleetwood Mac  11
Come On Over                3005     6         3005     Shania Twain   16
Man Against Machine         3006     8         3006     Garth Brooks   16
Bach                        3008     22        3008     Joshua Bell    14
Old Boots, New Dirt         3009     32        3009     Jason Aldean   16
Dark Side of the Moon       3010     27        3010     Pink Floyd     11
Kind of Blue                3011     21        3011     Miles Davis    15
```

The data returned by this query is now a lot more meaningful. Each CD is matched with the appropriate performer, and only 11 rows are displayed, rather than 110. However, even these query results include repetitive data (the PERF_ID column). In addition, you might find that not only do you want to eliminate duplicate columns, but you also want to display only certain columns and perhaps qualify your search condition even further.

Let's modify the SELECT statement we've been looking at by specifying column names in the SELECT clause to limit the columns returned and adding another predicate to the WHERE clause to limit the rows returned, as shown in the following example:

```
SELECT CD_INVENTORY.CD_NAME, PERFORMERS.PERF_NAME, CD_INVENTORY.IN_STOCK
  FROM CD_INVENTORY, PERFORMERS
 WHERE CD_INVENTORY.PERF_ID  = PERFORMERS.PERF_ID
   AND CD_INVENTORY.IN_STOCK < 15;
```

In this statement, I have specified that three columns should be included in the query results. Notice that I've qualified the column names by including the table names. Notice also that the WHERE clause includes an additional predicate, connected with the first predicate by the AND keyword. Now any rows that are returned must also have IN_STOCK values less than 15. If you execute this statement, you'll receive the following query results:

```
CD_NAME                PERF_NAME          IN_STOCK
--------------------   ----------------   --------
Drive All Night        Glen Hansard       12
Come On Over           Shania Twain       6
Man Against Machine    Garth Brooks       8
```

As you can see, we've refined the query results down to just the most essential information. Of course, you can create all sorts of queries, depending on your needs, as long as you follow the basic guidelines for creating a comma-separated join:

- The FROM clause must include all table names.
- The WHERE clause should define a join condition, avoiding a Cartesian product.
- The column references must be qualified when column names are shared among tables.

Aside from these guidelines, you're free to create whatever sort of SELECT statement is necessary to extract the information you need from the participating tables. And while using the WHERE clause to specify the join condition was the original way to do joins in SQL, later in this chapter you will see that there are now other syntax variations using the JOIN keyword, which most SQL programmers prefer over the original syntax. But no matter what syntax you use, always keep in mind that there needs to be some sort of logical connection between the tables. This connection is often seen in the form of a foreign key, but that doesn't have to be the case. (For more information about foreign keys, see Chapter 4.) Tables can be joined whether or not a foreign key exists. And although the equi-join is the most common, you may occasionally find a different join comparison operator useful, such as less than (<) or BETWEEN, in which case the join is referred to as a *theta-join*.

Using Correlation Names

As I stated earlier, you must qualify your column references by adding table names to those columns that share a name. However, as a general policy, it's a good idea to always qualify column references when joining tables, whether or not it's necessary. This makes referencing the code at a later time much easier if the statement is fully self-documented. However, as your queries become more complex, it can become increasingly tedious to reenter table names every time you reference a column. Because of this, SQL supports correlation names, or aliases, that can be used for the duration of a statement. A *correlation name* is simply a shortened version of the actual table name that is used to simplify code and make it more readable.

Take, for example, the last SELECT statement that we looked at. You can recast this statement by using correlation names for the two tables:

```
SELECT c.CD_NAME, p.PERF_NAME, c.IN_STOCK
  FROM CD_INVENTORY AS c, PERFORMERS AS p
 WHERE c.PERF_ID  = p.PERF_ID
   AND c.IN_STOCK < 15;
```

The SELECT statement produces exactly the same results as the preceding statement, only now the tables are referenced by different names, except in the FROM clause. In fact, you use the FROM clause to define the aliases that are used in the rest of the statement. In this case, the CD_INVENTORY table is renamed c, and the PERFORMERS table is renamed p. As a result, c and p must be used everywhere else in the SELECT statement when referring to those tables. Once a correlation name has been defined, you cannot use the actual table name. And yes, this can be confusing because you use the alias in the SELECT clause, but it is not defined until the FROM clause that follows the SELECT clause.

To better understand how the renaming process works, let's revisit the issue of how SELECT statements are processed. As you might recall from Chapter 7, the FROM clause is processed first and the SELECT clause is processed last. That is why the correlation names are defined in the FROM clause. Once they are defined, all other clauses can (and must) use those aliases when qualifying column references. The correlation names are used throughout the remainder of the statement, but they only apply to the statement in which they are defined. If you create a new SELECT statement, you must redefine those names in order to use them in the new statement.

As you can see in the previous SELECT statement, a correlation name is defined immediately after the actual table name. The new name follows the AS keyword. However, the AS keyword is not required. In most implementations, you can also use the following convention to rename the tables within a query:

```
SELECT c.CD_NAME, p.PERF_NAME, c.IN_STOCK
  FROM CD_INVENTORY c, PERFORMERS p
 WHERE c.PERF_ID  = p.PERF_ID
   AND c.IN_STOCK < 15;
```

Notice that only the new name is specified, without the AS keyword. This makes the SQL statement that much simpler. In fact, some implementations, such as Oracle, do not allow you to use the AS keyword at all, even though it is part of the SQL standard. Again, this last SELECT statement will provide the same query results that you saw in the two previous examples. Only the statement itself has been changed.

Creating Joins with More than Two Tables

Up to this point, the examples that we've looked at have joined only two tables. However, you can use a comma-separated join to display data from more than two tables. If you refer again to Figure 11-1, you'll see that the PERF_TYPE table is included in the illustration. You can, if you want, join all three tables in a single SELECT statement, as shown in the following example:

```
SELECT c.CD_NAME, p.PERF_NAME, t.TYPE_NAME
  FROM CD_INVENTORY c, PERFORMERS p, PERF_TYPE t
 WHERE c.PERF_ID = p.PERF_ID
   AND p.TYPE_ID = t.TYPE_ID
   AND TYPE_NAME = 'Country';
```

In this statement, the FROM clause includes all three tables. In addition, the WHERE clause provides two equi-join conditions: one that maps the PERF_ID columns and one that maps the TYPE_ID columns. If you execute this statement, you'll receive the following query results:

```
CD_NAME                   PERF_NAME      TYPE_NAME
------------------------  -------------  ---------
Come On Over              Shania Twain   Country
Man Against Machine       Garth Brooks   Country
Old Boots, New Dirt       Jason Aldean   Country
```

Notice that information from all three tables is included in the results: the name of the CD, the name of the performer, and the category of performer. Even though a relationship might exist between the CD_INVENTORY table and the PERFORMERS table, as well as between the PERFORMERS table and the PERF_TYPE table, your query results provide a seamless display that hides these relationships and shows only the information that you need.

Creating the Cross Join

In addition to the comma-separated join, SQL supports another type of operation called the cross join. The cross join is nearly identical to the comma-separated join. The only difference is that instead of separating column names with a comma, you use the CROSS JOIN keywords. For example, let's take a statement we used earlier and modify it by replacing the comma with the CROSS JOIN keywords:

```
SELECT c.CD_NAME, p.PERF_NAME, c.IN_STOCK
  FROM CD_INVENTORY c CROSS JOIN PERFORMERS p
 WHERE c.PERF_ID  = p.PERF_ID
   AND c.IN_STOCK < 15;
```

Ask the Expert

Q: If you're joining tables, it seems likely that in some cases you will return duplicate rows in your query results, depending on how your SELECT statement is constructed. How can you avoid duplicate rows?

A: As with most queries, it is possible to return duplicate rows. For example, the following statement will return duplicate performer names and types:

```
SELECT P.PERF_NAME, T.TYPE_NAME
  FROM CD_INVENTORY C, PERFORMERS P, PERF_TYPE T
 WHERE C.PERF_ID = P.PERF_ID
   AND P.TYPE_ID = T.TYPE_ID;
```

For those performers who made more than one CD, the query results will contain a row for each of those CDs. However, as with any other SELECT statement, you can add the DISTINCT keyword to your SELECT clause, as shown in the following example:

```
SELECT DISTINCT P.PERF_NAME, T.TYPE_NAME
  FROM CD_INVENTORY C, PERFORMERS P, PERF_TYPE T
 WHERE C.PERF_ID = P.PERF_ID
   AND P.TYPE_ID = T.TYPE_ID;
```

This statement will return fewer rows than the previous statement (10 compared to 11), and no rows will be duplicated. Also note that you can achieve the same results without the DISTINCT keyword by using a GROUP BY clause that lists both columns.

This statement returns three columns from two tables, and the WHERE clause contains an equi-join condition. If you execute the statement, you'll receive the same results as if you were using a comma-separated join. Using one over the other may simply be a matter of determining which statement your SQL implementation supports and, if both are supported, which provides better performance. In all likelihood, it will come down to a matter of personal preference, with little advantage of one over the other.

Creating the Self-Join

Another type of join that you can create is the self-join, which can be either a comma-separated join or a cross join. In a self-join, you create a join condition that references the same table two times, essentially joining the table to itself. This is almost always done to resolve a recursive relationship, finding other rows in the same table that are related to the selected rows. For example, suppose you add an EMPLOYEES table to your database, as shown in Figure 11-2. The EMPLOYEES table includes a list of employee IDs, employee names, and the employee IDs of their managers, who are also listed in the table. For example, the manager of Mr. Jones (EMP_ID 102) is Ms. Smith (EMP_ID 101).

EMP_ID: INT	EMP_NAME: VARCHAR(60)	MNGR: INT
101	Ms. Smith	NULL
102	Mr. Jones	101
103	Mr. Roberts	101
104	Ms. Hanson	103
105	Mr. Fields	102
106	Ms. Lee	102
107	Mr. Carver	103

Figure 11-2 Self-joining the EMPLOYEES table

To create a self-join on this table, you must create a join that treats the table as if it was two separate tables with the same name, same columns, and same data:

```
SELECT a.EMP_ID, a.EMP_NAME, b.EMP_NAME AS MANAGER
  FROM EMPLOYEES a, EMPLOYEES b
 WHERE a.MNGR = b.EMP_ID
 ORDER BY a.EMP_ID;
```

In this statement, each instance of the table is given a correlation name. As a result, you now have (in this example) table a and table b. You pull the EMP_ID value and EMP_NAME value from table a, but you pull the MANAGER value from table b. The equi-join condition is defined in the WHERE clause by equating the MNGR value in table a with the EMP_ID value in table b. This provides the link that treats one physical table as two logical tables. When you execute this statement, you receive the following query results:

```
EMP_ID  EMP_NAME     MANAGER
------  -----------  -----------
102     Mr. Jones    Ms. Smith
103     Mr. Roberts  Ms. Smith
104     Ms. Hanson   Mr. Roberts
105     Mr. Fields   Mr. Jones
106     Ms. Lee      Mr. Jones
107     Mr. Carver   Mr. Roberts
```

The results include the employee ID and name of each employee, along with the name of the employee's manager. As you can see, the self-join can be a handy tool to use in cases such as this where a table references itself.

Join Tables with Shared Column Names

SQL provides two methods for setting up joins that you can use when you're working with columns that have the same names. These two methods—the natural join and the named column join—allow you to easily specify a join condition between two tables when one or more columns within those tables are the same. In order to use either of these two methods, the tables must meet the following conditions:

- The joined columns must share the same name and have compatible data types.
- The names of the joined columns cannot be qualified with table names.

When you're using either the natural join or the named column join, each table must share at least one column in common. For example, the TITLES_IN_STOCK and the TITLE_COSTS tables, shown in Figure 11-3, have two columns that are the same: CD_TITLE and CD_TYPE. Notice that each set of matching columns is configured with the same data type.

You can use a natural join or a named column join to join these two tables. I describe each of these types of join operations in the next several sections, and I use the tables in Figure 11-3 to illustrate how each of these methods work.

Creating the Natural Join

The natural join automatically matches rows for those columns with the same name. You do not have to specify any sort of equi-join condition for natural joins. The SQL implementation determines which columns have the same names and then tries to form a match. The drawback

TITLES_IN_STOCK

CD_TITLE: VARCHAR(60)	CD_TYPE: CHAR(20)	INVENTORY: INT
Drive All Night	Alt. Rock	12
Different Shades of Blue	Blues	42
Innervisions (Remastered)	R&B	16
The Definitive Collection	R&B	34
Rumours (Reissued)	Rock	17
Come On Over	Country	6
Man Against Machine	Country	8
Dark Side of the Moon	Rock	27

TITLE_COSTS

CD_TITLE: VARCHAR(60)	CD_TYPE: CHAR(20)	WHOLESALE: NUMERIC(5,2)	RETAIL: NUMERIC(5,2)
Drive All Night	Alt. Rock	4.50	5.99
Different Shades of Blue	Blues	5.50	11.99
Bach	Classical	5.50	11.88
Innervisions (Remastered)	R&B	5.50	10.00
Old Boots, New Dirt	Country	5.50	11.88
The Definitive Collection	R&B	4.50	8.39
Kind of Blue	Jazz	4.50	7.29
Come On Over	Country	4.50	5.99
Man Against Machine	Country	5.50	9.99

Figure 11-3 Joining the TITLES_IN_STOCK and TITLE_COSTS tables

to this is that you cannot specify which columns are matched up, although you can specify which columns are included in the query results.

In the following example, a natural join is used to join the TITLES_IN_STOCK table to the TITLE_COSTS table:

```
SELECT CD_TITLE, CD_TYPE, c.RETAIL
  FROM TITLES_IN_STOCK s NATURAL JOIN TITLE_COSTS c
 WHERE s.INVENTORY > 15;
```

In this statement, the tables are joined through the CD_TITLE and CD_TYPE columns. Notice that neither column name is qualified—qualified names are not permitted in natural joins. If either of these column names had been included in the WHERE clause, they still would not be qualified. When you execute this statement, you receive the following query results:

```
CD_TITLE                  CD_TYPE  RETAIL
------------------------- -------  ------
Different Shades of Blue  Blues    15.99
Innervisions (Remastered) R&B      10.00
The Definitive Collection R&B      8.39
```

As you can see, only three rows are returned. These are the rows in which the CD_TITLE values in both tables are equal *and* the CD_TYPE values are equal *and* the INVENTORY values are greater than 15.

Creating the Named Column Join

Although natural joins can be handy for simple join operations, you might find that you do not always want to include every matching column as part of the join condition. The way around this is to use a *named column join*, which allows you to specify which matching columns to include. For example, suppose you want to include only the CD_TITLE in the join condition. You can modify the previous example as follows:

```
SELECT CD_TITLE, s.CD_TYPE, c.RETAIL
  FROM TITLES_IN_STOCK s JOIN TITLE_COSTS c
       USING (CD_TITLE)
 WHERE s.Inventory > 15;
```

In this statement, I've removed the NATURAL keyword and added a USING clause, which identifies the matching columns. Notice that the CD_TYPE column name has now been qualified, but the CD_TITLE column has not. Only the columns identified in the USING clause are not qualified. This statement returns the same results as the preceding example, although this does not necessarily have to be the case, depending on the data in the tables. If, however, you include both matching columns in the USING clause, you would definitely see the same results as you saw in the natural join. By identifying all matching columns in the USING clause, you are performing the same function as a natural join.

NOTE

Not all SQL implementations support natural joins or named column joins. For example, SQL Server does not support either of these methods, while MySQL and Oracle support both.

Use the Condition Join

So far in this chapter, we've looked at comma-separated joins, cross joins, natural joins, and named column joins. In comma-separated and cross joins, the equi-join condition is defined in the WHERE clause. In natural joins, the equi-join condition is automatically assumed on all matching columns. And in named column joins, the equi-join condition is placed on any matching columns defined in the USING clause. The *condition join* takes an approach different from any of these. In a condition join, the equi-join condition is defined in the ON clause, which works in a way very similar to the WHERE clause. However, despite the use of the ON clause, a basic condition join is similar in many ways to the previous join operations we've looked at, except that, unlike the natural join and named column join, the condition join allows you to match any compatible columns from one table against those in another table. Column names do not have to be the same. The condition join is the syntax preferred by most SQL programmers because of its clarity, flexibility, and wide support across SQL implementations.

A condition join can be separated into two types of joins: *inner joins* and *outer joins*. The difference between the two is the amount of data returned by the query. An inner join returns only those rows that meet the equi-join condition defined in the SELECT statement. In other words, the inner join returns only matched rows. This was the original join available in SQL, and thus is called a "standard join" by some SQL programmers, although this is a misnomer because all the joins presented in this chapter are described in the SQL standard. An outer join, on the other hand, returns matched rows and some or all of the unmatched rows, depending on the type of outer join.

NOTE

According to the SQL standard, natural joins and named column joins support both inner and outer joins. However, this can vary from SQL implementation to implementation, so be sure to check the product documentation. By default, a join is processed as an inner join unless specifically defined as an outer join.

Creating the Inner Join

Now that you have a general overview of the condition join, let's take a closer look at the inner join. The inner join is the most common of the condition joins and is specified by using the INNER JOIN keywords. However, the INNER keyword is not required. If JOIN is used alone, an inner join is assumed. In addition to the JOIN keyword (specified in the FROM clause), you must define an ON clause, which immediately follows the FROM clause. Let's take a look at an example to see how this works.

Suppose you want to join the CD_TITLES table and the TITLES_ARTISTS table, shown in Figure 11-4. In the following example, an inner join has been created that is based on the TITLE_ID columns in the two tables:

```
SELECT t.TITLE, ta.ARTIST_ID
  FROM CD_TITLES t INNER JOIN TITLES_ARTISTS ta
     ON t.TITLE_ID = ta.TITLE_ID
 WHERE t.TITLE LIKE ('%Blue%');
```

The statement uses the INNER JOIN keywords to join the CD_TITLES and TITLES_ARTISTS tables. The equi-join condition is defined in the ON clause, using the TITLE_ID column in each table. Notice that correlation names have been defined on both tables. The SELECT statement is further qualified by the WHERE clause, which returns only those rows

CD_TITLES

TITLE_ID: INT	TITLE: VARCHAR(60)
101	Drive All Night
102	Different Shades of Blue
103	Innervisions (Remastered)
104	The Definitive Collection
105	Rumours (Reissued)
106	Come On Over
107	Man Against Machine
108	Bach
109	Old Boots, New Dirt
110	Dark Side of the Moon
111	Kind of Blue
112	Thriller
113	The Endless River

TITLES_ARTISTS

TITLE_ID: INT	ARTIST_ID: INT
101	3001
102	3002
103	3003
104	3003
105	3004
106	3005
107	3006
108	3007
108	3008
109	3009
110	3010
111	3011
112	3012
113	3010

CD_ARTISTS

ARTIST_ID: INT	ARTIST: VARCHAR(60)
3001	Glen Hansard
3002	Joe Bonamassa
3003	Stevie Wonder
3004	Fleetwood Mac
3005	Shania Twain
3006	Garth Brooks
3007	J. S. Bach
3008	Joshua Bell
3009	Jason Aldean
3010	Pink Floyd
3011	Miles Davis
3012	Michael Jackson

Figure 11-4 Joining the CD_TITLES, TITLES_ARTISTS, and CD_ARTISTS tables

that contain Blue in the TITLE column of the CD_TITLES table. When you execute this query, you receive the following query results:

```
TITLE                      ARTIST_ID
------------------------   ---------
Different Shades of Blue   3002
Kind of Blue               3011
```

As you can see, the results include information from both tables: the TITLE column from the CD_TITLES table and the ARTIST_ID column from the TITLES_ARTISTS table. Although this information can be useful, it might be better for some users if they can view the actual names of the artists, rather than numbers. The way to achieve this is to include a third table in the join.

Let's return to the previous example and add a second join condition to the CD_ARTISTS table (shown in Figure 11-4). In the following example, the second condition is added immediately after the original ON clause:

```
SELECT t.TITLE, a.ARTIST
  FROM CD_TITLES t INNER JOIN TITLES_ARTISTS ta
         ON t.TITLE_ID = ta.TITLE_ID
       INNER JOIN CD_ARTISTS a
         ON ta.ARTIST_ID = a.ARTIST_ID
 WHERE t.TITLE LIKE ('%Blue%');
```

Notice that the INNER JOIN keywords are repeated, followed by the name of the third table, which is then followed by another ON clause. In this clause, the equi-join condition is defined on the ARTIST_ID columns in the TITLES_ARTISTS and CD_ARTISTS tables. Keep in mind that you do not need to include the INNER keyword, nor do the columns specified in the ON clause need to have the same name.

If you execute this statement, you'll receive the following query results:

```
TITLE                      ARTIST
------------------------   ---------------
Different Shades of Blue   Joe Bonamassa
Kind of Blue               Miles Davis
```

Notice that the artist names are now listed in the results. Also notice that the fact that three tables have been used to retrieve this information is invisible to whoever views the query results.

Creating the Outer Join

As I mentioned earlier in this chapter, an outer join returns all matched rows and some or all unmatched rows, depending on the type of outer join you create. SQL supports three types of outer joins:

- **Left** Returns all matched rows and all unmatched rows from the left table—the table to the left of the JOIN keyword.

- **Right** Returns all matched rows and all unmatched rows from the right table—the table to the right of the JOIN keyword.
- **Full** Returns all matched and unmatched rows from both tables.

NOTE

Oracle and SQL Server currently support full outer joins, but MySQL 5.7 does not.

An outer join follows the same syntax as an inner join, except that rather than using the INNER JOIN keywords (or just the JOIN keyword), you use LEFT OUTER JOIN, RIGHT OUTER JOIN, or FULL OUTER JOIN. Note that the OUTER keyword is optional. For example, you can specify LEFT JOIN instead of LEFT OUTER JOIN.

The best way to illustrate the differences between the types of outer joins is to show you examples of query results from each type. To illustrate the differences, I use the CD_INFO table and the CD_TYPE table, shown in Figure 11-5.

In the first example, I define an inner join on the two tables, just to show you how the query results would normally look:

```
SELECT i.TITLE, t.TYPE_NAME, i.STOCK
  FROM CD_INFO i JOIN CD_TYPE t
       ON i.TYPE_ID = t.TYPE_ID;
```

This statement returns the following query results:

```
TITLE                      TYPE_NAME          STOCK
-----------------------    ---------------    -----
Drive All Night            Alternative Rock   19
```

CD_INFO

TITLE: VARCHAR(60)	TYPE_ID: CHAR(4)	STOCK: INT
Drive All Night	ALTR	19
Different Shades of Blue	BLUS	28
Bach	CLAS	6
Man Against Machine	CTRY	8
Dark Side of the Moon	CROK	10
Kind of Blue	JAZZ	11

CD_TYPE

TYPE_ID: CHAR(4)	TYPE_NAME: VARCHAR(20)
ALTR	Alternative Rock
BLUS	Blues
CLAS	Classical
CTRY	Country
JAZZ	Jazz
RNBL	Rhythm and Blues
STRK	Soundtrack

Figure 11-5 Joining the CD_INFO and CD_TYPE tables

```
Different Shades of Blue  Blues             28
Bach                      Classical         6
Man Against Machine       Country           8
Kind of Blue              Jazz              11
```

In most cases, the inner join will provide all the information you need. But suppose you want to include the unmatched rows from the CD_INFO table. In that case, you would create a left outer join, as shown in the following example:

```
SELECT i.TITLE, t.TYPE_NAME, i.STOCK
  FROM CD_INFO i LEFT OUTER JOIN CD_TYPE t
       ON i.TYPE_ID = t.TYPE_ID;
```

Notice that I've replaced JOIN (for INNER JOIN) with LEFT OUTER JOIN. As I mentioned earlier, you can omit the OUTER keyword in most implementations. If you execute this statement, you'll receive the following query results:

```
TITLE                     TYPE_NAME         STOCK
------------------------  ----------------  -----
Drive All Night           Alternative Rock  19
Different Shades of Blue  Blues             28
Bach                      Classical         6
Man Against Machine       Country           8
Dark Side of the Moon     <null>            10
Kind of Blue              Jazz              11
```

As you may have noticed, the Dark Side of the Moon row is now included in the query results. Although this row doesn't include matched columns, it is still included in the query results because it is part of the *left* table. For this row, the TYPE_NAME column is assigned a null value because no logical value can be returned for this column. The null value serves as a placeholder.

You can also return the unmatched rows from the CD_TYPE table, which is the table to the right of the JOIN keyword:

```
SELECT i.TITLE, t.TYPE_NAME, i.STOCK
  FROM CD_INFO i RIGHT OUTER JOIN CD_TYPE t
       ON i.TYPE_ID = t.TYPE_ID;
```

This statement is nearly the same as the preceding statement, except that RIGHT has been specified. The statement returns the following query results:

```
TITLE                     TYPE_NAME         STOCK
------------------------  ----------------  -----
Drive All Night           Alternative Rock  19
Different Shades of Blue  Blues             28
Bach                      Classical         6
Man Against Machine       Country           8
Kind of Blue              Jazz              11
```

```
<null>                      Rhythm and Blues  <null>
<null>                      Soundtrack        <null>
```

This time the unmatched columns from the *right* table are included in the results, and null values are shown for the TITLE and STOCK column.

If you want to return all unmatched rows, you would need to modify the statement to define a full outer join:

```
SELECT i.TITLE, t.TYPE_NAME, i.STOCK
  FROM CD_INFO i FULL OUTER JOIN CD_TYPE t
       ON i.TYPE_ID = t.TYPE_ID;
```

This statement will return the following query results:

```
TITLE                       TYPE_NAME          STOCK
--------------------------  -----------------  -----
Drive All Night             Alternative Rock   19
Different Shades of Blue    Blues              28
Bach                        Classical          6
Man Against Machine         Country            8
Dark Side of the Moon       <null>             10
Kind of Blue                Jazz               11
<null>                      Rhythm and Blues   <null>
<null>                      Soundtrack         <null>
```

As you can see, all matched and unmatched rows are included in the query results. Notice that all six rows are included from the CD_INFO table and all seven rows are included from the CD_TYPE table.

NOTE

The SQL:2008 standard introduced an advanced type of outer join called a *partitioned join*, which can be used to fill in missing rows in a result set based on a column that forms a series. For example, an outer join of sales totals by department and month might have missing rows for departments that had no sales during some of the months. With a partitioned join, the missing rows can be generated in the result set with a zero in the sales column. As you might guess, the syntax for partitioned joins is complex and best tackled once you have experience writing less complicated outer joins. Also, partitioned joins are new enough that only a few SQL implementations, such as Oracle, currently support them.

Perform Union Operations

SQL provides yet one more method to combine data from different tables in a manner that is a bit different from the joins shown earlier in this chapter. The UNION operator is a method you can use to combine the results of multiple SELECT statements into a single result set, essentially concatenating rows from one query with rows from another. In contrast with

CDS_CONTINUED

CD_NAME: VARCHAR(60)	CD_TYPE: CHAR(4)	IN_STOCK: INT
Drive All Night	ALTR	19
Different Shades of Blue	BLUS	28
Bach	CLAS	6
Man Against Machine	CTRY	8
Dark Side of the Moon	CROK	10
Kind of Blue	JAZZ	11

CDS_DISCONTINUED

CD_NAME: VARCHAR(60)	CD_TYPE: CHAR(4)	IN_STOCK: INT
Architecture in Helsinki	CPOP	3
A.K.A.	CPOP	2
The Hunting Party	ALTR	2
Come On Over	CTRY	6
The Endless River	CROK	12
The Bodyguard	STRK	5

Figure 11-6 Combining the CDS_CONTINUED and CDS_DISCONTINUED tables

joins, which add columns from multiple tables side by side, unions add rows to the end of the result set. In order to use the UNION operator, each SELECT statement must produce *union-compatible* columns, meaning that each must produce the same number of columns, and corresponding columns must have compatible data types. For example, if the first column of a SELECT statement produces a character column, then other SELECT statements combined with it using the UNION operator must have a character data type in the first column rather than a numeric or datetime data type.

Let's take a look at an example to show you what I mean. Figure 11-6 shows two tables: the CDS_CONTINUED table and the CDS_DISCONTINUED table. The tables are identical in structure but serve two different purposes, which should be obvious from the table names.

Suppose you want to combine the data in these two tables so you can view information from both tables. You can, of course, execute two separate SELECT statements, or you can combine those statements into one statement that combines the information, as shown in the following example:

```
SELECT *
  FROM CDS_CONTINUED
UNION
SELECT *
  FROM CDS_DISCONTINUED;
```

As you can see, the two SELECT statements are combined using the UNION operator. If you execute this statement, you'll receive the following results:

```
CD_NAME                        CD_TYPE  IN_STOCK
-----------------------------  -------  --------
A.K.A.                         CPOP     2
```

```
Architecture in Helsinki      CPOP    3
Bach                          CLAS    6
Come On Over                  CTRY    6
Dark Side of the Moon         CROK    10
Different Shades of Blue      BLUS    28
Drive All Night               ALTR    19
Kind of Blue                  JAZZ    11
Man Against Machine           CTRY    8
The Bodyguard                 STRK    6
The Endless River             CROK    12
The Hunting Party             ALTR    2
```

The results include 12 rows of data, 6 rows from each table. You can limit the results even further by specifying search conditions in WHERE clauses. You can also specify that your search return only specific columns, as in the following statement:

```
SELECT CD_TYPE
  FROM CDS_CONTINUED
UNION
SELECT CD_TYPE
  FROM CDS_DISCONTINUED;
```

Now when you generate your query, only values from the CD_TYPE column are displayed:

```
CD_TYPE
-------
ALTR
BLUS
CLAS
CPOP
CROK
CTRY
JAXX
STRK
```

Notice that only 8 rows are returned rather than 12. This is because duplicate rows are filtered out by default when you use the UNION operator. If you want all rows included in the query results, regardless of whether there are duplicate values, you can add the ALL keyword after the UNION operator, as shown in the following example:

```
SELECT CD_TYPE
  FROM CDS_CONTINUED
UNION ALL
SELECT CD_TYPE
  FROM CDS_DISCONTINUED;
```

This statement will return 12 rows rather than 8, with several values duplicated.

As you can see, the UNION operator is useful only in very specific cases. If you want more control over your query results, you should use one of the several types of joins supported by SQL.

In addition, the SQL standard supports the INTERSECT and EXCEPT operators, which have syntax similar to UNION. INTERSECT works like UNION except it returns only rows that appear in the results of both SELECT statements. EXCEPT, on the other hand, returns only rows that appear in the results of the first SELECT statement but not in the results of the second one. SQL Server supports both INTERSECT and EXCEPT. Oracle supports INTERSECT but uses the operator MINUS instead of EXCEPT. MySQL supports neither INTERSECT nor EXCEPT.

Try This 11-1 Querying Multiple Tables

In this chapter, you have been introduced to a variety of join operations as well as the UNION operator, which, technically, is not considered a join. Now you will have the opportunity to practice several of these join techniques by querying data from the INVENTORY database. Specifically, you will query some of the tables that are configured with foreign key relationships, which are the sort of relationships that tie data from one table to data in another table. Because you will not be changing any data, you should feel free to try out various types of join operations beyond what we review in this Try This exercise. You can download the Try_This_11.txt file, which contains the SQL statements used in this Try This exercise.

Step by Step

1. Open the client application for your RDBMS and connect to the INVENTORY database.
2. The first type of operation you'll perform is a comma-separated join on the ARTISTS and ARTIST_CDS tables. The join will use the ARTIST_ID column to establish the equi-join condition. Enter and execute the following SQL statement:

   ```
   SELECT * FROM ARTISTS a, ARTIST_CDS c
    WHERE a.ARTIST_ID = c.ARTIST_ID;
   ```

   Your query results should include 16 rows and should include the ARTIST_ID columns from both tables as well as the ARTIST_NAME, PLACE_OF_BIRTH, and COMPACT_DISC_ID columns.
3. You will now modify the preceding statement so that it also joins the COMPACT_DISCS table. That way, you can display the actual name of the CDs. In addition, you will specify the names of the columns that should be returned. Enter and execute the following SQL statement:

   ```
   SELECT d.CD_TITLE, a.ARTIST_NAME, a.PLACE_OF_BIRTH
     FROM ARTISTS a, ARTIST_CDS c, COMPACT_DISCS d
   ```

```
  WHERE a.ARTIST_ID = c.ARTIST_ID
    AND d.CD_ID = c.CD_ID;
```

Your query results should again include 16 rows. However, this time the results will display only the CD_TITLE, ARTIST_NAME, and PLACE_OF_BIRTH columns.

4. Now let's turn the last SELECT statement into a cross join. Enter and execute the following SQL statement:

```
SELECT d.CD_TITLE, a.ARTIST_NAME, a.PLACE_OF_BIRTH
  FROM ARTISTS a CROSS JOIN ARTIST_CDS c
                 CROSS JOIN COMPACT_DISCS d
 WHERE a.ARTIST_ID = c.ARTIST_ID
   AND d.CD_ID = c.CD_ID;
```

You should receive the same query results as you did in the preceding SELECT statement.

5. The next type of statement that you'll try is a condition join. As you probably recall, a condition join can be either an inner join or an outer join. The first type you'll try is the inner join. In this statement, you'll join together three tables: COMPACT_DISCS, COMPACT_DISC_TYPES, and MUSIC_TYPES. Enter and execute the following SQL statement:

```
SELECT d.CD_TITLE, t.MUSIC_TYPE_NAME
  FROM COMPACT_DISCS d
       JOIN COMPACT_DISC_TYPES dt
         ON d.CD_ID = dt.CD_ID
       JOIN MUSIC_TYPES t
         ON dt.MUSIC_TYPE_ID = t.MUSIC_TYPE_ID;
```

Your query results should include 28 rows. Only the CD_TITLE column and the MUSIC_TYPE_NAME column should be displayed.

6. Now let's modify the last SELECT statement to create a full outer join on both join conditions. Enter and execute the following SQL statement:

```
SELECT d.CD_TITLE, t.MUSIC_TYPE_NAME
  FROM COMPACT_DISCS d
       FULL JOIN COMPACT_DISC_TYPES dt
         ON d.CD_ID = dt.CD_ID
       FULL JOIN MUSIC_TYPES t
         ON dt.MUSIC_TYPE_ID = t. MUSIC_TYPE_ID;
```

Your query results should still include 28 rows. This is because all the rows in the COMPACT_DISC_TYPES table have at least one matching row in the COMPACT_DISCS table, and all the rows in the MUSIC_TYPES table have at least one matching row in the COMPACT_DISC_TYPES table.

7. Close the client application.

(continued)

Try This Summary

In this Try This exercise, you created comma-separated, cross, and condition joins. The condition joins included inner and outer joins. As you can see, join operations provide a great deal of flexibility when querying data from the tables in your database. However, they're not the only solution when accessing data from more than one table. A subquery will often provide the same functionality as a join. In Chapter 12, I discuss subqueries in great detail. As you will see, they provide yet one more way for you to access data from multiple tables.

Chapter 11 Self Test

1. You are using a comma-separated join operation to join two tables. The first table contains five rows and the second table contains three rows. How many rows will the Cartesian product table contain?
2. What constitutes an equi-join condition in a WHERE clause?
3. Which clause contains the equi-join condition in a comma-separated join?
4. What basic guidelines should you follow when creating a comma-separated join?
5. You're creating a join on two tables. You assign correlation names to each of these tables. Which names should you use in the SELECT clause: the correlation names or the actual table names?
6. Which type of join is nearly identical to the comma-separated join?
   - **A** Condition join
   - **B** Natural join
   - **C** Cross join
   - **D** Named column join
7. How many tables are contained in a self-join?
8. What guidelines must you follow when creating natural joins or named column joins?
9. What is the difference between a natural join and a named column join?
10. Which type of join contains a USING clause to specify the equi-join condition?
11. What are the two types of condition joins?
12. What are the three types of outer joins?

13. Which type of condition join should you use if you want to return only matched rows?

    A Inner join

    B Left outer join

    C Right outer join

    D Full outer join

14. Which type of condition join returns all matched and unmatched rows?

    A Inner join

    B Left outer join

    C Right outer join

    D Full outer join

15. Which type of join contains an ON clause?

    A Cross join

    B Comma-separated join

    C Natural join

    D Condition join

16. A(n) ______________ operator allows you to combine separate SELECT statements into one statement in order to join data in a query result.

17. What keyword can you use with a UNION operator to return all rows in the query results, regardless of whether there are duplicate values?

Chapter 12

Using Subqueries to Access and Modify Data

Key Skills & Concepts

- Create Subqueries that Return Multiple Rows
- Create Subqueries that Return One Value
- Work with Correlated Subqueries
- Use Nested Subqueries
- Use Subqueries to Modify Data

Subqueries, like joins, provide a way to access data in multiple tables with a single query. A subquery can be added to a SELECT, INSERT, UPDATE, or DELETE statement in order to allow that statement to use the query results returned by the subquery. The subquery is essentially an embedded SELECT statement that acts as a gateway to data in a second table. The data returned by the subquery is used by the primary statement to meet whatever conditions have been defined in that statement. In this chapter, I discuss how subqueries are used in various statements, particularly SELECT statements, and provide examples that demonstrate how to create subqueries and what type of query results to expect.

Create Subqueries that Return Multiple Rows

In Chapter 9, I include several examples of subqueries that are used to demonstrate certain types of predicates, such as IN and EXISTS. This chapter, in many ways, is an extension of that discussion because of the way in which subqueries are most commonly implemented—in the WHERE clause of a SELECT statement. An understanding of these types of subqueries goes hand in hand with an understanding of how certain predicates are formulated to create specific search conditions, search conditions that rely on those subqueries to return data from a referenced table.

You can divide subqueries in a WHERE clause into two general categories: those that can return multiple rows and those that can return only one value. In this section, I discuss the first of these categories. In the next section, "Create Subqueries that Return One Value," I discuss the second category. As I expand on each subject, you'll no doubt recognize the statement formats from my discussion of predicates. Although this information might seem a bit repetitive (which is why I keep it brief), it is presented here not only to provide a cohesive overview of subqueries, but also to provide a different perspective. In other words, rather than looking at subqueries through the perspective of the predicate, we'll look directly at the subquery itself.

Despite the fact that my discussion focuses on subqueries that are implemented through the WHERE clause, the use of subqueries is not limited to that clause. Indeed, you can include subqueries in a SELECT clause or HAVING clause. However, using subqueries in a SELECT clause is not very common. In addition, you would use subqueries in a HAVING clause only when defining search conditions on grouped data. Even so, the principles for using subqueries in a HAVING clause are similar to using them in a WHERE clause. For these reasons, my discussion here focuses on using subqueries in the WHERE clause. As you become a more advanced SQL programmer, you will likely want to try using subqueries in other places within a SELECT statement.

Using the IN Predicate

The first type of subquery that we'll look at is the type used within the IN predicate. As you might recall from Chapter 9, the IN predicate compares values from a column in the primary table to values returned by the subquery. If the column value is in the subquery results, that row (from the primary table) is returned in the query results of the SELECT statement. For example, suppose you want to query data from the CD_STOCK table, shown in Figure 12-1.

Your query results should include only those rows whose CD_TITLE value matches one of the values returned by the subquery. The subquery results should include only those rows

CD_STOCK

CD_TITLE: VARCHAR(60)	STOCK: INT
Drive All Night	12
Different Shades of Blue	42
Innervisions (Remastered)	16
The Definitive Collection	34
Rumours (Reissued)	17
Come On Over	6
Old Boots, New Dirt	32
Dark Side of the Moon	27
Kind of Blue	21

CD_ARTISTS

TITLE: VARCHAR(60)	ARTIST_NAME: VARCHAR(60)
Drive All Night	Glen Hansard
Different Shades of Blue	Joe Bonamassa
Innervisions (Remastered)	Stevie Wonder
The Definitive Collection	Stevie Wonder
Rumours (Reissued)	Fleetwood Mac
Come On Over	Shania Twain
Man Against Machine	Garth Brooks
Bach	Joshua Bell
Old Boots, New Dirt	Jason Aldean
Thriller	Michael Jackson
The Endless River	Pink Floyd
Dark Side of the Moon	Pink Floyd
Kind of Blue	Miles Davis

Figure 12-1 Querying the CD_STOCK and CD_ARTISTS tables

that contain an ARTIST_NAME value of Stevie Wonder (from the CD_ARTISTS table). The following SELECT statement will return this data:

```
SELECT *
  FROM CD_STOCK
 WHERE CD_TITLE IN
    ( SELECT TITLE
        FROM CD_ARTISTS
      WHERE ARTIST_NAME = 'Stevie Wonder' );
```

Let's take a closer look at the subquery in this statement. As you can see, it is included in the IN predicate, after the IN keyword. The subquery is basically a SELECT statement that includes a search condition defined in the WHERE clause:

```
SELECT TITLE
  FROM CD_ARTISTS
 WHERE ARTIST_NAME = 'Stevie Wonder'
```

If you were to execute only the subquery, you would receive the following query results:

```
TITLE
-------------------------
Innervisions (Remastered)
The Definitive Collection
```

These results are then used by the IN predicate to compare them to the CD_TITLE values in the CD_STOCK table. When you execute the entire SELECT statement, you receive the following results:

```
CD_TITLE                   STOCK
-------------------------  -----
Innervisions (Remastered)  16
The Definitive Collection  34
```

Notice that only two rows are returned from the CD_STOCK table. These rows represent the two CDs performed by Stevie Wonder. Even though the CD_STOCK table does not include artist information, you can still tie data from the two tables together because they include similar columns, allowing you to use the data returned by a subquery.

NOTE

In the case of the example table shown in Figure 12-1, it is conceivable that a foreign key would be configured on the CD_TITLE column of the CD_STOCK table to reference the TITLE column of the CD_ARTISTS table. However, a foreign key relationship is not required. The primary requirement that a subquery must meet is that it return results that are logically comparable to the referencing column values. Otherwise, the subquery serves no purpose, and no rows will be returned by the primary SELECT statement because the condition of the IN predicate cannot be met.

Using the EXISTS Predicate

In some circumstances, you might want your subquery to return only a value of true or false. The content of the data itself is unimportant in terms of meeting a predicate condition. In this case, you can use an EXISTS predicate to define your subquery. The EXISTS predicate evaluates to true if one or more rows are returned by the subquery; otherwise, it evaluates to false.

For an EXISTS predicate to be useful, the associated subquery should include a search condition that matches values in the two tables that are being linked through the subquery. (I explain this type of subquery in more detail in the "Work with Correlated Subqueries" section later in this chapter.) This search condition is similar to the equi-join condition used in certain join operations. (See Chapter 11 for information about joins and equi-join conditions.) For example, returning to the CD_STOCK table and the CD_ARTISTS tables (shown in Figure 12-1), we can create a SELECT statement that uses an EXISTS predicate to query the CD_ARTISTS table:

```
SELECT *
  FROM CD_STOCK s
 WHERE EXISTS
    ( SELECT TITLE
        FROM CD_ARTISTS a
       WHERE a.ARTIST_NAME = 'Stevie Wonder'
         AND s.CD_TITLE    = a.TITLE );
```

In this statement, each row returned by the primary SELECT statement is evaluated against the subquery. If the condition specified in the EXISTS predicate is true, the row is included in the query results; otherwise, the row is omitted. When the specified condition is true, that means at least one row has been returned by the subquery. In this case, the row returned will include an ARTIST_NAME value of Stevie Wonder. In addition, the CD_TITLE value in the CD_STOCK table will be the same as the TITLE value in the CD_ARTISTS table. As a result, only two rows will be returned by the entire SELECT statement:

```
CD_TITLE                    STOCK
--------------------------- -----
Innervisions (Remastered)   16
The Definitive Collection   34
```

As was the case with the IN predicate, the EXISTS predicate allows you to use a subquery to access information in another table. Even though the CD_STOCK table doesn't include information about the performing artists, the subquery allows you to return data that is based on artist information.

NOTE

The manner in which an EXISTS predicate is processed can sometimes be a little unclear. Be sure to refer to Chapter 9 for a more complete discussion of that predicate.

Using Quantified Comparison Predicates

The IN and EXISTS predicates are not the only predicates that rely on the type of subqueries that can return one or more rows for the search condition to evaluate to true. Quantified comparison predicates—SOME, ANY, and ALL—also use subqueries that can return multiple rows. These predicates are used in conjunction with comparison operators to determine whether any or all returned values (from the subquery) meet the search condition set by the predicate. The SOME and ANY predicates, which perform the same function, check to see whether *any* returned values meet the search requirement. The ALL predicate checks to see whether *all* returned values meet the search requirement.

When a quantified comparison predicate is used, the values in a column from the primary table are compared to the values returned by the subquery. Let's take a look at an example to clarify how this works. Suppose your database includes the RETAIL_PRICES table and the SALES_PRICES table, shown in Figure 12-2.

Now suppose that you decide to query the RETAIL_PRICES table, but you want to return only those rows with an R_PRICE value greater than *all* values in the S_PRICE column in the SALES_PRICES table for those S_PRICE values less than 11.99. To set up this query, you can create a statement similar to the following:

```
SELECT CD_NAME, R_PRICE
  FROM RETAIL_PRICES
 WHERE R_PRICE > ALL
   ( SELECT S_PRICE
       FROM SALES_PRICES
      WHERE S_PRICE < 11.99 );
```

RETAIL_PRICES

CD_NAME: VARCHAR(60)	R_PRICE: NUMERIC(5,2)	AMOUNT: INT
Drive All Night	5.99	12
Different Shades of Blue	11.99	42
Innervisions (Remastered)	10.00	16
The Definitive Collection	8.39	34
Rumours (Reissued)	7.99	17
Come on Over	5.99	6
Man Against Machine	9.99	8

SALES_PRICES

CD_TITLE: VARCHAR(60)	S_PRICE: NUMERIC(5,2)
Drive All Night	5.99
Different Shades of Blue	11.99
Innervisions (Remastered)	8.99
The Definitive Collection	7.99
Rumours (Reissued)	7.99
Come on Over	5.99
Man Against Machine	9.99

Figure 12-2 Querying the RETAIL_PRICES and SALES_PRICES tables

Notice that the subquery returns only one column of data—the S_PRICE values that are less than 11.99. The values in the R_PRICE column are then compared to the subquery results. If a specific R_PRICE value is greater than *all* the subquery results, that row is returned. When you execute the entire SELECT statement, you receive the following results:

```
CD_NAME                           R_PRICE
------------------------------    -------
Different Shades of Blue          11.99
Innervisions (Remastered)         10.00
```

As you can see, only two rows are returned. For each row, the R_PRICE value is greater than the highest price returned by the subquery, which in this case would be 9.99.

Ask the Expert

Q: You state that a SELECT clause can include a subquery. How would you include the subquery in that clause?

A: You can include the subquery in a SELECT clause just as you would a column name. The values returned from the subquery are inserted in the query results in the same way column values would be inserted. For example, you can insert a subquery in a SELECT clause of a statement that is used to query the CD_STOCK table (shown in Figure 12-1). The subquery pulls data from the CD_ARTISTS table, as shown in the following example:

```
SELECT CD_TITLE,
       ( SELECT ARTIST_NAME
           FROM CD_ARTISTS a
          WHERE s.CD_TITLE = a.TITLE ) AS ARTIST,
       STOCK FROM CD_STOCK s;
```

In the main part of this statement, values are pulled from the CD_TITLE and STOCK columns. In addition to these values, a list of artists is returned by the subquery. The artists' names are matched up to their CDs by using a comparison predicate to compare values in the CD_TITLE and TITLE columns.

When using a subquery in a SELECT clause, you must be careful not to create a subquery that returns only one value when multiple values are needed. When you return only one value, that value might be inserted into all rows returned by the main SELECT statement, depending on how you've constructed your query.

Create Subqueries that Return One Value

So far, we have looked at subqueries that can return one or more rows of data. This is fine in many circumstances; however, there might be times when you want your subquery to return only one value so that you can compare the values in one column with a single subquery value. In these cases, you can use comparison operators.

As you learned in Chapter 9, the comparison operators include equal to (=), not equal to (<>), less than (<), greater than (>), less than or equal to (<=), and greater than or equal to (>=). For example, let's take another look at the RETAIL_PRICES and SALES_PRICES tables (shown in Figure 12-2). Suppose you want to retrieve data from the RETAIL_PRICES table. You want the R_PRICE values to equal the maximum price listed in the S_PRICE column of the SALES_PRICES table. The following query allows you to return the necessary data:

```
SELECT CD_NAME, R_PRICE
  FROM RETAIL_PRICES
 WHERE R_PRICE =
    ( SELECT MAX(S_PRICE)
        FROM SALES_PRICES );
```

Notice that the subquery returns only one value, which is 11.99 in this case. As a result, only rows with an R_PRICE value of 11.99 are returned by the SELECT statement, as shown in the following query results:

```
CD_NAME                            R_PRICE
---------------------------------  -------
Different Shades of Blue           11.99
```

You do not have to use an aggregate function (such as MAX) to return a single value in a subquery. For example, the subquery's WHERE clause might include a condition that will return only one value. The important point to remember is that you must be sure that your subquery returns only one value; otherwise, you will receive an error when using a comparison operator. However, if you've set up your subquery properly, you can use any of the comparison operators to compare column values. In addition, you're not limited to numbers. Character strings can also be compared in comparison predicates.

NOTE

In many cases, you can use predicates such as IN with subqueries that return only one value. However, it is usually more efficient to use predicates containing the conditions equal to (=) or not equal to (<>), not the conditions less than (<), less than or equal to (<=), greater than (>), or greater than or equal to (>=) with subqueries that return one value.

Work with Correlated Subqueries

In the "Using the EXISTS Predicate" section earlier in this chapter, I mention that for the EXISTS predicate to be useful, it should include in the subquery a search condition that matches values in the two tables that are being linked through the subquery. To illustrate this point, I include in that section an example SELECT statement that contains such a subquery. I'll repeat that statement here for your convenience:

```
SELECT *
  FROM CD_STOCK s
 WHERE EXISTS
   ( SELECT TITLE
       FROM CD_ARTISTS a
      WHERE a.ARTIST_NAME = 'Stevie Wonder'
        AND s.CD_TITLE    = a.TITLE );
```

This statement references the CD_STOCK and CD_ARTISTS tables in Figure 12-1. Notice that the subquery includes a predicate that matches CD_TITLE values in the CD_STOCK table to TITLE values in the CD_ARTISTS table. This matching of values is similar to the equi-join conditions you define when joining tables.

The reason I've returned to this statement is that it includes a type of subquery I have not discussed before—the correlated subquery. A *correlated subquery* is one that is dependent on the outer statement in some way. In this case, the outer statement is the main SELECT statement that includes a SELECT clause, a FROM clause, and a WHERE clause, which itself contains a subquery. Because that subquery references the CD_STOCK table, which is a component of the outer statement, the subquery is dependent on that statement in order to return data.

In most of the subquery examples we've looked at in this chapter, the subqueries have stood independent of the outer statement. For example, in the following SELECT statement (which was used as an example in the "Using the IN Predicate" section earlier in this chapter), the subquery is not dependent on the outer statement:

```
SELECT *
  FROM CD_STOCK
 WHERE CD_TITLE IN
   ( SELECT TITLE
       FROM CD_ARTISTS
      WHERE ARTIST_NAME = 'Stevie Wonder' );
```

In this case, the subquery merely returns results, which are then used in an outer statement. The subquery is evaluated (executed) just once, and the results are used by the main statement as necessary. However, with a correlated subquery, the subquery must be reevaluated for each row returned by the outer statement. The correlated subquery cannot be evaluated just once

Ask the Expert

Q: You state that creating a join might be a better alternative to creating a correlated subquery. How would you restate the preceding SELECT statement as a join?

A: In the preceding SELECT statement, you've already identified your equi-join condition in the subquery, and you already know the names of the two tables that are being joined. One way you can modify this statement is to use a comma-separated join, as shown in the following example:

```
SELECT CD_TITLE, STOCK
  FROM CD_STOCK s, CD_ARTISTS a
 WHERE a.ARTIST_NAME = 'Stevie Wonder'
   AND s.CD_TITLE    = a.TITLE;
```

Notice that the CD_TITLE and TITLE columns are still equated with each other. This statement produces the same results as the statement that included the correlated subquery, only the SQL implementation is not being forced to reprocess a subquery for each row returned by the outer statement. Instead, the WHERE clause merely takes the results returned by the FROM clause and applies the search conditions defined in the two predicates. For more information about join operations, see Chapter 11.

because at least one of the values changes for each row. For example, looking again at the SELECT statement that contains the correlated subquery (as part of the EXISTS predicate), you can see that the CD_TITLE value changes for each row returned by the outer SELECT statement. This can have a severe impact on performance, particularly when you are returning a large number of values. In these cases, you might find that creating a join provides better performance than a correlated subquery, but, of course, much depends on how your particular SQL implementation handles joins and correlated subqueries.

Use Nested Subqueries

Up to this point, we have looked at SELECT statements that include only one subquery. However, a SELECT statement can contain multiple subqueries. The SQL standard does not limit the number of subqueries that can be included in a statement, although practical application, performance, and the limitations of the SQL implementation all play an important role in determining what a reasonable number might be. Make certain that you refer to the documentation for your SQL implementation to determine what restrictions might apply to the use of subqueries.

One way you can include multiple subqueries in a SELECT statement is to include them as different components of the statement. For example, your WHERE clause might include two predicates, each of which contains a subquery. Another way in which multiple subqueries can be included in a SELECT statement is to nest one subquery inside the other. These are the types of subqueries we'll look at in this section.

A *nested subquery* is one that is a component of another subquery. The "outer" subquery acts as a primary SELECT statement that includes a subquery within one of its clauses. In most cases, the nested subquery will be part of a predicate in the WHERE clause of the outer subquery. Let's take a look at an example to help clarify this concept. The example uses the DISC_INVENTORY, DISC_ARTISTS, and DISC_TYPES tables, shown in Figure 12-3.

Suppose that you want to display the names of CDs and the amount in stock for CDs that are performed by country artists. The DISC_INVENTORY table contains the names of the CDs and the amount in stock for each one, the DISC_ARTISTS table contains the names of the artists, and the DISC_TYPES table contains the names of the artist types. The DISC_INVENTORY and DISC_ARTISTS tables are related through the ARTIST_ID column in each table. The DISC_ARTISTS and DISC_TYPES tables are related through the DISC_TYPE_ID column in each table. In order to return the information you need, you must query all three tables, as shown in the following SELECT statement:

```
SELECT DISC_NAME, STOCK_AMOUNT
  FROM DISC_INVENTORY
 WHERE ARTIST_ID IN
    ( SELECT ARTIST_ID
        FROM DISC_ARTISTS
       WHERE DISC_TYPE_ID IN
         ( SELECT DISC_TYPE_ID
             FROM DISC_TYPES
            WHERE DISC_TYPE_NAME = 'Country' ) );
```

DISC_INVENTORY

DISC_NAME: VARCHAR(60)	ARTIST_ID: INT	STOCK_AMOUNT: INT
Drive All Night	3001	12
Different Shades of Blue	3002	42
Innervisions (Remastered)	3003	16
The Definitive Collection	3003	34
Rumours (Reissued)	3004	17
Come On Over	3005	6
Man Against Machine	3006	8
Bach	3008	22
Old Boots, New Dirt	3009	32
Dark Side of the Moon	3010	27
Kind of Blue	3011	21

DISC_ARTISTS

ARTIST_ID: INT	ARTIST_NAME: VARCHAR(60)	DISC_TYPE_ID: INT
3001	Glen Hansard	10
3002	Joe Bonamassa	12
3003	Stevie Wonder	13
3004	Fleetwood Mac	11
3005	Shania Twain	16
3006	Garth Brooks	16
3007	J.S. Bach	14
3008	Joshua Bell	14
3009	Jason Aldean	16
3010	Pink Floyd	11
3011	Miles Davis	15

DISC_TYPES

DISC_TYPE_ID: INT	DISC_TYPE_NAME: CHAR(20)
10	Alternative Rock
11	Classic Rock
12	Blues
13	R&B
14	Classical
15	Jazz
16	Country
17	Pop
18	Soundtracks

Figure 12-3 Querying the DISC_INVENTORY, DISC_ARTISTS, and DISC_TYPES tables

In this statement, the primary SELECT statement queries the DISC_INVENTORY table. The statement includes a subquery in an IN predicate in the WHERE clause. The subquery is a SELECT statement that queries the DISC_ARTISTS table. The subquery, like the primary SELECT statement, includes an IN predicate in the WHERE clause, and this predicate also includes a subquery. As is the case with the outer subquery, the inner subquery includes a SELECT statement. However, in this case, the statement is querying the DISC_TYPES table.

To better understand how the entire SELECT statement works, let's first look at the inner subquery. If you were to execute this statement alone, it would return a value of 16, which is the DISC_TYPE_ID value for the DISC_TYPE_NAME value of Country. The outer subquery uses this value in the IN predicate to return those rows with a DISC_TYPE_ID value of 16. In this case, three rows are returned, containing ARTIST_ID values 3005 (Shania Twain), 3006 (Garth Brooks), and 3009 (Jason Aldean). The ARTIST_ID values are then used in the IN predicate of the primary SELECT statement to return only those rows that contain ARTIST_ID values of 3005, 3006, or 3009. If you execute the entire SELECT statement, you'll receive the following query results:

```
DISC_NAME              STOCK_AMOUNT
------------------     ------------
Come On Over           6
Man Against Machine    8
Old Boots, New Dirt    22
```

As you can see, only three rows are returned. Notice that the results don't include any information from the DISC_ARTISTS table or the DISC_TYPES table, although these two tables are integral to arriving at these results. If you had wanted, you could have nested additional subqueries in your statement. Each one would have been processed in the same manner as the subqueries shown in the previous example.

Use Subqueries to Modify Data

At the beginning of this chapter, I told you that you can use subqueries to modify data as well as query data. We'll now look at the three primary data modification statements—INSERT, UPDATE, and DELETE—and how they use subqueries to modify data in your database. For each statement, I provide an example that modifies data in the TITLE_TYPES table, shown in Figure 12-4. Each example includes a subquery that returns data from the TITLES_INVENTORY table. This information is used as a basis for the data modification in the TITLE_TYPES table.

NOTE

This section focuses on the subqueries used in the INSERT, UPDATE, and DELETE statements. For more information about the statements themselves, see Chapter 8.

TITLES_INVENTORY

TITLE_ID: INT	TITLE: VARCHAR(60)	STOCK: INT
101	Drive All Night	12
102	Different Shades of Blue	42
103	Innervisions (Remastered)	16
104	The Definitive Collection	34
105	Rumours (Reissued)	17
106	Come On Over	6
107	Man Against Machine	8
108	Bach	22

TITLE_TYPES

CD_TITLE: VARCHAR(60)	CD_TYPE: CHAR(20)
Drive All Night	Alt. Rock
Different Shades of Blue	Blues
Dark Side of the Moon	Rock
Innervisions (Remastered)	R&B
The Endless River	Rock
The Definitive Collection	R&B
Kind Of Blue	Jazz
Come On Over	Country
Man Against Machine	Country

Figure 12-4 Modifying the TITLE_TYPES table

Using Subqueries to Insert Data

An INSERT statement, as you no doubt recall, allows you to add data to an existing table. You can add that data directly to the table or through a view that allows you to insert data into the underlying table. If you use a subquery in an INSERT statement, you must include it as one of the values defined in the VALUES clause. For example, suppose you want to insert data into the TITLE_TYPES table. The VALUES clause should include a value for the CD_TITLE column and the CD_TYPE column. Now suppose that you know the TITLE_ID value (from the TITLES_INVENTORY table), but you don't know the exact name of the CD. You can create an INSERT statement that pulls the name of the CD from the TITLES_INVENTORY table and inserts that value into the TITLE_TYPES table, as shown in the following example:

```
INSERT INTO TITLE_TYPES VALUES
( ( SELECT TITLE FROM TITLES_INVENTORY WHERE TITLE_ID = 108 ), 'Blues' );
```

Notice that the subquery appears as one of the values in the VALUES clause. The subquery returns the value of Bach. This value and the value Blues are inserted into the TITLE_TYPES table. (The value Blues is incorrect but I use an UPDATE statement to correct the value in the "Using Subqueries to Update Data" topic later in this chapter.)

For the most part, using a subquery in an INSERT statement is a relatively simple process. However, you must be sure that your subquery returns only one value; otherwise, you will receive an error. In addition, the value must be compatible with the data type and any other constraints defined on the target column.

NOTE

Not all SQL implementations support the use of a subquery as a value in the INSERT statement. However, SQL Server, Oracle, and MySQL do.

Using Subqueries to Update Data

An UPDATE statement allows you to modify existing data in a table. As with an INSERT statement, you can modify data directly or through a view, if that view is updatable. To use a subquery in an UPDATE statement, you can include it in a predicate in the WHERE clause, as you did with the SELECT statements we looked at earlier in this chapter. For example, if you want to update the Bach row that was inserted in the preceding INSERT statement example (to correct the CD_TYPE value), you can create an UPDATE statement similar to the following:

```
UPDATE TITLE_TYPES
   SET CD_TYPE = 'Classical'
 WHERE CD_TITLE IN
   ( SELECT TITLE
       FROM TITLES_INVENTORY
      WHERE TITLE_ID = 108 );
```

In this statement, the IN predicate compares the values in the CD_TITLE column of the TITLE_TYPES table with the value returned by the subquery. The subquery is a simple SELECT statement that returns data from the TITLES_INVENTORY table. The subquery here works the same way as you saw in earlier SELECT statement examples. In this case, the subquery returns a value of Bach. This value is then used to determine which row in the TITLE_TYPES table to update. Once this row is determined, the CD_TYPE value is changed to Classical.

Subqueries are not limited to the WHERE clause of an UPDATE statement. You can also use a subquery in the SET clause to provide a value for the identified column. For example, suppose you want to once again update the Bach row that was inserted in the preceding INSERT statement example. You can pull a value from the TITLES_INVENTORY table to use as the new value for the TITLE_TYPES table, as shown in the following UPDATE statement:

```
UPDATE TITLE_TYPES
   SET CD_TITLE =
    ( SELECT TITLE
        FROM TITLES_INVENTORY
       WHERE TITLE_ID = 108 )
 WHERE CD_TITLE = 'Bach';
```

Notice that instead of specifying a value in the SET clause (to the right of the equals sign), you can specify a subquery. The subquery returns a value of Bach and uses that value to update the TITLE_TYPES table.

NOTE

In the preceding example, all we've done is write the same value over the existing one. The purpose of this statement is only to demonstrate how a subquery can be used in a SET clause. Even if a new value were being written into the row, the principles would be the same. For example, if the title had changed in the TITLES_INVENTORY table, the preceding statement would update the title in the TITLE_TYPES table.

Using Subqueries to Delete Data

A DELETE statement is similar to an UPDATE statement in terms of how a subquery can be used in the WHERE clause. You simply include a predicate that contains a subquery. In the following example, I delete the Bach row that I modified in the previous UPDATE statement example. To determine which row to delete, I use a subquery to return the appropriate TITLE value from the TITLES_INVENTORY table:

```
DELETE FROM TITLE_TYPES
 WHERE CD_TITLE IN
   ( SELECT TITLE
       FROM TITLES_INVENTORY
      WHERE TITLE_ID = 108 );
```

As you would expect, the subquery returns the value of Bach. The IN predicate compares this value to the values in the CD_TITLE column of the TITLE_TYPES table. Every row with matching values is deleted. In this case, only one row has a CD_TITLE value of Bach, so that is the row that is deleted.

Try This 12-1 Working with Subqueries

In this chapter, I discussed how you can use subqueries to query and modify data. The subqueries we looked at for the most part relied on the use of predicates to define the subquery condition. In this Try This exercise, you will create a number of SELECT statements that include WHERE clauses. These clauses will each include a predicate that defines a subquery, allowing you to access data from more than one table. You will also modify data by using an UPDATE statement that contains subqueries in the SET clause and the WHERE clause. For this exercise, as with previous Try This exercises, you will be using the INVENTORY database. You can download the Try_This_12.txt file, which contains the SQL statements used in this exercise.

(continued)

Step by Step

1. Open the client application for your RDBMS and connect to the INVENTORY database.

2. The first SELECT statement that you'll create allows you to return the name and number of CDs that are produced by Columbia. Enter and execute the following SQL statement:

```
SELECT CD_TITLE, IN_STOCK
  FROM COMPACT_DISCS
 WHERE LABEL_ID IN
    ( SELECT LABEL_ID
        FROM CD_LABELS
       WHERE COMPANY_NAME = 'Columbia' );
```

This statement uses a subquery to return the LABEL_ID value for Columbia, which is stored in the CD_LABELS table. The value is then used in the IN predicate to compare it to the LABEL_ID values in the COMPACT_DISCS table. Your query should return two rows.

3. In the next statement, you will use an EXISTS predicate to define a subquery. The predicate determines whether the COMPACT_DISCS table contains any rows with a CD_TITLE value of Dark Side of the Moon. Enter and execute the following SQL statement:

```
SELECT COMPANY_NAME
  FROM CD_LABELS l
 WHERE EXISTS
    ( SELECT *
        FROM COMPACT_DISCS d
       WHERE l.LABEL_ID = d.LABEL_ID
         AND CD_TITLE   = 'Dark Side of the Moon' );
```

The statement will return the name of the company that produces the Dark Side of the Moon CD, which in this case is Capitol Records. The Capitol Records row in the CD_LABELS table is the only row that evaluates to true for the subquery in the EXISTS predicate.

4. In the next statement you create, you'll determine the distributor names for those CDs in which the LABEL_ID value in the CD_LABELS table is equal to any LABEL_ID values returned by the subquery. Enter and execute the following SQL statement:

```
SELECT COMPANY_NAME
  FROM CD_LABELS
 WHERE LABEL_ID = ANY
    ( SELECT LABEL_ID
        FROM COMPACT_DISCS
       WHERE IN_STOCK > 30 );
```

The subquery returns only those LABEL_ID values for rows that contain an IN_STOCK value greater than 30. When you execute this statement, the names of only three companies should be returned.

5. Now you'll create a SELECT statement that uses a comparison predicate to define a subquery. The subquery returns the LABEL_ID value (from the CD_LABELS table) for Motown / Universal. That value is then compared to the LABEL_ID values in the COMPACT_DISCS table. Enter and execute the following SQL statement:

```
SELECT CD_TITLE, IN_STOCK
  FROM COMPACT_DISCS
 WHERE LABEL_ID =
   ( SELECT LABEL_ID
       FROM CD_LABELS
      WHERE COMPANY_NAME = 'Motown / Universal' );
```

   This statement should return only two rows.

6. Now let's redo the statement in step 5 and turn it into a comma-separated join. Remember that you should assign correlation names to the tables to simplify the code. Also remember that the WHERE clause should include an equi-join condition that matches up LABEL_ID values. Enter and execute the following SQL statement:

```
SELECT CD_TITLE, IN_STOCK
  FROM COMPACT_DISCS d, CD_LABELS l
 WHERE d.LABEL_ID    = l.LABEL_ID
   AND COMPANY_NAME = 'Motown / Universal';
```

   As you can see, this statement is a lot simpler than the subquery used in the preceding statement, and it returns the same results.

7. In the next statement that you'll create, you will use a nested subquery to return values to the outer subquery. Enter and execute the following SQL statement:

```
SELECT ARTIST_NAME
  FROM ARTISTS
 WHERE ARTIST_ID IN
   ( SELECT ARTIST_ID
       FROM ARTIST_CDS
      WHERE CD_ID IN
         ( SELECT CD_ID
             FROM COMPACT_DISCS
            WHERE CD_TITLE = 'Kind of Blue' ) );
```

   The inner subquery returns the CD_ID value for the Kind of Blue CD. The outer subquery then uses this value to determine the ARTIST_ID value for that CD. This value is then used in the main SELECT statement, which returns one value: Miles Davis. He is the artist on the Kind of Blue CD.

8. Now we're going to move on to using subqueries in an UPDATE statement. However, let's first take a look at the table we're going to update, which is the COMPACT_DISC_TYPES table. In order to know what to update, we're going to use values from the

(continued)

COMPACT_DISCS table and the MUSIC_TYPES table to help identify the IDs used in the COMPACT_DISC_TYPES table. Enter and execute the following SQL statement:

```
SELECT CD_TITLE, MUSIC_TYPE_NAME
  FROM COMPACT_DISCS d, COMPACT_DISC_TYPES t, MUSIC_TYPES m
 WHERE d.CD_ID           = t.CD_ID
   AND t.MUSIC_TYPE_ID = m.MUSIC_TYPE_ID
   AND CD_TITLE          = 'Dark Side of the Moon';
```

In this statement, you join three tables to return the CD_TITLE value and MUSIC_TYPE_NAME value for the Dark Side of the Moon CD. The CD is classified as Progressive Rock.

9. In this step, you will update the row in the COMPACT_DISC_TYPES table that matches the CD_ID for the Dark Side of the Moon CD with the MUSIC_TYPE_ID value for the Progressive Rock music type. You'll change the music type from Progressive Rock to Pop. Enter and execute the following SQL statement:

```
UPDATE COMPACT_DISC_TYPES
   SET MUSIC_TYPE_ID =
     ( SELECT MUSIC_TYPE_ID
         FROM MUSIC_TYPES
        WHERE MUSIC_TYPE_NAME = 'Pop' )
 WHERE CD_ID =
     ( SELECT CD_ID
         FROM COMPACT_DISCS
        WHERE CD_TITLE = 'Dark Side of the Moon' )
   AND MUSIC_TYPE_ID =
     ( SELECT MUSIC_TYPE_ID
         FROM MUSIC_TYPES
        WHERE MUSIC_TYPE_NAME = 'Progressive Rock' );
```

The statement uses a subquery in the SET clause to pull the MUSIC_TYPE_ID value from the MUSIC_TYPES table. The statement also uses two subqueries in the WHERE clause of the UPDATE statement to determine which row to update in the COMPACT_DISC_TYPES table. The first subquery in the WHERE clause returns the CD_ID value for the Dark Side of the Moon CD. The second subquery returns the MUSIC_TYPE_ID value for the Classical music type.

10. Now let's query the COMPACT_DISC_TYPES table to view the changes. Enter and execute the following SQL statement:

```
SELECT CD_TITLE, MUSIC_TYPE_NAME
  FROM COMPACT_DISCS d, COMPACT_DISC_TYPES t, MUSIC_TYPES  m
 WHERE d.CD_ID           = t.CD_ID
   AND t.MUSIC_TYPE_ID = m.MUSIC_TYPE_ID
   AND CD_TITLE          = 'Dark Side of the Moon';
```

The MUSIC_TYPE_NAME value should now be Pop.

11. Finally, you will return the COMPACT_DISC_TYPES table to its original state. Enter and execute the following SQL statement:

```
UPDATE COMPACT_DISC_TYPES
   SET MUSIC_TYPE_ID =
     ( SELECT MUSIC_TYPE_ID
         FROM MUSIC_TYPES
        WHERE MUSIC_TYPE_NAME = 'Progressive Rock' )
 WHERE CD_ID =
     ( SELECT CD_ID
         FROM COMPACT_DISCS
        WHERE CD_TITLE      = 'Dark Side of the Moon' )
          AND MUSIC_TYPE_ID =
          ( SELECT MUSIC_TYPE_ID
              FROM MUSIC_TYPES
             WHERE MUSIC_TYPE_NAME = 'Pop' );
```

This statement is similar to the preceding UPDATE statement that you used, only now the Progressive Rock music type will be used (which was the original music type).

12. Let's check the table one more time. Enter and execute the following SQL statement:

```
SELECT CD_TITLE, MUSIC_TYPE_NAME
  FROM COMPACT_DISCS d, COMPACT_DISC_TYPES t, MUSIC_TYPES  m
 WHERE d.CD_ID           = t.CD_ID
   AND t.MUSIC_TYPE_ID   = m.MUSIC_TYPE_ID
   AND CD_TITLE          = 'Dark Side of the Moon';
```

The COMPACT_DISC_TYPES table should now contain the same values as it did when you started this exercise.

13. Close the client application.

Try This Summary

In this Try This exercise, you created several SELECT statements that contained subqueries. These subqueries were included in predicates that permit the subqueries to return one or more rows. Specifically, the WHERE clauses included the IN, EXISTS, and ANY predicates. In addition, you created a SELECT statement that included a comparison predicate, which permits the subquery to return only one row. You also created a SELECT statement that included nested subqueries. These subqueries used the IN predicate. In addition to querying data in the INVENTORY database, you updated the COMPACT_DISC_TYPES table by using subqueries that accessed other tables. As you can see, subqueries provide you with a versatile tool for accessing data in your database. However, when creating statements that include subqueries, you should always try to determine whether a join would perform better in any given situation.

Chapter 12 Self Test

1. In which types of statements can you include subqueries?

   A SELECT

   B INSERT

   C UPDATE

   D DELETE

2. What is a subquery?

3. In which clauses of a SELECT statement can you include a subquery?

   A SELECT

   B WHERE

   C GROUP BY

   D HAVING

4. Into what two general categories can you divide subqueries in a WHERE clause?

5. Which types of predicates are you prevented from using with subqueries that return multiple rows?

   A IN and EXISTS predicates

   B SOME, ANY, and ALL predicates

   C Comparison predicates

   D Quantified comparison predicates

6. When does an EXISTS condition evaluate to true?

7. What should be included in a subquery's search condition when using an EXISTS predicate?

8. In addition to numbers, ________________ data can be compared in comparison predicates.

9. What are the three quantified comparison predicates?

10. Which types of predicates allow you to use subqueries that return multiple rows?

    A IN and EXISTS predicates

    B SOME, ANY, and ALL predicates

    C Comparison predicates

    D Quantified comparison predicates

11. What is a correlated subquery?
12. How often is a correlated subquery evaluated when a SELECT statement is processed?
13. A(n) ______________ is a subquery that is a component of another subquery.
14. How many subqueries can be included in a SELECT statement, as specified by the SQL standard?
15. Which clause in an INSERT statement can contain a subquery?
16. How many values can a subquery return if it is used in an INSERT statement?
17. Which clauses in an UPDATE statement can contain a subquery?

Chapter 13

Working with Temporal Data

Key Skills & Concepts

- Create and Use System-Versioned Tables
- Create and Use Application-Time Period Tables
- Create and Use System-Versioned Application-Time Period Tables

In this chapter, I discuss the temporal features that were added to the SQL:2011 standard. *Temporal data* is data that changes over time. In SQL, the term temporal data refers to any data that is defined with one or more associated time periods during which that data is considered to be effective or valid. You may find it helpful to visualize a timeline where each temporal data record (row) has a specific point on the timeline at which it becomes effective and a second point on the timeline when the record ceases to be effective. However, for records that are currently effective, the point at which it is no longer effective may be unknown.

It is perhaps an understatement to say the recent temporal data features of the SQL standard have been long awaited. The need to support temporal data in SQL was recognized in the early 1980s, as evidenced by books, research papers, and conference publications from that period. In 1995, the ISO SQL committee launched a project tasked with adding SQL language extensions to support temporal data. The project completed a proposed new part of the SQL standard known as SQL/Temporal in 1995. However, there were competing proposals from the American National Standards Institute (ANSI) and the UK, which led to considerable controversy and a failure to obtain adequate support for SQL/Temporal among the ISO SQL committee membership. The work on SQL/Temporal was canceled in 2001, not only because no new proposals had been submitted, but also because there was no indication that the DBMS vendors of the time were planning to implement any new extensions.

A second attempt at adding temporal features to the SQL standard was made in 2008, largely inspired by the earlier proposals, but with substantially different syntax. Rather than resurrecting SQL/Temporal, this proposal added "system-versioned tables" to SQL/Foundation (Part 2 of the SQL Standard). (I discuss system-versioned tables in the "Create and Use System-Versioned Tables" section of this chapter.) In 2010, another temporal feature known as "application-time period tables" was added to SQL/Foundation. (I discuss application-time period tables in the "Create and Use Application-Time Period Tables" section in this chapter.) Both system-versioned and application-time period were approved and published as part of the SQL:2011 standard. Although this may seem surprising at first, system-versioned tables and application-time period tables are not mutually exclusive, and thus it is possible to construct a system-versioned application-time period table. (I discuss these tables in the "Create and Use System-Versioned Application-Time Period Tables" section of this chapter.)

Create and Use System-Versioned Tables

As you learned in Chapter 3, system-versioned tables are one of five types of base tables supported by the SQL standard. A *system-versioned table* is a table that contains current rows as well as row history that is automatically maintained by the DBMS from a system (database) time perspective. System-versioned tables are useful in situations where an accurate history of data changes must be maintained for business and/or legal reasons. For example, a financial institution must keep previous versions of customer account information so that customers, auditors, and regulatory agencies can be provided a detailed history of account information. With system-versioned tables, previous versions of table rows are automatically preserved whenever an update or delete of a row is successfully processed by the DBMS. Furthermore, in order to maintain the integrity of the row history, only the DBMS is allowed to maintain the data values in the period begin and period end columns for each version of a row.

Here is the syntax for the CREATE TABLE statement, including the options required for defining a system-versioned table:

```
CREATE TABLE <table name>
( <table element> [ { , <table element> } . . . ] ,
  PERIOD FOR SYSTEM_TIME ( <period begin column name>,
                           <period end column name> ) )
[ WITH SYSTEM VERSIONING ]
```

Compared to the CREATE TABLE syntax you first saw in Chapter 3, you will likely notice these differences:

- The options for GLOBAL TEMPORARY and LOCAL TEMPORARY tables have been removed because system-versioned tables cannot be defined as temporary tables.
- The ON COMMIT clause has been removed because it only applies to temporary tables.
- The third line of the syntax contains the table period definition, which must be included in the table elements list for system-versioned tables. The table period definition contains the keywords PERIOD FOR SYSTEM_TIME followed by a comma-separated list containing the period begin column name and the period end column name, enclosed in a pair of parentheses. The period begin and period end column names must reference columns that are explicitly defined in the table. These columns must be defined with a datetime data type, such as DATE or TIMESTAMP, the NOT NULL clause, and the new GENERATE ALWAYS AS ROW BEGIN/END clause.
- The WITH SYSTEM VERSIONING clause implicitly adds the period begin column to the primary key constraint that was explicitly declared for the table. This prevents two rows with the same explicit primary key value from having the same period begin column value.

The best way to fully understand the definition of a system-versioned table is by looking at an example. Figure 13-1 shows the EMPLOYEE table, which contains the EMP_ID, EMP_NAME, SYS_BEGIN, and SYS_END columns. I have omitted the fractional seconds

EMPLOYEE

EMP_ID: INT	EMP_NAME: VARCHAR(50)	SYS_BEGIN: TIMESTAMP(12)	SYS_END: TIMESTAMP(12)
1	Kim I. Payne	2015-03-22 01:24:04	9999-12-30 00:00:00
2	Benjamin R. Vazquez	2015-03-22 01:24:04	9999-12-30 00:00:00
3	Agatha U. Lee	2015-03-22 01:24:04	9999-12-30 00:00:00

Figure 13-1 The EMPLOYEE system-versioned table

from the SYS_BEGIN and SYS_END timestamps for simplicity. The SYS_BEGIN column is the period begin column (the effective start date and time for each row) and the SYS_END column is the period end column (the effective end date and time for each row). You will likely notice that the SYS_END values for the three employees listed in the EMPLOYEE table all have the same value of midnight (zero hours, minutes, and seconds) on 12/30/9999. For current rows, the period end column will always contain a high value date or date and time. The system cannot know when a new row will cease to be effective, nor can the value be null, so a datetime value in the far future is the only sensible alternative.

NOTE

SQL implementations have different default display formats for date and time values. The formats shown in Figure 13-1 match the default format for TIMESTAMP columns in DB2 10. If you were to create the EMPLOYEE table on a different DBMS, you would likely see variances in the display format of the SYS_BEGIN and SYS_END column data. Also, as I already stated, I have omitted the fractional time components from Figure 13-1 for simplicity.

The TABLE CREATE statement for the EMPLOYEE table is as follows:

```
CREATE TABLE EMPLOYEE
(EMP_ID        INT             PRIMARY KEY NOT NULL,
 EMP_NAME      VARCHAR(50)     NOT NULL,
 SYS_BEGIN     TIMESTAMP(12)   GENERATED ALWAYS AS ROW BEGIN NOT NULL,
 SYS_END       TIMESTAMP(12)   GENERATED ALWAYS AS ROW END   NOT NULL,
 PERIOD FOR SYSTEM_TIME (SYS_BEGIN, SYS_END)
)
WITH SYSTEM VERSIONING;
```

The PERIOD FOR SYSTEM_TIME clause specifies SYS_BEGIN as the period begin column and SYS_END as the period end column. These columns specify the effective time period for each row in the table. Typically, the period begin and period end columns are defined with the TIMESTAMP data type and the precision specified by the SQL implementation, which is often the highest precision supported by the implementation. (Recall that TIMESTAMP precision specifies how many decimal places are carried in the fractional seconds included in the time component of the column.) In this example, I have specified TIMESTAMP(12), which is the precision required by DB2 10. Alternatively, a DATE data type can be used (if supported by the SQL implementation), which is appropriate when the data can have only one version per day. For example, insurance policies usually have effective dates without times because claims adjudication would be too confusing and difficult if insurance coverage were allowed to change multiple times per day.

The SYS_BEGIN column definition includes the GENERATED ALWAYS AS ROW BEGIN clause, as required by the SQL standard. This tells the DBMS to automatically populate the column with the period begin date and time when a new row is inserted. Once a row is inserted, the value of this column will never change. The SYS_BEGIN column is also defined with the NOT NULL clause, as required by the SQL standard.

Similarly, the SYS_END column is defined with the GENERATED ALWAYS AS ROW END clause and the NOT NULL clause, both of which are mandatory. The GENERATED ALWAYS AS ROW END clause tells the DBMS to automatically populate the column with a high datetime value for the specified data type when new rows are inserted. Essentially, this makes the new row valid forever. However, if the row is subsequently updated or deleted, the data value for this column will be automatically updated so that the row is no longer effective. I discuss this in more detail, including examples, later in this section.

NOTE

The SQL temporal features included in SQL:2011 are new enough that only a few SQL implementations currently support them. As of this writing, MySQL and SQL Server do not yet support SQL temporal features. Oracle 12*c* and Teradata support some of the SQL:2011 temporal features, but not system-versioned tables. IBM DB2 10 appears to support all the SQL:2011 temporal features. However, the DB2 10 syntax for system-versioned tables varies somewhat from the standard, and system-versioned tables must be created in three steps. First, the CREATE TABLE statement is run to create the base table. The WITH SYSTEM VERSIONING clause must be omitted at this point. DB2 10 also requires a transaction start date column (named TRANS_START in this example) in addition to the period begin and period end columns. This column may be hidden from normal queries using this IMPLICITLY HIDDEN clause. Also, the PERIOD FOR SYSTEM_TIME clause must be written as PERIOD SYSTEM_TIME (omitting the keyword FOR). Second, a history table must be created with a definition that is identical to the base table. Fortunately, the LIKE clause makes this statement very simple. Third, an ALTER statement must be run to link the base table and history table and to activate system versioning. Once the base table and history table are linked using the ALTER statement, the history table is automatically managed by the DB2 DBMS. For example, if you were to add a column to the base table, the DB2 DBMS would automatically add an identically defined column to the history table. The following example shows all three steps using DB2 10 syntax:

```
CREATE TABLE EMPLOYEE
(EMP_ID         INT             PRIMARY KEY NOT NULL,
 EMP_NAME       VARCHAR(50)     NOT NULL,
 SYS_BEGIN      TIMESTAMP(12)   GENERATED ALWAYS AS ROW BEGIN NOT NULL,
 SYS_END        TIMESTAMP(12)   GENERATED ALWAYS AS ROW END   NOT NULL,
```

```
 TRANS_START  TIMESTAMP(12) GENERATED ALWAYS AS TRANSACTION START ID
                                           IMPLICITLY HIDDEN,
 PERIOD SYSTEM_TIME (SYS_BEGIN, SYS_END)
);

CREATE TABLE EMPLOYEE_HISTORY LIKE EMPLOYEE;

ALTER TABLE EMPLOYEE ADD VERSIONING USE HISTORY TABLE EMPLOYEE_HISTORY;
```

Changing Data in a System-Versioned Table

As data is changed (inserted, updated and deleted) in a system-versioned table, the DBMS automatically manages history, keeping old versions of rows with an end effective date (or date and time) in the past. These historical rows are often referred to as "logically deleted" because they are invisible to normal queries. As you will see in the "Querying a System-Versioned Table" section later in this section, there are ways of exposing these logically deleted rows.

Inserts into system-versioned tables use normal SQL syntax. The period begin and period end columns are never referenced in the INSERT statement because they are always automatically maintained by the DBMS. For each new row, the period begin column is populated with the date and time the system (database) processed the INSERT statement, and the period end column is populated with a high datetime value, which is typically the highest date and time that the SQL implementation can represent. The following SQL statements were used to insert the three rows of the EMPLOYEE table illustrated in Figure 13-1:

```
INSERT INTO EMPLOYEE (EMP_ID, EMP_NAME)
       VALUES (1, 'Kim I. Payne');

INSERT INTO EMPLOYEE (EMP_ID, EMP_NAME)
       VALUES (2, 'Benjamin R. Vazquez');

INSERT INTO EMPLOYEE (EMP_ID, EMP_NAME)
       VALUES (3, 'Agatha U. Lee');
```

NOTE

The timestamp values are assigned automatically by the DBMS, so obviously you would see different values in the EFF_DATE column if you were to run these INSERT statements yourself. Figure 13-1 illustrates rows that were inserted on 3/22/2015 at 01:24:04 hours.

Updates of the data in system-versioned tables also use normal syntax. You can update only current rows—historical rows cannot be updated. Furthermore, you cannot explicitly update the period begin and period end columns—they are automatically updated by the DBMS as changes are made to the current rows in the table. When you update a row, the current row becomes history when the DBMS updates the period end column value to the date and time when the UPDATE statement was processed. The DBMS then inserts a new row with the period begin value also set to the date and time when the UPDATE statement was processed, and the period end value set to a high date and time. The rest of the column values look just the way they would if you had run the same UPDATE statement against a nontemporal table. To illustrate, the following statement changes the name of employee 3 to Agatha L. Chang:

```
UPDATE EMPLOYEE
   SET EMP_NAME = 'Agatha L. Chang'
 WHERE EMP_ID   = 3;
```

If you were to select all rows and columns from the EMPLOYEE table after the UPDATE statement was processed, you would receive query results similar to the following:

```
EMP_ID EMP_NAME            SYS_BEGIN           SYS_END
------ ------------------- ------------------- -------------------
     1 Kim I. Payne        2015-03-22 01:24:04 9999-12-30 00:00:00
     2 Benjamin R. Vazquez 2015-03-22 01:24:04 9999-12-30 00:00:00
     3 Agatha L. Chang     2015-03-22 12:20:48 9999-12-30 00:00:00
```

In the third row (EMPL_ID value of 3), we see the name was changed and the SYS_BEGIN date column value has changed. In this example, the update took place at 12:20:48 on 3/22/2015, almost 11 hours after the initial insert of the row for employee 3. The old row is no longer visible because it has been logically deleted. The row still exists—it is just invisible to a normal query because its period end date and time (SYS_END column) value has been set to the timestamp when the UPDATE statement was processed, which, as we can tell by looking at the period begin date and time (SYS_BEGIN column) of the current row, now has a value of 2015-03-22 12:20:48. Again, after an update takes place, the period end date and time of the old row will always have the same value as the period begin date and time of the new row. In the "Querying a System-Versioned Table" section later in this chapter, we will see how to write queries that expose both historical and current rows of data.

Deletions from system-versioned tables use normal SQL syntax. However, rather than physically removing rows, as would be done with deletes from a nontemporal table, the deleted rows are logically deleted by updating the period end date to the date and time at which the DELETE statement was processed. Once logically deleted, the rows are invisible to normal queries, which prevents you from trying to update them or delete them again. However, there is new SQL syntax that permits queries to expose the deleted rows. I discuss the new syntax for querying against historical (logically deleted) rows in the upcoming "Querying a System-Versioned Table" section. The following statement deletes the row for employee 2 (Benjamin R. Vazquez).

```
DELETE FROM EMPLOYEE
 WHERE EMP_ID = 2;
```

If you were to select all rows and columns from the EMPLOYEE table after the DELETE statement was processed, you would receive query results similar to the following:

```
EMP_ID EMP_NAME            SYS_BEGIN           SYS_END
------ ------------------- ------------------- -------------------
     1 Kim I. Payne        2015-03-22 01:24:04 9999-12-30 00:00:00
     3 Agatha L. Chang     2015-03-22 12:20:48 9999-12-30 00:00:00
```

Ask the Expert

Q: I find it confusing that after an update takes place, the end period timestamp of the old row has the exact same value as the begin period timestamp of the new row. Which of the two rows is considered effective at the exact moment in time indicated by the timestamp value that the two rows have in common?

A: The closed-open convention used for time periods in SQL temporal tables can be confusing at first. I find it easier to think of the time periods in SQL temporal tables as inclusive-exclusive, meaning that the effective lifespan of each record includes the period begin date and time, but excludes the period end date and time. It is important to use the same value for the period end timestamp of one row and the period begin timestamp of the next effective row so there is no chance of having a period of time, no matter how small, that falls in the gap between the end of one time period and the beginning of the next. The open-closed (inclusive-exclusive) convention is commonly used in application systems, particularly in the insurance industry where policy expiration dates are most often the same day as the effective date of the renewed policy.

As you will see in the upcoming "Querying a System-Versioned table" section, there is new SQL syntax to assist with queries that filter on time periods. The new syntax uses the keywords FROM and TO when referring to the period begin and period end columns, and once you learn that syntax, you should find it easier to remember the handling of time periods in SQL—a record is effective "from" the period begin date (inclusive) "to" the period end date (exclusive), rather than the "from" and "through" (inclusive-inclusive) comparison that the BETWEEN keyword supports.

Querying a System-Versioned Table

New syntax was added to SQL:2011 to allow for querying of historical rows as well as current rows. A new optional subclause in the table reference (FROM clause) can be used to specify the time period to be used when querying the table. As a reminder, the general syntax of the SELECT statement is as follows:

```
SELECT [ DISTINCT | ALL ] { * | <select list> }
FROM <table reference> [ { , <table reference> | <JOIN subclause> } . . . ]
[ WHERE <search condition> ]
[ GROUP BY <grouping specification> ]
[ HAVING <search condition> ]
[ ORDER BY <order condition> ]
```

Prior to SQL:2011, the <table reference> takes a relatively simple form—it contains a table name or a query. It can also contain an AS clause to assign an alias to the table or query.

The new <query system time period specification> was added in SQL:2011 to allow for specification of the time period to be used when querying the referenced table. The expanded syntax for the table reference is as follows:

```
<table name or query> [ AS <alias name> ]
 [ <query system time period specification> ]
```

The new <query system time period specification> subclause for system-versioned tables has the following possible forms:

```
FOR SYSTEM TIME AS OF <point in time 1> |
FOR SYSTEM TIME BETWEEN <point in time 1> AND <point in time 2> |
FOR SYSTEM TIME FROM <point in time 1> TO <point in time 2>
```

In all three forms, an expression that resolves to a datetime value is substituted for <point in time 1> and <point in time 2>. Let's explore some examples that use each form of the new FOR SYSTEM TIME syntax.

If we want to find the record for employee 2 as of 3/22/2015 at 02:00:00 hours, we can use the FOR SYSTEM TIME AS OF syntax, as shown in the following example:

```
SELECT EMP_ID, EMP_NAME, SYS_BEGIN, SYS_END
  FROM EMPLOYEE
   FOR SYSTEM_TIME AS OF TIMESTAMP '2015-03-22 02:00:00'
 WHERE EMP_ID = 2;
```

As the keywords imply, this form of the query system time period specification finds the rows that were effective as of the moment in time specified in the <point in time> expression. If there are no current records as of the specified point in time, then no rows are returned by the query; the same result you would expect if you searched for an employee who did not exist. If you were to run this query, the result would be similar to the following:

```
EMP_ID  EMP_NAME             SYS_BEGIN            SYS_END
------  -------------------  -------------------  -------------------
     2  Benjamin R. Vazquez  2015-03-22 01:24:04  2015-03-22 12:20:48
```

If you look back at the deletion example in the previous topic ("Changing Data in a System-Versioned Table"), you will see that we deleted this row, and when we subsequently attempted to select all rows in the EMPLOYEE table, the row did not appear in those results. However, we also know that the row was only logically deleted because the EMPLOYEE table is defined as a system-versioned table. With this query, we have been able to expose the deleted row from among the historical rows of the EMPLOYEE table because a current row existed at the point in time specified in the query.

If we want to see multiple versions of a row in the same query results, we can search records within a period of time. One method for doing this is to use the FOR SYSTEM TIME BETWEEN form of the query system time period specification. There is one caveat to this particular syntax—the time period includes both end points. In other words, the

BETWEEN used in this syntax works just like the BETWEEN keyword that can be used in the WHERE clause—the search condition is inclusive for both the beginning point in time and the ending point in time. The following example searches for employee 3 rows that were effective anytime between 3/22/2015 at midnight and 3/22/2015 at 2 P.M. (14:00):

```
SELECT EMP_ID, EMP_NAME, SYS_BEGIN, SYS_END
  FROM EMPLOYEE
   FOR SYSTEM_TIME BETWEEN TIMESTAMP '2015-03-22 00:00:00'
                       AND TIMESTAMP '2015-03-22 14:00:00'
 WHERE EMP_ID = 3;
```

If you were to run the query in this example with a time period that spanned the point in time when this employee's name was updated, the query results would contain multiple rows (the current row and one or more historical rows), similar to the following:

```
EMP_ID  EMP_NAME              SYS_BEGIN            SYS_END
------  --------------------  -------------------  -------------------
     3  Agatha W. Lee         2015-03-22 01:24:04  2015-03-22 12:20:48
     3  Agatha L. Chang       2015-03-22 12:20:48  9999-12-30 00:00:00
```

Note the SYS_END column value for the first row has a value other than a high timestamp, indicating that it is indeed a historical (logically deleted) row. The second row listed has a SYS_BEGIN datetime value that matches the SYS_END datetime value in the first row, so we can tell the second row is effective immediately after the effective time period for the first row. The SYS_END date value of 9999-12-30 00:00:00 in the second row tells us that it was the row currently in effect at the time the query was run.

The third form of the new query system time period specification is a slight, yet important, variation on the FROM SYSTEM TIME BETWEEN form that we just used. This form uses the keywords FROM and TO in place of BETWEEN, and as the keywords suggest, it includes the "from" datetime value in the selected range, but excludes the "to" datetime value. This matches the behavior of the closed-open (inclusive-exclusive) time period ranges used in SQL:2011. (Recall that a row in an SQL temporal table is valid from the datetime value stored in the period begin column up to, but not including, the datetime value stored in the period end column.) The following query uses a low timestamp and a high timestamp to find the full history of all rows in the EMPLOYEE table:

```
SELECT EMP_ID, EMP_NAME, SYS_BEGIN, SYS_END
  FROM EMPLOYEE
   FOR SYSTEM_TIME FROM TIMESTAMP '0001-01-01 00:00:00'
                     TO TIMESTAMP '9999-12-31 23:59:59'
 ORDER BY EMP_ID, SYS_BEGIN;
```

As we have seen in previous query results, currently effective rows have a period end column value of 9999-12-30 00:00:00 (the convention used in DB2 10). Since no row will have a value higher than midnight on 12/30/9999, using a TO TIMESTAMP with a higher value (one second before the end of 12/31/9999 in this example), every current and historical

Ask the Expert

Q: Can primary key and referential constraints be defined between system-versioned tables?

A: Yes. However, these constraints are enforced only on currently effective rows. Historical rows can be thought of as immutable snapshots of the past. When new rows are inserted into system-versioned tables, primary key and foreign key constraints in effect at the time of the insert are enforced. However, once a row has been logically deleted by an UPDATE statement (wherein the old version of the row is logically deleted and a new row is inserted as the current version) or a DELETE statement (wherein the old version of the row is logically deleted with no new version replacing it), the primary key and referential constraints no longer apply.

row will be returned. And the same is true if you use the BETWEEN TIMESTAMP form instead of the FROM/TO TIMESTAMP. The ORDER BY clause is included to make sure the rows in the result set are in proper chronological order within each primary key (EMP_ID) value. If you were to run the SELECT statement for this example, the query results would be similar to the following:

```
EMP_ID EMP_NAME             SYS_BEGIN            SYS_END
------ -------------------- -------------------- --------------------
     1 Kim I. Payne         2015-03-22 01:24:04  9999-12-30 00:00:00
     2 Benjamin R. Vazquez  2015-03-22 01:24:04  2015-03-22 12:20:48
     3 Agatha U. Lee        2015-03-22 01:24:04  2015-03-22 12:20:48
     3 Agatha L. Chang      2015-03-22 12:20:48  9999-12-30 00:00:00
```

Create and Use Application-Time Period Tables

An *application-time period table* is a table that contains rows with effective time periods that are assigned by the database user rather than the database system. (In this context, a database user is not always a human—it can be an application program that is connected to the database.) Unlike system-versioned tables, application-time period tables are considered regular persistent base tables, as defined in Chapter 3. In other words, they are ordinary, permanent tables. However, that only begins to describe the differences between application-time period tables and system-versioned tables. Rows of data can have time periods in the past, present, or future. However, row history is not rigorously maintained as it is with system-versioned tables, and period begin and end dates can be directly updated by the database user. Application-time period tables are most useful in situations where business application requirements call for capturing time periods when table rows are considered effective in the real world. For example, an insurance application must keep track of policy changes over time so that when a claim occurs, it can be processed against the policy as it existed on the date of the event that precipitated the need for the claim, such as the date of an auto accident or the date of a visit to a medical office.

Here is the syntax for the CREATE TABLE statement, including the options required for defining an application-time period table:

```
CREATE TABLE <table name>
( <table element> [ { , <table element> } . . . ] ,
  PERIOD FOR <time period name> ( <period begin column name>,
                                  <period end column name> ),
  PRIMARY KEY ( <column name> [ ( , <column name> ) ]
              [ , <time period name> WITHOUT OVERLAPS ]  )
```

While the syntax is similar to that of the system-versioned table, note the following differences:

- The time period name is user defined. It can be any unambiguous name (subject to the naming rules of the SQL implementation), *except* SYSTEM_TIME, which is reserved for use by system-versioned tables.
- The WITH SYSTEM VERSIONING clause (used with system-versioned tables) cannot be specified.
- The time period may be (and usually is) added as an element of the table's primary key by referencing the time period name followed by the keywords WITHOUT OVERLAPS. The WITHOUT OVERLAPS clause instructs the DBMS to prevent rows with identical primary key values (excluding the time period columns) from having overlapping time periods.

The best way to fully understand the definition of an application-time period table is by looking at an example. Figure 13-2 shows the CD_PROMOTION table, which contains the CD_ID, SALE_PRICE, BEGIN_EFF_DT, and END_EFF_DT columns. The BEGIN_EFF_DT column is the period begin column (the effective start date for each row), and the END_EFF_DT column is the period end column (the effective end date for each row). I have used the DATE data type for the BEGIN_EFF_DT and END_EFF_DT columns. However, the data types for the period begin and period end columns can be any valid datetime data type supported by the DBMS.

NOTE

SQL implementations have different default display formats for date and time values. The formats shown in Figure 13-2 match the default format for DATE columns in DB2 10. If you were to create the CD_PROMOTION table on a different DBMS, you would likely see variances in the display format of the BEGIN_EFF_DT and END_EFF_DT column data.

CD_PROMOTION

CD_ID: INT	SALE_PRICE: NUMERIC(5,2)	BEGIN_EFF_DT: DATE	END_EFF_DT: DATE
101	5.39	2015-01-01	2015-01-15
102	10.79	2015-03-01	2015-03-31
102	10.50	2015-03-31	2015-04-15
103	9.00	2015-01-01	2015-03-31
104	5.00	2017-01-01	9999-12-31

Figure 13-2 The CD_PROMOTION application-time period table

The TABLE CREATE statement for the CD_PROMOTION table is as follows:

```
CREATE TABLE CD_PROMOTION
 (CD_ID          INT            NOT NULL,
  SALE_PRICE     NUMERIC(5,2)   NOT NULL,
  BEGIN_EFF_DT   DATE           NOT NULL,
  END_EFF_DT     DATE           NOT NULL,
  PERIOD FOR BUSINESS_TIME (BEGIN_EFF_DT, END_EFF_DT),
  PRIMARY KEY (CD_ID, BUSINESS_TIME WITHOUT OVERLAPS)
);
```

The PERIOD BUSINESS_TIME clause specifies BEGIN_EFF_DT as the period begin column and END_EFF_DT as the period end column. These columns specify the effective application time period for each row in the table. The application time period columns must be defined with a datetime data type, such as DATE or TIMESTAMP, and they must be defined as NOT NULL. The exact data type and precision you select will depend on the application requirements. If the rows of data are always effective for full days, then the DATE data type is appropriate; otherwise, a data type such as TIMESTAMP can be used so the rows of data can be effective from some point in time on a given day to some point in time on the same or a different day. Unlike system-versioned tables, no special clauses are supplied with the period begin and period end column definitions. The data values for the period begin and period end columns are supplied by the user (or application) rather than being generated by the database system. Therefore, clauses such as GENERATED ALWAYS AS ROW BEGIN are not permitted because they simply are not applicable.

The PRIMARY KEY clause specifies CD_ID and the time period columns as the primary key columns, with the keywords WITHOUT OVERLAPS to prevent overlapping time periods for any given value of CD_ID.

NOTE

The SQL temporal features included in SQL:2011 are new enough that only a few SQL implementations currently support them. As of this writing, MySQL and SQL Server do not yet support SQL temporal features. DB2 10, Oracle 12*c*, and Teradata support application-time period table, with some syntax variations. For DB2 10, the syntax is per the SQL Standard, except DB2 uses the keyword PERIOD instead of the keywords PERIOD FOR, and the time period name must be BUSINESS_TIME. In other words, you cannot name the time period yourself. As a result, some people refer to DB2 10 application-time period tables as "business time" tables. In Oracle 12*c*, you may omit the period begin and period end columns from the table definition and the PERIOD clause, in which case the database engine will automatically add the columns to the table during the table creation process. Oracle refers to application-time period tables as "valid time temporal" tables. (Prior to version 12*c*, Oracle's Total Recall database option implemented temporal data by recording the system time or application time in the Flashback Data Archive.)

Inserting Data into an Application-Time Period Table

Normal syntax is used for inserting data into application-time period tables. Recall that, unlike system-versioned tables, the values for the period begin and period end columns must be specified. In other words, the time period values are neither generated by nor automatically supplied by the DBMS. The following example shows the INSERT statements that were used to populate the CD_PROMOTION table with the rows of data shown in Figure 13-2:

```
INSERT INTO CD_PROMOTION
       (CD_ID, SALE_PRICE, BEGIN_EFF_DT, END_EFF_DT)
VALUES (101, 5.39, '2015-01-01', '2015-01-15');

INSERT INTO CD_PROMOTION
       (CD_ID, SALE_PRICE, BEGIN_EFF_DT, END_EFF_DT)
VALUES (102, 10.79, '2015-03-01', '2015-03-31');

INSERT INTO CD_PROMOTION
       (CD_ID, SALE_PRICE, BEGIN_EFF_DT, END_EFF_DT)
VALUES (102, 10.50, '2015-03-31', '2015-04-15');

INSERT INTO CD_PROMOTION
       (CD_ID, SALE_PRICE, BEGIN_EFF_DT, END_EFF_DT)
VALUES (103, 9.00, '2015-01-01', '2015-05-01');

INSERT INTO CD_PROMOTION
       (CD_ID, SALE_PRICE, BEGIN_EFF_DT, END_EFF_DT)
VALUES (104, 5.00, '2017-01-01', '9999-12-31');
```

Keep in mind that SQL implementations vary in the way that date and datetime values are supplied as literal values in SQL statements. In this example, the BEGIN_EFF_DT and

END_EFF_DT are defined with the DATE data type, and the data values for those columns is provided in YYYY-MM-DD format, which is the most common default date format among current SQL implementations.

Updating Data in an Application-Time Period Table

Data in application-time period tables can be updated in the same way you update nontemporal tables, including updates to the period date columns themselves. Constraints on the period begin and period end columns prevent null values, overlapping time periods, or rows where the period end column value is earlier than the period begin column value. Furthermore, there is an additional feature that supports partial time period updates, which may cause existing rows to be split into two or even three rows.

The syntax for the UPDATE statement, including syntax added to support partial time period updates can be shown as follows:

```
UPDATE <table name>
[ FOR PORTION OF <time period name>
    FROM <point in time 1> TO <point in time 2> ]
SET <set clause expression> [ { , <set clause expression> } . . . ]
[ WHERE <search condition> ]
```

The optional FOR PORTION OF clause includes the time period name (the same name specified in the TABLE CREATE statement) along with the <point in time 1> and <point in time 2> expressions that are used to limit the update to a specific period of time. This adds considerable flexibility to your ability to update rows of data based on partial time periods, but as is often the case, this added flexibility comes with potentially complex side effects. These capabilities are best understood using some examples.

Looking at the CD Promotions shown in Figure 13-2, if a period begin and/or period end date is incorrect, it can easily be corrected using a simple UPDATE statement. The following example changes the period begin date (BEGIN_EFF_DT) for CD 104 to January 1, 2016:

```
UPDATE CD_PROMOTION
   SET BEGIN_EFF_DT = '2016-01-01'
 WHERE CD_ID = 104;
```

As you can see, an ordinary UPDATE statement is easily up to the task. If you were to run this query and then select all rows and columns from the CD_PROMOTION table, you would see a result similar to the following:

```
CD_ID  SALE_PRICE  BEGIN_EFF_DT  END_EFF_DT
-----  ----------  ------------  ----------
  101        5.39  2015-01-01    2015-01-15
  102       10.79  2015-03-01    2015-03-31
  102       10.50  2015-03-31    2015-04-15
  103        9.00  2015-01-01    2015-05-01
  104        5.00  2016-01-01    9999-12-31
```

For a more complex example, suppose you want the sale price for CD 103 to be 8.50 for the period of 4/1/2015 to 4/15/2015. If you tried to insert a new row using the following INSERT statement, you would receive an error because the time period would overlap with the existing row for CD 103 that has a time period of 1/1/2015 to 5/1/2015:

```
INSERT INTO CD_PROMOTION
       (CD_ID, SALE_PRICE, BEGIN_EFF_DT, END_EFF_DT)
VALUES (103, 8.50, '2015-04-01', '2015-04-15');
```

The required new time period falls in the midst of an existing time period, so ultimately we need three rows, dated 1/1/2015 to 4/1/2015, 4/1/2015 to 4/15/2015, and 4/15/2015 to 5/1/2015. We could get around this issue by deleting the existing row and inserting three new rows, or by updating the existing row and inserting two new rows. However, using the FOR PORTION OF clause, we can limit the scope of the update to the desired span of time (a partial time period). The UPDATE statement for this example is as follows:

```
UPDATE CD_PROMOTION
   FOR PORTION OF BUSINESS_TIME FROM '2015-04-01' TO '2015-04-15'
   SET SALE_PRICE = 8.50
 WHERE CD_ID = 103;
```

If you were to run the statement and then select all rows and columns from the CD_PROMOTION table, the results would be similar to the following:

```
CD_ID  SALE_PRICE  BEGIN_EFF_DT  END_EFF_DT
-----  ----------  ------------  ----------
  101        5.39  2015-01-01    2015-01-15
  102       10.79  2015-03-01    2015-03-31
  102       10.50  2015-03-31    2015-04 15
  103        9.00  2015-01-01    2015-04-01
  103        8.50  2015-04-01    2015-04-15
  103        9.00  2015-04-15    2015-05-01
  104        5.00  2016-01-01    9999-12-31
```

As you can see, the DBMS did exactly what we wanted. Where there had been one row in the table for CD 103 that spanned a period of 1/1/2015 to 5/1/2015 with a price of 9.00, there are now three rows, two with a price of 9.00 that represent the first and last portions of the original time period, and one with a price of 8.50 that spans the portion of the old time period where the lower price applies, specifically from 4/15/2015 to 5/1/2015. Always keep in mind that, like system-versioned tables, the time periods for application-time period tables include the point in time specified in the period begin column but exclude the point in time specified in the period end column.

Deleting Data from an Application-Time Period Table

Application-time period table data can be deleted in the same way you delete data from nontemporal tables. As with the UPDATE statement, there is an additional feature that supports partial time period deletion of application-time period table data. Deletion of partial time periods may cause insertion of one or two rows to preserve the information for the periods of time that lie outside the specified period.

The syntax for the DELETE statement, including syntax added to support partial time period deletion, can be shown as follows:

```
DELETE FROM <table name>
[ FOR PORTION OF <time period name>
      FROM <point in time 1> TO <point in time 2> ]
[ WHERE <search condition> ]
```

The optional FOR PORTION OF clause includes the time period name (the same name specified in the TABLE CREATE statement) along with the <point in time 1> and <point in time 2> expressions that are used to limit the update to a specified period of time. This adds great flexibility to your ability to delete data based on partial time periods, but this added flexibility comes with potentially complex side effects. These capabilities are best understood using a few examples.

Figure 13-3 shows the data in the CD Promotions table after applying the updates in the examples discussed in the "Updating Data in an Application-Time Period Table" topic earlier in this chapter.

Looking at the CD promotions shown in Figure 13-3, if we decide the promotion for the CD 101 should not take place as planned, we can simply delete the row. The DELETE statement for this example is as follows:

```
DELETE FROM CD_PROMOTION
 WHERE CD_ID = 101;
```

CD_PROMOTION

CD_ID: INT	SALE_PRICE: NUMERIC(5,2)	BEGIN_EFF_DT: DATE	END_EFF_DT: DATE
101	5.39	2015-01-01	2015-01-15
102	10.79	2015-03-01	2015-03-31
102	10.50	2015-03-31	2015-04-15
103	9.00	2015-01-01	2015-04-01
103	8.50	2015-04-01	2015-04-15
103	9.00	2015-04-15	2015-05-01
104	5.00	2016-01-01	9999-12-31

Figure 13-3 CD_PROMOTION table with updates applied

As you can see, an ordinary DELETE statement is a very simple way to accomplish the goal. If you were to run this query, you could run a simple SELECT statement to verify that the row has been removed from the table:

```
SELECT * FROM CD_PROMOTION
 ORDER BY CD_ID, BEGIN_EFF_DT;

CD_ID  SALE_PRICE  BEGIN_EFF_DT  END_EFF_DT
-----  ----------  ------------  ----------
  102       10.79  2015-03-01    2015-03-31
  102       10.50  2015-03-31    2015-04-15
  103        9.00  2015-01-01    2015-04-01
  103        8.50  2015-04-01    2015-04-15
  103        9.00  2015-04-15    2015-05-01
  104        5.00  2016-01-01    9999-12-31
```

Now suppose you want to delete the promotion for CD 102, but only for the period of 3/31/2015 to 4/5/2015. The required new time period falls at the beginning of an existing time period of 3/31/2015 to 4/15/2015. We could use an UPDATE statement to change the existing row for CD 102. However, we also have the alternative of using a DELETE statement with the FOR PORTION OF clause to limit the scope of the DELETE statement to the desired subset of time. The DELETE statement for this example is as follows:

```
DELETE FROM CD_PROMOTION
   FOR PORTION OF BUSINESS_TIME FROM '2015-03-31' TO '2015-04-05'
 WHERE CD_ID = 102;
```

If you were to run the statement and then select all rows and columns from the CD_PROMOTION table, the results would be similar to the following:

```
CD_ID  SALE_PRICE  BEGIN_EFF_DT  END_EFF_DT
-----  ----------  ------------  ----------
  102       10.79  2015-03-01    2015-03-31
  102       10.50  2015-04-05    2015-04-15
  103        9.00  2015-01-01    2015-04-01
  103        8.50  2015-04-01    2015-04-15
  103        9.00  2015-04-15    2015-05-01
  104        5.00  2016-01-01    9999-12-31
```

As you can see, the DBMS did exactly what we wanted. The second row in the table for CD 102 previously spanned a period from 3/31/2015 to 4/15/2015, but now spans the period from 4/5/2015 to 4/15/2015.

Finally, let's suppose we want to eliminate the promotion for CD 104 for the period of 03/01/2016 to 03/31/2016, which falls completely inside the time period of 01/01/2016 to 12/31/9999 that is covered by an existing row. (The END_EFF_DT value of 12/31/9999 is a work-around for a period end date that is unknown—remember, we cannot have nulls in the period dates of application-time period tables.) The DELETE statement for this example is as follows:

```
DELETE FROM CD_PROMOTION
  FOR PORTION OF BUSINESS_TIME FROM '2016-03-01' TO '2016-03-31'
WHERE CD_ID = 104;
```

If you were to run this statement and then select all rows from the CD_PROMOTION table, the result would look something like this:

```
CD_ID  SALE_PRICE  BEGIN_EFF_DT  END_EFF_DT
-----  ----------  ------------  ----------
  102       10.79  2015-03-01    2015-03-31
  102       10.50  2015-04-05    2015-04-15
  103        9.00  2015-01-01    2015-04-01
  103        8.50  2015-04-01    2015-04-15
  103        9.00  2015-04-15    2015-05-01
  104        5.00  2016-01-01    2016-03-01
  104        5.00  2016-03-31    9999-12-31
```

The previous row for CD 104 has been replaced by two rows, one for the period 1/1/2016 to 3/1/2016 and the other for the period 3/31/16 to 12/31/9999.

As you can see from these examples, UPDATE and DELETE statements are very powerful ways to manage time periods and related data in application-time period tables.

Ask the Expert

Q: Can relationships be defined between application-time period tables?

A: Yes, they can, and there is added syntax to assist in defining referential constraints where the foreign key references the primary key of the application-time period table. The syntax for the foreign key constraint (introduced in Chapter 4) with the added application-time period syntax can be shown as follows:

```
[ CONSTRAINT <constraint name> ]
FOREIGN KEY ( <referencing column > [ {, <referencing column> } . . . ]
            [ {, PERIOD <time period name> } ] )
REFERENCES <referenced table> [ ( <referenced columns> ) ]
            [ {, PERIOD <time period name> } ] )
[ MATCH { FULL | PARTIAL | SIMPLE } ]
[ <referential triggered action> ]
```

(continued)

For example, suppose we need to define an application-time period DEPARTMENT table and an application-time period EMPLOYEES table where the EMPLOYEES table contains a foreign key to the DEPARTMENT table. The CREATE TABLE statements might look like the following:

```
CREATE TABLE DEPARTMENT
(DEPT_ID             INT            NOT NULL,
 DEPT_NAME           VARCHAR(50)    NOT NULL,
 DEPT_BEGIN_EFF_DT   DATE           NOT NULL,
 DEPT_END_EFF_DT     DATE           NOT NULL,
 PERIOD FOR DEPT_PERIOD (DEPT_BEGIN_EFF_DT, DEPT_END_EFF_DT),
 PRIMARY KEY (DEPT_ID, DEPT_PERIOD WITHOUT OVERLAPS)
);

CREATE TABLE EMPLOYEES
(EMP_ID             INT            NOT NULL,
 EMP_NAME           VARCHAR(50)    NOT NULL,
 DEPT_ID            INT            NOT NULL,
 EMP_BEGIN_EFF_DT   DATE           NOT NULL,
 EMP_END_EFF_DT     DATE           NOT NULL,
 PERIOD FOR EMP_PERIOD (EMP_BEGIN_EFF_DT, EMP_END_EFF_DT),
 PRIMARY KEY (EMP_ID, EMP_PERIOD WITHOUT OVERLAPS),
 FOREIGN KEY (DEPT_ID, PERIOD EMP_PERIOD)
   REFERENCES DEPT (DEPT_ID, PERIOD DEPT_PERIOD)
);
```

NOTE

DB2 10 and Oracle 12*c* do not currently support the expanded foreign key constraint syntax.

Try This 13-1 Working with Application-Time Period Tables

In this chapter, I discuss the temporal features of SQL:2011, including application-time period tables. In this Try This exercise, you will create the CD_PRICES table and use INSERT, UPDATE, and DELETE statements to manipulate the data in the table. For this exercise, as with previous Try This exercises, you will be using the INVENTORY database, but you must have a DBMS that supports application-time period tables, such as Oracle 12*c* or DB2 10. You can download the Try_This_13.txt file, which contains the SQL statements used in this exercise.

Step by Step

1. Open the client application for your RDBMS and connect to the INVENTORY database. (DB2 limits database names to eight characters, so you will have to shorten the name to something like INVENT for DB2.)
2. In the first statement, you will create the CD_PRICES table to hold the wholesale and retail prices for CDs with application-effective dates. Enter and execute the following SQL statement:

```
CREATE TABLE CD_PRICES

 (CD_ID             INT           NOT NULL,
  WHOLESALE_PRICE   NUMERIC(5,2)  NOT NULL,
  RETAIL_PRICE      NUMERIC(5,2)  NOT NULL,
  BEGIN_EFF_DT      DATE          NOT NULL,
  END_EFF_DT        DATE          NOT NULL,
  PERIOD FOR BUSINESS_TIME (BEGIN_EFF_DT, END_EFF_DT),
  PRIMARY KEY (CD_ID, BUSINESS_TIME WITHOUT OVERLAPS)
);
```

NOTE

For DB2, change "PERIOD FOR BUSINESS_TIME" to "PERIOD BUSINESS_TIME."

3. In the next statement, you will use INSERT statements to create six rows in the CD_PRICES table. Enter and execute the following SQL statements:

```
INSERT INTO CD_PRICES
 VALUES (101, 4.50, 5.99, '2015-01-01', '9999-12-31');

INSERT INTO CD_PRICES
 VALUES (102, 5.50, 11.99, '2015-01-01', '9999-12-31');

INSERT INTO CD_PRICES
 VALUES (103, 5.50, 10.00, '2015-01-01', '9999-12-31');

INSERT INTO CD_PRICES
 VALUES (104, 4.50, 8.39, '2015-01-01', '9999-12-31');

INSERT INTO CD_PRICES
 VALUES (105, 4.50, 7.99, '2015-01-01', '9999-12-31');

INSERT INTO CD_PRICES
 VALUES (106, 4.50, 5.99, '2015-01-01', '9999-12-31');
```

(continued)

4. Now you will use an SQL update statement to update CDs with a wholesale price of 5.50 to increase the wholesale price to 5.75 and the retail price by 5 percent. Enter and execute the following UPDATE statement:

```
UPDATE CD_PRICES
   FOR PORTION OF BUSINESS_TIME FROM '2015-05-01' TO '9999-12-31'
   SET WHOLESALE_PRICE = 5.75,
       RETAIL_PRICE = RETAIL_PRICE * 1.05
 WHERE WHOLESALE_PRICE = 5.50;
```

5. After completing the price updates, you discover that CD 106 will be discontinued effective 7/1/2015 and you must remove any pricing information from that date forward. Enter and execute the following DELETE statement:

```
DELETE FROM CD_PRICES
   FOR PORTION OF BUSINESS_TIME FROM '2015-07-01' TO '9999-12-31'
 WHERE CD_ID = 106;
```

6. At this point, you want to see all the pricing information. Enter and execute the following SELECT statement:

```
SELECT CD_ID, WHOLESALE_PRICE, RETAIL_PRICE, BEGIN_EFF_DT, END_EFF_DT
  FROM CD_PRICES
 ORDER BY CD_ID, BEGIN_EFF_DT;
```

The query results should be similar to the following:

```
CD_ID  WHOLESALE_PRICE  RETAIL_PRICE  BEGIN_EFF_DT  END_EFF_DT
-----  ---------------  ------------  ------------  ----------
  101             4.50          5.99  2015-01-01    9999-12-31
  102             5.50         11.99  2015-01-01    2015-05-01
  102             5.75         12.58  2015-05-01    9999-12-31
  103             5.50         10.00  2015-01-01    2015-05-01
  103             5.75         10.50  2015-05-01    9999-12-31
  104             4.50          8.39  2015-01-01    9999-12-31
  105             4.50          7.99  2015-01-01    9999-12-31
  106             4.50          5.99  2015-01-01    2015-07-01
```

7. Close the client application.

Try This Summary

In this Try This exercise, you created an application-time period table named CD_PRICES; used INSERT, UPDATE, and DELETE statements to manipulate data in the table; and then used a SELECT statement to display all the rows of data, including the application time period dates. At this point, you should be fairly comfortable using the temporal features of SQL:2011.

Create and Use System-Versioned Application-Time Period Tables

As the name suggests, a *system-versioned application-time period table* combines the features of system-versioned and application-time period tables into a single structure with effective time periods (application time periods) assigned by the database user in addition to row change history with system time periods assigned by the database system. In recognition of the two different time periods that are tracked for each row of data, many practitioners use the term *bitemporal* when referring to system-versioned application-time period tables. Bitemporal tables are useful in situations where business application requirements call for capturing time periods when rows are considered effective in the real world combined with audit or regulatory requirements, which call for rigorous tracking of all changes made to rows of data in the table. For example, a financial account management application must keep track of the effective fiscal period for each transaction, as well as maintain an audit trail of all changes to the financial records.

Combining the SQL standard syntax for both system-versioned and application-time period tables, the CREATE TABLE syntax for defining a system-versioned application-time period table can be shown as follows:

```
CREATE TABLE <table name>
( <table element> [ { , <table element> } . . . ] ,
  PERIOD FOR <time period name> ( <period begin column name>,
                                  <period end column name> ),
  PERIOD FOR SYSTEM TIME ( <period begin column name>,
                           <period end column name> ),
  PRIMARY KEY ( <column name> [ ( , <column name> ) ]
              [ , <time period name> WITHOUT OVERLAPS ]  ) )
[ WITH SYSTEM VERSIONING ]
```

The syntax should be familiar to you from the syntax for system-versioned and application-time period tables I presented earlier in this chapter. Note the following:

- There are two PERIOD FOR clauses, one to define the application time period with a user-defined time period name, and the other to define the system time period using the name SYSTEM_TIME for the time period name.
- The application time period is added as an element of the table's primary key by referencing the time period name followed by the keywords WITHOUT OVERLAPS. The WITHOUT OVERLAPS clause instructs the DBMS to prevent overlapping application time periods.
- The WITH SYSTEM VERSIONING clause enables system versioning for the table.
- Two sets of datetime columns must be included in the table element list, one for the application time period begin and application time period end, and the other for the system time period begin and system time period end.

CD_PROMOTION_HISTORY

CD_ID: INT	SALE_PRICE: NUMERIC(5,2)	BEGIN_EFF_DT: DATE	END_EFF_DT: DATE	SYS_BEGIN: TIMESTAMP(12)	SYS_END: TIMESTAMP(12)
101	5.39	2015-01-01	2015-01-15	2015-03-28 13:23:36	9999-12-30 00:00:00
102	10.79	2015-03-01	2015-03-31	2015-03-28 13:23:36	9999-12-30 00:00:00
102	10.50	2015-03-31	2015-04-15	2015-03-28 13:23:36	9999-12-30 00:00:00
103	9.00	2015-01-01	2015-03-31	2015-03-28 13:23:36	9999-12-30 00:00:00
104	5.00	2017-01-01	9999-12-31	2015-03-28 13:23:36	9999-12-30 00:00:00

Figure 13-4 The CD_PROMOTION_HISTORY system-versioned application-time period table

Let's look at an example of a system-versioned application-time period table. Figure 13-4 shows the CD_PROMOTION_HISTORY table. For this example, I took the CD_PROMOTION table shown in Figure 13-2 and added system versioning in order to form a bitemporal table.

The TABLE CREATE statement for the CD_PROMOTION_HISTORY table is as follows:

```
CREATE TABLE CD_PROMOTION_HISTORY
 (CD_ID          INT            NOT NULL,
  SALE_PRICE     NUMERIC(5,2)   NOT NULL,
  BEGIN_EFF_DT   DATE           NOT NULL,
  END_EFF_DT     DATE           NOT NULL,
  SYS_BEGIN      TIMESTAMP(12) GENERATED ALWAYS AS ROW BEGIN NOT NULL,
  SYS_END        TIMESTAMP(12) GENERATED ALWAYS AS ROW END   NOT NULL,
  PERIOD FOR BUSINESS_TIME (BEGIN_EFF_DT, END_EFF_DT),
  PERIOD FOR SYSTEM_TIME (SYS_BEGIN, SYS_END)
  PRIMARY KEY (CD_ID, BUSINESS_TIME WITHOUT OVERLAPS)
 )
 WITH SYSTEM VERSIONING;
```

The PERIOD FOR BUSINESS_TIME clause defines the BEGIN_EFF_DT and END_EFF_DT columns as the application period begin and end dates. I used the DATE data type for these columns, but any datetime data type, such as DATE or TIMESTAMP, is acceptable for these columns. The PERIOD FOR SYSTEM_TIME clause defines the SYS_BEGIN and SYS_END columns as the system period begin and end timestamps. Again, any datetime data type is acceptable for these columns. The phrase BUSINESS_TIME WITHOUT OVERLAPS in the PRIMARY KEY clause adds the application time period to the primary key of the table with a directive to the DBMS to prevent any overlapping periods. The WITH SYSTEM VERSIONING clause activates system versioning for the table.

NOTE

As of this writing, MySQL, Oracle 12*c*, SQL Server, and Teradata do not yet support system-versioned application-time period tables. IBM DB2 10 supports system-versioned application-time period tables, but the DB2 10 syntax varies somewhat from the standard. As with DB2 system-versioned tables, system-version application-time period tables must be created in three steps. First, the CREATE TABLE statement is run to create the base time. However, the WITH SYSTEM VERSIONING clause must be omitted at this point. DB2 10 also requires a transaction start date column (TRANS_START) in addition to the application period begin and period end columns. Also, as with DB2 application-time period tables, DB2 uses the keyword PERIOD instead of the keywords PERIOD FOR, and the application time period name must be BUSINESS_TIME. Second, a history table must be created with a definition that is identical to the base table. Fortunately, the LIKE clause makes this statement very simple. Third, an ALTER statement is run to link the base table and history table and to activate system versioning. The following example shows all three steps using DB2 10 syntax:

```
CREATE TABLE CD_PROMOTION_HISTORY
 (CD_ID         INT           NOT NULL,
  SALE_PRICE    NUMERIC(5,2)  NOT NULL,
  BEGIN_EFF_DT  DATE          NOT NULL,
  END_EFF_DT    DATE          NOT NULL,
  SYS_BEGIN     TIMESTAMP(12) GENERATED ALWAYS AS ROW BEGIN NOT NULL,
  SYS_END       TIMESTAMP(12) GENERATED ALWAYS AS ROW END   NOT NULL,
  TRANS_START   TIMESTAMP(12) GENERATED ALWAYS AS TRANSACTION START ID
                              IMPLICITLY HIDDEN,
  PERIOD BUSINESS_TIME (BEGIN_EFF_DT, END_EFF_DT),
  PERIOD SYSTEM_TIME (SYS_BEGIN, SYS_END),
  PRIMARY KEY (CD_ID, BUSINESS_TIME WITHOUT OVERLAPS)
);

CREATE TABLE CD_PROMOTION_SYS_HISTORY LIKE CD_PROMOTION_HISTORY;

ALTER TABLE CD_PROMOTION_HISTORY
  ADD VERSIONING USE HISTORY TABLE CD_PROMOTION_SYS_HISTORY;
```

Inserting Data into a System-Versioned Application-Time Period Table

Normal syntax is used for inserting data into system-versioned application-time period tables. The values for the application period begin and period end columns must be specified, but as with system-versioned tables, you cannot specify values for the system period begin and end columns. The system time period values are automatically supplied by the DBMS, but the application time period values are not. The following example shows the INSERT statements that were used to populate the CD_PROMOTION_HISTORY table with the rows of data shown in Figure 13-4:

```
INSERT INTO CD_PROMOTION_HISTORY
       (CD_ID, SALE_PRICE, BEGIN_EFF_DT, END_EFF_DT)
VALUES (101, 5.39, '2015-01-01', '2015-01-15');

INSERT INTO CD_PROMOTION_HISTORY
       (CD_ID, SALE_PRICE, BEGIN_EFF_DT, END_EFF_DT)
VALUES (102, 10.79, '2015-03-01', '2015-03-31');

INSERT INTO CD_PROMOTION_HISTORY
       (CD_ID, SALE_PRICE, BEGIN_EFF_DT, END_EFF_DT)
VALUES (102, 10.50, '2015-03-31', '2015-04-15');

INSERT INTO CD_PROMOTION_HISTORY
       (CD_ID, SALE_PRICE, BEGIN_EFF_DT, END_EFF_DT)
VALUES (103, 9.00, '2015-01-01', '2015-05-01');

INSERT INTO CD_PROMOTION_HISTORY
       (CD_ID, SALE_PRICE, BEGIN_EFF_DT, END_EFF_DT)
VALUES (104, 5.00, '2017-01-01', '9999-12-31');
```

You probably noticed that these are essentially the same INSERT statements that I used to insert rows into the CD_PROMOTION application-time period table—only the table name has been changed. This should make sense because the system time period columns cannot be referenced in SQL INSERT statements. As before, I specified the application time period column values using literals in the YYYY-MM-DD format, which is the most common default format for date literals among SQL implementations.

Updating Data in a System-Versioned Application-Time Period Table

Data in system-versioned application-time period tables can be updated in the same way you update nontemporal tables, including updates to the application period date columns themselves. Constraints on the application period begin and period end columns prevent null values, overlapping time periods, or rows where the application period end column value is earlier than the application period begin column value. Furthermore, there is an additional feature that supports partial time period updates, which may cause existing rows to be split into two or even three rows. However, the system period begin and end column values are maintained automatically by the DBMS and cannot be explicitly updated by the database user.

The syntax for updating system-versioned application-time period tables is identical to the syntax for updating application-time period tables. If you need to review the syntax, refer to the "Updating Data in an Application-Time Period Table" section earlier in this chapter.

Let's apply updates to the CD_PROMOTION_HISTORY table that are equivalent to the ones we applied to the CD_PROMOTION application-time period table earlier in this chapter, so we can examine the results. Looking at the promotions shown in Figure 13-4, if a period begin and/or period end date is incorrect, it can easily be corrected using a simple UPDATE statement. The following example changes the period begin date (BEGIN_EFF_DT) for CD 104 to January 1, 2016:

```
UPDATE CD_PROMOTION_HISTORY
   SET BEGIN_EFF_DT = '2016-01-01'
 WHERE CD_ID = 104;
```

As you can see, an ordinary UPDATE statement is easily up to the task. If you were to run the UPDATE statement and then query the CD_PROMOTION_HISTORY table, you would see a result similar to the following:

```
SELECT CD_ID, SALE_PRICE, BEGIN_EFF_DT, END_EFF_DT, SYS_BEGIN
  FROM CD_PROMOTION_HISTORY
 ORDER BY CD_ID, BEGIN_EFF_DT;

CD_ID  SALE_PRICE  BEGIN_EFF_DT  END_EFF_DT  SYS_BEGIN
-----  ----------  ------------  ----------  -------------------
  101        5.39  2015-01-01    2015-01-15  2015-03-28 13:23:36
  102       10.79  2015-03-01    2015-03-31  2015-03-28 13:23:36
  102       10.50  2015-03-31    2015-04-15  2015-03-28 13:23:36
  103        9.00  2015-01-01    2015-05-01  2015-03-28 13:23:36
  104        5.00  2016-01-01    9999-12-31  2015-03-28 13:23:36
```

It may seem surprising that the system period begin timestamp (SYS_BEGIN column) did not change for CD 104. The DBMS did not count the update in this example as a change that needed to be tracked in history because we updated one of the application time period columns rather than an ordinary data column, such as SALE_PRICE.

For a more complex example, suppose you want the sale price for CD 103 to be 8.50 for the period of 4/1/2015 to 4/15/2015. If you tried to insert a new row using the following INSERT statement, you would receive an error because the time period would overlap with the existing row for CD 103 that has a time period of 1/1/2015 to 5/1/2015:

```
INSERT INTO CD_PROMOTION_HISTORY
      (CD_ID, SALE_PRICE, BEGIN_EFF_DT, END_EFF_DT)
VALUES (103, 8.50, '2015-04-01', '2015-04-15');
```

The required new time period falls in the midst of an existing time period, so ultimately we need three rows, dated 1/1/2015 – 4/1/2015, 4/1/2015 – 4/15/2015, and 4/15/2015 – 5/1/2015. This can be easily accomplished using the FOR PORTION OF clause to limit the scope of the update to the desired subset of time. The UPDATE statement for this example is as follows:

```
UPDATE CD_PROMOTION_HISTORY
   FOR PORTION OF BUSINESS_TIME FROM '2015-04-01' TO '2015-04-15'
   SET SALE_PRICE = 8.50
 WHERE CD_ID = 103;
```

If you were to run the UPDATE statement and then query the CD_PROMOTION_HISTORY table, you would see a result similar to the following:

```
SELECT CD_ID, SALE_PRICE, BEGIN_EFF_DT, END_EFF_DT, SYS_BEGIN
  FROM CD_PROMOTION_HISTORY
 ORDER BY CD_ID, BEGIN_EFF_DT;

CD_ID  SALE_PRICE  BEGIN_EFF_DT  END_EFF_DT  SYS_BEGIN
-----  ----------  ------------  ----------  -------------------
  101        5.39  2015-01-01    2015-01-15  2015-03-28 13:23:36
  102       10.79  2015-03-01    2015-03-31  2015-03-28 13:23:36
  102       10.50  2015-03-31    2015-04-15  2015-03-28 13:23:36
  103        9.00  2015-01-01    2015-04-01  2015-03-28 16:54:54
  103        8.50  2015-04-01    2015-05-15  2015-03-28 16:54:54
  103        9.00  2015-04-15    2015-05-01  2015-03-28 16:54:54
  104        5.00  2016-01-01    9999-12-31  2015-03-28 13:23:36
```

As you can see, the DBMS did exactly what we wanted. Where there had been one row in the table for CD 103 that spanned a period of 1/1/2015 to 5/1/2015 with a price of 9.00, there are now three rows, two with a price of 9.00 that represent the first and last portions of the original time period, and one with a price of 8.50 that spans the portion of the old time period where the lower price applies, specifically from 4/15/2015 to 5/1/2015. Always keep in mind that, like system-versioned tables, the time periods for system-versioned application-time period tables include the point in time specified in the period begin column but exclude the point in time specified in the period end column.

I omitted the SYS_END column in the previous examples because the values are always the same (9999-12-30 00:00:00). All the rows displayed are current rows and therefore have not been logically deleted by the DBMS. (Recall that the DBMS logically deletes rows by setting the system end period column to the date and time at which the statement that applied the update was run.) As with system-versioned tables, row history for system-versioned application-time period tables is selected only when the query requests it using one of the forms of the query system time period specification clauses (the clauses that begin with the keywords FOR SYSTEM_TIME). If you need to review retrieving row history, refer to the "Querying a System-Versioned Table" section earlier in this chapter. The following example selects all rows and columns from the CD_PROMOTION_HISTORY table, including row history.

```
SELECT CD_ID, SALE_PRICE, BEGIN_EFF_DT, END_EFF_DT, SYS_BEGIN, SYS_END
  FROM CD_PROMOTION_HISTORY
   FOR SYSTEM_TIME FROM TIMESTAMP '0001-01-01 00:00:00'
                     TO TIMESTAMP '9999-12-31 23:59:59'
 ORDER BY CD_ID, SYS_BEGIN, BEGIN_EFF_DT;
```

The results of this query are displayed in Figure 13-5, which shows four rows for CD 103: the three new rows inserted as a result of the UPDATE statement in the previous example plus

CD_PROMOTION_HISTORY

CD_ID: INT	SALE_PRICE: NUMERIC(5,2)	BEGIN_EFF_DT: DATE	END_EFF_DT: DATE	SYS_BEGIN: TIMESTAMP(12)	SYS_END: TIMESTAMP(12)
101	5.39	2015-01-01	2015-01-15	2015-03-28 13:23:36	9999-12-30 00:00:00
102	10.79	2015-03-01	2015-03-31	2015-03-28 13:23:36	9999-12-30 00:00:00
102	10.50	2015-03-31	2015-04-15	2015-03-28 13:23:36	9999-12-30 00:00:00
103	9.00	2015-01-01	2015-05-01	2015-03-28 13:23:36	2015-03-28 16:54:54
103	9.00	2015-01-01	2015-04-01	2015-03-28 16:54:54	9999-12-30 00:00:00
103	8.50	2015-04-01	2015-04-15	2015-03-28 16:54:54	9999-12-30 00:00:00
103	9.00	2015-04-15	2015-05-01	2015-03-28 16:54:54	9999-12-30 00:00:00
104	5.00	2016-01-01	9999-12-31	2015-03-28 13:23:36	9999-12-30 00:00:00

Figure 13-5 CD_PROMOTION_HISTORY table including row history

the original row, which has been logically deleted by the system. The logically deleted row has a SYS_END column value of 3/28/2015 at 16:54:54, which is shaded on Figure 13-5.

Deleting Data from a System-Versioned Application-Time Period Table

System-versioned application-time period table data can be deleted in the same way you delete data from nontemporal tables. However, deleted rows are logically deleted by the system instead of being physically removed from the table because the tables are system versioned. As with the UPDATE statement used with system-versioned application-time period tables, there is an additional feature that supports partial time period deletion of system-versioned application-time period table data. Deletion of partial time periods may cause insertion of one or two rows to preserve the information for the periods of time that lie outside the specified period. The syntax for the DELETE statement used with system-versioned application-time period tables is the same as the syntax used for application-time period tables. If you need to review the syntax, refer to the "Updating Data in a System-Versioned Application-Time Period Table" section earlier in this chapter.

Looking at the CD promotions shown in Figure 13-5, if we decide the promotion for the CD 104 should not take place as planned, we can simply delete the row. The DELETE statement for this example is as follows:

```
DELETE FROM CD_PROMOTION_HISTORY
 WHERE CD_ID = 101;
```

As you can see, an ordinary DELETE statement is a very simple way to accomplish the goal. If you were to run this query, you could run a simple SELECT statement to verify that the row has been logically deleted from the table:

```
SELECT * FROM CD_PROMOTION_HISTORY
 ORDER BY CD_ID, BEGIN_EFF_DT;

CD_ID  SALE_PRICE  BEGIN_EFF_DT  END_EFF_DT
-----  ----------  ------------  ----------
  102       10.79  2015-03-01    2015-03-31
  102       10.50  2015-03-31    2015-04-15
  103        9.00  2015-01-01    2015-04-01
  103        8.50  2015-04-01    2015-04-15
  103        9.00  2015-04-15    2015-05-01
  104        5.00  2016-01-01    9999-12-31
```

If you want to see the logically deleted row, you can use a query that requests row history, such as the one in the following example:

```
SELECT CD_ID, SALE_PRICE, BEGIN_EFF_DT, END_EFF_DT, SYS_END
  FROM CD_PROMOTION_HISTORY
   FOR SYSTEM_TIME FROM TIMESTAMP '0001-01-01 00:00:00'
                     TO TIMESTAMP '9999-12-31 23:59:59'
 WHERE CD_ID = 101;

CD_ID  SALE_PRICE  BEGIN_EFF_DT  END_EFF_DT  SYS_END
-----  ----------  ------------  ----------  -------------------
  101        5.39  2015-01-01    2015-01-15  2015-03-28 16:54:54
```

Now suppose you want to delete the promotion for CD 102, but only for the period of 3/31/2015 to 4/5/2015. The required new time period falls at the beginning of an existing time period of 3/31/2015 to 4/15/2015. We could use an UPDATE statement to change the existing row for CD 102. However, a better alternative is to use a DELETE statement with the FOR PORTION OF clause to limit the scope of the DELETE statement to the desired subset of time. If we were to update the BEGIN_EFF_DT for the existing row, we wouldn't have row history for the change, which is why using a DELETE statement with the FOR PORTION OF clause is a better alternative. The DELETE statement for this example is as follows:

```
DELETE FROM CD_PROMOTION_HISTORY
   FOR PORTION OF BUSINESS_TIME FROM '2015-03-31' TO '2015-04-05'
 WHERE CD_ID = 102;
```

If you were to run the statement and then select the rows for CD 102 from the CD_PROMOTION_HISTORY table, the results would be similar to the following:

```
SELECT CD_ID, SALE_PRICE, BEGIN_EFF_DT, END_EFF_DT
  FROM CD_PROMOTION_HISTORY
 WHERE CD_ID = 102;
```

```
CD_ID  SALE_PRICE  BEGIN_EFF_DT  END_EFF_DT
-----  ----------  ------------  ----------
  102       10.79  2015-03-01    2015-03-31
  102       10.50  2015-04-05    2015-04-15
```

As you can see, the DBMS did exactly what we wanted. The second row in the table for CD 102 that previously spanned a period of 3/31/2015 to 4/15/2015 now spans the period from 4/5/2015 to 4/15/2015.

If you want to see row history along with the current rows for CD 102, you could use the following query:

```
SELECT CD_ID, SALE_PRICE, BEGIN_EFF_DT, END_EFF_DT, SYS_END
  FROM CD_PROMOTION_HISTORY
   FOR SYSTEM_TIME FROM TIMESTAMP '0001-01-01 00:00:00'
                     TO TIMESTAMP '9999-12-31 23:59:59'
 WHERE CD_ID = 102;

CD_ID  SALE_PRICE  BEGIN_EFF_DT  END_EFF_DT  SYS_END
-----  ----------  ------------  ----------  -------------------
  102       10.79  2015-03-31    2015-04-15  2015-03-28 16:54:54
  102       10.79  2015-03-01    2015-03-31  9999-12-30 00:00:00
  102       10.50  2015-04-05    2015-04-15  9999-12-30 00:00:00
```

Finally, let's suppose we want to eliminate the promotion for CD 104 for the period of 3/1/2016 to 3/31/2016, which falls completely inside the time period of 1/1/2016 to 12/31/9999 that is covered by an existing row. (The END_EFF_DT value of 12/31/9999 is a work-around for a period end date that is unknown—remember, we cannot have nulls in the period dates of system-versioned application-time period tables.) The DELETE statement for this example is as follows:

```
 DELETE FROM CD_PROMOTION_HISTORY
   FOR PORTION OF BUSINESS_TIME FROM '2016-03-01' TO '2016-03-31'
 WHERE CD_ID = 104;
```

If you were to run this statement and then select all rows from the CD_PROMOTION_HISTORY table, the result would look something like this:

```
SELECT CD_ID, SALE_PRICE, BEGIN_EFF_DT, END_EFF_DT
  FROM CD_PROMOTION_HISTORY
 ORDER BY CD_ID, BEGIN_EFF_DT;

CD_ID  SALE_PRICE  BEGIN_EFF_DT  END_EFF_DT
-----  ----------  ------------  ----------
  102       10.79  2015-03-01    2015-03-31
  102       10.50  2015-04-05    2015-04-15
  103        9.00  2015-01-01    2015-04-01
  103        8.50  2015-04-01    2015-04-15
  103        9.00  2015-04-15    2015-05-01
```

```
104          5.00  2016-01-01     2016-03-01
104          5.00  2016-03-31     9999-12-31
```

The previous row for CD 104 has been replaced by two rows, one for the period 1/1/2016 to 3/1/2016 and the other for the period 3/31/16 to 12/31/9999. If you want to see all the current and historical rows, you can run a query like the following example, the results of which are shown in Figure 13-6:

```
SELECT CD_ID, SALE_PRICE, BEGIN_EFF_DT, END_EFF_DT, SYS_BEGIN, SYS_END
  FROM CD_PROMOTION_HISTORY
   FOR SYSTEM_TIME FROM TIMESTAMP '0001-01-01 00:00:00'
                    TO TIMESTAMP '9999-12-31 23:59:59'
 ORDER BY CD_ID, SYS_BEGIN, BEGIN_EFF_DT;
```

As you can see from these examples, UPDATE and DELETE statements are very powerful ways to manage time periods and related data in system-versioned application-time period tables.

CD_PROMOTION_HISTORY

CD_ID: INT	SALE_PRICE: NUMERIC(5,2)	BEGIN_EFF_DT: DATE	END_EFF_DT: DATE	SYS_BEGIN: TIMESTAMP(12)	SYS_END: TIMESTAMP(12)
101	5.39	2015-01-01	2015-01-15	2015-03-28 13:23:36	2015-03-28 16:54:54
10v	10.79	2015-03-01	2015-03-31	2015-03-28 13:23:36	9999-12-30 00:00:00
102	10.50	2015-03-31	2015-04-15	2015-03-28 13:23:36	2015-03-28 16:54:54
102	10.50	2015-04-05	2015-04-15	2015-03-28 16:54:54	9999-12-30 00:00:00
103	9.00	2015-01-01	2015-05-01	2015-03-28 13:23:36	2015-03-28 16:54:54
103	9.00	2015-01-01	2015-04-01	2015-03-28 16:54:54	9999-12-30 00:00:00
103	8.50	2015-04-01	2015-04-15	2015-03-28 16:54:54	9999-12-30 00:00:00
103	9.00	2015-04-15	2015-05-01	2015-03-28 16:54:54	9999-12-30 00:00:00
104	5.00	2016-01-01	9999-12-31	2015-03-28 13:23:36	2015-03-28 16:54:54
104	5.00	2016-01-01	2016-03-01	2015-03-28 13:23:36	9999-12-30 00:00:00
104	5.00	2016-03-31	9999-12-31	2015-03-28 13:23:36	9999-12-30 00:00:00

Figure 13-6 CD_PROMOTION_HISTORY table with complete history for updates and deletes (SYS_END column shaded for logically deleted rows)

Chapter 13 Self Test

1. The term temporal refers to data that ______________.
2. What types of temporal tables are described in the SQL:2011 standard?
   - **A** Application-versioned tables
   - **B** Application-time period tables
   - **C** System-versioned tables
   - **D** System-version application-time period tables
3. System-versioned tables are which type of SQL base table?
   - **A** Global temporary tables
   - **B** Local temporary tables
   - **C** System versioned tables
   - **D** Regular persistent base tables
4. Can the system time period columns in system-versioned tables be directly updated using SQL statements?
5. Can the system time period columns in system-versioned tables contain null values?
6. Is it possible to update system-versioned tables without the DBMS generating row history tables?
7. Is it possible to delete the row history for system-versioned or system-versioned application-time period tables?
8. Does the DBMS automatically provide values for the application time period columns of application-time period tables when inserting new rows?
9. You wish to update an application-time period table while limiting the application time period to 11/15/2015 to 12/31/2015. What clause should you add to the UPDATE statement to accomplish this?
10. You wish to see rows in a system-versioned or system-versioned application-time period table that were effective as of January 31, 2015. What clause should you add to the SELECT statement to accomplish this?

Advanced Data Access

Chapter 14

Creating SQL-Invoked Routines

Key Skills & Concepts

- Understand SQL-Invoked Routines
- Create SQL-Invoked Procedures
- Add Input Parameters to Your Procedures
- Add Local Variables to Your Procedures
- Work with Control Statements
- Add Output Parameters to Your Procedures
- Create SQL-Invoked Functions

Prior to the release of SQL:1999, the American National Standards Institute (ANSI) and the International Organization for Standardization (ISO) published an interim standard in 1996 that added procedures and functions, along with related language, to the existing SQL standard as Part 4. This new publication, also referred to as SQL/PSM, or PSM-96 (PSM standing for *persistent stored module*), represented the first step toward including procedural capabilities within SQL itself. Part 4 (SQL/PSM) was revised and incorporated into the SQL:1999 standard, revised again for the SQL:2003 standard, and corrections and revisions have taken place in subsequent versions of the SQL standard. These procedural capabilities define, among other components, the creation of SQL-invoked routines—specifically, SQL-invoked procedures and SQL-invoked functions. In this chapter, we'll take a close look at both procedures and functions, including how to create them and how to invoke them once they're created. We'll also take a look at a number of examples that demonstrate the various types of procedures and functions and the components that make up each.

Understand SQL-Invoked Routines

I first introduced you to the concept of SQL-invoked routines in Chapter 2, where I describe the schema objects that can exist within an SQL environment. As you might recall, an *SQL-invoked routine* is a function or procedure that can be invoked from SQL. Both functions and procedures are stored sets of predefined SQL statements that perform some sort of action on the data in your database. For example, you can define a SELECT statement and store it as an SQL-invoked procedure. Once you have created that procedure, you can invoke it simply by calling its name and, if appropriate, supplying the necessary parameters.

Unlike views, all SQL-invoked routines support the use of *parameters,* which are values passed to and from a routine when you invoke that routine. A function can receive input parameters and return a value based on the expression included in the function definition.

A procedure can pass input and output parameters. Regardless of whether it's a procedure or function, an SQL-invoked routine can be a schema object or can be embedded in an SQL server module, which is also a schema object. (A *module* is an object that contains SQL statements or routines.)

NOTE

The SQL standard also supports a third type of SQL-invoked routine—the SQL-invoked method. A method, which is used in user-defined types, is a type of function that performs predefined tasks. SQL supports two types of user-defined types: structured types and distinct types. Methods are used in structured types. The subject of structured user-defined types is beyond the scope of the book, so I won't be covering methods in this chapter.

Most SQL implementations support some form of the SQL-invoked routine in their products. Within various SQL implementations, SQL-invoked procedures are often referred to as *stored procedures,* and SQL-invoked functions are often referred to as *user-defined functions*. Regardless of the names used, the fundamental concepts are the same, and the basic functionality supported is similar from product to product. However, while concepts and functionality are similar, the implementation of SQL-invoked routines can vary widely, and the specifics of how SQL-invoked routines are created and called differ not only between the SQL standard and the individual product, but also between the products themselves. The main reason for this is that many products had already implemented PSM technology prior to the initial publication of the SQL/PSM standard in 1996. As a result, proprietary functionality has persisted among the different implementations, with few SQL products conforming to the actual SQL/PSM standard or, consequently, the PSM-related portion of the SQL standard.

Despite the product differences, it is still worthwhile to have a look at the basic concepts behind SQL-invoked routines as they are defined in the SQL standard. The standard provides insight into the underlying structure used by the various SQL implementations and can give you a cohesive overview of the basic concepts shared by all products that implement SQL-invoked procedures and functions. However, as with other SQL-related technology, you should refer to the product documentation for your specific SQL implementation. In few cases will you be able to use pure (standard) SQL to create an implementation-specific SQL-invoked routine.

SQL-Invoked Procedures and Functions

As I mentioned earlier, an SQL-invoked routine can be either an SQL-invoked procedure or an SQL-invoked function (or, in the case of user data types, an SQL-invoked method). SQL-invoked procedures and functions are similar in many ways, although there are some basic differences. Table 14-1 provides an overview of the main differences and similarities.

The easiest way to distinguish between SQL-invoked procedures and functions is to think of a procedure as a set of one or more stored SQL statements, similar to how a view stores a SELECT statement (as described in Chapter 5) and to think of a function as a type of

Procedures	Functions
Invoked from SQL statements, not from a programming language.	Invoked from SQL statements, not from a programming language.
Can be written in SQL or another programming language.	Can be written in SQL or another programming language.
Invoked by using the CALL statement.	Invoked as a value in an expression.
Support input and output parameters, although neither is required.	Support input parameters, although none are required. You cannot define output or input/output parameters for a function. The function returns a single output value.

Table 14-1 Differences and Similarities of SQL Procedures and Functions

operation that returns a value, similar to set functions such as SUM or AVG (as described in Chapter 10).

Working with the Basic Syntax

There are many similarities between the syntax used to create procedures and that used to create functions. In fact, they're defined as one syntactic element in the SQL standard. In addition, the syntax is, at its most basic level, similar to how procedures are created in most SQL implementations. Let's take a look at the syntax for each one to better understand their basic elements.

Using the CREATE PROCEDURE Statement

The first syntax we'll look at is that for creating a procedure. At its most basic, the CREATE PROCEDURE statement looks like the following:

```
CREATE PROCEDURE <procedure name>
( [ <parameter declaration> [ { , <parameter declaration> } . . . ] ] )
[ <routine characteristic> . . . ]
<routine body>
```

As you can see, you must provide a name for the procedure—in the CREATE PROCEDURE clause—followed by zero or more parameter declarations, which are enclosed in parentheses. If no declarations are defined, you must still provide the parentheses. If more than one declaration is defined, you must separate them using commas. Following the parameter declarations, you have the option of defining one or more routine characteristics. For example, you can specify whether the routine is an SQL routine or one written in another language such as C or Java.

NOTE

The type of routine characteristics that you can define vary greatly among the SQL implementations, not only in terms of which options are supported, but also with regard to how they're defined. Consequently, I will keep my discussion of these options short, so be sure to check the product documentation for more information. For example, the procedural extensions in Oracle are defined using a language that Oracle calls PL/SQL, while in SQL Server and Sybase, the procedural extensions are part of a language called Transact-SQL, both of which are significantly different from the SQL standard. On the other hand, MySQL and DB2 generally follow the SQL standard in defining functions and stored procedures.

After you've defined the procedure's characteristics, you're ready to add the SQL statements, which are represented by the <routine body> placeholder. Many of the statements you'll use in this section will be similar to those you've already seen in this book. However, the SQL/PSM standard introduced new language elements that make procedures more dynamic. As we continue through this chapter, we'll look at many of these elements and how they're used to extend the functionality of SQL-invoked procedures.

Using the CREATE FUNCTION Statement

Now let's take a look at the statement used for creating an SQL-invoked function. As you can see in the following syntax, a function contains a few more elements than a procedure:

```
CREATE FUNCTION <function name>
( [ <parameter declaration> [ { , <parameter declaration> } . . . ] ] )
RETURNS <data type>
[ <routine characteristics> . . . ]
[ STATIC DISPATCH ]
<routine body>
```

As with procedures, you must first provide a name for your function, followed by the parameter declaration list. Functions support only input parameters, and if none are provided, you must still use the parentheses. If more than one input parameter is provided, you must separate them using commas. Following the parameter declarations is the RETURNS clause. You must provide the data type for the value that's returned by the function. After that, you can include any of the optional routine characteristics, depending on what options your SQL implementation supports. Next is the STATIC DISPATCH clause. You must specify this clause if you use a user-defined type, a reference data type, or an array data type. Because these types are all beyond the scope of this book, you do not need to be concerned with the STATIC DISPATCH clause at this time.

The last thing that you must include in the procedure definition is, of course, the routine body. As with procedures, these are the SQL statements that make up the core of your procedure. However, there is one additional element you'll find in the routine body that is not included in a procedure's routine body—a RETURN statement (not to be confused with the RETURNS clause). The RETURN statement specifies the value that will be returned by the function. Later in this chapter, in the "Create SQL-Invoked Functions" section, I'll discuss the

RETURN statement and other elements of the CREATE FUNCTION statement in more detail.

Create SQL-Invoked Procedures

Now that you have an overview of SQL-invoked routines and the syntax used to create them, let's take a closer look at how to create SQL-invoked procedures. A procedure can perform most functions that you can perform by using SQL statements directly. In addition, procedures can be used to pass parameters and define variables, which we'll get into later in this chapter. For now, let's look at a procedure at its most basic, one that includes no parameters or special types of SQL statements.

Suppose you need to query the data in the CD_INVENTORY and CD_TYPES tables shown in Figure 14-1. You want your query results to return the CD names and number in stock for all New Age CDs.

To view this information, you can create a SELECT statement that joins the two tables, as shown in the following example:

```
SELECT CD_TITLE, CD_STOCK
  FROM CD_INVENTORY i, CD_TYPES t
 WHERE i.CD_TYPE_ID = t.CD_TYPE_ID
   AND CD_TYPE_NAME = 'Country';
```

Of course, every time you want to view this information, you would have to re-create the SELECT statement. However, another option is to store the SELECT statement within the

CD_INVENTORY

CD_TITLE: VARCHAR(60)	CD_TYPE_ID: CHAR(4)	CD_STOCK: INT
Drive All Night	ALTR	19
Different Shades of Blue	BLUS	28
Bach	CLAS	6
Man Against Machine	CTRY	8
Dark Side of the Moon	CROK	10
Kind of Blue	JAZZ	11
Old Boots, New Dirt	CTRY	22

CD_TYPES

CD_TYPE_ID: CHAR(4)	CD_TYPE_NAME: CHAR(20)
ALTR	Alternative Rock
BLUS	Blues
CLAS	Classical
CTRY	Country
JAZZ	Jazz
RNBL	Rhythm and Blues
STRK	Soundtrack

Figure 14-1 Using procedures to access the CD_INVENTORY and CD_TYPES tables

schema. That way, all you need to do is call that statement whenever you want to view the Country CDs. One way to store the SELECT statement is within a view definition:

```
CREATE VIEW COUNTRY_CDS AS
  SELECT CD_TITLE, CD_STOCK
    FROM CD_INVENTORY i, CD_TYPES t
   WHERE i.CD_TYPE_ID = t.CD_TYPE_ID
     AND CD_TYPE_NAME = 'Country';
```

Once the view is created, you can use a SELECT statement to call the view, as shown in the following statement:

```
SELECT * FROM COUNTRY_CDS;
```

However, views are very limited with regard to the types of statements and functionality that are supported. For example, you cannot include an UPDATE statement in a view, nor can you pass parameters to and/or from views. As a result, a better way to store this SELECT statement is as an SQL-invoked procedure. To do this, you must create a schema object by using the CREATE PROCEDURE statement, as shown in the following example:

```
CREATE PROCEDURE COUNTRY_CDS ( )
  SELECT CD_TITLE, CD_STOCK
    FROM CD_INVENTORY i, CD_TYPES t
   WHERE i.CD_TYPE_ID = t.CD_TYPE_ID
     AND CD_TYPE_NAME = 'Country';
```

This statement represents the minimum amount of information that you must provide in order to create a procedure. It includes a CREATE PROCEDURE clause that names the procedure (COUNTRY_CDS), a set of parentheses, and a routine body, which is the SELECT statement. If you were defining parameters, their declarations would be enclosed in the parentheses.

As you might well imagine, a CREATE PROCEDURE statement can be far more complex than what you see here. However, the statement in the example represents the basic structure on which you would build more extensive statements. Before I discuss more complicated procedures, let's first touch on the issue of how this statement is created in various SQL implementations.

Earlier in the chapter, I told you that SQL implementations can vary widely with regard to the specifics of how SQL-invoked routines are created and called. As a result, few implementations support pure SQL when attempting to define your procedures. For example, both SQL Server and Oracle require that you use the AS keyword before the routine body. In addition, SQL Server does not use parentheses after the procedure name, whether or not parameters are being defined. Oracle, on the other hand, does use the parentheses, and it also requires some additional statements that enclose executable statements in BEGIN...END blocks. As mentioned earlier, MySQL and DB2 closely follow the SQL standard. From this it should be clear that you simply *must* consult your product documentation whenever you're creating a procedure to determine how the product-specific language differs from the SQL standard.

Invoking SQL-Invoked Procedures

Once you've created your procedure, you can invoke (call) it by using a CALL statement. The basic syntax for the CALL statement is as follows:

```
CALL <procedure name>
( [ <value> [ { , <value> } . . . ] ] )
```

As you can see, you must identify the name of the procedure in the CALL clause and follow that with the values (in parentheses) that are passed into the procedure as parameters. If no parameters are defined for the procedure, you must still use the parentheses. If more than one parameter is defined for the procedure, you must separate them with commas. In addition, you must follow these guidelines when entering values:

- Your CALL statement must include the same number of values as the number of parameters defined in the procedure.
- The values must be entered in the same order as the order in which they are defined in the procedure.
- The values must conform to the data types that are assigned to the parameters.

I'll be discussing parameters in more detail in the next section, "Add Input Parameters to Your Procedures."

Now let's look at an example of the CALL statement. If you want to call the procedure that was created in the preceding example, you can use the following statement:

```
CALL COUNTRY_CDS( );
```

In this statement, the name of the procedure follows the CALL keyword. Notice the use of parentheses even though no parameters were defined for the procedure. Had parameters been defined, they would have been enclosed in the parentheses. When you execute this statement, you'll receive the same results as you would have if you had executed the SELECT statement separately, as shown in the following query results:

```
CD_TITLE              CD_STOCK
-------------------   ---------
Man Against Machine   8
Old Boots, New Dirt   22
```

The CALL statement, like the CREATE PROCEDURE statement, can vary from SQL implementation to implementation in how it is used and whether it is supported. In fact, you'll probably find that for most implementations, you must use an EXECUTE statement, rather than CALL, to invoke a procedure.

Add Input Parameters to Your Procedures

The COUNTRY_CDS procedure that we looked at in the previous examples can be very handy because it saves you having to create an SQL statement each time you want to view information about Country CDs. However, in order to return information about other types of CDs, such as Blues or Jazz, you must create a new query or set up a procedure for the specific type of music. But there is another alternative. You can create a procedure that does not specifically define the music type but instead allows you to enter that type whenever you call that procedure. That way, you need only one procedure to check any desired type of music.

To support this type of procedure, you must declare a parameter within the procedure definition that allows the procedure to accept input values when you call it. Let's return to the CD_INVENTORY table and CD_TYPES table shown in Figure 14-1. If we modify the language of the procedure we created earlier, we can create a new procedure that includes the necessary input parameter, as shown in the following CREATE PROCEDURE statement:

```
CREATE PROCEDURE CDS_BY_TYPE ( IN p_CD_Type CHAR(20) )
  SELECT CD_TITLE, CD_STOCK
    FROM CD_INVENTORY i, CD_TYPES t
   WHERE i.CD_TYPE_ID = t.CD_TYPE_ID
     AND CD_TYPE_NAME = p_CD_Type;
```

In the first line of code, a parameter is defined after the CREATE PROCEDURE clause. The parameter declaration includes the IN keyword, the name of the parameter (p_CD_Type), and the data type for that parameter (CHAR(20)), all of which are enclosed in parentheses.

NOTE

The "p_" convention used to name the parameters is not necessary. However, I like to use some type of naming convention to set parameters apart, making them easier to pick out in the code.

SQL supports three types of parameters: input, output, and input/output. The three types are represented by the parameter mode keywords IN, OUT, and INOUT, respectively. Input parameters allow you to provide values when you invoke a procedure. Those values are then used within the routine body when the SQL statements are executed. Output parameters allow your procedure to provide values as a result of invoking the procedure. Input/output parameters are those that provide the functionality of both input and output parameters. You do not have to specify one of the parameter mode keywords when you define your parameters. However, if you don't specify one of the keywords, SQL assumes that you're defining an input parameter.

NOTE

As with many other aspects of the CREATE PROCEDURE statement, parameter declarations can vary from product to product. In SQL Server, for example, parameter names must be preceded by the at (@) symbol, as in @p_CD_Type, the parameter declarations are not enclosed in parentheses, and the IN keyword is not used. Oracle, on the other hand, does not require the at symbol and does use parentheses. Oracle also uses the IN keyword, but it is positioned after the name of the parameter, as in p_CD_Type IN CHAR (20).

Now let's return to the CDS_BY_TYPE procedure that is defined in the previous CREATE PROCEDURE statement. Once you define your input parameter, you'll want to use it in some meaningful way within the routine body. In this case, the p_CD_Type parameter is used in the second predicate in the WHERE clause (CD_TYPE_NAME = p_CD_Type). This means that the value you enter when you invoke the procedure is compared to the CD_TYPE_NAME values of the CD_TYPES table when the SELECT statement is executed. As a result, your query results will include CD information about the specified music type.

Once you create your procedure, you can invoke it by using a CALL statement that specifies a value for the parameter. For example, if you want to return information about Jazz CDs, you can use the following CALL statement:

```
CALL CDS_BY_TYPE('Jazz');
```

Notice that you include the value for the parameter in parentheses after the name of the procedure. The value must conform to the data type assigned to the parameter, which in this case is CHAR(20). As with any other instance in which you're working with character string values, you must enclose the value in single quotes. When you invoke this procedure, the Jazz value is inserted into the predicate in the WHERE clause and the procedure returns the following query results:

```
CD_TITLE               CD_STOCK
---------------------  --------
Kind of Blue           11
```

As you can see, you now have a procedure that you can use to return CD information on any music type. You simply provide the name of the music type when you call the procedure. However, procedures are not limited to only one parameter. You can include multiple parameters in any procedure definition. For example, suppose you want to modify the preceding procedure definition to allow you to enter an amount. You want to use that amount to return CD information for only those CDs with a CD_STOCK value that exceeds the specified amount. At the same time, you still want to return CD information for only the specified music type. As a result, you need to define two parameters, as shown in the following CREATE PROCEDURE statement:

```
CREATE PROCEDURE CDS_BY_TYPE2 ( IN p_CD_Type CHAR(20), IN p_Amount INT )
  SELECT CD_TITLE, CD_STOCK
```

```
  FROM CD_INVENTORY i, CD_TYPES t
 WHERE i.CD_TYPE_ID = t.CD_TYPE_ID
   AND CD_TYPE_NAME = p_CD_Type
   AND CD_STOCK     > p_Amount;
```

Notice that the parameter declaration clause now includes two input parameters: p_CD_Type and p_Amount. The p_Amount parameter is configured with the INT data type. The p_Amount parameter, like the p_CD_Type parameter, is used in a predicate in the WHERE clause (CD_STOCK > p_Amount). As a result, the rows returned by the procedure must include CD_STOCK values greater than the amount specified when calling the procedure.

Once you've created the procedure, you can call it by using a CALL statement that includes values for both parameters, as shown in the following example:

```
CALL CDS_BY_TYPE2 ('Country', 5);
```

Now your CALL statement includes two values (separated by a comma) within the parentheses. The values must be listed in the order in which the parameters are defined in the CREATE PROCEDURE statement. When you invoke this statement, the p_C_Type is assigned the value Country, and the p_Amount parameter is assigned the value 5, making the SELECT statement embedded in the procedure definition behave as though you entered the values directly, as shown in the following example:

```
SELECT CD_TITLE, CD_STOCK
  FROM CD_INVENTORY i, CD_TYPES t
 WHERE i.CD_TYPE_ID = t.CD_TYPE_ID
   AND CD_TYPE_NAME = 'Country'
   AND CD_STOCK     > 5;
```

If you were to execute this statement, you would return the same query results as you would if you were to execute the CALL statement using the Country value and 5 value, as shown in the following results:

```
CD_TITLE              CD_STOCK
--------------------  ---------
Man Against Machine   8
Old Boots, New Dirt   22
```

Now let's modify the CALL statement to see how specifying a different value might affect the results. Suppose you use a numeric value of 8 rather than 5, as shown in the following statement:

```
CALL CDS_BY_TYPE2 ('Country', 8);
```

If you were to execute this statement, only one row would be returned:

```
CD_TITLE              CD_STOCK
--------------------  ---------
Old Boots, New Dirt   22
```

If you refer back to the CD_INVENTORY table in Figure 14-1, you'll see that only the Old Boots, New Dirt row is a Country CD with a CD_STOCK value that exceeds 8, the value you specified in your CALL statement. As you can see, using multiple parameters can provide you with a variety of options that make procedures a useful and flexible tool that can eliminate the need to write multiple statements that are meant to provide similar results. If you define the necessary parameters, users simply plug in the necessary values to achieve the results they desire.

Using Procedures to Modify Data

Up to this point, the SQL-invoked procedures that we've looked at have contained SELECT statements that query data. However, procedures are not limited to only SELECT statements. You can include data modification statements such as INSERT, UPDATE, and DELETE. Let's return to the CD_INVENTORY table and CD_TYPES table, shown in Figure 14-1. You might have noticed that the CD_INVENTORY table includes a row for the Dark Side of the Moon CD. The music type for that CD is Classic Rock, which is represented by CROK (the value in the CD_TYPE_ID column). You might also have noticed that there is no corresponding entry in the CD_TYPES table for the Classic Rock type. You can create a procedure that allows you to insert values into that table. You simply need to define that procedure with the appropriate input parameters and INSERT statement, as shown in the following example:

```
CREATE PROCEDURE INSERT_TYPE ( IN p_Type CHAR(4), IN p_Name CHAR(20) )
  INSERT INTO CD_TYPES VALUES ( p_Type, p_Name );
```

Notice that the procedure definition includes two input parameters: p_Type and p_Name, both of which are defined with the CHAR data type. These parameters are then used in the INSERT statement, in the same way in which you would normally specify values to be inserted into a table. Any parameter that you declare for this purpose must be defined with a data type that is compatible with the data type defined on the column that contains the data to be modified. Once you create the procedure, you can use a CALL statement similar to the following example to invoke the procedure:

```
CALL INSERT_TYPE('CROK', 'Classic Rock');
```

Notice that the CALL statement includes CROK and Classic Rock values. These values are passed to the two parameters defined in the INSERT_TYPE procedure. As a result, they are inserted into the CD_TYPES table as though you had executed the INSERT statement directly.

In the same way that you create the INSERT_TYPE procedure, you can create procedures that update and delete data by including the appropriate UPDATE and DELETE statement, rather than an INSERT statement. Simply create the necessary input parameters and assign

Ask the Expert

Q: Up to this point, you've shown us how to create SQL-invoked procedures, but not how to modify them. Is there a way to alter or delete procedures?

A: The SQL standard supports both an ALTER PROCEDURE statement and a DROP PROCEDURE statement. The ALTER PROCEDURE statement allows you to alter some of the routine characteristics of the procedure, but it does not allow you to alter the procedure body. However, the functionality supported by the ALTER PROCEDURE statement can vary so widely from one SQL implementation to another that you'll need to check the product documentation to see whether the statement is supported and what you can do with that statement. In SQL Server, for example, the ALTER PROCEDURE statement allows you to modify most aspects of the procedure, whereas the same statement in Oracle is used primarily to recompile the procedure to avoid runtime compiling (which saves on runtime overhead). However, Oracle and DB2 provide the CREATE OR REPLACE PROCEDURE syntax that replaces an existing procedure (including the procedure body) or creates a new procedure if it does not yet exist.

As for the DROP PROCEDURE statement, most implementations support this and it is usually fairly straightforward. You simply provide the name of the procedure in the statement and, depending on the SQL implementation, the RESTRICT or CASCADE keywords, as you've seen them used in other DROP statements. Note that the same is true for the ALTER FUNCTION and DROP FUNCTION statements. Although supported by many implementations, the ALTER FUNCTION statement can vary from one product to the next, and the DROP FUNCTION statement is fairly similar across implementations.

the appropriate values to those parameters when you call the procedure. However, keep in mind that the value you pass using the parameters must conform not only to the data types defined in the parameter declarations, but also to the data types and constraints on the columns that contain the data you're trying to modify.

Add Local Variables to Your Procedures

In addition to allowing you to pass parameters into a procedure, SQL provides a way for you to create local variables in the procedure definition that can be used within the body of the procedure. You can think of a *local variable* as a type placeholder that holds a value in memory during the execution of the statements in the routine body. Once the statements are executed, the variable ceases to exist.

When you define a local variable, you must first declare the variable and then set an initial value for it. You can then use that variable in the remaining block of statements. The basic syntax for defining a variable is as follows:

```
DECLARE <variable name> <data type>;
```

As you can see, the syntax is very straightforward. You must provide a name for the variable and assign a data type. Once you've declared the variable, you must then assign a value to it before it can be referenced. (However, some implementations automatically assign a null value to variables as they are defined.) You can use the SET statement to assign a value to a variable, which has the following syntax:

```
SET <variable name> = <value expression>;
```

In this statement, you must first provide the variable name and then provide the value, which can be any sort of value expression, such as a number, a character string, or a subquery.

After you've declared the variable and assigned it a value, you're ready to use the variable in your routine body. The best way to illustrate this is to show you an example of a procedure that uses a variable. For this example, we'll again use the CD_INVENTORY table, shown in Figure 14-1. The following statement creates a procedure that retrieves CD information for a specific music type:

```
CREATE PROCEDURE CD_AMOUNT ( IN p_Type_ID CHAR(4) )
  BEGIN
    DECLARE v_Amount INT;
    SET v_Amount = ( SELECT AVG(CD_STOCK)
                       FROM CD_INVENTORY );
    SELECT CD_TITLE, CD_STOCK
      FROM CD_INVENTORY
     WHERE CD_TYPE_ID = p_Type_ID
       AND CD_STOCK   < v_Amount;
  END;
```

Let's go through this statement line by line. In the first line, we create a procedure named CD_AMOUNT and an input parameter named p_Type_ID. The second line contains the keyword BEGIN. The BEGIN keyword is paired with the END keyword in the last line. Together they enclose a block of statements that are processed as a unit. We'll take a closer look at the BEGIN...END block later in the "Work with Control Statements" section.

The third line of the procedure definition includes a DECLARE statement that declares the v_Amount variable, which is defined with the INT data type. The next two lines use a SET statement to assign an initial value to the parameter. This value is derived from a subquery that finds the average for all the CD_STOCK values. The average in this case is about 15. In the next four lines of the procedure definition, a SELECT statement retrieves data from the CD_INVENTORY table based on the values supplied by the parameter and variable.

NOTE

Many SQL clients have difficulty interpreting SQL-invoked routines that contain multiple semicolons because they interpret the first semicolon as the end of a statement that should be run immediately. The usual remedy is to set the terminator (delimiter) for SQL statements to some other character and then use the new terminator character to mark the end of the SQL-invoked routine. For example, in MySQL you can use the DELIMITER command to set the statement delimiter to an alternative character and then change the END statement so that it is followed by the new delimiter. After the SQL-invoked routine is created, you can use the DELIMITER command to set the terminator back to the semicolon. The following example shows the CD_AMOUNT procedure modified for MySQL using the pipe (|) character as a statement delimiter.

```
DELIMITER |
CREATE PROCEDURE CD_AMOUNT ( IN p_Type_ID CHAR(4) )
  BEGIN
    DECLARE v_Amount INT;
    SET v_Amount = ( SELECT AVG(CD_STOCK)
                     FROM CD_INVENTORY );
    SELECT CD_TITLE, CD_STOCK
      FROM CD_INVENTORY
     WHERE CD_TYPE_ID = p_Type_ID
       AND CD_STOCK   < v_Amount;
  END |
DELIMITER ;
```

Once you've created your procedure, you can execute it by using a CALL statement and providing a value for the parameter, as shown in the following example:

```
CALL CD_AMOUNT('CTRY');
```

When the procedure is processed, it uses the CTRY value from the parameter and the CD_STOCK average from the variable in the SELECT statement defined in the procedure definition. It would be similar to executing the following statement:

```
SELECT CD_TITLE, CD_STOCK
  FROM CD_INVENTORY
 WHERE CD_TYPE_ID = 'CTRY'
   AND CD_STOCK   < 15;
```

This SELECT statement, like the procedure itself, will return the following query results:

```
CD_TITLE              CD_STOCK
-------------------   ---------
Man Against Machine   8
```

Notice that the row in the results contains a Country CD that has a CD_STOCK value less than the average amount (15).

You're not limited to only one variable in a procedure definition. You can create a DECLARE statement for each variable that you want to include. You can also include multiple variables in one statement if those variables are assigned the same data type. For example, suppose you want to declare several variables with an INT data type, as shown in the following DECLARE statement:

```
DECLARE Var1, Var2, Var3 INT;
```

This statement declares the Var1, Var2, and Var3 variables, and each one is assigned the INT data type. Once you assign initial values to the variables, you can use them in the routine body in the same way as any other local variables.

Work with Control Statements

When the SQL/PSM standard was released in 1996, it included not only language that supported SQL-invoked routines, but language that could be used within those routines to make them more robust. Such characteristics as grouping statements into blocks and looping statements so that they could be executed multiple times—behavior traditionally associated with procedural-type languages—made procedures and functions even more valuable to users needing to access and manipulate data in their databases. The SQL standard refers to these new language elements as *control statements* because they affect how you can control data in SQL-invoked routines. In this section, we'll look at several of these control statements, including those that allow you to group statements into a block, create conditional statements, and set up statements into a loop.

Create Compound Statements

The most basic of the control statements is the compound statement, which allows you to group statements into a block. The compound statement starts with the BEGIN keyword and finishes with the END keyword. Everything between the two keywords is part of the block. The compound statement is made up of one or more individual SQL statements, which can include statements such as DECLARE, SET, SELECT, UPDATE, INSERT, DELETE, or other control statements.

You've already seen an example of a compound statement in the preceding CREATE PROCEDURE statement that defines the CD_AMOUNT procedure. (This is the example shown in the "Add Local Variables to Your Procedures" section.) If you take another look at that example, you'll see that the procedure definition includes a compound statement. As you would expect, it starts with the BEGIN keyword and finishes with the END keyword. The block created by these keywords includes a DECLARE statement, a SET statement, and a SELECT statement. Notice that each statement is terminated with a semicolon. Although the BEGIN...END statement is considered one statement, the statements enclosed in the keywords are individual statements in their own right.

NOTE

In some SQL implementations, the compound statement might not be necessary under certain circumstances. In these cases, the semicolon terminator might be enough to signal to the implementation that one statement has ended and another has begun. Even those implementations that don't require the semicolon, such as SQL Server, will sometimes process multiple statements as a block even if the BEGIN...END construction has not been used. When the implementation reaches the end of one statement, it simply continues on to the next. However, as a general rule, you should use the compound construction to keep together those statements that should be processed as a unit. When you don't use it, you can sometimes experience unpredictable behavior, depending on the implementation.

You can use the compound statement wherever you need to keep SQL statements together. That means that they can be embedded within other compound statements or within other types of control statements. The BEGIN and END keywords do not affect how data might be passed from one statement to the next, as in the case of parameters.

The good news about compound statements and the BEGIN...END construction is that they're supported by most SQL implementations, although there can be slight variations from one product to the next in terms of the specifics of how they're implemented. Be sure to check the product documentation when using these statements.

Create Conditional Statements

The next type of control statement we'll look at is the conditional statement. This statement determines whether a statement (or series of statements) is executed based on whether a specified condition evaluates to true. The statement uses the IF, THEN, and ELSE keywords to establish the conditions and define the actions to take: *if* the condition is met, *then* the SQL statement is executed, or *else* another action is taken.

NOTE

The conditional statement is sometimes referred to as an IF statement, an IF...ELSE statement, an IF...END IF statement, or an IF...THEN...ELSE statement.

Let's take a look at an example that uses a conditional statement to define different courses of action, depending on the condition. In the following procedure definition, I modified the routine body of the CD_AMOUNT procedure (which we used in the preceding example) to include a conditional statement:

```
CREATE PROCEDURE CD_AMOUNT ( IN p_Type_ID CHAR (4) )
  BEGIN
    DECLARE v_Amount INT;
    SET v_Amount = ( SELECT SUM(CD_STOCK)
                       FROM CD_INVENTORY
                      WHERE CD_TYPE_ID = p_Type_ID );
    IF v_Amount < 20 THEN
```

```
    SELECT CD_TITLE, CD_STOCK
      FROM CD_INVENTORY
     WHERE CD_TYPE_ID = p_Type_ID;
  ELSE
    SELECT CD_TITLE, CD_STOCK
      FROM CD_INVENTORY;
  END IF;
END;
```

Notice that the BEGIN...END block now includes an IF...END IF statement. The IF clause introduces the statement and sets up the condition. For the condition to evaluate to true, the value of the v_Amount variable must be less than 20. If the condition evaluates to true, the first SELECT statement is executed. This is the SELECT statement that follows the THEN keyword. If the condition is false, then the second SELECT statement is executed. This is the statement that follows the ELSE keyword. To sum this all up, if v_Amount is less than 20, the CD_TITLE and CD_STOCK values from the CD_INVENTORY table are returned for those rows that contain the Type ID (column CD_TYPE_ID) specified by the p_Type_ID parameter. If v_Amount is not less than 20, the CD_TITLE and CD_STOCK values for all rows in the CD_INVENTORY table are returned.

Once you create your procedure, you can invoke it by using a CALL statement, as you have for previous procedures. For example, if you want to return Alternative Rock (ALTR) CDs, you can use the following CALL statement:

```
CALL CD_AMOUNT('ALTR');
```

This statement will return the Alternative Rock row: Drive All Night. This is because the total number of Alternative Rock CDs (19) is less than 20, so the first SELECT statement is executed. If you had specified the Country category (CTRY) when you invoked the CD_AMOUNT procedure, all rows would have been returned. This is because the total number of Country CDs (30) exceeds 20. As a result the IF condition would not be met, so the ELSE statement would be executed.

If you want to create a conditional statement that includes more than one SQL statement in either the IF clause or the ELSE clause, you can enclose those statements in a control statement. For example, if we add an UPDATE statement to the condition in the preceding example and use a control statement to enclose the UPDATE and SELECT statements, your procedure definition will look like the following:

```
CREATE PROCEDURE CD_AMOUNT ( IN p_Type_ID CHAR (4) )
  BEGIN
    DECLARE v_Amount INT;
    SET v_Amount = ( SELECT SUM(CD_STOCK)
                       FROM CD_INVENTORY
                      WHERE CD_TYPE_ID = p_Type_ID );
    IF v_Amount < 20 THEN
      BEGIN
        UPDATE CD_INVENTORY
```

```
          SET CD_STOCK = CD_STOCK + 1
        WHERE CD_TYPE_ID = p_Type_ID;
       SELECT CD_TITLE, CD_STOCK
         FROM CD_INVENTORY
        WHERE CD_TYPE_ID = p_Type_ID;
    END;
  ELSE
    SELECT * FROM CD_INVENTORY;
  END IF;
END;
```

The compound statement groups the two statements into one block of code. This way, the tables will be updated and the results of the update will be displayed in your query results.

Create Looping Statements

Now let's take a look at another type of control statement—the looping statement. SQL actually supports several types of looping statements. We'll be looking at two of them: the LOOP statement and the WHILE statement, both of which perform similar functions.

The LOOP statement uses the LOOP and END LOOP keywords to enclose a block of statements that are executed repeatedly until the loop is explicitly ended, usually through the use of the LEAVE keyword. Note that Oracle uses the EXIT keyword instead of LEAVE, and SQL Server does not support the LOOP statement. Let's take a look at an example to illustrate how this looks. Once again using the tables in Figure 14-1, we'll use a LOOP statement to update the CD_INVENTORY table.

Ask the Expert

Q: The condition statement in the preceding example shows only two conditions and courses of action: the condition/action defined in the IF clause and the condition/action defined in the ELSE clause. What if you want to include more conditions?

A: The SQL standard supports more than two condition/action constructions in a conditional statement. If more than two are needed, you treat the IF clause and the ELSE clause as shown in the example. The additional conditions are inserted between the two clauses by adding an ELSE IF clause or an ELSEIF clause. The syntax for this would be as follows:

```
IF <condition> THEN <action>
 ELSE IF <condition> THEN <action>
 ELSE <action>
```

The exact way you implement the third condition/action depends on your implementation. In addition, not all implementations support ELSEIF, and some use the ELSIF keyword. As always, be sure to refer to your product documentation.

NOTE

If you created and tested the CD_AMOUNT procedure in the preceding example, assume that the CD_INVENTORY table has been returned to its original condition shown in Figure 14-1 and that no data has been modified.

In the following procedure definition, I include a LOOP statement that continues to update the CD_STOCK column until it reaches an amount greater than 14:

```
CREATE PROCEDURE UPDATE_STOCK ( IN p_Title CHAR(40) )
  BEGIN
    DECLARE v_Amount INT;
    SET v_Amount = ( SELECT CD_STOCK
                        FROM CD_INVENTORY
                       WHERE CD_TITLE = p_Title );
    Loop1:
    LOOP
      SET v_Amount = v_Amount + 1;
      UPDATE CD_INVENTORY
         SET CD_STOCK = v_Amount
       WHERE CD_TITLE = p_Title;
      IF v_Amount > 14
        THEN LEAVE Loop1;
      END IF;
    END LOOP;
  END;
```

In this statement, the loop is first assigned a name (Loop1:), which is sometimes called a statement label. You must include a colon with the name when you first assign it. Next you create your loop block, which begins with the LOOP keyword and finishes with the END LOOP keywords. Within the block are SET and UPDATE statements. These two statements are executed until the loop is terminated. Notice that the CD_STOCK value is increased by an increment of 1 each time the statements in the loop are executed. These two statements are followed by an IF statement, which specifies the condition in which the loop is terminated. *If* the value for the v_Amount variable exceeds 14, *then* the loop is terminated (LEAVE Loop1). The IF statement is then ended with the END IF keywords.

NOTE

If you do not include the IF statement within the loop (with the LEAVE termination operator), the loop will continue to increase the CD_STOCK value until it fills all available storage or some other event terminates the operation. This is a common programming error known as an infinite loop.

You can then invoke the procedure by providing the procedure name and a value for the parameter. For example, suppose you want to update the Dark Side of the Moon row in the CD_INVENTORY table. You can invoke the procedure with the following CALL statement:

```
CALL UPDATE_STOCK('Dark Side of the Moon');
```

When the procedure is executed, a value of 1 is repeatedly added to the CD_STOCK column until the value reaches 15, and then the loop is terminated.

You can receive the same results more elegantly by using a WHILE statement. In the following example, I modified the UPDATE_STOCK procedural definition by replacing the LOOP statement with a WHILE statement:

```
CREATE PROCEDURE UPDATE_STOCK ( IN p_Title CHAR(40) )
  BEGIN
    DECLARE v_Amount INT;
    SET v_Amount = ( SELECT CD_STOCK
                       FROM CD_INVENTORY
                      WHERE CD_TITLE = p_Title );
    WHILE v_Amount < 15 DO
      SET v_Amount = v_Amount + 1;
      UPDATE CD_INVENTORY
         SET CD_STOCK = v_Amount
       WHERE CD_TITLE = p_Title;
    END WHILE;
  END;
```

NOTE

Again, if you tested the procedure created in the example preceding this one, assume that the table has been returned to its original condition shown in Figure 14-1 and that no data has been modified.

The WHILE statement sets up the same type of loop condition as the LOOP statement. However, instead of using an IF statement to terminate the loop, a condition is specified in the WHILE clause that terminates the loop automatically when the condition evaluates to false. In this case, the parameter value for v_Amount must be less than 15 for the WHILE condition to evaluate to true. As long as the condition evaluates to true, the SET statement and UPDATE statement are executed. If the condition evaluates to false, the WHILE loop is terminated. Note that many implementations, including Oracle and SQL Server, use a BEGIN block instead of the keyword DO to enclose the statements to be repeated by the WHILE loop. One more variance to be aware of is where the condition is evaluated in the looping logic. Some implementations evaluate the condition at the top of the loop. Others evaluate the condition at the bottom of the loop, which means that the statements in the loop will always execute at least once, even if the condition is false the first time the loop is initiated.

Try This 14-1 Creating SQL-Invoked Procedures

In this Try This exercise, you will apply what you have learned about creating SQL-invoked procedures to the INVENTORY database. You'll create procedures, invoke procedures, and drop procedures. One of the procedures will include a parameter and one will include a variable. For this exercise, even more so than most Try This exercises, you'll need to reference the product documentation for your SQL implementation to ensure that you take into account the variations in how a procedure is created, called, and dropped. As I said earlier in this chapter, procedure implementation can vary widely between the SQL standard and the individual product. You can download the Try_This_14_1.txt file, which contains the SQL statements used in this exercise.

Step by Step

1. Open the client application for your RDBMS and connect to the INVENTORY database.
2. The first procedure that you'll create is a very basic one that queries information from the COMPACT_DISCS, ARTIST_CDS, and ARTISTS tables. You'll join the three tables in order to display the CD names and artist names. Your procedure will include no parameters or variables. Enter and execute the following SQL statement:

```
CREATE PROCEDURE GET_CD_ARTISTS ( )
   SELECT cd.CD_TITLE, a.ARTIST_NAME
     FROM COMPACT_DISCS cd, ARTIST_CDS ac, ARTISTS a
    WHERE cd.CD_ID       = ac.CD_ID
      AND ac.ARTIST_ID = a.ARTIST_ID;
```

   You should receive a message indicating that the GET_CD_ARTISTS procedure has been created.
3. Next, you'll call the GET_CD_ARTISTS procedure. Enter and execute the following SQL statement:

```
CALL GET_CD_ARTISTS( );
```

   When you invoke the procedure, you should receive query results that include a list of all the CDs and their artists.
4. Now you'll drop the procedure from the database. Enter and execute the following SQL statement:

```
DROP PROCEDURE GET_CD_ARTISTS CASCADE;
```

   You should receive a message indicating that the GET_CD_ARTISTS procedure has been dropped from the database. Note that the CASCADE keyword may not be supported by your SQL implementation. For example, MySQL does not support the CASCADE option in a DROP PROCEDURE statement.

5. Your next step is to create a procedure similar to the last one, only this time you'll define a parameter that allows you to enter the name of the CD. The SELECT statement will include a predicate that compares the CD_TITLE value to the value in the p_CD parameter. Enter and execute the following SQL statement:

```
CREATE PROCEDURE GET_CD_ARTISTS ( IN p_CD VARCHAR(60) )
   SELECT cd.CD_TITLE, a.ARTIST_NAME
     FROM COMPACT_DISCS cd, ARTIST_CDS ac, ARTISTS a
    WHERE cd.CD_ID      = ac.CD_ID
      AND ac.ARTIST_ID = a.ARTIST_ID
      AND cd.CD_TITLE  = p_CD;
```

You should receive a message indicating that the GET_CD_ARTISTS procedure has been created.

6. Now you'll call the GET_CD_ARTISTS procedure. The CALL statement will include the Drive All Night value to insert into the parameter. Enter and execute the following SQL statement:

```
CALL GET_CD_ARTISTS('Drive All Night');
```

Your query results should now include only the Drive All Night row.

7. The next procedure that you'll create is one that uses a variable to hold a number based on the average of the IN_STOCK values. The procedure definition will include a compound statement that groups together the other statements in the routine body. Enter and execute the following SQL statement:

```
CREATE PROCEDURE GET_CD_AMOUNT ( )
  BEGIN
    DECLARE v_In_Stock INT;
    SET v_In_Stock = ( SELECT AVG(IN_STOCK)
                           FROM COMPACT_DISCS );
    SELECT CD_TITLE, IN_STOCK
      FROM COMPACT_DISCS
     WHERE IN_STOCK < v_In_Stock;
  END;
```

You should receive a message indicating that the procedure has been created.

8. Now you'll call the procedure. Enter and execute the following SQL statement:

```
CALL GET_CD_AMOUNT( );
```

Your query results should include a list of CDs that have an IN_STOCK value less than the average for all IN_STOCK values.

9. Close the client application.

(continued)

Try This Summary

In this Try This exercise, you created three procedures. The first procedure, GET_CD_ARTISTS, included no parameters or variables. After you dropped that procedure, you modified the original GET_CD_ARTISTS procedure to include a parameter. You then created a new procedure (GET_CD_AMOUNT) that included no procedures but did include one variable. The INVENTORY database should now contain these two procedures. Because both procedures only retrieve SQL data, you can invoke them at any time.

Add Output Parameters to Your Procedures

Up to this point, we've looked only at procedures that take input parameter values. However, SQL-invoked procedures also support output parameters. Output parameters provide a way to create a procedure that returns a value (or multiple values).

The process of defining an output parameter is similar to that of defining an input parameter, only you use the OUT keyword rather than IN. However, you must still provide a parameter name and assign a data type. In addition, you must assign a value to that parameter before the procedure ends by using a SET statement, although many implementations automatically return null values for output parameters that were not assigned a value.

A procedure definition can include both input and output parameters (and input/output parameters if your implementation supports them). You can also include variables or any other elements that we've looked at so far in this chapter.

Now let's take a look at an example of an output parameter. The following CREATE PROCEDURE statement creates a procedure that includes one output parameter (but no input parameters or variables):

```
CREATE PROCEDURE COUNTRY_TOTAL ( OUT p_Total INT )
  BEGIN
    SET p_Total = ( SELECT SUM(CD_STOCK)
                      FROM CD_INVENTORY i, CD_TYPES t
                     WHERE i.CD_TYPE_ID = t.CD_TYPE_ID
                       AND CD_TYPE_NAME = 'Country' );
  END;
```

The output parameter (p_Total) is assigned the INT data type. The SET statement defines a value for the parameter. In this case, the value is equal to the total number of Country CDs. This is the value that is returned by the procedure when you invoke it.

The process of invoking this procedure is different from what you've seen so far. When invoking a procedure with an output parameter, you must first declare a variable that is then used in the CALL statement, as shown in the following example:

```
BEGIN
  DECLARE p_Total INT;
  CALL COUNTRY_TOTAL( p_Total );
END;
```

In this case, I used the same name for the variable as the name of the parameter that was defined in the procedure definition. However, the variable and parameter are not required to have the same name, although they must be defined with the same data type.

NOTE

Some SQL implementations such as MySQL do not support BEGIN blocks outside of the definition of an SQL-invoked routine. In these cases, you can try using a temporary variable without declaring it. For example:

```
CALL COUNTRY_TOTAL (@p_Total);
```

Create SQL-Invoked Functions

Earlier in the chapter, in the "Understand SQL-Invoked Routines" section, I introduced you to the two types of SQL-invoked routines—procedures and functions—and I described the differences and similarities between the two. The main differences are that procedures support the definition of input and output parameters and are invoked by using the CALL statement. Functions, on the other hand, support the definition of input parameters only and are invoked as a value in an expression. The function's output is the value returned by the execution of the function and not through the explicit definition of an output parameter.

To create a function, you must use a CREATE FUNCTION statement. The statement is similar to a CREATE PROCEDURE statement, except for a few critical differences:

- The input parameter definitions cannot include the IN keyword.
- A RETURNS clause must follow the parameter definitions. The clause assigns a data type to the value returned by the function.
- The routine body must include a RETURN statement that defines the value returned by the parameter.

NOTE

SQL Server also uses a RETURNS clause to assign a data type to the returned value, while Oracle uses a RETURN clause for the same purpose. In both cases this clause is followed by the AS keyword. Both SQL Server and Oracle use a RETURN statement in the routine body to define the value returned by the parameter. Also, Oracle and DB2 support the CREATE OR REPLACE FUNCTION statement that can be used to redefine an existing function without having to first drop it.

A function definition can include many of the elements that have been described throughout this chapter. For example, you can define local variables, create compound statements, and use conditional statements. In addition, you can define and use input parameters in the same way you define and use input parameters in procedures (except that you do not use the IN keyword).

IN_STOCK_CDS

TITLE: VARCHAR(60)	STOCK: INT
Drive All Night	12
Different Shades of Blue	42
Innervisions (Remastered)	16
The Definitive Collection	34
Rumours (Reissued)	17
Come On Over	6
Man Against Machine	8
Endless River	12
Sonic Highways	27

PERFORMERS

TITLE: VARCHAR(60)	ARTIST_NAME: VARCHAR(60)
Drive All Night	Glen Hansard
Different Shades of Blue	Joe Bonamassa
Innervisions (Remastered)	Stevie Wonder
The Definitive Collection	Stevie Wonder
Rumours (Reissued)	Fleetwood Mac
Come On Over	Shania Twain
Bach	Joshua Bell
Old Boots, New Dirt	Jason Aldean
Man Against Machine	Garth Brooks
Dark Side of the Moon	Pink Floyd
Kind of Blue	Miles Davis
Endless River	Pink Floyd
Sonic Highways	Foo Fighters

Figure 14-2 Using functions to retrieve values from the IN_STOCK_CDS and PERFORMERS tables

Now that you have an overview of how to create a function, let's look at an example, which is based on the IN_STOCK_CDS and PERFORMERS tables, shown in Figure 14-2.

The following CREATE FUNCTION statement defines a function that returns the artist name for a specified CD, as it appears in the IN_STOCK_CDS table:

```
CREATE FUNCTION CD_ARTIST ( p_Title VARCHAR(60) )
  RETURNS VARCHAR(60)
  BEGIN
    RETURN
    ( SELECT ARTIST_NAME
        FROM IN_STOCK_CDS s, PERFORMERS p
       WHERE s.Title = p.Title
         AND s.Title = p_Title );
  END;
```

In the first line of the statement, the CD_ARTIST function and the p_Title parameter have been defined. In the next line, the RETURNS clause assigns the VARCHAR(60) data type to the value returned by the function. In the routine body, you can see that a RETURN statement has been defined. The statement includes a subquery that uses the value of the input parameter to return the name of the artist.

As you can see, defining a function is not much different from defining a procedure; however, calling the function is another matter. Instead of using the CALL statement to invoke the function, you use the function as you would any of the SQL predefined functions. (You saw some of these functions in Chapter 10.) For example, suppose you want to find the name of an artist based on the CD name and you want to know what other CDs that artist has made. You can create a SELECT statement similar to the one shown in the following example to retrieve the data:

```
SELECT TITLE, ARTIST_NAME
  FROM PERFORMERS
 WHERE ARTIST_NAME = CD_ARTIST('The Definitive Collection');
```

The CD_ARTIST function returns the Stevie Wonder value (the artist of the CD entitled The Definitive Collection), which is then compared to the ARTIST_NAME values. As a result, two rows are returned by the statement, as shown in the following query results:

```
TITLE                      ARTIST_NAME
-------------------------  ------------
Innervisions (Remastered)  Stevie Wonder
The Definitive Collection  Stevie Wonder
```

As you can see, functions help to simplify your queries by storing part of the code as a schema object (in the form of an SQL-invoked routine) and then invoking that code as necessary by calling the function as a value in your SQL statement. Functions provide you with a wide range of possibilities for returning values that make your queries less complex and more manageable.

Try This 14-2 Creating SQL-Invoked Functions

In this Try This exercise, you will create a function named CD_LABEL in the INVENTORY database. The function will provide the name of the company that publishes a specified CD. Once you create the function, you will invoke it by using it as a value in a SELECT statement. When you are finished, you will drop that function from your database. You can download the Try_This_14_2.txt file, which contains the SQL statements used in this exercise.

Step by Step

1. Open the client application for your RDBMS and connect to the INVENTORY database.

(continued)

2. You will create a function that returns the name of the company that publishes a specified CD. The function will include an input parameter that allows you to pass the name of the CD into the function. Enter and execute the following SQL statement:

```
CREATE FUNCTION CD_LABEL ( p_CD VARCHAR(60) )
  RETURNS VARCHAR(60)
  BEGIN
    RETURN ( SELECT COMPANY_NAME
               FROM COMPACT_DISCS d, CD_LABELS l
              WHERE d.LABEL_ID = l.LABEL_ID
                AND CD_TITLE   = p_CD );
  END;
```

You should receive a message indicating that the CD_LABEL function has been created.

3. Now that the function has been created, you can use it in your SQL statements as a value in an expression. The next statement that you'll create is a SELECT statement that returns the name of the CD and the company that publishes the CD for those CDs published by the same company as the specified CD. Enter and execute the following SQL statement:

```
SELECT CD_TITLE, COMPANY_NAME
  FROM COMPACT_DISCS d, CD_LABELS l
 WHERE d.LABEL_ID    = l.LABEL_ID
   AND COMPANY_NAME = CD_LABEL ('Kind of Blue');
```

Your query results should include a list of two CDs, both of which were published by Columbia, the company that publishes Kind of Blue.

4. Try executing the same statement by using various names of CDs to see what results are returned.

5. Now you can drop the CD_LABEL function from your database. Enter and execute the following SQL statement:

```
DROP FUNCTION CD_LABEL CASCADE;
```

You should receive a message indicating that the CD_LABEL function has been dropped from the database. (If your implementation does not support the CASCADE keyword in a DROP FUNCTION statement, simply omit the keyword.)

6. Close the client application.

Try This Summary

The Try This exercise had you create a function (CD_LABEL) that includes one parameter (p_CD). The parameter passes the value of a CD name to the SELECT statement defined in the RETURN statement of the parameter. The statement uses this information to determine the name of the company that publishes the CD. You then used the CD_LABEL function in a SELECT statement to retrieve the names of all CDs that are published by the same company that published the specified CD. After that, you dropped the function from the database. Now that you've completed this exercise, try creating other functions in the database, and then use the functions in SELECT statements to see what sort of data you can return.

Chapter 14 Self Test

1. Which are types of SQL-invoked routines supported by the SQL standard?

A CHECK constraint

B Function

C Trigger

D SQL-invoked procedure

2. Which types of parameters can you use in an SQL-invoked function?

A Input

B Output

C Input/output

D Variable

3. Which statement do you use to invoke an SQL-invoked procedure?

A RETURN

B CALL

C SET

D DECLARE

4. A(n) ________________ is a value passed to a statement in a procedure when you invoke that procedure.

5. Which types of parameters can you use in an SQL-invoked function?

   A Input

   B Output

   C Input/output

   D Variable

6. What is another name for an SQL-invoked procedure?

7. What are the two primary differences between procedures and functions?

8. What information must you include in a CALL statement when invoking a procedure?

9. Which types of statements can you include in a procedure?

   A SELECT

   B INSERT

   C UPDATE

   D DELETE

10. Which statement do you use to assign an initial value to a variable?

   A DECLARE

   B RETURN

   C SET

   D CALL

11. A(n) ________________ statement allows you to group SQL statements into blocks.

12. Which keyword do you use to begin a conditional statement?

   A IF

   B BEGIN

   C THEN

   D ELSE

13. What keyword do you use in a LOOP statement to end that loop?

14. What is the difference between a conditional statement and a compound statement?

15. What are two types of looping statements?

    A BEGIN...END

    B IF...END IF

    C LOOP...END LOOP

    D WHILE...END WHILE

16. Which type of parameter can return a value when you invoke a procedure?

17. What step must you take when calling a procedure that includes an output parameter?

18. How does a CREATE FUNCTION statement differ from a CREATE PROCEDURE statement?

19. You're calling a procedure named GET_TOTALS. The procedure does not include any parameters, but does include a SELECT statement that queries the CD_INVENTORY table. What SQL statement should you use to invoke this parameter?

20. You create a procedure named GET_CD_INFO that selects data about an artist from the CD_INFO table. The procedure includes one input parameter. You want to call that procedure with the value Fleetwood Mac. What SQL statement should you use to invoke the procedure?

21. What are two types of schema objects that you can use to store a SELECT statement?

Chapter 15

Creating SQL Triggers

Key Skills & Concepts

- Understand SQL Triggers
- Create SQL Triggers
- Create Insert Triggers
- Create Update Triggers
- Create Delete Triggers
- Create Instead Of Triggers

Up to this point in the book, you have learned to create a number of schema objects that you can access or invoke by using SQL statements. For example, you learned how to create tables, views, and SQL-invoked routines. In each case, once you create these objects, you need to take some sort of action to interact directly with them, such as executing a SELECT statement to retrieve data from a table or using a CALL statement to invoke a procedure. However, SQL supports objects that perform actions automatically. These schema objects, which are known as *triggers,* respond to modifications made to data within a table. If a specified modification is made, the trigger is automatically invoked, or *fired,* causing an additional action to occur. As a result, you never directly invoke the trigger—taking an action defined in the trigger implicitly causes the invocation. In this chapter, we'll explore triggers and how they're used when table data is modified. We'll also look at examples of how to create the three basic types of triggers—insert, update, and delete—and how they can be defined to extend your database's functionality and help to ensure the integrity of the data.

Understand SQL Triggers

If you've worked around any SQL products before, you've no doubt seen triggers implemented in one of your organization's databases, or at least heard the term tossed about. Most relational database management systems (RDBMSs) implemented triggers in their products long ago, although it wasn't until SQL:1999 that triggers were added to the standard. The result of the products preceding the standard is that trigger implementations are highly proprietary among the SQL products, and thus support different types of functionality and are implemented in different ways. For example, MySQL, DB2, SQL Server, and Oracle currently support triggers, but SQL Server triggers are somewhat limited in scope compared to the SQL standard, whereas Oracle triggers are more robust—yet neither product implements triggers according to the specifications of the SQL standard. Despite this, there are a number of similarities among the products (such as the use of a CREATE TRIGGER statement to create a trigger), and the implementations of triggers in the various products share some basic characteristics, particularly that of being able to fire automatically to perform an action secondary to the primary action that invoked the trigger. However, MySQL added support for triggers more recently (starting with release 5.1), so MySQL triggers closely match the syntax and capability spelled out in the SQL standard.

NOTE

The functionality supported by triggers is sometimes referred to as active database. In fact, this term is used to describe one of the optional packages that are included in the SQL standard. The package—PKG008—defines how triggers are implemented in SQL. (A package is a set of features to which a product can claim conformance in addition to Core SQL.) For more information about SQL conformance, see Chapter 1.

Before we get into the specifics of how to implement triggers, let's take a look at the trigger itself, which, as I said, is a schema object (in the same sense as a table, view, or SQL-invoked routine). A trigger definition defines the characteristics of the trigger and what actions are taken when the trigger is invoked. These actions, which are specified in one or more SQL statements (referred to as the *triggered SQL statements*), can include such events as updating tables, deleting data, invoking procedures, or performing most tasks that you can perform with SQL statements. Any limitations placed on those statements are usually the ones placed by the SQL implementation.

Triggers are invoked when you insert data, update data, or delete data. By defining one or more triggers on a table or view, you can specify which data-modification actions will cause the trigger to fire. The trigger is never invoked unless the specified action is taken. SQL supports three types of triggers: insert, update, and delete. As their names suggest, the insert, update, and delete types correspond with the applicable data modification statements made against tables. For example, an insert trigger is fired when the INSERT statement is executed against the specified table. The SQL:2008 standard introduced the *instead of* trigger, which is defined on a view rather than a table, along with the specific action to be taken in place of (instead of) the action defined by the data modification statement on the view. For example, an instead of trigger is fired when an UPDATE statement is executed against the specified view, but unlike triggers defined on tables, the view is not actually updated—the actions in the trigger take the place of the update of the view.

Although a trigger is a schema object, separate from table objects, it can be associated with only one table or view, which you specify when you create your trigger definition. When the applicable data modification statement is invoked against that table or view, the trigger fires; however, it will not fire if a similar statement is invoked against a different table or view, or if a statement other than the specified type is invoked against the same table. In this sense, a trigger can be thought of as a table object, despite the fact that it is created at the schema level.

If a trigger fails, raising an error condition, the SQL statement that caused the trigger to fire also fails and is rolled back. This is how triggers can be used to enforce complex constraints—the trigger is written to perform whatever tests are necessary to verify that the constraint conditions are met, and if not, ends by raising an error condition.

Trigger Execution Context

Before we move on to discussing how a trigger is created, I want to touch on the subject of how triggers are executed with regard to the *trigger execution context,* a type of SQL execution context. You can think of an *execution context* as a space created in memory that holds a statement process during the execution of that statement. SQL supports several types of execution contexts, triggers being one of them.

A trigger execution context is created each time a trigger is invoked. If multiple triggers are invoked, an execution context is created for each one. However, only one execution context can be active in a session at any one time. This is important when a trigger in one table causes a trigger in a second table to be fired. Let's take a look at Figure 15-1 to help illustrate this point.

Notice that the figure contains three tables. An update trigger is defined on Table 1, and an insert trigger is defined on Table 2. When an UPDATE statement is executed against Table 1, the update trigger fires, creating a trigger execution context that becomes active. However, the update trigger, which is defined to insert data into Table 2, invokes the insert trigger on Table 2 when the first trigger attempts to insert data into that table. As a result, a second execution context is created, which becomes the active one. When the second trigger execution has completed, the second execution context is destroyed, and the first execution context becomes

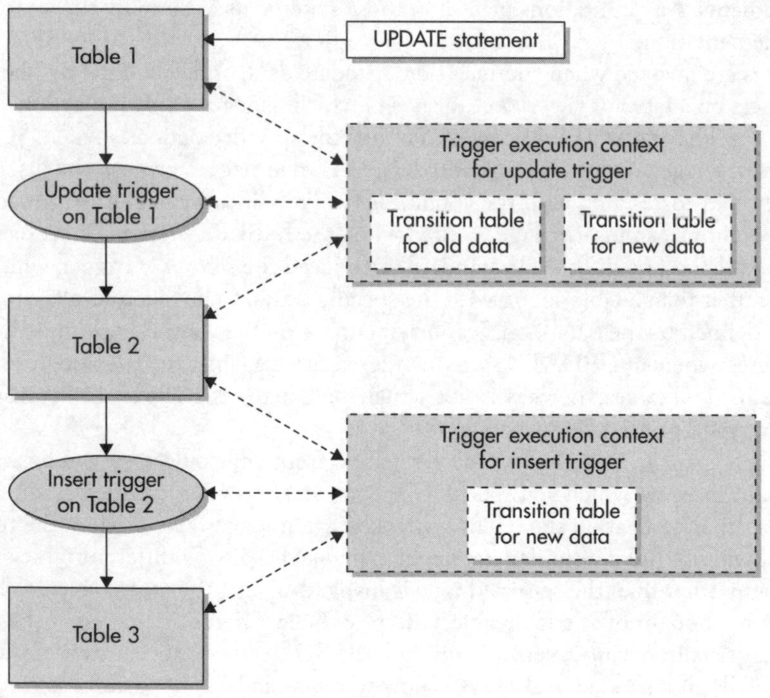

Figure 15-1 Trigger execution contexts for two triggers

active once more. When the first trigger execution has completed, the first trigger execution context is destroyed.

A trigger execution context contains the information necessary for the trigger to be executed correctly. This information includes details about the trigger itself and the table on which the trigger was defined, which is referred to as the subject table. In addition, the execution context includes one or two transition tables, as shown in Figure 15-1. The transition tables are virtual tables that hold data that is updated in, inserted into, or deleted from the subject table. If data is updated, then two transition tables are created, one for the old data and one for the new data. If data is inserted, one transition table is created for the new data. If data is deleted, one transition table is created for the old data. The transition tables and some of the other information in the trigger execution context are used by the SQL statements that perform the triggered action. You'll learn more about how this information is used in the following section, when we look at the CREATE TRIGGER syntax.

Create SQL Triggers

Now that you have a general overview of triggers, let's take a look at the syntax you use to create them. Most of the syntax is concerned with defining the characteristics of the trigger, such as the name of the trigger and the type. Only at the end of the statement do you define the triggered SQL statements that specify the actions taken by the trigger when it is invoked.

The basic syntax for creating a trigger definition is as follows:

```
CREATE TRIGGER <trigger name>
{ BEFORE | AFTER | INSTEAD OF }
{ INSERT | DELETE | UPDATE [ OF <column list> ] }
ON <table or view name> [ REFERENCING <alias options> ]
[ FOR EACH { ROW | STATEMENT } ]
[ WHEN ( <search condition> ) ]
<triggered SQL statements>
```

Let's take a look at each line of the syntax. The first line is fairly straightforward. You simply provide a name for the trigger following the CREATE TRIGGER keywords. In the second line, you must designate whether the trigger is invoked before, after, or instead of the data modification specified in the SQL statement that caused the trigger to fire. For example, if you're defining an insert trigger, you can specify whether the triggered SQL statements are executed before the data is inserted into the subject table (by using the BEFORE keyword), after the data is inserted into the subject table (by using the AFTER keyword), or instead of inserting data into the subject view (by using the INSTEAD OF keywords). The BEFORE option is particularly useful when one of the tables is configured with a referential integrity constraint and cannot contain data before that data exists in the other table. (For information about referential integrity, see Chapter 4.) Depending on the nature of the triggered action that is defined, it may not matter whether you designate BEFORE or AFTER because the triggered action may have no direct relation to the data modified in the subject table.

In the third line of syntax, you specify whether the trigger is an insert, delete, or update trigger. If it is an update trigger rather than an instead of trigger, you have the option of applying the trigger to one or more specific columns. If more than one column is specified, you must separate the column names with commas. In the next line of syntax, you must specify an ON clause that includes the name of the subject table or view. This is the table or view on which the trigger is applied. The trigger can be applied to only one table or view. Keep in mind that before and after triggers can be applied only to tables, while instead of triggers can be applied only to views. The syntax rules for instead of triggers vary quite a bit—see the "Create Instead Of Triggers" section of this chapter for more details.

Up to this point, all the syntax we've looked at is required, except for specifying column names in update trigger definitions, which is optional. However, the next several clauses are not mandatory, but they add important capabilities to your trigger. The first of these clauses is the REFERENCING clause. This clause allows you to specify how data that is held in the trigger execution context is referenced within the WHEN clause or the triggered SQL statements. We'll look at the REFERENCING clause in more detail in the following section, "Referencing Old and New Values."

The next line of syntax contains the FOR EACH clause, which includes two options: ROW or STATEMENT. If you specify ROW, the trigger is invoked each time a row is inserted, updated, or deleted. If you specify STATEMENT, the trigger is invoked only one time for each applicable data modification statement that is executed, no matter how many rows are affected. If you do not include this clause in your trigger definition, the STATEMENT option is assumed, and the trigger fires only once for each statement.

Next in the syntax is the optional WHEN clause, which is not supported for instead of triggers. The WHEN clause allows you to define a search condition that limits the scope of when the trigger is invoked. The WHEN clause is similar to the WHERE clause of a SELECT statement. You specify one or more predicates that define a search condition. If the WHEN clause evaluates to true, the trigger fires; otherwise, no trigger action is taken. However, this doesn't affect the initial data modification statement that was executed against the subject table; only the triggered SQL statements defined in the trigger definition are affected.

NOTE

MySQL 5.7 does not support the WHEN clause in the CREATE TRIGGER statement.

Finally, the last component that your CREATE TRIGGER statement must include is one or more SQL statements (sometimes called the trigger body) that are executed when the trigger is invoked and, if a WHEN clause is included, that clause evaluates to true. If the trigger definition includes more than one triggered SQL statement, or if you are using Oracle, those statements must be enclosed in a BEGIN...END block, like those you saw in Chapter 14. However, there is one difference from what you saw before. When used in a trigger definition, the BEGIN keyword must be followed by the ATOMIC keyword to notify the SQL implementation that the statements within the block must be handled as a unit. In other words, either all the statements must be executed successfully or none of the results of any statement executions can persist. Without the ATOMIC keyword, it would be possible for some statements to be executed while others fail to be executed.

NOTE

Many implementations do not support the use of the ATOMIC keyword in the BEGIN...END block of the triggered SQL statements. This includes MySQL, SQL Server, and Oracle. Also, with Oracle, all trigger and procedure bodies must be enclosed in BEGIN...END blocks, including those that include only a single SQL statement.

Aside from the issue of the ATOMIC keyword, the triggered SQL statements, including the BEGIN...END block, can consist of almost any SQL statements, depending on the limitations of your SQL implementation. Be sure to check the product documentation to determine what limitations might be placed on the triggered SQL statements and how triggers are generally created and implemented.

Referencing Old and New Values

Now let's return to the REFERENCING clause of the CREATE TRIGGER statement. The purpose of this clause is to allow you to define correlation names for the rows stored in the transition tables or for the transition tables as a whole. As you'll recall from the "Understand SQL Triggers" section earlier in this chapter, the transition tables hold the data that has been updated, inserted, or deleted in the subject table. The correlation names, or aliases, can then be used in the triggered SQL statements to refer back to the data that is being held in the transition tables. This can be particularly handy when trying to modify data in a second table based on the data modified in the subject table. (This will be made clearer when we look at examples later in the chapter.)

If you refer back to the syntax in the previous section, you'll notice that the optional REFERENCING clause includes the <alias options> placeholder. SQL supports four options for this clause:

- REFERENCING OLD [ROW] [AS] <alias>
- REFERENCING NEW [ROW] [AS] <alias>
- REFERENCING OLD TABLE [AS] <alias>
- REFERENCING NEW TABLE [AS] <alias>

Notice that in the first two options, the ROW keyword is not mandatory. If you don't specify ROW, it is assumed. Notice too that the AS keyword is optional in all cases. However, for the purposes of maintaining clear, self-referencing code, I recommend that you use the complete option whenever you include it in a trigger definition.

Depending on the type of trigger (update, insert, or delete) and the FOR EACH option (ROW or STATEMENT), you can include up to four REFERENCING options in your trigger definition, one of each type. However, you cannot include more than one of any single type. For example, you cannot include two OLD ROW options in your trigger definition.

When adding REFERENCING options to your trigger definition, you must follow these guidelines:

- You cannot use the NEW ROW and NEW TABLE options for delete triggers because no new data is created.
- You cannot use the OLD ROW and OLD TABLE options for insert triggers because no old data exists.
- You can use all four options in an update trigger because there is old data and new data when you update a table.
- You can use the OLD ROW and NEW ROW options only when you specify the FOR EACH ROW clause in the trigger definition.

Once you define your REFERENCING clauses and assign the appropriate aliases, you're ready to use those aliases in your triggered SQL statements, in the same way you used correlation names in your SELECT statements.

Dropping SQL Triggers

Although the SQL standard does not support any sort of statement that allows you to alter a trigger, it does support a way to delete a trigger, which you achieve by using the DROP TRIGGER statement. As you can see in the following syntax, this statement is quite basic:

```
DROP TRIGGER <name>
```

All you need to do is provide the name of the trigger, along with the DROP TRIGGER keywords. Because no other objects are dependent on the trigger, you do not need to specify any additional keywords, such as CASCADE or RESTRICT. When you execute the DROP TRIGGER statement, the trigger definition is deleted from the schema.

Create Insert Triggers

So far in this chapter, I've provided you with background information about triggers and the syntax used to create triggers. Now we'll look at examples of how triggers are created and what happens when they're invoked. We'll begin with the insert trigger, which, as you know, is invoked when an INSERT statement is executed against the subject table (the table on which the trigger has been defined). In the first example, we'll create a trigger on the RETAIL_INVENTORY table (subject table), shown in Figure 15-2. The trigger, when invoked, will insert data into the INVENTORY_LOG table.

The following CREATE TRIGGER statement defines an INSERT trigger that fires after the data is inserted into the subject table:

```
CREATE TRIGGER INSERT_LOG
  AFTER INSERT ON RETAIL_INVENTORY
  FOR EACH ROW
```

RETAIL_INVENTORY

CD_NAME: VARCHAR(60)	R_PRICE: NUMERIC(5,2)	AMOUNT: INT
Drive All Night	5.99	12
Different Shades of Blue	11.99	42
Innervisions (Remastered)	10.00	16
The Definitive Collection	8.39	34
Rumours (Reissued)	7.99	17
Come On Over	5.99	6
Man Against Machine	9.99	8

INVENTORY_LOG

ACTION_TYPE: CHAR(6)	DATE_MODIFIED: TIMESTAMP
INSERT	2015-04-02 10:58:05.120
UPDATE	2015-04-02 12:02:05.033
UPDATE	2015-04-02 16:15:22.930
DELETE	2015-04-03 11:29:14.223
INSERT	2015-04-03 13:32:45.547
INSERT	2015-04-03 15:51:15.730
UPDATE	2015-04-03 17:01:32.270
UPDATE	2015-04-04 10:46:35.123
DELETE	2015 04 04 12.19.13.843
UPDATE	2015-04-04 14:15:09.673

Figure 15-2 Creating an insert trigger on the RETAIL_INVENTORY table

```
BEGIN ATOMIC
  INSERT INTO INVENTORY_LOG (ACTION_TYPE)
    VALUES ('INSERT');
END;
```

NOTE

As I mentioned at the beginning of the chapter, SQL implementations can vary widely with regard to the semantics of the CREATE TRIGGER statement. For example, SQL Server does not allow you to specify a FOR EACH clause, nor does it support the use of the ATOMIC keyword in the BEGIN...END statement. On the other hand, the basic Oracle trigger definition is a lot closer to the SQL standard, although Oracle also does not support the use of the ATOMIC keyword in a trigger definition. MySQL trigger definition is nearly identical to the standard, except it also does not support the ATOMIC keyword.

Let's take a look at this statement one element at a time. In the first line, the CREATE TRIGGER clause defines a trigger named INSERT_LOG. In the next line, the AFTER keyword is used to specify that the triggered SQL statements will be executed *after* the data has been inserted into the subject table. The AFTER keyword is followed by the INSERT keyword, which defines the trigger as an insert trigger. Next is the ON clause, which specifies the name of the subject table. In this case, the subject table is RETAIL_INVENTORY.

As we move through the statement, we come to the FOR EACH clause, which specifies the ROW keyword. This clause, when used with ROW, indicates that the trigger will be invoked for each row that is inserted into the table, rather than for each INSERT statement that is executed against the table. Following the FOR EACH clause are the triggered SQL statements.

The triggered SQL statements include a BEGIN...END statement and an INSERT statement. I did not need to include the BEGIN...END statement in the trigger definition because, without it, there is only one triggered SQL statement. However, I wanted to demonstrate how the block would be used had there been more than one statement. Notice that the block includes the ATOMIC keyword following the BEGIN keyword. According to the SQL standard, ATOMIC is required, although it will depend on your SQL implementation whether the keyword is supported.

The BEGIN...END block encloses an INSERT statement that adds data to the INVENTORY_LOG table when the trigger is invoked. Each time a row is inserted into the RETAIL_INVENTORY table, a row is inserted into the INVENTORY_LOG table. The INVENTORY_LOG row will contain the INSERT value for the ACTION_TYPE column. A timestamp value is then added automatically to the DATE_MODIFIED column, which is defined with the default CURRENT_TIMESTAMP.

You can, if you want, create other triggers on the RETAIL_INVENTORY table. For example, you might want to create update and delete triggers that insert rows into the INVENTORY_LOG table when the applicable data modifications are made. In that case, you would simply create a trigger definition for each additional trigger that you need.

NOTE

The SQL standard does not place a limit on the number of triggers that can be defined on any one table; however, SQL implementations can have many restrictions, so check the product documentation. In addition to these limitations, various implementations might support different ways in which multiple triggers can be implemented. For example, SQL Server allows you to define an insert, update, and delete trigger in one statement.

Now let's take a look at what happens when you insert a row into the RETAIL_INVENTORY table. Suppose you want to insert information about the Bach CD. You would create an INSERT statement as you would normally do, as shown in the following example:

```
INSERT INTO RETAIL_INVENTORY
  VALUES ( 'Bach', 11.88, 22 );
```

If you were to execute the statement, the row would be inserted into the RETAIL_INVENTORY table. To verify this, you can execute the following SELECT statement:

```
SELECT * FROM RETAIL_INVENTORY;
```

The SELECT statement will return the same rows shown in the RETAIL_INVENTORY table in Figure 15-2, plus an additional row for the Bach CD, exactly as you would expect. The trigger has no effect on the data modifications you make to the RETAIL_INVENTORY table. However, as you'll recall from the trigger definition that was defined on the RETAIL_INVENTORY table, the triggered SQL statements should insert data into the INVENTORY_LOG table when the trigger is invoked, which should have occurred when you inserted a row into the RETAIL_INVENTORY table. To verify this, you can execute the following SELECT statement:

```
SELECT * FROM INVENTORY_LOG;
```

The query results should include not only the rows shown in the INVENTORY_LOG table in Figure 15-2, but also an additional row that includes an ACTION_TYPE value of INSERT and a DATE_MODIFIED value for the current date and time. Each time a row is inserted into the RETAIL_INVENTORY table, a row is inserted in the INVENTORY_LOG table. You could have defined your triggered SQL statements to take any sort of action, not just log events in a log table. Depending on your needs and the database in which you work, you have a great many possibilities for the type of actions that your triggers will support.

Create Update Triggers

Now that you've seen an example of an insert trigger, let's take a look at a couple of update triggers. The update trigger is invoked when an UPDATE statement is executed against the subject table. As with any other type of trigger, when the trigger is invoked, the triggered SQL statements are executed and an action is taken. To illustrate how the update trigger works, we'll use the TITLES_IN_STOCK and TITLE_COSTS tables shown in Figure 15-3.

TITLES_IN_STOCK

CD_TITLE: VARCHAR(60)	CD_TYPE: CHAR(20)	INVENTORY: INT
Drive All Night	Alt. Rock	12
Different Shades of Blue	Blues	42
Innervisions (Remastered)	R&B	16
The Definitive Collection	R&B	34
Rumours (Reissued)	Rock	17
Come On Over	Country	6
Man Against Machine	Country	8
Dark Side of the Moon	Rock	27

TITLE_COSTS

CD_TITLE: VARCHAR(60)	CD_TYPE: CHAR(20)	WHOLESALE: NUMERIC(5,2)	RETAIL: NUMERIC(5,2)
Drive All Night	Alt. Rock	4.50	5.99
Different Shades of Blue	Blues	5.50	11.99
Bach	Classical	5.50	11.88
Innervisions (Remastered)	R&B	5.50	10.00
Old Boots, New Dirt	Country	5.50	11.88
The Definitive Collection	R&B	4.50	8.39
Kind of Blue	Jazz	4.50	7.29
Come On Over	Country	4.50	5.99
Man Against Machine	Country	5.50	9.99

Figure 15-3 Creating an update trigger on the TITLES_IN_STOCK table

The first example that we'll look at is created on the TITLES_IN_STOCK table and includes triggered SQL statements that update the TITLE_COSTS table, as shown in the following CREATE TRIGGER statement:

```
CREATE TRIGGER UPDATE_TITLE_COSTS
  AFTER UPDATE ON TITLES_IN_STOCK
  REFERENCING NEW ROW AS New
  FOR EACH ROW
  BEGIN ATOMIC
    UPDATE TITLE_COSTS c
      SET RETAIL = ROUND(RETAIL * 0.9, 2)
  WHERE c.CD_TITLE = New.CD_TITLE;
END;
```

As you can see, this trigger definition is similar in many ways to the insert trigger we looked at in the preceding example. The update trigger definition includes the name of the trigger (UPDATE_TITLE_COSTS) and specifies the AFTER and UPDATE conditions. The ON clause then follows the UPDATE keyword and provides the name of the target table. Following all this is a line of code we did not see in the preceding example—a REFERENCING clause.

The REFERENCING clause uses the NEW ROW option to define a correlation name for the row that has been updated in the TITLES_IN_STOCK table. However, the REFERENCING clause, and subsequently the search condition or triggered SQL statements that might refer to the alias defined in this clause, are not directly referencing the TITLES_IN_STOCK table. Instead, they're referencing the transition table for new data in the trigger execution context. In other words, the correlation name defined in the REFERENCING clause references the updated row that is copied to the transition table. In this case, the correlation name is New. As a result, the New correlation name can be used in the search condition in the WHEN clause or in the triggered SQL statements to refer back to the data in the transition table.

Once you've defined the correlation name in the REFERENCING clause, you must use it to qualify the column names of the modified row when they are referenced in the WHEN clause or in the triggered SQL statements. In the CREATE TRIGGER statement in the preceding example, you can see that the alias is used in the WHERE clause of the UPDATE statement. Notice that the word New precedes the column name and that the two are separated by a period. This is typical of how you would qualify a name. It is similar to the way in which you use the qualified name c.CD_TITLE for the CD_TITLE column in the TITLE_COSTS table. If you had specified a different NEW ROW correlation name or used the name in the WHEN clause or in another part of the triggered SQL statement, you would still qualify the name of the column with the alias that references the rows in the transition table or the table itself.

NOTE

SQL Server does not support the REFERENCING clause. However, it supports similar functionality by automatically assigning the names Inserted and Deleted to the transition tables (Inserted for new data and Deleted for old data). In addition, there are some cases in which you must declare a variable to use values from the Inserted and Deleted tables, rather than qualifying column names, as you do in the SQL standard. Similarly, MySQL does not support the REFERENCING clause—it automatically assigns the names New for new data and Old for old data. Oracle, on the other hand, does support the REFERENCING clause, but it also automatically assigns the names New and Old to the transition tables, which you can use in the WHEN clause and triggered SQL statements without specifying a REFERENCING clause. When you do use the aliases in the triggered SQL statements of an Oracle trigger definition, you must precede the alias name with a colon, as in :New. This is not the case for the WHEN clause, in which the alias name is used without the colon. Also, you cannot use the keyword ROW in the REFERENCING clause of an Oracle trigger definition.

In addition to the REFERENCING clause, the CREATE TRIGGER statement includes a FOR EACH clause, which specifies the ROW option. Also notice that the triggered SQL statements include a BEGIN...END statement, which encloses an UPDATE statement. As you can see, the UPDATE statement modifies the RETAIL value in the TITLE_COSTS table for the CD that was updated in the TITLES_IN_STOCK table.

Now let's take a look at what happens when you update the TITLES_IN_STOCK column. The following UPDATE statement changes the INVENTORY value for the Man Against Machine row:

```
UPDATE TITLES_IN_STOCK
   SET INVENTORY = 16
 WHERE CD_TITLE = 'Man Against Machine';
```

When the UPDATE statement is executed, the UPDATE_TITLE_COSTS trigger is invoked, causing the TITLE_COSTS table to be updated. As a result, not only is the INVENTORY value in the TITLES_IN_STOCK table changed to 16, but the RETAIL value in the TITLE_COSTS table is reduced to 8.99 (RETAIL * 0.9, rounded to two decimal places). Any time you update the TITLES_IN_STOCK table, the corresponding row or rows in the TITLE_COSTS table will be reduced by 10 percent.

You might find that you want to limit when the triggered SQL statements are executed. For example, you might want to reduce the price of CDs only when the inventory exceeds a certain amount. As a result you decide to change your trigger definition to include a WHEN clause that defines the necessary search condition. However, as I said earlier, SQL does not support an ALTER TRIGGER statement (although Oracle supports CREATE OR REPLACE TRIGGER syntax that can be used to completely replace an existing trigger), so you would need to first delete the trigger from the database. The way to do that is to use the following DROP TRIGGER statement:

```
DROP TRIGGER UPDATE_TITLE_COSTS;
```

When you execute this statement, the trigger definition is removed from the schema and you can now re-create the trigger with the necessary modifications. The following example again creates the UPDATE_TITLE_COSTS trigger, but this time a WHEN clause has been added to the statement:

```
CREATE TRIGGER UPDATE_TITLE_COSTS
  AFTER UPDATE ON TITLES_IN_STOCK
  REFERENCING NEW ROW AS New
  FOR EACH ROW
  WHEN ( New.INVENTORY > 20 )
  BEGIN ATOMIC
    UPDATE TITLE_COSTS c
       SET RETAIL = ROUND(RETAIL * 0.9, 2)
     WHERE c.CD_TITLE = New.CD_TITLE;
END;
```

NOTE

This trigger cannot be created in MySQL 5.7 because the WHEN clause is not supported.

As you can see, the WHEN clause specifies that the INVENTORY value must be greater than 20; otherwise, the triggered SQL statements will not be invoked. Notice that the INVENTORY column name is qualified with the New correlation name in the same way that the CD_TITLE column name is qualified in the WHERE clause of the UPDATE statement. As a result, the WHEN clause will reference the transition table for new data in the trigger execution context when comparing values.

Now let's take a look at what happens when you update the TITLES_IN_STOCK table. The following UPDATE statement changes the INVENTORY value for the Different Shades of Blue row:

```
UPDATE TITLES_IN_STOCK
   SET INVENTORY = 40
 WHERE CD_TITLE = 'Different Shades of Blue';
```

As you would expect, the INVENTORY value in the TITLES_IN_STOCK column is changed to 40. In addition, because the condition specified in the WHEN clause is met (New.INVENTORY > 20), the triggered SQL statements are executed and the TITLE_COSTS table is updated. If you were to query the TITLE_COSTS table, you would see that the RETAIL value for the Different Shades of Blue row has been changed to 10.79.

Now let's take a look at an UPDATE statement that sets the INVENTORY value to an amount less than 20:

```
UPDATE TITLES_IN_STOCK
   SET INVENTORY = 10
 WHERE CD_TITLE = 'Drive All Night';
```

Ask the Expert

Q: When describing trigger execution contexts, you discussed how one trigger can cause another trigger to be invoked. Is there a point at which multiple triggers can become a problem if too many are invoked?

A: Problems can arise when multiple triggers are invoked and they cause a cascading effect from one table to the next. For example, an attempt to update one table might invoke a trigger that updates another table. That update, in turn, might invoke another trigger that modifies data in yet another table. This process can continue on as one trigger after the next is invoked, creating undesirable results and unplanned data modifications. The condition can be made even worse if a loop is created in which a trigger causes a data modification on a table for which another trigger has fired. For example, a data modification on one table might invoke a trigger that causes a second modification. That modification might invoke another trigger, which in turn invokes another trigger, which invokes yet another trigger. The last trigger might then modify data in the original table, causing the first trigger to fire again, repeating the process over and over until the system fails or an implementation-specific process ends the loop. The best way to prevent unwanted modifications or trigger loops is through careful planning in the database design. Triggers should not be implemented unless you're sure of their impact. In addition to careful planning, you should look to the SQL implementation to determine what sorts of safety nets might be in place to prevent trigger looping or unwanted cascading. For example, some implementations allow you to control whether cascading triggers are allowed, and some limit the number of cascading triggers that can fire. Make sure that you read your product's documentation before creating multiple triggers in your database.

Q: Earlier, you mentioned that SQL allows you to define multiple triggers on a table. How are triggers processed if multiple triggers are invoked?

A: In SQL, processing of multiple triggers is a concern only if the triggers are defined to fire at the same time (BEFORE or AFTER) and if they're the same type of trigger (INSERT, UPDATE, or DELETE). For example, a multiple trigger scenario would exist if two or more triggers are defined (on the same table) with the AFTER UPDATE keywords. If this condition exists, then the triggers are invoked in the order in which they were defined. Let's take a look at an example to show you what I mean. If you create Trigger1 and then create Trigger2 and then create Trigger3, Trigger1 is invoked first, then Trigger2, and then Trigger3. The problem with this is that SQL does not define any way in which you can change that order. For example, if you decide that you want Trigger3 invoked before Trigger1, your only option—based on the SQL standard—is to delete Trigger1 and Trigger2 from the schema and then re-create the triggers in the order you want them invoked. Because you did not delete Trigger3, it will move into the top spot and be the first to be invoked because it will then be seen as the first to have been created.

This statement will still update the INVENTORY value in the TITLES_IN_STOCK table, but it will not cause the triggered SQL statements to be executed because the search condition in the WHEN clause is not met. As a result, no changes are made to the TITLE_COSTS table, although the TITLES_IN_STOCK table is still updated.

Create Delete Triggers

The final type of trigger defined in the SQL standard is the delete trigger. As you would expect, the delete trigger is invoked when a DELETE statement is executed against the subject table, and as with other triggers, the triggered SQL statements are executed and an action is taken. Now let's take a look at an example that uses the CD_STOCK table and CD_OUT table, as shown in Figure 15-4.

Suppose you want to create a trigger on the CD_STOCK table. You want the trigger to insert the deleted values into the CD_OUT table. The following CREATE TRIGGER statement uses a REFERENCING clause to allow the triggered SQL statement to know which data to insert into the CD_OUT table:

```
CREATE TRIGGER INSERT_CD_OUT
  AFTER DELETE ON CD_STOCK
  REFERENCING OLD ROW AS Old
  FOR EACH ROW
    INSERT INTO CD_OUT
      VALUES ( Old.CD_NAME, Old.CD_TYPE );
```

In this statement, you are creating a trigger named INSERT_CD_OUT. The statement is defined with the AFTER DELETE keywords, meaning that the old values are inserted into the CD_OUT table after they have been deleted from the CD_STOCK table. The ON clause identifies the CD_STOCK table as the subject table.

CD_STOCK

CD_NAME: VARCHAR(60)	CD_TYPE: CHAR(4)	IN_STOCK: INT
Drive All Night	ALTR	19
Different Shades of Blue	BLUS	28
Bach	CLAS	6
Man Against Machine	CTRY	8
Dark Side of the Moon	CROK	10
Kind of Blue	JAZZ	11

CD_OUT

CD_NAME: VARCHAR(60)	CD_TYPE: CHAR(4)
Architecture in Helsinki	CPOP
A.K.A.	CPOP
The Hunting Party	ALTR
Come On Over	CTRY
The Endless River	CROK
The Bodyguard	STRK

Figure 15-4 Creating a delete trigger on the CD_STOCK table

Following the ON clause is the REFERENCING clause. The REFERENCING clause uses the OLD ROW option to assign a correlation name of Old. Remember that you can use only the OLD ROW and OLD TABLE options in the REFERENCING clause of a delete trigger definition. This is because there is no new data, only the old data that's being deleted.

The FOR EACH clause follows the REFERENCING clause. The FOR EACH clause uses the ROW option. As a result, a row will be inserted into the CD_OUT table for each row deleted from the CD_STOCK table.

Next is the triggered SQL statement. Notice that in this example, a BEGIN...END statement is not used. Because there is only one triggered statement, you do not have to use the BEGIN...END block (except Oracle always requires a block). The triggered statement in this case is an INSERT statement that specifies two values, each of which is based on the values deleted from the CD_STOCK table. The Old alias is used to qualify each column name. As a result, the deleted values can be inserted directly into the CD_OUT table.

Now let's take a look at an example of what happens when you delete a row from the CD_STOCK table. The following DELETE statement deletes the Bach row from the table:

```
DELETE FROM CD_STOCK
 WHERE CD_NAME = 'Bach';
```

Once you execute this statement, the row is deleted and the trigger is invoked. The row is then inserted into the CD_OUT table. You can verify the deletion by using the following SELECT statement to view the contents of the CD_STOCK table:

```
SELECT * FROM CD_STOCK;
```

The query results from this statement should no longer include the Bach row. However, if you execute the following SELECT statement, you'll see that a row has been inserted into the CD_OUT table:

```
SELECT * FROM CD_OUT;
```

Each time a row is deleted from the CD_STOCK table, two values from that row will be inserted into the CD_OUT table. As with other trigger definitions, you could have included a WHEN clause in your CREATE TRIGGER statement so that the triggered SQL statements are executed only when the search condition specified in the WHEN clause evaluates to true. Otherwise, the statements are not executed. The row will still be deleted from the CD_STOCK table, but nothing will be inserted into the CD_OUT table.

Create Instead Of Triggers

In this final topic on triggers, let's look at instead of triggers. While each instead of trigger falls into one of the three categories I have already discussed (insert triggers, update triggers, and delete triggers), there are several substantial differences between instead of triggers and triggers that specify the BEFORE and AFTER options. First, instead of triggers must be defined on a view (a viewed table using the SQL standard's terminology). Instead of triggers cannot be defined on tables. Second, instead of triggers intercept the action specified in the SQL statement that invoked them. In other words, the insert, update, or delete of the data in the view on which the trigger is based never takes place—the instead of trigger's actions *replace* the action specified in the INSERT, UPDATE, or DELETE statement that caused it to fire. Third, instead of triggers cannot specify the WHEN clause, so they cannot be fired conditionally. Instead of triggers will always fire when the triggering event takes place. For instead of triggers, the triggering event is an INSERT, UPDATE, or DELETE statement (depending on the trigger's type) executed against the view on which the trigger is defined. Fourth, instead of update triggers cannot specify the column list. An instead of update trigger will fire when any update attempt is made on the associated view, regardless of which columns are referenced by the UPDATE statement. Finally, the SQL implementation may place additional restrictions on the syntax of instead of triggers. For example, MySQL 5.7 does not support instead of triggers. As always, refer to your implementation's documentation for details.

The most common use of instead of triggers is to work around update restrictions on complex views. In situations where an insert, update, or delete is not supported on the view itself, you can often use one or more instead of triggers to apply equivalent updates to the data in the view's base tables. I discuss update restrictions on views in Chapter 5. Another possible, yet uncommon, use for instead of triggers is to intercept updates to views submitted by business users and to instead store the requested updates in staging tables that can be reviewed and either approved or disapproved by management.

In order to better understand instead of triggers, let's look at an example. Figure 15-5 shows the LABEL_STATUS and CD_INVENTORY tables along with the ACTIVE_LABEL_INVENTORY view.

The LABEL_STATUS table contains one row for each CD label, including the STATUS_CD column, which specifies whether the label is active (A) or inactive (I). The CD_INVENTORY table contains information pertaining to CDs, including the LABEL_ID column, which associates the CD with its label. The ACTIVE_LABEL_INVENTORY view shows the inventory (the total number of CDs) for each label. The CREATE VIEW statement for the ACTIVE_LABEL_INVENTORY is as follows:

```
CREATE VIEW ACTIVE_LABEL_INVENTORY AS
 SELECT  L.LABEL_ID, L.LABEL_NAME, SUM(I.CD_STOCK) AS TOTAL_STOCK
   FROM  LABEL_STATUS L
    JOIN CD_INVENTORY I ON L.LABEL_ID = I.LABEL_ID
 WHERE     L.STATUS_CD = 'A'
 GROUP BY L.LABEL_ID, L.LABEL_NAME;
```

The definition of the ACTIVE_LABEL_INVENTORY view contains the SUM function and the GROUP BY clause in order to add up the inventory amount (the CD_STOCK column) for each CD label, resulting in one row for each CD label. The view also contains a WHERE clause that filters labels so that only active labels are included. The JOIN clause included in the ACTIVE_LABEL_INVENTORY view definition is an inner join, so

LABEL_STATUS

LABEL_ID: INT	STATUS_CD: CHAR(1)	LABEL_NAME: VARCHAR(60)
827	A	Motown/Universal
828	A	J&R Adventures
829	I	Sony Classical
831	A	Mercury
832	A	Sony Music Nashville
834	A	Capitol Records
835	A	Columbia

CD_INVENTORY

CD_TITLE: VARCHAR(60)	LABEL_ID: INT	CD_STOCK: INT
Innervisions (Remastered)	827	16
Different Shades of Blue	828	28
The Definitive Collection	827	34
Man Against Machine	832	8
Bach	829	10
Kind of Blue	835	21
The Endless River	835	12

ACTIVE_LABEL_INVENTORY

LABEL_ID: INT	LABEL_NAME: VARCHAR(60)	TOTAL_STOCK: INT
827	Motown/Universal	50
828	J&R Adventures	28
832	Sony Music Nashville	8
835	Columbia	33

Figure 15-5 Creating an instead of trigger on ACTIVE_LABEL_INVENTORY

rows in the CD_INVENTORY table that do not match selected labels from the LABEL_STATUS table are excluded from the ACTIVE_LABEL_INVENTORY view.

The ACTIVE_LABEL_INVENTORY view has several update restrictions. First, we cannot insert rows into or delete rows from the ACTIVE_LABEL_INVENTORY view because each row in the view cannot be mapped to a single row in a base table. Second, we cannot update the TOTAL_STOCK column in the view because it is an aggregate (a sum, in this case) of the CD_STOCK column in the CD_INVENTORY table. Finally, while most SQL implementations will allow the LABEL_NAME column in the view to be updated because it can be easily mapped to the LABEL_NAME column in the LABEL_STATUS table, most implementations will not allow you to update the LABEL_ID column if is defined as a foreign key in the CD_INVENTORY table. (Some SQL implementations support the ON UPDATE CASCADE option in referential integrity constraint definitions, in which case an update to LABEL_ID in the view may be supported as well.)

Suppose we have a requirement to allow authorized business users to change CD labels to inactive status, but we do not want to grant them update privileges on the LABEL_STATUS table. (I discuss database object privileges in Chapter 6.) The following instead of trigger easily handles the task:

```
CREATE TRIGGER DELETE_ACTIVE_LABEL_INVENTORY
  INSTEAD OF DELETE ON ACTIVE_LABEL_INVENTORY
  REFERENCING OLD ROW AS Old
  FOR EACH ROW
    UPDATE LABEL_STATUS
       SET STATUS_CD = 'I'
     WHERE LABEL_ID = Old.LABEL_ID;
```

The DELETE_ACTIVE_LABEL_INVENTORY trigger fires whenever a DELETE statement is executed against the ACTIVE_LABEL_INVENTORY view. However, instead of attempting the delete operation directly on the view, the trigger updates the STATUS_CD column of the LABEL_STATUS table row for the corresponding LABEL_ID to inactive (data value I). As a convenient side benefit of this update, the row that is updated by the DELETE_ACTIVE_LABEL_INVENTORY trigger will no longer be displayed by the ACTIVE_LABEL_INVENTORY view because the view only displays active labels. This will appear to the business user who submits the delete against the view as if their statement actually deleted the row from the view.

Let's look at the functioning of the DELETE_ACTIVE_LABEL_INVENTORY using a sequence of SQL statements. First, we select all the rows from the ACTIVE_LABEL_INVENTORY view using the following statement:

```
SELECT * FROM ACTIVE_LABEL_INVENTORY
 ORDER BY LABEL_ID;
```

The result should look like the view as shown in Figure 15-5. Next, suppose a business user wants to change the label Sony Music Nashville to inactive status. By virtue of the DELETE_ACTIVE_LABEL_INVENTORY trigger, the business user can do so by issuing a delete statement like the following (assuming the business user has been granted the appropriate permissions):

```
DELETE FROM ACTIVE_LABEL_INVENTORY
 WHERE LABEL_NAME = 'Sony Music Nashville';
```

Alternatively, the WHERE clause in the DELETE statement could reference the LABEL_ID column instead of the LABEL_NAME column. The instead of trigger will carry out the same action provided the DELETE statement identifies the desired row in the ACTIVE_LABEL_INVENTORY view. If we were to again select all rows from the ACTIVE_LABEL_INVENTORY view, we would see that the Sony Music Nashville row no longer appears in the results. We can confirm that the row for Sony Music Nashville still exists in the LABEL_STATUS table, with its status changed to inactive, using the following SELECT statement:

```
SELECT * FROM LABEL_STATUS;
```

As we have seen, instead of, triggers are a convenient and powerful way of applying changes to views that would not otherwise be updatable. However, these triggers can be very powerful, perhaps more powerful than intended, if they are not created carefully. For example, a DELETE statement issued against the ACTIVE_LABEL_INVENTORY view without a WHERE clause to limit rows will cause every CD label displayed by the view to be changed to inactive. Fortunately, additional statements can be added to the trigger to restrict this behavior, but it takes additional planning and coding to do so.

Try This 15-1 Creating SQL Triggers

Throughout this chapter, we have looked at how to create the three basic types of triggers—insert, update, and delete triggers. You will now create your own triggers (one of each of the three types) in the INVENTORY database. The triggers will be defined to log data modification activity that occurs in the ARTISTS table. Whenever data is modified in the ARTISTS table, a row will be inserted into a log table, which you will create. The log table will record the type of action taken (insert, update, delete), the ARTIST_ID value for the modified row, and a timestamp of when the row was inserted into the table. As a result, whenever you execute an INSERT, UPDATE, or DELETE statement against the ARTISTS table, a row will be inserted into the new table for each row that is modified. As with other Try This exercises in this book (particularly Chapter 14, when you created stored procedures), you should refer to the documentation for your SQL implementation when creating triggers to make certain you follow that product's standards. There are a lot of variations among the SQL implementations. You can download the Try_This_15.txt file, which contains the SQL statements used in this exercise in standard syntax along with CREATE TRIGGER statements in the syntax required by MySQL and Oracle.

Step by Step

1. Open the client application for your RDBMS and connect to the INVENTORY database.
2. Before you create the actual triggers on the ARTISTS table, you must create a table that will log the data modifications you make to the ARTISTS table. The log table, named ARTIST_LOG, will include three columns to record data modification events. One of the columns will be configured with a default value that records the current date and time. Enter and execute the following SQL statement:

```
CREATE TABLE ARTIST_LOG
  ( ACTION_TYPE CHAR(6),
    ARTIST_ID   INT,
    MOD_DATE    TIMESTAMP DEFAULT CURRENT_TIMESTAMP );
```

   You should receive a message indicating that the table was successfully created.

(continued)

3. Now you will create an insert trigger on the ARTISTS table. The trigger definition will include a REFERENCING clause that specifies a correlation name (New) for the new row that is inserted into the ARTISTS table. That correlation name will then be used in the triggered SQL statement as a value inserted into the ARTIST_LOG table. Enter and execute the following SQL statement:

```
CREATE TRIGGER INSERT_LOG
  AFTER INSERT ON ARTISTS
  REFERENCING NEW ROW AS New
  FOR EACH ROW
  BEGIN ATOMIC
    INSERT INTO ARTIST_LOG ( ACTION_TYPE, ARTIST_ID )
      VALUES ( 'INSERT', New.ARTIST_ID );
  END;
```

   You should receive a message indicating that the trigger was successfully created.

4. Next you will create an update trigger. This trigger definition is similar to the one in step 3, except that you are specifying that it is an update trigger. Enter and execute the following SQL statement:

```
CREATE TRIGGER UPDATE_LOG
  AFTER UPDATE ON ARTISTS
  REFERENCING NEW ROW AS New
  FOR EACH ROW
  BEGIN ATOMIC
    INSERT INTO ARTIST_LOG ( ACTION_TYPE, ARTIST_ID )
      VALUES ( 'UPDATE', New.ARTIST_ID );
  END;
```

   You should receive a message indicating that the trigger was successfully created.

5. Now you will create a delete trigger. This trigger definition is a little different than the last two triggers because the REFERENCING clause specifies a correlation name for the old values rather than the new. This is because new values are not created when you delete data from a table. The correlation name (Old) is then used in the VALUES clause of the INSERT statement. Enter and execute the following SQL statement:

```
CREATE TRIGGER DELETE_LOG
  AFTER DELETE ON ARTISTS
  REFERENCING OLD ROW AS Old
  FOR EACH ROW
  BEGIN ATOMIC
    INSERT INTO ARTIST_LOG ( ACTION_TYPE, ARTIST_ID )
      VALUES ( 'DELETE', Old.ARTIST_ID );
  END;
```

   You should receive a message indicating that the trigger was successfully created.

6. Now you can begin to test the triggers that you created. The first step is to insert data into the ARTISTS table. In this statement, values are specified for the ARTIST_ID column and the ARTIST_NAME column, but not the PLACE_OF_BIRTH column. As a result, the default value of Unknown will be inserted in that column. Enter and execute the following SQL statement:

   ```
   INSERT INTO ARTISTS ( ARTIST_ID, ARTIST_NAME )
     VALUES ( 2019, 'John Lee Hooker' );
   ```

   You should receive a message indicating that the row was successfully inserted into the ARTISTS table.

7. Now you will update the row that you just inserted by providing a value for the PLACE_OF_BIRTH column. Enter and execute the following SQL statement:

   ```
   UPDATE ARTISTS
       SET PLACE_OF_BIRTH = 'Clarksdale, Mississippi, USA'
     WHERE ARTIST_ID = 2019;
   ```

   You should receive a message indicating that the row was successfully updated into the ARTISTS table.

8. Your next step is to delete the row that you just created. Enter and execute the following SQL statement:

   ```
   DELETE FROM ARTISTS
     WHERE ARTIST_ID = 2019;
   ```

   You should receive a message indicating that the row was successfully deleted from the ARTISTS table.

9. Now that you've modified data in the ARTISTS table, you will look at the ARTIST_LOG table to verify that rows have been entered into the table to record your data modifications of the ARTISTS table. Enter and execute the following SQL statement:

   ```
   SELECT * FROM ARTIST_LOG;
   ```

   Your query results should include three rows, one for each action type (INSERT, UPDATE, and DELETE). The rows should all have the same ARTIST_ID value (2019) and include the current dates and times.

10. Your next step will be to drop the triggers from the database. The first trigger that you'll drop is the insert trigger. Enter and execute the following SQL statement:

    ```
    DROP TRIGGER INSERT_LOG;
    ```

    You should receive a message indicating that the trigger was successfully dropped from your database.

(continued)

11. Next you will drop the update trigger. Enter and execute the following SQL statement:

```
DROP TRIGGER UPDATE_LOG;
```

You should receive a message indicating that the trigger was successfully dropped from the database.

12. Now drop the delete trigger. Enter and execute the following SQL statement:

```
DROP TRIGGER DELETE_LOG;
```

You should receive a message indicating that the trigger was successfully dropped from the database.

13. Finally, you will drop the ARTIST_LOG table that you created in step 2. Enter and execute the following SQL statement:

```
DROP TABLE ARTIST_LOG;
```

You should receive a message indicating that the table was successfully dropped from the database.

14. Close the client application.

Try This Summary

In this Try This exercise, you created the ARTIST_LOG table, which was set up to store information about data modifications to the ARTISTS table. Next you created three triggers on the ARTISTS table—an insert trigger, an update trigger, and a delete trigger. All three triggers used REFERENCING clauses to allow you to pass the ARTIST_ID value of the modified row to the ARTIST_LOG table. After the triggers were created, you inserted, updated, and deleted data in the ARTISTS table to test the triggers. You then viewed the contents of the ARTIST_LOG table to verify that the data modifications had been properly recorded. After that, you dropped the three triggers and the ARTIST_LOG table. By the time you completed the exercise, the INVENTORY database should have been returned to the same state it was in when you began.

Chapter 15 Self Test

1. What is a trigger?
2. What are the three types of triggers?
3. What types of actions can be performed by the triggered SQL statements?

4. Which actions can invoke a trigger?
   - A Updating data
   - B Querying data
   - C Deleting data
   - D Inserting data
5. When is an insert trigger invoked?
6. How does an instead of trigger differ from a before or after trigger?
7. A trigger can be defined on how many tables?
   - A Only one
   - B One or more
   - C One to three
   - D Any number of tables
8. A(n) ______________ is a space created in memory that holds a trigger process during the execution of that trigger.
9. You insert data into Table 1, which invokes an insert trigger defined on that table. The trigger updates information in Table 2, which invokes an update trigger defined on that table. The update trigger deletes information in Table 3, which invokes a delete trigger defined on that table. Which trigger execution context is active at this point?
   - A The trigger execution context for the insert trigger
   - B The trigger execution context for the update trigger
   - C The trigger execution context for the delete trigger
10. If three triggers are invoked during a session, how many trigger execution contexts are created in that session?
11. What information is included in a trigger execution context?
12. In which clause of the CREATE TRIGGER statement do you assign correlation names to old and new data?
    - A FOR EACH
    - B ON
    - C REFERENCING
    - D WHEN

13. In which clause of the CREATE TRIGGER statement do you specify whether the triggered SQL statements are executed once for each row or once for each statement?

    A FOR EACH

    B ON

    C REFERENCING

    D WHEN

14. You're creating a trigger definition for an insert trigger. Which REFERENCING clauses can you include in your CREATE TRIGGER statement?

    A REFERENCING OLD ROW AS Old

    B REFERENCING NEW ROW AS New

    C REFERENCING OLD TABLE AS Old

    D REFERENCING NEW TABLE AS New

15. A(n) ______________ trigger allows you to specify the column names of a subject table.

16. What keywords can you use to designate whether the triggered SQL statements are executed before, after, or instead of the data modification statement is applied to the subject table?

17. You're creating an update trigger on the CD_INVENTORY table. The table includes a column named IN_STOCK. You want the triggered SQL statements to be executed only when the IN_STOCK value of the updated row exceeds 20. Which clause should you include in your CREATE TRIGGER statement to restrict when the statements are executed?

    A WHERE

    B HAVING

    C FOR EACH

    D WHEN

18. What statement must you include in your CREATE TRIGGER statement if the trigger definition includes more than one triggered SQL statement?

19. Which statement can you use to delete a trigger from the schema?

20. What SQL statement do you use to alter a trigger definition?

Chapter 16

Using SQL Cursors

Key Skills & Concepts

- Understand SQL Cursors
- Declare a Cursor
- Open and Close a Cursor
- Retrieve Data from a Cursor
- Use Positioned UPDATE and DELETE Statements

As we have looked at different aspects of SQL throughout this book, we have used direct invocation to create and access various data objects. *Direct invocation,* or *interactive* SQL, is a type of data access method that supports the ad hoc execution of SQL statements, usually through some sort of client application. For example, you can use SQL Server Management Studio, Oracle's SQL Developer, or MySQL Workbench to interact directly with your SQL database. However, direct invocation generally represents only a small percentage of all database use. A far more common method used to access SQL databases is *embedded SQL,* a data access model in which SQL statements are embedded in an application programming language, such as C, Java, and COBOL. To support embedded SQL, the SQL standard allows you to declare cursors that act as pointers to specific rows of data in your query results. This chapter explains why cursors are used and how cursors can be declared, opened, and closed within an SQL session. You'll also learn how to retrieve data using the cursor so that your programming language can work with SQL data in a format that the application can process.

Understand SQL Cursors

One of the defining characteristics of SQL is the fact that data in an SQL database is managed in sets. In fact, query results returned by SELECT statements are often referred to as *result sets.* These result sets are each made up of one or more rows extracted from one or more tables.

When working with SQL data interactively, having data returned in sets rarely presents a problem because you can normally scroll through the query results to find the information you need. If the size of the results is too great to easily skim through, you can narrow the focus of your query expression to return a more manageable result set. However, most data access is through means other than direct invocation (despite the fact that we access data interactively throughout the book). One of the most common methods, embedded SQL, accesses data through SQL statements embedded in an application program. The data elements returned by the SQL statements are used by the outer programming language—the *host language*—to support specific application processes.

The problem we run into with this arrangement is that the application programming languages are generally not equipped to deal with data returned in sets. As a result, an impedance mismatch exists between SQL and the programming languages. *Impedance mismatch* refers to differences between SQL and other programming languages. As you might recall from Chapter 3, one example of impedance mismatch is the way in which SQL data types differ from data types in other programming languages. These differences can lead to the loss of information when an application extracts data from an SQL database. Another example of impedance mismatch is the fact that SQL returns data in sets but other programming languages cannot handle sets. Generally, they can process only a few pieces of data (a single record) at the same time. The way in which SQL deals with this type of impedance mismatch is through the use of cursors.

A cursor serves as a pointer that allows the application programming language to deal with query results one row at a time, much like the way these programming languages handle records from traditional (flat) data files. Although the cursor can traverse all the rows of a query result, it focuses on only one row at a time. A cursor still returns a full result set, but allows the programming language to call only one row from that set. For example, suppose your query results are derived from the following SELECT statement:

```
SELECT PERFORMER_NAME, PLACE_OF_BIRTH
  FROM PERFORMERS;
```

The query results from this statement will return all rows from the PERFORMERS table, which includes the PERFORMER_NAME column and the PLACE_OF_BIRTH column. However, your application programming language can deal with only one row at a time, so the cursor is declared as an embedded SQL statement within the application programming language. The cursor is then opened, much like the way these application languages open files, and a row is retrieved from the query results. Figure 16-1 illustrates how a cursor acts as a pointer to retrieve only one row of data.

In this case, the row that is retrieved through the cursor is the Shania Twain row. However, you can retrieve any row from the query results, and you can continue to retrieve rows, as long as they're retrieved one at a time and the cursor remains open. Once you close the cursor, you cannot retrieve any more rows from the query results.

Declaring and Opening SQL Cursors

Most application programming languages support the use of cursors to retrieve data from an SQL database. The cursor language is embedded in the programming code in much the same way you would embed any SQL statement. When using a cursor in a programming language, you must first declare the cursor—similar to how you would declare a variable—and then use the declaration name (the name you've assigned to the cursor) in other embedded SQL statements to open the cursor, retrieve individual rows through the cursor, and close the cursor.

NOTE

You can also use cursors in SQL client modules, which are sets of SQL statements that can be called from within an application programming language. Client modules, along with embedded SQL and interactive SQL, provide one more method to invoke SQL statements. Because client modules are not implemented as widely as embedded SQL, I focus on using cursors in embedded SQL. For more information about SQL client modules, see Chapter 18.

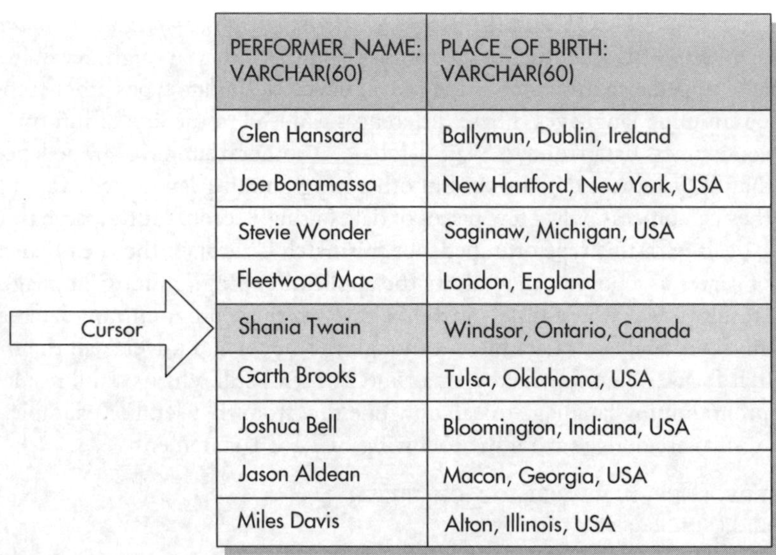

PERFORMER_NAME: VARCHAR(60)	PLACE_OF_BIRTH: VARCHAR(60)
Glen Hansard	Ballymun, Dublin, Ireland
Joe Bonamassa	New Hartford, New York, USA
Stevie Wonder	Saginaw, Michigan, USA
Fleetwood Mac	London, England
Shania Twain	Windsor, Ontario, Canada
Garth Brooks	Tulsa, Oklahoma, USA
Joshua Bell	Bloomington, Indiana, USA
Jason Aldean	Macon, Georgia, USA
Miles Davis	Alton, Illinois, USA

Figure 16-1 Using a cursor to access the PERFORMERS table

Although declaring a cursor is pivotal in using that cursor in your application, the declaration alone is not enough to extract data from an SQL database. In fact, full cursor functionality is supported through the use of four SQL statements, each of which are embedded in the application programming language, or host language. The following descriptions provide an overview of these four statements:

- **DECLARE CURSOR** Declares the SQL cursor by defining the cursor name, the cursor's characteristics, and a query expression that is invoked when the cursor is opened.
- **OPEN** Opens the cursor and invokes the query expression, making the query results available to FETCH statements.
- **FETCH** Retrieves data into variables that pass the data to the host programming language or to other embedded SQL statements.
- **CLOSE** Closes the cursor. Once the cursor is closed, data cannot be retrieved from the cursor's query results.

The four statements are called from within the host language. Figure 16-2 illustrates how the cursor-related statements are used. The embedded SQL statements are shown in the boxes that are shaded gray.

As you can see, you must first declare the cursor, and then you open it. Once you've opened the cursor, you can use the FETCH statement to retrieve rows of data. You can use this

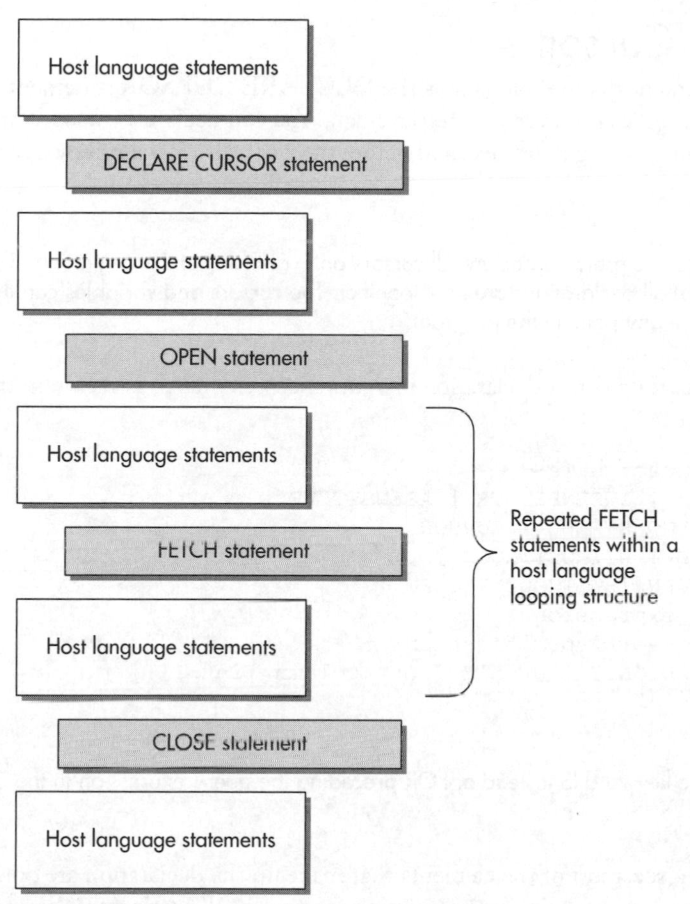

Figure 16-2 Embedding cursor-related SQL statements

statement as many times as necessary, usually within some sort of looping structure defined by the host language. Once you've retrieved the necessary data, you should close the cursor.

NOTE

For most application programming languages, an embedded SQL statement is preceded by EXEC SQL. This signals to a preprocessor that the following statement is SQL and must be processed separately from the host language. The preprocessor, provided by the RDBMS vendor, analyzes the SQL code and converts it into a form that can be used by the SQL implementation. The host language is compiled in the normal way. For more information about embedded SQL, see Chapter 18.

Declare a Cursor

The first statement that we'll look at is the DECLARE CURSOR statement. The cursor must be declared before you can use it to retrieve data. You can declare a cursor at any point in your application code, as long as it's declared before the cursor is referenced by any other statements.

NOTE

Many programmers prefer to declare all cursors and variables at the beginning of the program so that all declarations are kept together. The cursors and variables can then be referenced at any point in the program.

The syntax for a cursor declaration includes many elements, as shown in the following syntax:

```
DECLARE <cursor name>
[ SENSITIVE | INSENSITIVE | ASENSITIVE ]
[ SCROLL | NO SCROLL ] CURSOR
[ WITH HOLD | WITHOUT HOLD ]
[ WITH RETURN | WITHOUT RETURN ]
FOR <query expression>
[ ORDER BY <sort specification> ]
[ FOR { READ ONLY | UPDATE [ OF <column list> ] } ]
```

NOTE

Oracle uses the keyword IS instead of FOR preceding the query expression in the cursor declaration.

As you can see, most of the elements that make up the declaration are optional. And as always, you need to check the documentation for your SQL implementation to see which ones are supported. We'll look at these elements in greater detail in the following section. For now, let's focus on those elements that are required. To do so, we can synthesize the syntax down to the following basic elements:

```
DECLARE <cursor name> CURSOR FOR <query expression>
```

This syntax shows only those parts of the cursor declaration that are mandatory. As you can see, this is a much more manageable chunk of code. All you're required to provide is a name for the cursor and the query expression that is invoked when the cursor is opened. The name must be different from the name of any other cursor declared within the same program. The query expression is basically a SELECT statement, as you have seen throughout this book.

That's all there is to the basic syntax. In the following section, we'll take a look at each of the optional elements that make up the cursor declaration. After that, we'll look at some examples.

Working with Optional Syntax Elements

If you refer back to the full syntax for a cursor declaration (shown in the previous section), you'll see that the majority of the elements are optional. In this section, we'll look at each of these elements. Later in the chapter, after we've completed this discussion, you might find that you'll want to refer back to this section for details about specific options.

Cursor Sensitivity

The first optional element of the DECLARE CURSOR statement that we'll look at is cursor sensitivity, which is represented with the following syntax:

```
[ SENSITIVE | INSENSITIVE | ASENSITIVE ]
```

Cursor sensitivity is concerned with statements outside the cursor that affect the same rows as those returned by the cursor. For example, suppose your cursor returns rows from the CDS_IN_STOCK table. While the cursor is open, another statement within the same transaction deletes some of the same rows in the CDS_IN_STOCK table that were returned by the cursor. Whether or not the cursor can see these deletions depends on the cursor sensitivity.

As you can see in the syntax, SQL supports three cursor sensitivity options:

- **SENSITIVE** Significant changes made by statements outside the cursor immediately affect the query results within the cursor.
- **INSENSITIVE** Significant changes made by statements outside the cursor do not affect the query results within the cursor.
- **ASENSITIVE** Cursor sensitivity is implementation defined. Significant changes may or may not be visible within the cursor.

If no cursor sensitivity option is specified, ASENSITIVE is assumed, in which case the SQL implementation can take whatever action it has been designed to take.

NOTE

Some SQL implementations provide initialization or system parameters that alter the behavior of cursors. For example, Oracle provides the CURSOR_SHARING initialization parameter that specifies which kind of SQL statements can share the same cursors. As always, you should consult the documentation for your particular implementation.

Cursor Scrollability

The next optional element in the DECLARE CURSOR statement that we'll look at is cursor scrollability, as shown in the following syntax:

```
[ SCROLL | NO SCROLL ]
```

Scrollability is directly tied to the FETCH statement and the options that the FETCH statement can use to retrieve data. If the SCROLL option is specified, the FETCH statement can be defined with one of several options that extend its ability to move through the query results and return specific rows. The SCROLL option allows the FETCH statement to skip around through the query results as needed to retrieve the specific row. If NO SCROLL is specified in the cursor declaration, the FETCH statement cannot make use of the additional scrolling options and can retrieve only the next available row from the query results. If neither option is specified, NO SCROLL is assumed. For more information about the FETCH options, see the "Retrieve Data from a Cursor" section later in this chapter.

Cursor Holdability

The next item that we'll look at in the DECLARE CURSOR syntax is related to cursor holdability, as shown in the following syntax:

```
[ WITH HOLD | WITHOUT HOLD ]
```

Cursor holdability refers to a characteristic in cursors that is concerned with whether a cursor is automatically closed when the transaction in which the cursor was opened is committed. A *transaction* is an atomic unit of work. This means that all statements within the transaction must succeed or none of them can have any effect. If some statements within a transaction are executed and then one statement fails, all executed statements are rolled back and the database remains unchanged. (Transactions are discussed in more detail in Chapter 17.)

SQL provides two options that allow you to define cursor holdability: WITH HOLD and WITHOUT HOLD. If you specify WITH HOLD, your cursor will remain open after you commit the transaction, until you explicitly close it. If you specify WITHOUT HOLD, your cursor will be automatically closed when the transaction is committed. If neither option is specified, WITHOUT HOLD is assumed and your cursor is automatically closed.

NOTE

Even if your cursor is defined as a WITHOUT HOLD cursor—whether explicitly or by default—it is still generally considered good practice to explicitly close your cursor when it is no longer needed. This can free up system resources, and it helps to ensure that your code is clearly self-documenting. In SQL Server, a cursor must be deallocated after it is closed in order to free up all of its resources.

The advantage of defining a holdable cursor (one that is defined with the WITH HOLD option) is that there might be times after a transaction is committed when you want your cursor to persist in order to maintain its position within the query results returned by that cursor. Closing a cursor and reopening it can often make it difficult to restore conditions, including the cursor's position in the query results, to exactly what they were when you first closed the cursor.

Cursor Returnability

Cursor returnability, the next option we'll look at in the cursor declaration definition, uses the following syntax:

```
[ WITH RETURN | WITHOUT RETURN ]
```

The returnability option applies only to cursors that are opened in an SQL-invoked procedure. As you'll recall from Chapter 14, an *SQL-invoked procedure* is a type of routine that is invoked by using the CALL statement. The CALL statement is an SQL statement that invokes procedures and allows you to pass parameter values to those procedures. If the cursor is not opened within a procedure, the returnability option has no effect.

As the syntax shows, SQL supports two returnability options: WITH RETURN and WITHOUT RETURN. If you specify WITH RETURN, the cursor is considered a result set cursor. If you then open the cursor within an SQL-invoked procedure, the cursor's result set is returned to the procedure's invoker, which might be another SQL-invoked routine or a host language program. If you specify WITHOUT RETURN, the cursor's result set is returned in the normal manner, whether or not it is opened with an SQL-invoked procedure. If neither option is specified, WITHOUT RETURN is assumed.

Cursor Ordering

The DECLARE CURSOR statement includes an optional ORDER BY clause, as shown in the following syntax:

```
[ ORDER BY <sort specification> ]
```

You'll no doubt recognize this clause from Chapter 7, when we looked at the basic clauses of the SELECT statement. You might recall from that discussion that the ORDER BY clause can be used when directly invoking SQL, but not in an embedded SQL statement, unless that statement is contained within a cursor declaration.

The ORDER BY clause allows you to sort the query results returned by your query specification. In the clause, you can specify which columns form the basis for sorting the rows. Care must be taken regarding performance because a cursor with an ORDER BY may force the SQL engine to retrieve and sort the entire result set before the first row can be returned, and this can be a performance disaster for very large result sets. If you use an ORDER BY clause, your cursor's SELECT statement cannot contain a GROUP BY clause or a HAVING clause. In addition, the SELECT clause portion of the statement cannot specify the DISTINCT keyword or use a set function.

If your ORDER BY clause includes calculated columns in the query results (such as COLUMN_A + COLUMN_B), you should define an alias for the result column, as in (COLUMN_A + COLUMN_B) AS COLUMN_TOTALS. In addition, you can use the ASC and DESC keywords for any column included in the sort specification to specify that the column be sorted in ascending or descending order, respectively, with ASC being the default. (For more information about the ORDER BY clause, see Chapter 7.)

Cursor Updatability

The last optional element of the DECLARE CURSOR statement that we'll look at is cursor updatability, as shown in the following syntax:

```
[ FOR { READ ONLY | UPDATE [ OF <column list> ] } ]
```

Cursor updatability refers to the ability to use an UPDATE or DELETE statement to modify data returned by the cursor's SELECT statement. As you can see from the syntax, you must use the FOR keyword along with the READ ONLY or UPDATE option. Let's first go over the READ ONLY option. If you specify READ ONLY, you cannot execute an UPDATE or DELETE statement against the query results returned by the cursor's SELECT statement. On the other hand, if you specify UPDATE, you can execute the statements. If you specify neither option, UPDATE is assumed, unless another option overrides the UPDATE default.

NOTE

In some cases, even if no updatability option is specified, the cursor will be defined as a read-only cursor because other options might prevent the cursor from being updated. For example, if you specify the INSENSITIVE option, the cursor will be read-only. The same is true if you specify an ORDER BY clause or SCROLL keyword.

You'll notice that the UPDATE option also allows you to specify which columns in the underlying table can be updated. To do this, you must include the OF keyword, followed by one or more column names. If more than one column is specified, the column names must be separated by commas. If you do not specify any column names (with the OF keyword), the UPDATE option applies to all columns in the underlying table.

Creating a Cursor Declaration

Now that we've looked at each component of the DECLARE CURSOR statement, let's take a look at a few examples that help illustrate how to declare a cursor. For these examples, we'll use the CD_INVENTORY table, shown in Figure 16-3.

The first example that we'll review is a basic cursor declaration that includes only the required elements plus an ORDER BY clause, as shown in the following DECLARE CURSOR statement:

```
DECLARE CD_1 CURSOR
  FOR
    SELECT *
      FROM CD_INVENTORY
     ORDER BY COMPACT_DISC;
```

In this statement, I've declared a cursor named CD_1 and defined a SELECT statement. The cursor name follows the DECLARE keyword. After the cursor name, I've included the CURSOR keyword and the FOR keyword. The only additional element is the SELECT statement, which includes an ORDER BY clause. The statement returns all rows and columns from the CD_INVENTORY table. The rows are then ordered according to the values in the COMPACT_DISC column. Because I did not specify the ASC or DESC keyword, the rows are returned in ascending order.

COMPACT_DISC: VARCHAR(60)	CATEGORY: VARCHAR(15)	PRICE: NUMERIC(5,2)	ON_HAND: INT
Drive All Night	Vocal	5.99	12
Different Shades of Blue	Vocal	11.99	42
Innervisions (Remastered)	Vocal	10.00	16
The Definitive Collection	Vocal	8.39	34
Rumours (Reissued)	Vocal	7.99	17
Come On Over	Vocal	5.99	6
Man Against Machine	Vocal	9.99	8
Bach	Instrumental	11.88	22
Old Boots, New Dirt	Vocal	11.88	32
Dark Side of the Moon	Vocal	10.86	27
Kind of Blue	Instrumental	7.29	21
Thriller	Vocal	7.50	29
The Endless River	Vocal	13.39	12
Sonic Highways	Vocal	11.88	27

Figure 16-3 Declaring cursors on the CD_INVENTORY table

NOTE

In Chapter 7, when discussing the SELECT statement, I explain that although an asterisk can be used to return all columns from a table, it is a better practice to identify each column that you want returned. This is especially important in embedded SQL because the host language relies on certain values—a specified number in a specified order—being returned from the database. If the database should change, your application may not operate properly, and the application code would have to be modified. For the examples in this chapter, I often use an asterisk to simplify the code and conserve space, but know that in the real world, I would usually specify each column.

The ORDER BY clause is an important element because the order in which the rows are returned affects which rows are retrieved when using a FETCH statement. (I discuss the

FETCH statement later in the chapter, in the "Retrieve Data from a Cursor" section.) This is especially true if defining a scrollable cursor, such as the one in the following example:

```
DECLARE CD_2 SCROLL CURSOR
  FOR
    SELECT *
      FROM CD_INVENTORY
     ORDER BY COMPACT_DISC
       FOR READ ONLY;
```

Notice that I've added two new elements to this statement: the SCROLL keyword and the FOR READ ONLY clause. The SCROLL keyword signals to the FETCH statement that the cursor is scrollable. As a result, additional options can be used within the FETCH statement, which extend how your application can move through the cursor results. The FOR READ ONLY clause indicates that neither an UPDATE nor a DELETE statement can be used to modify data returned by the cursor. However, this clause is not necessary. Because the cursor declaration includes the SCROLL keyword and the SELECT statement includes an ORDER BY clause, the cursor is automatically limited to read-only operations. The use of either of these two options—or the use of the INSENSITIVE option—automatically overrides the cursor's default updatability.

The next type of read-only declaration that we'll look at also includes the INSENSITIVE keyword, as shown in the following example:

```
DECLARE CD_3 SCROLL INSENSITIVE CURSOR
  FOR
    SELECT *
      FROM CD_INVENTORY
     ORDER BY COMPACT_DISC
       FOR READ ONLY;
```

The CD_3 cursor declaration is exactly like the CD_2 cursor declaration except that CD_3 has also been defined as an insensitive cursor. This means that no modifications made to the data in the underlying table while the cursor is open will be reflected in the query results returned by the cursor. Of course, if you close the cursor and then reopen it, any modifications that had been made when the cursor was originally open will be reflected in the data returned by the reopened cursor.

The three preceding cursor declarations that we've looked at have all been read-only. Now let's take a look at an updatable cursor. In the following cursor declaration, the SELECT statement again returns all rows and columns from the CD_INVENTORY table:

```
DECLARE CD_4 CURSOR
  FOR
    SELECT *
      FROM CD_INVENTORY
       FOR UPDATE;
```

Notice that this DECLARE CURSOR statement does not include the SCROLL keyword, the INSENSITIVE keyword, or an ORDER BY clause, any of which would have prevented us from creating an updatable cursor. We could have specified the NO SCROLL and SENSITIVE options, but they're not necessary. Also notice, however, that the cursor declaration does include the FOR UPDATE clause. The clause is also not necessary in this particular statement because the cursor is, by default, updatable, since it contains no options to limit the updatability.

However, if you want your cursor to be updatable only for a certain column, you must include the FOR UPDATE clause, along with the column name, as shown in the following example:

```
DECLARE CD_5 CURSOR
  FOR
    SELECT *
      FROM CD_INVENTORY
       FOR UPDATE OF COMPACT_DISC;
```

Now the FOR UPDATE clause includes the OF keyword and the column name, COMPACT_DISC. If you were to try to modify data in the cursor results in columns other than the COMPACT_DISC column, you would receive an error.

Once you've declared your cursor, you can open it and retrieve data from the query results. However, as you have seen in the preceding cursor declarations, the actions that you can take are limited to the restrictions defined with the DECLARE CURSOR statement.

Open and Close a Cursor

The process of opening a cursor is very straightforward. You need to provide only the keyword OPEN and the name of the cursor, as shown in the following syntax:

```
OPEN <cursor name>
```

For example, to open the CD_1 cursor, you invoke the following SQL statement:

```
OPEN CD_1;
```

You cannot open a cursor until you have declared it. Once you've declared it, you can open it anywhere within your program. The SELECT statement within the cursor is not invoked until you actually open the cursor. That means that any data modifications made between the time the cursor is declared and the time the cursor is opened are reflected in the query results returned by the cursor. If you close the cursor and then reopen it, data modifications that took place between the time you close it and the time you reopen it are reflected in the new query results.

Once you have finished using your cursor, you should close it so that you can free up system resources. To close a cursor, you can use the CLOSE statement, as shown in the following syntax:

```
CLOSE <cursor name>
```

The CLOSE statement does nothing more than close the cursor, which means that the query results from the cursor's SELECT statement are released. For example, to close the CD_1 cursor, use the following SQL statement:

```
CLOSE CD_1;
```

Once you close the cursor, you cannot retrieve any more rows from the cursor's query results. In other words, you cannot use a FETCH statement to retrieve data from a closed cursor. If you reopen the cursor, you can again retrieve data, but you will get a new result set and (assuming no scrolling options) will start with the first row in the query results, which can mean retrieving rows that have already been processed by a prior invocation of the cursor.

Retrieve Data from a Cursor

So far, you've learned how to declare a cursor, open it, and then close it. However, these actions alone do not allow you to retrieve any of the data that is provided by the cursor. In order to do that, you must use a FETCH statement.

Before we take a look at the syntax for the FETCH statement, let's briefly review the purpose of a cursor and its related statements. As I said earlier, one of the problems with embedding SQL statements in a programming host language is the impedance mismatch. One form of that mismatch is that SQL returns data in sets, and traditional application programming languages cannot handle sets of data. In general, they can deal only with individual values. In order to address this form of impedance mismatch, you can use cursors to retrieve data one row at a time—regardless of how many rows are returned—from which you can extract individual values that can be used by the host language.

As you have seen, a cursor declaration includes a SELECT statement that returns a set of data. The OPEN statement executes the SELECT statement, and the CLOSE statement releases the query results from the SELECT statement. However, it is the FETCH statement that identifies individual rows within that set of data and extracts individual values from those rows, which are then passed to host variables. A *host variable* is a type of parameter that passes a value to the host language.

NOTE

Host variables are highly important in some SQL implementations in order to avoid serious performance issues. For example, with some versions of Oracle, if host variables are used within embedded SQL statements, the statement can be reused from the SQL cache when it is invoked again, which saves significant overhead. As always, check the documentation for your SQL implementation.

One or more FETCH statements can be executed while a cursor is open. Each statement points to a specific row in the query results, and values are then extracted from those rows. The following syntax shows the basic elements that make up the FETCH statement:

```
FETCH [ [ <fetch orientation> ] FROM ]
<cursor name> INTO <host variables>
```

As you can see by the syntax, you must specify the FETCH keyword, the name of the cursor, and an INTO clause that identifies the host variables that will receive the values returned by the FETCH statement. These values are derived from the query results that are generated by the cursor's SELECT statement when that cursor is opened. If your FETCH statement includes more than one host variable, you must separate the variables with commas.

In addition to the mandatory components of the FETCH statement, the syntax includes the optional <fetch orientation> placeholder and the FROM keyword. If you specify a fetch orientation option in your FETCH statement, you must include the FROM keyword, or you can specify FROM without the fetch orientation.

SQL supports six fetch orientation options that identify which row is selected from the cursor's query results. Most of these options are available only if you declare the cursor as scrollable. A scrollable cursor, as you'll recall, is one that extends the ability of the FETCH statement to move through the cursor's query results. A cursor is scrollable if the cursor declaration includes the SCROLL keyword. If you include a fetch orientation in your FETCH statement, you can choose from one of the following options:

- **NEXT** Retrieves the next row from the query results. If you use NEXT in your first FETCH statement after you open your cursor, the first row in the query results will be returned. A second FETCH NEXT statement will return the second row.
- **PRIOR** Retrieves the row directly preceding the one that had last been retrieved. If you use PRIOR in your first FETCH statement after you open the cursor, no row will be returned because no row precedes the first row.
- **FIRST** Retrieves the first row from your cursor's query results, regardless of how many FETCH statements have been executed since opening the cursor.
- **LAST** Retrieves the last row from your cursor's query results, regardless of how many FETCH statements have been executed since opening the cursor.
- **ABSOLUTE <value>** Retrieves the row specified by the <value> placeholder. The value must be an exact numeric, although it can be derived from a host variable. The numeric value identifies which row is returned by the FETCH statement. For example, ABSOLUTE 1 returns the first row, ABSOLUTE 2 returns the second row, and ABSOLUTE -1 returns the last row.
- **RELATIVE <value>** Retrieves the row specified by the <value> placeholder, relative to the cursor's current position. If you use RELATIVE in the first FETCH statement after you open the cursor, RELATIVE 1 returns the first row from the cursor's query results, and RELATIVE -1 returns the last row. However, if the cursor is not at the beginning of the query results, as it is when you first open the cursor, RELATIVE 1 and RELATIVE -1 return rows relative to the cursor position as it was left after the last executed FETCH statement.

Whenever you open a cursor, the cursor points to the beginning of the query results. The FETCH statement moves the cursor to the row designated by the fetch orientation option. If no option is specified, NEXT is assumed, and the cursor always points to the next row in the query results.

To help illustrate how the fetch orientation options work, let's take another look at a cursor we declared earlier in the chapter:

```
DECLARE CD_2 SCROLL CURSOR
  FOR
    SELECT *
      FROM CD_INVENTORY
     ORDER BY COMPACT_DISC
       FOR READ ONLY;
```

Notice that the SCROLL keyword is specified and that the SELECT statement retrieves all rows and columns from the CD_INVENTORY table. Also notice that the SELECT statement includes an ORDER BY clause that sorts the query results in ascending order according to the values in the COMPACT_DISC column. This is important because the FETCH statements move through the rows in the query results in the order specified by the ORDER BY clause, regardless of how rows are ordered in the underlying table.

Now let's take another look at the query results returned by the SELECT statement in the CD_2 cursor. The query results, in the form of a virtual table, are shown in Figure 16-4. Notice that the illustration includes pointers that represent the various types of FETCH statements (based on their fetch orientation). In each case, the pointer is based on a FETCH statement that is the first to be executed after the cursor has been opened.

Notice that the FETCH FIRST and FETCH NEXT pointers each point to the Drive All Night row. This is the first row in the cursor's query results. FETCH FIRST will always point to this row, assuming the data in the underlying tables doesn't change. FETCH NEXT will always point to the first row whenever it is the first FETCH statement executed after the cursor is opened. In addition, the FETCH LAST pointer will always point to the Sonic Highways row. However, the FETCH PRIOR pointer doesn't point to any row. It points instead to a space prior to the first row of the query results. This is because PRIOR cannot retrieve a row if it is used in the first FETCH statement after the cursor is opened.

Now let's take a look at the FETCH ABSOLUTE 5 pointer. As you can see, it points to the Rumours (Reissued) row, which is the fifth row in the cursor's query results. FETCH ABSOLUTE 5 will always return this row. On the other hand, FETCH RELATIVE 10 points to the Dark Side of the Moon row, which is the tenth row in the cursor's query results. However, if RELATIVE were used in a FETCH statement other than the first one, FETCH RELATIVE 10 would probably be pointing to a different row.

As you can see, the six fetch orientation options provide a great deal of flexibility in moving through a cursor's query results. Keep in mind, however, that most of these options can be used in read-only cursors only, such as the CD_2 cursor we've been looking at. The only option that can be used for updatable cursors is NEXT, which is the default fetch orientation. Now let's take a look at a few examples of FETCH statements so you can see how they can be used to retrieve data from your cursor's query results.

	COMPACT_DISC	CATEGORY	PRICE	ON_HAND
FETCH PRIOR				
FETCH FIRST FETCH NEXT	Drive All Night	Vocal	5.99	12
	Different Shades of Blue	Vocal	11.99	42
	Innervisions (Remastered)	Vocal	10.00	16
	The Definitive Collection	Vocal	8.39	34
FETCH ABSOLUTE 5	Rumours (Reissued)	Vocal	7.99	17
	Come On Over	Vocal	5.99	6
	Man Against Machine	Vocal	9.99	8
	Bach	Instrumental	11.88	22
	Old Boots, New Dirt	Vocal	11.88	32
FETCH RELATIVE 10	Dark Side of the Moon	Vocal	10.86	27
	Kind of Blue	Instrumental	7.29	21
	Thriller	Vocal	7.50	29
	The Endless River	Vocal	13.39	12
FETCH LAST	Sonic Highways	Vocal	11.88	27

Figure 16-4 The query results (virtual table) returned by the CD_2 cursor

The first FETCH statement that we'll look at uses the NEXT fetch orientation option to retrieve a row from the CD_2 cursor:

```
FETCH NEXT
 FROM CD_2
 INTO :CD, :Category, :Price, :On_Hand;
```

The statement identifies the fetch orientation and the cursor name. As you'll recall, the NEXT keyword is optional because NEXT is the default fetch orientation. The statement also includes the INTO clause, which identifies the host variables that will receive values returned by the FETCH statement. There are four host variables to match the number of values returned by the FETCH statement. The number of variables must be the same as the number of columns returned by the cursor's SELECT statement, and the variables must be listed in the same order as the columns returned. Notice that the host variables are separated by commas and their names begin with colons. According to the SQL standard, host variables must begin with a colon, although this can vary from one SQL implementation to the next.

Now that you've seen how a FETCH NEXT statement works, you can create any FETCH statement for whichever fetch orientation you want to specify. Simply replace one option with the other. For example, the following FETCH statement uses the ABSOLUTE fetch orientation:

```
FETCH ABSOLUTE 5
 FROM CD_2
 INTO :CD, :Category, :Price, :On_Hand;
```

Ask the Expert

Q: You mention that a cursor's SELECT statement is not executed until the cursor is opened. How does this affect special values such as CURRENT_USER or CURRENT_TIME?

A: Because a cursor's SELECT statement is not executed until the cursor is opened, special values are populated when the cursor is opened rather than when the cursor is declared. For example, if you include the CURRENT_TIME special value in your cursor's SELECT statement and declare that cursor at the beginning of your program code, the time assigned to the CURRENT_TIME value is the time when the cursor is opened, not the time when the cursor is declared. In addition, if you close and then reopen the cursor, the CURRENT_TIME value is that time when you again open the cursor, not when it was first opened.

Q: You state that host variables are a type of parameter that is used in embedded SQL. How do host variables differ from other types of parameters?

A: For all practical purposes, a host variable is just like any other parameter. The main distinction is that a host variable is used in embedded SQL to pass values between the host language and SQL. The only other real distinction is that a colon must be added to the name of the variable. The reason that a colon must be included when used in an embedded SQL statement is to indicate that the name is a host variable and not a column. As a result, you can use variable names that are meaningful to your application without worrying about accidentally naming a variable the same as a column name. The colon has nothing to do with the variable itself, only in distinguishing it as a variable. A colon must also be used in SQL client modules. However, values are passed to modules through parameters rather than host variables. Module parameters are essentially the same thing as host variables; only the names are different. If you were to refer to all of them as parameters, you would not be far off.

Notice that with the ABSOLUTE option, as with the RELATIVE option, you must specify a numeric value. In this case, the cursor will retrieve the fifth row from the cursor's query results. The ABSOLUTE, FIRST, and LAST options are the only fetch orientation options that will always return the same row from the cursor's query results, assuming that the data in the underlying table has not changed. On the other hand, the NEXT, PRIOR, and RELATIVE options return rows based on the cursor's last position. As a result, you want to be certain to design your cursors and your FETCH statements with positioning in mind.

Use Positioned UPDATE and DELETE Statements

Once you fetch a row from the query results of an updatable cursor, you might then want your application to update or delete that row. To do so, you must use a positioned UPDATE or DELETE statement. The positioned UPDATE and DELETE statements contain a special WHERE clause that references the opened cursor. Let's take a look at each of these two statements to show you how you can use them to modify data returned by your cursor.

Using the Positioned UPDATE Statement

The positioned UPDATE statement is, for the most part, the same as a regular UPDATE statement, except that it requires a special WHERE clause, as shown in the following syntax:

```
UPDATE <table name>
        SET <set list>
 WHERE CURRENT OF <cursor name>
```

A regular UPDATE statement, as you no doubt recall, contains the UPDATE clause and the SET clause, just as you see in the syntax for a positioned UPDATE statement. However, in a regular UPDATE statement the WHERE clause is optional, while in a positioned UPDATE statement, it is required. In addition, the WHERE clause must be defined with the CURRENT OF option, which identifies the opened cursor. By using the CURRENT OF option, you're telling your application to use the values returned by the most recent FETCH statement for the referenced cursor. For example, if your cursor is pointing to the Rumours (Reissued) row of the CD_INVENTORY table (the row most recently returned by the FETCH statement), it is that row that is being referenced by the WHERE clause of the positioned UPDATE statement.

Let's take a look at an example to demonstrate how this works. In the following set of SQL statements, we declare the CD_4 cursor, open that cursor, fetch a row from the cursor's query results, update that row, and close the cursor:

```
DECLARE CD_4 CURSOR
FOR
  SELECT *
    FROM CD_INVENTORY
     FOR UPDATE;
```

```
OPEN CD_4;

FETCH CD_4
 INTO :CD, :Category, :Price, :On_Hand;

UPDATE CD_INVENTORY
   SET ON_HAND = :On_Hand * 2
 WHERE CURRENT OF CD_4;

CLOSE CD_4;
```

I added some blank lines to improve readability, but, of course, they are not necessary, and if you include them, your SQL engine will simply ignore them. The first statement declares the CD_4 cursor and defines a SELECT statement that returns all rows and columns from the CD_INVENTORY table. Next, we open the cursor and then fetch the next row, which in this case is the first row, Drive All Night. After we fetch the row, we use a positioned UPDATE statement to double the amount of the ON_HAND value for that row. Notice that the UPDATE statement includes a WHERE clause that contains the CURRENT OF option, which identifies the CD_4 cursor. After we update the row, we close the cursor.

NOTE

Keep in mind that the statements shown in the preceding example would be embedded in a host language, so they are not likely to be grouped so closely together and there would likely be other host language elements, such as variable declarations, looping structures, and conditional statements.

In the preceding example, we were able to update the ON_HAND column because it was implicitly included in the FOR UPDATE clause of the cursor's SELECT statement. When no column names are specified, all columns are updatable. However, let's look at another example that explicitly defines a column. In the following set of SQL statements, I've declared the CD_5 cursor and used it to try to update a row in the CD_INVENTORY table:

```
DECLARE CD_5 CURSOR
FOR
  SELECT *
    FROM CD_INVENTORY
     FOR UPDATE OF COMPACT_DISC;

OPEN CD_5;

FETCH CD_5
 INTO :CD, :Category, :Price, :On_Hand;

UPDATE CD_INVENTORY
   SET ON_HAND = :On_Hand * 2
 WHERE CURRENT OF CD_5;

CLOSE CD_5;
```

As you can see, the cursor declaration specifies the COMPACT_DISC column in the FOR UPDATE clause. If you try to execute the UPDATE statement, you will receive an error indicating that the ON_HAND column is not one of the columns specified in the cursor declaration.

Using the Positioned DELETE Statement

The positioned DELETE statement, like the positioned UPDATE statement, requires a WHERE clause that must include the CURRENT OF option. (A regular DELETE statement, as you'll recall, does not require the WHERE clause.) A positioned DELETE statement uses the following syntax:

```
DELETE <table name>
WHERE CURRENT OF <cursor name>
```

As you can see, you need to define a DELETE clause that identifies the table and a WHERE clause that identifies the cursor. The WHERE clause in a positioned DELETE statement works just like the WHERE clause in a positioned UPDATE statement: The row returned by the last FETCH statement is the row that is modified. In this case, the row is deleted.

Now let's look at an example of a positioned DELETE statement. The following SQL statements declare the CD_4 cursor, open the cursor, return a row from the cursor, delete that row, and close the cursor:

```
DECLARE CD_4 CURSOR
FOR
  SELECT *
    FROM CD_INVENTORY
     FOR UPDATE;

OPEN CD_4;

FETCH CD_4
 INTO :CD, :Category, :Price, :On_Hand;

DELETE CD_INVENTORY
 WHERE CURRENT OF CD_4;

CLOSE CD_4;
```

You should be familiar with most of these statements. The only new one is the positioned DELETE statement. This statement deletes the row returned by the FETCH statement, which is the Drive All Night row. Once the row is deleted, the cursor is closed using a CLOSE statement. As stated previously, it is always a good idea to explicitly close cursors when they are no longer needed.

Try This 16-1 Working with SQL Cursors

In this chapter, we looked at how to declare cursors, open those cursors, retrieve data from them, and then close them. In addition, we reviewed positioned UPDATE and DELETE statements. However, as I said earlier, cursors are used primarily in embedded SQL, which makes it difficult to fully test cursor functionality if you're limited to directly invoking SQL statements (as we are in this Try This exercise). Ideally, it would be best to embed the cursor-related SQL statements in a host language, but that is beyond the scope of this book. What complicates this issue even further is the fact that different SQL implementations support the use of cursors in an interactive environment in different ways, which can make it difficult to directly invoke cursor-related statements. Still, you should be able to execute most cursor-related statements interactively, but know that cursors are designed for use in embedded SQL and SQL client modules, so you might have to modify the statements a great deal in order to execute them. You can download the Try_This_15.txt file, which contains the SQL statements used in this exercise.

NOTE

Ideally, it would be good to walk you through each step of declaring and opening a cursor, retrieving data, and closing a cursor, but because of the nature of direct invocation, we will use fewer steps and larger blocks of statements.

Step by Step

1. Open the client application for your RDBMS and connect to the INVENTORY database.
2. The first cursor that you'll declare and access is a basic read-only cursor that retrieves data from the COMPACT_DISCS table. The first thing you'll notice in the set of statements you'll be creating is that you'll declare a variable named v_CD_NAME. You'll need to create this variable in order to fully test the FETCH statement. Keep in mind that, depending on the situation, the host language, and the product, you may or may not use this method for defining your variable. Also notice that the variable name in the FETCH statement is not preceded by a colon. This is because you'll be using direct invocation to execute these statements and, for most implementations, the name of the variable in the FETCH statement will have to be the same as the name you declared at the beginning of this set of statements.

   As with any SQL statement, you will find that the exact language you use to create statements varies from one product to the next. In addition, the fact that you're invoking the statements directly rather than embedding the statements can lead to other variations between SQL and the implementation (such as not using a colon in the variable name). For example, if you execute these statements in SQL Server, you'll have to precede your variable names with the at (@) character. Oracle deviates from the standard even more. In Oracle, you declare the cursor and variable in one block of statements. In addition, the

CURSOR keyword precedes the name of the cursor, and you must use the IS keyword rather than FOR. You must also enclose the OPEN, FETCH, and CLOSE statements in a BEGIN...END block. You will also find that not all SQL options are supported in all SQL implementations, and many products include additional features not defined in the SQL standard. Be sure to check your product's documentation before trying to declare and access any cursors.

Now let's create the cursor-related statements. Enter and execute the following SQL statements:

```
DECLARE v_CD_NAME VARCHAR (60);

DECLARE CD_cursor_1 CURSOR
  FOR
    SELECT CD_TITLE
      FROM COMPACT_DISCS
     ORDER BY CD_TITLE ASC;

OPEN CD_cursor_1;

FETCH CD_cursor_1 INTO v_CD_NAME;

CLOSE CD_cursor_1;
```

In these statements, you first declared a variable named v_CD_NAME. Next, you declared a cursor named CD_cursor_1. The cursor definition contained a SELECT statement that was qualified with an ORDER BY clause. Because you included the ORDER BY clause, your cursor was read only. After you declared the cursor, you opened it, fetched a row from the cursor's query results, and then closed the cursor. The FETCH statement returned the value Bach, which could have then been used in some other operation, had you embedded these statements. After you executed the statements, you should have received a message saying that the statements were executed successfully.

3. Now you will declare and access a second cursor. This time you will specify that the cursor is insensitive and scrollable. In addition, you will specify that the cursor is read-only, although this clause is optional because you're making the cursor scrollable and insensitive. You will also fetch the last row from the cursor's query results rather than the first. Enter and execute the following SQL statements:

```
DECLARE v_CD_NAME VARCHAR(60);

DECLARE CD_cursor_2 SCROLL INSENSITIVE CURSOR
  FOR
    SELECT CD_TITLE
      FROM COMPACT_DISCS
     ORDER BY CD_TITLE ASC
       FOR READ ONLY;
```

(continued)

```
OPEN CD_cursor_2;

FETCH LAST FROM CD_cursor_2 INTO v_CD_NAME;

CLOSE CD_cursor_2;
```

This time the FETCH statement retrieved the value Sonic Highways because LAST was specified. This value was inserted into the v_CD_NAME variable. After you executed the statements, you should have received a message saying that the statements were executed successfully.

4. Your next cursor will be updatable, which means that it cannot include an ORDER BY clause and cannot be defined as insensitive or scrollable. Because the cursor is updatable, you will also create an UPDATE statement that doubles the value of the IN_STOCK column for the row returned by the FETCH statement. Enter and execute the following SQL statements:

```
DECLARE v_CD_NAME VARCHAR(60);

DECLARE CD_cursor_3 CURSOR
  FOR
    SELECT CD_TITLE
      FROM COMPACT_DISCS
       FOR UPDATE;

OPEN CD_cursor_3;

FETCH CD_cursor_3 INTO v_CD_NAME;

UPDATE COMPACT_DISCS
   SET IN_STOCK = IN_STOCK * 2
 WHERE CURRENT OF CD_cursor_3;

CLOSE CD_cursor_3;
```

Notice that your UPDATE statement includes a WHERE clause that contains the CURRENT OF option, which specifies the CD_cursor_3 cursor. This clause is mandatory. Because no ORDER BY clause was used, the first row in your cursor's query results was Drive All Night. This is the row that was updated. After you executed the statements, you should have received a message indicating that a row had been updated.

5. Now let's take a look at the COMPACT_DISCS table to verify that the change you made is correct. Enter and execute the following SQL statement:

```
SELECT * FROM COMPACT_DISCS;
```

The IN_STOCK value of the Drive All Night row should now be 24, double its original amount.

6. Let's return the database to its original state. Enter and execute the following SQL statement:

```
UPDATE COMPACT_DISCS
   SET IN_STOCK = 12
 WHERE CD_ID = 101;
```

You should receive a message indicating that the row has been updated.

7. Close the client application.

Try This Summary

In this Try This exercise, you declared and accessed three cursors, two that were read-only and one that was updatable. For all three cursors you declared a variable. The variable was then used in the FETCH statement to receive the value returned by that statement. For the updatable cursor, you created an UPDATE statement that modified the IN_STOCK value for the row returned by the FETCH statement. After you updated the COMPACT_DISCS table, you updated it once more to return the database to its original state. Because no other changes were made to the database, your data should be as it was before you started this exercise.

Chapter 16 Self Test

1. What is a cursor?
2. Which invocation methods support the use of cursors?
3. What form of impedance mismatch is addressed through the use of cursors?
4. A(n) ________________ serves as a pointer that allows the application programming language to deal with query results one row at a time.
5. When using cursors in embedded SQL, what is the first step you must take before you can retrieve data through that cursor?

   A Fetch the cursor.

   B Declare the cursor.

   C Close the cursor.

   D Open the cursor.

6. What are the four cursor-related statements that you can embed in a host language?

7. Which options can be used only in read-only cursor declarations?

   A SCROLL

   B WITH HOLD

   C ORDER BY

   D INSENSITIVE

8. What are the required elements of a DECLARE CURSOR statement?

9. What cursor type does not see changes made by statements outside the cursor?

10. Which option should you use in a cursor declaration to extend the retrieving capabilities of a FETCH statement?

    A WITHOUT HOLD

    B ASENSITIVE

    C SCROLL

    D FOR UPDATE

11. Cursor ________________ refers to a characteristic in cursors that is concerned with whether a cursor is automatically closed when the transaction in which the cursor was opened is committed.

12. You're creating a cursor declaration. The SELECT statement includes an ORDER BY clause. Which clauses cannot be included in the SELECT statement?

    A SELECT

    B HAVING

    C GROUP BY

    D WHERE

13. What option should you include in a cursor declaration to define that cursor as holdable?

14. Your cursor declaration includes a FOR UPDATE clause that does not specify any columns. Which columns in the underlying table can be updated?

15. What SQL statement should you use if you want to open the CD_ARTISTS cursor?

16. Which SQL statement executes the SELECT statement in a cursor?

17. A(n) ________________ statement retrieves rows from a cursor's query results once you open that cursor.

18. What type of cursor allows you to use all the fetch orientation options in a FETCH statement?

19. Which fetch orientation option should you use in a FETCH statement if you want to be sure to retrieve the first row in a cursor's query results?

    A PRIOR

    B NEXT

    C ABSOLUTE -1

    D FIRST

20. What clause is required in a positioned UPDATE statement in order to update a row returned by the most recent FETCH statement?

Chapter 17

Managing SQL Transactions

Key Skills & Concepts

- Understand SQL Transactions
- Set Transaction Properties
- Start a Transaction
- Set Constraint Deferability
- Create Savepoints in a Transaction
- Terminate a Transaction

In Chapter 4, I spend a considerable amount of time discussing data integrity and the methods supported by SQL to ensure that integrity. These methods include the creation of constraints, domains, and assertions, all of which are used by your database in one way or another to ensure that your SQL data remains valid. However, these methods alone are not always enough to maintain the integrity of that data. Take, for example, the situation that can arise when more than one user tries to access and modify data in the same table at the same time, or when their actions overlap and impact the same data. Actions may be taken by one user based on data that is no longer valid as a result of actions taken by the other user. Data might become inconsistent or inaccurate, without either user knowing that a problem exists. To address situations of this type, SQL supports the use of transactions to ensure that concurrent actions do not impact the validity of the data that is seen by any one user. In this chapter, I describe how transactions are implemented in an SQL environment and how you can control their behavior. You will learn how to set transaction properties, start transactions, terminate them, and use other options that extend their functionality.

Understand SQL Transactions

Relatively few databases exist in which only one user is trying to access data within that database at any given point in time. For the most part, databases are used by different types of users for many different purposes, and often these users are trying to access the same data at the same time. The greater the number of users, the greater the likelihood that problems will arise when users attempt to view or modify the same data at the same time. However, problems can arise even if only two users are accessing data at the same time, depending on the nature of their operations. For example, one user might view data in a table, take some sort of action based on that data, then return to the table to verify the data once more. However, if another user updates that table between the two times that the first user views it, the first user will see different data the second time, and might even notice that the action taken by the second user invalidated the change they made after they viewed the table the first time. For example, the first user might notice that a customer's phone number is incorrect and apply the correction. However, a second user might be looking at the same customer's data, and while updating the customer's credit status, might inadvertently put the old phone number back into the database record (because the data they were looking at contained the old number), overlaying the change that the first user made.

To address these sorts of data inconsistencies, SQL uses transactions to control the actions of individual users. A *transaction* is a unit of work that is made up of one or more SQL statements that perform a related set of actions. For example, your application might use a transaction to change the number of CDs in stock. The process of updating the applicable table or tables and reporting the updated information back to you is treated as a single transaction. The transaction might include a number of SQL statements, each performing a specific task.

In order for a set of actions to qualify as a transaction, it must pass the ACID test. ACID is an acronym commonly used when referring to the four characteristics of a transaction:

- **Atomic** This characteristic refers to the all-or-nothing nature of a transaction. Either all operations in a transaction are performed or none are performed. If some statements are executed, the results of these executions are rolled back if the transaction fails at any point before it is completed. Only when all statements are executed properly and all actions are performed is a transaction complete and the results of that transaction applied to the database.
- **Consistent** The database must be consistent at the beginning and at the end of the transaction. In fact, you can think of a transaction as a set of actions that takes the database from one consistent state to another. All rules that define and constrain the data must be applied to that data as a result of any changes that occur during the transaction. In addition, all structures within the database must be correct at the end of the transaction.
- **Isolated** Data that might temporarily be in an inconsistent state during a transaction should not be available to other transactions until the data is once again consistent. In other words, no user should be able to access inconsistent data during a transaction implemented by another user when the data impacted by the transaction is in an inconsistent state. In addition, for a transaction to be isolated, no other transactions can affect that transaction.
- **Durable** Once the changes made by a transaction are committed, those changes must be preserved, and the data should be in a reliable and consistent state, even if hardware or application errors occur.

If any problems arise at any time during a transaction, the entire transaction is rolled back and the database is returned to the state it was in before the transaction started. Any actions that were taken are undone, and the data is restored to its original state. If the transaction is successfully completed, all changes are implemented. Throughout the entire process, regardless of whether the transaction is successfully completed or must be rolled back, the transaction always ensures the integrity of the database.

SQL supports a number of statements related to transaction processing. You can use these statements to begin and end transactions, set their properties, defer constraint enforcement during the transaction, and identify places within a transaction that act as stopping points when you roll back transactions. Throughout the rest of this chapter, we'll examine how each of these statements is used within a transaction. However, before we go into a more detailed discussion of the statements, I want to provide you with a brief overview of each one in order to give you a better understanding of how transactions work.

The SQL standard defines seven statements related to transaction processing:

- **SET TRANSACTION** Sets the properties of the next transaction to be executed.
- **START TRANSACTION** Sets the properties of a transaction and starts that transaction.
- **SET CONSTRAINTS** Sets the constraint mode within a current transaction. The constraint mode refers to whether a constraint is applied immediately to data when that data is modified or whether the application of the constraint is deferred until later in the transaction.
- **SAVEPOINT** Creates a savepoint within a transaction. A *savepoint* marks a place within the transaction that acts as a stopping point when you roll back a transaction.
- **RELEASE SAVEPOINT** Releases a savepoint.
- **ROLLBACK** Terminates a transaction and rolls back any changes to the beginning of the transaction or to a savepoint.
- **COMMIT** Terminates a transaction and commits all changes to the database.

Although we'll be looking at all seven statements in more detail, some of them are pivotal in understanding the nature of a transaction. Let's take a look at Figure 17-1 to help illustrate this point.

Notice that the figure includes four of the SQL transaction-related statements: SET TRANSACTION, START TRANSACTION, COMMIT, and ROLLBACK. If a SET TRANSACTION statement is used, it is executed before the transaction begins. After that, a START TRANSACTION statement begins the transaction.

NOTE

As you'll see later in this chapter, it would be rare in a pure SQL environment that you would want to use both the SET TRANSACTION and START TRANSACTION statements because both statements set the same properties. However, you'll find that SQL implementations vary with regard to which transaction-related statements they support and how they implement those statements. Specific differences are pointed out throughout this chapter.

When you start the transaction, the database is in its original state—the data is consistent and correct. Next the SQL statements within the transaction are processed. If

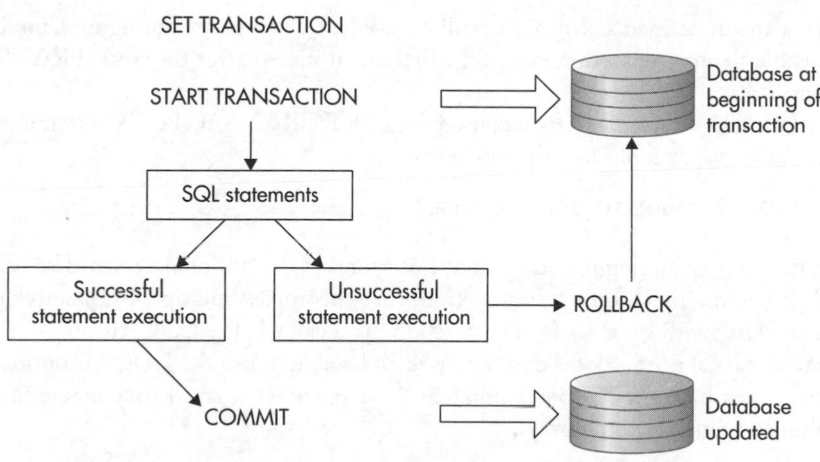

Figure 17-1 A basic SQL transaction

this process is successful, a COMMIT statement is executed. The COMMIT statement causes the SQL implementation to update the database and terminate the transaction. If the statement-execution process is not successful, a ROLLBACK statement is executed, and the implementation returns the database to its original state. An unsuccessful execution does not necessarily mean that the statements have failed. A ROLLBACK statement can be executed according to the conditions of a WHERE clause, a predefined error, or whatever other conditions are defined within the transaction. The point is, under certain circumstances, the ROLLBACK statement is executed and under other circumstances, the COMMIT statement is executed.

Set Transaction Properties

The first statement that we'll look at in detail is the SET TRANSACTION statement. The SET TRANSACTION statement allows you to configure several of the properties associated with transaction processing. You can execute this statement only when no transactions are active (or in the case of Oracle, only as the first statement after a COMMIT or ROLLBACK). When you do use a SET TRANSACTION statement, the settings configured within the statement are applied only to the next transaction that is initiated. The settings do not carry over from one transaction to the next.

The SET TRANSACTION statement is not required in order to initiate a transaction. If the statement is not executed, the transaction uses either the default settings or the settings supplied in the subsequent START TRANSACTION statement. If the SET TRANSACTION statement is executed, the transaction uses the settings specified in that statement. If the statement is executed but not all settings are defined, the transaction uses the defaults for the undefined settings. Regardless of which settings are configured, none of them are applicable to any transaction except the first one initiated after the SET TRANSACTION is executed.

Now let's take a look at the syntax used for a SET TRANSACTION statement. At its most basic, the syntax looks like the following:

```
SET [ LOCAL ] TRANSACTION <mode> [ { , <mode> } . . . ]
```

The first thing you might notice about this syntax is the optional keyword LOCAL. The LOCAL keyword applies only to transactions that encompass multiple SQL implementations. If you're working with these sorts of transactions, you can use the LOCAL option to apply settings to the local portion of the transaction. To be able to use the LOCAL option, the transaction must have been initiated on an SQL server other than the one where the local transaction settings are configured.

NOTE

The subject of encompassing transactions and local settings is beyond the scope of this book. I mention them here only to provide you with a complete picture of the SET TRANSACTION statement. As a beginning SQL programmer, you will most likely not be concerned with encompassing transactions. Furthermore, support of encompassing transactions varies across SQL implementations. For example, Oracle does not support them, and while MySQL does, it uses the terms global and session.

Returning to the SET TRANSACTION syntax, you can see that the only other type of option you need to specify is the one represented by the <mode> placeholder. There are three types of transaction modes you can specify:

- Access level
- Isolation level
- Diagnostics size

You must specify one or more transaction modes. If you specify more than one, you must separate them with commas. In addition, you cannot include more than one of any type of transaction mode. For example, you can specify an access level and an isolation level, but you cannot specify two isolation levels.

The SET TRANSACTION statement supports two access level options: READ ONLY and READ WRITE. If you select the READ ONLY option, you cannot include any statements within the transaction that modify the database. This includes statements that modify data (such as the UPDATE statement) and statements that modify the database structure (such as the CREATE TABLE statement). If you select the READ WRITE option, you can execute both types of statements in your transaction. As you will see in the next section, "Specifying an Isolation Level," the default access level depends on the isolation level. However, if no isolation level and no access level are specified, the default access level is READ WRITE.

Specifying an Isolation Level

When you create a SET TRANSACTION statement, you can specify zero or one isolation levels. An isolation level defines how isolated a transaction will be from the actions of other transactions. A SET TRANSACTION statement supports four isolation level options:

- READ UNCOMMITTED
- READ COMMITTED
- REPEATABLE READ
- SERIALIZABLE

The isolation levels are listed from least restrictive to most restrictive, with the READ UNCOMMITTED option being less effective in terms of isolating data, and the SERIALIZABLE option the most effective. If no isolation level is specified, SERIALIZABLE is assumed.

NOTE

Support for isolation levels varies across SQL implementations. For example, Oracle supports only the READ COMMITTED and SERIALIZABLE options, while SQL Server supports all four of the options defined in the SQL Standard, plus it adds a new one called SNAPSHOT that provides read consistency for all statements in a transaction as of the start of the transaction.

Data Phenomena

The best way to understand isolation levels is to take a look at the basic types of phenomena that can occur to data, depending on how isolated one transaction is from another. In general, three types of phenomena can occur:

- Dirty reads
- Nonrepeatable reads
- Phantom reads

The type of data phenomena that you might experience during a transaction depends on which isolation level you configure for your transaction. However, before we get into any more specifications about isolation levels, let's take a look at these three types of phenomena.

Dirty Reads The first phenomenon that we'll look at is the dirty read. A *dirty read* can occur when one transaction modifies data, a second transaction sees those modifications before they're actually committed to the database, and the first transaction rolls back the modifications, returning the database to its original state. However, the second transaction, having read the modified data, might have taken action based on the incorrect data. To help illustrate the concept of a dirty read, let's take a look at Figure 17-2, which shows two transactions operating concurrently.

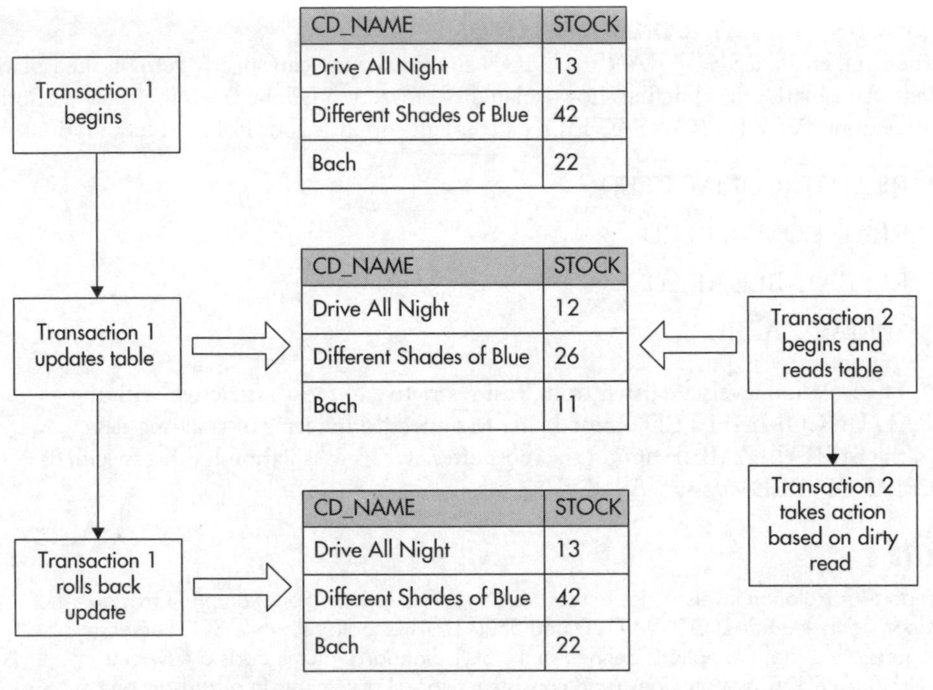

Figure 17-2 Concurrent transactions resulting in a dirty read

When Transaction 1 first begins, it reads the table in its original state. The transaction then updates the table, changing the STOCK value of each row. After those changes are made, Transaction 2 is initiated and reads the updated data. For example, Transaction 2 will see that the STOCK value for the Bach row is 11. Based on that information, Transaction 2 takes some sort of action, such as ordering additional Bach CDs. After Transaction 2 has read the table data, Transaction 1, for one reason or another, rolls back the update, and the database is returned to its original state. As a result, the Bach row actually has a STOCK value of 22, even though Transaction 2 thought that it had a value of 11. Transaction 2, then, is said to have experienced a dirty read.

Nonrepeatable Reads The next phenomenon that can occur when concurrent transactions are initiated is the nonrepeatable read. The *nonrepeatable read* can occur when one transaction reads data from a table, another transaction then updates that data, and the first transaction rereads the data, only to discover that the data has changed. As a result, the first read is not repeatable. Let's take a look at Figure 17-3 to better understand this concept.

When Transaction 1 is initiated, it reads the data in the table. At that point, the transaction might be involved in other processes or is waiting for a response from a user. For example, the user might receive a call from a manager who is trying to find out how many copies of a particular CD are in stock. The user checks for that information. The manager then puts the

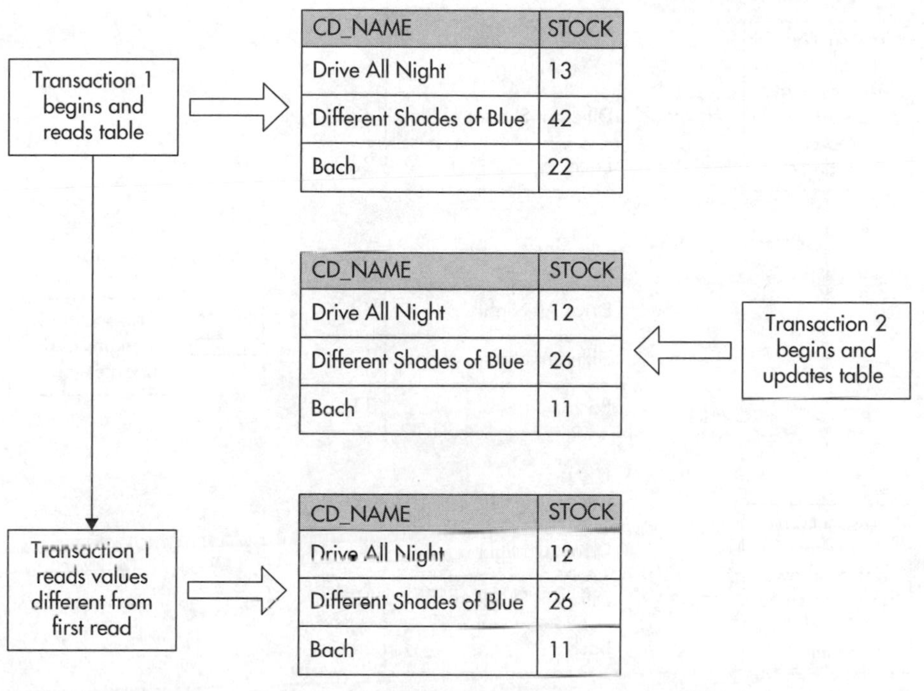

Figure 17-3 Concurrent transactions resulting in a nonrepeatable read

user on hold for a short time, so the user must wait to complete the transaction. During that time, Transaction 2 is initiated and it updates the table. After the update, Transaction 1 again reads the data (the manager returns to the phone) and finds different information from the first read, resulting in a nonrepeatable read.

Phantom Reads The last phenomenon that we'll look at is the phantom read. Although similar to the nonrepeatable read, the phantom read has some subtle differences, which are factors when trying to determine an isolation level. A *phantom read* can occur when a transaction reads a table based on some sort of search condition, then a second transaction updates the data in the table, and then the first transaction attempts to reread the data, only this time different rows are returned because of how the search condition is defined. To clarify this, let's take a look at Figure 17-4.

When Transaction 1 is initiated, it reads the data in the table by executing a SELECT statement that queries the data. The statement includes a WHERE clause that returns only those rows with a STOCK value greater than 20. That means that the Different Shades of Blue row and the Bach row are returned. After Transaction 1 retrieves (reads) the data, Transaction 2 begins and updates the table. Now when Transaction 1 rereads the data (using the same search criteria), only the Drive All Night row is returned because it is now the only

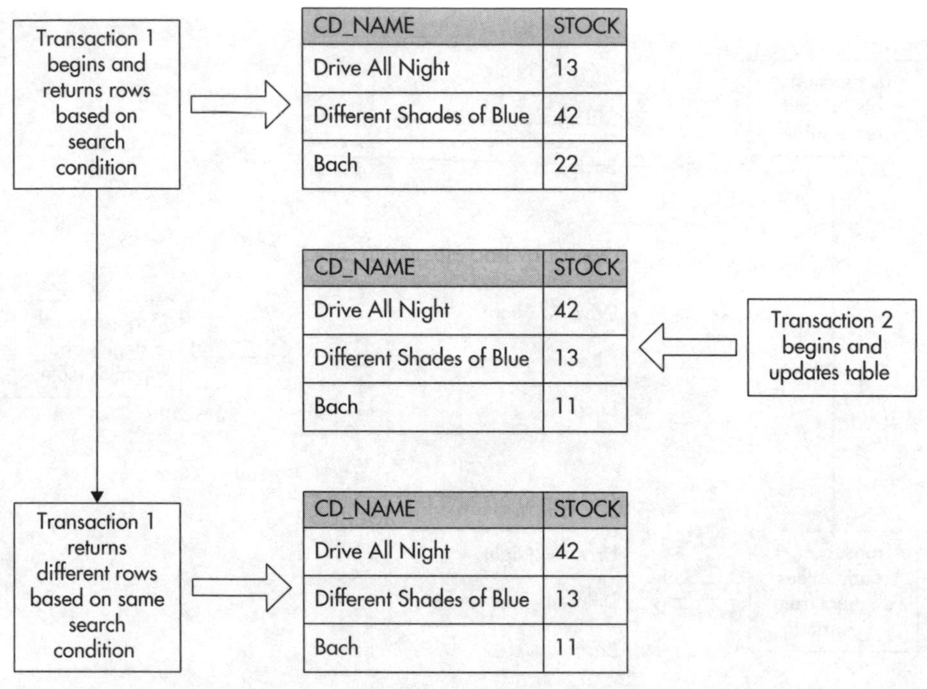

Figure 17-4 Concurrent transactions resulting in a phantom read

row with a STOCK value greater than 20. As a result, the transaction has experienced a phantom read; the rows that it's reading are not the same rows as it saw earlier.

Choosing an Isolation Level

Now that you have an overview of the type of data phenomena that you can run into when you have concurrent transactions, you should be better equipped to choose an isolation level for your transaction. The important point to remember is that the more restrictive the isolation level, the more types of phenomena you can eliminate.

Let's take a look at the READ UNCOMMITTED isolation level, the least restrictive of the four levels. A transaction that's configured with this option may experience any of the data phenomena that we've looked at (dirty read, nonrepeatable read, and phantom read). As you can imagine, this is normally not a desirable state. In fact, if you define a transaction with the READ UNCOMMITTED option, the transaction cannot include statements that modify data. These transactions, by default, have a READ ONLY access level, and you cannot specify a READ WRITE level. (All other isolation levels have a default access level of READ WRITE.) You should use the READ UNCOMMITTED isolation level only for transactions that generate approximate information, such as some types of statistical data in which the results are not critical in terms of precise accuracy.

The READ COMMITTED isolation level is only slightly more restrictive than READ UNCOMMITTED. The READ COMMITTED option prevents dirty reads, but nonrepeatable reads and phantom reads can still occur. The next option, REPEATABLE READ, is even more restrictive than READ COMMITTED. It prevents dirty reads and nonrepeatable reads, but does not prevent phantom reads. The only option that prevents all three types of data anomalies is SERIALIZABLE.

A transaction that is defined with the SERIALIZABLE isolation level fully isolates that transaction from all other transactions. As a result, the transaction is said to be *serializable,* meaning that it interacts with concurrent transactions in a way that orders transactions sequentially so that one transaction cannot impact the other. This does not mean that one transaction must close before another can open, but it does mean that the results of those transactions have to be the same as the results of operations that do operate one at a time. As long as no serializable transaction can influence another serializable transaction, the transactions are in conformance to the SERIALIZABLE isolation level.

Table 17-1 provides an overview of the phenomena that can occur for each isolation level. For example, notice that for the READ UNCOMMITTED option, it's possible that all three data anomalies can occur.

As you can see from the table, the SERIALIZABLE isolation level provides the greatest data protection, and the READ UNCOMMITTED isolation level provides the least protection. This is why SERIALIZABLE is the default isolation level if no other level is defined.

NOTE

You may be wondering why you don't simply use the SERIALIZABLE isolation level for all transactions. There is a trade-off: the more restrictive the isolation level, the greater the effect on performance, so although you want to be sure to use an isolation level restrictive enough to meet your needs, you don't want to define a level that's more restrictive than necessary.

Specifying a Diagnostics Size

As you'll recall from the SET TRANSACTION syntax, one type of transaction mode that you can define is the diagnostics size. The diagnostics size refers to a diagnostics area that is used

Isolation Level	Dirty Read	Nonrepeatable Read	Phantom Read
READ UNCOMMITTED	Yes	Yes	Yes
READ COMMITTED	No	Yes	Yes
REPEATABLE READ	No	No	Yes
SERIALIZABLE	No	No	No

Table 17-1 Possible Data Anomalies for Isolation Levels

for conditions raised when an SQL statement is executed. A *condition* is a warning, exception, or other type of message generated by a statement execution. The diagnostics size actually refers to the number of conditions that will be stored for the execution of an SQL statement. For example, if the diagnostics size is 10, up to 10 conditions will be stored for the executed statement. If more than 10 conditions are raised for that statement, only 10 conditions are saved to the diagnostics area.

NOTE

You cannot assume that any specific conditions will be saved to the diagnostics area if more conditions are raised than the number defined by the diagnostics size. For example, if the diagnostics size is 15 and your statement raises 20 conditions, you cannot assume that the first 15 or last 15 conditions will be recorded. For more information on how conditions are handled for your particular SQL implementation, see the product documentation. Incidentally, the use of SET TRANSACTION to set diagnostics size is not supported by SQL Server, Oracle, MySQL, or most other current SQL implementations.

If you do not specify a diagnostics size in your SET TRANSACTION statement, the SQL implementation determines the size of the diagnostics area.

Creating a SET TRANSACTION Statement

Now that you've looked at the various components of the SET TRANSACTION statement, let's take a look at a couple of examples. The first example defines a transaction with an access level of READ ONLY, an isolation level of READ UNCOMMITTED, and a diagnostics size of 5:

```
SET TRANSACTION
     READ ONLY,
     ISOLATION LEVEL READ UNCOMMITTED,
     DIAGNOSTICS SIZE 5;
```

Notice that the transaction modes are separated by commas. Also notice that the isolation level option includes the keywords ISOLATION LEVEL, and the diagnostics size option includes the keywords DIAGNOSTICS SIZE. The transaction is configured with the least restrictive isolation level, which is why the access level must be READ ONLY. You cannot define a READ WRITE access level for this statement. Because the isolation level is READ COMMITTED, the statement does not have to specify the READ ONLY access level—it would have been assumed. However, including it causes no problems and better documents the code.

In the next example, the SET TRANSACTION statement defines a transaction with an access level of READ WRITE, an isolation level of SERIALIZABLE, and a diagnostics size of 8:

```
SET TRANSACTION
    READ WRITE,
```

```
    ISOLATION LEVEL SERIALIZABLE,
    DIAGNOSTICS SIZE 8;
```

Because SERIALIZABLE is the default isolation level, you do not have to specify it in your SET TRANSACTION statement. In addition, because the READ WRITE access level is the default level for serializable transactions, you do not have to specify that either. Your statement, then, might have looked like the following:

```
SET TRANSACTION
    DIAGNOSTICS SIZE 8;
```

This SET TRANSACTION statement will produce the same results as the preceding one.

As you can see, the SET TRANSACTION statement is a relatively simple statement to execute. However, be sure to check the documentation for your SQL implementation to determine the exact syntax used to set transaction properties. For example, SQL Server supports a SET TRANSACTION ISOLATION LEVEL statement that allows you to set only the isolation level. You cannot set the access level or diagnostics size. Oracle, on the other hand, supports a SET TRANSACTION statement that allows you to set a transaction's access and isolation level (but not a diagnostics size) and assign the transaction to a rollback segment. Similarly, MySQL supports a SET TRANSACTION statement that allows you to set a transaction's access and isolation level (but again without a diagnostics size). However, MySQL supports transactions only for tables defined to use the InnoDB storage engine, which is the default starting with MySQL 5.5. (Storage engines are unique to MySQL and not mentioned in the SQL standard. Consult your MySQL documentation for more details.)

Start a Transaction

In SQL, a transaction can be started either implicitly or explicitly. A transaction starts implicitly when certain types of SQL statements are executed, such as the SELECT, DELETE, UPDATE, and CREATE TABLE statements. These types of statements must be executed within the context of a transaction. If a transaction is not active, one is initiated.

Transactions can also be initiated explicitly by using the START TRANSACTION statement. The START TRANSACTION statement serves two purposes: to set the transaction's properties, and to initiate the transaction. In terms of setting the properties, the START TRANSACTION statement works just like the SET TRANSACTION statement. You can set the access level, the isolation level, and the diagnostics size. As for initiating a transaction, you simply execute the START TRANSACTION statement.

The syntax for the START TRANSACTION statement is similar to the SET TRANSACTION statement, as you can see in the following syntax:

```
START TRANSACTION <mode> [ { , <mode> } . . . ]
```

After you specify the START TRANSACTION keywords, you must specify one or more transaction modes. As with the SET TRANSACTION statement, you can include only one mode for each type.

Now let's take a look at an example that defines an access level of READ ONLY, an isolation level of READ UNCOMMITTED, and a diagnostics size of 5:

```
START TRANSACTION
      READ ONLY,
      ISOLATION LEVEL READ UNCOMMITTED,
      DIAGNOSTICS SIZE 5;
```

As you can see, this looks almost identical to a SET TRANSACTION statement. The transaction modes are applied in the same way, and if more than one transaction mode is specified, they're separated with commas. The basic difference between a START TRANSACTION statement and a SET TRANSACTION statement is that the START TRANSACTION statement will initiate the transaction and set its properties.

NOTE

The START TRANSACTION statement was added to SQL with the release of SQL:1999. As a result, not all SQL implementations support a START TRANSACTION statement or any statement that explicitly initiates a transaction. Transactions in Oracle, for example, can only be initiated implicitly. On the other hand, SQL Server supports a BEGIN TRANSACTION statement, but it does not allow you to define any transaction modes. MySQL supports a START TRANSACTION statement that closely follows the standard.

Ask the Expert

Q: Does it matter whether your transaction includes data definition language (DDL) statements or data manipulation language statements?

A: SQL allows you to include both types of statements in your transaction, but this is not the case for all SQL implementations. Some implementations do not allow you to mix the two types of statements in a single transaction. Other products allow you to mix the two types of statements, but limit which statements can be combined in one transaction. And still other implementations do not allow data definition language statements to be executed within the context of a transaction. For example, Oracle implicitly ends any current transaction when it encounters a DDL statement, and never handles DDL as part of a transaction. The restrictions that various implementations place on mixing statement types can vary widely. The reason for this is that the interactions between the two types of statements can be complicated, so each implementation determines what statement mixtures it will support in its own database environment. Be sure to check the product documentation to determine what types of statements can be included in a transaction and how they can be mixed.

Set Constraint Deferability

There can be times in a transaction when you want to modify data in a table that temporarily violates a constraint placed on that table. For example, you might have a table that includes a column configured with the NOT NULL constraint. It is possible that, during the course of the transaction, you want to insert a row in the table but don't yet have a value for the NOT NULL column. For this reason, the SQL standard allows you to define a constraint as deferrable. That means that the constraint does not have to be applied to the data immediately (when the modifying SQL statement is executed); it can be postponed until a later point in a transaction, such as after you were able to insert a value into the NOT NULL column.

If a constraint is defined as deferrable, you can use the SET CONSTRAINTS statement within the transaction to defer the application of the constraint or to apply the constraint immediately. (Defining a constraint as deferrable doesn't automatically defer the application of that constraint. You must still explicitly defer it within the transaction.) If you explicitly defer a constraint, you can then temporarily violate the deferred constraint until the constraint is explicitly applied or the transaction ends. For a better understanding of how this works, let's take a look at Figure 17-5.

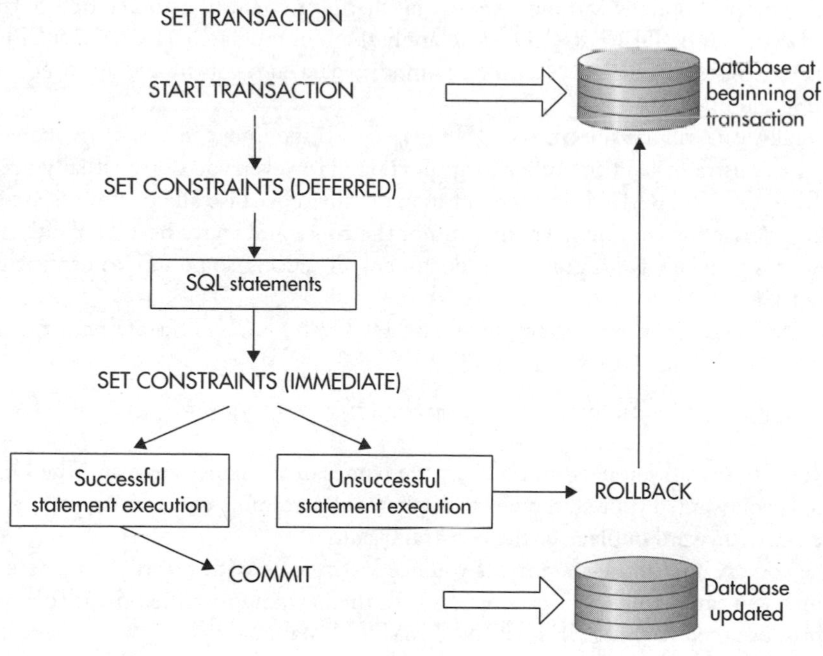

Figure 17-5 Deferring constraints in a transaction

In this illustration, you'll notice that after the transaction has been started, you can set the constraints to deferred. You don't have to defer the constraints right after the transaction starts, but you must defer them before executing any SQL statements that could violate the constraints. Once the applicable SQL statements have been executed and you're sure that no SQL data violates any of the deferred constraints, you can then apply the constraints to the applicable data. If the constraints are violated at this point, the transaction is considered unsuccessful and any updates are rolled back. Otherwise, the updates are committed to the database.

In order to defer or apply the constraints within a transaction, you must use the SET CONSTRAINTS statement, as shown in the following syntax:

```
SET CONSTRAINTS { ALL | <constraint names> }
{ DEFERRED | IMMEDIATE }
```

As you can see from the syntax, you must choose from two sets of options. The first set of options allows you to specify the deferrable constraints that will be affected by the statement. If the statement should apply to all deferrable constraints, you can use the ALL keyword; otherwise, you must list the constraint names, separated by a comma. You can specify only deferrable constraints in the SET CONSTRAINTS statement.

The next set of options you must specify is whether to defer the application of the identified constraints (DEFERRED) or to apply them immediately (IMMEDIATE). You should defer constraints before you insert or modify data, and you should apply constraints after you've modified that data.

Normally, you will use the SET CONSTRAINTS statement in sets of two: one statement to defer the constraints and the other to apply them. However, you don't actually need to use the SET CONSTRAINTS statement to apply them because all constraints are applied before the transaction commits, whether or not the constraints have been explicitly applied. However, it is generally good practice to document all actions, so be sure to explicitly apply your constraints.

Now let's take a look at an example of a SET CONSTRAINTS statement that defers CONSTRAINT_1 and CONSTRAINT_2:

```
SET CONSTRAINTS CONSTRAINT_1, CONSTRAINT_2 DEFERRED;
```

As you can see, all you need to do is list the names of the constraints and the DEFERRED keyword. If you wanted your statement to apply to all deferrable constraints, you could have used the ALL keyword in place of the constraint names.

Once you execute all the statements you need to execute with regard to the deferred constraints, you can then apply the constraints to the new and modified data. To apply the constraints, use the following SET CONSTRAINTS statement:

```
SET CONSTRAINTS CONSTRAINT_1, CONSTRAINT_2 IMMEDIATE;
```

The only difference between this statement and the one that preceded this is that the IMMEDIATE keyword is used rather than DEFERRED.

NOTE

In order for you to use the SET CONSTRAINTS statement, your SQL implementation must support both the statement (or a similar statement) and deferrable constraints. If you cannot define deferrable constraints in your SQL database, the statement is not very useful. Oracle currently supports the SET CONSTRAINTS statement, but MySQL and SQL Server do not.

Create Savepoints in a Transaction

Often when you're setting up your transactions, you'll find that the set of actions you need to perform is straightforward and easily treated as a unit. However, there might be times when some of your transactions are not as simple as others, and different degrees of complexity between actions makes treating them as one unit a little more difficult, even though you still want to keep them all within the same transaction. One way to deal with this type of situation is through the use of *savepoints,* which are designated markers within your transaction that act as rollback points for portions of your transaction.

NOTE

Support for savepoints varies across SQL implementations. Oracle and MySQL support the SAVEPOINT statement, but SQL Server uses a SAVE TRANSACTION statement instead.

Say, for example, that the first part of your transaction contains relatively straightforward code that, although not particularly complicated, can still demand a heavy load on your system's performance. Now suppose that later in your transaction you must perform more complex actions, actions that are more likely to cause a rollback than the first set of actions. However, you don't want your rollbacks to cause you to lose the work performed by the first set of actions because of the hit on performance. If you insert a savepoint between the two sets of actions and then the second set needs to be rolled back, it will roll back only to the savepoint rather than to the beginning of the transaction, thus making it unnecessary to perform the first set of actions over again. To help illustrate how savepoints work, let's take a look at Figure 17-6.

As you can see from the diagram, a savepoint can be inserted wherever you want to preserve a set of actions. Any changes made prior to the savepoint are preserved. In this case, two savepoints have been defined, each after a set of SQL statements has been successfully executed. If a rollback is necessary at any point after the savepoint has been defined, the database can be rolled back to that savepoint, without having to go back to the beginning of the transaction, and the actions prior to the savepoint will not have to be repeated. In addition, SQL allows you to name savepoints so that, if necessary, you can roll back the transaction to a specific savepoint rather than to the one directly preceding the rollback. As a result, you can be more specific about which operations to preserve and which to roll back in the event that problems arise in your transaction.

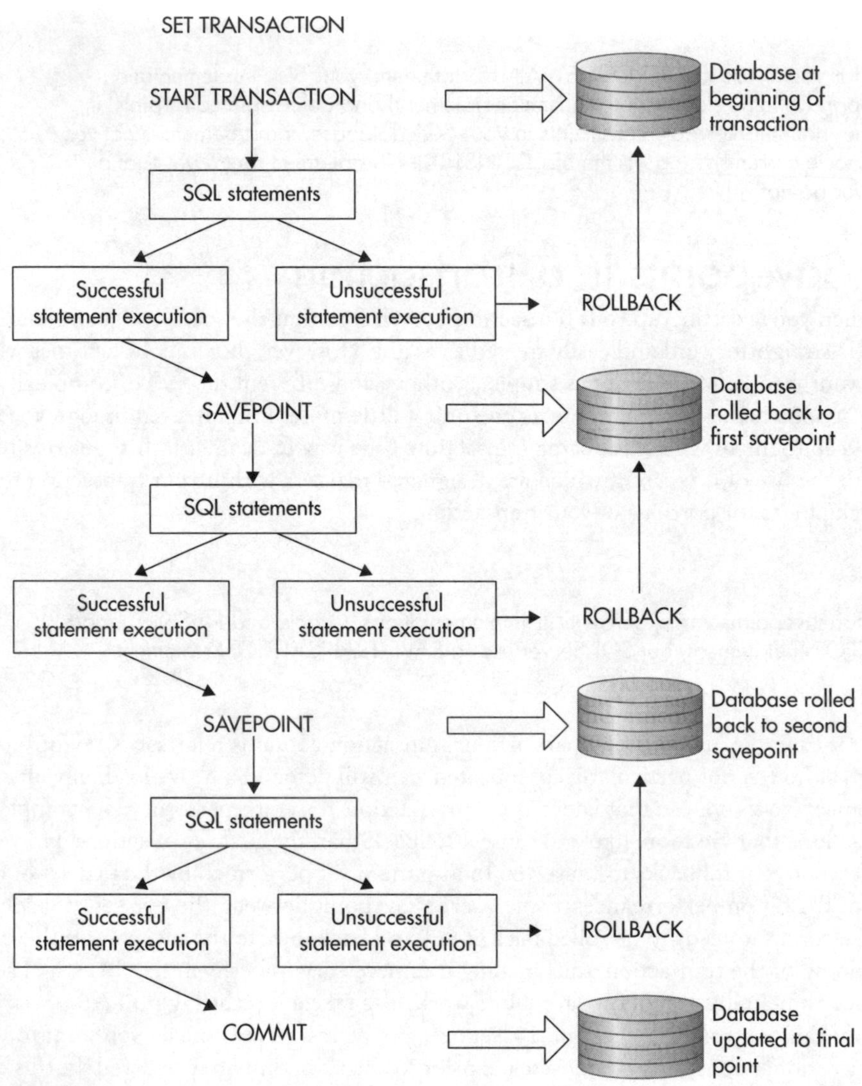

Figure 17-6 Deferring constraints in a transaction

NOTE

As you'll see in the "Terminate a Transaction" section later in this chapter, a transaction is rolled back to a savepoint only if the savepoint is identified in the ROLLBACK statement. Otherwise, the entire transaction is rolled back, the transaction is terminated, and the database is returned to its original state before the transaction was initiated.

Creating a savepoint in your transaction is very simple, as shown in the following syntax:

```
SAVEPOINT <savepoint name>
```

All you need to do is use the SAVEPOINT keyword, followed by a name for the savepoint. For example, to create a savepoint named SECTION_1, you would use the following statement:

```
SAVEPOINT SECTION_1;
```

Once the savepoint is created, you can use the SECTION_1 name to identify the savepoint later in your transaction.

Releasing a Savepoint

After some operations within a transaction, you might find that you want to release a savepoint. If a savepoint is released, you can no longer roll back the transaction to that savepoint. Releasing a savepoint removes it from the transaction. In addition, all savepoints defined subsequent to the released savepoint are released. This means that if your transaction includes three savepoints and you release the first savepoint, all three are removed from the transaction. The syntax used to release a savepoint is as follows:

```
RELEASE SAVEPOINT <savepoint name>
```

As you can see, this statement is similar to the SAVEPOINT statement. For example, to release the savepoint created in the preceding example, you would use the following statement:

```
RELEASE SAVEPOINT SECTION_1;
```

When you execute this statement, the SECTION_1 savepoint is removed from the transaction, along with any other savepoints defined subsequent to the SECTION_1 savepoint. MySQL 5.7 supports the RELEASE SAVEPOINT statement, but Oracle 12*c* and SQL Server do not.

Terminate a Transaction

Earlier in this chapter, you learned that a transaction can be initiated either explicitly or implicitly. The same thing is true for ending a transaction. You can explicitly commit or roll back a transaction, which then terminates the transaction, or the transaction is terminated implicitly when circumstances force that termination.

In SQL, there are four primary circumstances that will terminate a transaction:

- A ROLLBACK statement is explicitly defined in the transaction. When the statement is executed, actions are undone, the database is returned to the state it was in when the transaction was initiated, and the transaction is terminated. If the ROLLBACK statement references a savepoint, only the actions taken after the savepoint are undone, and the transaction is not terminated.

- A COMMIT statement is explicitly defined in the transaction. When the statement is executed, all transaction-related changes are saved to the database, and the transaction is terminated.
- The program that initiated the transaction is interrupted, causing the program to abort. In the event of an abnormal interruption, which can be the result of hardware or software problems, all changes are rolled back, the database is returned to its original state, and the transaction is terminated. A transaction terminated in this way is similar to terminating a transaction by using a ROLLBACK statement.
- The program successfully completes its execution. All transaction-related changes are saved to the database, and the transaction is terminated. Once these changes are committed, they cannot be rolled back. A transaction terminated in this way is similar to terminating a transaction by using a COMMIT statement.

As you can see, the ROLLBACK and COMMIT statements allow you to explicitly terminate a transaction, whereas a transaction is terminated implicitly when the program ends or is interrupted. These methods of termination ensure that data integrity is maintained and the database is protected. No changes are made to the database unless the transaction is complete.

Now let's take a closer look at the two statements that you can use to explicitly end a transaction.

Committing a Transaction

Once all the statements have been executed in a transaction, the transaction must be terminated. The preferable type of termination is one that commits all the changes to the database. After all, why try to make changes if you don't want to commit them? To explicitly commit the changes and end the transaction, you must use the COMMIT statement, as shown in the following syntax:

```
COMMIT [ WORK ]  [ AND [ NO ] CHAIN ]
```

At its most basic, the COMMIT statement requires only the COMMIT keyword. All other statement elements are optional. If you want, you can include the WORK keyword, which is simply a carryover from earlier versions of SQL. In other words, COMMIT and COMMIT WORK perform the same function. The only reason to use the WORK keyword is if your SQL implementation requires it.

The next optional element in the COMMIT statement is the AND CHAIN clause, which is not widely supported in current SQL implementations. The clause tells the system to start a new transaction as soon as the current transaction ends. The new transaction uses the same transaction modes as the current transaction. If you use the AND CHAIN option, you do not need to use the SET TRANSACTION or the START TRANSACTION statements for the next transaction unless you want to specify different modes.

Rather than specify AND CHAIN in your COMMIT statement, you can specify AND NO CHAIN, which tells your system not to start a new transaction based on the settings of the current transaction. If AND NO CHAIN is specified, a new transaction will not be initiated automatically when the current transaction is terminated. You must start a new transaction by using an implicit method or explicit method. If neither the AND CHAIN clause nor the AND NO CHAIN clause is specified, AND NO CHAIN is assumed.

In all likelihood, your commit statement will look like the one in the following example:

```
COMMIT;
```

As you can see, the COMMIT keyword is the only required element. However, if you want a new transaction to be initiated after the current one, you should use the following COMMIT statement:

```
COMMIT AND CHAIN;
```

If you don't want a new transaction to be initiated, do not include the AND CHAIN clause.

Rolling Back a Transaction

Although the goal of any transaction is to commit the changes made by the statements in that transaction, there will no doubt be times when you want to roll back those changes. To be able to control these rollbacks, you must use a ROLLBACK statement to undo changes and terminate the transaction or to undo changes back to a specified savepoint. The following syntax shows the various elements that can be included in a ROLLBACK statement:

```
ROLLBACK [ WORK ] [ AND [ NO ] CHAIN ]
[ TO SAVEPOINT <savepoint name> ]
```

The first line of syntax is very similar to the COMMIT statement. You must specify the ROLLBACK keyword. In addition, you can specify WORK, AND CHAIN, or AND NO CHAIN, all of which work the same way they did in the COMMIT statement, with AND NO CHAIN once again being the default.

However, the ROLLBACK statement, unlike the COMMIT statement, includes the optional TO SAVEPOINT clause. The TO SAVEPOINT clause specifies a savepoint that is used if changes have to be rolled back. This applies to any changes made after the specified savepoint. If you include the TO SAVEPOINT clause in your ROLLBACK statement, the transaction will be rolled back to the savepoint, but it will not be terminated. If the TO SAVEPOINT clause is not included, all changes are rolled back and the transaction is terminated.

The most basic type of ROLLBACK statement is one that includes no optional elements, as in the following example:

```
ROLLBACK;
```

You could have included the WORK keyword and the AND NO CHAIN clause, and the statement would have performed the same function. If you want a new transaction to be initiated when the current transaction is terminated, you must specify the AND CHAIN clause. Keep in mind, however, that you cannot specify the AND CHAIN clause and the TO SAVEPOINT clause because AND CHAIN relies on the transaction being terminated in order to start a new transaction.

If you do specify the TO SAVEPOINT clause, you must include the name of the savepoint. For example, the following ROLLBACK statement specifies the SECTION_1 savepoint:

```
ROLLBACK TO SAVEPOINT SECTION_1;
```

If this statement is executed, all changes that occurred after the SECTION_1 savepoint was created are rolled back to the state the database was in when the SAVEPOINT statement was executed. Even if other savepoints were created after the SECTION_1 savepoint, changes are still rolled back to SECTION_1.

Ask the Expert

Q: Are there any performance implications to using transactions?

A: Indeed there are. The DBMS must carefully log the effects of every SQL statement inside a transaction so that changes can be rolled back when needed. And it is possible to fill the memory areas set aside for tracking transactions. To counter this, SQL programmers sometimes break processes that apply lots of changes to the database into multiple transactions using commits. Check your DBMS documentation to see if there are restrictions on using commits during program loops, particularly when cursors are open.

Q: Earlier in the chapter, you state that statements such as the SELECT, DELETE, UPDATE, and CREATE TABLE statements must be executed within the context of a transaction. However, we have not been using transactions in the examples and Try This exercises throughout the book. When are transactions used?

A: Throughout the book, we have been using interactive SQL (direct invocation) to communicate with the database. Most of the SQL statements that we have been executing within this environment have been done within the context of a transaction, even though you weren't aware of that happening. For most SQL implementations, each SQL statement is considered its own transaction, a processing mode that is often called autocommit. When you execute the statement, a transaction is initiated. If the statement is successful, any changes made are committed to the database and the transaction is terminated, in much the same way as if you had executed a COMMIT statement. If the statement is not successful, the changes are rolled back, the database is returned to the state it was in when the statement was first executed, and the transaction is terminated as though you executed a ROLLBACK statement. Although interactive SQL tends to treat each statement as its own transaction, you can usually execute transaction-related statements in this environment. However, which statements you can execute and what options they support vary from product to product, so make sure you check the documentation. In general, it is not necessary to specifically define a transaction in interactive SQL.

Try This 17-1 Working with Transactions

In this Try This exercise you will create several transactions that execute statements against the INVENTORY database. For each transaction, you will explicitly start the transaction and execute one or more SQL statements. For this exercise, you will work with the COMMIT statement and ROLLBACK statement in separate transactions because you're working with directly invoked SQL (in your client application). However, if you were initiating transactions from within an application programming language, you would no doubt be using COMMIT and ROLLBACK together in some sort of conditional structure. In that way, certain results would cause the transaction to roll back, and other results would cause the transaction to commit, depending on how you set up the conditions in the programming language. However, for this exercise, we keep them separate so that you can effectively run through these steps. You can download the Try_This_17.txt file, which contains the SQL statements used in this exercise.

Step by Step

1. Open the client application for your RDBMS and connect to the INVENTORY database.
2. The first transaction that you'll create uses a START TRANSACTION statement to set the isolation level to READ UNCOMMITTED, retrieves information from the ARTISTS table, and then commits the transaction. Enter and execute the following SQL transaction:

   ```
   START TRANSACTION
         ISOLATION LEVEL READ UNCOMMITTED;

   SELECT *
     FROM ARTISTS;

   COMMIT;
   ```

   The transaction should return all the rows and columns from the ARTISTS table.
3. The next transaction that you'll create also uses a START TRANSACTION statement to set the isolation level. But this time you'll be setting the level to SERIALIZABLE. Because SERIALIZABLE is the default, you aren't required to define it; however, for the purposes of this exercise, we're going to include it. After you start the transaction, you'll attempt to update the COMPACT_DISCS table by increasing the IN_STOCK value by 2 for all rows with a LABEL_ID value equal to 827. After the UPDATE statement, you'll roll back the

(continued)

transaction so that no data is modified in the database. Enter and execute the following SQL transaction:

```
START TRANSACTION
      ISOLATION LEVEL SERIALIZABLE;

UPDATE COMPACT_DISCS
   SET IN_STOCK = IN_STOCK + 2
 WHERE LABEL_ID = 827;

ROLLBACK;
```

You should receive some sort of message acknowledging the termination of the transaction.

4. Now you'll confirm that the update you attempted in the preceding step was indeed rolled back. Enter and execute the following SQL statement:

```
SELECT CD_TITLE, IN_STOCK
  FROM COMPACT_DISCS
 WHERE LABEL_ID = 827;
```

The SELECT statement should return the following query results:

```
CD_TITLE                        IN_STOCK
----------------------------    --------
Innervisions (Remastered)       16
The Definitive Collection       34
```

The IN_STOCK values shown in these results are what were contained in the COMPACT_DISCS table before you executed the transaction. If the transaction had not been rolled back, each of these values would have been increased by 2.

5. Now you're going to add a savepoint to the transaction we created in the previous step. You want to be sure to reference the savepoint in the ROLLBACK statement. You will also add a SELECT statement before the savepoint. Enter and execute the following SQL transaction:

```
START TRANSACTION ISOLATION LEVEL SERIALIZABLE;

SELECT CD_TITLE, IN_STOCK
  FROM COMPACT_DISCS
 WHERE LABEL_ID = 827;

SAVEPOINT SECTION_1;

UPDATE COMPACT_DISCS
   SET IN_STOCK = IN_STOCK + 2
 WHERE LABEL_ID = 827;

ROLLBACK TO SAVEPOINT SECTION_1;
```

Now your transaction will roll back only to the point preceding the UPDATE statement. In addition, because your transaction included a SELECT statement, you should receive the query results that you received in the previous step.

6. In the preceding transaction, the SELECT statement came before the savepoint, which means that the SELECT statement was executed before the UPDATE statement. If the transaction did not roll back the update, the query results would not reflect the correct information. As a result, you should verify that the UPDATE statement was rolled back. Enter and execute the following SQL statement:

```
SELECT CD_TITLE, IN_STOCK
  FROM COMPACT_DISCS
 WHERE LABEL_ID = 827;
```

   Your query results should show the same IN_STOCK values as the query results returned in the previous two steps.

7. Close the client application.

Try This Summary

In this Try This exercise, you created and initiated three transactions. In the first one, you simply queried data and committed the transaction. In the next two, you updated data and then rolled back the updates. However, as you saw in the third transaction, it is possible to roll back a transaction to a specified savepoint. This allows you to protect certain portions of your transaction without having to reprocess statements that have been executed successfully. Because you rolled back the updates that you made, the INVENTORY database should have been left in the same state it was in when you began this exercise.

Chapter 17 Self Test

1. Which transaction characteristic refers to the all-or-nothing nature of a transaction?

   A Atomic

   B Consistent

   C Isolated

   D Durable

2. A(n) ______________ is a unit of work that is made up of one or more SQL statements that perform a related set of actions.

3. What statement can you use to explicitly initiate a transaction?

4. Which SQL statements will terminate a transaction?
   - **A** SAVEPOINT
   - **B** SET TRANSACTION
   - **C** ROLLBACK
   - **D** COMMIT
5. What are the three types of transaction modes that you can specify in a SET TRANSACTION statement?
6. Which access level options can you include in a START TRANSACTION statement?
   - **A** READ ONLY
   - **B** UPDATE
   - **C** LOCAL
   - **D** READ WRITE
7. Two concurrent transactions are active in your system. The first transaction modifies data in a table. The second transaction sees those modifications before they're actually committed to the database. The first transaction then rolls back the modifications. Which type of data phenomenon has occurred?
   - **A** Phantom read
   - **B** Repeatable read
   - **C** Dirty read
   - **D** Nonrepeatable read
8. A(n) ____________ read can occur when a transaction reads a table based on some sort of search condition, then a second transaction updates the data in the table, and then the first transaction attempts to reread the data, but this time different rows are returned because of how the search condition is defined.
9. What type of constraint can you specify in a SET CONSTRAINTS statement?
10. Which isolation level fully isolates one transaction from another transaction?

11. You're using a SET TRANSACTION statement to configure transaction modes. You want to ensure that no nonrepeatable reads and no dirty reads can occur within that transaction. However, you're not concerned about phantom reads. Which isolation level should you use?

    A READ UNCOMMITTED

    B READ COMMITTED

    C REPEATABLE READ

    D SERIALIZABLE

12. You're setting up a transaction that defers the application of the CK_CD_STOCK constraint until you execute several SQL statements. After you execute the statements, you want to explicitly apply the constraint to the changes you made to the database. What SQL statement should you use to apply the constraints?

13. A(n) _______________ is a designated marker within your transaction that acts as a rollback point for a portion of your transaction.

14. You want to create a savepoint named svpt_Section2. What SQL statement should you use?

15. You create a transaction that includes four savepoints: Section1, Section2, Section3, and Section4. Near the end of the transaction, after all four savepoints, you define a RELEASE SAVEPOINT that specifies the Section2 savepoint. Which savepoint or savepoints are removed from the transaction when the RELEASE SAVEPOINT statement is executed?

    A Section1

    B Section2

    C Section3

    D Section4

16. What circumstances will terminate a transaction?

17. You're creating a ROLLBACK statement in your transaction. You want the rollback to undo changes back to the svpt_Section2 savepoint. What SQL statement should you use?

18. You're creating a COMMIT statement in your transaction. After the transaction is terminated, you want a new transaction to be initiated. The new transaction should be configured with the same transaction modes as the first transaction. How should you create your COMMIT statement?

Chapter 18

Accessing SQL Data from Your Host Program

Key Skills & Concepts

- Invoke SQL Directly
- Embed SQL Statements in Your Program
- Create SQL Client Modules
- Use an SQL Call-Level Interface

Throughout this book, you have been performing Try This exercises and testing examples by using a client application to work interactively with your SQL database. For example, you might have been using SQL Server Management Studio to access a SQL Server database, SQL Developer to access an Oracle database, MySQL Workbench to access a MySQL database, or perhaps a command-line SQL client. This method of data access is referred to as direct invocation, or interactive SQL. The SQL standard also provides for the use of other types of data access, including embedded SQL, SQL client modules, and the call-level interface (CLI); however, the types of data access supported by an SQL implementation often vary from product to product. Some, for example, do not support embedded SQL, and few support SQL client modules. In this chapter, I introduce you to the four types of data access methods and explain how they can be used to retrieve and modify data in your SQL database. Because SQL and CLI are the two methods most commonly used by programs to access SQL data, I cover these two topics in greater detail than direct invocation and SQL client modules, although I do provide a foundation in all four access types.

Invoke SQL Directly

If you've gotten this far in the book, you should already be very comfortable with interactive SQL. By using your client application, which comes with most database management products, you've been able to create ad hoc SQL statements that return immediate results to the application. These results are normally displayed in a window separate from where you executed your SQL statement. For example, let's take a look at Figure 18-1, which shows SQL Server Management Studio. Notice that the top window includes a SELECT statement and the bottom window includes the query results from executing that statement. Most direct invocation client applications behave in a manner similar to this.

The types of SQL statements supported by the direct invocation method can vary from one SQL implementation to the next. Although most implementations will allow you to execute basic types of statements, such as SELECT or UPDATE, they might not allow you to execute statements specific to another method of data access. For example, some implementations might not allow you to declare a cursor within an interactive environment.

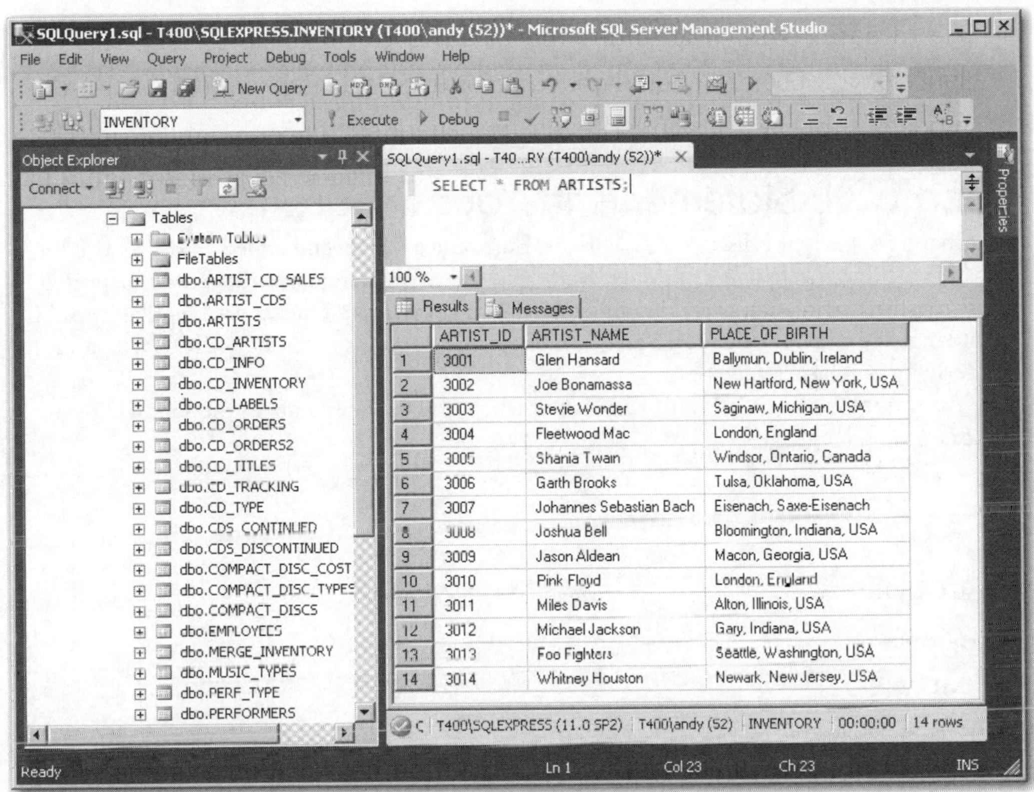

Figure 18-1 SQL Server Management Studio

Despite the differences among SQL implementations, the SQL standard does define which types of statements should be supported in an interactive environment. These include SELECT, INSERT, UPDATE, and DELETE statements and statements related to schema definitions, transactions, connections, and sessions. You should also be able to declare temporary tables in an interactive environment. In fact, nearly any actions critical to the maintenance of data and of the underlying database structure should be supported by direct invocation.

One of the main advantages to interactive SQL—in addition to the ability to execute ad hoc statements—is the elimination of any impedance mismatch. As you'll recall from earlier discussions, an impedance mismatch can occur because of differences in data types between SQL and application programming languages and in how query results (result sets) are handled between SQL and those languages. However, interactive SQL is a pure SQL environment, which means that only the data types supported by the implementation can be used, and result sets pose no problems to the client application because you can simply scroll through query results. It is also common for application developers to use interactive SQL to test the SQL statements they intend to embed in other modules. Even so, direct invocation represents only a small percentage of users. You'll find that most data access is through embedded SQL and CLI-type mechanisms, and some through SQL client modules, but relatively few users rely solely on interactive SQL.

Embed SQL Statements in Your Program

In Chapter 16, when I discuss SQL cursors, I introduce you to embedded SQL. As you'll recall from that discussion, embedded SQL refers to SQL statements that are interspersed in some type of application programming language. The SQL statements are blended into the host language to allow the source program to be able to access and modify SQL data and the underlying database structure.

According to the SQL standard, you can embed SQL statements in the following programming languages:

- Ada
- C
- COBOL
- Fortran
- MUMPS
- Pascal
- PL/I

Although the standard supports embedded SQL statements in these languages, SQL implementations rarely support embedding statements in all these languages. An implementation might be limited to only one or two programming languages, and some implementations might not support embedded SQL at all (although most implementations provide embedded SQL for at least one language). In addition, many implementations support embedded SQL in languages other than those specified in the SQL standard. For example, Oracle offers SQLJ, which supports embedded SQL in Java programs.

When a program contains embedded SQL statements, it must be compiled in a manner different from regular programs. Figure 18-2 illustrates the process followed when compiling these programs.

As you can see from the figure, we start with a program file that contains the host programming language and the embedded SQL statements. Before the program is compiled, it is submitted to a precompiler that is specific to the host programming language and the SQL implementation. The precompiler strips the SQL statements out of the host language code, often converting them into comments to document the original statements, and replaces them with calls to vendor-supplied library routines that access the SQL statements. As a result, two files are created, one for the host language and one for the SQL statements.

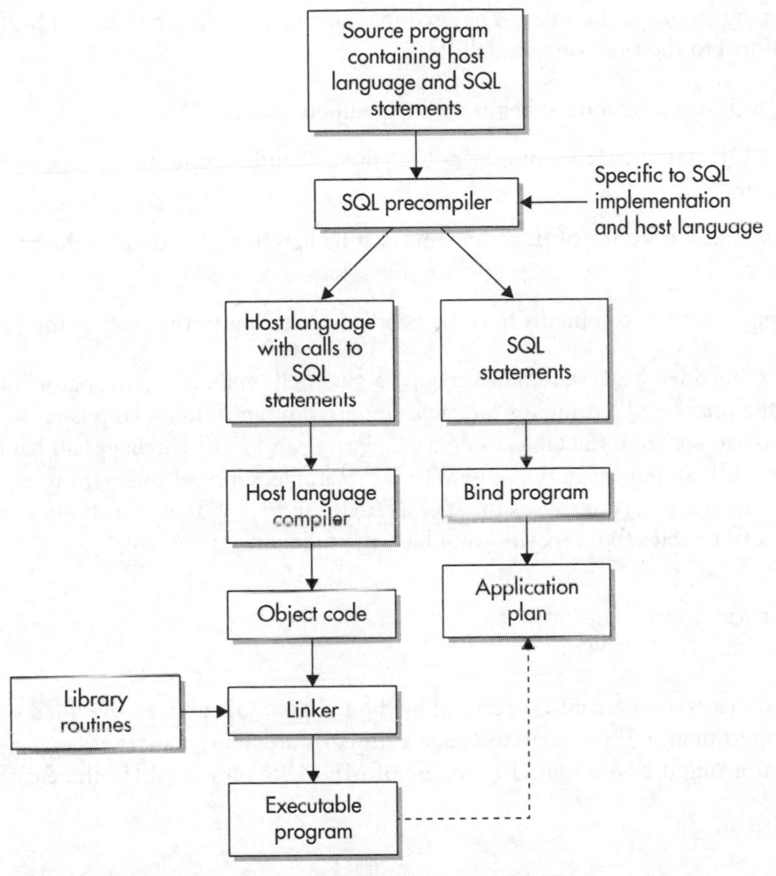

Figure 18-2 Compiling programs that contain embedded SQL

Once a file is created for the host language, the source program is compiled in its normal way, as would be expected from a specific language. The output from the host language compiler is the object code, which is linked to various library routines. From this, an executable program is generated that links to the application plan. The application plan is created by a bind utility that validates and optimizes the SQL statements. The plan contains the SQL statements and information that the program needs to access the database.

Creating an Embedded SQL Statement

When you develop a program that contains embedded SQL, you must follow specific conventions that determine how the SQL code is added to the program. These conventions are based on a combination of special SQL language elements and the requirements of the host programming language. In order to be used in a host language, an embedded SQL statement must conform to the following guidelines:

- Each SQL statement must begin with a qualified prefix.
- Each SQL statement may or may not require a qualified terminator, depending on the host language.
- Line breaks within the SQL statement must be handled according to the style of the host language.
- The placement of comments must be handled according to the style of the host language.

Most embedded SQL statements require a qualified prefix and terminator. Table 18-1 provides the prefix and terminator for each supported programming language.

As you can see from the table, the Ada, C, Pascal, and PL/I languages all handle an embedded SQL statement in the same way. For example, suppose you want to embed a SELECT statement that retrieves the CD_NAME and IN_STOCK columns from the CD_INVENTORY table. To do so, you would use the following statement:

```
EXEC SQL
  SELECT CD_NAME, IN_STOCK
    FROM CD_INVENTORY;
```

Notice that the statement is preceded by the EXEC SQL prefix and ended with the semicolon terminator. If you were to create a similar statement in another language, your prefix or terminator might be different. In the case of MUMPS, they would both be different.

Language	Prefix	Terminator
Ada	EXEC SQL	;
C	EXEC SQL	;
COBOL	EXEC SQL	END-EXEC
Fortran	EXEC SQL	(no terminator)
MUMPS	&SQL(	)
Pascal	EXEC SQL	;
PL/I	EXEC SQL	;

Table 18-1 Beginning and Ending an SQL Statement

NOTE

Normally, it doesn't matter whether your embedded SQL statements appear in uppercase or lowercase. Programmers generally follow the conventions of the host language. However, for the purposes of this chapter, I'll treat embedded SQL statements as I have other SQL statements throughout the book: I'll use uppercase for both SQL keywords and SQL identifiers.

Using Host Variables in Your SQL Statements

In order to use embedded SQL effectively, you must be able to pass values between the host program and the SQL statements. For example, your embedded SQL statement might include a WHERE clause that requires a specific value in order to evaluate the search condition. The value might be supplied by a user or by an operation within the host program. In either case, that value must in some way be passed from the program to the SQL statement.

To pass values to and from an SQL statement, you can use host variables. A *host variable* is a type of parameter that is declared within the host language and is then referenced within the embedded SQL statement. When a host variable is used within an SQL statement, the name of the variable must be preceded by a colon. The colon signals to the precompiler that the named item is a variable and not a database object, such as a table or a column. As a result, you do not have to worry about whether the host variable shares the same name as a database object.

You can use a host variable in an embedded SQL statement in any place where you might expect to define a value. For example, the following SELECT statement can be embedded in a C program:

```
EXEC SQL
  SELECT CD_NAME, IN_STOCK
    FROM CD_INVENTORY
   WHERE CD_ID = :v_CD_ID;
```

Notice that the v_CD_ID host variable is preceded by a colon. The colon is used only within the SQL statement. When the variable is declared—earlier in the host program—no colon is used.

NOTE

The preceding example begins with EXEC SQL and ends with a semicolon. In addition, no specific continuation character is required to indicate a line break in the SQL statement. These conventions are consistent with what you would expect to find in a C program. For the examples in this chapter, I will be using embedded SQL statements as they would appear within a C program. Embedded SQL is well supported in C by a number of SQL implementations.

You're not limited to referencing a host variable in the WHERE clause of a SELECT statement. For example, you can reference a variable in the SET clause of an UPDATE statement, the VALUES clause of an INSERT statement, or the WHERE clause of a

DELETE or UPDATE statement. However, you cannot use a host variable in place of an SQL identifier. In other words, you cannot pass an object name, such as a table name or column name, through a host variable.

Declaring Host Variables

As I mentioned earlier, you must declare your host variables within the host program. You can declare them anywhere in the program where you would normally declare variables in a particular language. In addition, you must declare the variables according to the conventions of the host language. The only difference is that you must begin the declarations with the BEGIN DECLARE SECTION statement and end the declarations with the END DECLARE SECTION statement. These two statements notify the precompiler that the variables enclosed in the statements are to be used in the other embedded SQL statements.

Let's take a look at an example of what I mean. Suppose you want to declare two variables, one to receive a value that identifies the CD and one that receives the name of the CD. Your variable declaration in C might look like the following:

```
EXEC SQL
  BEGIN DECLARE SECTION;
    long     v_CD_ID;          /* compact disc ID */
    varchar  v_CD_NAME[60];    /* compact disc name */
EXEC SQL
  END DECLARE SECTION;
```

As you can see, the variable declarations are enclosed in the two declaration-related SQL statements. Notice that these statements are treated just like any other embedded SQL statements in C. Each statement begins with EXEC SQL and ends with a semicolon.

Two host variables are being declared in this section. The first one, v_CD_ID, is declared with the long data type, and the second variable, v_CD_NAME, is declared with the varchar data type. The two variable declarations follow the conventions of the host language. Notice that a comment follows each declaration. The comments also adhere to the conventions of the host language.

When host variables are used in SQL statements, an impedance mismatch can occur as a result of the differences between host language data types and SQL data types. As you can see in the preceding example, the variables are declared with C data types; however, the variables will be used in SQL statements to pass data to columns that are configured with SQL data types. If the data types are compatible, then data can be passed through the variables; otherwise, the impedance mismatch between the data types prevents values from being passed. For example, the v_CD_ID variable is configured with the long data type, which is compatible with the INTEGER data type in SQL, and the v_CD_NAME variable is configured with the varchar data type, which is compatible with the CHARACTER VARYING data type (usually abbreviated as VARCHAR) in SQL. As a result, you can pass data through these variables as long as the receiving columns are configured with the compatible data types.

Ask the Expert

Q: You state that data can be passed from the variable to the SQL statement if the data types are compatible. How do you pass data if they're not compatible?

A: Most programming languages contain at least some data types that do not match up with SQL data types. If this situation arises, you can use the CAST value expression within the SQL statement to convert the variable value into a value that can be used by the SQL statement. In effect, the CAST value expression changes the data type of the value. For example, we can modify the previous embedded statement to convert the v_CD_ID host variable, as shown in the following example:

```
EXEC SQL
  SELECT CD_NAME, IN_STOCK
    FROM CD_INVENTORY
   WHERE CD_ID = CAST(:v_CD_ID AS INT);
```

As you can see, CAST is used to convert the value in the host variable to an INTEGER data type. (For more information about CAST, see Chapter 10.) To determine which data types in a host language are compatible with data types in SQL, you should refer to the SQL standard, language-specific documentation, or product-specific documentation.

Retrieving SQL Data

As you have seen throughout this book, the process of querying data in an SQL database involves executing a SELECT statement that in turn retrieves data from the applicable table or tables and returns that data in a result set. A result set can be made up of one or more rows and one or more columns. When you are querying data interactively, the multiple rows present no problems because your client application can handle more than one row. However, when querying data from an embedded SQL statement, multiple rows have to be handled through a cursor in order to allow that host language to work with one row at a time. A cursor, as you'll recall, acts as a pointer to specific rows in the result set. The cursor declaration defines the SELECT statement that retrieves data from the database, and cursor-related statements are then used to retrieve the individual rows from that result set. (For more information about cursors, see Chapter 16.)

Cursors, then, provide a solution to one type of impedance mismatch that can occur between SQL and the host language. Specifically, SQL returns data in sets, and most programming languages cannot handle sets. By using some sort of looping construct within the programming language and then using the SQL FETCH statement, you can cycle through each row in the result set to retrieve the data that you need.

Despite the availability of cursors to embedded SQL, there are often times when you know that your database query will return only one row. For example, you might want to retrieve data about a specific CD or performing artist, in which case a cursor is unnecessary. To facilitate single-row retrievals, embedded SQL supports the *singleton* SELECT statement. A singleton SELECT statement is similar to a regular SELECT statement except in two ways:

- You do not include a GROUP BY, HAVING, or ORDER BY clause.
- You include an INTO clause that specifies the host variables that will receive the data returned by the SELECT statement to the host program.

For example, suppose your SELECT statement returns the name of the CD and the number in stock, as shown in the following embedded statement:

```
EXEC SQL
  SELECT CD_NAME, IN_STOCK
    INTO :v_CD_NAME, :v_IN_STOCK
    FROM CD_INVENTORY
   WHERE CD_ID = :v_CD_ID;
```

As you can see in this statement, the v_CD_ID variable is used to specify which CD should be returned. The value is entered by the user, and the variable passes that value from the host program into the SELECT statement.

Now let's take a look at the INTO clause. Notice that the clause contains two variables, the same number of variables as the number of columns retrieved from the CD_INVENTORY table. These variables are declared in the same way as the other host variables that we've seen. Because this SELECT statement returns only one row and two columns, only two values are returned. These values are transferred to the variables. The variables must be specified in the same order as the column names are specified.

NOTE

The v_CD_ID variable in the WHERE clause is an input host variable, and the v_CD_NAME and v_IN_STOCK variables in the INTO clause are output host variables. The only difference is in how they are used by the SQL statement—they are defined in exactly the same manner within the host language.

Handling Null Values

In Chapter 4, I discussed null values and how they're used to represent unknown or unavailable data. As you'll recall from that discussion, most SQL columns, by default, permit null values, although you can override the default by defining a NOT NULL constraint on the column. However, if you don't override the default and null values are permitted, you can run into a problem with the host language because most application programming languages do not support null values.

To work around this issue, SQL allows you to declare indicator host variables. An *indicator host variable* is a type of variable that accompanies a regular host variable, also referred to as a *data host variable*. For simplicity, I refer to these two types of host variables as just *indicator variables* and *data variables*. The indicator variable contains a value that specifies whether or not the value in the associated data variable is null. Indicator variables are declared in the same way as other host variables.

Let's take a look at an example of indicator variables to illustrate how they work. In the following embedded SELECT statement, an indicator variable has been added to each of the data variables in the INTO clause:

```
EXEC SQL
  SELECT CD_NAME, IN_STOCK
    INTO :v_CD_NAME :ind_CD_NAME, :v_IN_STOCK :ind_IN_STOCK
    FROM CD_INVENTORY
   WHERE CD_ID = :v_CD_ID;
```

The INTO clause includes two indicator variables: ind_CD_NAME and ind_IN_STOCK. Notice that each indicator variable follows the associated data variable. The placement of the indicator variable is the only indication the SQL implementation has that a particular host variable is an indicator variable. There is nothing in the variable declaration or naming that distinguishes indicator variables from data variables. When the implementation sees that one variable follows the other and that no comma separates the two, the implementation assigns a value of 0 to the indicator variable if the associated variable contains a real value (is not null). If the associated variable contains a null value, the implementation assigns a value of -1 to the indicator variable. The host program then takes the appropriate action based on this information. It is *essential* that the host program test the indicator variables for null values *before* attempting to use the values in the host variable because when nulls are encountered, the value of the corresponding host variable *is not changed* and thus could contain leftover values from a previous statement or unknown data that programmers call garbage.

NOTE

When you declare an indicator variable, be sure to use a numeric data type that supports the 0 and -1 values. The value 0 is logically a false condition because all bits will be set to a binary 0, while the value -1 is logically a true condition because all bits will be set to a binary 1.

Error Handling

When you embed SQL statements into your host language, you should provide a way to take specific actions if you receive error or warning messages when you try to access data. SQL provides a relatively straightforward method that you can use to monitor errors and warnings and take actions depending on the results of that monitoring. By embedding WHENEVER statements in your host language, you can provide your program with an effective level of error handling that works alongside your other embedded statements.

The WHENEVER statement includes two sets of options, as shown in the following syntax:

```
WHENEVER
{ SQLEXCEPTION | SQLWARNING | NOT FOUND }
{ CONTINUE | GOTO <target> }
```

As you can see, you must first specify the WHENEVER keyword and then specify the necessary options. The first set of options indicates the condition to which the WHENEVER statement applies. If that condition is met, a specified action is taken. A WHENEVER statement can include one of three conditions:

- **SQLEXCEPTION** The condition is met whenever an SQL statement generates an exception. For example, an exception might be generated when you try to insert invalid data into a column.
- **SQLWARNING** The condition is met whenever an SQL statement generates a warning. For example, a statement might generate a warning if a number has been rounded off.
- **NOT FOUND** The condition is met whenever a SELECT statement cannot return data in its query results. This can apply to a singleton SELECT statement or to a FETCH statement at the end of the cursor's result set.

Once you specify a condition in your WHENEVER statement, you must specify an action. The WHENEVER statement supports two actions:

- **CONTINUE** The program will continue running at the next statement.
- **GOTO <target>** The program will jump to a section within the host language that is named in the <target> placeholder.

Now that we've looked at the options available in the WHENEVER statement, let's take a look at an example. Suppose that you want your SQL statements to go to a certain part of the program if an error occurs. In the following WHENEVER statement, an exception will cause the program to move to the Error1 section:

```
EXEC SQL
  WHENEVER SQLEXCEPTION GOTO Error1;
```

Notice that the SQLEXCEPTION option and the GOTO option are specified in this statement. The SQLEXCEPTION option tells the program to take a specified action if an SQL statement generates an exception. The GOTO option defines the action that should be taken. In this case, the option specifies that the program should move to the Error1 section of the host language.

A WHENEVER statement applies to the embedded SQL statements that follow it. You can embed as many WHENEVER statements in your host language as necessary. The last statement to appear is the one that is applied to the other statements.

Try This 18-1 Embedding SQL Statements

In most of the Try This exercises in this book, you used a client application to access your SQL database interactively. However, because of the subject matter of this chapter, particularly with regard to embedded SQL, this exercise will take a different approach from previous Try This exercises. For this exercise, you will use some type of text editing program (such as Microsoft Notepad) to complete the steps. Because programming in a host language is beyond the scope of this book, you will create only the SQL statements that are embedded in the host language. The statements will conform to C, although they might apply to other host languages. In the exercise, you will set up variable declarations, create an error-handling statement, and embed an SQL SELECT statement that queries data from the INVENTORY database. You can download the Try_This_18_1.txt file, which contains the embedded SQL statements used in this Try This exercise.

Step by Step

1. Open a text editing program such as Microsoft Notepad.
2. The first step is to create one input host variable and two output host variables. The purpose of the input host variable is to be able to receive a CD identifier from the user. That identifier can then be used in the WHERE clause of the SELECT statement to determine which row of data will be returned from the COMPACT_DISCS table. Along with declaring the variables, you will include comments that identify the purpose of those variables. Type the following embedded SQL statements and variable declarations into your text document:

```
EXEC SQL
  BEGIN DECLARE SECTION;
    long      v_CD_ID;          /* input variable for CD identifier */
    varchar   v_CD_TITLE[60];   /* output variable for CD title */
    long      v_IN_STOCK;       /* output variable for IN_STOCK value */
EXEC SQL
  END DECLARE SECTION;
```

Notice that the variable declaration section is required, so you had to include the BEGIN DECLARE SECTION statement and the END DECLARE SECTION statement. These statements are necessary to notify the precompiler that the variable declarations will be used in the embedded SQL statements.

(continued)

3. After you create your declaration section, you realize that you want to include indicator variables for the output data variables. As a result, you must add two declarations to your declaration section. Type the following declarations into your text document:

```
short ind_CD_TITLE; /* indicator variable for v_CD_TITLE */
short ind_IN_STOCK; /* indicator variable for v_IN_STOCK */
```

You can add the declarations anywhere in your declaration section. However, for clear coding, I suggest you add them close to each of their associated data variables, as shown in the following declaration section:

```
EXEC SQL BEGIN DECLARE SECTION;
  long     v_CD_ID;          /* input variable for CD identifier */
  varchar  v_CD_TITLE[60];   /* output variable for CD title */
  short    ind_CD_TITLE;     /* indicator variable for v_CD_TITLE */
  long     v_IN_STOCK;       /* output variable for IN_STOCK value */
  short    ind_IN_STOCK;     /* indicator variable for v_IN_STOCK */
EXEC SQL END DECLARE SECTION;
```

Notice that the two new declarations have been inserted beneath their respective data variables.

4. Now let's include an error-handling statement into your test document. The statement will represent a section named Error1 in your host language. The assumption will be that if an embedded SQL statement generates an exception, the program will jump to the Error1 section and take whatever action is defined in that section. Type the following embedded SQL statement into your text document:

```
EXEC SQL
  WHENEVER SQLEXCEPTION GOTO Error1;
```

Notice that the embedded SQL code contains a WHENEVER statement that specifies the SQLEXCEPTION and GOTO options.

5. Now you're ready to create the embedded SELECT statement. The statement will contain the variables defined in your declaration section. In addition, a singleton SELECT statement will be used because the statement will retrieve only one row at a time. The WHERE clause is based on a specified CD_ID value, and each value is unique within the COMPACT_DISCS table. (The CD_ID column is the primary key, so values must be unique within that column.) Type the following embedded SQL statement into your text document:

```
EXEC SQL
  SELECT CD_TITLE, IN_STOCK
    INTO :v_CD_TITLE :ind_CD_TITLE, :v_IN_STOCK :ind_IN_STOCK
    FROM COMPACT_DISCS
   WHERE CD_ID = :v_CD_ID;
```

Notice that an INTO clause is included in this statement. The INTO clause contains the output data variables and their associated indicator variables. Your text document should now look like the following code:

```
EXEC SQL
  BEGIN DECLARE SECTION;
    long     v_CD_ID;           /* input variable for CD identifier */
    varchar  v_CD_TITLE[60];    /* output variable for CD title */
    short    ind_CD_TITLE;      /* indicator variable for v_CD_TITLE */
    long     v_IN_STOCK;        /* output variable for IN_STOCK value */
    short    ind_IN_STOCK;      /* indicator variable for v_IN_STOCK */
EXEC SQL
  END DECLARE SECTION;
EXEC SQL
  WHENEVER SQLEXCEPTION GOTO Error1;
EXEC SQL
  SELECT CD_TITLE, IN_STOCK
    INTO :v_CD_TITLE :ind_CD_TITLE, :v_IN_STOCK :ind_IN_STOCK
    FROM COMPACT_DISCS
   WHERE CD_ID = :v_CD_ID;
```

If this were an actual C program, you would also see the C code surrounding the embedded SQL statements. The C code would represent that actual program and would take actions appropriate to that program. For example, the host language would include code that would allow the program to receive the CD identifier for the user. That identifier would be passed to the v_CD_ID variable to be used in the embedded SELECT statement.

6. Save the file and close the application.

Try This Summary

In this Try This exercise, you created a host variable declaration section, declared five host variables, added an error-handling statement, and embedded a singleton SELECT statement. If this were a complete C program, the host language would have used the data in the output variables to take any actions appropriate to the program. The C program would also include a section named Error1 that would specify an action to take should an exception be raised when the SQL statement is executed. You can, of course, include many more embedded SQL statements than those used in this exercise, and you can include other types of statements such as UPDATE or DELETE. However, the purpose of this exercise was to provide you with a foundation in embedded SQL. For more details on embedding SQL statements, you should refer to documentation specific to the host language and documentation for the applicable SQL implementation.

Create SQL Client Modules

Now that you have a basic understanding of embedded SQL, let's take a look at SQL client modules. SQL client modules are self-contained collections of SQL statements. Unlike embedded SQL, in which the SQL statements are inserted into the host programming language, SQL client modules are separate from the host language. The host language contains calls that invoke the module, which in turn executes the SQL statements within that module.

An SQL client module is made up of the properties that define the module, temporary tables, cursors, and the procedures that contain the SQL statements. Each procedure can contain only one SQL statement. The following syntax provides the basic elements of an SQL client module:

```
MODULE <module name> [ NAMES ARE <character set> ]
LANGUAGE { ADA | C | COBOL | FORTRAN | MUMPS | PASCAL | PLI }
[ SCHEMA <schema name > ] [ AUTHORIZATION <authorization identifier> ]
[ <temporary table declarations> ] [ <cursor declarations> ]
PROCEDURE <procedure name> ( <parameter declarations> )
<SQL statement>;
```

Let's take a look at each clause within the syntax so that you have a better understanding of all the elements that make up an SQL client module. The MODULE clause specifies a name for the module. This is followed by the optional NAMES ARE clause, which is used to specify a character set for the identifiers in the module. If the NAMES ARE clause is not specified, the default character set for the SQL implementation is used. The next element in the syntax is the LANGUAGE clause, which specifies the host language that will be calling the module. You must specify a language.

After you've defined the LANGUAGE clause, you must define a SCHEMA clause, an AUTHORIZATION clause, or both. The SCHEMA clause identifies the default schema to be used by SQL statements in the module. The AUTHORIZATION clause identifies the authorization identifier to be used for executing the statements within the module. If no AUTHORIZATION clause is specified, the current authorization identifier is assumed.

You can also declare temporary tables and cursors within a module. Temporary tables must be declared before any cursors or procedures. You can declare as many temporary tables as necessary. Unlike temporary table declarations, cursor declarations can be mixed in between procedures; however, a cursor declaration must always precede the procedure that references that cursor.

The final portion of the module statement is the procedure. As I mentioned earlier, your module can contain one or more procedures. However, each procedure can contain only one SQL statement and *must* contain at least one parameter declaration, which is the status parameter SQLSTATE.

NOTE

The procedure in an SQL client module is sometimes referred to as an externally invoked procedure.

The SQLSTATE status parameter provides a way to report errors back to your host language. Like any other host parameter, values are passed between the SQL database (the DBMS) and the host program. In the case of SQLSTATE, the values are related to the status of SQL statement execution. By including the SQLSTATE parameter in your modules, you're allowing your host program to see the status of your statement execution. As a result, the program can monitor for errors and take appropriate actions if those errors occur.

In addition to the SQLSTATE status parameter, you must declare all other host parameters used in the procedure's SQL statement. Parameter names (except SQLSTATE) must be preceded by a colon when being declared and when used in the SQL statement. As you can see in the syntax, parameter declarations must be enclosed by parentheses. In addition, if more than one parameter is declared, those declarations must be separated with commas.

Defining SQL Client Modules

Now that we've reviewed the syntax for an SQL client module, let's take a look at an example of how to create one. In the following statement, I create a module that contains one procedure:

```
MODULE QUERY_CD_INVENTORY
  LANGUAGE C
  SCHEMA INVENTORY AUTHORIZATION Sales
  PROCEDURE QUERY_1
  ( SQLSTATE, :p_CD_ID INT, :p_CD_NAME VARCHAR(60) )
    SELECT CD_NAME
      INTO :p_CD_NAME
      FROM CD_INVENTORY
     WHERE CD_ID = :p_CD_ID;
```

As you can see in this example, we're creating a module named QUERY_CD_INVENTORY. The module will be called by a C program (LANGUAGE C). The SQL statement within the module will access a table in the INVENTORY schema and will be executed under the context of the Sales authorization identifier. The MODULE statement includes only one procedure, which is named QUERY_1. If more than one procedure were defined, they would each be terminated by a semicolon. Now let's take a closer look at the QUERY_1 procedure.

The first thing you might notice is that three host parameters have been declared. The SQLSTATE parameter provides status information to the host program. The p_CD_ID parameter is an input parameter that will receive a value from the host program. The p_CD_NAME parameter is an output parameter that will take the value returned by the SELECT statement and pass it to the host program. Notice that both the p_CD_ID and p_CD_NAME parameters are preceded by a colon and declared with a data type. The SQLSTATE parameter does not require a semicolon or data type.

Once we declare the parameters, we can define the SELECT statement. As you can see, the input parameter is used in the WHERE clause, and the output parameter is used in the INTO clause. The use of the parameters in this way allows the module to interact with the host program. A value for the input parameter is passed to the module when the module is called within the host language, and the output parameter is returned to the host language to be used by the program as necessary.

NOTE

The process of calling a module within a host program and passing a parameter to the module is language specific. Be sure to check the documentation for the specific programming language and for the applicable SQL implementation.

As you can see, an SQL client module can be a handy tool for developing the SQL component of an application without having to embed the SQL statements within the host language. Unfortunately, SQL client modules are not widely supported in SQL implementations, and if they are supported, they are often not well documented. However, whether or not they're widely implemented is becoming beside the point as the industry moves away from embedded SQL and SQL client modules toward CLI and CLI-like data access, which I cover in the next section.

Use an SQL Call-Level Interface

As you have seen so far in this chapter, a program can access an SQL database by using embedded SQL and SQL client modules. In embedded SQL, SQL statements are inserted directly into the host programming language. For SQL client modules, the host program calls modules that contain executable SQL statements. The statements are separate from the host language. SQL provides yet another method for accessing SQL data from within a programming language—the call-level interface, or CLI.

A CLI is an application programming interface (API) that supports a set of predefined routines that allow a programming language to communicate with an SQL database. The programming language calls the routines, which then connect to the database. The routines access data and status information from the database, as required, and return that information to the program. Figure 18-3 provides an overview of how a CLI allows a program to communicate with an SQL database.

The program invokes CLI routines through the use of functions. When calling a function, the program must specify values for the function's arguments. These values define what actions to take and what data to access. The function passes the values to the designated routine, which acts as an interface between the program and the SQL database. The CLI, in effect, hides the details of accessing the database from the program, making it possible for the program to access databases in different management systems.

One of the most well-known implementations of the CLI model is Microsoft's Open Database Connectivity (ODBC) API, although other vendors have released CLI-like products that support similar types of database access. In addition, new generations of data-access APIs are gaining popularity, such as Microsoft's OLE-DB, which is more efficient than ODBC and supports access to SQL data sources and other types of data sources. For Java programmers, there is a similar API called JDBC. You'll also find that such products as ActiveX Data Object (ADO) provide an object-oriented interface between scripting languages or object-oriented languages and the OLE-DB API. Many development tools also make accessing an SQL data source easier than ever. For example, Visual Studio .NET allows you to build data-driven

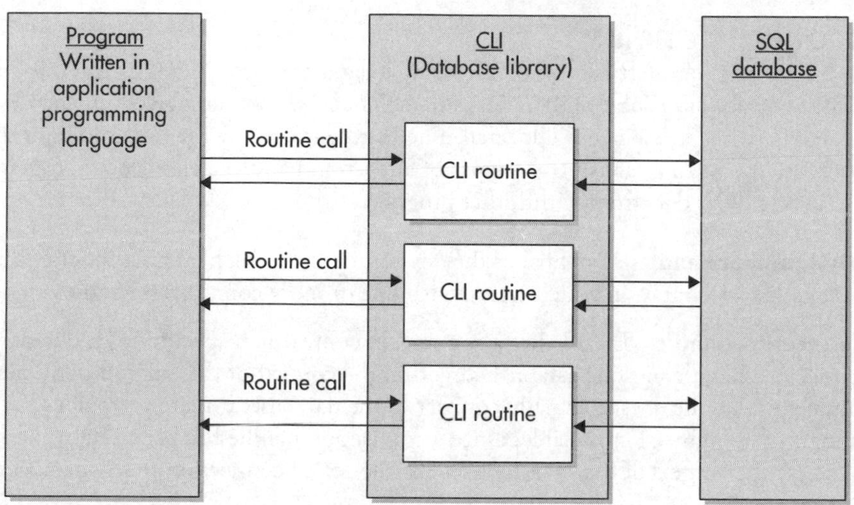

Figure 18-3 Using a CLI to access data in an SQL database

applications in such languages as Visual Basic, C++, and C#. By using the built-in ADO.NET tools, you can create applications that can access a variety of data sources, such as SQL Server and Oracle.

NOTE

Although Microsoft is generally given credit for ODBC, it was developed by Microsoft in partnership with Simba Technologies, and is based on CLI specifications from the SQL Access Group, X/Open (now part of The Open Group), and the ISO/IEC.

The key to all these products is to provide a uniform method of database access from within the programming language. The CLI specifications in SQL standardize the database access interface by providing a set of predefined CLI functions that allow your program to connect to a database, modify and retrieve data, pass information to and from the database, and obtain status information about statement execution. In this section, we'll look at several CLI functions and how they can be used in a programming language to access SQL data.

NOTE

Despite how extensively the SQL standard has defined the CLI model, applications can vary greatly in the methods they use to access a data source. As a result, you'll find that you'll want to use a data access method that is supported in your environment. For example, if you're developing a C application that connects to a data source via ODBC, the specifics of data access described in this section will be very useful to you. However, if you're developing a C# application or an Active Server Pages (ASP) application using VBScript and you're connecting to a data source via ADO, you'll want to refer to documentation related to that particular technology as well as reviewing the information in this section.

Allocating Handles

The first step that you must take when accessing a database through a CLI interface is to establish the necessary allocation handles. An *allocation handle* is an object returned by the SQL database when a resource is allocated. The handle is used by the host program to access the database. You must establish three types of allocation handles in your host program in order to access SQL data from within that program:

- **Environment handle** Establishes the environment in which all CLI functions are called and provides a context in which to establish one or more connection handles.
- **Connection handle** Establishes a connection context to a specific SQL database. The connection handle must be established within the context of the environment handle. A connection handle doesn't actually connect to the database. It merely provides the context to make that connection possible. Once a connection handle has been established, you must use the context of that handle to make the actual connection to the database.
- **Statement handle** Establishes a context in which SQL statements can be executed. Any statement invoked through the CLI must be executed within the context of a statement handle, and the statement handle must be defined within the context of a connection handle.

To better understand how allocation handles operate, let's take a look at Figure 18-4. As you can see in the figure, two connection handles are allocated within an environment handle, and one statement handle is allocated within each connection handle. Each SQL statement is executed within the context of a statement handle.

Establishing an Environment Handle

To establish an environment handle in which to support database access, you can use the AllocHandle( ) function, which requires three arguments. The first argument (SQL_HANDLE_ENV) specifies the type of handle (environment) that is being allocated. The second argument (SQL_NULL_HANDLE) indicates that the environment handle does not depend on any existing handle. The third argument is a host variable that identifies the environment handle. When a host variable is used in this context, it is preceded by an ampersand (&).

NOTE

Host variables are declared according to the conventions of the host language. In addition, the host program might contain other elements that support CLI functionality. For example, a C program might require special include files necessary to interact with the CLI API. Also be aware that language libraries can vary from vendor to vendor; for instance, there are several known inconsistencies between the C libraries provided by Microsoft and Borland. In addition, the host program might contain special error-handling functions that can monitor the success or failure of a CLI routine call. For information about language-specific elements that should be included in your host program, be sure to check the documentation for the specific language, CLI API, and SQL implementation.

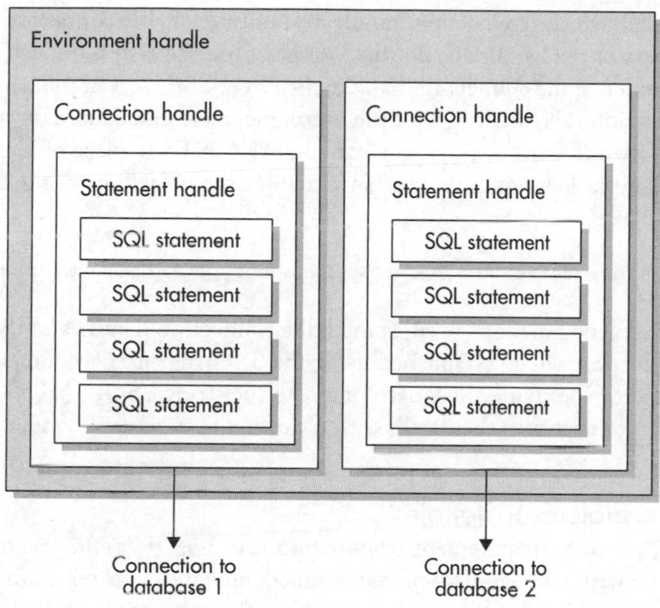

Figure 18-4 Establishing allocation handles

Now that we've reviewed the individual elements necessary to establish an environment handle, let's take a look at the AllocHandle( ) function as it would be included in your C program:

```
SQLAllocHandle ( SQL_HANDLE_ENV, SQL_NULL_HANDLE, &henv );
```

The first thing you'll notice is that the AllocHandle function is preceded by the SQL prefix. In C programs, the SQL prefix is added to all CLI functions. The prefix can vary according to the host language. You'll also notice in this statement that the three arguments are enclosed in parentheses and separated by commas. In addition, the host variable that identifies the handle is preceded by an ampersand.

Establishing a Connection Handle

Once you've established your environment handle, you can establish one or more connection handles within the context of that environment. To do so, you will again use the AllocHandle( ) function, along with three arguments. The first argument (SQL_HANDLE_DBC) specifies the type of handle (connection) that is being allocated. The second argument identifies the environment in which the connection is being established. (This is the host variable identified when you established the environment handle.) The third argument is a host variable that identifies the connection handle. Again, it is preceded by an ampersand, as shown in the following function statement:

```
SQLAllocHandle ( SQL_HANDLE_DBC, henv, &hdbc );
```

After you establish the connection handle, you must explicitly connect to the database within the context of the handle. To do this, you must use the SQLConnect( ) function, which takes seven arguments: the connection handle, the target SQL server, the length of the server name, the connection user, the length of the username, the connection password, and the length of the password. For C strings, you can use SQL_NTS in place of length arguments to indicate that a length does not have to be specified for the preceding string, as shown in the following example:

```
SQLConnect ( hdbc, server01, SQL_NTS, SaleMngr, SQL_NTS, SalesPW, SQL_NTS );
```

As you can see, the function specifies the hdbc connection handle and the server01 SQL server. The connection will be established using the SaleMngr user account and the SalesPW password. Instead of specifying the length of any of the strings, SQL_NTS is used.

Once you've connected to the database, you can create statement handles and execute SQL statements.

Establishing a Statement Handle

In order to execute an SQL statement from within your host program, you must create a statement handle within the context of your connection handle. As with other types of handles, you can use the AllocHandle( ) function to establish the statement handle.

As you have seen, the AllocHandle( ) function requires three arguments. In the case of a statement handle, those arguments are SQL_HANDLE_STMT, the host variable that identifies the connection handle, and the host variable that identifies the statement handle. The host variable that identifies the statement handle is preceded by an ampersand, as shown in the following example:

```
SQLAllocHandle ( SQL_HANDLE_STMT, hdbc, &hstmt );
```

In this function, the connection handle referenced is hdbc, and the variable identifying the statement handle is hstmt.

Executing SQL Statements

Now that you've established your allocation handles and connected to the database, you can set up functions that allow you to execute the SQL statements. The CLI model supports two methods that you can use to execute SQL statements. The first is direct execution and the second is preparing the statement for later execution.

Using the ExecDirect( ) Function

The first method you can use to execute an SQL statement is the ExecDirect( ) function. The function takes three arguments. The first argument is the name of the statement handle in whose context you'll be executing the statement. The second argument is the actual SQL statement, enclosed in double quotation marks. The third argument is the length of the statement. In a C program, you generally use SQL_NTS to indicate that you do not have to specify the length of the string.

Let's take a look at an example of the ExecDirect( ) function to demonstrate how you can use it to execute an SQL statement. The following function references the hstmt statement handle and defines a DELETE statement:

```
SQLExecDirect ( hstmt, "DELETE FROM CD_INVENTORY WHERE CD_ID = 115", SQL_NTS );
```

As you can see, the SQL statement is passed as an argument to the CLI routine. In this case, any rows with a CD_ID value of 115 will be deleted from the CD_INVENTORY table. Notice that the SQL_NTS value is used to indicate that you do not have to specify the length of the string (the actual SQL statement).

Using the Prepare( ) and Execute( ) Functions

Another method that you can use to execute a statement is to first prepare the statement and then later execute it. You would use this method if you need to execute your statement more than one time.

The first function that you use in the two-step process is the Prepare( ) function, which requires the same three arguments as the ExecDirect( ) function, as shown in the following example:

```
SQLPrepare ( hstmt, "DELETE FROM CD_INVENTORY WHERE CD_ID = 115", SQL_NTS );
```

Notice that we reference the same statement handle and define the same SQL statement as in the preceding ExecDirect( ) example. The only difference is that in the case of the Prepare( ) function, the statement isn't actually executed, but is instead prepared for execution. When a statement must be executed multiple times, this process saves on overhead because the statement has to be analyzed and optimized only once.

Once you've prepared the statement, you can then use the Execute( ) function to execute the statement. The Execute( ) function takes only one argument—the statement handle that contains the prepared statement, as shown in the following example:

```
SQLExecute ( hstmt );
```

Because the statement was already prepared, you merely need to reference the statement handle to execute the statement. You can execute the statement as often as necessary simply by invoking the Execute( ) function and specifying the statement handle.

Working with Host Variables

In the preceding examples, the SQL statements that we executed were relatively straightforward because no host variables were used in the statement. However, if you plan to pass host variable values into or out of an SQL statement, you must take an extra step to bind those host variables to the SQL statement.

For example, suppose you want to set up a DELETE statement that takes an input variable identifying the row to be deleted. Your Prepare( ) function would be similar to the following:

```
SQLPrepare ( hstmt, "DELETE FROM CD_INVENTORY WHERE CD_ID = ?", SQL_NTS );
```

Notice that a question mark is used to indicate the position of the variable. The question mark is used in place of the host variable. This is often called a *placeholder*.

Once you've prepared your SQL statement, you must now bind the host variable to the statement. To do so in a C program, you must use a BindParameter( ) function that identifies the statement handle, the position of the host variable within the SQL statement, the name of the host variable, and a number of other arguments, as shown in the following example:

```
SQLBindParameter ( hstmt, 1, SQL_PARAMETER_MODE_IN, SQL_INT,
  SQL_INT, 4, 0, &v_CD_ID, 4, &ind_CD_ID );
```

As you can see, the BindParameter( ) function takes 10 arguments. Table 18-2 lists the arguments used in the preceding example and provides a description of each of those arguments.

If more than one host variable is included in your SQL statement, a BindParameter( ) function statement should be defined for each variable, and the position (the second argument) should be incremented by one for each additional variable. Once you bind the host variables to your SQL statement, you can execute the statement by using the Execute( ) function.

Argument	Example	Description
1	hstmt	Identifies the statement handle that provides the context for the SQL statement execution
2	1	Identifies the position of the host variable in the SQL statement
3	SQL_PARAMETER_MODE_IN	Specifies whether the host variable is an in, out, or in/out variable
4	SQL_INT	Identifies the data type of the value supplied
5	SQL_INT	Identifies the data type of the host variable
6	4	Specifies the column size of the host variable
7	0	Specifies the number of digits to the right of the decimal required by the host variable
8	&v_CD_ID	Identifies the name of the host variable, as declared in the host program
9	4	Specifies the length in octets (bytes) of the host variable
10	&ind_CD_ID	Identifies the name of the indicator variable, as declared by the host program

Table 18-2 Arguments Used in the BindParameter( ) Function

Retrieving SQL Data

Up to this point, the SQL statements that we've executed in the CLI environment have not returned any data. However, you'll often run into situations where your program will need to query the database and process the values that are returned by that query. As a result, you'll need some sort of mechanism to bind the output from your query to variables that you declared in the host language.

For example, suppose that you want to execute the following SELECT statement:

```
SQLExecDirect ( hstmt, "SELECT CD_NAME, IN_STOCK FROM CD_INVENTORY",
   SQL_NTS );
```

As you can see, the statement will return a list of CD_NAME values and IN_STOCK values from the CD_INVENTORY table. In order to deal with those values, you must bind them to the applicable host variables. To do this in a C program, you should use the BindCol( ) function. The BindCol( ) function is a little simpler than the BindParameter( ) function and takes only six arguments, as shown in the following example:

```
SQLBindCol ( hstmt, 1, SQL_CHAR, &v_CD_NAME, 60, &ind_CD_NAME );
SQLBindCol ( hstmt, 2, SQL_INT,  &v_IN_STOCK, 5, &ind_IN_STOCK );
```

Table 18-3 lists the arguments used in the first statement of this example and provides a description of each of those arguments.

Notice that two function statements have been defined, one for each column retrieved by the SELECT statement. You must define a function statement for each column that is listed in the SELECT clause of the SELECT statement. Once you bind the column values to the host variables, you can use those variables in the host program to process the data within the program as necessary.

Argument	Example	Description
1	hstmt	Identifies the statement handle that provides the context for the SQL statement execution
2	1	Identifies the column as it is listed in the SELECT clause of the SELECT statement
3	SQL_CHAR	Identifies the data type of the host variable
4	&v_CD_NAME	Identifies the name of the host variable, as declared in the host program
5	60	Specifies the length in octets of the host variable
6	&ind_CD_NAME	Identifies the name of the indicator variable, as declared by the host program

Table 18-3 Arguments Used in the BindCol( ) Function

Try This 18-2 Using the SQL Call-Level Interface

In Try This 18-1, you used a text editing program to create embedded SQL statements. In this Try This exercise, you will perform similar actions except that you'll be defining the functions necessary to make CLI routine calls. As part of this process, you will establish the necessary allocation handles, create a connection to the database, set up SQL statement execution, bind host variables to SQL statements, and bind statement output to host variables. The CLI functions that you'll be using are those typically used in a C program. Keep in mind, however, that the CLI model supports many more functions than what we've covered in this chapter, so be sure to check the appropriate documentation for details on functions other than those described here. You can download the Try_This_18_2.txt file, which contains the CLI function statements used in this exercise.

Step by Step

1. Open a text editing program such as Microsoft Notepad.
2. The first step that you must take is to establish an environment handle. You'll use the henv host variable to set up the handle. Type the following function statement into your text document:

   ```
   SQLAllocHandle ( SQL_HANDLE_ENV, SQL_NULL_HANDLE, &henv );
   ```

   Notice that your functions include three arguments, enclosed in parentheses and separated by commas. Also notice that an ampersand is used for the host variable.
3. Now you can establish your connection environment. The connection environment will be established within the context of the environment handle that you created in step 2. Type the following function statement into your text document:

   ```
   SQLAllocHandle ( SQL_HANDLE_DBC, henv, &hdbc );
   ```

   As you can see, the henv host variable is used to indicate the environment handle, and the hdbc host variable is used to identify the connection handle.
4. Now that you've established a connection handle, you can create the actual connection. For this connection, you'll use DBServer as your SQL server, DBAdmin as the user account, and AdminPW as the password for that account. Type the following function statement into your text document:

   ```
   SQLConnect ( hdbc, DBServer, SQL_NTS, DBAdmin, SQL_NTS, AdminPW, SQL_NTS );
   ```

   Notice that the statement includes the SQL_NTS value to indicate that a string length does not have to be specified.
5. Next you'll establish your statement handle within the context of the connection you created in step 3. Type the following function statement into your text document:

   ```
   SQLAllocHandle ( SQL_HANDLE_STMT, hdbc, &hstmt );
   ```

As you can see, the hdbc host variable is used to identify the connection handle, and the hstmt variable is used to identify the statement handle.

6. Now that you've established your allocation handles and created your connection, you're ready to execute an SQL statement. You'll use the ExecDirect( ) function to specify a DELETE statement. Type the following function statement into your text document:

```
SQLExecDirect ( hstmt, "DELETE FROM COMPACT_DISCS
  WHERE COMPACT_DISC_ID = 115", SQL_NTS );
```

The DELETE statement is included as one of the function's arguments. Notice that it is enclosed in double quotation marks. Also notice that the statement is being prepared within the context of the hstmt host variable, which is assigned to the statement environment.

7. In the last step, you executed your SQL statement in one step by using the ExecDirect( ) function. In this step, you will prepare an SQL statement for execution, but you will actually execute it in a later step. Type the following function statement into your text document:

```
SQLPrepare ( hstmt, "SELECT CD_TITLE, IN_STOCK FROM COMPACT_DISCS
  WHERE COMPACT_DISC_ID = ?", SQL_NTS );
```

Notice that the WHERE clause of the SELECT statement includes a question mark to indicate that a value will be passed into the statement through a host variable.

8. In order to execute the statement in the previous step, you'll need to bind the host variable to the statement. Type the following function statement into your text document:

```
SQLBindParameter ( hstmt, 1, SQL_PARAMETER_MODE_IN, SQL_INT,
   SQL_INT, 3, 0, &v_CD_ID, 4, &ind_CD_ID );
```

As you can see, the v_CD_ID host variable is being bound to the SQL statement in the context of the statement environment created earlier. Because only one host variable is referenced in the SQL statement, only one BindParameter( ) function statement is required.

9. Now you can execute the statement prepared in step 7. Type the following function statement into your text document:

```
SQLExecute ( hstmt );
```

The statement will be executed in the context of the hstmt statement environment.

10. Next you must bind the query results to the host variables. Because two columns are identified in the SELECT clause of the SELECT statement, you must include two BindCol( ) function statements. Type the following function statements into your text document:

```
SQLBindCol ( hstmt, 1, SQL_CHAR, &v_CD_TITLE, 60, &ind_CD_TITLE );
SQLBindCol ( hstmt, 2, SQL_INT,  &v_IN_STOCK,  5, &ind_IN_STOCK );
```

(continued)

Your C program should now be able to use the values returned by your SELECT statement. If you review the document that you created, it should contain the following code:

```
SQLAllocHandle ( SQL_HANDLE_ENV, SQL_NULL_HANDLE, &henv );
SQLAllocHandle ( SQL_HANDLE_DBC, henv, &hdbc );
SQLConnect ( hdbc, DBServer, SQL_NTS, DBAdmin, SQL_NTS, AdminPW, SQL_NTS );
SQLAllocHandle ( SQL_HANDLE_STMT, hdbc, &hstmt );
SQLExecDirect ( hstmt, "DELETE FROM COMPACT_DISCS
  WHERE COMPACT_DISC_ID = 115", SQL_NTS );
SQLPrepare ( hstmt, "SELECT CD_TITLE, IN_STOCK FROM COMPACT_DISCS
  WHERE COMPACT_DISC_ID = ?", SQL_NTS );
SQLBindParameter ( hstmt, 1, SQL_PARAMETER_MODE_IN, SQL_INT,
   SQL_INT, 3, 0, &v_CD_ID, 4, &ind_CD_ID );
SQLExecute ( hstmt );
SQLBindCol ( hstmt, 1, SQL_CHAR, &v_CD_TITLE, 60, &ind_CD_TITLE );
SQLBindCol ( hstmt, 2, SQL_INT,  &v_IN_STOCK,  5, &ind_IN_STOCK );
```

11. Save the file and close the application.

Try This Summary

This Try This exercise introduced the basic functions necessary to use CLI to access an SQL database from a host program. What the exercise did not cover is the actual C code that would provide the foundation for your program. For example, a C program would usually include variable declarations, include files, error-handling capabilities, user-related operations, and conditional language that allow you to use the values returned by the SQL database. The CLI functions that we covered in this exercise would usually be interspersed into and work in conjunction with the host language. Still, this exercise should have helped you understand the basic concepts involved in using CLI and better prepared you for working in the host language environment when trying to access SQL data.

Chapter 18 Self Test

1. Which data access method should you use if you want to create and execute ad hoc SQL statements?

A CLI

B SQL client modules

C Direct invocation

D Embedded SQL

2. What is embedded SQL?

3. What does the precompiler do with the program file?

4. Which files are created by an SQL precompiler?

   A A file for the CLI functions

   B A file for the host language

   C A file for the CLI calls

   D A file for the embedded SQL statements

5. Which clause in a MODULE statement do you use to specify the host programming language?

6. Which prefix should embedded SQL statements use when those statements are embedded in the MUMPS programming language?

   A &SQL(

   B EXEC SQL

   C START-EXEC

   D Statements embedded in MUMPS do not require a prefix.

7. A(n) ______________ is a type of parameter that is declared within the host language and is then referenced within the embedded SQL statement.

8. What statement should you use at the beginning of the declaration section for host variables?

9. Which prefix must you provide for a host variable when it is included in an SQL statement?

   A Question mark

   B Ampersand

   C Semicolon

   D Colon

10. You plan to embed SQL statements in your host program. You want to declare several host variables to be used in the SQL statements. Which SQL statement should you use to terminate the declaration section of your program?

    A TERMINATE DECLARE SECTION

    B END DECLARE SECTION

    C TERMINATE DECLARATIONS

    D END DECLARATIONS

11. What can cause an impedance mismatch to occur when passing a variable from a host program to an SQL statement?

12. What type of SELECT statement can you use in embedded SQL when retrieving only one row of data?

13. A(n) ________________ is a type of variable that specifies whether an associated data variable contains a null value.

14. Which statement can you use in embedded SQL to provide your host program with exception and warning information?

A WHENEVER

B INTO

C CAST

D PROCEDURE

15. A(n) ________________ is a self-contained collection of SQL statements that are separate from a host programming language but that can be called from within that language.

16. What allocation handles must you establish in order to execute an SQL statement through a CLI API?

17. How many SQL statements can you include in a procedure in an SQL client module?

18. Which function should you use to establish a CLI connection handle?

A ExecDirect( )

B Connect( )

C Prepare( )

D AllocHandle( )

19. You're allocating an environment handle within a C program and associating the handle with the henv host variable. What function statement should you use?

20. You're creating the following Prepare( ) function statement in your host program:

```
SQLPrepare ( hstmt, "SELECT CD_ID, CD_TITLE, IN_STOCK FROM COMPACT_
DISCS WHERE COMPACT_DISC_ID = ?", SQL_NTS );
```

How many BindCol( ) function statements should you create?

A One

B Two

C Three

D Four

21. What CLI function should you use if you want to execute an SQL statement in one step?

Chapter 19

Working with XML Data

Key Skills & Concepts

- Learn the Basics of XML
- Learn About SQL/XML

The Extensible Markup Language (XML) is a general-purpose markup language used to describe documents in a format that is convenient for display on web pages and for exchanging data between different parties. The specifications for storing XML data in SQL databases were added to the SQL standard in SQL:2003 as Part 14 (arguably the most significant enhancement to that version of the standard). Part 14, also known as SQL/XML, was expanded in SQL:2006, and some error corrections were published in 2007.

NOTE

SQL/XML is not at all the same as Microsoft's SQLXML, which is a proprietary technology used in SQL Server. As you can imagine, the unfortunate similarity in names has caused much confusion. Microsoft participated in the standards proceedings for SQL/XML, but then chose not to implement it.

Learn the Basics of XML

In order to understand SQL/XML, you must first understand the basics of XML. While a complete explanation of XML is well beyond the scope of this book, this topic provides a brief overview. You can find a lot more information by searching on the Internet.

You may already be familiar with HTML, the markup language used to define web pages. If so, the syntax of XML will look familiar. This is because both are based on the Standard Generalized Markup Language (SGML), which itself is based on Generalized Markup Language (GML), which was developed by IBM in the 1960s. A *markup language* is a set of annotations, often called *tags*, which are used to describe how text is to be structured, formatted, or laid out. The tagged text is intended to be human readable. One of the fundamental differences between HTML and XML is that HTML provides a predefined set of tags, while XML allows the author to create their own tags.

Let's look at a sample XML document that contains the results of an SQL query. Figure 19-1 shows two artists from the PERFORMERS table and four of their CDs from the CD_INVENTORY table. As you learned in Chapter 11, we can easily join the two tables using an SQL SELECT statement like this one:

```
SELECT a.PERF_NAME, a.PERF_ID, b.CD_NAME, b.IN_STOCK
  FROM PERFORMERS a JOIN CD_INVENTORY b
       ON a.PERF_ID = b.PERF_ID
 ORDER BY a.PERF_NAME, b.CD_NAME;
```

PERFORMERS

PERF_ID: INT	PERF_NAME: VARCHAR(60)
3003	Stevie Wonder
3010	Pink Floyd

CD_INVENTORY

CD_NAME: VARCHAR(60)	PERF_ID: INT	IN_STOCK: INT
Innervisions (Remastered)	3003	16
The Definitive Collection	3003	34
Dark Side of the Moon	3010	27
The Endless River	3010	12

Figure 19-1 The PERFORMERS and CD_INVENTORY tables

Note that I used the ORDER BY clause to specify the order of the rows in the result set. The query results should look something like this:

```
PERF_ID  PERF_NAME          CD_NAME                    IN_STOCK
-------  ----------------   -------------------------  --------
3010     Pink Floyd         Dark Side of the Moon      27
3010     Pink Floyd         The Endless River          12
3003     Stevie Wonder      Innervisions (Remastered)  16
3003     Stevie Wonder      The Definitive Collection  34
```

The query results are well suited for display or printing, but they are not in a form that would be easy to display on a web page or to pass to another computer application for further processing. One way to make this easier is to convert the query results into XML as shown here:

```
<artists>
   <artist id="3010">
      <name>Pink Floyd</name>
         <CDs>
            <CD stock="27"><name>Dark Side of the Moon</name></CD>
            <CD stock="12"><name>The Endless River</name></CD>
         </CDs>
   </artist>
   <artist id="3003">
      <name>Stevie Wonder</name>
         <CDs>
            <CD stock="16"><name>Innervisions (Remastered)</name></CD>
            <CD stock="34"><name>The Definitive Collection</name></CD>
         </CDs>
   </artist>
   <!-- Additional artists available soon -->
</artists>
```

As you can see in the code listing, tags are enclosed in angle brackets, and each start tag has a matching end tag that is identical except that the name has a slash (/) in front of it. HTML uses an identical convention. For example, the tag <artists> starts the list of recording artists, while the end tag </artists> ends it. Within the artists list, the information for each individual artist begins with the <artist> tag, which includes a data value for the artist id attribute, and ends with the </artist> tag. It is customary (and considered a best practice) to name a list using the plural of the tag name used for each item in the list. Comments can be added using a special tag that begins with <!-- and ends with --> as shown in the next-to-last line of the example.

Data items and values, such as those that would be stored in a relational table column, can be coded as name and value pairs in one of two ways. The first way is using an XML *attribute* by naming the attribute inside another tag, followed by the equals sign and the data value enclosed in double-quote characters, such as I did with the id and stock attributes. The second way is using an XML *element* by creating a separate tag for the data item with the data value sandwiched between the start and end tags, such as I did with both the artist name and CD name attributes. The question of which form to use has been the subject of much debate among XML developers. However, the general consensus is to use elements whenever the data item might later be broken down into additional elements, such as splitting the artist name into first name and last name, or dividing a single data element containing a comma-separated

Ask the Expert

Q: Is there a standard for the XML language itself?

A: While ISO does not currently publish a standard for XML, ISO 8879 provides a standard for SGML (Standard Generalized Markup Language), and XML is based on SGML. More importantly, the World Wide Web Consortium (W3C) publishes XML specifications that comprise the generally accepted standard throughout the IT industry.

Q: You mentioned that XML is a convenient way for different parties to exchange information. Does that mean that two companies can freely exchange data without having to create elaborate interface software so long as they both use XML?

A: Well, not exactly. XML only provides a standard way to format the data. In order for one company to correctly interpret the XML data that another company has sent them, they must know the names and definitions of the tags the other company formatted for them, particularly the elements and attributes that contain the data. Fortunately, there are a number of industry standards that help. For example, HR/XML provides a standard for exchanging human resources (HR) data so that a company can, for example, send employee data to a vendor that provides medical insurance to those employees. In some industries, XML has virtually replaced an older standard known as EDI (Electronic Data Interchange).

list of backup artist names into a list of elements. An additional consideration is whether you want to allow the XML processor to ignore insignificant whitespace, as it would do for attributes, but not for elements.

You likely noticed that, unlike the SQL result set, XML can show the hierarchy of the data. In this case, the list of CDs recorded by each artist is nested within the information about the artist. I have indented the XML statements to make the nesting more obvious. And while indentation of nested tags is a best practice, it is not significant because whitespace between tags is ignored when the XML is processed.

XML coding can be quite tedious. Fortunately, there are tools available to convert between XML and plain text and SQL/XML functions (covered later in this chapter) to convert relational database (SQL) data into XML. For a time, specialized databases for storing and retrieving XML were gaining popularity, but the major relational database vendors added features to permit native XML to be stored directly in their databases. At the same time, the SQL standard was expanded to include provisions for XML data, as I discuss in the remainder of this chapter.

Learn About SQL/XML

As already mentioned, XML is commonly used to represent data on web pages, and that data often comes from relational databases. However, as you have seen, the two models are quite different in that relational data is stored and presented in tables where neither hierarchy nor sequence have any significance, while XML is based on hierarchical trees in which order is considered significant. The term *forest* is often used to refer to a collection of XML tree structures. XML is used for web pages because its structure so closely matches the structure that would be used to display the same data in HTML. In fact, many web pages are a mixture of HTML for the static portions, and XML for the dynamic data. It is perhaps this widespread implementation that has led many of the major vendors, including Oracle and IBM, to support XML extensions.

SQL/XML can be divided into three main parts: the XML data type, SQL/XML functions, and SQL/XML mapping rules. I cover each of these as the major topics in the remainder of this chapter.

The XML Data Type

The XML data type is handled in the same general way as all the other data types I had discussed in Chapter 3. While storing data in XML format directly in the database is not the only way to use SQL and XML together, it is a very simple way to get started because it is a logical extension of the earliest implementations where SQL developers simply stored the XML text in a column defined with a general character data type such as CHARACTER VARYING (VARCHAR). However, it is far better to tell the DBMS that the column contains XML and the particular way the XML is coded so that the DBMS can provide additional features tailored to the XML format.

The specification for the XML data type has this general format:

```
XML ( <type modifier> {( <secondary type modifier> )} )
```

The type modifier is required and must be enclosed in a pair of parentheses as shown, while the secondary type modifier is optional, and in fact is not supported for all type modifiers. The standard is not specific about how a particular SQL implementation should treat the various types, but some conventions and syntax rules are specified. The valid type modifiers are:

- **DOCUMENT** The DOCUMENT type is intended for storage of text documents formatted using XML. In general, the data values are expected to be composed of human-readable characters such as letters, numbers, and symbols as they would appear in an unstructured text document.
- **CONTENT** The CONTENT type is intended for more complex data that can include binary data such as images and sound clips.
- **SEQUENCE** The SEQUENCE type is intended for XQuery documents, which are often called XQuery sequences. XQuery is an advanced topic that is beyond the scope of this book.

The secondary type modifier, used only with the DOCUMENT and CONTENT primary type modifiers, can have one of these values:

- **UNTYPED** The XML data is not of a particular type.
- **ANY** The XML data is of any of the types supported by the SQL implementation.
- **XMLSCHEMA** The XMLSCHEMA type refers to a registered XML schema that has been made known to the database server. The two most common are as follows:

Common Prefix	Target Namespace URI (Uniform Resource Identifier)
Xs	http://www.w3.org/2001/XMLSchema
sqlxml	http://standards.iso.org/iso/9075/2003/sqlxml

For SQL implementations that do not support the secondary type modifier, ANY is assumed as a default.

NOTE

Because SQL/XML is a relatively new standard, vendor implementation support varies. Oracle supports an XMLType data type instead of the XML type. IBM's DB2 UDB supports an XML type, but without the type modifiers. As already mentioned, Microsoft SQL Server supports XML and an XML data type, but in a manner a bit different from the SQL/XML standard. While MySQL 5.7 does not support an XML data type, it does support a set of XML functions that can be used in formatting and manipulating character strings that contain XML data.

Suppose we want to add a biography of the artist that can be displayed on a web page to our artists table. If the biographical sketch could come from several different sources, and thus be formatted differently depending on the source, XML might be a good way to store the data in our artists table. In the following example, I have added the column to the definition of the ARTISTS table that appeared in Chapter 3:

```
CREATE TABLE ARTISTS
( ARTIST_ID         INT,
  ARTIST_NAME       VARCHAR(60),
  ARTIST_DOB        DATE,
  POSTER_IN_STOCK   BOOLEAN,
  ARTIST_BIOGRAPHY XML(DOCUMENT(UNTYPED)) );
```

SQL/XML Functions

An SQL/XML function (also called an XML value function) is simply a function that returns a value as an XML type. For example, a query can be written that selects non-XML data (that is, data stored in data types other than XML) and formats the query results into an XML document suitable for display on a web page or transmission to some other party. Table 19-1 shows the basic SQL/XML functions.

There are more functions than those I have listed, and SQL/XML functions can be used in combination to form extremely powerful (if not complicated) queries. Also, the functions available vary across SQL implementations. Let's look at a simple example to clarify how these functions can be used. In this example, I will list the CDs by artist Stevie Wonder from the PERFORMERS and CD_INVENTORY tables shown in Figure 19-1. Here is the SQL statement, using the XMLELEMENT and XMLFOREST functions:

```
SELECT XMLELEMENT(NAME "ArtistCD",
       XMLFOREST(a.PERF_NAME as Artist, a.PERF_ID, b.CD_NAME,
b.IN_STOCK))
  FROM PERFORMERS a JOIN CD_INVENTORY b
       ON a.PERF_ID = b.PERF_ID
 WHERE a.PERF_ID = '3003'
   AND a.PERF_ID = b.PERF_ID
 ORDER BY b.CD_NAME;
```

The results returned should look something like this:

```
<ArtistCD>
  <Artist>Stevie Wonder</Artist>
  <PERF_ID>3003</PERF_ID>
  <CD_NAME>Innervisions (Remastered)</CD_NAME>
  <IN_STOCK>16</IN_STOCK>
</ArtistCD>
<ArtistCD>
  <Artist>Stevie Wonder</Artist>
  <PERF_ID>3003</PERF_ID>
```

Function	Value Returned
XMLAGG	A single XML value containing an XML forest formed by combining (aggregating) a collection of rows that each contain a single XML value
XMLATTRIBUTES	One or more attributes in the form name=value within an XMLELEMENT
XMLCOMMENT	An XML comment
XMLCONCAT	A concatenated list of XML values, creating a single value containing an XML forest
XMLDOCUMENT	An XML value containing a single document node
XMLELEMENT	An XML element, which can be a child of a document node, with the name specified in the name parameter
XMLFOREST	An XML element containing a sequence of XML elements formed from table columns, using the name of each column as the corresponding element name
XMLPARSE	An XML value formed by parsing the supplied string without validating it
XMLPI	An XML value containing an XML processing instruction
XMLQUERY	The result of an XQuery expression (XQuery is a sublanguage used to search XML stored in the database; it is beyond the scope of this book)
XMLTEXT	An XML value containing a single XML text node, which can be a child of a document node
XMLVALIDATE	An XML sequence that is the result of validating an XML value

Table 19-1 SQL/XML Functions

```
  <CD_NAME>The Definitive Collection</CD_NAME>
  <IN_STOCK>34</IN_STOCK>
</ArtistCD>
```

Notice that the XML element names are taken from the column names in uppercase with underscores as is customary in SQL. However, using the column alias, as I did for the PERF_NAME column, you can change the column names to just about anything you want.

SQL/XML Mapping Rule

Thus far I have not discussed how SQL values are translated and represented as XML values and vice versa. The SQL standard describes in detail how SQL values can be mapped to and from XML values. This topic contains an overview of the SQL/XML mapping rules.

Mappings from SQL to XML

The mappings in this topic apply to translating data in SQL data types to XML.

Mapping SQL Character Sets to Unicode *Unicode* is an industry standard that allows computer systems to consistently represent (encode) text characters expressed in most of the world's written languages. XML is often encoded as Unicode characters to allow for text in multiple languages. SQL character data is stored in whatever character set is specified when the table or database is created, and while many SQL implementations support Unicode, many other character sets can also be used. The SQL standard requires that each character in an SQL character set have a mapping to an equivalent Unicode character.

Mapping SQL Identifiers to XML Names It is necessary to define a mapping of SQL identifiers, such as table and column names, to XML names because not all SQL identifiers are acceptable XML names. Characters that are not valid in XML names are converted to a sequence of hexadecimal digits derived from the Unicode encoding of the character, bracketed by an introductory underscore and lowercase x and a trailing underscore. For example, a colon (:) in an SQL identifier might be translated to _x0003A_ in an XML name.

Mapping SQL Data Types to XML Schema Data Types This is perhaps the most complicated of the mapping forms. For each SQL type or domain, the SQL implementation is required to provide a mapping to the appropriate XML schema type. Detailed mapping of standard SQL types to XML schema data types is provided in the standard in exhaustive detail. I summarize them in Table 19-2.

Mapping Values of SQL Data Types to Values of XML Schema Data Types For each SQL type or domain, with the exception of structured types and reference types, there is also a mapping of values for the type to the value space of the corresponding XML schema type. Null values are represented using either absence (skipping the element) or using the facet xsi:nil="true" to explicitly set the null value.

Mapping an SQL Table to an XML Document and an XML Schema Document The SQL standard defines a mapping of an SQL table to one or both of two documents: an XML schema document that describes the structure of the mapped XML, and either an XML document or a sequence of XML elements. This mapping applies only to base tables and viewed tables, and only columns visible to the database user can be mapped. The implementation may provide options for the following:

- Whether to map the table to a sequence of XML elements or as an XML document with a single root name derived from the table name.
- The target namespace of the XML schema to be mapped.
- Whether to map null values as absent elements or elements marked with facet xsi:nil="true".
- Whether to map the table into XML data, an XML schema document, or both.

SQL Type	XML Schema Type	Notes
CHARACTER CHARACTER VARYING CHARACTER LARGE OBJECT	xs:string	The XML facet xs:length is used to specify length for fixed-length strings. (A *facet* is an element used to define a property of another element.)
NUMERIC DECIMAL	xs:decimal	Precision and scale are specified using XML facets xs:precision and xs:scale.
INTEGER SMALLINT BIGINT	xs:integer	This mapping is listed as implementation defined, meaning it is optional.
FLOAT REAL DOUBLE PRECISION	xs:float, xs:double	For precisions up to 24 binary digits (bits) and an exponent between −149 and 104 inclusive, xs:float is used; otherwise, xs_double is used.
BOOLEAN	xs:Boolean	
DATE	xs:date	The xs:pattern facet is used to exclude the use of a time zone displacement.
TIME WITH TIME ZONE TIME WITHOUT TIME ZONE	xs:time	The xs:pattern facet is used to exclude or specify the time zone displacement, as appropriate.
TIMESTAMP WITH TIME ZONE TIMESTAMP WITHOUT TIME ZONE	xs:dateTime	The xs:pattern facet is used to exclude or specify the time zone displacement, as appropriate.
Interval types	xdt:yearMonthDuration, xdt:day-TimeDuration	
Row type	XML schema complex type	The XML document contains one element for each field of the SQL row type.
Domain	XML schema data type	The domain's data type is mapped to XML with an annotation that identifies the name of the domain.

Table 19-2 Mapping of SQL Data Types to XML Schema Types *(continued)*

SQL Type	XML Schema Type	Notes
SQL distinct type	XML schema simple type	
SQL collection type	XML schema complex type	The complex type has a single element named *element*.
XML type	XML schema complex type	

Table 19-2 Mapping of SQL Data Types to XML Schema Types

Mapping an SQL Schema to an XML Document and an XML Schema Document The SQL standard defines the mapping between the tables of an SQL schema and either an XML document that represents the data in the tables or an XML schema document, or both. Only tables and columns visible to the database user can be mapped. The implementation may provide options for the following:

- Whether to map each table as a sequence of XML elements or as an XML document with a single root name derived from the table name.
- The target namespace of the XML schema to be mapped.
- Whether to map null values as absent elements or elements marked with facet xsi:nil="true".
- Whether to map the schema into XML data, an XML schema document, or both.

Mapping an SQL Catalog to an XML Document and an XML Schema Document The SQL standard defines the mapping between the tables of an SQL catalog and either an XML document that represents the data in the catalog's tables or an XML schema document, or both. However, this part of the standard specifies no syntax for invoking such mapping because it is intended to be used by applications or referenced by other standards. Only schemas visible to the SQL user can be mapped. The implementation may provide options for the following:

- Whether to map each table as a sequence of XML elements or as an XML document with a single root name derived from the table name.
- The target namespace of the XML schema and data to be mapped.
- Whether to map null values as absent elements or elements marked with facet xsi:nil="true".
- Whether to map the catalog into XML data, an XML schema document, or both.

Mappings from XML to SQL

This topic contains two mappings from XML back to SQL.

Mapping Unicode to SQL Character Sets As with the mapping of SQL character sets to Unicode, the SQL standard requires that there be an implementation-defined mapping of Unicode characters to the characters in each SQL character set supported by the SQL implementation.

Mapping XML Names to SQL Identifiers This is the reverse of the mapping of SQL identifiers to XML names where characters that were converted because they were not valid in XML names are converted back to their original form. So, if a colon in an SQL identifier was converted to _x003A_ when translating the SQL identifier into XML, it would be converted back into a colon when the process was reversed. The SQL standard further recommends that the SQL implementation use a single algorithm for translation in both directions.

Try This 19-1 Using SQL/XML Functions

In this Try This exercise, you will use XML functions to select XML-formatted data from the INVENTORY database. Obviously, your SQL implementation has to provide XML support in order for you to complete the exercise, and as usual, you may have to modify the code included in this exercise in order to run it on your DBMS. You can download the Try_This_19.txt file, which contains the SQL statements used in this Try This exercise.

Step by Step

1. Open the client application for your RDBMS and connect to the INVENTORY database.
2. You are going to create an SQL query that uses the three SQL/XML functions to format XML that contains an element for each CD in the COMPACT_DISCS table, with each element including the ID of the CD, followed by a separate element containing the title of the CD. Enter and execute the following statement:

```
SELECT XMLELEMENT(NAME "CD",
       XMLATTRIBUTES(COMPACT_DISC_ID AS "ID"),
       XMLFOREST(CD_TITLE AS "Title"))
  FROM COMPACT_DISCS
 ORDER BY COMPACT_DISC_ID;
```

3. The output produced should look something like the following listing. Note that in the interest of space, only the first two CDs are shown.

```
<CD ID='101'>
  <Title>Drive All Night</Title>
</CD>
<CD ID='102'>
  <Title>Different Shades of Blue</Title>
</CD>
```

4. Close the client application.

Try This Summary

In this Try This exercise, the SQL SELECT statement used three SQL/XML functions to format data from the COMPACT_DISCS table into XML. The XMLELEMENT function was used to create an element for each CD. The XMLATTRIBUTES function was used to include the COMPACT_DISC_ID value with the name ID as a value within the CD element. Finally, the XMLFOREST function was used to create an element for the CD_TITLE column.

Chapter 19 Self Test

1. What is XML?
2. Which of the following are common uses of XML?
   - **A** Displaying database data on a web page
   - **B** Creation of static web pages
   - **C** Transmission of database data to another party
   - **D** Enforcement of business rules on documents
3. How do SQL databases and XML documents vary in terms of data structure?
4. If two organizations are both using XML, does that mean that they have a standard way of exchanging data without having to create interface software?
5. Which of the following are valid type modifiers for the XML data type?
   - **A** DOCUMENT
   - **B** SEQUENCE
   - **C** SQLXML
   - **D** CONTENT
6. What are the valid secondary type modifiers for the SEQUENCE type modifier?
7. Which of the following SQL/XML functions creates an element based on a table column?
   - **A** XMLQUERY
   - **B** XMLELEMENT
   - **C** XMLFOREST
   - **D** XMLDOCUMENT
   - **E** XMLPARSE

8. Which XML schema type is mapped from the SQL NUMERIC data type?
   - **A** xs:integer
   - **B** xs:float
   - **C** xs:decimal
   - **D** xs:double

9. Which XML schema type is mapped from the SQL DATE data type?
   - **A** xs:dateTime
   - **B** xdt:yearMonthDuration
   - **C** xs:time
   - **D** xs:date
   - **E** xdt:dat-TimeDuration

10. What are the two ways that null values from the database can be represented by SQL/XML?
    - **A** Absent document
    - **B** Absent element
    - **C** xsi:null= "true"
    - **D** xsi:nil= "true"
    - **E** <elementname=nil>

Part IV

Appendices

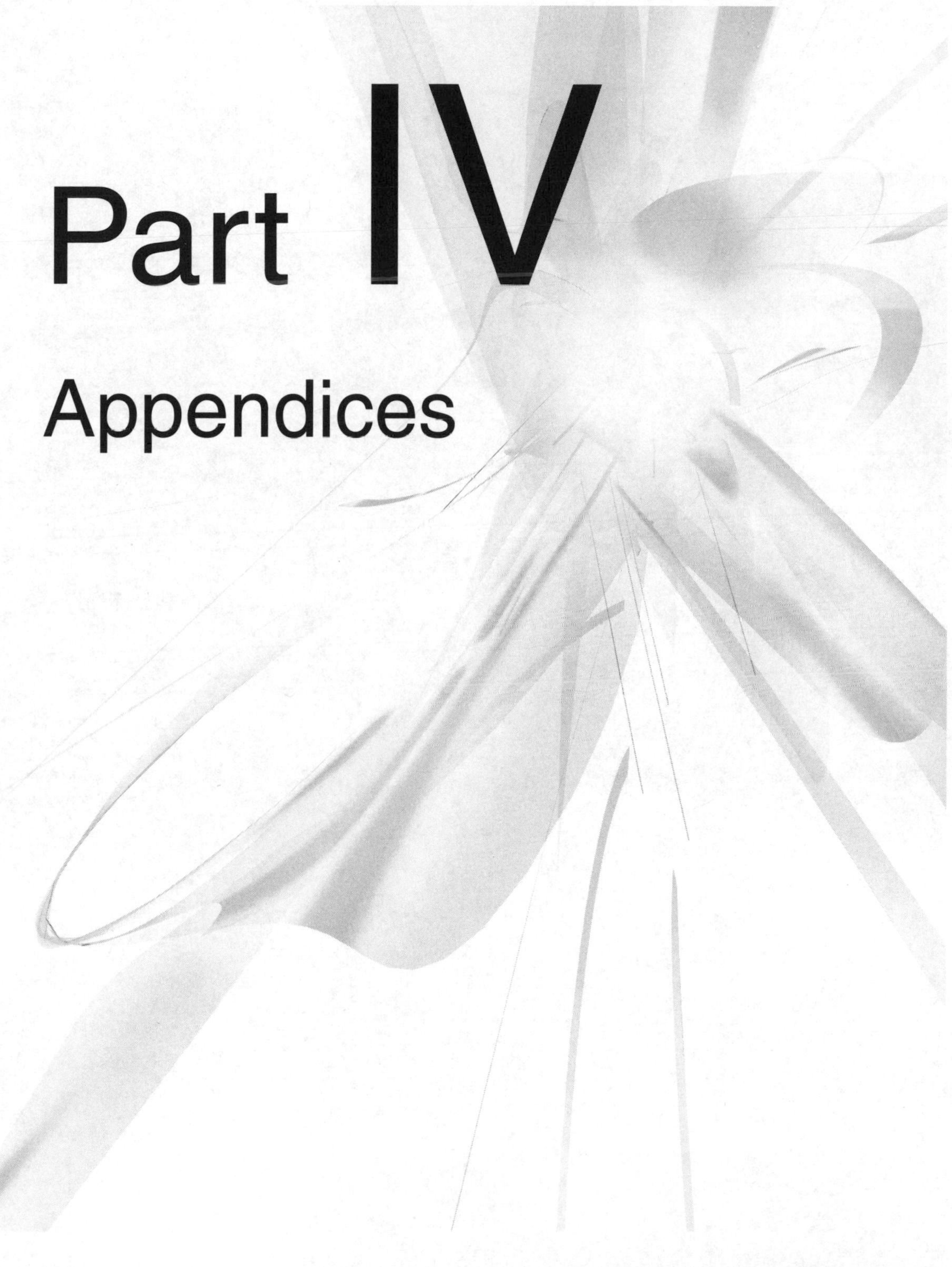

Appendix A

SQL Keywords

The SQL standard defines a set of reserved keywords and nonreserved keywords that are used within your SQL statements. You cannot use reserved keywords as identifiers. In addition, it is generally a good idea to avoid using nonreserved keywords. Note that the SQL standard warns that it makes no guarantees about what keywords might be added to the standard in the future. As a result, an identifier you use in a current database might not be usable in future releases of SQL. You can avoid conflicts with future reserved keywords by adding a digit or an underscore to your identifiers, especially those composed of only a single word, and by not beginning an identifier with current_, session_, system_, or timezone_, or ending an identifier with _length.

NOTE

Various SQL implementations include additional keywords and reserved words that cannot be used as identifiers. Always check your product documentation.

SQL Reserved Keywords

Table A-1 lists SQL reserved keywords.

ABS	ALL	ALLOCATE	ALTER
AND	ANY	ARE	ARRAY
AS	ARRAY_AGG	ARRAY_MAX_CARDINALITY	ASENSITIVE
ASYMMETRIC	AT	ATOMIC	AUTHORIZATION
AVG	BEGIN	BEGIN_FRAME	BEGIN_PARTITION
BETWEEN	BIGINT	BINARY	BLOB
BOOLEAN	BOTH	BY	CALL
CALLED	CARDINALITY	CASCADED	CASE
CAST	CEIL	CEILING	CHAR
CHAR_LENGTH	CHARACTER	CHARACTER_LENGTH	CHECK
CLOB	CLOSE	COALESCE	COLLATE
COLLECT	COLUMN	COMMIT	CONDITION
CONNECT	CONSTRAINT	CONVERT	CORR
CORRESPONDING	COUNT	COVAR_POP	COVAR_SAMP

Table A-1 SQL Reserved Keywords *(continued)*

CREATE	CROSS	CUBE	CUME_DIST
CURRENT	CURRENT_CATALOG	CURRENT_DATE	CURRENT_DEFAULT_ TRANSFORM_GROUP
CURRENT_PATH	CURRENT_ROLE	CURRENT_ROW	CURRENT_SCHEMA
CURRENT_TIME	CURRENT_TIMESTAMP	CURRENT_TRANSFORM_ GROUP_FOR_TYPE	CURRENT_USER
CURSOR	CYCLE	DATE	DAY
DEALLOCATE	DEC	DECIMAL	DECLARE
DEFAULT	DELETE	DENSE_RANK	DEREF
DESCRIBE	DETERMINISTIC	DISCONNECT	DISTINCT
DOUBLE	DROP	DYNAMIC	EACH
ELEMENT	ELSE	END	END_FRAME
END_PARTITION	END-EXEC	EQUALS	ESCAPE
EVERY	EXCEPT	EXEC	EXECUTE
EXISTS	EXP	EXTERNAL	EXTRACT
FALSE	FETCH	FILTER	FIRST_VALUE
FLOAT	FLOOR	FOR	FOREIGN
FRAME_ROW	FREE	FROM	FULL
FUNCTION	FUSION	GET	GLOBAL
GRANT	GROUP	GROUPING	GROUPS
HAVING	HOLD	HOUR	IDENTITY
IN	INDICATOR	INNER	INOUT
INSENSITIVE	INSERT	INT	INTEGER
INTERSECT	INTERSECTION	INTERVAL	INTO
IS	JOIN	LAG	LANGUAGE
LARGE	LAST_VALUE	LATERAL	LEAD
LEADING	LEFT	LIKE	LIKE_REGEX

Table A-1 SQL Reserved Keywords *(continued)*

LN	LOCAL	LOCALTIME	LOCALTIMESTAMP
LOWER	MATCH	MAX	MEMBER
MERGE	METHOD	MIN	MINUTE
MOD	MODIFIES	MODULE	MONTH
MULTISET	NATIONAL	NATURAL	NCHAR
NCLOB	NEW	NO	NONE
NORMALIZE	NOT	NTH_VALUE	NTILE
NULL	NULLIF	NUMERIC	OCTET_LENGTH
OCCURENCES_ REGEX	OF	OFFSET	OLD
ON	ONLY	OPEN	OR
ORDER	OUT	OUTER	OVER
OVERLAPS	OVERLAY	PARAMETER	PARTITION
PERCENT	PERCENT_RANK	PERCENTILE_CONT	PERCENTILE_DISC
PERIOD	PORTION	POSITION	POSITION_REGEX
POWER	PRECEDES	PRECISION	PREPARE
PRIMARY	PROCEDURE	RANGE	RANK
READS	REAL	RECURSIVE	REF
REFERENCES	REFERENCING	REGR_AVGX	REGR_AVGY
REGR_COUNT	REGR_INTERCEPT	REGR_R2	REGR_SLOPE
REGR_SXX	REGR_SXY	REGR_SYY	RELEASE
RESULT	RETURN	RETURNS	REVOKE
RIGHT	ROLLBACK	ROLLUP	ROW
ROW_NUMBER	ROWS	SAVEPOINT	SCOPE
SCROLL	SEARCH	SECOND	SELECT
SENSITIVE	SESSION_USER	SET	SIMILAR

Table A-1 SQL Reserved Keywords *(continued)*

SMALLINT	SOME	SPECIFIC	SPECIFICTYPE
SQL	SQLEXCEPTION	SQLSTATE	SQLWARNING
SQRT	START	STATIC	STDDEV_POP
STDDEV_SAMP	SUBMULTISET	SUBSTRING	SUBSTRING_REGEX
SUCCEEDS	SUM	SYMMETRIC	SYSTEM
SYSTEM_USER	TABLE	TABLESAMPLE	THEN
TIME	TIMESTAMP	TIMEZONE_HOUR	TIMEZONE_MINUTE
TO	TRAILING	TRANSLATE	TRANSLATE_REGEX
TRANSLATION	TREAT	TRIGGER	TRIM
TRIM_ARRAY	TRUE	TRUNCATE	UESCAPE
UNION	UNIQUE	UNKNOWN	UNNEST
UPDATE	UPPER	USER	USING
VALUE	VALUES	VALUE_OF	VAR_POP
VAR_SAMP	VARBINARY	VARCHAR	VARYING
VERSIONING	WHEN	WHENEVER	WHERE
WIDTH_BUCKET	WINDOW	WITH	WITHIN
WITHOUT	YEAR		

Table A-1 SQL Reserved Keywords

SQL Nonreserved Keywords

Table A-2 lists SQL nonreserved keywords.

A	ABSOLUTE	ACTION
ADA	ADD	ADMIN
AFTER	ALWAYS	ASC
ASSERTION	ASSIGNMENT	ATTRIBUTE

Table A-2 SQL Nonreserved Keywords *(continued)*

ATTRIBUTES	BEFORE	BERNOULLI
BREADTH	C	CASCADE
CATALOG	CATALOG_NAME	CHAIN
CHARACTER_SET_CATALOG	CHARACTER_SET_NAME	CHARACTER_SET_SCHEMA
CHARACTERISTICS	CHARACTERS	CLASS_ORIGIN
COBOL	COLLATION	COLLATION_CATALOG
COLLATION_NAME	COLLATION_SCHEMA	COLUMN_NAME
COMMAND_FUNCTION	COMMAND_FUNCTION_ CODE	COMMITTED
CONDITION_NUMBER	CONNECTION	CONNECTION_NAME
CONSTRAINT_CATALOG	CONSTRAINT_NAME	CONSTRAINT_SCHEMA
CONSTRAINTS	CONSTRUCTOR	CONTINUE
CURSOR_NAME	DATA	DATETIME_INTERVAL_CODE
DATETIME_INTERVAL_ PRECISION	DEFAULTS	DEFERRABLE
DEFERRED	DEFINED	DEFINER
DEGREE	DEPTH	DERIVED
DESC	DESCRIPTOR	DIAGNOSTICS
DISPATCH	DOMAIN	DYNAMIC_FUNCTION
DYNAMIC_FUNCTION_ CODE	ENFORCED	EXCLUDE
EXCLUDING	EXPRESSION	FINAL
FIRST	FLAG	FOLLOWING
FORTRAN	FOUND	G
GENERAL	GENERATED	GO
GOTO	GRANTED	HIERARCHY
IGNORE	IMMEDIATE	IMMEDIATELY

Table A-2 SQL Nonreserved Keywords *(continued)*

IMPLEMENTATION	INCLUDING	INCREMENT
INITIALLY	INPUT	INSTANCE
INSTANTIABLE	INSTEAD	INVOKER
ISOLATION	K	KEY
KEY_MEMBER	KEY_TYPE	LAST
LENGTH	LEVEL	LOCATOR
M	MAP	MATCHED
MAXVALUE	MESSAGE_LENGTH	MESSAGE_OCTET_LENGTH
MESSAGE_TEXT	MINVALUE	MORE
MUMPS	NAME	NAMES
NESTING	NEXT	NFC
NFD	NFKC	NFKD
NORMALIZED	NULLABLE	NULLS
NUMBER	OBJECT	OCTETS
OPTION	OPTIONS	ORDERING
ORDINALITY	OTHERS	OUTPUT
OVERRIDING	p	PAD
PARAMETER_MODE	PARAMETER_NAME	PARAMETER_ORDINAL_POSITION
PARAMETER_SPECIFIC_ CATALOG	PARAMETER_SPECIFIC_ NAME	PARAMETER_SPECIFIC_SCHEMA
PARTIAL	PASCAL	PATH
PLACING	PLI	PRECEDING
PRESERVE	PRIOR	PRIVILEGES
PUBLIC	READ	RELATIVE
REPEATABLE	RESPECT	RESTART
RESTRICT	RETURNED_CARDINALITY	RETURNED_LENGTH

Table A-2 SQL Nonreserved Keywords *(continued)*

RETURNED_OCTET_LENGTH	RETURNED_SQLSTATE	ROLE
ROUTINE	ROUTINE_CATALOG	ROUTINE_NAME
ROUTINE_SCHEMA	ROW_COUNT	SCALE
SCHEMA	SCHEMA_NAME	SCOPE_CATALOG
SCOPE_NAME	SCOPE_SCHEMA	SECTION
SECURITY	SELF	SEQUENCE
SERIALIZABLE	SERVER_NAME	SESSION
SETS	SIMPLE	SIZE
SOURCE	SPACE	SPECIFIC_NAME
STATE	STATEMENT	STRUCTURE
STYLE	SUBCLASS_ORIGIN	T
TABLE_NAME	TEMPORARY	TIES
TOP_LEVEL_COUNT	TRANSACTION	TRANSACTION_ACTIVE
TRANSACTIONS_ COMMITTED	TRANSACTIONS_ROLLED_ BACK	TRANSFORM
TRANSFORMS	TRIGGER_CATALOG	TRIGGER_NAME
TRIGGER_SCHEMA	TYPE	UNBOUNDED
UNCOMMITTED	UNDER	UNNAMED
USAGE	USER_DEFINED_TYPE_ CATALOG	USER_DEFINED_TYPE_CODE
USER_DEFINED_TYPE_NAME	USER_DEFINED_TYPE_ SCHEMA	VIEW
WORK	WRITE	ZONE

Table A-2 SQL Nonreserved Keywords

Index

B

C

G

H

I

N

O

P

Q

R

S

T

U

V

W

X

Y